UNDER THE EDITORSHIP OF

Dayton D. McKean

UNIVERSITY OF COLORADO

Capitol
Courthouse
and
City Hall

Readings in American State and Local Government

THIRD EDITION

Robert L. Morlan

UNIVERSITY OF REDLANDS

HOUGHTON MIFFLIN COMPANY · BOSTON

New York · Atlanta · Geneva, Ill. · Dallas · Palo Alto

Preface to the Third Edition

One of the incidental and rarely noted benefits of revised editions of a book is that the prefaces become progressively more brief. One seeks of course in a revision to make the end product as current and relevant as possible, to incorporate the most useful recent writings, and to stress those matters which have emerged as central elements of controversy in the field (notably in this edition the reapportionment question, for example). The basic goals and approach, as indicated in the preface to the first edition, remain unchanged.

R.L.M.

Preface to the First Edition

FOLLOWING the years of depression and war, when the focus of attention was quite naturally upon the national government, there has come a resurgence of interest on the part of both students of government and civic groups in the affairs of the states and local governments. A number of excellent up-to-date textbooks are now available in this field, but the wealth of valuable materials in periodicals and other publications has remained accessible only through extensive and complex library assignments, often not feasible with even moderately sized classes. This collection of readings is offered in an effort to provide these needed teaching materials. It is designed primarily to be used as a supplement to a text, though some instructors may wish to use it, in conjunction with other assignments, in lieu of the traditional type of textbook.

In the view of the editor of this volume a collection such as this should serve principally to bring the student directly to grips with the actual problems of government and to make concrete and meaningful through graphic illustrations issues which may otherwise seem distant and unreal to readers whose contacts with state and local government have so far been largely via the printed page. The selections reprinted here have been carefully chosen on the basis of two primary criteria: (1) competent treatment of a significant segment of the subject-matter field, and (2) a style which is readable and understandable to college students. There is little point in providing articles which cannot be read with genuine interest. Documentary materials have been avoided and the sprightliest writing available, consistent with soundness, has been utilized, on the assumption that the purpose here is less a display of scholarship than an effort to get the subject "across" to the student in the most effective manner possible. A wide range of both popular periodicals and books and specialized publications is represented — from *Colliers,* the *Saturday Evening Post,* and the *American Mercury* to the *National Municipal Review,* the *Western Political Quarterly,* and the *Annals of the American Academy of Political and Social Science.*

The problem of elimination of a multitude of worthwhile items in order to stay within manageable scope is a difficult one. For the most part purely descriptive materials, which instructors and texts will adequately cover, have not been included. Nor has it seemed feasible to include articles dealing with the functional services of state and local governments, most of which are fields of study in themselves that must perforce be handled largely by descriptive summary in a general course in this area.

The emphasis has been placed on the important contemporary issues in government at this level, especially where these are at all controversial. In such cases varying (and often opposite) points of view are presented, insofar as they are available. It is hoped, therefore, that in addition to the purposes already mentioned many of these articles may serve as springboards for fruitful class discussions. The entire collection is presented not as a reference volume of "basic data," but as a de-

vice for more effective teaching and study of a most important field of political science.

A sincere expression of thanks is due the authors and publishers who have so generously consented to the use of the writings which make up this volume, to Dayton D. McKean, editorial adviser in Political Science to Houghton Mifflin Company, and to my students of the past few years who have not only served as a testing ground for these materials but have frequently provided helpful suggestions and criticisms.

Robert L. Morlan

Contents

CHAPTER ONE

The Theory of Local Self-Government

MOST WRITERS on the theory of democracy have assumed that institutions of local self-government, if not absolutely essential to democratic government, at least make a major contribution to its success. There are values in self-government at this level, it is contended, which are nowhere else obtainable. In the opening selection the classic statement of the theoretical basis for local self-government is presented in the words of one of the most distinguished foreign observers of American institutions, Lord Bryce. Dr. Morgan, former chairman of the board of TVA, then argues that in this age of giantism smallness itself is a virtue; in the close personal relationships of the small community alone can we even approach the realization of some of our most cherished social ideals.

1

The Values of
Local Self-Government

By James Bryce

THE BEGINNINGS of popular government were in small areas, rural communities and tiny cities, each with only a few hundreds or possibly thousands of free inhabitants. The earliest form it took was that of an assembly in which all the freemen met to discuss their common affairs, and in which, although the heads of the chief families exerted much influence, the mind and voice of the people could make itself felt. Such assemblies marked the emergence of men from barbarism into something approaching a settled and ordered society. In many places these communities lay within a monarchy, in others (as in Iceland)

James Bryce, *Modern Democracies* (New York: The Macmillan Company, 1921), Vol. I, pp. 129, 131–133; Vol. II, pp. 435–437. Reprinted by permission of the publisher.

they were independent, but everywhere they accustomed the people to cherish a free spirit and learn to co-operate for common aims. . . .

The small communities here described may be called the tiny fountain-heads of democracy, rising among the rocks, sometimes lost altogether in their course, sometimes running underground to reappear at last in fuller volume. They suffice to show that popular government is not a new thing in the world, but was in many countries the earliest expression of man's political instincts. It was a real misfortune for England — and the remark applies in a certain sense to Germany also — that while local self-government did maintain itself in the county and borough it should in both have largely lost the popular character which once belonged to it, as it was a misfortune for Ireland and for France that this natural creation of political intelligence should not have developed there. Many things that went wrong in those four centuries from the end of the sixteenth century onwards might have fared better under institutions like those of Switzerland or the Northern United States.

. . . A few words may be said as to the general service which self-government in small areas renders in forming the qualities needed by the citizen of a free country. It creates among the citizens a sense of their common interest in common affairs, and of their individual as well as common duty to take care that those affairs are efficiently and honestly administered. If it is the business of a local authority to mend the roads, to clean out the village well or provide a new pump, to see that there is a place where straying beasts may be kept till the owner reclaims them, to fix the number of cattle each villager may turn out on the common pasture, to give each his share of timber cut in the common woodland, every villager has an interest in seeing that these things are properly attended to. Laziness and the selfishness which is indifferent to whatever does not immediately affect a man's interests is the fault which most afflicts democratic communities. Whoever learns to be public-spirited, active and upright in the affairs of the village has learnt the first lesson of the duty incumbent on a citizen of a great country, just as, conversely, "he that is unfaithful in the least is unfaithful also in much." The same principle applies to a city. In it the elector can seldom judge from his own observation how things are being managed. But he can watch through the newspapers or by what he hears from competent sources whether the mayor and councillors and their officials are doing their work, and whether they are above suspicion of making illicit gains, and whether the taxpayer is getting full value for what he is required to contribute. So when the election comes he has the means of discovering the candidates with the best record and can cast his vote accordingly.

Secondly: Local institutions train men not only to work for others but also to work effectively with others. They develop common sense, reasonableness, judgment, sociability. Those who have to bring their minds together learn the need for concession and compromise. A man has the opportunity of showing what is in him, and commending himself to his fellow-citizens. Two useful habits are formed, that of recognizing the worth of knowledge and tact in public affairs and that of judging men by performance rather than by professions or promises.

Criticisms are often passed on the narrowness of mind and the spirit of parsimony which are visible in rural local authorities and those who elect them. These defects are, however, a natural product of the conditions of local life. The narrowness would be there in any case, and would affect the elector if he were voting for a national representative, but there would be less of that shrewdness which the practice of local government forms. Such faults must be borne with for the sake of the more important benefits which self-government produces. The main thing is that everybody, peasant and workman as well as shopkeeper and farmer, should join in a common public activity, and feel that he has in his own neighborhood a sphere in which he can exercise his own judgment and do something for the community. Seeing the working, on a small scale, of the principle of responsibility to the public for powers conferred by them, he is better fitted to understand its application in affairs of larger scope....

It is enough to observe that the countries in which democratic government has most attracted the interest of the people and drawn talent from their ranks have been Switzerland and the United States, especially those northern and western States in which rural local government has been most developed. These examples justify the maxim that the best school of democracy, and the best guarantee for its success, is the practice of local self-government....

In countries which, like France, Britain, and Australia, are governed by representative assemblies it is desirable to relieve, as far as possible, the strain upon the Central Government. A practically omnipotent legislature is liable to sudden fluctuations of opinion, and the fewer are the branches of administration which such fluctuations disturb, the more regular and stable will be the general course of affairs. Those of national importance must of course be dealt with by the National legislature, but there are many matters in which uniformity is not required, and the more these are left to local control the less will representatives be drawn away from national work. Where local discontents arise, it is better for them to find vent in the local area rather than encumber the central authority. Under a federal system of government, such as that of the United States, Canada, Switzerland, where many matters are left to be settled by State, or Provincial, or Cantonal assemblies, controversial issues are divided between those assemblies and the central national legislature, and a political conflict in the latter need not coincide with other conflicts in the former. The same principle holds true with regard to local authorities in smaller areas, such as the county or municipality. Men opposed in national politics may work together harmoniously in the conduct of county or municipal business, as happens in Switzerland and England, and to a large extent in the United States also.

The wider the scope of a central government's action, so much the larger is the number of the persons employed in the administrative work it directs, and the larger therefore the patronage at its disposal. Patronage is a powerful political engine, certain to be used for party purposes wherever admission to the civil service and promotion therein are not controlled by rules which secure competence through examinations administered by a non-partisan authority. The fewer temptations to the abuse of patronage are left within the grasp of the central authority, necessarily partisan in all the countries we have been studying, the fewer abuses will there be. The United States suffered until recent years from the so-called spoils system, applied in municipalities as well as in the Federal service, but the evils would have been even greater had the same party been steadily supreme at the same time in the National Government and in the local government areas....

In some countries possessing a highly trained civil

service each department tends to lay undue stress upon uniformity, becomes attached to its settled habits, dislikes novelties, contracts bureaucratic methods, and may assume towards the private citizen a slightly supercilious air. Progress is retarded because experiments are discouraged. Popular interest flags because popular interference is resented, and officials fall out of touch with general sentiment. The more the central bureaucracy controls local affairs, the wider will be the action of these tendencies.

Lastly we come to another benefit, of a more theoretical aspect, yet with real value, which local self-governing institutions may secure. They contribute to the development of local centres of thought and action. Many a country has had reason to dread the excessive power of its capital city. There ought to be many cities, each cherishing its own traditions, each representing or embodying a certain type of opinion, and each, instead of taking its ideas submissively from the capital, supporting journals of the first excellence in point of news supply and intellectual force. Such cities will be all the more useful in forming independent centres of opinion if they have also strong local governments which enlist the active service of their leading citizens of all classes. . . .

2

The Significance of the Small Community

By Arthur E. Morgan

IN MODERN TIMES the small community has played the part of an orphan in an unfriendly world. It has been despised, neglected, exploited, and robbed. The cities have skimmed off the cream of its young population. Yet the small community has supplied the lifeblood of civilization, and neglect of it has been one of the primary reasons for the slowness and the interrupted course of human progress. It is high time that the fundamental significance of the small community be recognized.

Over most of the world the village is an ancient institution, often with a history extending into the dim past, sometimes thousands of years, outlasting kingdoms and dynasties. Modern and ancient ways

Arthur E. Morgan, *The Small Community* (New York: Harper & Brothers, 1942), pp. 3–19. Footnotes in original omitted. Reprinted by permission of the publisher.

exist there side by side. Often existing informal democratic village government, well adapted to its purpose, differs little from that of the dawn of history.

The village has played a dominant part in the destinies of men. Anthropologists ascribe a million to four million years to the life of mankind. So far as we know, most of our ancestors during this long period lived in small groups of from a few dozen to a few hundred persons. Only when necessity compelled did they resort to isolated dwellings. . . .

Cities have existed only during the past ten or twenty thousand years — for perhaps one per cent of the life of the race — and many of them were but overgrown villages. During the Middle Ages most "cities" of Europe were self-sustaining agricultural villages. Even Rome was then a town of about ten thousand, and for centuries scarcely a city in all Europe had a greater population.

Even today most city dwellers are children or grandchildren of rural people. When the writer's grandfather was born, only six American cities had as many as eight thousand inhabitants. Even now probably three quarters of the human race live in villages. There are estimated to be two million villages in Asia, while probably more than half of all Europeans are villagers.

Small communities are the sources of city population. Large cities have such low birth-rates that if their population were not renewed from outside they would almost disappear in four or five generations. Latest census reports indicate that American city families have less than three quarters as many children as would be necessary to maintain their population. The rural fertility rate is more than twice as great as that of cities of more than one hundred thousand.

The community also is the chief source of leadership. A leader is a person of unusual native vigor, intelligence, or personality, who uses that superiority to give expression to the character he acquired from family and community. Great men may make history, but the kind of history they make is determined chiefly by their childhood environment. Napoleon as a boy on the faction-ridden, brigand-infested island of Corsica learned the local ways of intrigue, feud, and ambition. When he was well-nigh master of Europe, enthroning and dethroning kings, the ways of the Corsican village ruled his life. A similar story might be told of nearly every present-day European dictator. . . .

Controlling factors of civilization are not art, business, science, government. These are its fruits. The roots of civilization are elemental traits — good will, neighborliness, fair play, courage, tolerance, open-minded inquiry, patience. A people rich in these qualities will develop a great civilization, with great art, science, industry, government. If the basic qualities fade, then no matter how great the wealth, how brilliant the learning, how polished the culture, that civilization will crumble.

These finer underlying traits, which we recognize as the essence of civilization, are not inborn; neither are they best acquired in rough-and-tumble business or political life. They are learned in the intimate, friendly world of the family and the small community, usually by the age of ten or twelve, and by unconscious imitation, as we learn the mother tongue. Only as such traits have opportunity to grow in the kindly, protective shelter of family and small community, or in other groups where there is intimate acquaintance and mutual confidence, do they become vigorous and mature enough to survive. Unless supported by the surrounding community, the single family is too small a unit to maintain fine standards.

When we say that human nature does not change, what we generally mean is that this chain of teaching or conditioning seldom is broken from generation to generation. Each generation acquires while very young the elemental incentives which preceding generations learned in the same way. This basic human culture is of very slow growth. Apparently simple attitudes such as honesty or courtesy have required thousands of years to originate and to be refined and established. Those from whom we learned them, be they parents, neighbors, teachers or companions, did not originate them, but caught them from others, and so on, from time immemorial. If the social threads of community, by which they are preserved and transmitted, should be broken, equally long periods might be necessary to re-create them. The traits of refined culture can be passed by contagion from one individual to another, but that does not mean that they can be quickly originated. The displacement of a lower culture by a higher, such as took place when European culture replaced that of the bushmen in Australia, does not mean that a new culture has been created, but only that an existing culture has been transferred or diffused. That the dandelion has spread all over North America from Europe in a very short time does not nullify the fact that millions of years were necessary for its evolution. If we eliminate a type of plant or animal or of human culture, thousands of years might be necessary for the re-creation of its equivalent. . . .

Today is not the first time that more excellent human cultures have been threatened with submergence by crude violence on the part of less excellent societies. During the very long periods when the prevailing type of social organization was the small community, a high degree and fine quality of social adjustment was achieved within the limits of the ancient village.

The age of force and strategy, of conquest, of empire, and of feudalism, swept over and submerged this ancient community life. The democratic equality, the good-will and co-operativeness, of communities the world over were largely displaced by dictatorship and serfdom. Men's minds were subjected to indoctrination and propaganda. The common man became the tool of his master, bound to the soil. Deceit, intrigue, and shrewdness — the spirit of Machiavelli — often prevailed over simple honesty. Yet the ancient spirit of community was not killed. Nearly everywhere it survived in small groups and close to the soil. Feudal society could exploit that quality, but could not live without it. Community traits of good will and mutual confidence constituted the very life-principle of society. Without them society would disintegrate. . . .

Many of the ideals which the Western world holds as most precious are survivals from the ancient community way of life. The burden of the Hebrew prophet's message, good will and brotherhood, which flowered in Christian teaching, was not a new revelation, but a resurgence and extension of ancient community ways in the hills of Palestine. The democracy of Switzerland, which became a beacon light to the modern world, did not originate when men of the forest cantons tore down the baron's castle six hundred and fifty years ago. Those Swiss communities were fighting to preserve their ancient democratic way of life, which in their mountain retreats never had succumbed to feudalism. Religious democracy, which has been a potent school for political democracy, has a similar history. The pre-Reformation reformers did not start a new kind of church government or a new way of life. They chiefly persisted in ancient community ways which they found strikingly in accord with primitive Christianity. When we trace democratically governed religious groups to their origins we find that in most cases they lead back to small communities where the traditions of political and religious democracy had never been wholly extinguished.

Today, as in the ancient past, the small community is the home, the refuge, the seed bed, of some of the finest qualities of civilization. But just as the precious values of the ancient community were submerged and largely destroyed by empire and feudalism, so the present-day community with its invaluable cultural tradition is being dissolved, diluted, and submerged by modern technology, commercialism, mass production, propaganda, and centralized government. Should that process not be checked, a great cultural tradition may be largely lost. . . .

World events of today and tomorrow took their determining directions further back in the past than we realize; and the work of today, if in accord with fundamental realities, will come to full fruition further in the future than we supposed. When events are full grown, herculean effort may change them but slightly. How little change in the current of human affairs, except in spiritual disorganization and exhaustion, was made by the prodigious efforts of the first World War!

Yet very moderate powers, wisely used in harmony with the nature of things, may have profound effect on the more distant future. The free men in obscure Swiss valleys who kept alive the ancient tradition of democratic life may have had more enduring influence than the heads of the Holy Roman Empire. Excellence may be more significant than bigness.

Should people of serious purpose realize the extent to which the local community is the seed bed of civilization, the source of basic character and culture, as well as the medium for their preservation and transmission, then, within their communities, they might be sowing the seeds and cultivating the growth of a better future. The slowness of this process may seem discouraging, yet to expect quicker results may be wishful dreaming — a common cause of cynical despair. One sees everywhere frustration and disillusionment among young people as they measure their small individual powers against vast world currents. Could they see clearly the process by which the future is made and the opportunities they have to share in the making, they would have compelling reasons for a sense of significance and validity for their lives.

Great civilizations rise and fall, and when they fall it is to the level of the small rural communities. . . .

Many times in history urban civilizations have broken down, leaving society to rebuild, largely from the village level. Should there be a breakdown in the present social order, the small community is the seed bed from which a new order would have to grow. If it now deteriorates by neglect and by being robbed of its best quality, the new order will not be excellent. Whoever increases the excellence and stability of small communities sets limits to social retrogression.

Though the art and practice of community life are vital to social progress, during historic times the small community nearly always has been neglected. All rural America has been skimmed of its material wealth and of its human quality to feed the insatiable city. The small community has been despised as something to escape from to the larger, better life of the city. The typical American farm village has become little more than a local market, and a location for church and school. The mining town has been drearier still — rows of shacks along the sides of a gully; and the usual factory town, or quarry, fishing, or lumbering village, has been little better. That is an epitome of the old story of neglect and exploitation of the small community, the killing of the goose that lays the golden egg. Do we not have here one of the major causes of the slow progress of humanity in civilization?

Many an American small town or village is no longer a community. Too often it is only a small city, the citizens largely going their individual ways. This progressive disappearance of the community in present-day life is one of the most disturbing phenomena of modern history. It constitutes an historic crisis.

The community need not disappear. The very changes which are destroying it have put into our hands means for re-creating it in a finer pattern. Seldom in modern times has the small community caught a glimpse of its possibilities. Today for the first time it can be abreast or ahead of the city in convenience of living. If we use the present time of social and economic transition as an opportunity, the disappearance of the old community need be no disaster. But there is little time to lose, for with its passing some fine cultural traditions are being broken; and with human culture as with the human breed, if we have no children we cannot transmit our inheritance to grandchildren.

If many young people, searching for careers of significance and adventure, should see the small community as the place where basic human culture is preserved and transmitted, and should seek careers there, the results might be more important than failure or success of any present political or economic movement; and enduring satisfactions along the way might be very real. Many rural callings provide economic footholds of such careers.

In every phase of community life there is room for research, invention, discovery, and for the patient development of community spirit. There one deals with basic realities. There, as a rule, no false appearance of success blinds one to the necessity and the difficulty of the elemental process of developing good will, mutual respect, fair play, co-operation, thrift, and competence.

Suppose a man or woman living in a small community wishes to work for its development. What can he or she do? First it is necessary to get a clear vision of the new community as an all-round, well-proportioned society in which human relations are fine and sound, and where all the elemental needs of men can be met, together with a vision of the place of such communities in larger societies. The poverty of the average small American town or village is not wholly due to shortcomings of economic and political systems. In large part it results from lack of such a vision.

There are many opportunities for community service. Much work is needed in community economics. Fine culture does not thrive best amid starvation or squalor. The community needs help to appraise its economic needs and resources, to plan through the years to achieve sound economic balance. There are unfilled needs for community services, the supplying of which would provide community careers. There are similar opportunities in vocational guidance, in recreation, in developing community libraries, in musical and dramatic programs, in working out recognized community ethics and standards, in promoting community health, and in improving public administration.

America is waking to the meaning of the community, and to its present danger. During the last decade about three hundred communities in the United States, nearly half of them in California, have established "community councils." Each socially-minded organization in a community — such as the Parent-Teachers Association, the Chamber of Commerce, the service clubs, the trades and the labor councils, the Y.M.C.A., the several churches, the juvenile court, and the school board — appoints one member to a central council. Through suitable committees this organization keeps in touch with all vital community interests, brings neglected issues to the attention of those responsible or to the public, or directly undertakes the necessary service. This new invention of democracy promises to be a powerful instrument for community welfare, though as yet its workings are often crude, superficial, and restricted. . . .

Many country ministers are helping to build up their communities in health, housing, and income, and especially in neighborly community spirit. . . .

The community, by means of free inquiry and common aspiration, must achieve a common view of a total way of life, and a common discipline. Only to the extent that it does so is it actually a community. That way of life must grow by the democratic process of voluntary general agreement. It will be influenced by leadership, both local and general, by knowledge of what other communities have done, by literature, art, science, and religion, and by everyday experience. Never will a community be united on everything, yet it must be aware of the standards on which it is substantially united, and which its members can be expected to support. In the ancient community the common way of life was fully understood, deeply entrenched, and generally observed; so questions arose in marginal cases only. The flux of modern life has largely erased these common values from the community mind. They must be re-established by conscious, intelligent, critical search, by example, and by teaching.

Community well-being requires a spirit of open, full, free inquiry, with no organization or sect claiming supreme merit, authority, or revelation, or plotting to capture community loyalty for its peculiar doctrines. Many an American community has had its unity disrupted by the strategy of political or religious ideologies, some claiming to be sole repositories of truth. A real community can emerge only when there is sincere recognition of the fact that ultimate truth or wisdom is not given to any sect or class or organization, but that all alike should be open-minded seekers.

The new community can be something new under the sun. It can recover the precious qualities of the old, the fellow feeling, acquaintance, good will, mutual respect, planning and working together for common ends. But it need not lose the contributions of the new day. It can escape the narrowness and provincialism of the old village. It must have clearing-houses for the exchange of ideas and experience.

The new community will not try to monopolize the whole life of its members, as did the ancient village. While it endeavors to satisfy those cravings for common purpose and united neighborly effort which modern life neglects, its members will use many other forms of association — national societies, trade unions, churches, universities, nation-wide industries, and the national government. While co-operating heartily with various federal agencies, it will firmly maintain its individuality and autonomy, and will not be swallowed up in grasping, characterless uniformity of far-flung, centralized government bureaucracy. The community, if it is wise and vigorous, need not be eclipsed, but can be richer, sounder, finer, for its contacts with the wide world. For thousands of young people who seek a way to leave their imprint on their own and on future times, there is room to take part in such adventures. But neither that vision, nor general interest in it, will come suddenly. It must be slowly won.

For the preservation and transmission of the fundamentals of civilization, vigorous, wholesome community life is imperative. Unless many people live and work in the intimate relationships of community life, there never can emerge a truly unified nation, or a community of mankind. If I do not love my neighbor whom I know, how can I love the human race, which is but an abstraction? If I have not learned to work with a few people, how can I be effective with many?

While recognizing that there are at least potential social and political values inherent in local self-government, as set forth by the writers of the preceding selections, there are those who suggest that this theorizing can be carried too far. Changing times and circumstances inevitably demand changes in political institutions which, though different, need not be less democratic. Surely, they say, there must at least be a minimum limit of size and population for a community which can claim significant advantages. Professor Martin here casts a critical eye upon our practice of unquestioning acceptance of traditional doctrines. The authors of the next selection then argue vigorously that the much discussed problems and shortcomings of the American states are not primarily institutional or structural, but in fact result from a lack of "timeliness" — the unrealistic persistence of the small-town approach to the needs of an urbanized mid-twentieth century America.

3

Grass Roots Government:

An Appraisal

By Roscoe C. Martin

IN THIS ESSAY it is proposed to evaluate rural government in terms of structure, administration, and the practice of democracy. Due to the long-standing habit, especially among those predisposed toward local government, of confusing grass-roots government with local democracy, and even of identifying the one with the other, it is necessary to emphasize that it is *rural government* which is under appraisal. There is a distinct tendency to construe a criticism of local government as an attack on democracy, and so by a not unnatural inversion to defend democracy in terms of the prevailing structure and practice of local government. This habit of thought, which stems direct from the tenets of Jeffersonian agrarianism, straitjackets democracy in a mold which was set a century and a half ago, and precludes discussion of that subject as a live and vital thing.

It is the thesis here that democracy and rural local government not only can be analyzed independently but that they are indeed completely separate things. Democracy is to be weighed in terms appropriate to a particular day or age. So is rural government, if it is to be viewed realistically. To the extent that grass-roots government has adapted itself to changing social, economic, and political requirements, it has, it may be supposed, equipped itself to serve positively the cause of democracy; but to the extent that it has resisted adaptation to mid-twentieth century needs, it may well have become anti-democratic in content and effect. In any event, the champions of grass-roots government must not be allowed to identify themselves as being *ipso facto* the defenders of de-

mocracy, and the only true defenders. Such champions, in fact, often will be discovered on examination to be defenders of the *status quo*. The marriage between little government and democracy thus becomes a device, though sometimes an unconscious one, by which the rural "fortress of anachronistic privileges" is defended in terms of principles dear to the nation. The principles of democracy are indeed traditional and enduring, but their invocation in defense of a particular political institution is a dangerous thing.

Apart from the unwarranted employment of democracy in defense of rural government, there is credible authority for the proposition that democracy and local government are mutually antagonistic. De Tocqueville was among those who early maintained that the government in a democratic nation ". . . must be more uniform, more centralized, more extensive, more searching, and more efficient than in other countries." A present-day student developed this thesis in a recent article, maintaining that democracy is by definition broad in view, equalitarian, majoritarian, unitarian; it emphasizes the social whole, avoiding the atomization which necessarily follows the interposition of any intermediary between the state and the individual. Local government, on the other hand, is a phenomenon of differentiation and individualization; it represents and seeks to strengthen separate social groups enjoying a measure of autonomy which sometimes becomes virtual independence. Democracy and local government are therefore in an important sense antithetical; ". . . the incompatibility of democratic principle with the practice of decentralization is a phenomenon so evident that it may be considered as a kind of sociological law."*

It is not necessary to accept this view in order to justify question of the logic by which rural government is equated with democracy. One may stop far short of the position assumed by Langrod and still conclude that the arrogation of all democratic virtues by the champions of grass-roots government is presumptuous and indefensible. The focus of the present discussion is on rural government, not on democracy. If the practice of rural government emerges somewhat the worse from this analysis, as almost inevitably it must, it will be well always to remember where the emphasis lies. . . .

. . . The great majority . . . [of rural local governments] find all excepting the most rudimentary services, and these performed in quite elementary fashion, beyond their resources. . . .

The outlook for rural government is no brighter with respect to administrative organization and procedure. Sound fiscal administration is beyond the reach

From Roscoe C. Martin, *Grass Roots* (University, Alabama: University of Alabama Press, 1957), pp. 42–44, 54–70. Three footnotes in original omitted. Reprinted by permission of the publisher.

---

* Georges Langrod, "Local Government and Democracy," *Public Administration,* Vol. XXXI (Spring, 1953), 25–34.

of the minor units. The part-time, amateur character of the rural functionary militates against development of a professional public service. So does the method of compensation, which would be totally inadequate if competent service were demanded or expected. Nor is the method of selection calculated to ensure choice of competent personnel. Local officers and employees, including specifically most of the chief administrative officials of the county, are chosen by popular vote, which virtually all students agree is not the best way to fill a position whose duties require technical competence. The system by which the duties and responsibilities of office are divided, both through the fragmentation of functions within a unit and through duplication with overlying areas, likewise is destructive of the environment in which a competent and professionally motivated public service might thrive. Another aspect of the same problem is found in the lack of integration among the various segments of the administrative organization. In short, there is regrettably little of professional spirit or conduct in the affairs of grass-roots government. The administrative structure is ill-organized and poorly manned, while the procedures and systems of public management are largely alien to the rural scene.

What is required more than any other one thing for the administrative rehabilitation of rural government is a system which will command the confidence and respect of the citizen. A government which has no important services to perform, or which does not have resources adequate to its needs, or which is so inconsequential that it must content itself with part-time and amateur service, or which is satisfied to drift along an administrative channel marked out a century ago and not changed since, or which approaches the public's problems timidly and half-heartedly, or which shares responsibilities with a dozen or a hundred other units and agencies—such a government will not enjoy because it will not have earned the confidence of the people. The first and most important lesson to be learned about grass-roots democracy is that local government, like government at other levels, must be strong, energetic, and well supported if it is to discharge with satisfaction the duties which modern conditions impose upon it. Grass-roots government unhappily does not now answer that description, notwithstanding the pervasive mythology to the contrary.

Rural government and democracy

It appears from the foregoing that very large numbers of local governments are too small and weak to operate efficiently in administrative terms. It is appropriate to inquire whether these same units may not also be too small to be effectively democratic. What

could the towns of Glastonbury (population seven) and Somerset (population twenty), Vermont, do that would be of any real significance? Each was dominated by one family, and each was entitled to its representative in the state legislative body. The representative of one failed to put in an appearance for the whole of a legislative session; the representative of the other, however, was on hand every meeting day to protect his family's right to representation — and to the taxes paid (nominally to the town, but actually to the family) by the power company. Both of these towns were disestablished by the General Assembly twenty years ago, but not until long after they (and others like them) had brought the honorable tradition of town government in New England to disrepute. One of the things most needed to permit a reasoned judgment of the grass-roots practice of democracy is an examination of the folklore enveloping the subject.

It will prove useful to begin with an analysis of the tacit (sometimes the explicit) assumption of the devotees of agrarian democracy that Lilliputian government is more democratic *per se* than big government. The argument runs thus: government to be democratic must be close to the people; little government is close to the people, and the smaller it is the closer it is; therefore the smaller the units of government and the larger their number the greater the degree of democracy. A companion line holds that little government tends to be more democratic than big government because it lacks the incentive, the resources, and the power to be otherwise; it is democratic, so to speak, by default.

A 1955 Census publication (*State Distribution of Public Employment in 1954*) provides an interesting basis for speculation on this subject. It reads in part:

The range for State governments (full-time equivalent) in October 1954 was from 45 [employees] per 10,000 [inhabitants] for Illinois up to 177 per 10,000 for North Carolina. The range for local government employment was from 58 per 10,000 in North Carolina up to 265 per 10,000 in New York State.

In 1952 North Carolina had 106 special districts, Illinois 1,546, New York 968; North Carolina had no school districts, while Illinois had 3,484 and New York 2,915; North Carolina had no township governments, Illinois had 1,433 and New York 932. The conclusion to be drawn from these figures, within the framework of traditional thinking about rural government, is clear: North Carolina's government is less close to the people and therefore is less democratic than that of either Illinois or New York.

One who looks beneath the surface will reject this proposition both as being too pat and as resting upon inadequate evidence. It is true that in relation to population North Carolina has the largest number of state employees and the smallest number of local employees of any state in the union. This is attributable largely to the fact that in North Carolina the state government has assumed primary responsibility for a number of important functions traditionally left largely to the localities, among them public school administration and road construction and maintenance. With the passing of administrative responsibility from the local units (principally the counties) to the state has gone a shift in the incidence of public employment, though so far as the testimony at hand reveals without adverse effect on the practice of democracy in the state. It is also true that North Carolina has comparatively few units of government (608 as compared with Illinois' 7,723 and New York's 5,483). This fact, however, will hardly support the generalization that government in that state is less democratic than elsewhere—than in Illinois or New York, specifically. On the contrary, students of local government would maintain that North Carolina has taken a significant step along the path leading to local democracy by moving to clear away the undergrowth to make government visible to the citizen.

It must be concluded that smallness in size and multiplicity in number of rural governments provide neither a guarantee of the existence of nor a standard for measuring the effectiveness of local democracy. There are other and more meaningful criteria, among them the nature of popular participation, the representativeness of policy-making bodies, and the kind and efficacy of the control exercised over administrative officials. The relationship between the degree of democracy and the complexity of local governmental machinery is much more likely to be inverse than direct.

Second among the hallowed articles of faith is the tradition that the local community serves as the "schoolroom for democracy."* As a writer in a recent issue of the *National Municipal Review* put it, "The value of democracy is not open to question in this discussion. Assuming its virtue, there is little doubt that the most effective training ground for democracy lies in the field of local self-government." Here is the doctrine, naked and unadorned. It is worthy of analysis.

The author makes two basic assumptions. The first, that democracy is virtuous, few will wish to challenge; but the second, concerning the effectiveness of local self-government as a training ground for democracy, may be open to question. The assumption is that the citizen learns about democracy from participation in the affairs of local government. But what does he learn and how does he learn it? What is the curriculum offered? Who are the faculty?

What are the teaching and learning materials? To answer some of these questions, let it be noted that the citizen learns only about local affairs — that is, provincial and parochial affairs, that his teachers are small-time politicians and part-time functionaries, and that the courses of study are village pump politics and strictly amateur administration. The value of this kind of knowledge imparted in this fashion to the students of democracy is doubtful. The citizen so schooled in local government may develop a keen sense for sectional and special interests, but except by accident he will not graduate with a perceptive grasp of government in any broad or meaningful sense. Further, he is more than likely to emerge with a permanent bias against big government, and particularly against the federal government of the United States. The average grass-roots government as a schoolroom for democracy may be compared with the one-room public school, which is assailed on every hand by professional educators and which is sharply on the decline.

An important aspect of the "training ground" argument is found in the notion that persons trained in the rural arena go on to achieve renown on larger stages and before greater audiences. This assumption may be valid up to a point: it may well be that large numbers of state legislators gain their initial experience in public life from local office. Of the 31 state governors listed in *Who's Who* in 1954, however, only eleven confessed to previous local experience. Two-thirds therefore came to the gubernatorial office through other than local channels. Of the 96 United States senators in 1955, more than two-thirds (67) reported no experience in local government. Among the members of the House of Representatives, 71 per cent had had no experience as local office-holders. These figures do not dispose of the onward-and-upward argument, but they do suggest that the assumption on which the point rests deserves to be questioned. Grass-roots government as the Little Green Schoolhouse of democracy is another aspect of the agrarian mythology which requires re-examination.

Yet another phase of the myth concerns citizen participation in local affairs, both as candidate for public office and as voter. It appears to be generally assumed that non-participation poses no problem at the grass roots. A spokesman of the United States Department of Agriculture recently opined that "if all farmers could be members of a county land-use planning committee, planning would be entirely democratic as it is in some New England town meetings." In some town meetings maybe, but not in all, and perhaps in simple fact not in many. The New England town has played a prominent role in song and story for more than three centuries as America's chief exemplar of local democracy. Yet even in colonial times some of the towns found cause to question the

---

* The Little Green Schoolhouse, shall we call it, in succession to the Little Red Schoolhouse.

presumed warmth of local patriotism. Boston, as a single example, was driven to levy a fine of ten pounds on any person who without good cause refused, having been elected, to serve as constable. In latter days, the problem of non-participation in town affairs has in many instances been acute. A credible reporter describes a town meeting which, with 700 adult citizens qualified to take part, was attended by 110 citizens who came and stayed most of the day. That is a participation figure of 15.7 per cent. An additional ninety citizens dropped by during the day to cast a vote on this or that issue and, having voted, went away. If these ninety are added to the original 110, total participation comes to 29 per cent; but were the ninety casual droppers-by participants in town affairs in any real sense? They were instead special pleaders who came in to vote on a single issue; their concern was a particular, fragmental one, and it may be argued with some logic that the cause of town government would have been better served and a consensus of citizen opinion more accurately recorded had these ninety remained at home with their special interests and left the decisions to those who came and stayed through the day.

It would, of course, be erroneous to suppose that the problem of non-participation is a sectional one. An article in the *New York Times Magazine* some time ago carried the telling title, "Nobody Wants to be Town Clerk." "The people don't seem to understand the problems of town government," the author said of his Ohio town of 3,500 inhabitants. "Ninety-five per cent of the people don't even know who is on the Town Council. All official meetings are open to the public, but they seldom come to see what's going on." It is invidious to cite a particular illustration, for the reason that citizen non-participation is an almost universal phenomenon. Note was made earlier of the fact that farmer participation in the various local committees sponsored by the United States Department of Agriculture fell off sharply after the novelty of the committee system wore off. The apathy of the voter is widespread, and is alleviated only where an occasional scandal finds its way into the campaign or a flamboyant individual emerges as a candidate.

This does not mean that the attempted practice of democracy should be abandoned; it does not necessarily mean, indeed, that democracy does not exist even in the localities where citizen non-participation is most pronounced. A recent article in *Harper's Magazine* bore the provocative title, "Let's Not Get Out The Vote." The burden of its argument was that the citizen is not duty-bound to vote, but that he is obligated to acquaint himself with the candidates and the issues if he does vote. Voter action or inaction is only one of the several criteria appropriate to an evaluation of the workings of democracy. For pres-

ent purposes, however, attention is centered on the fact that there is a marked lack of citizen enthusiasm for voting at the grass-roots level. The Little Green Schoolhouse is badly in need of a truant officer.

Another cause for concern over democracy as it is practiced in rural government arises from the representative system, and on two principal counts. First, the legislative bodies are not representative; and second, the procedures are neither democratic themselves nor productive of democratic results. As to the first, most legislative bodies, local and otherwise, consist of representatives elected by districts. This is true, for example, of the typical rural county court (or board of commissioners or supervisors). In the states of the Middle West the township is the election district; in the South it is the precinct, or "beat." Everywhere, however, the result is the same: district-sized men are elected to the county governing body, with the consequence that a "county legislature" prevails. This means that county problems are viewed through myopic local eyes. It means, for example, that bridges must be scattered about the county in accordance with the residence of the commissioners; it means that roads are parceled out the same way; it means that a commissioner will seize "his" road machinery with a firm grasp and refuse to allow it to be used outside his own district. It means finally, and of course most importantly, that the interests of the county are lost in those of the individual election districts.

Other illustrations of faulty representative bodies can be found both below and above the county: the state legislature is a prime example of an important body normally dominated by district-minded members. . . . The rural-urban inequity is more striking in the case of the state legislature than in that of local representative bodies, but is by no means without example in grass-roots government.

Yet another aspect of the representative system which is worthy of note concerns the procedures employed in the legislatures. In South Carolina, to cite a single example, the state legislature is dominated by the various county delegations, as it is, indeed, in most states where the county is an important unit. In South Carolina, however, the hold of the counties on their representatives and of the county delegations in turn on the legislature appears to be particularly strong. As evidence, it may be noted that most of the measures passed by the legislature are local in import: of all bills passed over a period of 24 years recently ended, 83.9 per cent were local measures. Friday is the day set aside during a legislative session for consideration of local and uncontested matters. The question of a quorum by general agreement is never raised on that day, and a mere handful in each house proceeds to enact local measures. According to a recent count of a number of Friday meetings, the median meeting time for the House was six minutes.

The Senate normally met for somewhat longer, though there was no effort in either house to give local bills any real consideration. They were passed by courtesy at the request of local delegations. Among the measures proposed by the 46 county delegations are the annual supply bills, one for each county. These bills are drafted by the delegations after local hearings and are passed as a matter of routine action by the legislature, almost always without question.

How democratic is a government whose legislative body is palpably unrepresentative in any real sense and whose practice is deliberately designed to serve the desires of ward and district delegates? Such a body is in fact more a congress of ambassadors than a legislative assembly. The system operates on the unspoken premise that what the five (or 25) county commissioners desire individually will add up to what is best for the county as a whole, that the 46 particularistic programs of the several county delegations in the aggregate will constitute a sound general legislative program for the state. It is not clear where responsibility for the welfare of the county or the state as a whole lies under this theory of representative government, but clearly it does not reside in any real sense in the representative body.

Concerning politics at the grass roots, it must be emphasized that political activities are in no wise the exclusive preserve of big government. In popular fancy the ultimate in politics is found in the manipulation of "the machine" by "the boss." The very concepts suggest the local character of machine politics. It is difficult to imagine the existence of either a national political machine or a national boss; statewide machines and bosses, indeed, have been rare phenomena. The natal place of party is the locality, where political organizations find a hospitable environment and where the phrase grass roots, in respect of politics, has tangible meaning. The notorious organizations in the past have been typically the big city (and county) machines, their managers the "bosses" of the muckrakers and their followers. Not less than three times in the last five years have the newspapers characterized a particular politician (a different one in each instance) as "the last of the big city bosses." The implication is clear that the supply of old-line urban machine politicians is running low.

Not so the supply of rural bosses, who continue in full production — and often in full command of tightly organized, highly disciplined machines. There must be, and there must always have been, a hundred nameless grass-roots bosses for every big city boss who found his way into the headlines. The case of the judge of a small southern county (1950 population somewhat more than 20,000) is instructive. That official, who had held a variety of local offices over a period of years and had served as county judge for twelve years at the time these facts were recorded, was complete and unquestioned arbiter of local affairs. He arranged candidates for county offices, supervised elections to the end that there should be no recorded defections, referred patronizingly (but accurately) to "his" tax collector and "his" commissioners' court, operated his own personal system of poor relief, and so conducted the business of the county and the affairs of the local Democratic Party that they were virtually indistinguishable. So great was the faith of his associates in his leadership that there had not been a single dissenting vote on a matter brought before the commissioners' court in the twelve years of his tenure as county judge. "In every village," Sir Robert Peel once foretold, "there will arise some miscreant, to establish the most grinding tyranny by calling himself the people." This is a harsh prophecy, and one hardly confirmed by our example; but it sounds a warning not to be ignored. Grass-roots governments have their machines and their bosses, too. And to paraphrase a Chinese proverb, a small black spot is not less black than a large black spot.

Machines and bosses apart, rural government is permeated by politics. One of the Public Administration cases relates the story of a county agricultural conservation program committee which crossed swords with an influential rancher on the question of the latter's compliance or non-compliance with a ranch management plan previously approved by the committee. The local contest ended in a draw, and the rancher's neighbors of the county committee were glad enough to buck the case up to the state committee for final decision. In the *Rutland Herald* (Vermont) of November 10, 1946, the writer of a letter to the editor made some remarks on the subject of politics in Vermont town government. In the first place, he said, with 525 voters (in the town of Danby) and only thirty town officers to be elected, one would think that it would not be necessary to elect one man to two offices. Not so, however, for two or three justices of the peace also serve as selectmen. This means that, as holders of one office, they count the ballots for the other, for which they themselves are candidates. This struck the writer as not wholly democratic. He had yet a second cause for complaint: that the Republican candidates for justice of the peace were nominated at a party caucus which was so secret that he (the letter writer) had been unable to find out when and where it was to be held, though as a Republican and prospective participant he had made a special effort to learn. The effect of this disclosure was so unpleasant, the writer continued, that when ". . . one of our town officers informed me that I had been appointed as assistant ballot-clerk for Tuesday's election, . . . I told him I wanted to accommodate a fellow I am working for who is building a barn" and so could not serve. What more graceful way to "take a walk" in rural Vermont?

A contemporary observer has written revealingly of politics in the conduct of the affairs of a rural irrigation district of the Far West. The first three years of a recent five-year period, he reports, ". . . witnessed a county grand jury probe and indictment, a recall election, an outbreak of fisticuffs at a board session, numerous mass meetings, hirings, firings, charges and counter-charges. In the fourth year there were demands for reinstatement of a dismissed bookkeeper and accusations by him regarding the . . . holding of tea parties on district time, overcharges of a considerable number of water users, and negligence in the collection of . . . bills. Meanwhile his successor was jailed on the charge of grand theft. . . . Soon thereafter a recall was started against a director. . . . In the fifth year the manager was dismissed and the post filled on a temporary basis. . . ."

It is clear that the traditional concept of intimate, tranquil, personal, "non-political" little government by friends and neighbors, while an idyllic one, is not always or necessarily in accord with fact. The rural atmosphere is such, indeed, as to invite the familiar personal relationships which, whether so recognized or so called, form the essence of grass-roots political ties. Among larger units, the requirements of a budget, an accounting system, maintenance of detailed records, competitive purchasing, and (often) appointment by merit under civil service regulations tend to regularize and record these relationships. So does the lively competition of active political organizations, which makes access to public favor both more systematic and more difficult. There are relatively few trammels on political activity at the grass roots, where the lack of formal restraints is matched by the absence of political inhibitions. The difference between politics in big government and politics in little government is largely quantitative in character: in kind, politics in rural government is pretty much like politics everywhere else. It may not be any worse in its consequences for democracy, generally speaking, but almost certainly it is no better.

In general summary, the shibboleths which surround the whole subject of rural government and democracy need to be called into question. Some of the more pervasive among them may be listed:

1. That frequent elections will result in a more democratic government than infrequent elections; that short terms of office will ensure a democratic system.

2. That the closer to the people a government is, the more democratic it is; that the popular election of many administrative officials, together with a frequent turnover in appointive officers, will bring about the desired closeness to the people and so will be conducive to democracy.

3. That a representative body elected by districts is more democratic than one whose members are elected at large.

4. That a representative chosen from a small district will more truly represent his constituency than one elected from a large district.

5. That a large legislative or governing body (for example, a county board) is more representative (that is, more democratic) than a small one.

6. That big politics is more subject to boss control and therefore is more to be feared than little politics.

7. That big government is (a) more impersonal and less human; (b) less subject to popular control; (c) more subject to political control; (d) more out of touch with local conditions; (e) less flexible; (f) more bureaucratic; and therefore for all these reasons, (g) less democratic than grass-roots government.

These propositions, or some of them, may have been sound at one time, as indeed some (or all) may be valid now; but their validity is no longer to be granted without question. The assumption of the mantle of virtue in the name of grass-roots democracy has gone too long unchallenged. That there is much that is virtuous in rural government may be allowed, but a realistic appraisal places grass-roots performance at least a step this side of the perfection claimed for it by its more unrestrained admirers.

Virtually all who write and speak of democracy agree on the proposition that "government must be kept close to the people." Accepting this dictum, a question nevertheless must be raised as to how the desired end is to be accomplished. By what standards of measurement may government, or a given unit of government, be said to be close to or far from the people? What units and what organization shall be reckoned adequate to represent and to speak for the people? What are the procedures for bringing and keeping the government close to the people? Of equal importance is the question, how may government "close to the people" be made viable in operational terms? The nature of the challenge is clear enough: it is to contrive a system of rural government that will be able to render prompt and energetic service without loss of responsibility to or contact with the people, that will be both efficient and democratic.

4

Why Our State Governments Are Sick

*By Charles Press and
Charles R. Adrian*

STATE GOVERNMENTS ARE SICK. In recent years there have been exposés of prison riots, snake-pit mental facilities, "death trap" and "speed trap" highway traffic regulations, state mining regulations, court and police procedures, and out-dated divorce laws. Almost every year someone attracts attention by writing a book critical of one of the activities for which state government has responsibility. Those who defend state governments must apologize for such practices as those of legislators in New Hampshire who hire out as ushers at race tracks; or for the wholesale turnover of state personnel that occurs after an election in border states such as Kentucky and West Virginia; or for the generally weak performance of Southern governors (as compared with many Southern mayors) in response to the school integration order of the Supreme Court. These examples are not representative of universal state practices, but they are common enough to place state government a poor second when specialists make a comparison of quality between it and Federal or most municipal government operations. A decade ago President Eisenhower said he wished to return a number of governmental functions to the states. Not only professional Democrats greeted his proposal as a "give-away" of the nation's resources; many others assumed that substituting state for Federal supervision would mean a shift from regulation in the interest of consumers to that of producers.

Certainly the weaknesses plaguing state governments can not all be traced to one source. Some result from the operation of a federal system. Competition among states tends to drive standards to the level of the lowest common denominator and encourages cut-rate practices such as Nevada's gambling and divorce industries. A good many of the worst weaknesses of state government, however, are unnecessary.

These recognized shortcomings, we believe, are traceable to the failure of state governments to reflect the modern viewpoints held by a large majority of their citizens. We charge that ideas dominant among the decision makers for state governments lack *timeliness*. By this we mean that the ideology to which decision makers are beholden is not appropriate as a yardstick against which to judge proposed public policies for today because it is appropriate for a rural, small town, pre-industrial society rather than for our contemporary urban society. Furthermore, it is outmoded because many of its assumptions are based on folk beliefs rather than on the scientific study of psychology, psychiatry, economics, engineering, and other fields that have advanced rapidly in recent decades. (Advocates of the archaic small-town ideology, we should add, are not necessarily themselves small-town dwellers. They may live in large cities or in suburbs. Despite their urban life experiences, some persons, because of career success which they attribute to the older ideology, to childhood teachings, to early life in a small town, to a deliberate revolt against urbanism, or to lack of education, subscribe to the belief system of the small town.) The concepts of reality that dominate policy making in most states are out-of-date by at least half a century.

Crisis amid plenty

Daily headlines announce that a number of states are in financial difficulties. Indiana and Ohio recently cut back services severely to live within their income, while in New Jersey until a short time ago both parties had planks in their platforms opposing any new taxes. The posture of state legislatures in respect to taxes illustrates well the quality of their guiding ideologies. Meat-axe economizing is occurring at a time when, as John Kenneth Galbraith has illustrated, the private economy is full of frills. But to hear some state politicians tell it, one would imagine their state park, library, and water pollution budgets must be cut to the bone to head off widspread starvation, to keep tax-impoverished citizens out of soup lines, to prevent the ride over the hill to the poorhouse. To argue this way is patent foolishness in an economy where motor boat sales are skyrocketing, people feel deprived unless they own a movie camera, and student cars on high school and university parking lots are shinier and newer than those owned by many of their teachers. The last time such nonsense was taken seriously was in the 1920's.

Michigan has received a good deal of publicity for its financial sickness, and it provides a case study for the diagnosis of the disease. The state entered the post-war period with a tidy treasury surplus. In 1946 a constitutional amendment took two and one-half cents of the three-cent state sales tax and handed it

Charles Press and Charles R. Adrian, "Why Our State Governments Are Sick," *Antioch Review*, Summer, 1964, pp. 149–165. Reprinted by permission of the authors and the publisher.

over to the cities, villages, townships, and school districts, which were then in serious financial trouble. Within a few years, however, the state encountered financial difficulties. Several times attempts were made to increase state revenues, but almost always the governor and the state Senate could not agree on a tax program. In 1959, when crisis could no longer be sidestepped, they fought each other in a year-long, nationally publicized battle. State bills went unpaid, and some state employees had a paycheck delayed. After a year of struggle, one cent was added to the state sales tax. It is clear that this was not enough, for the state immediately began to suffer from an austerity budget under which universities turned away qualified students, the mental health program (especially rehabilitation of patients) was seriously set back, and a reduction in personnel was made necessary in many agencies, including the state police.

Common explanations for these developments include the argument that there was "too much" party competition, or that the state was a "welfare paradise," or that Michigan had a worker-oriented government which lacked "good business sense." At the heart of the deadlock, however, was an ideological clash. A spokesman for one side was Governor G. Mennen Williams, who was first elected in 1948 and who served an unprecedented six terms in office. He and his Democratic cohorts ran on a platform calling for personal and corporate income taxes. Steadily through the 1950's the Democrats gained strength in state government. After the election in 1958 the score on state offices filled by election was as follows: the Democrats had captured every executive office, held a top-heavy majority on the four statewide boards dealing with education, a majority on the Supreme Court, and an even split in the House, which was apportioned so as to give smaller districts roughly an eight-seat bonus. Few party organizations can claim a popular mandate of this extent, and perhaps for this reason Williams and his Democratic following felt justified in fighting for their program. Nevertheless, the state Senate had a twenty-two to twelve Republican majority. Democrats pointed out that their twelve members represented more citizens than the twenty-two Republicans and that the twelve Democrats had received more total votes than the twenty-two Republicans, but this line of argument did not make the latter more willing to compromise.

The Senate battled mightily with the Governor in the manner of the House of Lords fighting the wrong-headed popular majority—and easily won the war. A legislative sales-tax plan was finally adopted because the state desperately needed more funds.

Representation of political traditions

The composition of most state legislatures is defended because it is representative of both area and population. (The idea is, incidentally, one borrowed from the Federal government where it seems to work well.) Yet, almost every state can provide startling examples of "rotten boroughs" based on area representation. In Vermont, a town with less than a hundred residents has the same representation as the state's largest city, a difference in representation of about 600 to one. New Jersey provides a classic case, for the price of its post-war constitution of 1947 was leaving the state Senate undisturbed. In this body each county has one representative: Cape May, with a population of less than 40,000 has the same number of legislators as Essex County, with a population approaching one million.

Why is the national government not faced with the same problem concerning timeliness? Each state has two senators. The 1960 ratio at its extreme between New York and Nevada was 122 to one. As League of Women Voters spokeswomen are fond of saying, when 122 voters in New York equal one in Nevada, the situation is "obviously unfair and undemocratic." Yet the system works reasonably well in terms of the timeliness of legislation, and few seriously suggest changing it. The usual justification for the Senate's representative ratio takes the form of legal mumbo-jumbo; states, the argument goes, are semi-sovereign, while counties or other sub-units of a state are not. But this seems to us to sidestep the crucial point.

The United States Senate, despite its lack of mathematical equality in representation, comes fairly close to representing the mood of the nation—closer, many would argue, than the House of Representatives, which was intended to represent population. The United States Senate is, in fact, *timely*. Only a minority of its members could be described as of the group that had to be "dragged, kicking and screaming, into the twentieth century," as Adlai Stevenson once put it.

Turning to the states, one finds a different picture. There the unapportioned house commonly is dominated by "the old guard," which is likely to boast that its members are "watch-dogs of the treasury." In an inspired phrase, the journalist and lobbyist Olga Moore once described a legislator from among this group in her home state of Wyoming as having a "look of consecrated negativism." Most of these long-time stalwarts probably have little to worry about in elections. Leon Epstein, in a study of Wisconsin, found that the safe districts (which he defined as consistently favoring one party by over sixty per cent of the vote) were also those districts that had few primary fights. These are generally the kinds of districts the legislative old guard represents.

Because of a lack of apportionment, a small minority in the state becomes a top-heavy majority in its legislature. What kind of minority is over-represented? Clearly it is that of the small-town and agricultural minority devoted to a belief system that was popularly dominant prior to the Great Depression, but that has since become an atypical ideology. Duane Lockard, writing of Rhode Island, noted that its state Senate was the last bastion of conservative Republican strength, but argued that this situation produced an advantage gained only by putting a millstone around the neck of the party. In Northern states this dominant legislative bloc is generally Republican while in Southern and Border states it is Democratic. In neither case, however, does it co-operate well with the state-wide leaders of its own party. In Florida, former Governor Leroy Collins faced the same kind of problem as did Governor Nelson Rockefeller in New York, though each was—on paper—being supported by a legislative majority from his own party.

Sometimes legislative leaders devoted to the small-town ideology test their personal strength in state-wide races. The results are revealing. In Michigan, for example, the state senator who quite appropriately claimed to have masterminded in 1959 the legislative torpedoing of an income tax sought to run for governor in 1960. He put a large mock torpedo on the top of his car and toured the state seeking votes in the Republican primary. The first election-year opinion poll published by the Detroit *News* reported he was the favorite of less than ten per cent of the Republican voters. Shortly afterwards he decided to drop out of the gubernatorial primary and leave the "modern" Republican unchallenged. Meanwhile the majority floor leader of the Senate announced that he was a member of the John Birch Society, a revelation that was not greeted with great enthusiasm by Republicans who were interested in seeking state-wide office.

The type of archaic ideology legislative leaders express is often carelessly defined and ascribed to farmers who are sometimes said to constitute a "hayseed brigade." The image is misleading. Most legislative leaders were born in and reside in small towns. They are lawyers, real estate dealers, insurance men, and merchants. Even where districts are primarily agricultural, the dirt farmer, who is himself unable to run for an office that would take him away from the land for increasingly long periods each year, often votes for a candidate from a nearby trading center. Most such legislators seem to have gotten their start in small-town government and at some time have held a county office. The county-seat connection may explain why so many of them are from one of the smaller rather than the middle-sized towns in the district. The distinction made here between farmer and small-town dweller is, we believe, of importance. The legislative oligarchy is recruited in most states from small-town fish who reflect a large image while cruising around in little ponds. The political traditions of the small-town environment have had a notable effect on state government, and they have consistently supported archaic beliefs. The farmer, unlike the village merchant, has for more than a century seen government as an institution that can aid the citizen with his problems. And while he is often suspicious of the big-city businessman and factory worker, he is also far more of an experimental empiricist than is the small-town dweller.

In the 1930's, a fight over the Supreme Court raged at the national level. The justices were attacked as "nine old men," though in fact some of the most conservative were not among the oldest. But after 1937, the Supreme Court became *timely* without changing its structure. It did so as a reaction to the Roosevelt "packing" plan and the blandishments of the Chief Justice, Charles Evans Hughes. It became much too timely, in fact, for the tastes of some observers. The legislatures need a similar kind of change toward timeliness if states are to take their place with national and municipal governments as units reflecting contemporary popular concerns. The problem is not necessarily one of apportioning on the basis of strict population. We can settle for some consideration of area in apportionment if only the viewpoints represented are evolved in response to twentieth-century conditions and problems. As matters now stand, most contemporary state legislatures have inherited the discarded mantle and way of thinking of the pre-1937 Supreme Court.

The choice of political traditions

The problem we have been discussing is one of viewpoint or political tradition. A political tradition is not easily changed; the ideas that are part of it have been formed as a result of life's experiences. When a political generation has undergone a period of trial under a novel set of conditions, the mood that results is worked into political programs, and if that political generation becomes a national majority, it is espoused by one of the major parties. This program is their definition of social justice and at the time of its birth purports to liberate the common man. Each of the important political eras of our history can be interpreted as the breakthrough of a new political generation, of its view of desirable public policies and of social justice.

An early political perspective that still has some relevance for state government was that formed on the frontier in the period of Andrew Jackson. Jackson, in 1824, received the most popular votes for the presidency but was denied the office by what he and his followers regarded as another manipulation of an Eastern Seaboard aristocracy. In 1828, he marshalled the newly enfranchised electorate of the common man to swamp the candidate of the East, John Quincy Adams. Jackson and his followers fashioned a political viewpoint that was meant to smash all political oligarchies before they had a chance to develop by applying the principle of rotation in office. State governments still bear the marks of this view: in the requirements for a great number of elected officials; frequent elections; short terms of office; laws against succession in office; and the spoils system of patronage, the moral justification of which is that no bureaucrat should ever feel he owns his office and that any citizen of ordinary intelligence is capable of handling any government job. Most people still respond somewhat favorably to the old Jacksonian rallying cries. They have lost most of their attractiveness, however, under the impact of changing conditions. Today we pay lip service to, but do not uncritically accept, these old theories, and this skepticism is but one step away from complete unbelief. We have reorganized most of our municipal governments, and the "little Hoover commissions" of the 1950's supported the rejection of Jacksonianism on the state level. The last remnants of the frontier view are to be found in the complex, much criticized governments of villages, townships, and counties.

The development of each new political ideology seems to follow the movement of the population frontier. Each set of ideas reflects the views of those who at the moment of its creation were the dynamic part of American society. By the end of the Civil War, a great part of the population had shifted from the wilderness to the small towns. As the potentialities of industrial society were revealed, their possibilities were seized upon by the new American majority, those living in the smaller cities and villages. The young men from these places built a new and mighty society for America and in the process formed a new political ideology.

The key to the small-town tradition is the Horatio Alger myth. Many a small-town boy has re-enacted it in detail: Thomas Edison, Will Rogers, Henry Ford, Harvey Firestone, together with an impressive number of presidents, governors, generals, and writers. The promise of this new ideology was that a young man could make good on nothing more than personal ability, pluck, thrift, hard work, and moral worth, with perhaps a little—but only a little—luck thrown in. The objective was not to find a safe and secure spot in some large organization but to be one's own boss and to succeed on one's own merits.

The attitude toward government that followed from this belief system was, of course, that government should not spoil the process by interfering with it or by making wasteful expenditures that would deplete the capital of the entrepreneur. If government did little more than its traditional functions of keeping order and enforcing civil contracts, leaving other decisions in private hands, the land would flow with milk, honey, and useful industrial artifacts such as automobiles, zippers, and packaged breakfast foods.

This political perspective blended with the older frontier view of distrust of the expert or professional.

It placed heavy reliance on conventional wisdom or "common sense." Especially in government, the virtuous amateur, or jack-of-all-trades, was trusted over the specialist with professional concepts or standards.

The small town is no longer dominant, however. The descendants of its entrepreneurs are now living in the metropolis or its suburbs. The cream of small-town creativity has soured as small-town vitality has diminished. The importance of this fact is so great for our subject that it will shortly be dealt with in more detail.

After the Horatio Alger ideology, the next political breakthrough came as Americans moved to the large city during and after World War I. The political budding of this majority was brought about by such men as Al Smith; it flowered in the New Deal. Samuel Lubell, in the *Future of American Politics,* has described how the elements of the Roosevelt coalition merged once they had been given impetus by the Great Depression. The experiences of those who lived in the cities led them to reject the small-town view as irrelevant and impractical. Urbanites embraced a social-service state ideology. The sons and daughters of urbanite immigrants believed that failure was not simply the consequence of personal inability or immorality. They felt that sweatshops, dumbbell tenements, Jim Crow regulations, city streets serving as children's playgrounds, or monopolies could be changed ony by government. The traditional social controls of the small town—neighborhood gossip and personal morality—no longer were sufficient in the city. The urbanite wanted workmen's compensation, wages-and-hours legislation, abolition of child labor, inspection of milk and food, adequate control of the conditions of work for women, fire and safety regulations in factories, and a host of other public policies that could only be accomplished through state action.

This welfare or social-service viewpoint has not yet spent itself. The Kennedy campaign of 1960 echoed the slogans of the New and Fair Deals. The unsolved problem of medical care remains, as do the unfinished battle over civil rights, and the expanding problems of the technologically unemployed (President Johnson's war on poverty). However, American life styles have changed again since the end of World War II. America has discovered the suburbs. The emerging majority now consists of white-collar organization men from nation-wide corporations rather than blue-collar workers and small-business entrepreneurs. The new majority has yet to make its dramatic breakthrough into the national political scene, but the outlines of its political slant are already familiar on the local level. It is evidenced in a desire to avoid conflict and partisanship, a preference for political independence, and a willingness to split party tickets, a taste for blandness, a championing of the technical efficiency of civil service, a deference to the opinions of the "expert," and an emphasis on selected welfare functions such as education and mental health. Probably the greatest impact of the new political viewpoint on the state level will be in the encouragement it gives to professionalism in government.

The fruits of the small-town political tradition

To return to the major point of analysis, our argument is that state government is suffering from an overdose of the small-town political ideology, a viewpoint that no longer is appropriate for contemporary society and business. Legislators who hold this viewpoint are occasionally used by large industry to avoid government regulation and to secure preferred labor laws. The legislative laissez-faire viewpoint is not, however, one that is purchased; anyone so cynical as to think so seriously misjudges the situation. The small-town contingent sincerely believes in its traditions. To the beleaguered small-town legislators in an unfriendly modern world of cities, it often seems as if they are themselves the last stronghold of sanity and morality. These men grew up in the last days of glory for the small-town viewpoint and they accepted it wholeheartedly. Herbert Hoover once said that the years before World War I were the best time to be alive in America or to be alive, in fact in any nation at any point in history—which is, everything considered, quite a broad statement. But the world Hoover idolized could not survive in the face of the even greater demand for the material goods the American Way seemed to offer to citizens. In 1916, as Henry Ford applied the assembly-line approach to mass production in Detroit's suburban Highland Park, the present generation of small-town legislators was passing through adolescence. To these men, small-town values were very real. As is the case with all of us, the ideas adopted at this period of one's life are among the hardest to change. They still color the small-town concept of reality.

During World War I and in the 1920's, population shifts tipped the scales in favor of the industrial cities. The presidency fell to the Democrats in 1932, and the New Deal followed. Big Steel, General Motors, and the Supreme Court surrendered in 1937, and within five years even Ford was unionized. The axis of the world, as Oliver Wendell Holmes once said, continued to be driven through every small town in America. But by the end of World War II, these places consisted mainly of those who did not want to try to advance under the new rules. (We hasten to concede that there continued to be many individual exceptions.) The small-town viewpoint, now on the defensive, sometimes achieves a shrill note with irrational overtones. Low taxes and simplicity in state government are the goal for a group of legislators who see most modern-day conditions as a mammoth conspiracy against their views of truth and beauty. Big-city schemers seem to surround them. Legislators of the small town paint pictures—in a day of widespread prosperity and the most conspicuous forms of consumption—of the beleaguered and almost bankrupt taxpayer who cannot afford to have rivers unpolluted, or mental institutions with rehabilitation facilities for their patients, or highway systems designed to minimize the danger of head-on crashes.

One political analyst, describing the small-town legislative bloc in his own state said, "They have 'tantrums' for a platform." And this nicely sums up the decline of what once was the most dynamic political viewpoint in America. A querulousness about governmental "frills" is almost all that remains of the once proud doctrine of small-town individualism. State legislatures, as currently established, are made to order for a group with this ideology. To gain their ends, they do not need to formulate alternative programs; they need only the power to block action and hence to stagnate government.

Because legislation and, in more than two-thirds of the states, constitutional amendments as well can be proposed only with its approval, the small-town bloc will often levy a special price when it agrees to act. This is the most obvious result of its control. A study in Connecticut, for example, described a state-aid formula constructed so that towns with less than 500 population received $27.19 per student while cities of over 100,000 received $4.95 per student. In Colorado, Denver schools with an enrollment of 90,000 received $2,300,000 under the state-aid formula while the schools of nearby Jefferson County with 72,000 fewer children enrolled received $100,000 more in state aid. The same pattern is frequently repeated in state aid for local roads, welfare grants, police protection, library facilities, and almost every other purpose. Richard Neuberger, when he was a state senator in Oregon, noticed that a bill to exempt rural mail carriers (usually residents of small towns) from state gasoline taxes passed overwhelmingly. When he proposed that some help be given urban mailmen who were more underpaid and had to walk, he was greeted with guffaws. This pattern of special gimmicks for the over-represented is repeated in the drawing of representative district lines for the United States Congress. Urban areas are seriously shortchanged in a way that has its effect on the national scene as well. A 1964 decision of the United States Supreme Court calling for equal population in House districts may change this pattern. It is now too early to know.

This self-interest aspect of small-town dominance is often irritating, but this is the least important of the effects. Urban areas are rich enough to carry small-town residents on their backs, and to some extent such a pattern is justified. Just as New York taxes are spent in Mississippi and North Dakota, so taxes from urban areas should probably be spent to bring facilities in smaller communities up to modern standards. But there is another more serious set of issues that represents a mixture of small-town morality and small-town selfishness. The opposition to the child-labor amendment sprang from such mixed motives. Children were a source of labor in small towns and on farms, Federal control was considered wrong, and besides, work for children was thought to be "character building." Probably the most obvious issue is the reluctant recognition of the need for government regulation. The price of small-town leaders' support for new legislation is often a rider that exempts towns of less than some figure acceptable to them. One study of Alabama by Murray Havens found small-town legislators exempting from regulation those barbers who worked only on Saturdays, presumably those working in the county seat when the farmers came in. In matters affecting the small-town businessmen, the mixed motives of the small-town attitude are frequently manifested. Legislators have valiantly tried to handicap chain-stores, both in order to help the small-town merchant and because they regard chains a threat to small businessmen generally. The Utah legislature in the 1940's passed anti-chain legislation. When put to a state-wide vote on a referendum, the bill was defeated by a four to one margin. The small-town crusade against trading stamps and the refusal of legislatures in states like New York to accept Federal funds at the price of eliminating billboards on freeways are examples. In the latter case, the fear was openly expressed that without billboards motorists would pass the small town by.

However, probably the most debilitating effect of the small-town ideology on stage government today is the attempt to apply to all citizens the morality of small-town life of a half-century ago. At base, this morality holds that those who succeed will do so without help because they deserve to succeed. Those who do not, then, deserve to fail. In Minnesota, for example, a small-town representative once announced that he opposed a civil rights bill, explaining that when he was young he had been orphaned and he felt all citizens should make their own way by themselves, as he had done, for this would "build character." In the South, as an Alabama study of legislative voting has illustrated, it is the small-town legislator who favors last stands on segregation. His urban colleagues, for the most part, have reluctantly concluded that the South must, as best it can, move into the twentieth-century world. The news stories of small-town violence over civil rights confirm this finding. The same attitudes are frequently reflected on prohibition and Sunday "blue" laws. Repeal is the only amendment to the United States Constitution that has been submitted to specially elected state conventions. This procedure was followed primarily because the Roosevelt administration felt state legislatures might not agree to repeal, despite the fact that repeal was able to secure two-thirds majorities in each house of Congress and was quickly adopted by the state conventions.

Small-town morality is particulary harsh on matters involving labor, welfare, and crime, where the fear is one of coddling the undeserving. During the Great Depression, the principal small-town spokesman in the Minnesota Senate announced that "there is no need for a wide-open relief allowance in this state." He argued for state loans rather than grants to counties, even though thousands of families were on the edge of starvation and the counties were virtually bankrupt. He favored a bill granting *one-tenth* of the amount requested by the urban, liberal governor, Floyd B. Olson. It need scarcely be added that while governors do tend to inflate their budget requests, none comes close to padding 1000 per cent. In Franklin Roosevelt's term as Governor of New York, professional criminologists at the Governor's suggestion proposed revision of the criminal code. Leading the fight against the revision was a state Senator who favored a tough approach because, he said, there was "too much sentiment for the convict class." The outrage expressed in the California Senate when Governor Edmund (Pat) Brown stayed the execution of Caryl Chessman is another illustration of this attitude. One of the legislators with a small-town background argued that Brown's action provided grounds for impeaching the Governor. His stance offered no direct economic payoff for him — he acted from deep belief and tradition. The same attitude is reflected in the treatment of mental health patients. The small-town legislators generally favor custody over treatment — that is, locking up mental patients and criminals rather than spending funds on expensive psychiatric rehabilitation. The condition of our mental hospitals and prisons often reflects this judgment. Small-town morality finds no place for suspected academic or intellectual dreamers. In Maine, legislators refused a grant for legislative assistants who would be of help to themselves because the college instructor supervising the program has "extreme ideas." The suspect was, in fact, a Republican and his "extreme ideas" appear to have existed only in a proposal he had made for reorganizing Maine's archaic county governments.

Alcoholism in the small-town view should not be viewed as an illness. Rather, alcoholics are "drunks" and every small town has at least one specimen; he is regarded as morally weak. The small town's ideological bias also favors right-to-work laws, fights public housing, and works to ferret out "parlor pinks" from the universities. In welfare matters, non-urban legislators produce such legislation as Nebraska's homestead lien law, which confiscates all or part of the value of the home of the old-age assistance recipient at his death, or the means test to demonstrate need before aid is given, or the requirement of publication of lists of recipients as was once devised by the Indiana legislature. In Louisiana, the legislature — over the protest of professionals — sought to deny aid for dependents of unwed mothers who had any additional children out of marriage. All of these laws are aimed at what is considered to be the moral "slacker."

A distrust of the professional is also basic to the concepts of small-town moralism. The trained specialist is regarded as a "fuzzy-minded" idealist, an over-educated fool, rather than a practical worker. State legislatures are notorious for gutting civil service systems. More is involved than the simple desire to provide jobs for the county courthouse gangs; there is a deepfelt ideological distrust of government employees who attempt, through specialized skills, to handle the complex problems facing urban America. This attitude is potentially among the most destructive to effective state government, for it involves a notion that urban problems are imagined rather than real, that they can be best handled if government does nothing and if those who do not live moral, upright lives are allowed to suffer until they change their ways.

No industrial corporation could flourish if a group on its board of directors with this attitude towards professionalism held a veto, and no state government that uses the simple and archaic morality of the small town as a point of departure can cope effectively with modern problems.

Action related to the problem

The commonplace reform proposal is one for re-apportioning state legislatures strictly by population. . . .

We believe there is a solution to state archaism short of the mammoth efforts required to achieve apportionment strictly according to population. The problem is one of representing political views formed in response to twentieth-century urban conditions and problems. To do this not every district need necessarily be mathematically equal in size. If other viewpoints receive representation enough to offset the antedeluvian small-town ideology, the necessary result would be achieved. Adding to the representation of cities or suburbs would achieve this. Another method of diluting the small-town viewpoint in the legislature would be to increase the size of legislative districts so that each legislator would have some urban constituents. This is what has kept the United States Senate timely, even though that body is not selected on the basis of representation by population. House districts, on the other hand, have been planned by state legislative leaders to over-represent small towns. A third method for helping offset the small-town viewpoint in state legislatures might be to leave present districts as they are but to elect in addition a half dozen or more legislators on a state-wide, at-large basis. This would have the advantage of preserving the old district lines and sense of community while breaking down the disproportionate small-town hold. Another method — most drastic — would simply be to abolish the unapportioned house of the legislature and base the other on population.

The most important of all strategies, we believe, is to focus public attention on the real problem. Once the stakes are clear to the urban majority, a change will occur, for the tools are at hand. It is quite possible that along the way the urban areas may lose individual battles but in the end win the war, just as Franklin Roosevelt did in his 1937 fight with the Supreme Court. Gordon Baker has pointed out that suburbanites are even more drastically under-represented than are voters in the core cities of metropolitan area. The 1960 census showing population losses in many large cities has emphasized this fact. The emerging majority fights some of the battles of the last great majority as well as its own.

We think timeliness is the major problem facing state government. Today our legislatures over-represent a political tradition devised for small-town living in the last century. This viewpoint does not fit the wants of most members of today's society. Old-fashioned political cures for modern problems work about as well as do the medical home remedies of the 1890's. The followers of the small-town political tradition must be given the status of a legitimate minority rather than being enthroned as the dominant policy makers. Until such a change in the political balance of power is made, our state governments will remain sick, sick, sick.

CHAPTER TWO

Intergovernmental Relations— The Nation and the States

FUNDAMENTAL IN THE STUDY of American state and local government is an understanding of the constitutional framework within which they exist, and the conflicting interpretations of the proper relationship between the national and state governments. The claims of "national supremacy" as against "states' rights" have been an enduring theme in American history, although the controversy has reached a level of bitterness only spasmodically, and the terms themselves have not had a constant meaning. The states' rightist view, with reference to the Supreme Court's school integration decisions, is presented with vehemence in the words of Congressman Williams of Mississippi, with an assist by colleagues representing South Carolina and Georgia constituencies. In the second selection Professor William Anderson, one of the nation's most distinguished students of federalism and the sole political scientist member of the Commission on Intergovernmental Relations, discards the compact theory of the Constitution as not in accord with the facts. Examining the "intent of the Framers" and the meaning of national supremacy and reserved powers of the states, he contends that the states' rights theory is a "deviation" and that the proper relationship of the national and the state governments lies in a special kind of partnership in serving the needs of the people, who, rather than governments, are sovereign.

5

Interposition: The Barrier Against Tyranny

By John Bell Williams

The SPEAKER pro tempore. Under previous order of the House, the gentleman from Mississippi (Mr. Williams) is recognized for 60 minutes.

In the House of Representatives, January 25, 1956, *Congressional Record,* 84th Congress, 2nd Session, Vol. 102, Pt. 1, pp. 1291–1297.

Mr. WILLIAMS of Mississippi. Mr. Speaker, on May 17, 1954, the Supreme Court of the United States drove a knife into the heart of the American Constitution. On that date the Supreme Court delegated unto itself and the federal government certain powers in excess of those granted under the Constitution. On that date, nine appointed Justices assumed unto themselves the power to amend the Constitution in the absence of approval by the people or the several states in the manner which is provided in the Constitution. Willfully and wantonly, they violated every principle of established law. They usurped the legislative powers of the Congress, and contributed affirmatively to the destruction of our dual sovereignty form of government. . . .

For the states of this Union, North or South, to permit the Supreme Court's brazen act of usurpation to stand unchallenged is for them to surrender meekly their sovereignty to the central government. For the states to permit their sovereignties to be so usurped would be to provide the foundation on which oligarchies are built.

Because some states do not have segregation laws, their people may think that the Court's illegal ruling is of no importance to them. They may even believe conscientiously that the federal government would be morally justified in the employment of its full force and power against the southern states in order to compel integration of the races.

If they believe either, they are overlooking the disastrous effects of the Court's action of May 17, 1954.

If the Supreme Court has the inherent right, under its judicial powers — which are not clearly defined in the Constitution — to amend the Constitution in this instance, the Court may likewise amend the Constitution by interpretation in cases affecting other states, and in matters equally as vital to them. . . .

In their attempt to destroy the lines that separate the states and to compound the American people into one common mass, the present court found it necessary to go outside the law. They found it necessary to use, as the basis for their ruling, various sociological documents, some actually written by foreigners whose information on the subject was gained from abstract sources. The Black Monday decisions violate every principle of established law. There is no basis for such rulings in statutory law, nor can a substantial premise be found throughout the entire history of Anglo-Saxon common law.

Mr. Speaker, let us recall for a moment why the Constitution came into being and how the Union was formed. From a convention of patriots representing 13 independent colonies, there emerged a document forming a Federal Union. . . .

In that convention each colony voluntarily surrendered to the Union certain powers which they regarded as necessary to the purposes and function of the central government. These powers so surrendered were specifically enumerated and carefully limited. The individual states reserved to themselves all powers not expressly delegated to the Union nor prohibited to themselves in accordance with the terms of their compact.

In spite of the cautious wording of the original document, the states refused to ratify the Constitution until ample assurance was given to the states and the people that the central government so created could never devour its creators, or deprive the people of their inalienable rights. As a result, the Bill of Rights, the first ten amendments were added to the Constitution.

These ten amendments did not expand the authority of the central government. On the contrary, they further restricted its authority. Like the Ten Commandments, our Bill of Rights are "thou shalt nots," directed to the federal government. They shield the people and the states from an oppressive and tyrannical government born of overconcentration of powers. They were, and are now, the basis for individual liberty and state sovereignty.

The Tenth Amendment clarified the matter of delegated and reserved powers — in the simplest of language. It reads:

The powers not delegated to the United States by the Constitution, nor prohibited by it to the states, are reserved to the states respectively, or to the people. . . .

Is the Supreme Court of the United States, consisting of nine men holding office by appointment, and answerable not to the people but to their respective consciences if such they have, to exercise final and absolute dominion over every phase of society? Are they to be recognized as the sole and only judges of the limits to which the federal agency may go in the exercise of its powers, the Constitution to the contrary notwithstanding? Are we to assume that the States and the people are helpless and without recourse against unconstitutional usurpations of authority by the federal establishment? Are the states defenseless? Must they yield to federal authority, when the exercise or assumption of that authority is beyond the limitations imposed on the federal establishment in the Constitution?

If these premises are to be recognized as sound, then we have already changed our form of government, and no longer live under a constitutional republic. If these premises are sound, we are wasting the fruits of the peoples' labors in maintaining state governments and in supporting county and municipal governments.

The federal government, being a creature of the several states, through usurpation, is slowly but surely cannibalizing its creators, to the end that it and it alone shall sit in exclusive judgment of the acts of the citizens of the several states. . . .

As God-fearing people, we are obligated to resist tyranny, no matter what form it may take. If we are true to ourselves, we must resist it even when it wears the sheep's clothing of judicial robes, if freedom is to be the legacy we leave to our children.

The resolving of this crisis does not call for complacency, timidity, or cowardice. It will call for taxing new reservoirs of courage, and will demand sacrifices that will test the strength of our convictions. In the face of the Supreme Court's brazen usurpation of authority, its flagrant disregard of constitutional limitations, its wilful flaunting of judicial precedents, its wanton contempt for the doctrine of *stare decisis* and recognized principles of established law, we must resort to drastic measures if we are to preserve the structure of our republic. This will mean suffering and sacrifice on the part of liberty-loving

Americans, and it means seizing the offensive from the conscienceless self-seeking elements who seek to destroy our republic. It means that we must seek and find the courage that distinguished our great American ancestors in their struggle to build this republic, and there can be no retreating from principle for any cause whatsoever.

Mr. Speaker, inasmuch as the federal government is a creature of the states, it is the solemn duty of the states to protect themselves from encroachments upon their sovereignty. No machinery for this is set up in the Constitution. No relief is available in the statutes. Yet the law teaches us that for every wrong there must be a remedy.

The Black Monday decisions of the federal judiciary go beyond the limits of delegated powers and therefore are an invasion of powers reserved to the states, but the states have a remedy. It was first used by Georgia in the 1790's. It was used by Kentucky and Virginia in the same decade. Other states used it in the nineteenth century. Jefferson, Madison, and Calhoun were its authors and originators. It was called the doctrine of interposition. . . .

The right of the states to check encroachments of the federal government must, of necessity, be an integral part of our system of dual sovereignty, and vice versa. What happens when a state encroaches on the federal government's delegated powers? The federal government immediately interposes its sovereignty between the encroachment and the citizens affected. Does anyone believe that our Founding Fathers would confer such power on the creature and withhold it from the creator? No, Mr. Speaker, the principle of interposition is a fundamental part of our system of dual sovereignty. . . .

In the present case, the Supreme Court is clearly attempting to destroy the Constitution itself. It has made an abortive attempt to amend the Constitution. It is attempting to nullify the powers reserved to the states under the Constitution. Through acts of interposition, the states would merely be seeking to nullify the action of the nullifiers.

By design, the Supreme Court has committed a deliberate, palpable, and dangerous invasion of the field of sovereignty exclusively reserved to the states. The nine justices have committed an act of treason against the Constitution of the United States.

It is the duty of the states, in the face of such flagrant and illegal assumption of power by the federal judiciary, to interpose their sovereignty and nullify the decision. In doing so, the states are protecting the Constitution against nullification by the courts, and are protecting the liberties of the American people.

The time is at hand when the states must reassert their constitutional rights or suffer their own destruction. The zero hour for state governments has ar-

rived, and it might well be the zero hour also, for our republican form of government.

Mr. Speaker, I have heard many say that they favor interposition, but are opposed to nullification. This is the same thing as saying that we favor the aiming and firing of our guns but we are against hitting the target.

The very purpose of interposition is to nullify. If that is not to be the purpose, the act of interposition becomes merely an expression of disfavor and is meaningless.

Mr. Speaker, interposition is the act by which a state attempts to nullify. Interposition without nullification is a knife without an edge, a gun without bullets, a car without an engine, a body without life.

If the states are to preserve their sovereignties, if they are to preserve the Constitution, they must interpose and declare the Black Monday decisions to be illegal and invalid and of no force and effect within the territorial limits of their respective jurisdictions. This position I believe the states have the right and duty to take and to maintain until such time as this question of contested powers has been settled legally and finally by constitutional amendment. . . .

It is quite apparent that we can expect more and more such abortive invasions of state sovereignties, and more and more usurpation of power by the federal establishment. The question of whether the states are sovereign in the matter of reserved powers should be settled now, once and for all.

What will be the object of the Supreme Court's next act of usurpation? What among Jefferson's inalienable rights will be next to suffer destruction by judicial legislation?

Will it be the police power of the states? Intrastate transportation and commerce? Will it be state and local regulatory powers? Will it be property rights, marriage laws, contract laws, criminal laws? If we surrender to this trend, where will it end: Can anyone say? . . . .

Mr. Speaker, the same God that watched over Jefferson and inspired him to swear eternal hostility to tyranny watches over us. With His divine guidance and help we shall not fail.

Mr. RIVERS [of South Carolina]. Mr. Speaker, will the gentleman yield?

Mr. WILLIAMS of Mississippi. I yield.

Mr. RIVERS. Mr. Speaker, I want to congratulate the gentleman on this scholarly discussion of this unconstitutional decision by the politico-sociologically minded outfit known as the Supreme Court. The Supreme Court has invited and dared the states of the Union to interpose between them and law and order — yea, even riots and bloodshed in the states. To maintain their self-respect, Mr. Speaker, the states have no alternative in the absence of this action by this Congress in amending the Constitution or referring it to the people for amendment to interpose and follow out all the orderly processes in nullifying that unwarranted, unconstitutional, and unprecedented act of that politico-socialistic outfit up there. . . .

Mr. FLYNT [of Georgia]. Mr. Speaker, will the gentleman yield?

Mr. WILLIAMS of Mississippi. I yield to the gentleman from Georgia.

Mr. FLYNT. Mr. Speaker, I should like to congratulate and commend my distinguished friend and colleague from Mississippi on his masterful and scholarly open support of and reaffirmation of faith in the Constitution of the United States of America. . . .

Before I go any further, lest some of my statements may be misunderstood, I want to say without any reservation or evasion that I am here and now willing to take a solemn oath that I hold no malice, hatred, or prejudice whatsoever in my heart, in my mind, or in my soul, against any man or any group of men, living or dead, because of his race or the color of his skin. . . .

Yet I am just as willing to take another solemn oath that if necessary I will expend every ounce of my strength, every drop of my blood, even my life itself, to resist the efforts of the United States Supreme Court to usurp the power to amend the Constitution of the United States.

The skeptics and the wild-eyed dreamers may say with regard to the school decisions handed down on the 17th day of May, 1954, "What difference does it make whether those decisions were constitutional or not?" I will just as quickly reply that it makes all the difference in the world. If the Supreme Court of the United States can usurp the power to amend the Constitution of the United States of America and to write into it by judicial legislation that which was never intended by those who wrote the Constitution or by those who live under it today, then that same Court or any other similarly constituted group could just as easily abolish habeas corpus, trial by jury, freedom of speech and press, freedom of religion, the greatest of all freedoms — the freedom of choice, and every other personal right and emblem of liberty, which no human being in the world ever had guaranteed to him by the basic instrument of government of any country until the American Bill of Rights was added to the United States Constitution. If and when the time ever comes when the Supreme Court of the United States, or any other court, can usurp the amendatory powers which lie solely in not fewer than three-fourths of the states, then when that time comes we will become serfs under a totalitarian government even as Germany was under Hitler or as Russia is under the Communist conspiracy today. . . .

If that time ever comes there will be no one left to stop it because the supposed defenders of the Constitution, the black-robed justices of the United States Supreme Court, will be leading the carnival parade riding the chargers of dictatorship and tyranny like the Four Horsemen of the Apocalypse. I hope that time never comes and I humbly pray that it will not.

Mr. Speaker, I believe that our Constitution of the United States of America is a sacred thing. The most sacred and divinely inspired instrument produced by the brain and purpose of man since God gave the Ten Tablets of the Law to Moses on Mount Sinai, and since the Man of Galilee delivered His sermon on another mountain nearly 2,000 years ago.

Yes, the United States Constitution is a sacred thing. It protects and defends the weak and the oppressed against tyrants and would-be tyrants of strength and power. It protects minorities from vastly greater majorities. It protects the humblest cottage and the most stately mansion with equal sanctity. It protects the least of us from the powers of tyranny and despotism. It has caused us to have the greatest way of life ever experienced, or ever known, or ever dreamed of by the mind of man. . . .

Let us as American citizens explicitly declare that the powers of the federal government result solely from the compact to which the states are parties and that the powers of the federal government in all of its branches and agencies are limited by the terms of the instrument creating that compact and by the plain sense and intention of those provisions. . . .

. . . whenever the federal government attempts deliberately, palpably and dangerously to exercise powers not granted to it, the states who are parties to the compact have a right, and are in duty bound, to interpose for preserving the authorities and rights and liberties pertaining to them.

Failure on the part of the states thus to assert the clearly reserved powers would be construed as tacit consent to the surrender thereof and such submissive acquiescence to powerful and dangerous encroachment upon one power would, in the end, lead to the destruction and surrender of all powers, and inevitably to the obliteration of the sovereignty of the sovereign states, contrary to the sacred compact under which this Union of States was created. . . .

Let us take renewed courage as we try to preserve the greatest instrument the world has ever known, the Constitution of the United States. We know we are right. We shall not falter, and we shall not fail.

6

Rivals or Partners?

By William Anderson

CONCERNING THE NATURE of the federal system and of the Constitution there are in general terms two opposing philosophies. On the one hand there are the states' righters, the bring-the-government-back-home group. To the extent that they hold a theory on the origin of the federal system it is that sovereign states came together to form the union, that even in indissoluble and perpetual union these states retained their sovereignty, and that therefore the central government is the mere creature of the states. They believe that in order to preserve personal liberties and local government the national government must be kept at a minimum, and that the assumption of new activities by the federal government is "unconstitutional." They express fears of "centralization" and of "big government." They want the powers of the various governments "strictly defined and separated." Some of them oppose any suggestion of the "welfare state" at whatever level; others believe that the state governments can handle welfare functions more democratically and efficiently than the national government.

In opposition are those who believe that the people are sovereign; that the people created both state and national governments and that therefore both levels of government are merely the agencies of the people. They believe that the Constitution is a flexible document which cannot be read solely in terms of what the framers of 1787 intended but must be interpreted in the light of changing conditions and needs. They are not afraid of centralization or big government as such, as long as democratic processes are preserved to control government. They do not believe that recent increases in the national government's activities have taken any powers away from the states; on the contrary, they believe that the state governments are stronger and more active than ever before. Finally, they are convinced that it is in the best interests of the nation as a whole not to limit to any great extent the powers of the central government.

From William Anderson, *The Nation and the States: Rivals or Partners?* (Minneapolis: University of Minnesota Press, 1955), pp. 13–14, 65–67, 70–72, 75–77, 80–82, 84, 88–90, 95, 116, 123–124, 126–127, 134–135. Reprinted by permission of the publisher.

Admittedly these contrasts are oversimplified. Not all in either camp hold all the related views. In many cases individuals are not consciously aware of holding one philosophy or the other; they merely react to specific actions and proposals with approval or disapproval. I do not intend to suggest that the differences of opinion are clear-cut and easy to define; rather I would have us use these generalized characterizations merely as convenient points of reference.

Neither do I mean to imply that the nation is once again a "house divided," this time on the issue of intergovernmental relations, and doomed to be rent asunder. Certainly there are significant and basic differences of opinion, as I have outlined; there are tensions and frictions and even animosities among government officials at the various levels; there is a good deal of "viewing with alarm" and shaking of skeletons by numerous nonofficial groups. But there are wide areas of agreement, on purpose if not always on procedure. Excellent cooperation and smooth functioning mark many of the programs in which national, state, and local governments join hands. . . .

The intent of the Framers

The Constitution of the United States, after it was adopted, soon became a symbol of national unity, strength, and achievement. It took on for prideful Americans some of the aspects of the "crown" of the United Kingdom — that great symbol of British national and even imperial strength and unity. The framers of the Constitution were accordingly praised then and later by many patriotic speakers and writers as an assembly of demigods, or at least of men who were very near that level of ability, high purpose, and integrity. The bickerings, disagreements, and compromises of the Federal Convention were passed over in silence, while the Constitution was exalted into an almost sacrosanct and untouchable symbol of national greatness.

Along with this fetishism arose the feeling that everything about the interpretation and operation of the Constitution must be tested by the touchstone of "the intentions of the framers." This began even before the publication in 1843 of Madison's notes on the debates in the Convention, one of the best sources of evidence as to what was intended. And today, more than one hundred and sixty-five years after the drafting of the Constitution, there are still frequent references to the framers and their "intentions." . . .

The Constitution simply did not spring forth perfect, complete, and self-explanatory. Most likely it never will be complete and perfect. Men disagreed about it when it was being drafted, when it came up for adoption, and when it was being put into effect.

Many of the framers were participants in the early national government and in some of the state governments of that day, and they did not all agree as to what the Constitution meant or what its framers intended. Indeed, it is merely vain imagining to assume that such a thing as "the intention" of "the framers" in the full sense ever existed or ever can be discovered. Fifty-five delegates took part in the Federal Convention, and thirty-nine signed the final document. Hundreds of persons participated in the thirteen state ratifying conventions, while many other citizens engaged in written and oral discussions of the Constitution.

Many questions that came up later probably never were considered by the framers. Consequently they can hardly be said to have had any intentions on these issues. The record of what they did discuss is quite incomplete, obviously, but what is available provides voluminous evidence of differences of opinion as to what was intended and as to what might be expected from the Constitution on the points that men did discuss. There were differences of opinion not only between the proponents of the Constitution and the opponents, but also among the proponents themselves. Even *The Federalist,* the essays published in New York in 1787 and 1788 to help bring about the adoption of the Constitution by the people of New York, displays a noticeably "split personality." In fact each of the two principal authors of these essays revealed within his own writings some vagueness, confusion, and even contradiction — perhaps Madison more than Hamilton.

This is not to say that nothing at all can be determined about the intentions of the framers. There obviously were areas of agreement among the sponsors of the Constitution. That document is itself the best evidence of what they agreed upon. . . .

. . . the Constitution contains no term to suggest a treaty or agreement among the ratifying states — neither confederation, nor confederacy, not federation, nor federal. The complete omission of any and every such word from the Constitution can hardly have been a mere oversight of inadvertence. . . .

The framers of the new plan called it a constitution. The word was already in use among the states to designate the written document that sets forth the framework of the government of a single state. There is in this word no idea of a treaty or of a plighting of faith among various individuals or states, rather it suggests integration or unity.

On the other hand the Articles of Confederation were cast more clearly in the form of a treaty or compact among states. . . .

The Articles were drawn up by "Delegates of the States in Congress assembled," and were ratified by the legislatures of the several states on behalf of the states as units. On the other hand the famous words with which the Constitution begins are "We the People of the United States . . . do ordain and establish this Constitution for the United States of America." Furthermore, the Constitution was ratified by special conventions of the people in each state, not by the legislatures.

This is surely one of the most significant verbal and structural differences between the Constitution and the Articles.

The "sovereignty" of the states. One of the most notable clauses in the Articles of Confederation reads: "Article II. Each state retains its sovereignty, freedom and independence, and every Power, Jurisdiction and right, which is not by this confederation expressly delegated to the United States, in Congress assembled."

This seems to imply that the states were separately sovereign and independent before the Articles were adopted, that by their act of confederating they delegated to Congress whatever powers it was to have, and that all powers not expressly so delegated, plus the essence of sovereignty and independence, were retained by the states. This clearly put or left the states in the driver's seat.

The framers of the Constitution left out the word "sovereignty" entirely. It does not appear at all, to describe either the nation or the states. Since other words from the Articles were included in the Constitution, the presumption must be that the framers purposely and deliberately omitted the idea that the states were sovereign. In short, sovereignty was assumed by the people of the United States and this means popular supremacy over both the national government and the states.

Supreme law of the land. The only words in the Constitution that imply sovereignty or supremacy, outside of the preamble wherein the people take over the reins of authority, are to be found in the second paragraph of Article I, "the supreme law of the land" clause, which reads: "This Constitution, and the laws of the United States which shall be made in pursuance thereof; and all treaties made, or which shall be made, under the authority of the United States, shall be the supreme law of the land; and the judges in every state shall be bound thereby, any thing in the constitution or laws of any state to the contrary notwithstanding."

This clause, taken along with other phrases of the Constitution, has the obvious effect of putting the Constitution, laws, and treaties of the United States above the constitutions and laws of the several states. It is reinforced by the requirement that an official oath "to support this Constitution," must be taken by all members of Congress, all state legislators, "and all executive and judicial officers, both of the United States and of the several states . . ." (Article VI, paragraph 3).

Together these provisions illustrate the completeness of the overturn in authority that took place when the Constitution replaced the Articles of Confederation. The former residual "sovereignty" of the states was eliminated, and in place of it the people of the United States established the supremacy of the United States Constitution and of the proper laws and treaties of the United States government. . . .

. . . [The framers] planned to and did create a full-fledged national government, to be based on the people and to legislate for and serve the people, without requiring the consent of the state governments and without being dependent upon them in any way when legislating, taxing, making treaties, and enforcing laws for the nation as a whole. This national government was to be officered by men who held no state offices, and who were not to be delegates of the state governments as such, but whose attachments would be to the Union, to the United States as a whole, and to its national government. So organized, the central government would be able to act autonomously, upon its own initiative, in the national interest, without regard to what the state governments might be doing in their respective territories. . . .

Despite the broad range of powers granted to the national government, no one, except for Hamilton in the early days of the Federal Convention, seems to have advocated the abolition of the states. The states were to be left, though in a reduced role, and were actually to have some part in helping to conduct the new national government (the state legislatures were to elect United States senators; to regulate elections for the United States as well as for themselves; to provide for appointing presidential electors; and so on). The primary intention was to create a new, effective, autonomous national government for all the people and for the whole territory of the United States, and to set it down over the states to serve the people directly. In effect a dual system of government came into existence, the national government established for the whole country and the state governments left to carry on their local functions within their respective territories. . . .

Finally, the framers did not desire that the Constitution they proposed should be rigidly binding on all future generations. It has remained for later protagonists of various political and economic causes, when appealing from the present Constitution — which they think they don't like — to the original Constitution — which they think they do like — to urge that the intentions of the original framers must be respected and obeyed no matter what changes in thought or in circumstances have taken place since then.

This attempt to turn back, as it were, the clock of constitutional interpretation and practice in order to be guided by an earlier view finds little support in the writings and reasonings of the original framers. For one thing, the framers inserted in the Constitution an article that provided for future amendments. This certainly showed that they expected the Constitution might require amendments in the future. Indeed, Hamilton, Washington, and other leading supporters among the members expressed disappointment with various provisions of the Constitution as it went before the people. The existence of the amending article was one reason why Washington thought it best to adopt the Constitution as it was and then proceed to get amendments later. . . .

In short, the framers and proponents of the Constitution realized that the Constitution was a manmade and imperfect instrument; that its meaning was not entirely clear but would call for interpretations; that it probably would be found in practice to be deficient in a number of respects, and so would call for formal amendments. They did not claim superhuman wisdom or skill for themselves, or set themselves up as wiser than those who would come after them. They were content to leave the interpretation and the necessary modification of the Constitution to future congresses, legislatures, and supreme courts, and to the people of the United States. They recognized that constitutions are made "for posterity as well as ourselves," and that they must be adaptable to the "exigencies of ages" yet unknown (*The Federalist*, No. 34). . . .

The changes that have taken place in the Constitution since its adoption have not all been in one direction, nor have all been fully consistent one with another. On every constitutional issue that arises there are likely to be two or more positions that can be taken. Which of these will be approved as the basis for action will depend upon a variety of circumstances, of which the political views of those who must make the decision are highly important. It is largely a matter of chance whether those in office when a particular constitutional decision is to be made hold one set of political views or another.

In point of fact, however, there has been from the beginning one dominant trend, at least in the constitutional relations between the national government and the states — a trend toward spelling out and solidifying the supremacy of the national government.

This does not mean that the states have suffered an exactly corresponding loss in authority, or that they are actually less important, less active, or less serviceable than they used to be . . . the activities of the states after the Revolution were largely limited to legislating. As the functions and services of government have increased all along the line, and at all levels of government, national, state, and local, . . . the states have actually increased in importance. . . .

Reserved powers and the Tenth Amendment

To many leaders in state government the Tenth Amendment has appeared to be the most important provision among the first ten amendments. Its words and its consequences deserve much attention. It reads: "The powers not delegated to the United States by the Constitution, nor prohibited by it to the States, are reserved to the States respectively, or to the people." . . .

. . . some of the proponents of the Constitution thought that an express reservation of powers to the states was unnecessary, since it was patent on the face of the Constitution that the states were to remain in existence and that they would, therefore, continue to exercise powers not delegated by the Constitution to the United States government and not denied by the Constitution to the states.

As I see the situation, if the original states had been content to let well enough alone they might have been able to argue that each original state retained for itself, and by its own authority, the powers not delegated or denied, as seemed to be the situation under the Articles of Confederation. As it was, they desired the greater security that might come from having the reservation made explicit in the United States Constitution by an amendment. But a constitutional amendment like any other provision of the Constitution is ordained by the people of the United States. In seeking a constitutional amendment the states in effect acknowledged the supremacy of the people of the United States and submitted to receiving their powers from the people through the medium of the Constitution. . . .

The amendment, it seems to me, should be read with the enacting clause of the preamble as follows: "We the people of the United States . . . do ordain . . . [that] The powers not delegated to the United States by the Constitution, nor prohibited by it to the States, are reserved to the States respectively, or to the people."

In other words, it is the people of the United States who, in ordaining the Constitution, delegate some powers to the United States government, reserve other powers to the states or to the people, and place restrictions on both the national government and the states in the interests of the people. This carries out logically the idea expressed by Madison in *The Federalist,* No. 46, that "The federal and State governments are in fact but different agents and trustees of the people."

This view, I believe, is consonant also with the fact that nearly three fourths of the states have been subsequently brought into the Union under the Constitution, and they could not have had any prior "inherent" or "sovereign" powers as states which they could have retained for themselves by their own authority upon admission to the Union. The people of the United States surely are the source of the powers of all the states subsequently brought into the Union, which states had to accept the Constitution as a condition of their admission, so that the Constitution is for them both the means of conveying power to them and the measure of the powers conferred on them by the "reservation" in Amendment 10. And since all the states in the Union are constitutionally equal, I hold that all the states receive their powers from the people of the United States speaking through the Constitution. . . .

In short, at present, the reserved powers of the state are not a limit on or a bar to the exercise by Congress of the powers delegated to it. Indeed, the Tenth Amendment itself has been held to state "but a truism that all is retained which has not been surrendered" (Darby case). "From the beginning and for many years the amendment has been construed as not depriving the national government of authority to resort to all means for the exercise of a granted power which are appropriate and plainly adapted to the permitted end."

But Tenth Amendment or no Tenth Amendment, the states exercise under the Constitution a wide range of important powers. If state laws lack supremacy over the acts of Congress, they are nevertheless, from the individual's point of view, enforceable laws and laws that must be obeyed, just as fully as any act of Congress, as long as they do not violate any provisions of the Constitution or any valid act of Congress . . .

"States' rights"

The struggle for states' rights — as against the supremacy of the national government — has been like a fire that smolders for a time and then flares up anew, in new places and with new combustibles, but which never really dies out. . . .

It is interesting to notice . . . that outside of Virginia and Kentucky the 1798 "resolves" of these two states [nullification] fell on deaf ears in the other southern states, and were vigorously condemned in the states north of the Mason and Dixon line. The Federalists opposed the resolutions strongly, and they actually gained in political strength in 1799 at the expense of the Republicans. Both Madison and Jefferson dropped the idea of state nullification as the means of wiping out the Alien and Sedition Acts, and returned to their more congenial and constitutional political weapons, the attempt to get the people to elect Anti-Federalists to Congress.

Although both Jefferson and Madison were successively elected to the presidency (1800 and 1808), this fact cannot be attributed to their utterances in the Virginia and Kentucky Resolutions. And by

1830 Madison was clearly once more in the anti-nullification camp.

Another claim to the right of nullification arose a generation after the Virginia and Kentucky Resolutions, when South Carolina claimed the right to nullify a tariff law passed by Congress. Actual nullification was prevented by President Jackson's stern position against it. Nevertheless the slavery controversy soon thereafter raised a similar issue, and the conflict over federal control of slavery in the territories led on to southern secession and civil war.

Southern historians have discovered in the publications and utterances of some of the secession leaders statements that were almost lyrical in praise of states' rights. John C. Calhoun and other theorists of the South accepted as a historical fact that each of the thirteen original states had at the beginning been completely independent and sovereign in the full international sense of sovereignty. Calhoun further claimed that this sovereignty was by nature inalienable and indivisible, and that the Constitution was therefore only a compact among states, each of which continued to be fully sovereign. . . .

This theory was made explicit in the constitution of the Confederate states. As a practical matter the framers of that document followed rather closely the Constitution of the United States, but they began the preamble differently: "We, the people of the Confederate States, each State acting in its sovereign and independent character, in order to form a permanent federal government. . . ."

Ironically, the recalcitrancy of some of the states, which even in wartime pursued their theories of states' rights, is considered by many historians to be a major cause of the Confederacy's defeat. . . .

Since the Civil War, the states' rights doctrine — based on what Hamilton called "the inordinate pride of state importance" — has not led to bloody violence. As we have seen, however, it has in one form or another remained a factor in the politics of this nation. Although the Union victory in the War of Secession pretty well laid to rest Calhoun's theory of *absolute* sovereignty of each state, the "state-sovereignty theory," as Owsley termed it, which insists on a rigid reservation of powers to the states, is resuscitated regularly by those who oppose some extension or other of national powers.

But I believe and have tried to show that there is no constitutional basis for this theory. The people cannot be assumed to have undone with the left hand what they did with the right, to have reserved to the separate states powers that would defeat the powers conferred on the national government to promote the national security and the national welfare. If in the original Constitution they were not sufficiently clear about national objectives and national supremacy, by their subsequent actions they have done much to remove the uncertainty and doubt. . . .

The constitutional essentials

"The Constitution, in all its provisions, looks to an indestructible Union, composed of indestructible States."

This statement in a Supreme Court decision of 1869 sets forth succinctly the basic fact about national-state relations under the Constitution of the United States — the importance and permanence of both the national and the state governments.

It is true, of course, as we have seen, that the national government has been established as supreme. No state may constitutionally nullify or obstruct the acts of the national government. Every state stands under the compulsory jurisdiction and process of the nation's Supreme Court to decide on the state's rights and duties under the United States Constitution and laws. The constitutional acts of Congress are also binding on the states. National citizenship is the primary citizenship for all the people in the United States — above state citizenship — and the national government may reach with its laws any and every citizen (as well as all aliens and other persons) in any state. The national Constitution is the highest written law for all the people of the United States, for the nation as a whole and for each of its parts — for the national government and for the state and local governments as well. The Constitution is without qualification the "supreme law of the land." . . .

One aspect of this complex system of government that many foreign observers and perhaps many Americans also do not understand is defined approximately by the terms "autonomy" and "free initiative." Congress and the President, the national policy-making authorities, may go ahead and act for the general welfare upon their own interpretation of the national powers without consulting or getting the consent of either the United States Supreme Court or the state governments. Each state government may do the same in acting for the welfare of its state without consulting the President, Congress, or the Supreme Court. If not sovereign the states are at least autonomous.

This apparent looseness of governmental structure strengthens the importance of each part of the system: each part, though subordinate to the whole, has certain "checks" on the other parts and on the whole. At the same time, paradoxical though this seems, it also ties the nation and its parts permanently together. For the threads between the President and the Congress, Congress and the Supreme Court, the Supreme Court and the state legislatures, the state legislatures and the Congress, Congress and the state governors, state governors and national executive agencies, national executive agencies and state divisions, state executive divisions and state legislatures, and so on, are so intricately interwoven that a break at any point would only temporarily snarl the threads; it cannot unravel the whole.

The relationship between the states and the nation that emerges from the complex governmental structure of the United States is sometimes called a partnership. I have used the term "partners" in the title of this volume, and in a way I believe it is a very apt term. But I want to make perfectly clear the sense in which I am using "partners" and "partnership."

It seems to me that there is between the nation and the states nothing like an ordinary business-partnership arrangement in which the partners have equal status and voting powers. Each state, being but a part of the entire people, is not an equal partner of the nation; at the same time, all the states combined *are* the nation and cannot be called its partners.

On the other hand the national government and the state governments are the agents of the nation and for its several parts, the states. They share the responsibility to promote the general welfare of all the people. In this sense they form a partnership, though not a partnership of equals, and not a partnership in any transient sense.

For what I have in mind it would be hard to find a more eloquent expression than that of Edmund Burke when he was criticizing the contract theory of the state. Said he:

Society is, indeed, a contract. . . . [B]ut the state ought not to be considered as nothing better than a partnership agreement in a trade of pepper and coffee, calico or tobacco . . . to be dissolved by the fancy of the partners. It is to be looked upon with other reverence. . . . It is a partnership in all science, a partnership in all art, a partnership in every virtue and in all perfection. As the ends of such a parnership cannot be obtained in many generations, it becomes a partnership not only between those who are living, but between those who are living, those who are dead, and those who are to be born.

As the distinct and separate agents of the people of the United States, a great nation among nations and one that we hope will endure to promote human welfare through many generations, the national government and the state governments have joint responsibility to respect each other, to consult with each other, and to cooperate with and assist each other to promote the national security and the general welfare. It is in this broad meaning that I speak of a partnership in national-state relations. . . .

The attitude of public officials toward the current status of national-state relations is much more likely to reflect their personal political philosophies and the circumstances of the area they represent than their positions in national or state government. (Congressman Williams is, after all, technically a national official.) Here the former Republican Governor of West Virginia and the former Democratic Governor of Michigan suggest that the real reason for the presumed trend toward centralization is more likely the failure of the states to serve the needs of their populations than any "power-hungry" character of the national government. Professor Odegard then follows with a thoughtful analysis of the changing nature of intergovernmental relations in modern society and of the possible steps needed to restore greater vitality to local political institutions.

7

Usurpation — or Abdication?

★

Usurpation's a Myth

By Cecil H. Underwood

. . . RECENTLY we have heard an old and familiar cry, one of anguish, desperation and, perhaps too frequently, hypocrisy, a cry which we recognize as "states' rights." Again in our nation's history, certain states feel themselves violated by an oppressive federal government. And in spite of our opinion of the right they clamor for, the right to practice local prejudices, we too must consider states' rights.

For states' rights is a term of protest in the federal system — our system of government and a truly American creation. The federal system, like so much that is considered "typically American," is a process irritatingly undefinable and unmeasurable. It is practice itself. No matter how hopefully we retrace its more than 150 years of functioning, we cannot tell exactly what it is. We can only tell what it was and sometimes not even that. . . .

. . . The federal plan is first another guarantee of freedom because it assures broad, representative participation in government. Such participation in a complex, many leveled federal system trains leaders, preserves local autonomy, provides working laboratories for experimentation in government, and serves as an outlet for local grievances and political aspirations. It further allows for the multiformity in government to match the size and diversity of our country.

Cecil H. Underwood. "Usurpation's a Myth," *National Municipal Review,* November, 1958, pp. 504–508. Reprinted by permission of the publisher.

I firmly believe that the federal system strengthens our capacity to govern ourselves, the very essence of a democracy. It further produces a better government, one flexible enough internally to endure. . . .

There are those, of course, who see the federal government as a monster, devouring innocent states, which in turn are hampering struggling municipalities. To be candid we must admit that certain elements of such devouring and hampering are not so distasteful, like federal aid for a favorite project. Most states covet such financial aid; it allows us to evade the responsibility of paying for our actions. What we do not like is to surrender any authority or power to Washington. Nothing is so true as the statement that whoever holds the purse strings holds the power.

. . . .

It is such surrender of authority to the federal government that people fear. To this point, though, the actions of the central government have been for the better. It has done things, established standards which states themselves were unable or, more often, unwilling to do.

But a danger does exist and one that we cannot ignore. It is useless, however, to attempt to return to the Arcadian simplicity which we imagine we once had. The states and other local units of government must take the initiative and responsibility to keep the powers they exercise best. If some of such power has changed hands, it is generally the fault of the states. There has been little usurpation of power in this country; there has been instead abdication of power. I do not fear that the federal government will take away any further the autonomy of the states but that the states will give it away. . . .

. . . We cannot go back and redo what has been done. We cannot even undo most of it. There are too many people involved in already established programs, too many set patterns of procedure, too many expectations — in short, too many established interests and too much fear of failure in change. . . .

My first and basic conclusion is that we cannot alter materially the relationships already existing between units of the federal system which we now have. We can only try to consider each new problem as it arises, guided by a realistic understanding of federal-state-local relationships.

My second conclusion — one that is both encouraging and challenging — is the preoccupation of the national government with foreign affairs. By strengthening the state and local governments we can increase the effectiveness of the national government. The fullest possible utilization of state and local resources is desirable to supplement national action in domestic affairs and to relieve the national government of the unnecessary diversion of its resources and energies.

All responsibility for domestic affairs does not rest with the states. Local governments must share this obligation. In the third place then, it is necessary to conclude that municipal and other local governments must be free to act in their respective spheres of influence. Too often the states have jealously held to power at the expense of effective local government. By granting more home rule, by encouraging greater municipal and metropolitan autonomy, the states can strengthen themselves and the nation as a whole. . . .

Federal-State Relations

By G. Mennen Williams

. . . IT IS MY BELIEF that in an age of Madison Avenue and machine-made uniformity we need to strengthen every bit of creative diversity we possess. Our many great cities and our . . . fifty great and differing states can provide a rich variety of thought and action no single-centered nation can hope to attain.

It is true, as any candid observer must agree, that our pattern of state and local government may fail to meet the challenge of creative action and relapse into futile frustration and eventual national centralization. Certainly such a gloomy view was prevalent and seemed justified in the dark days of the thirties when bankruptcy faced every level of government below the nation and it alone possessed the fiscal strength to shoulder the burden of relief and combat the giant evils of unemployment and economic stagnation. Happily that storm was weathered and a series of measures we know as the New Deal and Fair Deal built stabilizers into the American economy and put a ceiling on human misery.

Many thought the states obsolete, a kind of vestigial remnant of our national evolution, impotent to help but powerful to hinder the national effort to solve our pressing problems. Certainly in that period mayors learned to beat a path to Washington without even a stop-over in their state's capitol. Cities on the front line of the battle against human misery found sympathetic ears and hard cash in Washington when state governments seemed bleakly negative.

Some of this situation stemmed from superior resources at the disposal of the national treasury but

G. Mennen Williams, "Federal-State Relations," *Public Administration Review,* Autumn, 1957, pp. 225–230. Reprinted by permission of the publisher, the American Society for Public Administration. An address at the annual meeting of the American Political Science Association, September 5, 1957.

all too much from a built-in lack of sympathy with urban problems in state legislatures. The well worn trail to Washington will become a four lane super-highway if urban areas now containing the great majority of our people are given the cold shoulder or asked to come hat in hand to beg for scraps from rural-oriented state governments still unaware of, or hostile to, their needs.

But all too unnoticed, there has been more recently, in the decade following the war, a revitalization of state government. While most public attention has been directed to events in Washington, many state capitols have been the scene of ferment and surprising accomplishment. . . .

As a Governor, I have found the powers of the state impressive and their opportunities for service challenging in the highest degree. Public service in the states and in local government need be no trivial thing; rather it can command to the full creative and moral imagination. . . .

State political parties can be built and they can quicken civic energies now dormant. The states can regain stature as significant political communities through a rebirth of responsible parties. And thousands who now know democracy only as the threadbare slogans of textbook or preachment will know the manly satisfaction of pulling their weight at the civic oar rather than sitting idly by as supercargo or dead weight.

The reason for the present condition of state government is well summed up in Adlai Stevenson's phrase: "States' rights would not be an issue if there were not so many states' wrongs."

The sad truth of the matter is not that the federal government has forcibly divested the states of functions that they were manfully performing but rather that it has had to do those things for the citizens of the states that their state governments were refusing or neglecting to do. . . .

It says in the books and the orators profess, with some truth I suspect, that people like their chores done by the government closest to them. But I strongly suspect that a good many citizens are more interested in *getting* their chores *done* than in *what* government does them. In other words, it may turn out that the government closest to the people is not so much the government that is closest geographically but the government that is closest sympathetically. . . .

. . . I am sure that each of you can recall some instance where a citizen or group of citizens who wanted something done started with their local government. If their local government failed them they as likely as not went to their state government. If relief was not forthcoming from that state, they went on to Washington. Then the next time they wanted something, they just didn't bother with their state or local government; they went where they got service the last time. . . .

States' rights has become a cult, with a sometimes strange and incomprehensible litany. All of us have watched the politicians who would die for states' rights but then dazzle you with footwork to get at the head of the line for federal handouts. . . .

A mad rush by political leaders to divest the federal government of power purely for the sake of divestment can create a vacuum in which progress will halt. It will not be enough to determine that the states are theoretically capable of performing certain duties now done by the federal government. There will have to be a firm guarantee that the states *will* perform these tasks, so that the problems of the people will not go unsolved. . . .

But after the experts have determined the solutions, the real task will have just begun. It is then that the art of politics will be tested to its fullest. None of the solutions will be worth a jot if they are not accepted by the people. No prefashioned, theoretical framework can be forced upon an unwilling public. The difficult job of achieving this public acceptance will be left to the political parties and their leaders. As throughout the history of democracy, final success rests in the wisdom and energy of the men and women who have chosen the public life.

As Jefferson said of the ward republics and as Pericles said in an earlier society, democracy is a way of life that has to be lived, and lived actively, not just by the few but by the many. It is a quality of human life not to be measured in its success merely by the economy and efficiency of government, but by what it does to lift and ennoble the human spirit. The true role of the states and local government is not the decentralization of power to achieve some eighteenth century clockmaker's dream of political equipoise, or even the higher goal of defeating the dangers of tyranny. Rather, their role is to provide as many of us as possible with the moral opportunity to be citizens, to participate in significant political decisions, to be lifted out of the pettiness of merely private cares to the ennoblement of shared civic life. Governments are no mere utilitarian enterprises. When they become such, they lose their holds on the souls of men.

It is for this reason that we must approach the task that confronts us in the re-fashioning of our federal system. This is no mere problem of transportation, comfort, convenience, economics, or foreign policy. It means building a governmental structure in which men may not merely live, but live well.

Jefferson feared the multitudes piled one on top of the other in great cities. Fortunately, he erred in his time. We, too, have cause to fear a faceless mass, a mere human heap, however well administered, that cannot govern itself, cares not to govern itself, passes this worksome task to authorities, commissions, or other divisions of what Erich Fromm calls the "escape from freedom."

We are facing an era when our powers of production will permit human leisure which Greek philosophers thought the privilege of the few — and that only at the expense of slavery. To be worthy of this leisure, we must plan not merely for the recreation of parks and beaches, but the recreation of the human spirit to be found in a vigorous civic life. Our governments of the future can be either convenient human heaps for commerce and mass entertainment, or hopeful partnerships in all art, all culture, all that ennobles the spirit of man. This is no vain dream. A brilliant age of cities and states is within our grasp if we have the heart and will. This is the promise of American politics. I ask that you who know best this promise do all you can to insure its fulfillment.

8

Freedom and Federalism

By Peter H. Odegard

IT IS AN AXIOM of a free society that the individual shall have maximum freedom to choose his way of life. Subject only to the influences or conditions of his cultural environment, he ought to be free to choose his religion, his politics, his job, his school, his friends — even his wife.

And it is characteristic of a free, pluralistic society — as distinguished from a monolithic-authoritarian one — that the alternatives among which he is free to choose are many rather than few. A free society strives to encourage diversity, knowing that only a pluralistic culture is compatible with the manifold differences that distinguish individuals from one another. And knowing also that it is open-eyed diversity and not blind conformity that gives to a free society its dynamic quality.

It is in the competion of ideas, patterns of behavior, multiple power centers and value systems that that fugitive mistress, Truth, is most likely to be found. Indeed, the late Oliver Wendell Holmes went so far as to say that the best test of an idea is its capacity to win its way in a free market of ideas.

Holmes was but repeating what had been said by

Peter H. Odegard, "Freedom and Federalism," *National Civic Review,* December, 1962, pp. 598–603, 650. Reprinted by permission of the publisher.

many wise men before him, from Socrates to Seneca and Justinian to Jefferson. John Milton put it most eloquently in his essay *Areopagitica:*

Though all the winds of doctrine were let loose to play upon the earth, so Truth be in the field, we do injuriously by licensing and prohibiting to misdoubt her strength. Let Her and Falsehood grapple whoever knew Truth put to the worse, in a free and open encounter.

There are many Americans in these days of continuing crisis who seem to have forgotten this simple notion — that without diversity there is no choice and without choice, no freedom. To speak of safeguarding freedom by denying or impairing the individual's capacity to choose among different and even conflicting alternatives is, of course, a contradiction in terms. . . .

The basic goals of the American Republic are set forth in the Preamble to the Constitution: (1) "To form a more perfect union," (2) "establish justice," (3) "insure domestic tranquility," (4) "provide for the common defense," and (5) "secure the blessings of liberty to ourselves and our posterity."

All that follows in the Constitution concerning the structure and powers of government has no meaning apart from the goals outlined in the Preamble. The relation between the Preamble and Articles I through VII of the Constitution, including the 23 amendments, is a relation of means and ends. The structure and powers of Congress, the President and the courts, the outline of intergovernmental relations in Article II and Section 10 or Article I, the process of amendment described in Article II, the Bill of Rights and the other amendments have no purpose or meaning but to achieve the goals outlined in the Preamble.

The terms in which these goals are outlined are highly ambiguous. What is a more perfect union? What does it mean to establish justice or to promote the general welfare? To point to this ambiguity is to emphasize that these are political terms designed to unite people of highly diverse interests upon common goals, leaving to the political process — that complex interplay of personal, partisan and interest-group competition — to define them more precisely and to agree upon appropriate means for their realization.

The broader goals themselves are quite ambiguous, but they are not meaningless. On the contrary, they provide a basic consensus within which the political process of definition and discovery can go on without resort to violence. It is in this sense that the political process may be defined as a continuous exercise in the logic of ambiguity. Because they are ambiguous, value propositions admit of a variety of definitions as to particular ends and means at particular times and places. That is to say, they admit of various alternatives among which reasonable men may choose. And because they admit of choice, they admit of freedom to choose — and thus help to preserve the blessings of liberty to ourselves and our posterity.

Some of the choices to be made are within the span of control, as it were, of the individual; others are made by individuals as members of some private group or organization like the family, the corporation or the trade union. Still others are made by individuals as members of some political community, i.e., as citizens. In all these situations people make decisions affecting their way of life as it relates to the broad goals outlined in the Preamble to the Constitution. But it is as a citizen that the individual is most directly caught up in the web of government as it reaches from the town meeting to the Security Council of the United Nations.

Because the central purpose of a free society is to secure and promote the freedom and welfare of individuals it strives also to maintain the greatest possible measure of decentralization in the decision-making process.

Freedom, it can be argued, is more secure where each individual himself is able to make the basic decisions affecting his own life. And for those which are beyond his own span of control, a free society requires that the individual participate as directly as possible in the making of decisions for the community in which he lives. To the extent that these decisions are made by authorities remote from the individual, or by a process in which he cannot significantly participate, to that extent he is not free. By this test it is argued that human freedom is most secure when political decisions are made at the lowest possible level of the total web of government — presumably by that unit closest to the people concerned and in which they can most directly and effectively take part. Hence, if we value freedom, we must constantly strive to maintain in the highest possible degree a decentralized system for making political decisions.

Yet increasing centralization is one of the most obvious facts of our political life. Some measure of the trend may be seen in one statistic from President Eisenhower's Commission on Intergovernmental Relations. Whereas in 1929 state and local taxes represented approximately 75 per cent of all taxes collected as against about 25 per cent for the federal government, by 1955 these positions are almost exactly reversed — with state and local taxes comprising only 24 per cent of the total and federal taxes 76 per cent. As our society becomes more closely integrated, this trend will no doubt continue. Presidents deplore it, governors and congressmen view it with alarm; but specific proposals for reversing the trend seem never to get off the drawing-boards.

President Eisenhower's Commission on Intergovernmental Relations (the so-called Kestnbaum Commission), reporting in July 1955, made numerous recommendations for the improvement of federal-state relations and for an increase in state and local responsibility in a number of areas. But so little came of this effort that, in 1958, a subcommittee on Intergovernmental Relations was set up by the House Committee on Government Operations "to evaluate the recommendations of the Kestnbaum Commission and to ascertain what action is being and should be taken concerning them." And in 1959 a permanent Advisory Commission on Intergovernmental Relations was established.

Many of the proposals that have been made involve not merely a reallocation of functions and finances, not merely questions of organization and administration, but questions of policy, i.e., of politics. Consequently, discussion often proceeds on a high level of ambiguity. The following statement of the President's commission will serve to illustrate:

Leave to private initiative all the functions *that citizens can perform privately,* use the *level of government closest to the community for all public functions it can handle,* utilize cooperative intergovernmental arrangements *where appropriate* to attain economical performances and popular approval, reserve national action for residual participation where state and local governments are not fully adequate and for the continuing responsibilities that only the national government can undertake.

Few people will quarrel with these basic objectives. Conflict ensues when we undertake to translate these ambiguous terms into specific proposals. Not many years ago most folks would have said that unemployment and poor relief and the support of the aged were matters more properly left to the family or to private charity. Today an important body of opinion believes that even medical care should be as much a public responsibility as unemployment insurance, poor relief and old age pensions now are. The expansion of the public sector of our economic and social life continues to be a subject of heated debate. For those who regard social security legislation, medical care for the aged or massive support for public education as avoidable, undesirable and even malicious, it makes little difference whether these new public responsibilities are assumed by local, state or national governments. States' rights, local self-government and other slogans used to resist federal action in these areas are often a kind of semantic screen to conceal campaigns of opposition not to centralization as such but to the substance of the particular policies proposed.

Businessmen who talk solemnly about the evils of big government are singularly complacent as they contemplate the growth of big business. The most strident plea to "restore the states to their rightful place in our federal union," by keeping the federal government out of such fields as education, health and welfare, housing or urban renewal, is rarely accompanied by opposition to monumental defense expenditures, highway programs or subsidies to business enterprise. The leaders of the fight against welfare legislation in Washington more often than not also lead the fight against welfare legislation at the state capitol and the city hall.

Nevertheless, these conflicts over particular policies are not unrelated to our basic assumption that human freedom and welfare will be most secure under a system based on the greatest possible decentralization of decision-making. Political decisions, it is said, should ideally be made at the "lowest possible level." But the lowest possible level will vary not only with time and place but with the kind of decisions to be made. The lowest possible level at which decisions affecting police, fire protection, garbage disposal, water supply, stream pollution, reclamation, mass communication or transportation, national defense, war and peace, will vary from the town meeting to the city council, the metropolitan area, the state legislature, the regional council or authority, the Congress of the United States or a summit meeting in Geneva.

What is the lowest possible unit for making decisions concerning smog control, mass transportation and a dozen other problems that confront our great metropolitan areas — especially those that overlap state boundaries and include dozens of towns, cities, counties and special districts?

What is the lowest possible unit for making decisions concerning the regulation of oligopolies, with headquarters in New Jersey or Delaware but with branches reaching not only into nearly every state but into many foreign countries? To say that these decisions should be made by the cities, counties and states within which these giants operate is to set David against Goliath with the cards all stacked against David.

The fact is, of course, that under the impact of irresistible centripetal forces — population growth, density and mobility, technological developments reducing barriers of time and space, hot wars and cold wars, etc. — major political decisions will increasingly be made at higher and higher levels in the great web of government.

Does this centralization of decision-making necessarily imply a threat to freedom? Does centralized decision-making by great corporations under conditions of monopolistic competition threaten freedom and welfare or has large scale enterprise accelerated economic growth, increased our standard of living and expanded our freedom in our range of choice? When the Supreme Court decides that states are not free to enforce racial segregation in public schools, will not this decision, in spite of temporary setbacks, give to both Negroes and whites greater freedom in choosing the schools to which they may send their children? Is freedom jeopardized or restricted when Congress, through grants-in-aid, enables states and municipalities to undertake programs of education, housing and urban rehabilitation, public health, transportation and welfare that in the absence of such grants would be impossible? Do not these programs, in fact, expand the scope of individual freedom by multiplying the alternatives among which he may realistically choose?

But, it will be said, even if the centralization of political decision-making poses no serious threat to freedom, it may threaten our democratic institutions by making participation in the decision-making process more difficult and thus undermining our will and capacity for self-government. "Municipal institutions," said de Tocqueville, "constitute the strength of free nations. Town meetings are to liberty what primary schools are to science: they bring it within the people's reach, they teach men how to use and how to enjoy it." This model of democracy with its roots and its strength in local assemblies has much to commend it.

Unfortunately, de Tocqueville's model had a closer fit to the comparatively stable agrarian society of 1832 than to the highly integrated, mobile society of 1962. There was a singular vitality in local assemblies when the major problems of government were local and could be met by decisions made at the village, town or county level. But as the scope and complexity of the major problems increased, as it became clear that local units of government — even when endowed with home rule by the state — were unable to deal with them, the center of power and the focus of civic interest moved away from the town to the county, the state and the nation.

The fact is that, to thousands of our citizens, the state and even the federal government seem closer and more visible than the city or the county. Indifference and apathy characterize democracy at the grass roots and may, in time, as de Tocqueville said it would, undermine our will and capacity for self-government. A recent study of elections for governing boards of local special districts says that "voter turnout is low, it being quite common for only 1 per cent to 5 per cent of the voters to participate." If we are to do something about this more constructive than wringing our hands, we shall have to take some radical measures to restore power and vitality to local political institutions. For civic interest follows power. A few things we might consider include:

1. A reform in the structure of our state governments is needed. State constitutions are almost models of what constitutions ought not to be. State legislatures are unrepresentative of the most dynamic forces in society and attract at best but mediocre talents. Recent court decisions may help to make legislatures at least more representative. The size, organi-

zation and procedures of most state legislatures inhibit honest discussion and debate, obscure responsibility for policy decisions and invite excessive influence, if not domination, by special interests.

2. Part of the problem arises from the inability of the governor to assume leadership and responsibility for policy and administration. He is normally but one of several elected executive officers—a hydra-headed monster often going in different directions at the same time. Moreover, the long ballot which this system entails, made longer by direct legislation, makes the voters' task all but impossible.

3. Congress and the states might seriously explore establishment of more regional authorities on the order of the TVA, where decisions can be made in the region with closer and continuous ties to local communities rather than in Washington, thus achieving decentralization on terms compatible with demography and common sense. Some of these results can be attained under interstate regional compacts provided Congress is prepared to give the necessary financial assistance at the beginning.

4. The reorganization of government in our great metropolitan areas can do much to revitalize interest in local affairs. The application of the federal principle to the government of these areas might make possible a maximum of decentralization of truly local functions with areawide authority over others.

5. The consolidation of thousands of special district authorities with the county, city or metropolitan area government to which they are properly related might help to stop the progressive Balkanization of local governments.

6. Independent authorities for air pollution, transit, etc., now engaged in performing special services in metropolitan areas should be brought under an area-wide government owing political responsibility to the citizens of the area.

7. Partisanship in state and metropolitan government should be restored and revitalized so that major issues of public policy can be debated by leaders responsible to effective political parties rather than to clandestine combines of pressure groups. There is, in fact, a Republican, Democratic or Socialist way to run a great city.

8. A continuous review by the permanent Advisory Commission on Intergovernmental Relations of state-federal-local fiscal relations can explore more equi-

table and realistic allocation of functions and sources of revenue.

These are but a few of the problems that confront the American web of government in the United States as it seeks to respond to the demands of a society in the midst of almost cataclysmic change. Part of this change is in the structure of the American economy and American society, part of it in the transformation of our federal system. For American federalism wears a new face and has a new orientation. The new orientation is toward closer and more cooperative relations between federal, state and local governments — through grants-in-aid, cooperative law enforcement, interstate compacts and regional authorities. This new orientation includes also a growing realization of the importance of the federal principle in the government of metropolitan areas.

The web of government in the United States, moreover, reflects a new and more affirmative relation between public and private power structures. The freedom which federalism was designed to conserve has come to mean not merely freedom from monolithic, arbitrary power but also freedom to take affirmative action to provide for the common defense, promote the general welfare and preserve the blessings of liberty to everyone regardless of race or class or creed. The new federalism, says Robert Hutchins, "tends to look upon law [not so much] as an invasion of freedom . . . [but] as a means of establishing, extending or confirming freedom."

If the decentralization of decision-making among federal, state and local governments is important to freedom and welfare, so too is the decentralization of decision-making in business and industry, the learned professions and labor, in education and other organized groups which compose the private power structure of our society. But centripetal forces are in the saddle, both in public and in private life, not because evil men have conspired to put them there but because a common market of continental and even world dimensions demands decision-making on a continental scale. The future of our federal system and of our freedom and welfare as individuals will depend upon our success in reconciling this fact with that degree of decentralization that will release in the greatest possible measure the creative initiative and energies of our people.

CHAPTER THREE

Intergovernmental Relations—
State-Local and Interstate

ALTHOUGH NATIONAL-STATE RELATIONS may be more sensational and are certainly better publicized, state-local relations are also of tremendous importance in our federal system. For many years local governments and their spokesmen have argued for establishment and later liberalization of home rule provisions, designed to let them draft their own charters and operate somewhat more independently of the state. The case for greater home rule is made here by a veteran member of the New York State Senate. It remains true that there is also a case for a reasonable degree of uniformity within a state, for coordination of efforts, and for a variety of assistance to local units from the state level. Without disputing the desirability of the home rule principle, Professor Grumm in the second article suggests the possible utility of a state agency concerned specifically with local government affairs.

9

The States
Eclipse the Cities

By Thomas C. Desmond

A PERPLEXED councilman of a city in upstate New York telephoned me not long ago to ask, "What kind of pipes will the state let us use for our city sewers?"

Although I am chairman of the New York State Senate Committee on Affairs of Cities, I was unaware that the state regulates sewer pipes. Since the question was solemnly put, I answered, just as solemnly, that I would look into it. Inquiries at several state agencies turned up a sanitary engineer who informed

me that his bureau in the State Health Department most certainly does have the power to approve or veto the use of various types of pipe by cities.

This is one example — and not a far-fetched one — of how our states keep a tight, often choking rein on our cities in a variety of matters, from sewer pipes to tax rates, from bond issues to hiring a stenographer for the fire commissioner.

This year 46 state legislatures have held or are holding sessions, and headlines in newspapers across the country have echoed charges and countercharges of state and city officials on the issue of state control of municipal affairs. The clash between the city's desire — and need — for more self-government and the state's attempt to retain its dominant position over the city has once more been brought to the fore as a major problem of government. It is a major problem because although minor abuses by the states might be tolerated, when the states strangle local initiative, curb local responsibility, foist unnecessary expenses on local taxpayers and block new services needed in an age of urbanism, the cities have strong arguments for home rule.

What is the nature of the controls the states have over cities? How are they exercised? And what, specifically, are the results?

Thomas C. Desmond, "The States Eclipse the Cities," *New York Times Magazine,* April 24, 1955, pp. 14, 42, 44. Reprinted by permission of the author and publisher.

The controls are both legislative and administrative, and are applied and enforced in three ways. One is by passing laws that affect cities. Another is by judicial decisions. The third is by administrative curbs.

In theory the states can grant — or withhold — municipal home rule to any degree they wish. In practice they restrict home rule by enacting or not enacting laws — either special laws applying locally or so-called general laws containing restrictive clauses aimed at certain cities. They can also do it by repealing or changing city charters. Like domineering mothers, the states refuse cities the right to run their own lives. Only 21 states make so much as a gesture toward granting some form of home rule to their cities, and even this is usually meaningless.

Thus, although cities have the right to elect their own officers and to carry out duties assigned to them by state legislatures, in most states they do not have the authority to determine their own form of government or the powers they may exercise. Many do not even have the right to choose which revenue sources they can tap to support local services.

Courts rule against cities

The judicial form of control stems from the fact that the courts have repeatedly ruled against cities and for legislatures. Judges have denied cities any inherent right to self-government; cities are deemed the legal creatures of the state, with no powers except those granted by the state. Moreover, courts have ignored repeated evasions of constitutional prohibitions against laws applying to a single city.

As with legislative controls, so with administrative restrictions. States view the cities at best as irresponsible, unruly children capable of an amazing amount of mischief; therefore, they must be held to firm standards, if necessary by an occasional fiscal spanking. Today, nearly half the states force cities to follow state-prescribed budget systems and require periodic probes of city accounts, either by state agencies or state-approved accountants. The feeling is: spare the regulations and spoil the city.

States do aid cities in various ways. One is by providing technical assistance. For example, Joseph Watkins, as a career personnel technician in the New York Civil Service Department, works in city halls throughout the state to help install modern personnel procedures. He also keeps a sharp eye out for violations of the merit system by job-hungry politicians. When such services are voluntarily accepted by the localities, neither local responsibility nor home rule is violated. But many states attempt to impose efficiency and virtue by restrictive state legislation which does more harm than good.

Another way states aid cities is by financial contributions. One out of every five dollars of the annual income of our cities comes from the states. But unfortunately the grants are usually hedged with many restrictions. Moreover, the cities must depend upon the real estate tax, a relic of the eighteenth century, for two out of every three tax dollars.

The states, viewing the cities as competitors for the taxpayer's dollar, not only force cities to rely on the property tax but also tightly limit the amount they can raise from this source. They have refused municipal pleas for the right to impose a payroll or an income tax, or to levy or increase taxes on local utilities — although the states themselves levy such taxes for statewide use. This further shrinks the cities' tax base. In addition, legislatures often yield to pressure groups and pass laws that force cities to raise the salaries of some categories of employees or to take on other fiscal burdens.

Thus, city officials, trapped between expensive demands for airports, roads, hospitals, schools or salary increases, and inadequate funds to pay the bills, are today walking a perilous economic tightrope. Yet in all the quarrels between cities and states, the cities usually have to battle with both hands tied behind their backs.

The net result of these methods of state control is that our cities must beseech legislators for their basic right to exist, to govern, to police their streets, to provide water for their people. Unless they obtain legislative authorization from the states, they cannot establish parking lots, regulate intracity buses, stop slaughterhouses from opening up in residential areas, or do any of a thousand things a modern city must do for its people.

How it happened

The city dweller who is the victim of the system may wonder how state controls became so thoroughly clamped on municipal affairs. One reason was the powerful position which the states assumed at the beginning of our national history. After the Revolution the states inherited all the authority formerly held by royal governors. At that time the legislatures dominated both the executive and judicial branches of the state governments. The constitution later confirmed many of the powers the states had assumed under the confederation. But, in those early years, the efforts of state control were not too onerous, for cities were small.

The cities' real troubles began with the growth of urbanism. As cities increased in size, political power passed from the farm to the tenement. The "city vote" became a prime target for ambitious politicians. Lawmakers discovered that more votes were usually to be gained by sponsoring local bills than by campaigning for even the most desirable statewide legislation. (In all state capitols, local bills are passed or killed on the basis of "legislative courtesy." Customarily no bill affecting a city will be introduced or voted down without advance approval of the legislator representing that community.)

This has led to a seeming paradox. The short-changing of cities by states is traditionally attributed to over-representation of rural areas in our legislatures. Yet the rural representatives are by and large disinterested and do not mix in city affairs. The worst offenders in the strangulation of cities by states are legislators from the cities. In New York State, for example, 45 out of 58 state senators either live or work in cities.

In the course of time the growth of urban political power in the legislatures raised, in practice, the local legislative delegations to the position of superior governing bodies over the municipal officials. Without the approval of the local legislators the city authorities were unable to carry out needed programs. This proved especially troublesome when the legislative delegation was of one party and the municipal officials were of another, or when the delegation belonged to the minority party in the legislature.

In the resulting stalemates the failure of cities to plan in advance to meet clearly emerging problems of traffic congestion, slum clearance and crime has created a recurring series of emergencies. Clutching at any straw, the cities have often turned to the states for what aid they can get. In addition, weak local officials have often evaded responsibility and passed on to the states the solution of sensitive issues. All of these factors have tended to put and keep the state in the driver's seat.

What, more specifically, is wrong with this system of state control over cities? In what ways does it harm the cities?

It has been argued in behalf of the system that the cities have brought some of their woes upon themselves. That is true. Corruption has been no stranger in city halls. To cite a minor but illuminating instance, one "H. Bell" was on Jersey City's payroll for years before someone discovered that he was a horse in the public works department and that a foreman had been collecting the "employee's" weekly pay check.

There have been many far greater municipal scandals. Yet cities are not as corrupt as some believe. William Embler, former deputy controller of New York State, informs me that the state's audit of the books of eight thousand localities every two years has disclosed remarkable official probity. Sums misappropriated in a recent year have totaled no more than $7,800.

The main thing wrong with the state control system is that cities are now too big and too complicated to have their affairs handled by outsiders who may not be as familiar as they should with city problems.

Half our people now live in cities with populations of 100,000 or more. Our cities have become giant diversified businesses, operating airports, hospitals and water plants. They are often the largest employers in their respective regions. They need freedom to regulate their growth and the increasing physical and social problems caused by their size.

Our cities have gained maturity. But instead of recognizing what they can and must do for themselves, the states continue to pass laws interfering with them, often for reasons of spite. Legislators can punish opposing cliques, grant concessions and act as benign overlords or petty tyrants.

Time and effort wasted

Another evil of the system is its waste of time and effort. Before my committee recently were bills to permit Poughkeepsie to sell some land it had acquired for hospital purposes and no longer needs, to authorize Ogdensburg to spend $5,000 on publicity, to let Newburgh turn over a dead-end street to a factory that needs it to expand. In some legislatures hundreds of local bills, of no concern to anyone except the single sponsor, must be considered and passed at each session.

Even when states, out of the best of motives, substitute arbitrary regulations for local flexibility, the end result is often waste and sometimes danger. Because cities are required to accept "the lowest responsible bid" when buying material, they must often purchase machinery from a distant source which cannot service it, rather than from a nearby source which can. There is no leeway, no discretion. Thus, some fire trucks in one city today carry different sets of hose connections to every fire because the lowest bidder on hose connections did not have connections to fit the fire hydrants in that city.

Another thing wrong with such strong state control is that lobbies can often use the state's power over cities to enrich themselves. For example, a bill was passed at the recent session of the New York legislature to require cities to equip each fire truck with two sets of gas masks of a type apparently made by only a few manufacturers. The bill, amazingly, had been passed twice before but was vetoed by Governor Dewey. Now it had been passed a third time.

What is solution?

What can be done to improve the state-city relationship? How can the cities gain some independence?

I do not propose that cities be cut loose to operate on their own. Local affairs are too intermingled with those of other levels of government for cities to become wholly autonomous. Arterial highways, control over courts, wage and hour regulations, annexation of land, war against communicable diseases — these are things which transcend local interest and call for state action. But if the delineation of state and local problems is difficult at times, it is hardly insuperable.

The standard should be this: what the states can do better than the cities should be done by the states; what the states and cities can do best together should be done jointly; what the cities can do better than the states should be done by the cities.

There remains the problem of how to achieve this method of operation. Professor Rodney Mott of Colgate University outlined for the American Municipal Association three conditions necessary to obtain home rule: (1) lively public support, (2) aggressive leadership by state leagues of municipalities, and (3) a change in the attitude of judges.

In rotary clubs and chambers of commerce, in women's clubs and welfare organizations, our people will have to voice demands that the states yield their authority over the cities. A rallying point could be a demand for the simple requirement that in every case where states force new expenses upon cities, the states would have to indicate how the expenses are to be met and authorize new tax levies if required. This would be a powerful influence in imposing a sense of responsibility on legislatures.

In states where the people have the right of initiative and referendum the voters can place freedom clauses in state constitutions which the lawmakers would not be able to skirt. In other states the campaign will have to be waged in constitutional conventions or by frontal attacks on the legislatures.

At future sessions bills should be introduced to provide that cities shall have all powers that legislatures are legally capable of granting to cities — subject to reasonable limitations. This would serve immediately to broaden the area of home rule. In addition, cities should be granted the power to draft and amend their own charters.

Not all public action, however, should be aimed at the states. The "buck-passers" on the local city councils who, when confronted with a politically hot issue, leave responsibility to the states, must be shown that the voters will not tolerate such supine behavior.

In the free association of cities the municipalities have opportunities to develop standards and employ experts without domination by the states. State leagues of municipalities need to be strengthened to bolster technical services available to cities and to withstand state intrusion. There is no basic need for conflict. The well-being of the states and cities depends upon the vitality and integrity of both. . . .

10

Do We Need a State Agency for Local Affairs?

By John G. Grumm

THE STEADY GROWTH of urban population has become an accepted fact of national life in the United States. The move to the cities has proceeded with virtually no interruption during the present century, and it would appear safe to anticipate a continued rising population in almost all major urban areas. Accompanying this has been a spreading out of urban population so that geographic expansion of urban areas also has shown a great increase.

One of the basic problems caused by the population movement is the absence of local governmental organizations broad enough geographically and functionally to cope with metropolitan matters. Instead, in most areas, there is a great multiplicity of governmental units which have not proven capable of making a concerted and coordinated attack on the pressing problems at hand. As a result, governmental services within the metropolitan region as a whole often present a chaotic picture. City streets, for example, may be laid down in an uncoordinated fashion with little relation to metropolitan traffic patterns. Within the same area, there may be great differences in the quality of services provided. The interests of the metropolitan area as a whole may easily be disregarded in the planning and zoning functions.

Still other problems are presented in the large unincorporated urban fringe areas surrounding the cities. In order to meet their needs, the unincorporated communities have either called upon the county to furnish services, or have set up a series of special districts for that purpose, or both. Under these circumstances the resulting standards of service often tend to be lower than in the cities, and the aggregate local tax load tends to be higher. . . .

In addition to the problems of the larger urban areas, small cities outside the major metropolitan regions are experiencing other problems because of their limited size and lack of resources. Many small and medium-sized cities have lost population in the rush

John G. Grumm, "Do We Need a State Agency for Local Affairs?" *Public Management*, June, 1961, pp. 129–133. Footnotes in original omitted. Reprinted by permission of the publisher.

to the larger urban centers. And even where there has been no loss, numerous incorporated places have remained very small in size and limited in their ability to finance governmental services.

These small cities need assistance of various types. Some cannot employ a full-time city attorney and need additional legal help. Many do not have adequate systems of personnel administration. Often small cities could use advice and assistance in budgeting, accounting, and debt management. Almost all of the smaller cities need help in city planning.

Role of the state

Although the problems of large metropolitan communities are vastly different from those of small municipalities, the state government has a vital role to play in the solution of both kinds of problems. Legally, the responsibility of the states in this regard cannot be ignored. From a practical standpoint, also, the state governments are the only institutions capable of handling some of these problems.

The activities of the state and of its local governments are, in essence, a joint endeavor, and many of the functions are shared functions. There are a few matters that can be considered *purely* local, but most of the activity of local government has an impact beyond local boundaries. Since the state is the more inclusive and legally superior entity, it is generally recognized that the state has primary responsibility for a well-ordered system of state-local relations. The state also is superior to the localities in its ability to raise revenue. In the words of the Committee on State-Local Relations of the Council of State Governments, "This dual dominance of states — in law and finance — is an incontrovertible fact. It places a heavy obligation upon the states to create an orderly and effective system of state-local relations."

State-local relations

The role of the states in meeting urban problems would seem to be three-fold. First they must provide the legal framework necessary for *effective* local government. This is a matter that might well be examined by most state legislatures. Second, the state's responsibility for the soundness and adequacy of local finances requires it to exercise a degree of supervision over local fiscal procedures but at the same time avoid making limitations on local revenue sources too restrictive. Where local units cannot properly finance their operations from local sources, state money must be provided through grants-in-aid. Finally, the states need to improve local administrative practice through supervision, encouragement, and assistance. Many types of supervision and control are employed, but a more fruitful approach in many respects is the provision of expert advice, information, research, and technical services to local governments.

With a few notable exceptions, the states have not been meeting their responsibilities toward their local governments. A major difficulty is that the states have generally not sought to concentrate their local services, research, and supervisory activities in one agency. Characteristically almost every agency of state government is involved in relations with the local units in some way.

How concentrated?

A national authority on local government, Harold F. Alderfer, has argued that, since the responsibility for maintaining a sound system of local government constitutes a major state function, *all* of the activities related to this responsibility should be placed in one agency which would have departmental or cabinet status.

Another significant proposal, though less far-reaching, advocated a separate state *research and service agency* which would "aid in determining the present and changing needs of its metropolitan and non-metropolitan areas."

Existing state agencies

A small number of states have established agencies primarily concerned with local government. The New Jersey Division of Local Government is one. Its most important functions are examining municipal and county budgets and auditing municipal and county accounts. It also publishes guides and statistical reports for local units and is authorized to study the whole field of local government, to render advice to municipalities when requested, and to recommend plans for the improvement of local administration.

In Pennsylvania the Bureau of Municipal Affairs is responsible both for a wide range of services to localities and for some supervisory functions. In the breadth and variety of its activities, it is probably unique in the United States. Its activities are organized into four divisions which are responsible for: (1) research and information regarding local units, (2) the collection and dissemination of local government financial statistics, (3) providing assistance in city planning and landscape architecture to local public bodies, and (4) the approval of local bond issues and bond proceedings.

Another type of local government agency exists in Tennessee — the Municipal Technical Advisory Service. Attached to the University of Tennessee, it offers direct services in such areas as municipal management, finance and accounting, engineering and public works, fringe areas, municipal law, municipal information, and ordinance codification. In addition, its publication program includes directories, handbooks, statistical compilations, and analyses of state laws and constitutional amendments affecting local government.

The recently established New York Office for Local Government is primarily a staff agency to the governor, but a list of its powers suggests a potential of some magnitude. It is empowered to assist the governor in coordinating the activities and services of 20 state agencies having relationships with local governments, to provide advice and assistance to local units, to make studies of urban and metropolitan problems, to serve as a clearinghouse for information about local matters, and to encourage and assist cooperative efforts toward the solution of metropolitan problems.

A number of other states have agencies for local affairs that are somewhat more narrow in scope. The North Carolina Local Government Commission has the basic responsibility of controlling municipal borrowing. The Minnesota Municipal Commission and the Alaska Local Boundary Commission are concerned primarily with review and approval of municipal incorporations, annexations, and consolidations.

It should be noted also that most of the provincial governments of Canada have an agency concerned exclusively with local affairs. Some of their powers and responsibilities are quite comprehensive. . . .

Desirability of state agency

Would the establishment of agencies responsible for the major state activities relating to its local government lessen the many problems which beset our urban communities? Agencies of this sort in Canada apparently have performed satisfactorily, and the few in the United States have done a good job within the limits of their authority. There are, however, a number of considerations that must be borne in mind before such a step is taken.

In listing the arguments in favor of a state agency for local affairs, one should first point out that the problems of urban areas are bound to increase and that only the state, by virtue of its superior legal position, can provide the positive measures that are needed. Therefore, a new state agency is advisable for the purpose of administering new local assistance and service programs and for coordinating some of the established local services that the state now provides.

Even without the addition of new functions, coordination of state-local relations is needed in most states. Generally a variety of agencies and officials administers existing aids and controls. This can lead to confusion and possibly to duplication of state efforts. From the standpoint of the city official, there

is no central place where he can go in the state government to get information or help.

Second, it is argued that there should be a recognition of the central importance of state-local relations in the state system, and that creation of such an agency would achieve this. It is also consistent with this view that the agency should have departmental or "cabinet" status. Thus a focus would be created in the state government for policy leadership on local matters. Many urban states have "cabinet" level departments devoted to agriculture, but none has such a department devoted to urban matters. This is inequitable, it is argued, and puts the more populous urban areas at a disadvantage in relation to the rural sections. According to this view, cities need an effective representative of their interests in the executive branch of the state government.

One other factor is the increasing role of the federal government in urban matters. . . . Undoubtedly the trend will not be reversed until the states become better organized to deal with their own local governments. According to this argument, the establishment of effective agencies for local affairs in most of the states, especially the heavily urbanized ones . . . would reduce the influence of the federal government in local matters.

On the other side, there are generally three objections to a state agency for local affairs. First, it would introduce an incongruity into the state's administrative structure and might disrupt a well-established relationship. State programs affecting local governments cut across the jurisdiction of many existing agencies and departments (highways, social welfare and public health, for example). The *internal* coordination of each of these major functional programs by the existing agencies is probably more important than close coordination *among* all the agencies having contact with local government. In addition, many of the relationships between the functional departments and the local units have been built up over a long period of time, are well established, and would be difficult to change even if it were considered desirable to do so.

Second, it can be argued that a new state agency of this kind might tend to increase the dependence of the local units on the state. It is suggested that the cities and counties can solve their own financial and administrative problems and that at the present time the state need only give local governments sufficient leeway through enabling legislation to permit them to seek their own solutions.

Third, local governments already have many sources of outside help. In almost all states a league of municipalities can help with legal and technical advice and information. In some states local governments can rely on bureaus and institutes connected with state universities. In fact, it is argued that the existing services and aids offered by the various state agencies constitute, in the aggregate, an extensive program of assistance, research, and service for local units.

Functions of state agency

Despite the objections raised, a properly constituted state agency for local affairs probably can play a significant role in many of the more urbanized states.

It would appear advisable, however, that the agency engage primarily in service and facilitative functions, rather than control or supervision, and that there be a minimum of interference with well-established programs of other departments dealing with local units.

Examples of some of the services that might be performed by the new agency would include planning assistance, personnel and civil service aids, assistance with budgeting and accounting procedures, aid in engineering and public works, and legal advice.

In addition the new agency almost certainly should be charged with conducting extensive research on urban problems. The research program would not seek to supplant those carried on by state leagues of municipalities or university bureaus of research but should be designed to complement them. General studies might be emphasized rather than studies of specific conditions in individual communities.

A final function of the new agency would be to assist the governor and legislature in coordinating state activities affecting local communities and in formulating policies with respect to urban areas. The agency could also serve as a central point of contact in the state government for local officials and representatives of municipal leagues and other local governmental associations.

The location of the agency within the state administrative structure is an important consideration. In many respects the best arrangement would be to establish it as a staff agency closely associated with or in the office of the governor. If it had no control functions, it would not have to be in the line structure of the executive branch. Close association with the governor's office would emphasize the agency's potential advantages as a source of information, research, and policy formulation in local affairs.

Relations between the states pose many vexing problems, these problems being of course peculiar to a federal system of government. That clause of the United States Constitution which requires each state to give "full faith and credit" to the public acts, records and judicial proceedings of every other state has been a sufficient bone of contention to merit Mr. Justice Jackson's label, "the lawyers' clause of the Constitution." In Williams v. North Carolina, the court comes to grips with the frequently recurring migratory divorce problem, and in the process establishes, over vigorous dissents, the conditions under which a demand to accept the proceedings of another state may be refused. Robert S. Rankin then describes, with illuminating anecdotes, the problems surrounding the interstate rendition of fugitives from justice, and suggests some possible solutions.

11

Williams et al.

v.

State of North Carolina

Mr. Justice FRANKFURTER delivered the opinion of the Court.

This case is here to review judgments of the Supreme Court of North Carolina, affirming convictions for bigamous cohabitation, assailed on the ground that full faith and credit, as required by the Constitution of the United States, was not accorded divorces decreed by one of the courts of Nevada. Williams v. North Carolina, 317 U.S. 287, 63 S.Ct. 207, 87 L.Ed. 279, 143 A.L.R. 1273, decided an earlier aspect of the controversy. It was there held that a divorce granted by Nevada, on a finding that one spouse was domiciled in Nevada, must be respected in North Carolina, where Nevada's finding of domicil was not questioned though the other spouse had neither appeared nor been served with process in Nevada and though recognition of such a divorce offended the policy of North Carolina. The record then before us did not present the question whether North Carolina had the power "to refuse full faith and credit to Nevada divorce decrees because, contrary to the findings of the Nevada court, North Carolina finds that no bona fide domicil was acquired in Nevada." Williams v. North Carolina, supra, 317 U.S. at page 302, 63 S.Ct. at page 215, 87 L.Ed. 279, 143 A.L.R. 1273. This is the precise issue which has emerged after retrial of the cause following our reversal. Its obvious importance brought the case here. . . . .

The essence of the matter was . . . put in what Thompson v. Whitman adopted from Story: " 'The Constitution did not mean to confer (upon the

325 U.S. 226, 65 S.Ct. 1092, 89 L.Ed. 1577 (1945)

States) a new power or jurisdiction, but simply to regulate the effect of the acknowledged jurisdiction over persons and things within their territory.' " 18 Wall. 457, 462, 21 L.Ed. 897. In short, the Full Faith and Credit Clause puts the Constitution behind a judgment instead of the too fluid, ill-defined concept of "comity."

But the Clause does not make a sister-State judgment a judgment in another State. The proposal to do so was rejected by the Philadelphia Convention. 2 Farrand, The Records of the Federal Convention of 1787, 447,448. "To give it the force of a judgment in another state, it must be made a judgment there." McElmoyle v. Cohen, 13 Pet. 312,325, 10 L.Ed. 177. It can be made a judgment there only if the court purporting to render the original judgment had power to render such a judgment. A judgment in one State is conclusive upon the merits in every other State, but only if the courts of the first State had power to pass on the merits — had jurisdiction, that is, to render the judgment. . . .

Under our system of law, judicial power to grant a divorce — a jurisdiction, strictly speaking — is founded on domicil. . . . The framers of the Constitution were familiar with this jurisdictional prerequisite, and since 1789 neither this Court nor any other court in the English-speaking world has questioned it. Domicil implies a nexus between person and place of such permanence as to control the creation of legal relations and responsibilities of the utmost significance. The domicil of one spouse within a State gives power to that State, we have held, to dissolve a marriage wheresoever contracted. . . . Divorce, like marriage, is of concern not merely to the immediate parties. It affects personal rights of the deepest significance. It also touches basic interests of society. Since divorce, like marriage, creates a new status, every consideration of policy makes it desirable that the effect should be the same wherever the question arises. . . .

The State of domiciliary origin should not be bound by an unfounded, even if not collusive, recital in the record of a court of another State. As to the truth or existence of a fact, like that of domicil, upon which depends the power to exert judicial authority, a State not a party to the exertion of such judicial authority in another State but seriously affected by it has a right, when asserting its own unquestioned authority, to ascertain the truth or existence of that crucial fact. . . .

If a finding by the court of one State that domicil in another State has been abandoned were conclusive upon the old domiciliary State, the policy of each State in matters of most intimate concern could be subverted by the policy of every other State. This Court has long ago denied the existence of such destructive power. . . .

In short, the decree of divorce is a conclusive adjudication of everything except the jurisdictional facts upon which it is founded, and domicil is a jurisdictional fact. To permit the necessary finding of domicil by one State to foreclose all States in the protection of their social institutions would be intolerable.

But to endow each State with controlling authority to nullify the power of a sister State to grant a divorce based upon a finding that one spouse had acquired a new domicil within the divorcing State would, in the proper functioning of our federal system, be equally indefensible. No State court can assume comprehensive attention to the various and potentially conflicting interests that several States may have in the institutional aspects of marriage. The necessary accommodation between the right of one State to safeguard its interest in the family relation of its own people and the power of another State to grant divorces can be left to neither State. . . .

What is immediately before us is the judgment of the Supreme Court of North Carolina, 224 N.C. 183, 29 S.E. 2d 744. We have authority to upset it only if there is want of foundation for the conclusion that that Court reached. The conclusion it reached turns on its finding that the spouses who obtained the Nevada decrees were not domiciled there. The fact that the Nevada court found that they were domiciled there is entitled to respect, and more. The burden of undermining the verity which the Nevada decrees import rests heavily upon the assailant. But simply because the Nevada court found that it had power to award a divorce decree cannot, we have seen, foreclose reexamination by another State. Otherwise, as was pointed out long ago, a court's record would establish its power and the power would be proved by the record. Such circular reasoning would give one State a control over all the other States which the Full Faith and Credit Clause certainly did not confer. . . .

When this case was first here, North Carolina did not challenge the finding of the Nevada court that petitioners had acquired domicils in Nevada. For her challenge of the Nevada decrees, North Carolina rested on Haddock v. Haddock, 201 U.S. 562, 26 S.Ct. 525, 50 L.Ed. 867, 5 Ann. Cas. 1. Upon retrial, however, the existence of domicil in Nevada became the decisive issue. The judgments of conviction now under review bring before us a record which may be fairly summarized by saying that the petitioners left North Carolina for the purpose of getting divorces from their respective spouses in Nevada and as soon as each had done so and married one another they left Nevada and returned to North Carolina to live there together as man and wife. Against the charge of bigamous cohabitation under

§14–183 of the North Carolina General Statutes, petitioners stood on their Nevada divorces and offered exemplified copies of the Nevada proceedings. . . . If the jury found, as they were told, that petitioners had domicils in North Carolina and went to Nevada "simply and solely for the purpose of obtaining" divorces, intending to return to North Carolina on obtaining them, they never lost their North Carolina domicils nor acquired new domicils in Nevada. Domicil, the jury was instructed, was that place where a person "has voluntarily fixed his abode . . . not for a mere special or temporary purpose, but with a present intention of making it his home, either permanently or for an indefinite or unlimited length of time."

The scales of justice must not be unfairly weighted by a State when full faith and credit is claimed for a sister-State judgment. But North Carolina has not so dealt with the Nevada decrees. She has not raised unfair barriers to their recognition. North Carolina did not fail in appreciation or application of federal standards of full faith and credit. Appropriate weight was given to the finding of domicil in the Nevada decrees, and that finding was allowed to be overturned only by relevant standards of proof. There is nothing to suggest that the issue was not fairly submitted to the jury and that it was not fairly assessed on cogent evidence.

State courts cannot avoid review by this Court of their disposition of a constitutional claim by casting it in the form of an unreviewable finding of fact. Norris v. Alabama, 294 U.S. 587, 490, 55 S.Ct. 579, 580, 79 L.Ed. 1074. This record is barren of such attempted evasion. What it shows is that petitioners, long-time residents of North Carolina, came to Nevada, where they stayed in an auto-court for transients, filed suits for divorce as soon as the Nevada law permitted, married one another as soon as the divorces were obtained, and promptly returned to North Carolina to live. It cannot reasonably be claimed that one set of inferences rather than another regarding the acquisition by petitioners of new domicils in Nevada could not be drawn from the circumstances attending their Nevada divorces. It would be highly unreasonable to assert that a jury could not reasonably find that the evidence demonstrated that petitioners went to Nevada solely for the purpose of obtaining a divorce and intended all along to return to North Carolina. Such an intention, the trial court properly charged, would preclude acquisition of domicils in Nevada. See Williamson v. Osenton, 232 U.S. 619, 34 S.Ct. 442, 58 L.Ed. 758. And so we cannot say that North Carolina was not entitled to draw the inference that petitioners never abandoned their domicils in North Carolina, particularly since we could not conscientiously prefer, were it our business to do so, the contrary finding of the Nevada court.

If a State cannot foreclose, on review here, all the other States by its finding that one spouse is domiciled within its bounds, persons may, no doubt, place themselves in situations that create unhappy consequences for them. This is merely one of those untoward results inevitable in a federal system in which regulation of domestic relations has been left with the States and not given to the national authority. But the occasional disregard by any one State of the reciprocal obligations of the forty-eight States to respect the constitutional power of each to deal with domestic relations of those domiciled within its borders is hardly an argument for allowing one State to deprive the other forty-seven States of their constitutional rights. Relevant statistics happily do not justify lurid forebodings that parents without number will disregard the fate of their offspring by being unmindful of the status of dignity to which they are entitled. But, in any event, to the extent that some one State may, for considerations of its own, improperly intrude into domestic relations subject to the authority of the other States, it suffices to suggest that any such indifference by a State to the bond of the Union should be discouraged not encouraged. . . .

We conclude that North Carolina was not required to yield her State policy because a Nevada court found that petitioners were domiciled in Nevada when it granted them decrees of divorce. North Carolina was entitled to find, as she did, that they did not acquire domicils in Nevada and that the Nevada court was therefore without power to liberate the petitioners from amenability to the laws of North Carolina governing domestic relations. And, as was said in connection with another aspect of the Full Faith and Credit Clause, our conclusion "is not a matter to arouse the susceptibilities of the states, all of which are equally concerned in the question and equally on both sides." Fauntleroy v. Lum, 210 U.S. 230, 238, 28 S.Ct. 641, 643, 52 L.Ed. 1039.

Affirmed.

[The CHIEF JUSTICE and Mr. Justice JACKSON joined in a concurring opinion by Mr. Justice MURPHY.]

Mr. JUSTICE RUTLEDGE, dissenting.

Once again the ghost of "unitary domicil" returns on its perpetual round, in the guise of "jurisdictional fact," to upset judgments, marriages, divorces, undermine the relations founded upon them, and make this Court the unwilling and uncertain arbiter between the concededly valid laws and decrees of sister states. From Bell and Andrews to Davis to Haddock to Williams and now back to Haddock and Davis through Williams again — is the maze the Court has travelled in a domiciliary wilderness, only to come out with no settled constitutional policy where one is needed most. . . .

I do not believe the Constitution has thus confided to the caprice of juries the faith and credit due the laws and judgments of sister states. Nor has it thus made that question a local matter for the states themselves to decide. Were all judgments given the same infirmity, the full faith and credit clause would be only a dead constitutional letter. . . .

Mr. JUSTICE BLACK, dissenting.

Anglo-American law has, until to-day, steadfastly maintained the principle that before an accused can be convicted of crime, he must be proven guilty beyond a reasonable doubt. These petitioners have been sentenced to prison because they were unable to prove their innocence to the satisfaction of the State of North Carolina. They have been convicted under a statute so uncertain in its application that not even the most learned member of the bar could have advised them in advance as to whether their conduct would violate the law. In reality the petitioners are being deprived of their freedom because the State of Nevada, through its legislature and courts follows a liberal policy in granting divorces. They had Nevada divorce decrees which authorized them to remarry. Without charge or proof of fraud in obtaining these decrees, and without holding the decrees invalid under Nevada law, this Court affirms a conviction of petitioners, for living together as husband and wife. I cannot reconcile this with the Full Faith and Credit Clause and with congressional legislation passed pursuant to it.

It is my firm conviction that these convictions cannot be harmonized with vital constitutional safeguards designed to safeguard individual liberty and to unite all states of this whole country into one nation. The fact that two people will be deprived of their constitutional rights impels me to protest as vigorously as I can against affirmance of these convictions. Even more, the Court's opinion today will cast a cloud over the lives of countless numbers of the multitude of divorced persons in the United States. . . .

The Constitution provides that "Full Faith and Credit shall be given in each State to the public Acts, Records, and judicial Proceedings of every other State. And the Congress may by general Laws prescribe the Manner in which such Acts, Records and Proceedings shall be proved, and the *Effect thereof.*" [Emphasis added.] Acting pursuant to this constitutional authority, Congress in 1790 declared what law should govern and what "Effect" should be given the judgments of state courts. That statute is still the law. Its command is that they "shall have such faith and credit given to them in every court within the United States as they have by law or usage in the courts of the State from which they are taken." 28 USCA 687, 8 FCA title 28, § 687. If, as the Court today implies, divorce decrees should be given less effect than other court judgments, Congress alone has the constitutional power to say so. We should not attempt to solve the "divorce problem" by consti-

tutional interpretation. At least, until Congress has commanded a different "Effect" for divorces granted on a short sojourn within a state, we should stay our hands. A proper respect for the Constitution and the Congress would seem to me to require that we leave this problem where the Constitution did. . . .

[Subsequent decisions have resulted only in modifications. For example, in *Sherrer* v. *Sherrer*, 334 U.S. 343, 68 S.Ct. 1087, 92 L.Ed. 1429 (1948), the court defined one limitation on the ability of a state to question the jurisdiction of a sister state. If both parties to the suit appear or are represented in the state in which the divorce is granted, there is deemed to have been an opportunity to challenge jurisdiction on the basis of domicil, and that question may not be raised later in the courts of a sister state.

A few states have adopted a "uniform divorce recognition act," which provides a definition of domicil. —— Ed. note.]

12

Fugitives from Justice

By Robert S. Rankin

THE AMERICAN PEOPLE in their scrutiny of the existing loopholes in the law that permit a criminal to evade justice should not carelessly pass over the rules governing interstate rendition of fugitives from justice. It is true that many criminals are at liberty today simply because they have been able to remove their bodily presence to another state. An illustration of this fact occurred at the beginning of the present century. At that time there was a contested election in Kentucky as to whether Goebel or Taylor was the duly elected governor of the state. The election was finally thrown into the legislature. While the contest was being heard, Goebel was assassinated while on the grounds of the executive mansion. After serving for a few days as governor of the state, Taylor was finally, along with others, indicted for murder. Before he could be arrested, he, and some of his followers, fled from Kentucky into Indiana. The Lieutenant Governor was immediately sworn in as governor of the state and he requested the governor

Robert S. Rankin, "Fugitives from Justice," in Rankin (ed.), *Readings in American Government* (New York: D. Appleton-Century, 1939), pp. 389–394. Reprinted by permission of the author and publisher.

of Indiana to return Taylor to the state to be tried for murder. The governor of Indiana refused this request, and Taylor remained in the asylum state until 1909, when the governor of Kentucky, being of the same political faith as Taylor, pardoned him. Demand was then made to change the rules governing interstate rendition but nothing was done. In recent years there have been several cases where criminals escaped trial and probable punishment by the crossing of state lines. Again a demand for a change has been made. This demand has had little effect upon the state, but the federal government has passed several acts that have for their purpose the removal of many evils of interstate rendition.

The constitutional fathers placed the duty of returning fugitives upon the state governments themselves, for in Article IV, Section 2, of the Constitution appears this statement:

A person charged in any state with treason, felony, or any other crime, shall, on demand of the executive authority of the state from which he has fled, be delivered up to be removed to the state having jurisdiction.

During the administration of President Washington and under his direction Congress passed an act which was an attempt to give some degree of uniformity to the procedure under this section of the Constitution and to provide means for its execution.

In the absence of state legislation, court interpretation has formulated the rules of interstate rendition. Briefly, the chief rules are as follows:

1. A person may be extradited for any offense made punishable by the law of the demanding state and it is immaterial whether the offense charged is a crime under the laws of the state upon which the demand is made. In other words, Mr. X can be extradited from Pennsylvania to West Virginia even though the offense that he has committed in West Virginia is not an offense in Pennsylvania.

2. The person whose custody is demanded must be a fugitive from justice. This simple statement has caused much trouble, for at times it is difficult to determine when a person becomes "a fugitive from justice." Back in the '90's a certain mountaineer in North Carolina shot across the state line into Tennessee and there killed another mountaineer named Bryson. For this offense he was tried in the North Carolina courts. The Supreme Court of North Carolina decided, however, that no North Carolina court could legally have jurisdiction of the case since the crime occurred where the bullet entered the victim's body — and this was in Tennessee. The Governor of Tennessee then requested the rendition of Hall so that he could be tried in the proper Tennessee court. Hall fought extradition and the Supreme Court of North Carolina decided that since Hall had never

been in the State of Tennessee he could not be "a fugitive from justice." In the words of the court "no one can in any sense be alleged to have fled from the justice of a state in the domain of whose territorial jurisdiction he has never been corporally present since the commission of the crime. — A fugitive from justice is one who having committed a crime in one jurisdiction flees therefrom in order to evade the law and escape punishment." In most cases the determination of whether the accused is a fugitive from justice is much easier although we frequently find criminals successfully evading punishment by proving to the court that they are not legally fugitives from justice.

3. The chief executive of the state from which the accused has fled must send a written demand to the governor of the state where the criminal is alleged to be, demanding him as a fugitive from justice.

4. The duty of the executive of the state to which the accused has fled is to arrest the fugitive. This duty is discretionary and is not ministerial, and there is no power residing in any governmental body to compel the executive to act. He can refuse to return the fugitive for any reason, or for no reason, although there is a strong moral obligation to honor the request of his fellow governor. Many fugitives are at liberty today because one governor does not like another one, or because a former governor of the demanding state refused to honor a previous request of the governor to whom the present request was made. In one case the failure was due to the fact that the Governor of New Jersey did not think that the courts of Georgia had given or would give justice to the fugitive. While it is true that in certain instances the refusal of a governor to return the fugitive gives justice to the alleged criminal, on the other hand it is a dangerous precedent for one governor to set himself up as a judge of the court system of another state. It permits retaliation, and often defeats the ends of justice.

5. The accused may appeal to the judiciary in order to secure his liberty — or justice. A fugitive always has the opportunity of recourse to the courts on a writ of habeas corpus and if he can show that he was not in that state at the time the crime was committed or that it was a case of mistaken identity or some other equally convincing evidence, the court will not permit his return to the state in which he was charged with the crime.

The case of Colonel Luke Lea and his son brings out many points that have been stressed in this brief account of the perils of interstate rendition. The different steps in this case show clearly the intricate maze of the law, the legal technicalities existing in the courts, and the many opportunities given by our legal system to a criminal to delay, if not eventually to dodge, justice. In 1931 Colonel Luke Lea and his son were sentenced in Buncombe County, North Carolina, for conspiracy to defraud the now defunct Central Bank and Trust Company of Asheville, the father to six to ten years, and the son to two to six years in the North Carolina penitentiary. They immediately appealed their case and were permitted to remain at liberty on a bond amounting to $50,000. Having failed to get the Supreme Court of the United States to review the case, they were called upon to surrender to the North Carolina officials. It must be remembered that the Leas were citizens of Tennessee and that their residence was in Nashville. On their failure to appear in North Carolina, their bonds were declared forfeited but, unfortunately for North Carolina, the bonding company in the meantime had failed. When the Leas failed to return to North Carolina, Governor Ehringhaus requested Governor Hill McAllister of Tennessee to return the Leas to North Carolina. In the meantime the legal counsel for the Leas announced that they would fight extradition on the ground that the Leas were not fugitives from justice since they were not in North Carolina at the time the crime was supposed to have been committed. This point was brought to the attention of Governor McAllister, but instead of upholding their contention Governor McAllister, fulfilling campaign promises and indirectly aiding the ends of justice, issued fugitive warrants for the arrest of the Leas.

After some clever jockeying between the Leas and the officials from North Carolina who were sent to Tennessee to secure the custody of the "fugitives," the Leas were finally arrested but a writ of habeas corpus was granted. The main contention of the Leas before the Supreme Court of Tennessee was that they were not fugitives from justice since they were not in North Carolina at the time the alleged crime was committed. It will be remembered that the original charge against the Leas was that of conspiracy and this conspiracy was conducted by the Leas from Nashville, Tennessee, and not in Asheville, North Carolina. Therefore, the Leas held that since they were not in North Carolina at the time the alleged conspiracy took place they could not be fugitives from justice. The decision of the Supreme Court of Tennessee held that the petition for a writ of habeas corpus should not be granted and that the Leas should be remanded to the North Carolina authorities. In giving this decision, the court maintained that, since the Leas gave themselves up for trial and went back to Asheville and appeared in the court, they relinquished all rights that they might have had to fight extradition. In the words of the court,

When petitioners voluntarily appear in a foreign state to answer criminal charges of conspiracy, were tried and convicted, and were released on bail pending appeal, petitioners having thereafter left foreign state and failed to appear upon affirmance of conviction held 'fugitives from justice,' although not present in the demanding state at time crime was committed.

This opinion was upheld by the Supreme Court of the United States.

Other instances show how alleged criminals by simply crossing state lines complicate the entire judicial process and give the criminal another opportunity of evading justice. These evils being apparent, several attempts have been made in recent years to improve the system of interstate rendition. The first suggested reform is to have the different states adopt a uniform extradition act. Such an act has been prepared and has been adopted by approximately one-third of the states. The failure of many states to adopt this measure may be due to the fact that the law itself is not what it should be and to the lethargy of state legislatures. . . .

The other method of improving the process of interstate rendition is to establish federal control and regulation. In 1932 Congress passed the "Lindbergh Law" which concerns the rendition of fugitives. The transportation of a kidnapped person across a state line by this act becomes a federal offense. Formerly, if the governor of an asylum state refused to return a fugitive, an officer of the demanding state might kidnap the fugitive, carry him back to his own state and there try him. In the case of Ponzi, a self-styled financier, the above method was used. Ponzi escaped from Massachusetts on an Italian ship. When the ship touched at New Orleans, Ponzi, by fraud, was induced to go ashore where he was forcibly arrested by a Texas officer, taken to Texas and there extradited to Massachusetts. However, since the passage of the "Lindbergh Law" kidnapping as an effective means of gaining custody of a fugitive has lost its appeal to state officers. By so doing they are subject to arrest by federal officers, and the state is unable to give protection to these "public spirited" officers.

A more recent act that directly affects interstate rendition has been styled the "Federal Fugitive Felon Act" or the "Fleeing Felon Law." . . . By its power to regulate interstate commerce, Congress enacted this measure which makes it a federal offense for a person to move or travel in interstate commerce to avoid state prosecution for certain felonies. The measure also included those individuals who cross state lines to avoid giving testimony in trials. The maximum penalty provided for those who break this law is $5,000 fine, or five years' imprisonment, or both. The testimony taken at the hearings conducted before the passage of the measure, and the statements of the advocates of the bill show that it was enacted for the purpose of securing the return of fugitives who cross state lines in order to avoid arrest and trial. Senator Vandenberg, one of the sponsors of the bill, contended that when the criminal was returned for trial in the federal court, he should be turned over to the state for trial of his original offense.

. . . one case [that] has arisen over the constitutionality of this measure . . . concerned an individual named McClure who was about to be arrested for a traffic violation in Virginia, and, in order to avoid arrest, intentionally sideswiped another car in an attempt to dislodge a state officer from the running board of his car. This officer was severely injured. McClure escaped to Tennessee and extradition proceedings were instituted. While these proceedings were taking place, a federal grand jury in Virginia indicted McClure for fleeing Virginia to escape prosecution for the violation of the Virginia statute. McClure fought his return by contesting the validity of this act. However, the federal district court in Tennessee, the court to which McClure appealed, held that fugitives from justice were fit subjects for regulation by Congress under the commerce clause, and that the law was not an encroachment upon the powers reserved to the states. The court would not look behind the wording of the measure in order to ascertain its purpose. In the words of the judge,

It has been repeatedly decided that the courts are not to impugn the motives of Congress, but may alone consider the question of the validity of the statute giving it the construction the language employed requires.

Notwithstanding this decision, many lawyers believe that the court could have found "the ulterior purpose" — the regulation of interstate rendition — the true objective of the bill and not the regulation of interstate commerce. Particularly is this [true] when consideration is given the testimony secured by the hearings and the statements of the sponsors of the measure in Congress. . . .

. . . the measure shows, however, a growing desire for the improvement of the rules governing interstate rendition and a threat of federal intervention if the states fail to improve existing conditions.

CHAPTER FOUR

Powers and Legal Status of State and Local Governments

LOCAL GOVERNMENTS are by no means independent units in the sense that the states may be so considered. In a legal view they remain the "creatures of the state" which gave them being, and rights which a citizen may have against a state are not ordinarily applicable to municipal corporations. The relationships between a state and its local governments are not officially those between equals but between superior and subordinate. In the first selection, the township of Bridgie seeks to prevent its being dissolved by the county in which it is located. In this case, the court has the opportunity to examine several of the common legal issues of state-local relations, presenting the traditional view concisely and vigorously. Court decisions, incidentally, are really not as forbidding reading as they may appear to the uninitiated. They provide us concrete illustrations dealing with real-life situations and with all the interest inherent in a contest.

13

Town of Bridgie, et al.

v.

County of Koochiching

THOMAS GALLAGHER, Justice.

Plaintiff towns in Koochiching county challenge the constitutionality of M.S.A. 368.47, whereunder they were dissolved by resolution of the board of county commissioners of defendant county of Koochiching. Section 368.47 in part provides:

. . . When the assessed valuation of any town drops to less than $40,000, . . . the county board by resolution may declare any such town, naming it, duly dissolved and no longer entitled to exercise any of the powers or functions of a town. . . .

227 Minn. 320, 35 N.W. 2d 537 (1948)

When a town is dissolved under the provisions of sections 368.47 to 368.49 the county shall acquire title to any telephone company or any other business being conducted by such town and such business shall be operated by the board of county commissioners until such time as a sale thereof can be made; provided that the subscribers or patrons of such businesses shall have the first opportunity of purchase. If such dissolved town has any outstanding indebtedness chargeable to such business, the auditor of the county wherein such dissolved town is located shall levy a tax against the property situated in the dissolved town for the purpose of paying the indebtedness as it becomes due.

Section 368.49 provides for the disposal of road or bridge funds of any such dissolved town by the county board wholly within the limits of such town and for the crediting of any other funds to the general fund of the county.

Plaintiffs challenge the power of the legislature to enact the above legislation upon the grounds (1) that provision for dissolution of such towns *without* notice to or consent of the residents thereof is in excess of the legislative power and violative of the due process clause, Minn. Const. art. 1, section 7; (2) that the classification therein based upon an assessed valuation of less than $40,000 is unfair and arbitrary and hence special legislation in contravention of Minn. Const. art. 4; sections 33 and 34; and (3) that it constitutes an unlawful delegation of power from the legislature to the county board, in violation of Minn. Const. art. 3, section 1, providing for the separation of the legislative, executive, and judicial branches of the government.

From the trial court's order sustaining a demurrer to the complaint, which had attacked the constitutionality of the enactment, this appeal is taken.

1–2. We do not regard the challenged statute as in excess of the power of the legislature. As stated in State ex rel. Simpson v. City of Mankato, 117 Minn. 458, 463, 136 N.W. 264, 266:

We must not forget that the voice of the legislature is the voice of the sovereign people, and that, subject only to such limitations as the people have seen fit to incorporate in their Constitution, the legislature is vested with the sovereign power of the people themselves. In other words, the provisions of a state Constitution do not and cannot confer upon the legislature any powers whatever, but are mere limitations in the strict sense of that term, and the legislature has all the powers of an absolute sovereign of which it has not been divested by the Constitution.

It has frequently been stated that municipal corporations have no rights, privileges, or immunities within the protection of the usual constitutional guaranties against legislative interference or control. They are merely governmental agencies, and legislation regulating or affecting them does not amount to a contract, the obligation of which may not be impaired by legislative action. 4. Dunnell, Dig. & Supp. Section 6548. Our constitution, art. 11, section 3, gives to the legislature the power to create and establish towns; and the power thus to create implies the power to curtail. The powers of such townships are derived solely from the legislature, and they may be enlarged and extended, or abridged and entirely withdrawn by legislative action. There is no constitutional restriction binding the legislature in this respect. 4 Dunnell, Dig. & Supp. Section 6548, and cases cited.

3. This rule is not altered by the fact that such a municipal corporation has been allowed to acquire property. Provision is made in the challenged statute for disposition thereof. The power of the legislature over the property which a municipal corporation has acquired in its public or governmental capacity and which is devoted to public or governmental uses is complete. It may take control thereof from the officers of the corporation and turn it over to other officers under the direct supervision and control of the state. There are no constitutional limitations or restrictions in this respect. Monaghan v. Armatage, 218 Minn. 108, 15 N.W. (2d) 241; 4 Dunnell, Dig. & Supp. Section 6548.

4. As to property held in a proprietary or private capacity, in trust for the benefit of township inhabitants for certain designated purposes, the legislature may provide for the transfer thereof from the officers of such municipality to different trustees, with or without compensation to it. Monaghan v. Armatage, supra.

Based upon these well-established principles, we are compelled to hold that the legislature did not exceed its constitutional authority in the enactment of section 368.47.

5. Likewise, we are of the opinion that the legislative classification of towns with less than $40,000 in assessed valuation, for the purpose of the act, is not unfair and arbitrary so as to constitute a violation of Minn. Const. art. 4, sections 33 and 34, prohibiting special legislation for counties, cities, villages, and towns. Our function with reference to this issue is merely to determine whether the classification provided for bears a reasonable relationship to the subject matter of the legislation. Classification is so much a question of policy that the legislature should be allowed a large measure of discretion in the matter. If the basis of classification is proper, the act is general although it operates on only one class of municipalities and makes no provision for those not falling within its classification. It must be based upon some natural, apparent reason of public policy growing out of the condition to which the legislation is limited.

Here, it is obvious that the purpose of the legislation is to prevent the expenditure of funds or the incurring of liabilities by townships lacking assessed valuations permitting them to raise funds therefor through legal taxation rates. When such circumstances appear, the county may, by resolution, dissolve the town and take over its functions and provide for the necessary services. Likewise, it may become trustee for any property held by the township officers in trust for the inhabitants thereof for specific services, such as telephone exchanges and like matters. The assessed valuation bears a direct relationship to the subject matter of the legislation, i.e., the dissolution of towns which, for financial reasons, may find it impossible to finance themselves. In Nichols v. City of Eveleth, 204 Minn. 352, 355, 283 N.W. 539, 541, where classification was based upon assessed valuation, we stated:

In the case at bar we have no difficulty in seeing a relation between the assessed valuation and the practical ability of the city for an extended period to maintain a pension fund of this character. . . . Obviously this would be a hardship upon cities of small population and low assessed valuation, and consequently the legislature empowered only those cities having an assessed valuation of $8,000,000 to bring themselves within the act. . . . In the wisdom of the legislature some other point of demarcation between cities of the fourth class which could afford and those which could not afford a retirement fund of this character might have been made, but the legislature exercised its wisdom in selecting $8,000,000 assessed valuation as the point of demarcation. It had to place that point somewhere, and we see nothing arbitrary or special in its action in placing it at the amount which it did.

We hold here that the classification based upon assessed valuation bears a direct relationship to the objects of the legislation, and that it is not unfair or arbitrary so as to constitute a violation of Minn. Const. art. 4, sections 33 and 34.

6. It is urged that the act, though otherwise within the power of the legislature, is violative of the provisions of Minn. Const. art. 3, section 1, providing for the separation of the three branches of the government, under which it has frequently been held that the legislature may not delegate its powers to the executive or judicial departments of the government.

The law seems well established that this prohibition does not extend to a grant of power from the legislature to a division of the government likewise within the legislative department.

It is well settled that a legislature may delegate part of its power over local subjects to county boards and other public bodies within the legislative classification. 11 Am. Jur., Constitutional Law, Section 223, citing Wright v. May, 127 Minn. 150, 149 N.W. 9, L.R.A. 1915B, 151, and Searle v. Yensen, 118 Neb. 835, 226 N.W. 464, 69 A.L.R. 257.

As stated in the Searle case (118 Neb. 842, 226 N.W. 466):

The power of the legislature to delegate a part of its legislative functions to municipal corporations or other governmental subdivisions, boards, commissions, and tribunals, to be exercised within their respective jurisdictions, cannot be denied; but the recipient of such powers must be members of the same governmental department as that of the grantor. . . .

As stated in 14 Am. Jur., Counties, Section 30:

. . . There is a well-settled rule that inhibitions against the delegation of legislative power do not apply to statutes vesting local bodies such as county boards with authority to legislate upon matters purely of local concern.

We find no constitutional prohibition here against the delegation of legislative powers to counties. Minn. Const. art. 11, section 1, provides that the legislature may from time to time establish and organize new counties. Section 4 of said article states:

Provision shall be made by law for the election of such county or township officers as may be necessary.

And Section 5 states:

Any county and township organization shall have such powers of local taxation as may be prescribed by law.

There is nothing contained therein which denies to the legislature power to delegate to counties the capacity to act upon matters such as those here involved. It is obvious that the statute here in question relates to matters of purely local concern. We hold that under the above authorities the legislature violated no constitutional restriction in delegating to counties the power to act in connection with the dissolution of towns falling below certain standards of classification.

The order is affirmed.

The powers possessed by municipal corporations are usually interpreted in a restrictive fashion by the courts. Perhaps the most striking statement of the traditional official view is that expressed many years ago by Judge John F. Dillon and reiterated constantly by later courts as "Dillon's Rule."

One of the underlying principles in the determination of the scope of municipal powers is to the effect that public funds may be spent only for a "public purpose," a matter not always easy to define. This question is tackled with reference to a highly controversial issue in Albritton v. Winona. *The decision is not necessarily typical, but the case illustrates the kinds of questions in this area with which courts must grapple and points up dramatically the impact of differing political-economic opinions held by the judges.*

The Arlen Service Stations *and* Dutton Phosphate Co. *cases indicate some of the rules which circumscribe one of the most significant municipal powers — the power to regulate, as well as the normal attitude of self-restraint on the part of courts in interpreting this power.*

14

Dillon's Rule

IT IS A GENERAL and undisputed proposition of law that a municipal corporation possesses and can exercise the following powers, and no others: First, those granted in express words; second, those necessarily or fairly implied in or incident to the powers expressly granted; third, those essential to the accomplishment of the declared objects and purposes of the corporation — not simply convenient, but

John F. Dillon, *Commentaries on the Law of Municipal Corporations* (5th ed., 1911), Vol. I, p. 448.

indispensable. Any fair, reasonable, substantial doubt concerning the existence of power is resolved by the courts against the corporation, and the power is denied.

15

Albritton

v.

City of Winona

SMITH, C. J. This is an appeal from a decree validating a proposed issue by the appellee of serial bonds aggregating $35,000 rendered in a proceeding authorized for that purpose by section 313, Code 1930. The bonds are to be issued under chapter 1, Laws of First Extraordinary Session of 1936, and the appellant's claim is that the provision of the statute authorizing the levy of taxes for the payment of the bonds violates the due process of law provision of the Fourteenth Amendment to the Federal Constitution and of section 14 of our State Constitution, and also violates sections 17, 183, and 258 of our State Constitution.

The preamble to the statute sets forth the reason for the enactment of the statute and the purposes sought to be accomplished by it. . . . The statute then creates the Mississippi Industrial Commission and charges it with certain duties, section 2 et seq., among which are to make effective the "declared public policy of this state to balance agriculture with industry, and for that purpose is hereby authorized and empowered to determine, under the provisions of this act, whether the public convenience and necessity require that any municipality shall have the right to acquire lands and thereon to erect industrial enterprises and to operate them and to dispose of such lands and industrial enterprises." Section 7. To this end it is authorized, when requested by a municipality, to investigate and determine, in the manner provided by the statute, whether the public convenience and necessity require that the municipality be authorized "to acquire, to own, and to operate the particular type of industry found suited to the needs of that municipality under the provisions of this act." Section 8. If and when the commission grants this certificate of public convenience and necessity, the municipality is authorized to acquire,

own, and operate the particular industry set forth in the certificate, and "when and to the extent authorized by said commission . . . to sell, lease or otherwise dispose of such industrial enterprise or enterprises, in whole or in part, on such terms and conditions and with such safeguards as will best promote and protect the public interest." Section 18. The municipality may not operate the industry itself unless authorized by the commission so to do, but if the commission so authorizes, it may acquire the facilities for the operation of the industry and lease them, as hereinbefore said, to individuals or private corporations.

When so authorized by the commission, a municipality may issue serial bonds, with the approval of two-thirds of its qualified electors. The commission "shall determine the amount of taxes necessary to be levied and collected annually to retire the bonds and pay interest coupons and to create a sinking fund for the payment of said bonds and interest so that the annual tax levy shall be uniform throughout the period for which the bonds are issued," section 14, which annual tax the municipality must levy. Section 18 of the act provides that "all income from any lease or contract for the operation or from the disposition of said industrial enterprise shall be paid into the bond sinking fund provided for the bonds issued under the provisions of this act for the retirement of said bonds and the interest thereon, and such income or proceeds shall not be used by the municipality for any other purpose except as to disposition of surplus income authorized above, and shall be subject to all of the provisions hereof relative to said sinking fund."

A certificate of public convenience and necessity was issued by the Mississippi Industrial Commission in the manner provided by the statute to the City of Winona "to acquire, to own and to operate, subject to the hereinafter limitations, a hosiery, knitting and wearing apparel manufacturing plant." The certificate then provides for the acquisition by the city of not less than 20,000 square feet of land within the city limits, and that "the said City of Winona, Montgomery County, Mississippi, may construct on said land a municipal factory building containing not less than fourteen thousand (14,000) square feet of floor space, and expend therefore not exceeding the sum of thirty-five thousand dollars ($35,000), but no part of said amount shall be expended for machinery or equipment, and said municipality shall not operate said industrial enterprise, but is authorized to lease or rent said lands and building after acquirement and construction to some person, firm or corporation, for a period of not less than twenty-five (25) years on terms and conditions to be submitted to this Commission for approval before any such contract for lease, rental and operation shall become finally bind-

181 Miss. 19, 178 So. 799 (1938)

ing upon said municipality. Provided, however, if for any reason the plant cannot be leased or said lease shall for any reason terminate, then the municipality may operate the same under the direction of the municipal authorities."

Another order was made by the commission reciting that the municipal officers of the City of Winona "are not presently suitable, competent, or fit persons to direct and control the operations of said industrial enterprise, but for the best municipal public interests and welfare said enterprise should be operated under lease or contract for the general municipal welfare by some private individual, firm or corporation, which said contract, however, must be approved by this Commission under provisions of said Mississippi Industrial Act, before the same is effective."

The proposed bond issue was submitted to and approved by more than two-thirds of the city's qualified electors. The record relating thereto was then, under the provisions of section 313, Code 1930, submitted to the state's bond attorney, who certified that in his opinion "the proposed bonds are legal and should be validated." The record was then filed, in accordance with section 313, in the court below, and after the notice to the taxpayers, required thereby, had been given, the appellant appeared on the day fixed for hearing objections to the issuance of the bonds, and objected thereto; and from the decree validating the bonds has brought the case to this court. . . .

The state's taxing power can be resorted to only for a constitutionally valid public or governmental purpose, so that the question here is whether the purpose for which the tax is to be levied is constitutionally valid. . . .

The ownership by municipalities of business enterprises that are usually designated as public utilities has long been recognized as valid, but the enterprise here is not within that category and belongs to the class usually owned and operated by private individuals. That fact is not an insuperable obstacle, for the state and its subdivisions have long been permitted to engage in such enterprises, provided the public interest requires. . . . This state owns a very large farm on which it produces and sells a large quantity of cotton and other crops — a business usually engaged in by private individuals — the necessity and, therefore, the justification therefor being to give its convicts employment. But the validity of the exercise of the taxing power does not rest alone on necessity, as Judge Cooley has admonished us in People v. Township of Salem, 20 Mich. 452, 4 Am. Rep. 400, where in holding that taxes can be levied only for public purposes he said: "I do not understand that the word public, when employed in reference to this power, is to be construed or applied in any narrow or illiberal sense, or in any sense which would preclude the Legislature from taking broad views of State interest, necessity or policy, or from giving those views effect by means of the public revenues. . . ." "The end being legitimate [here, the relief of unemployment and the promotion of the state's agricultural and industrial welfare], the means is for the legislature to choose." Carmichael v. Southern Coal & Coke Co., 301 U.S. 495, . . . the only limitation thereon under due process being that the means chosen must not be so far beyond the necessity of the case as to be arbitrary exercise of governmental power.

Manufacturing enterprises, as all will agree, will tend to relieve unemployment and both directly and indirectly furnish markets for agricultural and other products. . . .

But it is said, in effect, that the engaging by a state, or its political subdivisions, in manufacturing enterprises, is a complete departure from the concept our forefathers had of the powers and duties of the state and is a step towards socialism. This ambiguous and ill-defined word, which is given an "exceedingly wide range of specific connotations," according to the use desired to be made of it, came first into use in its modern sense in 1827. 14 Ency. of The Social Sciences, 188. Every intervention of any consequence by the state and national governments in the economic and social life of the citizen has been so branded, beginning in the latter part of the last century with governmental control and regulation of industries usually owned and operated by private individuals and which have come to be recognized as public utilities. We must not permit ourselves to be subjected to the tyranny of symbols. The due process of law provisions of our constitutions do not enact Adam Smith's concept of the negative state, one of the main functions of which would be to stand aloof from intervention in the social and economic life of its citizens. This concept of the state was probably acted upon in the early history of this country but has long since been discarded, beginning with the social and economic security statutes of the latter part of the last century, and evidenced today by numerous such statutes of the state and federal governments. "It is manifest," in the language of the Supreme Court of the United States in Home Building & Loan Association v. Blaisdell, 290 U.S. 398, 442, 54 S.Ct. 231, 241, 78 L.Ed. 413, 431, 88 A.L.R. 1481, from a "review of our decisions that there has been a growing appreciation of public needs and of the necessity of finding ground for a rational compromise between individual rights and public welfare. . . ."

Again it is said that, if the state and its subdivisions can own and operate a manufacturing enterprise, it can then take over and operate every business and industry, thereby bringing all its citizens into direct dependence on the state. This, of course, under due process of law could not be done, for the liberty of the citizen to acquire, own, and use private property cannot thereunder be destroyed or arbitrarily interfered with. The statute here under consideration does not create a state or municipal monopoly nor interfere with the right of individuals to engage in the business of manufacturing raw materials into finished products. The due process clauses of our constitutions must not be construed so as to put the state and federal governments into a straitjacket and prevent them from adapting life to the continuous change in social and economic conditions. That the framers of our constitutions may not have visualized the present public needs is of no consequence, for, as the Supreme Court of the United States further said in Home Building & Loan Association v. Blaisdell, supra, "it is no answer to say that this public need was not apprehended a century ago or to insist that what the provision of the Constitution meant to the vision of that day it must mean to the vision of our time. . . ."

We must never forget that, in the words of John Marshall, a constitution is "intended to endure for ages to come, and consequently, to be adapted to the various crises of human affairs. . . ." McCulloch v. Maryland, 4 Wheat. 316, 415, 4 L.Ed. 579. While the Federal Constitution was in process of adoption by the states, Alexander Hamilton, in No. 32 of the Federalist, said: "We are not to confine our view to the present period, but to look forward to remote futurity; constitutions of civil government are not to be framed upon a calculation of existing exigencies, but upon a combination of these with the probable exigencies of ages, according to the natural and tried course of human affairs. . . ."

Growth is the life of the law, and when it ceases to grow and to keep pace with social and economic needs it becomes a hindrance instead of an aid to the public welfare. . . . We must not be influenced by vague notions of natural law, nor decide due process of law cases in accordance with our own particular economic theories — by what Dean Pound designates as "an idealized political picture of the existing social order." The Theory of Judicial Decision, 36 Harvard Law Review, 641, 656. So to do would frequently result in deciding cases "upon an economic theory which a large part of the country does not entertain" (Holmes, J., in Lochner v. New York, 198 U.S. 45, . . .), "prevent the making of social experiments that an important part of the community desires" (Holmes, J., in Truax v. Corrigan, 257 U.S. 312, 344, . . .), and in the "exercise of the powers of a super-Legislature — not the performance of the constitutional function of judicial review" (Brandeis, J., in Jay Burns Baking Co. v.

Bryan, 264 U.S. 504, 534, . . .). In the oft-quoted language of Mr. Justice Holmes, "The Fourteenth Amendment does not enact Mr. Herbert Spencer's Social Statics. . . . A Constitution is not intended to embody a particular economic theory, whether of paternalism and the organic relation of the citizen to the state or of laissez faire. It is made for people of fundamentally different views." Lochner v. New York, supra.

Cases from other jurisdictions may be cited holding statutes somewhat similar to the one here under consideration invalid under due process, but cases holding such a statute valid thereunder may also be cited. We will not pause to discuss these cases, with one exception that will hereinafter appear, for the reason that they were decided (1) on social and economic facts from which we must draw our own conclusions (West Coast Hotel Co. v. Parrish, 300 U.S. 379); (2) under the social and economic conditions then existing, which conditions are ever changing and each case must be decided on the social and economic conditions that exist when the statute was enacted or, probably, at the time the case is decided; and (3) under social and economic theories which are no longer universally entertained. . . .

Leases of an analogous character are generally held not to violate constitutional provisions similar to the one here under consideration. . . . The language of the Supreme Court of Ohio in Taylor v. Commissioners, supra, 23 Ohio St. 22, at page 77, dealing with the lease of a municipally owned railroad, mutatis mutandis, applies here: "It is the road 'owned' by the municipality that is authorized to be leased. The public use for which the road was built, is to be preserved, and the power of leasing the right to use and operate it, is designed only as a mode of making such use available to the public. If, under color of this authority, it should be attempted to divert the work from the purposes for which it was authorized, and to subordinate the public to private interests, the attempt would be unwarranted, and the courts would be open to prevent or redress the wrong. . . . The constitution does not forbid the employment of corporations, or individuals, associate or otherwise, as agents to perform public services; nor does it prescribe the mode of their compensation. And if it should be deemed wise and economical to authorize municipalities, who own water-works, or gas-works, to lease them as a means of supplying the public needs, we know of no constitutional impediment. . . ."

Affirmed.

GRIFFITH, J. (Specially concurring).

We all agree that, when a challenged statute is susceptible of a construction which will bring it within the Constitution, the duty of the court is to put that construction upon it, and thereupon to sustain it. Looking at the statute, here in question, in the light of that principle, I concur in the result reached that (1) the act is constitutional and (2) that the acquisition, and the proposed lease, of "a hosiery, knitting and wearing apparel manufacturing plant," is within constitutional allowance, provided the terms of the lease shall vest in the public authorities the ultimate control as regards the employment of the labor in said plant. But in my judgment the opinion as written by the CHIEF JUSTICE goes too far as respects the grounds upon which the act is sustained, and not far enough in regard to the terms of the proposed lease. For that reason, and also because there is a dissent, it becomes my duty to briefly state my views, matured as a result of an examination of the entire field of the authorities on the subject.

One of the purposes expressed within the act is the alleviation of unemployment. From the earliest times in our history it has been regarded as a public purpose, and within the power of direct taxation, to keep the poor from starvation. Cooley's Constitutional Limitations, 8th Ed., 1026. Ordinarily, a man will break in and take before he will starve, and all will do this for their families. They will do so singly and in groups. Thus the public duty and purpose to furnish food and necessaries to the famished is traceable directly to the police power of the state. And since in such cases the state, or its authorized subdivisions, may afford direct relief or aid of money or supplies, or both, it may provide work, and if to do so it becomes necessary to enter within the confines of that which has always heretofore been considered the domain of private enterprise, nevertheless the legislative power may so direct, under the established principle that whenever there is a constitutional power to accomplish a certain object the power includes, by implication, the authority to avail of all the necessary and proper means for the accomplishment of the particular object. Brister v. Leflore County, 156 Miss. 240, 248, 125 So. 816.

But when it is said that, without express constitutional provision to that effect, the field of private enterprise, the domain of the general manufacturing business, may be directly entered as a public purpose because, and because only in so doing, other businesses and other occupations will be incidentally benefited and thereby the public welfare promoted, this, I think, goes too far and has no support in any adjudicated case in this country and is against the fundamentals of a free constitutional system. . . .

Since the field of industrial enterprise, or the domain of the general manufacturing business, may be entered as a public purpose for the alleviation of unemployment, but for that object only, there comes into operation here, and unavoidably so, the principle that public money raised by taxation for the benefit of the indigent or unemployed must be spent under the direction and control of the public authorities. It cannot be turned over to a private agency to do with it as that agency may please. . . .

ANDERSON, J. (dissenting).

In my judgment the majority opinion drives a steam shovel through our Constitution, not only sections 183 and 258 but others to be referred to. It holds that a municipality may either own and operate a garment factory or own and lease it to a private person, association of persons, or a corporation, provided it retains and exercises supervision and control over its operation, which, of course, carries with it the necessary power to fix the wages and hours of labor of the employees. To that extent the right to contract is destroyed. We all agree that ownership and lease by a municipality without supervision and control would violate due process, in that it would result in taxation in aid of a private enterprise and not for a public purpose.

Can the Legislature make a public utility out of a private business? The court knows, as everybody knows, that according to universal acceptance an industrial plant is a private enterprise and not a public utility. How far can the Legislature go in balancing industry with agriculture for the purpose of relieving unemployment — where is the stopping place? If 10 per cent of the adult population of the state is unemployed where is the limit? The same question might be asked if 25 per cent or 50 per cent were unemployed.

The logic of the majority opinion leads to this: The Legislature, if it found necessary to relieve the unemployment, could authorize a municipality to take over, under the power of eminent domain, all property and all business of every kind within its corporate limits, and to manage and operate it as a public utility. And, of course, what the state could authorize municipalities to do, it could do itself. In other words, the state could take over all property and business of every kind within its boundaries and manage and control it as a public utility. That would indeed be giving Soviet Russia an approving handshake. Mississippi would be safe not for democracy but for communism. The valuable rights of contract and of private ownership of property would be gone. We would have a commonwealth of serfs instead of freemen — parasites instead of patriots. There would be no such thing as taxation for public purposes, for neither the municipalities nor the state could tax their own property. Section 112 of the Constitution, providing for a uniform tax for the support of the government, would be destroyed, and so would section 206 providing for a school fund tax, as well as section 236 providing for a levee tax. The only income would be from rentals and from operation of business. That would certainly be a new definition of democracy.

Going now to sections 183 and 258 of the Constitution: Section 183 provides, among other things, that municipalities shall not subscribe to the "capital stock or any railroad or other corporation or association, or make appropriation, or loan its credit in aid of such corporation or association." Section 258 provides that "the credit of the state shall not be pledged or loaned in aid of any person, association, or corporation; and the state shall not become a stockholder in any corporation or association," etc. It will be noted that the word "person" is included in section 258 and omitted from section 183. However, construing the two sections together, it is manifest that section 183 covers persons as well as corporations and associations. Furthermore, without section 183, section 258 would prohibit municipalities and other political subdivisions of the state from doing what the state itself could not do.

Hinds & Adams Counties v. Natchez, Jackson & Columbus R. Co., 85 Miss. 599, 38 So. 189, 107 Am. St. Rep. 305, throws light on what those two sections of the Constitution mean. In the 1870's and 1880's Adams County, Hinds County, and the City of Natchez owned the majority of the stock of the Natchez, Jackson & Columbus Railroad Company and had a majority of the directors of the corporation. The aggregate of their stock was something over $700,000. In several other counties and municipalities of the state like conditions existed. . . . Some of them are yet levying taxes to meet those railroad ventures. These sections of the Constitution were intended to prevent, among other things, a repetition of that history.

Under the statute here involved, a lease with supervision and control by the municipality would be giving aid to the lessee, even though he paid value therefor, for it is manifest that the lessee would build his own plant if he were able and thought it more profitable to own than to lease it. In other words, he leases because he thinks it is to his advantage — it is in his aid. Sections 183 and 258 plainly prohibit such aid. They apply to public utilities as well as private business. . . .

The majority opinion cites as a precedent the state convict system, which provides for the working of convicts on a farm owned by the state, in competition with the farming interests generally. That is not a precedent, it is expressly authorized by section 225 of the Constitution.

Furthermore, it is a matter of common knowledge that industrial plants like the one here involved are owned and operated by corporations, not individuals or partnerships. Sections 182 and 192 of the Constitution limit the powers of the Legislature with reference to such corporations. The former authorizes an exemption from state taxation for a period of not exceeding five years, and the latter authorizes munici-

palities to encourage the establishment of factories, gasworks, waterworks, and other enterprises of a public utility, other than railroads, within their limits by exempting them from municipal taxation for ten years. These two sections deal with the subject and in State v. Henry, 87 Miss. 125, 40 So. 152, 154, 5 L.R.A., N.S., 340, the court held that, where the Constitution deals with the subject, its words are the sole boundary "and sacred from the Legislatures"; that where powers are scheduled in the Constitution, giving or taking away, it must be presumed to have scheduled all, and it only must be looked to with its necessary implications for the limit of authority. So it appears plain to me that this scheme is absolutely cut off by our Constitution. This is not a case of stretching the Constitution to meet new conditions, but it is a case of breaking it.

16

People
v.
Arlen Service Stations, Inc.

LEWIS, J. The single question presented by this appeal is the constitutionality of Local Law No. 141, p. 288, adopted by the Council of the City of New York August 10, 1939. . . .

The defendant corporation, which operates a service station at 594 Jamaica avenue in the borough of Brooklyn, concedes that it violated section B36—101.0 of the Administrative Code on November 2, 1939, when it failed to post on each of four pumps from which it sold gasoline a sign stating the retail price per gallon of gasoline sold therefrom; and by posting on two other pumps maintained on the premises, three signs of dimensions sixty inches in height and from thirty to thirty-six inches in width on which were letters twenty-four to twenty-five inches in height. . . .

Section B36—101.0 of the Administrative Code, quoted above, bears upon its face clear indication that it was designed to prevent fraud in the retail sale of gasoline. In our present inquiry, however, we may not give weight to the fact that fraud was neither charged nor proved against the defendant. A business, however honest in itself, may be the subject of governmental regulation if it may become a medium

284 N.Y. 340, 31 N.E. (2d) 184 (1940)

of fraud. "It is not enough to say that the business may be honestly conducted." People v. Beakes Dairy Co., 222 N.Y. 416, 427, 119 N.E. 115, 118, 3 A.L.R. 1260. Nor may we extend the field of our judicial inquiry into the realm of expediency where legislative judgment alone dictates the necessity for statutory regulation and its wisdom.

The defendant asserts that the law here in question is an improper exercise of power and violates the due process clauses of the Federal Constitution (Fourteenth Amendment) and the Constitution of New York (Art. 1, §6). But we know that "A reasonable regulation governing the use of property offered for sale so as to prevent fraud does not destroy that property nor deprive the owner of its use in a constitutional sense." People v. Luhrs, 195 N.Y. 377, 383, 89 N.E. 171, 173, 25 L.R.A., N.S., 473. We also have in mind the rule that "A legitimate public purpose may always be served without regard to the constitutional limitations of due process and equal protection." People v. Perretta, 253 N.Y. 305, 309, 171 N.E. 72, 73, 84 A.L.R. 636 (and other N.Y. cases).

Accordingly we are concerned only as to whether section B36 — 101.0 of the Administrative Code is a legislative measure reasonably adapted to accomplish its purpose.

From the arguments of counsel we understand that, as in a case before this court more than fifty years ago, which involved the adulteration of food products, so today when we consider a local regulatory measure which governs the retail sale of gasoline, "Ingenuity keeps pace with greed, and the careless and heedless consumers are exposed to increasing perils." People v. Kibler, 106 N.Y. 321, 324, 12 N.E. 795, 796. Those perils, including the exceptional facilities which the retail sale of gasoline affords for imposition upon the public, are not, however, a matter for our consideration. We may assume they were the subject of investigation and study by the City Council during its consideration of the necessity for and wisdom of the local law in question. Our inquiry goes only to the reasonableness of the resulting enactment.

It cannot be said of this local legislation that it impairs the defendant's freedom to determine the price at which it will sell the gasoline which it offers to the public, nor does it prohibit the defendant from advertising that price. True, there are restrictions as to the location and size of the sign which the City Council has determined must be posted upon each pump as a means of imparting to customers information upon factors which enter into each retail sale of motor fuel — the amount of governmental tax to be collected in connection with the sale; the trade name, if any, by which the gasoline is marketed and the grade or quality by which it is classified. Likewise a restriction is made effective by the prohibition against the posting upon the premises of any other sign which states the price or prices of gasoline sold.

Restriction is implicit in police power however exercised. The problem is to ascertain whether the restriction, as an incident to the accomplishment of the legislative purpose, is reasonable in degree. We have said that "Any trade, calling, or occupation may be reasonably regulated if 'the general nature of the business is such that unless regulated many persons may be exposed to misfortunes against which the Legislature can properly protect them.'" Biddles, Inc. v. Enright, 239 N.Y. 354, 363, 146 N.E. 625, 628, 39 A.L.R. 766. In the present instance we do not regard the restriction as to the placement, size or limitation of signs, or the requirement of a uniformity in size of the retail sale price figures thereupon, as being more drastic than is reasonable to accomplish the end for which the law was adopted.

It follows that the enforcement of the local law does not deprive the defendant of its property without due process. Cf. Slome v. Godley, 304 Mass. 187, 23 N.E. 2d 133.

Nor can we say upon the present record that the defendant has been deprived of the equal protection of the laws. There is no proof of discrimination or of arbitrary action. The local law affects alike all in a given class — the retail dealers in motor fuel — and calls for the uniform enforcement of the act itself. People v. Beakes Dairy Co., supra, page 429, . . .

The . . . judgment of conviction [is] affirmed.

17

Dutton Phosphate Co.

v.

Priest

WHITFIELD, J. . . . The provisions of the organic law that no person shall be deprived of life, liberty, or property without due process of law, nor denied the equal protection of the laws, are not intended to hamper the states in the discretionary exercise of any of their appropriate sovereign governmental powers, unless substantial private rights are arbitrarily invaded by illegal or palpably unjust, hostile and oppressive exactions, burdens, discriminations or deprivations. . . .

67 Fla. 370, 65 So. 282 (1914)

Under the American system of laws and government, everyone is required to so use and enjoy his own rights as to not injure others in their rights or to violate any law in force for the preservation of the general welfare. This principle does not conflict with the express constitutional right that all persons have of "acquiring, possessing and protecting property. . . ."

. . . All property rights are held and enjoyed subject to the fair exercise of the state's police power to establish regulations that are reasonably necessary to secure the general welfare of the state. The selection and classification of the subjects of statutory regulation are within the lawmaking discretion of the Legislature. See King Lumber & Mfg. Co. v. Atlantic Coast Line R. Co., 58 Fla. 292, 50 So. 509; Atlantic Coast Line R. Co. v. Goldsboro, 232 U.S. 548, . . .

Courts have no power to annul a legislative enactment on the ground that it is unreasonable in its terms or in its operations, when the statute does not, because of arbitrary unreasonableness, conflict with the superior force of the Constitution as the higher law. . . .

The Legislature has a wide discretion in classifying the subjects of police regulation, and a legislative classification will not be annulled by the court unless it is wholly without a reasonable or practical basis. . . .

The wisdom and necessity, as well as the policy, of a statute are authoritatively determined by the Legislature. Courts may inquire only into the power of the Legislature to lawfully enact a particular statute; and all doubts as to its constitutionality are resolved in favor of the statute. . . .

The ancient doctrine that "the king can do no wrong" has been carried over into American law in the prohibition of private damage suits against the states. Insofar as they perform state functions, at least, local governments have also benefited from this immunity, but the courts have developed what often appears to be a highly artificial distinction between what are called "governmental" and "proprietary" functions of local units. When engaging in the former type of function the local government is not liable for torts (civil wrongs other than breach of contract), but in the case of "proprietary" functions it may be. Many students of this problem have suggested that the solution lies in doing away with present damage suit procedure in such instances and establishing special courts or administrative tribunals to handle claims. Change is under way, however slowly: some state courts are taking the position that all municipal acts are governmental, while others have ruled that in no instances will local governments be considered immune. Hoggard v. City of Richmond is a typical municipal tort liability case, but one in which the court vigorously points out the inconsistencies of the situation in which it finds itself.

In the following article Rufus Jarman combines careful investigation with a sense of humor to illustrate graphically the scope and seriousness of this problem for a major city.

18

Hoggard

v.

City of Richmond

HUDGINS, J. This is an action to recover $5,000, alleged to be due plaintiff for injuries sustained when her left hand struck a barbed-wire fence while bathing in Shield's Lake, a swimming pool owned and operated by the city of Richmond. In the first count of the notice of motion, defendant is charged with non-feasance — that is, negligence in maintaining the resort. In the second count, defendant is charged with misfeasance in erecting a barbed-wire fence above and under the waters of the lake, thereby creating a dangerous place to which plaintiff and other inhabitants of the city were invited. The trial court sustained the city's demurrer to the motion, on the ground that the city "in maintaining and operating the bathing and swimming resort, known as Shield's Lake, was engaged in the exercise of a governmental function."

The question of plaintiff's contributory negligence is negatived in her notice of motion. Hence the single question presented is whether the municipality is liable for negligence in the maintenance of a bathing resort, or negligence in erecting an unsafe and dangerous instrumentality at a place designated for the use of bathers and swimmers.

The general law, as interpreted by the courts in all but two states (South Carolina and Florida), is that a municipality is clothed with two-fold functions; one governmental, and the other private or proprietary. In the performance of a governmental function, the municipality acts as an agency of the state to enable it to better govern that portion of its people residing within its corporate limits. To this end there is delegated to, or imposed upon a municipality, by the charter of its creation, powers and duties to be performed exclusively for the public. In the exercise of these governmental powers a municipal corporation is held to be exempt from liability for its failure to exercise them, and for the exercise of them in a

172 Va. 145, 200 S.E. 610 (1939)

negligent or improper manner. This immunity is based on the theory that the sovereign can not be sued without its consent, and that a designated agency of the sovereign is likewise immune.

There is granted to a municipal corporation, in its corporate and proprietary character, privileges and powers to be exercised for its private advantage. In the performance of these duties the general public may derive a common benefit, but they are granted and assumed primarily for the benefit of the corporation. For an injury resulting from negligence in their exercise or performance, the municipality is liable in a civil action for damages in the same manner as an individual or private corporation. . . .

While this distinction is generally recognized, the difficulty arises in the application of the rule to various municipal activities.

This court has held that a municipal corporation acts in its governmental capacity in operating a hospital (City of Richmond v. Long's Adm'rs, 17 Grat., 375, 58 Va. 375, 94 Am. Dec. 461); in regulating the use of sidewalks and streets (Terry v. City of Richmond, 94 Va. 537, 27 S.E. 429, 38 L.R.A. 834; Jones v. City of Williamsburg, 97 Va. 722, 34 S.E. 883, 47 L.R.A. 294); in maintaining a jail (Franklin v. Richlands, 161 Va. 156, 170 S.E. 718); and in maintaining a police force (Burch v. Hardwicke, 20 Grat. 24, 71 Va. 24, 33, 34, 32 Am. Rep. 640; Lambert v. Barrett, 115 Va. 136, 140, 78 S.E. 586, Am. Cas. 1914D, 1226; City of Winchester v. Redmond, 93 Va. 711, 716, 25 S.E. 1001, 57 Am. St. Rep. 822).

In Maia's Adm'r v. Eastern State Hospital, 97 Va. 507, 34 S.E. 617, 618, 47 L.R.A. 577, it was held that the Eastern State Hospital was a public corporation, governed and controlled by the state, and acted exclusively as an agency of the state for the protection of society, and for the promotion of the best interests of the unfortunate citizens, hence it was not liable in damages for personal injuries inflicted on one of its inmates in consequence of the negligence or misconduct of the persons administering the powers, or their agents or employees. . . .

In Ashbury v. Norfolk, 152 Va. 278, 147 S.E. 223, it was held that a municipality, in removing garbage, acted in a governmental capacity. Judge Prentis, speaking for the court, said: "There is some conflict in the cases, but the weight of authority quite certainly is to the effect that the removal of garbage by a municipality is a governmental function, which is designed primarily to promote public health and comfort, and hence that the municipality is not liable therefor in tort when the negligence which is charged occurred in the performance of that particular function, and no nuisance is thereby created."

In the City of Lynchburg v. Peters, 156 Va. 40, 157 S.E. 769, Justice Holt said: "The city, in the establishment of this park and playground, was act-

ing in its governmental capacity and committed no legal wrong. . . ."

The following are a few of the cases in which this court held that a municipal corporation, while engaged in the construction, repair, improvement or maintenance of its streets and sidewalks, in the operation of a wharf, in changing the grade of its street level, and in controlling surface water, acts in a private or proprietary capacity, and is liable to the individual for injuries resulting from the negligence of its officers or servants employed in the activities enumerated. City of Petersburg v. Applegarth's Adm'r, 28 Grat. 321, 69 Va. 321, 26 Am. Rep. 357 (and others cited).

The same rule applies to the activity of a municipality in conducting public utilities, such as water, sewerage systems, gas, light, etc. Chalkley v. City of Richmond, 88 Va. 402, 14 S.E. 399, 29 Am. St. Rep. 730 (and others cited).

This general line of demarcation between immunity and liability of a municipal corporation for torts has been followed with more or less consistency in this jurisdiction for more than a century. Judge Prentis, in . . . Ashbury v. Norfolk, . . . quoted Chief Justice Rugg, in Bolster v. City of Lawrence, 225 Mass. 387, 390, 114 N.E. 722, L.R.A. 1917B, 1285, as follows: "The difficulty lies not in the statement of the governing principles of law, but in their application to particular facts. The underlying test is whether the act is for the common good of all without the element of special corporate benefit, or pecuniary profit. If it is, there is no liability, if it is not, there may be liability. That it may be undertaken voluntarily and not under compulsion of statute is not of consequence."

Near the conclusion of the opinion, Judge Prentis said: "In a modern instance (Scibilia v. Philadelphia, supra, p. 796), it has been suggested that, as local governments are so constantly assuming or being vested with new duties, the distinction between purely public functions which are certainly within the police power, and those private business enterprises which are not is becoming increasingly difficult to maintain. This may be true, but, if so, it is doubtless because of our bad habit of counting cases instead of adhering to fundamental rules."

Notwithstanding the reference to fundamental rules, the decision of this court in that case was in direct conflict with the following statement of Judge Cardwell in Portsmouth v. Lee, 112 Va. 419, 71 S.E. 630, 632: "It is to be borne in mind that it is as much the duty of a municipal corporation to take due and proper precautions for the health and welfare of its citizens as it is to keep its streets and all parts of them in reasonably safe condition for public travel, and the principles of law fixing the liability or non-liability of the city in damages, where an injury on the street is sued for, and where the suit is for neglect of duty in the protection of health and general welfare, are the same and apply alike in both cases."

These quotations from the opinions delivered or prepared by two members of this court show the inconsistency of the application of the rule, and illustrate the difficulty of basing the distinction of the two functions on any logical reasoning. The same inconsistent and illogical holding of courts from other jurisdictions is apparent from a study of the cases. (Citing cases.)

The Connecticut court, in 1927, held that the city of Waterbury was acting in a governmental capacity in maintaining a swimming pool, and hence the city was not liable for negligence in maintaining a locker room at the pool. Hannon v. Waterbury, 106 Conn. 13, 136 A. 876, 57 A.L.R. 402. The same court, some four years later, in Hoffman v. City of Bristol, 113 Conn. 386, 155 A. 499, 75 A.L.R. 1191, held that the city of Bristol was guilty of maintaining a nuisance in that it erected a diving board four feet above the surface of the water which was only three feet deep at that point, and that the city was liable to plaintiff, who was injured in diving off the board into shallow water. . . . Sometimes recovery under the nuisance doctrine is restricted to property damage to the exclusion of liability for personal injuries. City of Louisville v. Hehemann, 161 Ky. 523, 171 S.W. 165, L.R.A. 1915C, 747 (and other cases).

South Carolina recognized the confusion in its own jurisdiction and the confusion in other jurisdictions, and finally held that a municipality, in the absence of statute, was not liable for tort in any event. Irvine v. Town of Greenwood, 89 S.C. 511, 72 S.E. 228, 36 L.R.A., N.S., 363. . . .

The A.L.R. annotator, in 75 A.L.R. 1196, among other criticisms, said: "It is almost incredible that in this modern age of comparative sociological enlightenment, and in a republic, the medieval absolutism supposed to be implicit in the maxim, 'the King can do no wrong,' should exempt the various branches of the government from liability for their torts, and that the entire burden of damage resulting from the wrongful acts of the government should be imposed upon the single individual who suffers the injury, rather than distributed among the entire community constituting the government, where it could be borne without hardship upon any individual, and where it justly belongs.

". . . The doctrine has been severely criticized by recent writers, and the courts have frequently been revolted by the hardships resulting therefrom in individual cases, and have introduced 'fictions, artificial distinctions and concessions to expediency,' in order to avoid the full rigor of the 'legal anachronism canonized as a legal maxim.' " . . .

Nothing so promotes public health as a supply of pure water for domestic use to all citizens. The same, to a more limited extent, may be said of water furnished by the city for the purpose of public swimming and bathing. . . . The expense of owning and maintaining a municipal water system or a public swimming pool is borne by the community group. A different method may be adopted in collecting the necessary funds to defray the expense of conducting the two activities. Usually the expense of operating the water system is met by a tax upon the amount of water used by each householder. Frequently, the expense of erecting and maintaining a swimming pool is paid out of the general municipal tax fund. To say that one activity is governmental and the other private or proprietary is arbitrary. Such classification of the two activities is not based on sound, logical reasoning. However, it is quite generally held that a municipal corporation is exercising a proprietary function when it acquires and operates a water works system for the benefit of its inhabitants. On the other hand, the courts are hopelessly divided as to whether the establishment and operation of a swimming resort is a governmental or a proprietary function. (Citing cases.) . . .

Confronted as we are by inconsistent statements in our own decisions as to what is and what is not a governmental function, and a sharp conflict in the decisions of other jurisdictions, we feel free to decide the question of tort arising from the activity of the municipality in maintaining an artificial swimming pool, as one of first impression.

Furnishing water to the inhabitants of a municipality for domestic purposes, and furnishing water to inhabitants to be used for the purpose of public swimming and bathing, are closely allied activities. Each activity tends to promote the health and happiness of its inhabitants. To hold a municipality liable for tort when engaged in one of these activities, and immune from liability when engaged in the other, is obviously unsound. This illogical distinction, with the harsh results inflicted upon the individual who has suffered personal injury through the negligence of the municipality or its servants, by which these activities are conducted, has been severely criticized. . . .

When the Commonwealth or a municipal corporation, whether acting in its governmental or proprietary capacity, seizes or damages the property of a citizen for public good, compensation, under a constitutional mandate (Const. §§6 and 58), must be made to the owner. Common justice demands that the right to be safe in life and limb should be as sacred to the citizen as his property rights. The rule that results in this unfairness of the community group to the individual citizen has become apparent to many courts, hence the tendency of all recent decisions is not to extend the immunity of municipalities. Canada, Minnesota, California, New York, Washington and other states have recognized the evils mentioned, and have, by statute, to some extent at least, enlarged the liability of both the municipality and the state for the wrongful conduct of their officers and agents acting within the scope of their employment.

Under the circumstances stated, we hold that the operation of a swimming and bathing pool by a municipality under the provisions of its charter, or the general law, is a ministerial act, and that where a wrongful act causing injury is committed by the servants of a municipality in the performance of a purely ministerial act, the municipal corporation is liable as any other private corporation, even though it does not derive any pecuniary advantage from such activity.

Applying these principles to the facts alleged in plaintiff's notice of motion, we hold that it states a cause of action, and that the municipal corporation has a right to offer any and all defenses that a private corporation would have under the same circumstances. The application of these rules for the determination of liability will sufficiently safeguard the municipality and will have a tendency to induce greater caution in the maintenance of swimming pools for the safety of invited guests.

For the reasons stated, the judgment of the trial court is reversed, and the case remanded for further proceedings in accord with the principles herein announced.

Revised and remanded.

EGGLESTON, J. (dissenting).

The majority opinion holds that the operation by a municipality of a swimming pool for the free use of its citizens is a ministerial and not a governmental function, and that consequently the municipality is liable in damages for the tortious acts of its servants and employees in such operation.

It is true, as the majority opinion states, that there is a division of authority in the question, but I think the great weight of authority, as well as the better reasoning, favors the view that the operation of such a facility for the gratuitous use of its citizens is a governmental function, and that therefore the municipality is immune from liability in connection with such operation.

It is a matter of common knowledge that all branches of the government — national, state, and local — now engage in many functions for the common good of the people which only a short time ago were undreamed of. In this State we have beautiful parks and playgrounds maintained by the national, state, and municipal governments for the common enjoyment of our citizens. No one questions the view that in establishing and operating these recreational centers the respective branches of the government are acting in a governmental capacity. See City of Lynchburg v. Peters, 156 Va. 40, 48, 157 S.E. 769: . . . Why is the same not true of a swimming pool operated without profit by a city as a part of one of its public playgrounds?

We had thought that these things, so obviously for the common good, should be encouraged, but the majority opinion is notice to the cities of this State that such playgrounds and parks are to be henceforth established and maintained at their peril. If the majority view is to prevail, then every municipal playground will henceforth be a fruitful source of both litigation and liability.

Moreover, the majority opinion is contrary to the principles heretofor laid down by this court.

In Ashbury v. Norfolk, supra, we held that the collection of garbage . . . is a governmental function. To my mind, the operation of free parks or playgrounds and swimming pools . . . is just as essential to the common good as the collection of garbage.

But that is not all. In the Ashbury Case we cited with approval the reasoning of the court in Bolster v. City of Lawrence, supra, in which it was expressly held that the operation of a bath house for the free use of the public was a governmental function. Other cases to this same effect will be found in the annotations in 41 A.L.R. 370 and 57 A.L.R. 406.

For these reasons I cannot agree with the majority opinion.

CAMPBELL, C. J., and HOLT, J., concur in this dissent.

19

Let's Sue the City

By Rufus Jarman

ON DECEMBER 26, 1947, beginning at 3:20 A.M. and lasting almost twenty-four hours, 25.8 inches of snow fell in New York City, which was the heaviest snowfall and the most paralyzing and upsetting experience from natural causes that New York had ever had. The way some of the local newspapers talked about it at the time made the event sound like the coming of another ice age, while accounts by New Yorkers of their personal hardships during the ordeal were reminiscent of the experiences of Washington's army at Valley Forge.

Rufus Jarman, "Let's Sue the City," *Saturday Evening Post,* April 22, 1950, pp. 31, 171–174. Copyright, 1950, by The Curtis Publishing Company. Reprinted by permission of the author and publisher.

Well, as bad as it all may have seemed, practically everybody and everything affected have long since recovered from the "Big Snow," as it is now called — all, that is, except the city of New York itself. The city government's 1947–48 snow woes are being resumed currently in the form of some 1500 suits against the city by citizens who are demanding about $28,000,000 damages for broken bones, lacerations, abrasions, contusions and sundry other injuries and indignities suffered from falls upon the slippery pavements.

These cases, which are just coming to trial because the crowded New York courts customarily run about two years behind schedule, constitute probably the greatest number of actions ever brought by its citizens against a municipality because of any one situation. They are also the largest group of worries ever thrust in one bundle upon the New York corporation counsel's office, which is the city's law department.

With a staff of 650 lawyers, engineers, accountants, investigators, clerks, stenographers, and process servers, the Corporation Council has the largest corporation law office in the world. In a year it represents the city in perhaps 25,000 cases, ranging from condemnation proceedings involving millions of dollars down to curious and baffling suits such as "breach of library tranquility" — a singular type of action, unknown until the time it was brought.

This remarkable charge was made by one Nathaniel Becker, a library-reading-room habitué, who became enraged when attendants at the New York Public Library tossed him out because he snored so loudly that others using the reading room could not concentrate . . . or sleep. Becker was even more infuriated when he lost his case in court, and proceeded to sue the judge. He lost that too.

Some people have the mistaken notion that a citizen must obtain municipal permission before he can sue the city. . . . Any citizen can sue the city of New York for any cause, without paying a filing fee or hiring a lawyer. He can make his own charges, file his brief and argue his case, which he frequently does.

Not long ago, a woman who listed her residence as the subway sued the city for $1,000,000,000, charging that the Police Department had robbed her of her husband, her family's real estate and certain valuable patents. Wacky as her charges were, they were solemnly entered upon the books, and no doubt will be disposed of eventually according to formal court procedure.

There was one bent, wrinkled crone, living hard by the City Hall, who once filed suit for $1000 against the city, charging that she was injured when she tripped over a hole in a sidewalk. By securing continuances in court she was able to keep her suit alive for seven years. She used the judgment she said she expected to obtain from the city as collateral for seventy-five-cent loans from friends along the Lower East Side. Her suit was dismissed eventually, to the chagrin of her creditors.

A man in Brooklyn sued the city on the ground that New York's radio broadcasting station, WNYC, produced cosmic rays that irritated his arthritis, while a woman in the Bronx sued for injuries received when she leaped from a window of a burning building. She claimed that the Fire Department should have arrived before she jumped.

But we digress from the incidents growing out of the Big Snow, or the Cases of the 1500 Sore Backsides. Now, during an ordinary year there are about 3500 suits filed against New York City for torts, or wrongs, done to citizens by the city. About 80 per cent of these concern falls people had, or said they had, upon the sidewalks. These include falls upon snow and ice, but usually the majority of sidewalk falls are blamed on the city because of holes in the pavement when there is no snow or ice underfoot.

Judging from the number of such cases, it sometimes appears that the sidewalks of New York afford the most treacherous footing in the world, with the possible exceptions of the Fens of Lincolnshire and the quicksands of the Amazon country. But in 1948 the great majority of falls were of the snow-and-ice variety, traceable to the Big Snow.

The one case growing out of the Big Snow that had been tried at this writing was lost by the city, although the corporation counsel's men asserted with great emphasis that such a snowfall was an act of God with which no city could cope immediately. It was pointed out that there are 17,130 miles of sidewalks and roadways, including 35,000 intersections, within Greater New York, and the 1947 storm deposited 21,692,086 tons of snow over these areas. The city hired 30,000 snow-clearance workers with shovels, besides its regular sanitation department force of some 10,000, and spent $9,000,000 clearing away the snow. This is five times as much as New York usually spends for snow clearance in an entire year.

The corporation counsel's staff feels that sympathy influences juries in many cases, particularly if the injured party happens to be a child or an aged person.

"Whenever a blizzard hits the city, with the wind howling down the Hudson, with blinding snow and sleet in the air and ice underfoot," one official of the department mused recently, "it appears that all young people with strong, healthy bones remain indoors by the fire, reading good books. The people who venture out into the storm are decrepit old grandmothers with tissue bones and brittle pelves. On a cold, still, icy night you can hear their bones breaking and snapping all over town."

Regardless of how the Big Snow cases turn out, assistant corporation counsels who handle them will doubtless emerge as authorities on the weather. This is not unusual. The city's legal eagles become experts on a great many things, such as geology, psychiatry, rare diseases, laws of the sea, engineering, water power, the milk industry and anatomy — particularly anatomy. They handle so many cases involving bodily injury that some assistant corporation counsels spout anatomical terms in ordinary conversation. . . .

Most cases . . . concern the woes and complaints of small people, unknown outside of their own block, and they never make the news columns. Perhaps the most important part in handling them is played by the corporation counsel's corps of investigators — a group of some thirty slightly rumpled-looking men whose headquarters are on the seventeenth floor of the New York Municipal Building, which towers officiously over the sedate City Hall.

The haunt of the investigators, or examiners as they are called officially, is a group of dismal offices, bare except for some scuffed desks, uncomfortable chairs and dusty filing cases. From this stronghold the investigators fare forth daily to learn the true facts of how Mrs. O'Slattery got her ankle sprained, for which she is suing the city.

Twenty-five or so such cases turn up in New York every day. On last July fourth, for instance, the Police Department reported about eighty accidents that might result in suits against the city. Some of them included the following:

Nine persons were injured in falls on streets, and twenty-three were hurt in city pools. Five fell while exercising on athletic bars and swings in city parks. A cat bit a man while on city property; a tombstone fell upon another man on city property. A tree limb landed on a woman's neck while she was drinking from a fountain in a city park, and the wind blew a man into a lake in Central Park, where he drowned. A boy was hit with a baseball bat in a park. Three automobiles were wrecked when they struck fire hydrants. Three people were drowned in city pools. A man was knocked down and injured when a city ferry jarred into her slip. And a Sanitation Department employee, while flushing a fire hydrant, thoughtlessly turned the hose upon a family from the Bronx that was dressed in holiday attire, and, lunch baskets in hand, was heading for Riverside Park.

Accidents reported by police are usually simple for examiners to investigate, since the police have the facts firsthand, and, in serious accidents, summon the corporation counsel's men to the scene. The tough investigations are accidents that are not reported until the complaint against the city is filed, perhaps a month afterward. By that time witnesses are hard to locate, and in cases of fraudulent claims

the plaintiff has had time to manufacture a strong case. The corporation counsel's examiners have to go after these with plodding patience.

Each examiner has a certain section of the city for his beat, where he cultivates friendships with shopkeepers, householders who keep abreast of local gossip, letter carriers, policemen and bartenders. The latter are particularly valuable, since most neighborhood events are threshed out at the local pub. Investigators assigned to racial sections speak Yiddish, German, Italian, French and Spanish.

Some time ago a man sued the city for $200,000 because of a broken hip he said he suffered from tripping over a hole in the sidewalk near his home on Staten Island. His attorney produced in court a photograph of the hole, which was some five inches deep and a foot square. The photograph was a clear one, showing shadows made by sunlight, and it was testified that it had been made the day the accident happened.

However, a corporation counsel's examiner had learned through local gossip that it had rained part of that day in that part of Staten Island, and there had been no sun at all; a freak of nature, since most of the city was sunny. The Weather Bureau corroborated this, and the case was thrown out of court. It was learned later that the man actually had fallen in his home. Friends or relatives had quickly made the hole in the sidewalk, photographed it and proceeded to sue the city.

Although they are men of infinite patience, the city's examiners sometimes grow restless on drawn-out investigations, and resort to methods of their own to smoke out the facts. This happened in the case of a woman who claimed she was made a permanent invalid from a fall she had when alighting from a trolley car. The car had moved, she contended, before she left the step. The resultant fall, she said, had caused complete paralysis of both legs. The trolley-car motorman agreed that the accident had happened the way the woman said.

The corporation counsel, however, was not convinced, and an investigator for the division attached to the Board of Transportation was sent to the woman's neighborhood to watch the apartment building in which she lived. It was thought that if the woman was exaggerating her paralysis, the investigator might catch her leaving or entering the building. He watched the building for weeks, saw nothing and finally got tired.

The examiner procured a smoke pot, which he fired up in the basement of the apartment building. He put it on the dumb-waiter and pulled the waiter up its shaft until it was near the floor where the woman lived. Then he mounted to that floor, and, giving the smoke time to be seen and smelled, ran down the hall, shouting, "Fire!"

It was observed that the supposed paralytic was the first person in the building to race down the stairs and gain the street. It developed later that the trolley-car motorman who had substantiated her story about the fall was the woman's brother.

Occasionally, when the city goes to trial in a personal-injury case that it is likely to lose, Fate, in the form of coincidence, steps in on the side of the municipality. Along that line, the legal staff recalls fondly the case of a woman who sued for injuries she alleged she received on a city-owned ferry because of the captain's negligence.

According to the city's version, the woman debarked from a City Island-Astoria ferry, and asked a policeman on duty at the Astoria landing to find her a doctor. The policeman testified that the woman was obviously in pain, adding that she told him she had been injured before boarding the ferry when she fell on a street called Lovers' Lane.

However, when the woman filed suit against the city some weeks later, she claimed that she was injured while riding on the ferry. Undoubtedly, if she could prove that she had been hurt while a passenger on one of the city's boats, she would stand to collect heavier damages than if her injuries had resulted from a mere fall on the street.

The city's only defense was the policeman's statement, but its big weakness was that in all New York there could be found no street named Lovers' Lane. The post-office people had never heard of it. Neither had the Borough President's office, the Sanitation Department, the Police Department, or the city engineer. Old maps dating back almost to the days of Peter Stuyvesant were consulted. But it appeared that, although almost every city, village and town in the United States has its Lovers' Lane, New York City did not.

Apparently the plaintiff's lawyer knew this, and made much of it. He brought a huge mounted map of the city into court, and challenged the city's lawyers to show the jury a Lovers' Lane. He said that it was a fine thing when a city, in order to defeat a proper claim by one of its citizens, would go so far as to make one of its policemen manufacture the name of a nonexistent street. Since there was no such street, he contended, the woman's injuries clearly resulted from negligence by the ferry's captain and crew.

He was interrupted in the midst of his oration by the timid voice of a woman juror. "I beg your pardon, your honor," she said, addressing the court, "but there is a Lovers' Lane in New York. I know, because I live there."

Naturally, the plaintiff's suit blew up with that. Later, some curious assistant corporation counsels, amazed at this break, questioned the woman privately. They learned that Lovers' Lane was a tiny street with only three houses, located near the extreme northern edge of the Bronx.

Actually, it was an offset of a more prominent street, and went by the name of the street from which it was offset on the city maps and in post-office records. It was known as Lovers' Lane to only a handful of old residents living in the immediate vicinity. . . .

Of all the strange cases the corporation counsel handles, probably the strangest come from the Board of Transportation, which operates in New York 6868 city-owned subway and elevated cars over 738.37 miles of track. There are 2692 trolley cars and busses owned by the city that operate over routes totaling 577.40 miles. During the fiscal year ending last June thirtieth, these vehicles traveled a total of 466,737,395 miles and hauled a total of 2,402,339,432 passengers.

All those people going all that distance can get into an awful lot of trouble — so much, in fact, that the corporation counsel has a special division, under a veteran transit attorney, Joseph E. Murphy, which has its own staff of examiners and handles its cases separately from those in the regular torts division.

Over the past nine years, an average of 2034 cases a year has been filed against the city for accidents occurring in the transportation system alone. They range from the tragic to the ridiculous. In the latter line, there was a man in Brooklyn who cultivated a flower garden in his back yard that adjoined an open subway cut. One day, after toiling among his plants, he turned up with a case of ivy poisoning. He claimed that he trailed the vine into the subway cut, which was owned by the city, so naturally he sued.

The city sent out an assistant corporation counsel to look over the garden, and he got ivy poisoning too. In spite of all that itching, it was never determined just where the noxious vine originated, but the flower grower lost his suit.

On the tragic side, there are a hundred or so people killed yearly in transportation accidents, including those who fall from subway platforms or from trains in the roaring tunnels. In a year, two dozen or more people will attempt suicide by jumping in front of trains. The corporation counsel's men have observed that more of these cases occur around Christmas than at any other time of the year. Those who are not killed in suicide attempts, but lose a limb or so, frequently sue the city on grounds that it was an accident and the city was to blame.

Then there are people who, for reasons completely beyond the wildest imagination of the corporation counsel, try to walk from one station to another along the subway tracks — a narrow, dark, howling area where the live third rail is located, and where trains miss them only by inches, even when the adventurers squeeze tightly against the tunnel walls. They are usually brought out dead or maimed.

Again, there are people who just get drunk and fall on or even deliberately lie down on the subway tracks. Some time ago a man walked into the claims department and inquired how he should go about filing a suit against the city for personal injuries. When asked what had happened to him, he replied that he did not know, but had been told that a few days before he had somehow been involved in a subway accident. He added that he personally had no recollection of the matter.

A check of accidents reported for the day that he mentioned revealed that this man had been found in a drunken sleep, lying in the trough between the subway tracks, after a ten-car train had passed over him. When awakened, he showed no signs of injury, only annoyance that his sleep had been disturbed. The city talked him out of bringing that suit.

With so many New Yorkers getting into trouble, and as conscious of suing the city as they are, it is apparent why the corporation counsel has to maintain the huge staff he does. Otherwise, the city would go bankrupt paying claims to its citizens.

As it is, the corporation counsel will win in a year maybe one third of the personal-injury suits for the city. He will lose perhaps one fifth, and settle the remainder for a fraction of what had been demanded.

Over the past five years the corporation counsel's office had to pay out an average of $4,173,725.25 a year in judgments lost and for out-of-court settlements, which is a good average, considering the huge number of cases filed against the city and the prodigious amounts demanded.

The corporation counsel has a good many excellent lawyers on his staff, who, in private practice, could command salaries several times larger than what the city pays them. . . . Unlike many other cities, New York does not allow them to augment their salaries by taking private cases.

It is sometimes puzzling, therefore, to other lawyers, why some of these men stick on, year after year, with the city. The answer was expressed not long ago by Bernard Richland, a sharp-eyed, enthusiastic man who is head of the opinions division of the corporation counsel's office. He points out that in important cases the city lawyers sometimes have to face a battery of high-priced legal talent on the other side, who get for that one day's work more than an assistant corporation counsel draws in salary for the whole year.

"It's the thrill of going up against the big shots that appeals to some of us," Richland said. "We have a lot of little two-bit cases, but we also have cases of such magnitude that a lawyer would rarely get them in private practice. I have found myself before the Court of Appeals, the only one on our side of the table, facing half a dozen of the cream of the New York Bar. It makes me feel that I am on the field of Armageddon fighting the battle of the Lord."

CHAPTER FIVE

Constitutions and Charters

MOST STATE CONSTITUTIONS are lengthy documents containing a vast amount of detail which has made them extremely inflexible. Despite the need for occasional revision, amendment or rewriting has usually been most difficult to accomplish. The first two articles in this chapter point up the handicaps found in the constitutions themselves, and the other legal, political, and psychological "roadblocks" which must be hurdled. The political realities of the constitutional convention process are then presented in an article by Professor Sturm, giving us an inside view of the Michigan convention of 1961–62.

20

The Urgent Need for State Constitutional Revision

THERE IS INCREASING AWARENESS of the need to modernize state constitutions, an awareness that would swell to a crescendo of demand if some public relations genius could find the way to show the citizenry how urgent is the need.

The truth is that there is a vast ignorance of what is in state constitutions and why, how well the provisions are suited for today and tomorrow, how tragically they prevent communities, counties, metropolitan areas and even the states themselves from dealing self-reliantly and competently with their problems.

Few people, including many authorities on constitutional law, ever have sat down to read critically the complete constitutions of their own states. When

"Trust in State Government," (Editorial) *National Civic Review,* January, 1959, pp. 4–5. Footnotes in original omitted. Reprinted by permission of the publisher.

a group of legal scholars performed this operation on the constitution of the state of New York earlier this year, they declared themselves "literally amazed" and were harsh in their condemnation of the document which, by the way, is generally considered to be among the better ones. The group termed the constitution badly written, too detailed and involved, frequently self-defeating and often an obstacle to progress.

During the last several years the Commission on Intergovernmental Relations, the national and regional meetings arranged by The American Assembly, and virtually all other thoughtful studies of the problem have deplored the "self-imposed constitutional limitations [that] make it difficult for many states to perform all of the services their citizens require, and consequently have frequently been the underlying cause of state and municipal pleas for federal assistance."

Yet the very men of influence who worry aloud about the trend toward big government in Washington are often the ones who make it impossible for their own states to resist this alleged trend because they either actively oppose the strengthening of state government or withhold their leadership in such efforts. They shirk this moral obligation, it should be added, more often because they have failed to do their homework than because of any positive wish to weaken state and local government.

"Most of the states are using constitutions adopted

in the nineteenth century," it was pointed out by Allan R. Richards, who added, "That was not a century of genius for constitution-making."

Age in itself is not a proper basis for condemnation, of course. The United States constitution, quite old itself, is a fine document; but unlike the state constitutions it has not been smothered in a mass of restrictive amendments that are essentially legislative detail designed for the benefit of special interests rather than in the broad public interest.

Despite the impressive evidence of the need for updating constitutions, demagogues seem to find it distressingly easy to pose as the defenders of "the American way" by resisting improvement. Several years ago a Wisconsin legislator delivered a frenzied oration in which he said he would rather trust the genius of the simple hunters and trappers who (he said) drafted the original document than he would the long-haired theorists who would be involved in a present day revision. It might be interesting to check back on the simplicity and occupations of the original draftsmen.

This is just one of many indications that people tend to sanctify a constitution and, when something goes wrong in state government, to make the governor or legislature the culprit, failing to see that these officials may be the hapless prisoners of outworn constitutional provisions.

Actually there is relative unanimity of opinion among those who know the most about constitutions that widespread revision is needed to strengthen state and local governments. No rational person would suspect dangerous radicalism in the Council of State Governments, an organization founded and maintained by the states themselves, which has advised the states to revise their constitutions, modernize their legislative processes, reorganize their executive branches, maintain adequate planning and resource agencies, and free their political subdivisions from crippling straitjackets.

The simple truth is that the people of few states seem to trust their elected representatives to govern and have expressed their distrust with a mass of complicated restrictions. Executive responsibility is diffused among too many officials. Legislative power and effectiveness of operation are so hampered by the dead hand of the past that few legislatures command popular respect.

The urge to seek protection against arbitrary official action is basically to blame for these and numerous other weaknesses. Ideally, the constitution, short and general, should reflect citizen trust of government. It is better to give power to government and then to hold that government responsible than to manacle it through detailed constitutional restraint.

It is no simple task to revise a state's constitution

and not one to be approached lightly. Ideally, the calling of a constitutional convention should be preceded by a thorough examination of the existing document that would result in the identification of weaknesses, suggestions for its improvement and, above all, in an understandable report to the people to insure widespread knowledge of the evils and the cures.

An obviously sound way to provide this is to create a commission with financial capacity to employ competent staff and with time to do its job thoroughly. Without this background, the convention itself, with a real or psychological timetable and without an atmosphere conducive to statesmanship, is as likely as not to fall short of its potentialities.

21

Road-Blocks to Conventions

By Wilbert L. Hindman

IT IS COMMONPLACE to point out that America is the land of the written constitution, and that we have had some two hundred constitutional conventions since the revolution. This statement is generally made in a spirit of complacency, not to say smugness.

Actually, it is a remarkable achievement that the number of constitutional assemblies in this country has reached such a substantial total. For in order to be held at all, constitutional conventions must overcome a host of interrelated hurdles, ranging from the legal through the political to the psychological.

Once result is that, despite all the revisions which have taken place, there are many state constitutions in substantial need of modification and rewriting. These include the famous unamended document of Tennessee and California's constitutional colossus. (Alas for Hollywood — we have to concede to Louisiana the right to use the term "supercolossal" in describing that state's basic law.) The instances of Tennessee and California are typical demonstrations

Wilbert L. Hindman, "Road-Blocks to Conventions," *National Municipal Review,* March, 1948, pp. 129–132, 144. Footnote in original omitted. Reprinted by permission of the publisher.

that constitutional change is needed both to modernize the archaic and to organize the chaotic.

If the need for revision can be regarded as self-evident in many states, the three factors which stand in the way of change — legal, political and psychological — require careful analysis.

Without commenting upon the elaborate legal restrictions imposed in many states on submission of individual amendments, it is important to note that the question of calling a constitutional convention may be submitted to the people in nineteen states only after a two-thirds vote of the legislature, and in four states a majority of all the legislators must support such a measure. In ten states ordinary majorities suffice and in eight there must be submission of the question at definite intervals, ranging from seven to twenty years.

Interestingly enough, twelve states have no specific provisions in their constitutions for calling conventions. It is now generally held in these states that authority to establish conventions exists, stemming from the provisions found in many bills of rights asserting that the people may "alter their government as they deem proper."

Actually more important than legal limitations, although related to them, are political barriers to conventions. The precise nature of these obstacles will differ in each state, but it is important to understand that substantial political opposition to constitutional change exists everywhere and will, if possible, take advantage of any and all legal impediments to revision of the basic law. Minority groups hostile to constitutional modernization are greatly fortified by any requirement of a two-thirds vote in each house of a legislature as a prerequisite to submitting the question to the people.

While political opposition to constitutional change varies from state to state, one may safely generalize to the extent of asserting that change will be opposed by interest groups afforded special protection in the existing basic law. Such groups are easily discerned where tax limits are severe, where taxes are earmarked by constitutional fiat for such specific purposes as highway construction, or where there is inadequate constitutional support for existing regulations. Groups profiting from such weaknesses will fight change with every device at their command. On the one hand they will fall back upon legal restrictions and on the other hand they will use every technique they can muster to bolster a psychology which will defeat reform.

One political problem in many states [has been] the relationship between the reapportionment issue and constitutional revision. . . .

. . . . It is ordinarily the case . . . that constitutional conventions are made up of members elected or otherwise chosen from existing legislative districts. . . .

Where this is true, the rural voice [. . . has been] strong enough in a convention to cry down urban insistence upon the creation of representative assemblies. . . .

It must be stressed at this point that the district system of choosing delegates, even if supplemented as in New York and Missouri by a number of delegates chosen at large, not only overweights the convention in favor of the rural elements — upstate, downstate, or outstate as the case may be — but in any event makes no provision, except by chance, for the representation of the principal interests of the state. So long as the legislatures cannot cope directly with this problem of interest group, or functional representation, it is of course too much to expect it to be solved in constitutional conventions.

Conventions commonly operate under closer public scrutiny than legislatures do, however, and they also tend to bring out in the delegates an unusually strong sense of public responsibility. This means that the excesses of the lobby are more likely to be restrained at conventions, while the services of the lobby such as affording useful technical as well as political information, are likely to be given full play.

It might be mentioned in passing that at least partial functional representation in constitutional revision is most likely to be secured under present circumstances through the creation of appointive constitutional commissions. Appointments to these commissions, however, seem to go largely to lawyers who may or may not represent points of view beyond those of their vocation. . . .

The psychological barrier to conventions is made up again of a number of attitudes. On the one hand there is the citizen who has the approach indicated in Kentucky: "If it was good enough for grandfather it is good enough for me." Related to this is the point of view reported from Missouri in the slogan: "Why rewrite the Bible?" There was an example of this in the Los Angeles press recently, where one newspaper argued that California did not need constitutional revision. After all, it said, the state has grown big (that's our chief criterion of success, of course) under the 1879 constitution, and certainly its . . . [hundreds of] amendments have kept it up to date!

People are conservative

Another psychological obstacle, and probably the major one, is mistrust of the people themselves. That sounds strange in a democracy but it is true. This is simply to ignore history, however, for the record of constitutional change in this country shows that if there is one thing above all else calculated to bring out in the electorate a sense of cautious responsibility, it is the selection of delegates to a constitutional convention.

The people will not support moves for revision of basic law on trivial grounds, nor will they ordinarily approve a constitution that embodies matters currently regarded as radical or unsound. Although the written constitution itself was a radical and experimental device at the time of the American Revolution, today the people will not depart too markedly from the basic constitutional pattern established in any state. Professor McIlwain refers to constitutions as the "appeal from the people drunk to the people sober," and the public adopts a temperate attitude toward all aspects of constitution-making.

So, whatever the fears may be in some quarters that constitutional conventions may produce a document tinged with pink instead of red, white and blue, the principal psychological fact about such conventions is that they are constrained by the community and the dignity of their responsibility to be sincere, cautious and moderate. This, rather than ill-advised mechanical impediments to change, is the greatest check on unwarranted constitutional revision.

I am thoroughly in favor of provisions permitting the people to call constitutional conventions with reasonable ease and frequency. The people in each generation are entitled to solve their own political problems, or even to make their own mistakes, rather than to be saddled with the errors of the past or suffer from the consequences of the fact that no earlier convention, however distinguished its membership, possessed divine omniscience.

Not only, then, do most constitutional provisions for calling conventions require liberalization, but a decision of the people favoring a convention should be supported by a self-executing clause clearly setting forth the essentials involved in electing and holding the gathering. . . .

We make much these days, and rightly so, of the importance of strengthening our democracy in an era of renewed external challenge. Certainly we must do this, and one effective phase of the program is to modernize the basic laws of our states instead of letting them be diluted with statutory content or permitting them to weaken from inapplicable and dead sections which do not apply in the atomic age.

As believers in democracy we should have sufficient confidence in our own people to give them the utmost freedom to decide when to have constitutional conventions and whether or not to approve the changes recommended. This is one sure way to combine the enduring fundamentals of the past with a dynamic adjustment to the needs of today. Constitutional flexibility is fundamental in insuring a system of government responsive to constructive suggestions and therefore impregnable in the face of subversive attack.

22

Making a Constitution

By Albert L. Sturm

A SIGNIFICANT DATE in the political development of Michigan was January 1, 1964, on which the fourth constitution of the state became effective. Drafted by Michigan's fifth constitutional convention, the new document was approved by the voters on April 1, 1963, by a margin of 7,424 votes in a total vote of 1,614,296. It is the twelfth constitution to be adopted in the 50 states since 1900 and the first general revision of an existing organic document since the New Jersey Constitution of 1947.

Steps leading to the 1961–1962 convention

The 1908 constitution of Michigan, which the new instrument replaces, had been subject to an increasing number of amendments reflecting mounting dissatisfaction with its provisions. Although it contained a few measures characteristic of the progressive movement, this document generally had retained the philosophy of its immediate predecessor, the constitution of 1850, which reflected the Jacksonian and pre-Civil War emphasis on elective officers, frequent rotation in office, and dispersion and limitation of governmental powers. Growing desire of the electorate for constitutional reform was reflected in the five popular votes on the question of calling a constitutional convention during the effective period of the 1908 constitution. The voters rejected a convention in 1926 and 1942; in 1948 and 1958 a majority of those voting on the question approved, but in each case the favorable vote failed to meet the constitutional requirement of a majority participating in the election. Significantly, the vote favoring general constitutional revision increased in each succeeding referendum on the question from 1926 to 1958.

During the 1940s and 1950s a distinct pattern of constitutional issues emerged — partly from immediate and pressing problems confronting the state, and partly reflecting reform efforts in other states. Michigan's cash crisis of 1959 dramatized the need for reform and helped focus public attention on emerging constitutional issues.

Albert L. Sturm, "Making a Constitution," *National Civic Review,* January, 1964, pp. 14–26. Reprinted by permission of the publisher.

The Jaycees and the League of Women Voters, joined later by Citizens for Michigan and other groups, prepared and collected the signatures for the constitutional initiative proposal that opened the door to basic legal reform. This Gateway Amendment, approved by the voters in November 1960, provided for approval of general constitutional revision by a simple majority of those voting on the question, somewhat liberalized the basis of representation in a constitutional convention and made other lesser changes. Michigan electors voted April 3, 1961 for general constitutional revision, but only by a narrow margin of about 23,000 votes. Only four of the 83 counties, located in the greater Detroit area, registed affirmative majorities.

The legislature appropriated $2 million for the constitutional convention and laid down rules for the selection of delegates. Legislative implementation of the popular mandate for a convention, however, did not include financial support for preparation. An $85,000 grant from the W. K. Kellogg Foundation provided the necessary funds for preparation of a series of research studies and for physical facilities to accommodate the convention and its staff. This work was directed by an eighteen-member Constitutional Convention Preparatory Commission appointed by Governor John Swainson, who had previously designated six citizens' advisory committees to develop recommendations in major areas of the constitutional system. The governor had also reconstituted the Constitutional Reform Study Commission appointed by his predecessor, Governor G. Mennen Williams, in anticipation of a convention call. All of these groups submitted useful reports which were augmented by studies prepared by private organizations such as the Citizens Research Council of Michigan and the Michigan Municipal League.

Convention organization and procedure

Con-Con delegates, as they were popularly called, were nominated on a partisan basis in the primary election on July 25, 1961. The voters selected 286 nominees from more than 1,100 candidates. The result of the election on September 12, in which only approximately 20 per cent of the state's registered voters participated, was a landslide victory for the Republicans. They won 99 of the 144 seats — a ratio of more than two to one. Except for four Democratic delegates from the Upper Peninsula, all Democrats were from the Detroit metropolitan area. Republican representation in the convention was distributed over both urban and rural areas of outstate Michigan, with fewer of them from the southeastern urban counties.

A profile analysis by the University of Michigan's Institute of Public Administration characterizes the delegates as predominantly male white Protestants with education and annual incomes well above average. Women participated for the first time in the writing of a Michigan constitution. There were eleven in the convention — six Republicans and five Democrats. All thirteen Negro delegates were Democrats from Wayne County. Ages of delegates ranged from 25 years upward. As a delegation, the Democrats were younger than the Republicans. Largest occupational groups in convention were 59 attorneys of whom six were former circuit judges, fourteen farmers and thirteen educators, including five Ph.Ds. The profile showed also that most of the delegates were deeply involved in the public affairs of their respective communities; many had held public offices, both elective and appointive, on national, state and local levels. . . .

By unanimous vote the delegates ratified the preconvention selections by the Republican caucus for major convention offices and approved the Democrats' nominee for the vice presidency allocated to the minority. As its presiding officer, the convention selected Stephen S. Nisbet, retired vice president and director of public relations of the Gerber Products Company, former president of the Michigan Education Association and member of the State Board of Education. The three vice presidents represented major blocs in the convention: Edward Hutchinson, attorney — the conservative rural Republicans; George Romney, president of the American Motors Corporation and president of Citizens for Michigan — the moderate Republican wing; and Tom Downs, attorney for the AFL-CIO — the Democratic minority.

This "troika" organization on the second executive level reflected generally the two-to-one ratio of Republicans to Democrats in the convention and was applied in the designation of committees and in other organizational phases of the convention's activities. The only nonmember of the convention elected as a permanent officer was the secretary, Fred I. Chase, retired secretary of the Michigan Senate and consultant of the preparatory commission.

The staff, which totaled about 90 persons during the seven and a half months of the convention, was organized in three major divisions: research, drafting and public information; administration and housekeeping; and the police and guide division. Headed by three co-directors from the three largest universities, the research division provided invaluable staff services to both committees and individual delegates.

Initially, the rules provided for nine substantive committees and four operational or housekeeping committees. Substantive committees were on rights, suffrage, and elections; legislative organization; legislative powers; executive branch; judicial branch; local government; finance and taxation; education; and miscellaneous provisions and schedule. The convention later increased this number to ten with the creation of the committee on emerging problems. Operational committees named were on administration, rules and resolutions, style and drafting, and public information. Initial committee assignments by President Nisbet totaled 243, allocated to the two party delegation on a two-to-one basis. Committee leadership in all cases included a Republican as chairman and as first vice chairman, and a Democrat as second vice chairman.

The convention maintained formal procedural controls mainly through the standing rules, the work of the committee on rules and resolutions, and establishment of a convention schedule. The original timetable resulted from a ruling by the attorney general that failure of the convention to adjourn finally before April 1, 1962, would mean that the work of the convention could not be submitted to the voters before April 1963. The original schedule was revised three times before the final version was adopted. Adjournment on May 11 suggests that possibly the termination of pay at the end of seven and a half months may also have been an important factor in controlling the length of the convention.

There were three distinct phases in the work of the 1961–62 convention: (1) The organizational and staffing period of two to three weeks; (2) the committee phase of intensive study of existing and proposed constitutional provisions, hearings, and formulation and submission of proposals to the plenary body, which took approximately three months; and (3) plenary convention consideration and action involving three readings. First reading in committee of the whole covered two and a half months of long debate and frequent partisan conflict. Second reading was accomplished in two weeks; third reading required only three days.

Politics and the convention

Understanding of the constitution-making process requires attention to the forces and influences that motivate delegates in reacting to issues and in making decisions on the structuring, allocation and limitation of governmental power. We turn now to a brief examination of the power structure of the Michigan convention and the forces that appeared to control its major basic decisions.

Michigan is a strong two-party state and many Michiganders take their politics seriously. The two party delegations in the convention reflected the vigor of party activity. Of the two groups the Democrats were the more homogeneous, although there were intra-party factions in both the Democratic and Republican delegations. Most observers distinguished three principal factions among the Republicans: the conservatives from rural outstate districts; the moder-

ates, who comprised the largest group in the convention, mainly from suburban Detroit and outstate urban areas; and a relatively small group of liberals or progressives. Besides these groups, distinct blocs developed on particular constitutional issues, often cutting across party lines when personal and group interests became involved.

As the majority, the Republicans bore not only the principal responsibility for organizing the convention but also for providing policy leadership. No single faction, however, commanded a majority of all delegates which would have enabled it to direct the course of constitution-making. Nor did the Republican State Central Committee attempt to lay down a party line so far as could be determined. There was too much heterogeneity in Republican ranks. The Democrats, in contrast, received definite guidance from party leaders on policy issues.

Party caucuses afforded some direction but they fell short of providing firm policy leadership. They proved to be most useful in informing delegates and in developing greater consensus on issues. The Democratic caucus appeared more effective, on the whole, in producing party discipline and affording guidance than its Republican counterpart.

An informal steering committee, composed of officers and committee chairmen, was a useful decision-making device during the early months of the convention. In the later decisive stages, however, major policy decisions tended to be made under the guidance of factional leaders rather than through more formal channels.

A number of significant political developments during debate of the committee of the whole greatly influenced the course of proceedings and the convention's final product. Three are particularly noteworthy.

First, the Romney announcement of candidacy for the governorship quickly melted the thin veneer of bipartisanship that characterized the early proceedings. Even before the announcement, Democratic leaders both within and outside the convention reacted strongly. Two Democratic delegates, for example, introduced a resolution calling for the resignation of any delegate who announced his candidacy for state office, and Democratic State Chairman John J. Collins declared: "Con-Con is in grave danger of becoming no more than background noise to the political ambitions of one man." The prospect of a Republican vice president and prominent leader in the movement for constitutional reform running for governor on a platform of which the new constitution would be an important part did much to inject partisan considerations into basic decisions and to alienate Democratic support for the emerging document. President Nisbet expressed the opinion that the Romney candidacy had "hurt the convention."

The candidacies of other delegates for public office also affected the convention's work. Many legislators considered their seats to be jeopardized by the political ambitions of Con-Con delegates; this feeling of insecurity among some legislators led to outright hostility toward potential rivals. Press reports indicated also that political candidacies of delegates affected the convention's image in the minds of some citizens, who feared that aspirations for political office sometimes weighed too heavily in the voting on important constitutional issues.

The third major political development was the package compromise agreement between the conservative and moderate Republican factions. The agreement was stimulated by a threatened potential alliance of the outstate Republican conservatives with the Democrats in mid-March. The coalition expected by many observers to develop between the Democrats and the moderate Republicans, both predominantly from urban areas, failed to materialize. Instead, the Democrats found their views more congenial with those of the Republican conservatives on a number of issues. The agreement between the Republican moderates and conservatives, however, forestalled an alliance of Democrats and Republican conservatives and afforded the basis for majority action that had not previously been possible. Major controversial areas covered in the package compromise were apportionment, the executive branch and finance.

Writing the new Michigan Constitution involved many interest groups, organizations and individuals. Although only 70 persons, representing some 59 organizations, registered as convention agents hundreds of persons appeared before committees on behalf of an estimated minimum of 150 interest groups. There were, naturally, innumerable other personal contacts of the delegates with interested groups. The convention maintained communication with the people through its committee on information, extensive press, radio and television coverage, as well as through public relations activities of the delegates themselves. A number of events and developments during the convention drew national publicity, such as ex-President Eisenhower's visit to the convention in December and the potential candidacy of Romney for national office.

Major issues and decisions

Evaluation by the Michigan Constitutional Convention delegates of the relative importance of principal issues as revealed by responses to a questionnaire before the convention, coincided closely with subsequent developments. First by far was apportionment. Financial issues of tax and debt limitations and earmarking of revenue came next. Lowest in ranking were reduction of the voting age and uni-

cameralism. Except for apportionment, organizational changes in the three branches tended to fall in the middle range. . . .

Completion of the work

The convention completed action on the new constitution and approved it by a vote of 99 to 44 on May 11, after rejecting a substitute document proposed by the Democrats. Five Democrats joined 94 Republicans in approving the new basic instrument of government for submission to the voters; two Republicans voted with the remaining 42 Democrats and one Republican abstained. . . .

From the early stages of the convention, both the method and time of submission of the new document to the voters were to be the subject of debate. As partisan differences developed among delegates, these submission issues became deeply enmeshed in party maneuvering in the convention. On both issues the great majority of Democrats and Republicans took opposing positions. The method of submission was resolved on May 1 against the Democrats, who preferred separate submission of controversial and noncontroversial items, in favor of a single proposal embodying the entire constitution to be accepted or rejected as a whole by the electorate. . . .

Some appraisals

The following capsule appraisals are based mainly on interviews with, and questionnaire responses from, Con-Con delegates, and on personal observation of the convention and study of the document that it produced.

The Convention. The delegates on the whole were satisfied with the convention and the manner in which it functioned. Although many delegates thought that political considerations played an excessively important role in deliberations, a number of proposals seeking to divorce delegates from politics were rejected. Over substantial and vigorous opposition a majority of the delegates affirmed their belief in a political basis for convention membership.

Although opinion differed among delegates about the optimum size of a constitutional convention, majority registered its decision for no change in the plan providing for a number of delegates equal to the total authorized membership of both houses of the state legislature. Although in some recent state constitutional conventions a smaller membership produced new constitutions in a shorter time, these states differed greatly from Michigan. Large population, wide diversity of interests, long political tradition, and a complicated and diversified political system are factors that would appear to justify a broadly based and widely representative organ for constitution-making.

As for organization and procedure, most delegates agreed that the number of committees should be kept small; no delegate should serve on more than one substantive committee; care should be exercised to avoid overloading committees with specialists, who will probably be unable to agree among themselves; and it is best to remove a constitutional convention as far as possible from elections and legislative sessions.

Most of the convention delegates who originally were skeptical of the need for constitutional reform and opposed the calling of a convention soon became enthusiastic supporters of this method of constitutional change. Few disputed the far-reaching value of seven and a half months' intensive study of Michigan's government by a group of present and potential leaders in both major parties. Few denied the immense value of the convention, not only as a school for statesmen but also as a vehicle for general education of the citizenry on basic state problems. President Nisbet voiced the opinion of the great majority in asserting that "Con-Con has been good for Michigan regardless of the fate of its document at the polls."

The constitution. The new constitution of Michigan reflects the political environment in which it was written. Such features as the apportionment plan, establishment of a civil rights commission, the provision on county home rule, creation of a five-tiered, unified court system and earmarking of revenues developed from Michigan problems and issues.

The new constitution is on the whole a conservative instrument. Current and traditional practices are continued in such sections as those providing for a bicameral legislature, the four-cent limitation on the sales tax and retention of traditional forms of local government. Michigan Con-Con delegates, like those in other recent state constitutional conventions, displayed conservatism in making changes. Few delegates favored radical departure from well established forms and principles.

A number of innovations are nevertheless contained in the new constitution. Some have been recommended for years by specialists in state government and by organizations such as the National Municipal League. Others were adopted in response to pressing needs that could no longer be met adequately by traditional methods. Illustrative are the sections providing for administrative consolidation, cooperative inter-governmental relations, longer terms of office, a legislative auditor, abolition of justice of the peace courts and more liberal debt limitations. Some of these and other new features were accepted in a form substantially modified from that advocated by model documents. For example, although many delegates gave lip service to the short ballot principle,

it was applied only to a limited extent in the 1963 constitution.

Like the constitution of the United States, which is often referred to as "a bundle of compromises," the Michigan document contains many provisions on which agreement was possible only because of concessions and willingness to compromise. Concessions occurred within party delegations, as well as between these groups. On some issues, alignment of forces and votes was determined on a partisan basis; others involved geography and some developed from a desire to maintain political advantage. Thus, for example, wide ideological differences between rural conservative Republicans and urban Democrats proved on occasion to be secondary to hard realities concerning retention of political power. Political parties thrive by gaining control of public offices; this fact of life is implicit in the decisions written into the Michigan document.

Politics in writing the constitution accounts not only for substantive decisions on policy issues but also in large measure for the length of the document. Michigan Con-Con delegates were well aware of the standard of brevity emphasized by authorities on constitutions and constitution-making, but the product of their labors retains many provisions of a statutory character. Responsibility for the statutory content belongs both to party delegations and to interparty special interest blocs and alliances. The desire of every special interest group for constitutional status, prestige, and sanction for its particular function and program accounts for much verbiage. As one delegate put it when interviewed: "On the one hand, we want to make the constitution simple, flexible and brief; on the other hand, the politician in us, the realist, tells us that, unless reforms are spelled out in the document, they probably will not be achieved." With the knowledge that the legislature cannot be forced to act on matters within its power, delegates tended to spell out their intent in the basic law.

The 1963 Michigan Constitution contains 19,203 words, as compared with 21,790 words in the 1908 constitution. It is half again as long as the new basic laws of Alaska and Hawaii and the 1947 New Jersey Constitution. Two of these documents, however, were written in new states without long-established constitutional systems. In form, style and phraseology, the Michigan Constitution is unquestionably superior to its predecessor, mainly because of the excellent work of the committee on style and drafting.

The Michigan experience clearly indicates that constitution-making, like other forms of lawmaking in American states, is a very practical process necessarily molded by tradition and experience and political forces. Even though it is lawmaking on the highest level, it cannot be removed from politics, the very essence of which is the acquisition of power to determine public policy and to control its execution. No matter how liberal or progressive the personal views of delegates to a constitutional convention, their collective decisions and votes tend to reflect prevailing opinion. Delegates are representatives, and they weigh proposed decisions in terms of their acceptability to voters. Contrary to a popular notion, few American constitutional conventions have taken radical action far in advance of public expectations. The 1961–62 Michigan Constitutional Convention was no exception. Michigan's experience in constitution-making affords an excellent case study of democracy at work in establishing a sound foundation for government in a modern American state.

Although revision of city charters may not ordinarily be quite as difficult as the writing of a state constitution, it poses many of the same problems. One of the greatest shortcomings of many charter reform movements is to assume that the job is done when a new charter has been drafted. The best charter in the world is of little value if it is not accepted by the voters and does no more than collect dust on a shelf. An excellent "model" campaign is presented here by Dr. Charlton F. Chute, who served as consultant to the Philadelphia Charter Commission, as he describes the main features of the successful campaign in that city.

23

How to Get a New City Charter

By Charlton F. Chute

THE MEMBERS of the Philadelphia Charter Commission began their work two years ago with their friends warning them of the futility of their efforts. Yet nineteen months later the voters, by nearly two to one (65 per cent), adopted the charter they had drafted! Planned public relations was the key to the victory.

A definition of good public relations is that it is a function of two parts: (1) doing the right thing and (2) telling about it. This precisely describes the story of Philadelphia's first home rule charter.

The effort to win public understanding and ac-

Charlton F. Chute, "How to Get a New City Charter," *National Municipal Review,* September, 1951, pp. 403–410. Footnotes in original omitted. Reprinted by permission of the publisher.

ceptance started from the day the charter commission was named. Thus the foundation for the formal appeal for public approval was built solidly into the charter itself. It would be fair to rate writing the charter at about 50 per cent of the job and building an attitude favorable toward adoption at about 50 per cent.

Frequently charter commissions have ended their work in failure because they misinterpreted their goal. They thought that writing a charter was 100 per cent of the job and neglected to do those things necessary to secure the document's adoption at the polls.

Charter commissions sometimes make a second mistake in defining their goal. They say, "We are here to write the best possible charter." This can be dangerous business! The goal for most commissions should be, "We are here to write the best possible charter that we think the voters will adopt on election day."

If you say, "This is the attitude of a cynic and it will not lead to Utopia," my reply would be, "A charter commission is justified in writing a Utopian charter when it has voters that will adopt such a charter!"

There is room, however, for a different viewpoint in some communities where the existing charter is a fairly good one. A commission in such circumstances may wish to write the best possible charter, realizing that it may be defeated at the polls but that a subsequent charter along the same lines may be adopted.

Just what voters will be willing to adopt is frequently far from clear in the early stages of a commission's work. The commission members in their talks and methods of operation can and should do a great deal to raise public attitudes on what to include in a charter.

The public relations program used so successfully in winning a new charter for Philadelphia was based on considerable observation of successes and failures in other cities and states, including campaigns for new state constitutions because they are remarkably similar.

The more important background factors in the Philadelphia situation may be classified as either favorable or unfavorable.

Unfavorable factors:

1. Futility — the belief that government in big cities is corrupt and must remain so.

2. Machine hostility — Philadelphia voters are partisans, not independents. The dominant party organization has retained power for 80 years. It was widely believed the organization would be hostile to a good new charter and that would spell defeat.

3. Philadelphia voters were said to be apathetic, particularly on issues involving good government.

4. It was said that the civic groups would not pull together.

5. Philadelphians do not understand home rule and have had no experience in how to go about getting such a charter.

6. The present charter is a good one and a new charter could not possibly correct the real problem in in city government — getting honest officials.

These unfavorable factors were, to a large extent, widely held beliefs without much factual basis.

Favorable factors:

1. By far the most important was the series of city hall scandals which started in May 1948 with the discovery of an embezzler in the city's purchasing department and the suicide of the head of the amusement tax division, who left a note stating all the men in his unit were guilty of embezzlement. In succeeding months one scandal followed another, more embezzlements were disclosed, several extortionists were convicted and three more suicides occurred.

The earlier events led to creation of the home rule charter commission; the later ones added emphasis and focused public attention on the imperative need for corrective measures. The cumulative effect led many voters of the dominant party to lose faith in their political organization and its leaders, as shown by the party's defeat in November 1949. . . .

2. The city hall scandals provided clear evidence of the failure of the existing charter to provide safeguards. For example, the city controller had certain broad auditing powers. A special grand jury, after nearly a year's study, concluded that the operations of the receiver of taxes had not been audited for at least five or six years! Here was a clear breakdown in financial control.

3. The personnel of the charter commission appointed by the mayor and president of city council, following passage of a home rule act for Philadelphia by the state legislature, was of high caliber. All were of fine reputation, of recognized ability and public spirit and representative of the community.

The strategy of home rule is based on the ultimate appeal to all the voters. In Philadelphia this meant a million people. It calls for full and free discussion, much publicity and education and much public participation. It requires the organized effort of many people of ability, understanding and untiring energy — and it takes time. A charter commission of outstanding citizens, representative of various groups in the community and taking a year or so to write a charter, is a "natural" for a successful public relations program.

For the most part, leaders recruited were present or former officers of groups in the community — civic clubs and associations; vocational, professional, business, religious, political groups; neighborhood clubs, labor unions, and so on. Over 500 such groups were active.

Hearings are public

Shortly after the charter commission organized, it held a series of public hearings once a week for about two months in three-hour afternoon sessions. To these meetings were invited representatives of the newspapers and leading civic groups.

It is flattering to a group and its officers to be invited to explain their point of view to the charter commission. Later, if the commission adopts some of the suggestions — as they must do because nearly everything conceivable will be suggested — the groups will take pride in their participation.

But in educating the members of the charter commission, group leaders educate each other! In listening to arguments for opposing points of view they gain a new appreciation of the magnitude of the commission's task and the difficulty of making sound decisions on controversial issues. They become less dogmatic and more inclined to recognize the need for justifiable compromise. As the seats of the chairs grow harder they gain an increased admiration for the ability of commission members to "take" such punishment week after week.

If the newspapers think well enough of some of the comments to carry them in their columns, the authors walk with a new spring in their step. Friends and acquaintances congratulate them on the important role they are playing in civic affairs and the reading public learns that improvements are being suggested at city hall — maybe there is hope after all!

If the political leaders in the community have traditionally received group leaders with disrespect, hostility, or evident insincerity, there is an opportunity for the charter commission to show the value of a good public relations policy.

So far, the leaders of the community were being educated — first, on what was needed in a new charter and, secondly, on the complexities of the job. Meanwhile the charter commission built good will for itself and made friends.

The heads of participating groups usually reported back to their membership that they appeared before the commission and presented recommendations. This educated additional people. Frequently committees on the new charter were set up to render further assistance to the commission. The matter was in many instances reported in the group's publication and so still more people learned that a good city charter was in the making — and that the commission was composed of a pretty intelligent group of sincere and hard working people.

One difficulty was that the voters were largely in-articulate in the early stages. This was demonstrated by a letter of the Greater Philadelphia Youth Movement, a group of former presidents of high school student bodies, who had discussed the need for a new city charter. The letter said:

The question, "What method for selecting a city council would you favor under the new city charter?" was most frequently answered by these replies:
1. How do they select the council now?
2. What do you mean by a "new city charter"?
3. I don't know; what do you think?

In this situation recourse was had to the trial balloon technique. If the voters could not state what they wanted, speakers for the commission would formulate a statement of the needs and then let the voters tell where they were wrong.

Many voters expect too much in a new charter or constitution. Some look for action beyond the legal powers of the commission or convention. Others expect perfection. Speakers explained the legal scope of the project and pointed out that the charter could not be a perfect document. Undoubtedly, members of the commission could point to parts of it which they did not favor. The main objective, it was said, was to produce a charter that would be as great an improvement as fifteen outstanding citizens could agree upon.

In the early months of the commission's life, both leading newspapers published articles on the commission and its problems which were most helpful. Reprints were made available. Radio and television broadcasts were given. Local magazines told the story.

Education in civics

The schools did a splendid job of making the charter a practical project for education in civics. The school children took the problem home. Some asked their parents what they thought should go into a new charter! One political worker announced he was in an embarrassing spot because his ward leader wanted him to help defeat the charter while his son, a schoolboy, wanted him to work for adoption!

When the preliminary draft was released on September 6, 1950, members of the commission stated that, as far as they were concerned, all provisions were tentative and subject to change if changes would bring improvement. Again, many public hearings were held, many sound changes were accepted by the commission.

By such means the commission built confidence in its work and made an impregnable case against charges of "trying to jam something down the people's throats."

Another advantage of hearings on a preliminary draft was that it forced the opposition to come into the open with its criticisms. If it failed to do so, preferring to wait for the final campaign, it was open to the charge of bad faith in that it was more concerned with the defeat of the charter than in cooperating to draft a good one.

By the time final campaigning began, the opposition found it difficult to organize for lack of outstanding leaders, good arguments and funds. It was thus forced to rely on absurdities and distortions.

Opposition forestalled

Everything that went into the new charter was carefully scanned to see what aid and comfort it might give the opposition. It was not known who would be in the opposition camp but experience showed that their arguments would not relate to the provisions they disliked but would be based on those provisions from which they thought they could make the most political capital. These provisions usually have a high emotional content — race relations, tax provisions, etc. The most important reason for the defeat of the proposed home rule charter of St. Louis on August 1, 1950, was the wage tax provision.

Sometimes it is good public relations to insert a few words in a charter, even though they are not necessary from the legal point of view. Here is an example:

In the closing days of the charter commission's work, there was general agreement on the following wording on the jurisdiction of the Civil Service Commission over appeals from employees who had been dismissed or demoted: "Findings and decisions of the commission and any action taken in conformance therewith as a result thereof shall be final and there shall be no further appeal on the merits."

This was attacked by some laymen as denying to an employee "his day in court." The lawyers on the commission were quick to point out that, of course, an employee could appeal to the courts on jurisdictional or procedural grounds. While this was true, the proposed charter language did not say so and was sure to be used as an argument against the charter by ignorant or unscrupulous opponents. For this reason there was added, "but there may be an appeal to the courts on jurisdictional or procedural grounds." These words were highly useful from a public relations standpoint, although contributing nothing legally.

It is fortunate that it is not necessary to develop a thorough understanding of a proposed new charter because many voters have neither the training, the time nor the inclination to master its technical provisions. The approach to such people is by means of endorsements by individuals as well as groups.

Consequently outstanding men in whom the public had confidence were selected as co-chairmen to run the Philadelphia campaign. One was a former judge, a Republican of splendid reputation who had resigned from the Municipal Court only a few months earlier. The other was a prominent and equally highly regarded Democrat, a former U.S. senator. This backing was strengthened by the endorsements of the heads of the Republican and Democratic city committees. It was also pointed out that the members of the charter commission were both Republicans and Democrats, but that in votes within the commission there had never been a division along party lines.

Influence by endorsement

Members of the commission also helped by endorsement. The chairman was also president of city council and one of the most highly regarded men in city hall. The only woman member was a fluent speaker with a sense of humor, who had been active in women's club and church activities.

Seven were outstanding members of the Philadelphia Bar who were of tremendous importance in both drafting and public relations. Three members were prominent business men. The local head of the American Federation of Labor was invaluable in winning the confidence and support of labor. Two outstanding members representing the Negro community helped effectively among their people. A city councilman contributed his good judgment based on years of political experience.

A charter commission cannot be satisfied with merely writing a new charter. It owes to the public brief statements, in laymen's language, describing problems and the answers it proposes. Such a written statement for the 1917 charter of Boulder, Colorado, was called a *Prefatory Synopsis*. In Missouri, by long tradition, it was called *Address to the People*. In Philadelphia the commission selected what is probably the best title yet, *Report to the Voters*. It was released at the same time the final draft was filed and helped the press and public to interpret the commission's work fairly. This was only one of several printed pieces put out by the commission to explain the charter's highpoints.

The magnitude of the campaign is demonstrated by the more than 600 speeches listed in the speakers' bureau register during its last months. Toward the end there was an average of about 30 speeches per day. Much of the speaking burden was carried by the commission's executive secretary, Edgar B. Cale, and its legislative draftsman, Paul Wolkin, as well as members of the Citizens Charter Committee and of the commission.

Printed publicity materials were produced on a large scale. Some 1,250,000 sample ballots and 600,000 four-page tabloid newspapers with cartoons, called *Charter Express,* were distributed by a pro-

fessional organization to each householder. Other literature included 150,000 *Philadelphia Charter Observers* distributed through the schools and the Citizens Charter Committee, 100,000 accordion folders, 100,000 *Be Sure to Vote On Charter Day,* 100,000 *Comparisons,* 85,000 *Report to the Voters,* 25,000 *Comments of the Drafting Committee.* The commission realized, of course, what so many public relations specialists have emphasized for years, that there is not one public but many publics variously interested in efficiency, economy, good race relations, more democratic control, better personnel in city hall, greater financial control, better city services, a more representative council, and so on.

Charter campaign committee

The heavy work of the campaign was carried on by the Citizens Charter Committee, organized in November 1949 shortly after the charter commission began its work. Starting with members from about 70 organizations, it began the final campaign with 522 cooperating organizations.

Under sponsorship of the Greater Philadelphia Movement, one of the city's newer civic groups, this committee set up a ward and district organization, a speakers' bureau, a publicity organization, and the other campaign activities familiar to every community. It had on its staff four technicians in public relations.

The Chamber of Commerce staged a rally at the historic old Academy of Music and filled it for speeches from business, labor and campaign leaders. The president of the chamber raised $80,000 to finance the campaign.

The Committee of 70, a well known local civic group, held a successful luncheon, the highlights of which were speeches by the titular heads of the Republican and Democratic organizations.

The Pennsylvania Economy League, in addition to supplying the consultant to the charter commission, organized a statement of facts that was distributed by many large companies to their employees and also prepared a series of bulletins analyzing certain aspects of the charter. A story on the Pennsylvania Economy League was carried by the *Saturday Evening Post* in its issue of April 14, 1951, on sale six days before the election. It contained the challenging statement that the vote on April 17 "should indicate whether Philadelphia is really awake or has merely turned over in its sleep."

The Bureau of Municipal Research, in addition to publishing charter information in its weekly bulletin, prepared a booklet analyzing the charter, which was widely distributed. The Citizens Council on City Planning alerted its more than a hundred civic betterment associations to the advantages to be gained.

The two daily newspapers, the *Inquirer* and the *Bulletin,* vigorously endorsed the charter day after day with news items, cartoons and strong editorials, while the *Daily News* covered both sides generally without taking a position. The powerful hammering of the *Inquirer* and the *Bulletin,* each having a circulation of over 600,000 daily, was perhaps the most important single factor in the campaign. Many neighborhood newspapers also helped.

It would be a mistake to assume, however, that vigorous newspaper support alone will result in adoption, as was shown by the defeat of the proposed St. Louis charter in 1950.

The campaign developed three novelties: (1) An editorial on the front page of the *Inquirer* on April 10, one week before the election, printed in blue surrounded by a red border! (2) A daily series of cartoons in comic strip form which the *Bulletin* carried on its editorial page for several weeks. This concerned a mythical Philadelphia family called "The Philbys," who discussed various charter problems within the family circle. (3) An eight-page tabloid newspaper printed for the public schools in an edition of 100,000 and later reprinted for general distribution, called the *Philadelphia Charter Observer.*

The usual last minute campaign of distortion developed but, because of the long and thorough campaign of education, it did not prove fatal.

Public relations is not the whole story. No program of publicity or other public relations techniques can bring a new charter into being unless a real need for a new charter exists.

Checklist for a good public relations program to secure a new city charter

1. Remember that many well written charters have been lost at the polls for lack of a good public relations policy.
2. Start the public relations program of getting understanding and acceptance when the charter commission is selected.
3. Determine from a study of the community, as well as from experience in other well governed cities, just what a new charter should contain.
4. Determine what are the favorable and unfavorable factors for the success of a new charter at the polls.
5. Develop a continuing program to inform the voters about the charter commission and its work by talks, radio and television programs, magazine and newspaper articles and other media. Have reprints available.
6. Encourage the thought that the proposed charter will be a compromise that will not completely satisfy all interests, but that it will be a great improvement over the old document.
7. To the fullest extent possible have charter commission meetings open to the public.
8. Invite and encourage individuals and groups to appear before the charter commission to present suggestions — encouraging participation by all citizen groups is important.
9. Pay special attention to the newspapers and the schools because they can be among the most important factors in success.
10. If possible, release a preliminary draft of the proposed charter for public criticism and comment.
11. Beware of wording charter provisions in such a way as to aid the opposition.
12. Allow a period of from two to six months for the final campaign.
13. After the proposed charter is filed, do not relax on the job of public education, for this is the best insurance against a last-minute campaign of distortion.
14. Secure endorsements of the proposed charter from as many groups and important individuals in the community as possible.
15. The charter commission should print and distribute a brief "Report to the Voters" in laymen's language, explaining the high points of the charter.
16. Realize throughout that your appeal is to many publics interested in efficiency, economy, better personnel, greater financial control, more effective democratic control, improved city services, etc., etc.

CHAPTER SIX

The Problem of Representation

NO DECISION OF THE U. S. SUPREME COURT in modern history, with the exception of the anti-segregation decision of 1954, has created the political furor touched off by the series of decisions on apportionment of state legislatures, beginning with Baker *v.* Carr in 1962. The implications of these rulings for the future of state and local government are indeed far-reaching, although there is little agreement on precisely what all the effects will be, let alone on the desirability of the representation principle established, or on what the proper role of the judiciary should be in this matter. Typical of the complaints about rural over-representation in most state legislatures, leavened in this instance by a sense of humor, is the opening article by a city editor of the *Detroit Times*. The next selection, by a prominent authority on constitutional law, features a survey of the leading decisions, an evaluation of the reasoning of the judges, and a vigorous defense of the "rightness" of the court majority's position. Another outstanding professor of law raises serious questions, however, about the court's arithmetical approach to the highly complex issue of reapportionment, arguing that it by no means solves the basic problems of fair representation and that it may be politically naive. Although most of the arguments at the moment deal with the state legislatures, it is worth noting that the logic of the "one man, one vote" principle applies equally to the legislative bodies of cities, counties, and other units of local government, and that in a few states the courts have already begun to enforce such requirements.

24

Inflation in Your Ballot Box

By John Creecy
Drawings by Stanley Stamaty

AS A CITY DWELLER, I'm becoming rather piqued at my rural neighbors' stolid conviction that I'm not fit to be trusted with a full vote in matters of state government.

John Creecy, "Inflation in Your Ballot Box," *Harper's,* August, 1953, pp. 66–69. Reprinted by permission of the author and publisher.

I'm from Michigan, where Joe Smith who traps muskrats in the Keweenaw Peninsula has nine times as much representation in the State Senate, and three times as much in the House, as his brother Jim who moved to Detroit a couple of years ago and got a job in an auto plant.

Before you squander any sympathy on me or Jim, allow me to point out that if you live in a big city you're probably in pretty much the same fix. In most states our country cousins have the legislature sewed up tighter than Joe Smith's winter underwear and seem to regard this as a natural and socially desirable condition. In many cases the framework of representative democracy with which the states began has been subtly wrenched and prodded out of shape, the better to protect the special interests of the rural people. City dwellers pay an increasingly major share of the taxes, but the benefits they receive therefrom seem gauged by a sort of state law of diminishing returns.

Perhaps the most candid expositor of the rural viewpoint in Michigan is State Senator Alpheus P. Decker of Deckerville (Pop. 719, including numerous Deckers). He has argued that "it would be a crime to the state of Michigan to give Detroit full representation on a population basis."

In seeking to prevent this misdeed he has zealously circulated, among citizens pondering reapportionment, reprints of an article by Roger W. Babson uttering the complaint that "Large cities are the main sources of poverty, gangsters, and immorality" and that "most big city voters are ignorant about government and are controlled largely by unscrupulous ward heelers."

On the other hand, the author concludes, "rural people have much better character and more time to think and read than do large-city people. . . . the votes of people in small cities and rural communities should count more than the vote of the ordinary city man."

This statement, with its apparent implication that full franchise might be permissible for the *extraordinary* city man, appears rather on the daring side when contrasted with usual apportionment practice as followed by our rustic lawgivers.

Most legislatures are supposed to be reapportioned every few years on a population basis. Actually this seldom gets done, despite great and continuing shifts from rural to urban areas. . . .

Even where the constitutions are obeyed the city people are often deprived of an even break by sly clauses foresightedly inserted by the country slickers. Sometimes — as in California, New York, and Pennsylvania — it is an arbitrary limit on the amount of representation any one city or county can have. Sometimes — as in Michigan — it is the granting of a seat to any county or group of counties which can muster *half* the regular population ratio.

Such gimmicks add up to a form of ballot box inflation, which cuts the value of a vote as effectively as monetary inflation cuts the value of a dollar.

AND if, as a desperate measure, the issue is carried to the voters as it was in Michigan last fall, it becomes clear that the embattled farmers still have a trick or two up their sleeves to pull on the city voters.

It also becomes disillusioningly clear that full representation for city dwellers is the last thing that some city dwellers want, and that when the chips are down the farmers are able to find powerful allies in the camp of the enemy.

Early in the year, in Michigan, there was an ominous flourish of initiatory petitions for reapportionment. The rural legislators, having — as Mr. Babson pointed out — ample time to read, were quick to decipher the handwriting on the wall. They undertook to quell the reapportionment uprising by getting there fustest with the leastest.

They broached, under the plausible title of "The Citizens' Plan for a Balanced Legislature," a proposal which would give the city people a slightly increased voice in the House but would even further muffle their feeble whisper in the Senate.

The city papers showered it with abuse, one terming it an "anti-Detroit plan" that the rural leaders were attempting to "jam through on grounds that Detroit citizens do not deserve a voice in government."

A few weeks later, however, the papers reexamined the plan and discerned merit in it.

Their change of heart followed the launching of a rival plan, sponsored jointly by the League of Women Voters, the AF of L, and the CIO, which called for restoring both houses to a strict population basis. The early public reaction to it was encouraging. But a flurry of alarm swept through the corps of lobbyists at Lansing. Most of them, including those for some groups which had no reason to fear that greater urban representation would harm their cause, were apprehensive about swapping known quantities for unknown.

Even greater apprehension was felt, in some quarters, over the added legislative strength that equal

urban representation would give to employee groups on matters in which their interests diverge from those of their employers.

For support of their legislative interests, as against those of their employees, industrialists are inclined to look to the rural members. City delegates are more likely to be under obligation to the labor vote. Hence such elite urban organizations as the Detroit Board of Commerce and the Michigan Manufacturers Association speedily took up positions abreast the pitchfork platoons. Aligned with them were many urban Republican leaders, actuated by the fact that their party's strength is greater in the countryside than in the cities.

The reasoning which had convinced these groups that unlimited representative democracy would not be a wholesome thing for Michigan had also converted the major elements of the city press, which began to see in the new plan a nefarious CIO plot to dominate the state (despite the fact that a big-business-sponsored research organization had pronounced it "the best plan that has been advanced" for placing the legislature on a population basis).

As the campaign reached its climax, the rival proposals came to be designated in the press as "The CIO Plan" and "The Citizens' Plan."

With the issue thus simplified, a decisive block of urban citizens agreed at the polls that, while reapportionment was desirable, it would be better in the hands of "citizens" rather than the CIO. The "balanced" plan thus became part of the state constitution. . . .

THERE are enough urban citizens in Michigan, not closely connected with top-level business management, to have adopted the plan which would have

given us full representation. If the fact that we failed to support it is not to be written down as a triumph of the rural strategy of confusion, it would seem we are entitled to be credited with a high-minded, philosophical renunciation of our selfish interests — an acceptance of the arguments that we are not rightfully entitled to equal representation.

Aren't we? What is there to these arguments?

It was claimed that city voters are often influenced by labor leaders; and it is true.

It was claimed that city voters are often less well informed and less thoughtful about the candidates and election issues than are rural voters. This could be disputed on the ground the city voter generally has more candidates to select from, and less opportunity to know them.

But, assuming the claim to be valid — what of it? Is the extent of our franchise to be governed by the degree to which we can be expected to vote wisely? Is a citizen's vote to be cut in half or less because he is likely to vote Democratic, or Republican, or Vegetarian? Or because he belongs to the United Auto Workers or the Detroit Board of Commerce? And if so, who is to be the arbiter of these qualifications?

It was claimed that area and socio-economic factors, rather than population, should be the base of at least one house of the legislature, in order to provide the checks and balances which are essential to good government.

If the legislature were merely a business or industrial council this might make a good deal of sense. But it is of course far more than that. It deals with interests that transcend area and economic classification.

If interests, rather than numbers of people, are to be fairly represented, some definite formula would have to be found for doing so. But how would you go about it? Everybody has legislative interests and many of them have no connection with the way in which he makes his living.

It is true that the city taxpayer in states such as Michigan, if given representational equality, could outvote the country taxpayer. And it may be true that rural interests would suffer. But I still can't see why this entitles the rural minority to a majority vote.

Obviously a fine solution for the problems of any minority is for it to acquire a majority voice in the government. It is a solution that has been employed effectively in many lands, in many centuries; but I do not believe it is one to be thoughtfully endorsed by many people in this century, in this land where men are created free and equal. . . .

25

Equal Protection and
the Urban Majority

C. Herman Pritchett

THIS YEAR MARKS the tenth anniversary of the Supreme Court's decision in *Brown* v. *Board of Education*. On May 17, 1954, nine judges, sworn to defend a Constitution which guarantees equal protection of the laws, speaking for a country which declared its independence on the proposition that all men are created equal and which is fighting for moral leadership in a world predominantly populated by people whose skin color is other than white — these nine men unanimously concluded that segregated educational facilities are "inherently unequal."

Most of the members of this audience can probably still recall their feelings when they heard what the Supreme Court had done. Even those who were in full sympathy with the holding must nevertheless have been awed by the responsibility the Supreme Court had undertaken and shaken by some doubts whether the judicial institution could engage in a controversy so charged with emotion and bitterness without running the risk of political defeat and possible permanent impairment of judicial power.

Ten years later, we know that they made the right decision. The decision was right because it got the United States on the right side of history at a crucial time in world affairs. By its action the Court raised a standard around which men of good will might rally. Under the Court's leadership the issue of racial segregation was forced on the American conscience. Segregation could persist only if it could be ignored; once the case for segregation had to be examined, it was lost. Without either the purse or the sword, the weakest of the three branches of government proved to be the only one with the conscience, the capacity, and the will to challenge the scandal, the immorality, the social and economic waste, and the positive international dangers of racial discrimination. Eventually the Executive, through Presidents Kennedy and Johnson, and the Congress began to assume their responsibilities for achieving the broad purposes of racial

C. Herman Pritchett, "Equal Protection and the Urban Majority," *American Political Science Review,* December, 1964, pp. 869–875. Footnotes in original omitted. Reprinted by permission of the author and the publisher.

equality. But if the Court had not taken that first giant step in 1954, does anyone think there would now be a Civil Rights Act of 1964?

Today, the Supreme Court stands with respect to the issue of legislative districting and apportionment where it stood in 1954 on the issue of racial segregation. Though the differences are substantial, I suggest that the similarities are even greater. Now, as then, the Court has taken sides in the crisis of our times. Where the Court in 1954 was demanding a social revolution, today it is presiding over a political revolution. Once again the Court has unlocked the explosive potentialities of the equal protection clause, staking its prestige and its reputation on its ability to remake the nation in the image of its constitutional concepts.

I

The Supreme Court has never been detached from the major political issues of the times. As Edward S. Corwin once said: "Constitutional law has always a central interest to guard." Under John Marshall the central interest was in the heroic task of legitimizing a strong national government. Under Roger Taney the Court's attachment was to narrower, more fragmented goals, principally the economic interests of the South and West. In the latter part of the nineteenth century the Court's role was to encourage the economic freedom which a rapidly expanding economy demanded. In the New Deal period the Court was striving toward a balance of governmental power, strong enough to prevent depressions yet restrained enough not to threaten individual freedom.

When we come to the recent past, we stand in our own light and may not see what will be obvious from a longer perspective. But certainly a central focus of constitutional law since World War II has been on problems of what may be called "the urban majority." The census of 1920 revealed that rural America, which from the beginning of the nation had dominated American politics and social values, had become a minority. Since that time white, Protestant, rural America has been on the defensive, seeking to maintain in race, religion and politics its former superiority. Urban America, the new majority, has offered to the Negro the opportunity to escape from the bondage of rural peonage, as it had earlier permitted European immigrants to rise in economic and social status. Urban America has had to develop a tolerance which did not exist in rural America, so that various races and religions could live together in peace. Urban America has needed the political power which would make possible governmental recognition of its staggering problems of housing, transportation, recreation, juvenile delinquency, disease, and social disintegration.

Faced with this challenge, the rural minority could preserve its political power and its social system only by a denial of that equality which had been a major tenet of the American *credo,* though often "honored in the breach" rather than the observance. Conversely, the drive of the urban majority required the assertion and the practice of equality in race, equality in religion, equality in political power. As Alan Grimes says in his thoughtful book on *Equality in America,* the urban majority has proved to be "a liberating force in American politics, redistributing freedom by equalizing the claims of the contestants." He continues:

American politics has always made a pragmatic adjustment to its immediate needs, tempering its idealism with expediency. Today, ironically, the imperatives of urban life are making expedient the fulfillment of the historic ideal of equality.

II

The idea of equality indeed has roots deep in Western political thought. It reaches back to the Greek and Roman Stoics and the Christian fathers, and was carried forward by seventeenth and eighteenth century political philosophers such as Hobbes and Locke. The Declaration of Independence announced the "self-evident" truth that "all men are created equal," but no language specifically reflecting egalitarian concern found a place in the Constitution. In fact, that document in several provisions accepted and guaranteed the institution of human slavery.

The idea of equality finally appeared in the Constitution when the Fourteenth Amendment was adopted in 1868, forbidding the states to deny to any person within their jurisdiction "the equal protection of the laws." This formulation was conceived primarily as a protection for the newly freed slaves. Justice Miller in *The Slaughter-House Cases* said that this was "the one pervading purpose" of the Civil War amendments. Speaking specifically of the equal protection clause, he doubted very much "whether any action of a State not directed by way of discrimination against the negroes as a class, or on account of their race, will ever be held to come within the purview" of the clause.

This expectation was doubly confounded. The Court proved very reluctant to use the equal protection clause as an instrument for the protection of the civil rights of the "newly made freemen," and at the same time eager to invent uses for it as a bar to business regulation. Robert J. Harris, in his fine study of the equal protection clause, located some 544 decisions of the Supreme Court up to 1960 in which this provision was invoked and passed upon by the Court. Of these, 426 (77 per cent) dealt with legislation affecting economic interests, while only 78 (14 per

cent) concerned state laws allegedly imposing racial discrimination or acts of Congress designed to eliminate it.

The generally low regard in which the equal protection clause was held as late as 1927 is indicated by Justice Holmes's deprecatory characterization of equal protection in *Buck* v. *Bell as* "the usual last resort of constitutional arguments." It was not until the early 1930s that the Supreme Court "returned to the Constitution," as Harris puts it, and began the rehabilitation of the equal protection clause in a series of cases dealing with racial discrimination which finally led in 1954 to the epoch-making decision in *Brown* v. *Board of Education.*

In the meantime there had been a tentative exploration on the Court of the possible application of the equal protection clause to legislative districting and apportionment. Serious complaints had accumulated in most of the states as to inequality of population in congressional and state legislative districts. Inequality resulted both from failure to redraw district lines as population changes occurred, and from provisions in many states basing legislative districts on factors other than population. The problem of unequal congressional districts was raised in the 1946 case of *Colegrove* v. *Green,* and three members of the Court asserted there for the first time that equal protection required the election of congressmen from districts generally equal in population. But there was no follow-up on this suggestion. Over the next fifteen years efforts to get the Court to intervene in other kinds of legislative election problems were met, in Harris' words, with "bland unconcern for equitable representation." Consequently it came as a considerable surprise in 1962 when the Court in *Baker* v. *Carr* by a 6 to 2 vote reversed the result of the *Colegrove* case and directed a federal court to hear a challenge to the constitutionality of Tennessee's legislative arrangements, where no reapportionment of seats in the state legislature had taken place since 1901.

While this decision did not indicate what standards the judiciary should apply in passing on complaints about legislative apportionment, that was soon to come. In 1963 the Court in *Gray* v. *Sanders* by a vote of 8 to 1 invalidated the Georgia county unit system of primary elections for statewide offices, a system deliberately designed to give control of the electoral process to rural minorities. The Court held:

Once the geographical unit for which a representative is to be chosen is designated, all who participate in the election are to have an equal vote — whatever their race, whatever their sex, whatever their occupation, whatever their income, and wherever their home may be in the geographical unit. This is required by the Equal Protection Clause of the Fourteenth Amendment.

This was Court's first approach to the rule of one-man-one-vote. *Gray* v. *Sanders* was not, of course, a legislative apportionment case. But in 1964 the Court held that the same principle covered election of representatives in Congress and the apportionment of seats in the state legislatures. In *Wesberry* v. *Sanders* the Court by a vote of 6 to 3 applied the one-man-one-vote principle to the congressional districts of Georgia, holding that the Constitution had the "plain objective of making equal representation for equal numbers of people the fundamental goal for the House of Representatives." Four months later the rule of one-man-one-vote was responsible for holding unconstitutional the legislatures in no less than fifteen states, as the Court decided *Reynolds* v. *Sims* and fourteen other cases by varying majorities of from six to eight justices. Probably more than forty state legislatures in all are vulnerable to challenge under the principle of *Reynolds* v. *Sims*.

III

The apportionment decisions have been bitterly criticized on many grounds, but there are two basic objections to the constitutional position asserted by the Court. First, it is argued that the equal protection clause has no relevance to and does not control matters of political representation, and consequently that there are no constitutional limits on legislative arrangements. Second, even if there are some limits, it is alleged that they are not judicially enforceable. So this is partly an argument about constitutional standards for apportionment systems, and partly an argument about the proper role of the courts.

Let us examine first the question of constitutional standards. Only Justices Frankfurter and Harlan on the recent Court contend that there are no constitutional limitations on legislative discretion in setting up apportionment arrangements. With Frankfurter's retirement, the Court's position is eight to one against Harlan on this score.

Six members of the Court majority say that the proper standard is one-man-one-vote. In *Wesberry* v. *Sanders* Justice Black derived the principle of equal congressional districts from certain of Madison's statements at the Constitutional Convention and in *The Federalist,* and from the provisions in Article I for the choosing of representatives "by the people of the several States." In *Reynolds* v. *Sims* Chief Justice Warren relied on general principles of representative government and majority rule to support the Court's conclusion that "the Equal Protection Clause guarantees the opportunity for equal participation by all voters in the election of state legislators." "Legislators represent people, not trees or acres," he said, adding: "To the extent that a citizen's right to vote is debased, he is that much less a citizen."

Obviously the Court is here creating new law, just as it did in the *Brown* decision. The Court never likes to admit that it is creating new law. In *Brown* the Court had hoped that it could find some support for overruling its precedents in the "intention of the framers," some definite indication of concern with segregated education when the Fourteenth Amendment was adopted, and so it had asked counsel to undertake research on the historical background of the amendment. But no clear voice spoke from the past, and consequently the Court had to ground its interpretation of equal protection on the "present place" of public education in American life and present psychological knowledge and present standards of morality. In the same way the Court in *Reynolds* v. *Sims* relates equal protection to present concepts of representative government.

It is charged, however, that these are simply the concepts of a "particular political philosophy" which seems wise to the present majority of the Supreme Court, and without constitutional standing. Justices Stewart and Clark deny that the rule of one-man-one-vote can be logically or historically drawn out of the equal protection clause, and they contend that the rule is much too rigid in its effect on systems of representation. Holding every state to the one-man-one-vote rule, they say, would deny "any opportunity for enlightened and progressive innovation in the design of its democratic institutions." The goal of equal protection as they see it is a broader one, "to accommodate within a system of representative government the interests and aspirations of diverse groups of people, without subjecting any group or class to absolute domination by a geographically concentrated or highly organized majority."

This is a rather vague standard. How is one to judge whether it has been achieved? There are two tests, according to Stewart. First, the plan of representation must be "rational," in the light of the state's own characteristics and needs. Second, "the plan must be such as not to permit the systematic frustration of the will of a majority of the electorate of the State." Determining whether a state is meeting this test might seem to require the employment of whole cadres of political scientists, but Stewart suggests that a liberal arrangement for use of the initiative and referendum in approving or reviewing apportionment plans should be regarded as an acceptable guarantee against frustration of the basic principle of majority rule.

Application of this two-fold test led Stewart and Clark to uphold the legislative apportionments of New York, Colorado, Illinois, and Michigan, all of which were condemned by the six-judge majority as violative of one-man-one-vote. In addition, Stewart, but not Clark, would have approved the Ohio apportionment. The Stewart-Clark standard gave the same result as one-man-one-vote in the ten other states which the Court considered in the spring of 1964.

Which of these standards has the better claim to validity? The Stewart-Clark rule of rationality has the pragmatic merit of flexibility. It does not clamp down so strictly on the discretion the states have traditionally exercised in making representation decisions, and consequently it may be more politically acceptable.

By contrast, one-man-one-vote is a rigorous rule. But I believe that it comes closer to summarizing current notions of democracy in representation than any other. For example, the Twentieth Century Fund in 1962 assembled a conference of sixteen distinguished research scholars and political scientists to discuss the problems of legislative apportionment. With only one dissent, they concluded that "the history of democratic institutions points compellingly in the direction of population as the only legitimate basis of representation today."

Moreover, the Court's one-man-one-vote rule may not be as rigorous as it sounds. Chief Justice Warren's opinion in *Reynolds* v. *Sims* specifically disclaimed the intention "to spell out any precise constitutional tests." All that the Court asked was that apportionments be "based substantially on population and the equal-population principle was not diluted in any significant way." He also granted that "a State can rationally consider according political subdivisions some independent representation in at least one body of the state legislature, as long as the basic standard of equality of population among districts is maintained." It therefore appears possible that one-man-one-vote may in practice be tempered by some of the same rationality which is the foundation of the Stewart and Clark approach.

IV

Fortunately for us, however, this comparison of the Court's two standards can be left to another occasion. For present purposes their similarity is more important than their differences. The significant fact is that eight members of the Court, though disagreeing as to the standard, have agreed that the Court must assume responsibility for bringing legislative apportionments under the coverage of the equal protection clause. And the more lenient of the two standards is still strict enough to invalidate ten of the first fifteen state legislatures to which it has been applied.

The basic division on the Court, then, is not over standards but over the proper role of the Court in handling political questions. In *Colegrove* v. *Green,* Justice Frankfurter first made the argument that legislative districting and apportionment was a "political thicket" which courts must shun. When he lost this

argument in *Baker* v. *Carr,* he had to develop a positive justification for inequality of voting and representation arrangements in order to continue his posture of judicial non-intervention. His argument was that population had never been the sole basis for representation systems, either in the past or the present, and so it could not be part of the concept of equal protection. He presented a long historical review of the various systems of representation, and wound up with the conclusion that there had been "a decided twentieth century trend away from population as the exclusive base of representation." Only twelve state constitutions, he reported, provided for a substantially unqualified application of the population standard for even a single chamber. This appeared to Frankfurter to constitute a conclusive case against one-man-one-vote.

Frankfurter is of course correct on the mathematics. There *has* been a trend away from population as the exclusive base of representation in state legislatures. Such a trend has manifested itself, for example, in the state of Illinois, which affords an interesting commentary on Frankfurter's statistics. The Northwest Ordinance of 1787, the Illinois Enabling Act of 1818, the Illinois Constitution of 1848, and the present Constitution of 1870 all provided for two houses based on population. From 1818 to 1901 both houses were redistricted fourteen times in conformity with population changes. In 1870 Cook County contained only 14 per cent of the state's population. But by 1900 it had grown to 38 per cent, and 1901 was the last reapportionment that could be put through the legislature, because the population growth of Cook County would have had to be recognized. Efforts to force remapping in the courts failed. Finally, in 1954 a compromise constitutional amendment was presented to the voters — the lower house to be redistricted every ten years on a population basis, the senate to be drawn permanently with area the prime consideration to guarantee downstate control. The amendment was ratified by 87 per cent of Illinois voters.

This is a sample of how Frankfurter's trend was established. It is a trend resulting from rural legislators' persistent refusal to recognize state constitutional requirements and metropolitan expansion, and final acquiescence by city dwellers in permanent under-representation as the price of getting any reapportionment at all. Somehow Frankfurter's trend seems less impressive when put in this light. The principle of representation which his research has discovered is simply the principle that power holders do not willingly give up power.

Since Frankfurter did not recognize this as the operative principle of representation in the twentieth century, he did not have to defend it. But his colleague Justice Harlan did in fact do so in his several opinions. In *Baker* v. *Carr,* supplementing Frankfurter's dissent, he announced that he would not regard it as unconstitutional for a state legislature to conclude (a) "that an existing allocation of senators and representatives constitutes a desirable balance of geographical and demographical representation," or (b) "that in the interest of stability of government it would be best to defer for some future time the redistribution of seats in the state legislature," or (c) that "an electoral imbalance between its rural and urban population" would be desirable "to protect the State's agricultural interests from the sheer weight of numbers of those residing in the cities."

Bear in mind that in *Baker* v. *Carr* the legislature which was making these decisions was a legislature elected from districts drawn in 1901 and not subsequently revised, in defiance of the state constitution. So what Harlan was saying was that legislators representing the state as it was in 1901 could legitimately decide in 1962 that the 1901 balance of geography and demography had been preferable, that the political situation in the state would be more stable if the clock had been stopped in 1901, and that the rural interests as of 1901 could themselves decide, contrary to the state constitution, that they deserved protection against the cities and that it should take the form of keeping city representation in a minority.

Justice Harlan did not even stop with this. In the 1963 case of *Gray* v. *Sanders,* he was,, alone on the Court, rash enough to argue that Georgia's county unit caricature of a representation system was not irrational. He said in its defense:

Given the undeniably powerful influence of a state governor on law and policy making, I do not see how it can be deemed irrational for a State to conclude that a candidate for such office should not be one whose choice lies with the numerically superior electoral strength of urban voters. By like token, I cannot consider it irrational for Georgia to apply its County Unit System to the selection of candidates for other statewide offices in order to assure against a predominantly 'city point of view' in the administration of the State's affairs.

The amazing doctrine here announced is that a state can rationally, and therefore lawfully, set up an electoral system under which the governor and other statewide officers must be chosen by the minority because if they represented the majority they might abuse the "legitimate interests" of the minority. By the same logic it could be argued that Negroes, who are in every state a minority more abused than rural interests ever were, could rationally be given the right to control the naming of public officials. Actually, Harlan suggests in his *Baker* dissent that he would accept as rational *any* legislative plan of allotting representatives short of throwing dice.

V

Justice Harlan would have been better advised not to try to find rational excuses for misrepresentation, and simply to confine himself to stating the case against judicial involvement in political questions. He does elaborate on Frankfurter's *Colegrove* reasoning, as in the following statement from the *Wesberry* case:

What is done today saps the political process. The promise of judicial intervention in matters of this sort cannot but encourage popular inertia in efforts for political reform through the political process, with the inevitable result that the process is itself weakened.

My response is that it is a naive, static view of politics which holds that if the courts do more, the legislature and executive will do less. If the courts act, it is quite possible that they will stimulate others to act. In fact, within four days after the *Wesberry* decision was handed down, the Georgia legislature, its political process not sapped but invigorated, passed a bill redistricting the state's congressional seats for the first time since 1931 and giving Atlanta the representation in Congress to which it was entitled by population.

The *Wesberry* decision also motivated the House Judiciary Committee to take up a long pending measure drafted by Representative Celler providing that congressional districts must be composed of compact and contiguous territory, varying not more than 15 per cent from the average population of the state's congressional districts. . . . Representative William McCulloch (Rep., Ohio) was quoted as saying, when the bill was being considered in committee: "With hindsight, we probably would have been well-advised to have taken some action heretofore." Now that the Supreme Court has said that there is no defense for unequal congressional districting, everyone agrees and the districts are being made equal. But until the Supreme Court acted, there was no legislative action and no prospect of legislative action.

Justice Harlan puts his objection to judicial activism in a somewhat different way when he castigates the "current mistaken view . . . that this Court should 'take the lead' in promoting reform when other branches of government fail to act." Stated this broadly, Harlan's criticism must include the Court's historic accomplishment achieved by "taking the lead" in *Brown* v. *Board of Education.* The Court in 1954 could have decided that ending racial segregation was not a task for them — indeed, not a task for a court at all. The justices could have said, this is a job for Congress, which is specifically authorized by section 5 of the Fourteenth Amendment to enforce the equal protection clause by "appropriate legislation." They could have said, this is a job for the President, who has resources for marshalling opinion and providing the leadership and quite possibly the coercion that will be required to make equal protection a reality in many parts of the nation. The *Brown* Court could have said these things — but it did not. It took the lead.

Now, in 1964 the Court has taken the lead to achieve equality in the representative process at the state level. It has taken the lead in demanding that the naked power struggle, which up to the present has determined how state legislatures are composed, be subjected to the rule of law — specifically, equal protection of the laws. The Court has stirred the stagnant waters in the rotten boroughs. It has challenged the beneficiaries of the various systems of malapportionment and underrepresentation to justify if they can their privileged status. The Court has cut through the sophistry that to prevent the problems of rural minorities from being ignored, it is necessary to ignore the problems of urban majorities.

But stirring the waters is not enough, of course, and here is where Justice Harlan's reservations about judicial leadership have some relevance. Courts cannot lead unless some one will follow. The burden of achieving racial integration was too heavy for the courts to bear alone; they needed the executive and legislative assistance they have recently received. Just so the Supreme Court cannot expect to carry through a massive reform of American state legislatures unless there is substantial legislative support for the goals it has announced. It is true that some courts, when reapportionment deadlines imposed on state legislatures have not been met, have themselves carved up a state into legislative districts. But few can be happy to see courts assume such functions, for which they have so little qualification.

The Supreme Court, needing legislative support, must anticipate the possibility that this support may be less than complete. Many proposals for constitutional amendments have been put forward to modify in one respect or another the impact of the Supreme Court decisions on state legislatures. . . .

In a very real sense, then, the Court's decision in *Reynolds* v. *Sims* is not an order. It is an opinion offering itself for belief; it is a recommendation proposing action. The Court proposes, but politics disposes.

The Court was justified in taking the lead on reapportionment in state legislatures because no other channels of protest were open to an aggrieved citizenry. The Court was justified in concluding that the stalemate of legislative representation could be broken only by holding one-man-one-vote to be a constitutional mandate. In a nation which is seventy

per cent urban, the Court is saying to rurally dominated legislatures that the way to regain the position and prestige the states once had is to establish contact with the real world of the second half of the twentieth century. The Court is opening the way for state legislatures, which all too often have seemed engaged in an organized conspiracy against the future, to play a positive role in dealing with the staggering problems of metropolitan America.

"Courts are not representative bodies," said Justice Frankfurter in his concurring opinion in *Dennis* v. *United States*. "They are not designed to be a good reflex of a democratic society." It is one of the strengths of the American system that this is not necessarily true. Not all elective institutions are representative, and not all representative institutions are elective. Students of public administration have demonstrated how much we rely on the representative character of the American civil service. Now *Brown* and *Baker* have again reminded us that judges who endeavor to speak for the constituency of reason and justice may truly represent the enduring principles of a democratic society.

26

Reapportionment:
What the Court Didn't Do

By Robert G. Dixon, Jr.

THE SUPREME COURT'S recent reapportionment decisions on the structure of state legislatures are a major event in America's long romance with the principle of egalitarianism. There is no doubt that much change was overdue in some states, and at least some change was overdue in most states. We are a democratic people and our institutions presuppose according population a dominant role in formulas of representation.

The court ruled that the members in both houses of state legislatures must be elected from districts of approximately equal population. At the same time,

Robert G. Dixon, Jr., "Reapportionment: What the Court Didn't Do," *The Reporter*, October 8, 1964, pp. 39–41. Copyright 1964 by The Reporter Magazine Company. Reprinted by permission of the author and the publisher.

by its intensive focus on numbers, the court may have transformed one of the most intricate, fascinating, and elusive problems of democracy into a simple exercise of applying elementary arithmetic to census data.

Like so many of the Constitutional issues that have split the Supreme Court, the reapportionment decisions lend themselves to superficial characterization in simple, moral terms, but are devilishly difficult to assess in terms of political realism, political philosophy, and long-run implications. Chief Justice Warren's majority opinions in the reapportionment decisions find support in the oral argument, which the states, frankly, botched rather badly. But his opinions, and particularly the far-reaching opinion in the Colorado case, have not found universal support among legal writers. Among the general commentators there were many who hailed the decisions as a new charter of liberty, signaling a new majoritarianism that could yield fresh political force for more effective approaches to urbanism, civil rights, social welfare, and even international relations. They heard the death knell on a rule of rural virtue rooted in the mystique of the settler tradition, the log cabin, and the family farm. Several of the more perceptive columnists, however, such as Walter Lippmann and Max Freedman, have been sober and restrained in their praise, hesitating not so much over the need for reapportionment as the sweep of the decisions, as Anthony Lewis reported in the New York *Times* a few days after the decisions. "Even some liberal-minded persons, admirers of the modern Supreme Court, found themselves stunned by last Monday."

Ideals and reality

The difficulty lies not so much in the results of these cases as in the court's absolutistic approach. None of the apportionment opinions, except Justice Stewart's, showed an adequate awareness of the complexity of representative government in a pluralistic society. This complexity involves trying to achieve fair representation of the many interests and groupings and shades of opinion in a multimembered body chosen from geographic districts. In any election in any district system, there is a minority that is weighted at zero and a majority that elects its man or its slate and so is weighted, at least until the next election, at one hundred per cent. Some vote weighting necessarily is involved in any election system of a multimembered body from separate districts. To talk of "equal votes" in this context simply is not responsive to the issue. The important thing, in assessing the Constitutional fairness of the system, is how these "equal votes" producing one hundred per cent majorities and zero minorities add up across a state.

Actual examples of this complexity and the insufficiency of a simple "equal-population" formula are not hard to find. For example, a few days after the equal-population rule was announced for Congressional districts last February, in a Supreme Court case that preceded and foreshadowed the reapportionment decisions, Maryland's old-line legislative leaders demonstrated their resilience. They unveiled a plan for new arithmetically equal districts which actually would have worsened the position of the underrepresented suburbs that had brought the redistricting suit. The gerrymandering plan, which was narrowly defeated in the final days of the session, would have carved and regrouped the populous counties without regard to community of interest to yield equal-population districts that preserved the traditional power structure.

A second cause of the inequities even under an equal-population standard is the familiar balance-of-power factor. Significant interest-group overrepresentation can occur whenever a minority group — religious, racial, or other — holds the balance of power in a series of districts. The prohibitionists proved this by actually obtaining a Constitutional amendment. Fear of this balance-of-power factor may be one explanation for the outcome of the Colorado referendum that selected the apportionment plan subsequently nullified by the Supreme Court.

The Colorado case had attracted special attention and was thought to raise deeper philosophic issues than any others in the group of fifteen apportionment cases on the Supreme Court's calendar. It presented an apportionment plan placing the lower house on a straight population basis and the upper house on a modified population basis. This plan had been approved by every county in Colorado in a referendum. In the same statewide referendum, an alternative plan placing both houses on a straight population basis had been resoundingly rejected. Although Justices Clark and Stewart had given limited concurrence to Chief Justice Warren's basic opinion for the court in the Alabama case, they joined Justice Harlan in dissent in this case.

A third potential cause of gross inequities even under an equal-population standard is the possible operation of multimember districts. The South provides interesting examples of this in regard to two minorities in the populous urban-suburban centers: the Republicans and the Negroes. If single-member districts are used, the housing patterns in some populous areas will produce some Republican seats and some Negro seats. But if the legislators are chosen in large plural-member districts, the Negroes and the Republicans will be swamped, despite their substantial numbers.

In short, numbers are easy to play with so long

as they remain mere numbers. If, as Aristotle said, "Law is reason unaffected by desire," the reapportionment opinions of Chief Justice Warren show up well as an ideal prescription for a theoretical society. But if what the Founding Fathers called "factionalism" rears its ugly head, and if, as Justice Holmes said, "The life of the law has not been logic; it has been experience," then the Warren opinions are inadequate. The basic difficulty seems to be that the court views all these cases as being simply civil-rights cases involving the personalized right of the individual voter to cast a vote that theoretically will have "equal weight" with the votes of all other voters. In one sense, of course, these cases do involve voting. But this simple characterization by the court misses the crucial point that in apportionment cases the personal civil right of the voter is intertwined with large, overriding questions concerning representation.

Unresolved issues

Perhaps the first need is to perceive what these cases are all about, and the effect the court order unavoidably will have. In reapportionment, courts sit in judgment on the structure of political power, even effect a judicial transfer of political power. To speak thus in terms of distribution of political power is to talk not of legislative acts, and not of judicial acts in the previously accepted concept of judicial review, but of constitutive acts. Reapportionment restructures government at the core.

Although the judiciary is deeply immersed in reapportionment litigation that the various measures before Congress will not be able to halt, there is not nearly enough information available for intelligent decision. One recent study of the House of Representatives, in which congressmen's votes on four issues were weighted by the population of their districts and recomputed, rather surprisingly suggests that the liberals benefit from such Congressional maldistricting as now exists. A similar recomputation of twenty-two roll-call votes in two sessions of the Texas legislature indicates that the outcome would have differed on only one measure. This is an area where political science, unfortunately, has let us down rather badly. We are just beginning to compile studies of the actual operation of legislatures and the relationships between legislators and their constituencies.

Another critically important aspect, the matter of standards, will need perpetual refinement as legislators develop new patterns of apportionment under which some identifiable group has disproportionate representation. It is a problem of putting real meaning into Chief Justice Warren's admonition that "fair and effective representation for all citizens is concededly the basic aim of legislative apportionment."

To achieve this goal, the court will have to move forward in two directions beyond the equal-population principle. It will have to join Justice Stewart in his concern for "ultimate effective majority rule." And it will have to be disposed to act against gerrymandering devices whereby a minority political party spreads its voters over enough districts in a state to control a majority of seats. Conversely, it should be disposed also to act against gross and continued underrepresentation of a minority party or group which finds itself so distributed and "locked into" a district system that its votes, though substantial, always achieve zero representation.

On the latter point, two lower Federal courts already have suggested that the equal-protection clause, on which the reapportionment decisions rest, may require breaking up multimember districts into single-member districts. Under a statute voided by a lower Federal court in Georgia last March, some voters had their own state senator in a single-member district. Other voters in populous counties having more than one senator were under a system whereby each senator was chosen at large in the county even though assigned for representation purposes to a subdistrict in the county, where he also had to reside. The court found unconstitutional discrimination between the single-member-district voters who "owned their man," so to speak, and the voters in the subdistricts in the plural-member counties who might be represented by a man elected at large but not favored by the very subdistrict he represented. It does not take much imagination to see that this system could operate, and perhaps was designed to operate, to overcome sub-district majorities that were contrary to the county-wide majority.

In Pennsylvania a lower Federal court last April held that both political philosophy and Constitutional law prohibited the use of multimember districts along with single-member districts. "One man, one vote" means, the court said, that each voter must vote for the same number of legislators. Otherwise, some voters would have only one legislator looking out for their interests; others would have two, three, or four, although of course their districts might be two, three, or four times larger. The court added the more respectable rationale that "minority groups living in particular localities may well be submerged in elections at large but can often make their voting power much more effective in the smaller single-member district in which they may live.". . .

In devising remedies for malapportionment, the courts also should guard against undue haste. How anomalous is the contrast between the "hell-bent for election" speed with which some courts approach reapportionment and the lengthy delay and procrastination in desegregation of public education! Desegregation is conceptually far more simple than legislative apportionment, and is a moral issue as well. It is almost exclusively a matter of vindicating a personalized civil right. And yet in desegregation we have had "all deliberate speed" over a ten-year period, whereas in reapportionment we have been treated to the spectacle of courts pressuring and threatening legislators and fixing exact deadlines measured in months or even weeks.

The "political thicket" that Justice Frankfurter warned the courts not to enter is no less political because the courts are in it. But the highest commitment is to the viability of the system and to maintenance of popular faith in it. With political avenues for redress of malapportionment blocked in many states, with protests mounting, the court has concluded that some judicial participation in the politics is a precondition to there being any effective politics.

Unfortunately, there are no simple formulas for making power just, and politics clean. An equal-population-district system will be no exception to the tendency of all district systems to exaggerate the strength of the dominant party, and may even heighten the tendency. As courts go forward in this new era of "one man, one vote," the task will be to assure both majority rule and equitable minority representation.

Whatever the abstract justice to a system of equal representation, it is true that there is little solid research to back up contentions on one side or the other as to the actual results of malapportionment. It does not appear, for example, that all rural controlled legislatures do in fact discriminate against the cities. Even if true, that of course would still not justify inequity, but we do need much more information on the effects of various representational systems. In the following selection the staff of the Advisory Commission on Intergovernmental Relations presents some data on the effects of population-area systems and the very limited prospects for city dominance even under straight population formulas. Senator Wesberry, who represents Atlanta in the Georgia legislature and initiated the suit Wesberry v. Sanders, *then portrays satirically the effects of "non-people factors" in representation. The concluding selection represents the consensus of a conference of political scientists and others with particular experience and interest in the apportionment field, assembled by the Twentieth Century Fund. In the process of supporting the "one man, one vote" principle, this group examines and evaluates the major arguments of those holding the opposing view, and contends that in the long run equal representation will strengthen the states as viable elements of our federal system. The influential character of this report is partially evident from strong similarities of language appearing in the majority report of the Advisory Commission on Intergovernmental Relations and in the landmark case of* Reynolds v. Sims.

27

Effects of Reapportionment on Political Power

IF PERSONS RESIDING in rural and urban areas, assuming they can be divided into two separate groups, sought the same legislative goals there might be no issue raised by the fact that legislative seats are not apportioned according to population. While no absolute dichotomy of interests exists between urban and rural residents, there are apparently enough differences affecting enough interests to say that some type of a conflict exists. Whether this conflict can be analyzed in concrete terms when applied to specific issues is another question. . . .

To quantify the extent of the underrepresentation of population in state legislatures . . . is one matter, but to determine what particular segment of the population actually is underrepresented in a particular state requires much more careful analysis. The 1960 Census revealed that 112.9 million individuals or 63.0 per cent of the nation's population reside in the Standard Metropolitan Statistical Areas. While the residents of SMSA's are usually the people who are most underrepresented in state legislatures, they do not form a single homogeneous group. On a national scale approximately half of these people reside outside the central cities. . . . In the present distribution of seats in many state legislatures it is the suburban area and not the city that is most underrepresented. In Maryland, for instance, the city of Baltimore has 30 per cent of the state's population and it elects 20 per cent of the members of the state senate, while the three largest counties, all within SMSA's, have 35 per cent of the state's population but elect only 10 per cent of the state senators . . . since the views of the central city and its suburban area often are in conflict, they cannot reach agreement on a particular approach to . . . [a] problem. This disagreement or conflict is often transferred to the state legislature.

Apportionment of State Legislatures. A Report of the Advisory Commission on Intergovernmental Relations (Washington, D.C., December, 1962), pp. 23–28, 44–46.

The 1955 apportionment of the Illinois house according to population shows this clearly:

It is interesting that in the 1957 House, after reapportionment had placed all Cook County districts either completely inside or completely outside the city of Chicago, there were only four of the 332 contested roll calls displaying a cohesion of more than 67 per cent for the combined Chicago-Cook County group which had a numerical majority in the House.*

Derge also notes that disagreement within the delegation from the Chicago metropolitan area occurred more frequently than any other disagreement in the state legislature. Many have said that in most instances where the representatives of the urban area could agree among themselves as to what they want, the state legislature would be more than happy to give it to them.

Obviously this reflects only part of the picture. . . . Taking the states as a whole, it is difficult to determine the overall effect of the present structure on the political composition of state legislatures. It is assumed by many that underrepresented cities outside the southern and border states are basically strongholds of the Democratic Party, but that the underrepresented suburbs in these states tend to support the Republican Party. In the southern and border states the Republican Party has tended to be strongest in the urban areas. In view of the fact that the urban area population of the nation is divided almost equally between the central city and the suburbs, it is difficult to arrive at any overall national consensus as to the party gaining or suffering most from present apportionment practices . . .

Perhaps the most significant feature of the relationship of population to apportionment of legislative seats is how the people from a small number of political units would be able to elect a majority of the legislative body. . . .

In 24 states the residents of Standard Metropolitan Statistical Areas would elect a majority of members to the state legislature, if population were the only factor in apportioning legislative seats. . . . But in only two states (Arizona and New York) would residents of the central cities of the Standard Metropolitan Statistical Areas elect a majority of representatives to the legislature. In Arizona, it would require the cities of two SMSA's to elect a majority and in New York, the three largest SMSA central cities would be necessary. . . .

In only five states (Hawaii, Nevada, Rhode Island, New York, and Arizona) do the three largest cities contain over 40 per cent of the state's population. In 36 states the combined populations of each state's three largest cities constitute less than 30 per cent of the state's total population. The danger of large cities controlling state legislatures if apportionment was based strictly on population only appears at this time to be extremely remote in most states. . . .

One problem that has concerned many who are interested in state government is the impact of a substantial number of representatives from one city in the delegation of the majority party in the state legislature. In some instances, the city may be in a position to control the majority party in the state legislature, even though it may not be in a position to control the legislature in an absolute sense. Examples of this potential situation are the impact of the Democratic Party leadership of New York City and Chicago on all the party's representatives in the state legislature. This matter is probably more acute in New York than in Illinois because the procedure for electing members of the Illinois House of Representatives almost guarantees one Democratic Party representative from each legislative district outside the city of Chicago. This problem can be of even greater impact in those states such as Ohio where all seats apportioned to a single county must be elected at large. Thus, the dominant political party in the county or central city of such county may have an extremely significant impact in the legislature.

The above type situation, as a practical matter, could occur only in those states where the population of a city constitutes a significant portion of the state's population. If an apportionment were based strictly on population, a single city probably would have to have at least 25 per cent of the state's population before this problem could possibly occur. Such a population center, if one party could "deliver the vote," could elect 50 per cent of the majority party members of a legislative body. . . . Only in four states — Arizona (Phoenix, 33.7 per cent), Colorado (Denver, 28.1 per cent), Hawaii (Honolulu, 47.2 per cent), and Maryland (Baltimore, 30.3 per cent) — in addition to Illinois and New York would these conditions for central city political dominance of the state legislature be present. While these factors may have different political significance within each state, it is interesting to note that the mayors of the cities involved in the six states meeting the party control criteria set forth above are evenly split between the parties, though the Democratic Party elected the mayors in the three largest cities.

If apportionment were based strictly on population, a small number of counties would elect a majority of legislators in a significant number of states. In 15 states, three counties or less would elect over 50 per cent of the State legislature. These 15 states, of course, include those with a small number of counties. If states with fewer than 15 counties were omitted,

* David R. Derge, "Urban-Rural Conflict: The Case in Illinois," *Legislative Behavior, A Reader in Theory and Research,* ed. John C. Wahlke and Heinz Eulau (The Free Press, 1959), p. 227.

in only eight of the remaining 42 states would three or less counties elect a majority of the legislature.

These figures have significance beyond showing that in relatively few states would two or even three population centers be in a position to elect a majority of state legislators. These figures reflect a somewhat different view than that generated by the statement that over two-thirds of the nation's population live in urban areas. Certainly a majority of the nation's population now resides in urban areas, but this population is split evenly between central cities and suburbia. As a matter of fact, the nation's population is distributed fairly evenly — 32.3 per cent in central cities of Standard Metropolitan Statistical Areas; 30.7 per cent outside the central city but within SMSA's; and 37.0 per cent who do not live in SMSA's. The percentages differ greatly within individual states. . . .

28

"Non-People Factors"

By James P. Wesberry, Jr.

EVERY FIFTEEN MINUTES this year a unique ritual occurs in the Georgia House of Representatives. The clerk reads a resolution which usually does little less than call for abolition of the United States Constitution and restoration of the Articles of Confederation. Then some red-faced member makes a fiery speech, most of which is unintelligible to one whose native language is English but which unmistakably indicates that the Supreme Court of the United States has, upon its own initiative, overhauled the U.S. constitution from top to bottom. The speaker calls on his fellows to "restore the constitution." They do — by clapping, yelling, turning redder than the speaker and voting for the resolution which barely passes by a vote of about 194 to 8 (not counting rebel yells).

This unforgettable orgy, which would bring a glow of anticipation to the eye of any psychiatrist, is common not only to Georgia. It is called a "reapportionment session" and it may be found going on in a similar form in the legislative chambers of most of the states of what we hopefully continue to call the Union. Any resemblance between a reapportionment session and a cannibal ritual can be easily distin-

James P. Wesberry, Jr., " 'Non-People Factors,' " *National Civic Review*, April, 1965, pp. 188–190. Reprinted by permission of the publisher.

guished by noting that in the former the men in the pot are all dressed in long black robes. Also, the man selling "Earl Warren dolls" and hat pins looks suspiciously like former Georgia Governor Marvin Griffin's purchasing agent.

To one unschooled in modern legislative processes, the proceedings of the Georgia House might appear unorderly, unorthodox and unrelated to the making of laws for the state. Enlightenment is gained by the following explanation:

The Georgia House members are representing "factors other than people."

This should fully explain their actions. After all, shouldn't an elected official reflect the views of his constituents? If his constituency consists primarily of factors other than people, why then should he give regard to old-fashioned human thinking? Indeed, why shouldn't men who represent factors other than people act in a non-human manner? So they do.

The "non-people factor" has recently been exposed in House Resolutions 9, 47 and 135 and Senate Resolution 14 in the Georgia General Assembly, in which the authors seek to insert it into the Constitution of the United States.

Perhaps we should now forgive all our previous legislatures for the poor laws they passed. They weren't really representing people. Prior to reapportionment of the Senate, senators were actually representing 78.6 per cent of factors other than people. The House, right up to the present day, contains 158 members out of its 205 total who represent factors other than people. Stated as a percentage, 77.5 per cent of the members represent such factors.

Now that we people have had the non-people factor explained to us fully, we can understand the political history of Georgia. We can understand the logic of the county-unit system, the white primary, the speed trap, the fee system. We can understand why Georgia government was for so many years run by political hacks, cronies and their relatives. We can see how it is possible for the state to enter into long-term leases for non-existent property which neither begin nor end within some of our lifetimes. We can understand the awarding of purchases without bids, the kickbacks, the graft — in short — the wholesale disregard of the people.

We may still wonder just what factors other than people are but, even if we never get an explanation, the exposure of the non-people factor in state government certainly answers a lot of questions we have been asking for some time. We can even see that until 1962 the selection of our governor was prescribed by the non-people factor, thus explaining the actions of many of our former governors selected by the county-unit system.

Now, who has rewritten the Constitution of the United States?

The original constitution started out: "We the people of the United States, in order to form a more perfect Union, establish justice, insure domestic tranquility, provide for the common defense, promote the general welfare, and secure the blessings of liberty to ourselves and our posterity, do ordain and establish this Constitution for the United States of America." There was no mention here of factors other than people — and no thought was given it by the framers of the constitution.

When the Union was formed, only four states (Maryland, New Jersey, Connecticut and Rhode Island) utilized apportionments based on anything other than population and their plans deviated little from truly representative government. The fact is that the legislative apportionment of the thirteen original states makes our present-day situation look pitiful by comparison.

The same Congress which adopted, ratified and began to function under the constitution passed the Northwest Ordinance in 1789. It guaranteed inhabitants of the Northwest Territory, soon to become states, proportionate representation in their future legislatures. A similar pattern prevailed in the admission of all states, from 1789, except Vermont, until Montana in 1889. Thus, population equity was the main criterion for apportionment in 30 of the 36 states during the first century of our nation's existence. No one ever mentioned factors other than people.

In the early years, Thomas Jefferson criticized what today would be a minor malapportionment in his own beloved Virginia legislature and stated, "Equal representation is so fundamental a principle in a true republic that no prejudices can justify its violation."

Our Georgia constitution says that, "All government, of right, originates with the people." No non-people factor can be found in it.

Georgia's first legislature was unicameral and was based upon population. Today's Supreme Court would have upheld it. . . .

Factors other than people began to creep into the federal constitution in the latter part of the nineteenth century. No one can actually say when the constitution was revised in this manner, but, in general, it quietly occurred between 1890 and 1960. This perversion of our constitution did not come about through formal amendment, nor through judicial or legislative fiat. It came about through the failure of state legislatures to recognize the large-scale and rapid urbanization of the country by reapportioning themselves. Their failure to act was contrary, in many cases, to their own constitutions. It was successful because the courts bent over backward to avoid entering the "political thicket."

Thus was the Constitution of the United States changed — thus were the principles of the founding fathers altered — not by courts but by the inaction of legislatures. Thus, representation in our great country was transferred from people to factors other than people — the great unwritten amendment to the constitution.

When the Supreme Court ruled on March 26, 1962, and again on June 15, 1964, that factors other than people should be stricken from the constitution, it was not changing the constitution of 1789 — it was restoring it. The 70 per cent of Americans living in urban areas — the twelve thousand people who leave rural areas each day to live in our urban areas — should be everlastingly grateful that the United States Supreme Court had the courage, the wisdom and the will to stand up against the petty politicians, against unrepresentative legislatures throughout the country and declare in decisions that will ring throughout the pages of history that "factors other than people" have no place in the land of the free and home of the brave — that "one man" deserves "one vote" and that in America he will get it.

29

One Man — One Vote

Background

In many countries with a long tradition of representative government, legislative apportionment is no longer a political issue. In Great Britain and some Commonwealth nations, for example, there is general agreement that parliamentary districts should contain approximately equal populations, and redistricting is accomplished regularly and on a non-partisan basis. But in the United States apportionment remains a vexing problem, politically divisive and significantly affecting the way the people are governed.

The shape of the problem has become increasingly clear: In the last three-quarters of a century the United States has changed from a country two-thirds rural in population, according to Census Bureau standards, to one two-thirds urban and suburban. But

One Man — One Vote (New York: The Twentieth Century Fund, 1962). (Reduced by about one-third.) The conference reporter who prepared the statement was Anthony Lewis, but the conclusions were those reached by the conferees as a group. Reprinted by permission of the Twentieth Century Fund.

the legislatures have not reflected the change. Either because of state constitutional provisions freezing apportionments or because of simple refusal to redistrict, the legislatures have become less and less representative of population. . . .

The statistics of malapportionment are well known. So are some of the effects on state government. The mushrooming problems of cities and suburbs are often ignored, and fast-growing areas tend to look to Washington for relief. Public confidence in state government falls; cynicism sets in. As President Eisenhower's Commission on Intergovernmental Relations concluded, the decline in the influence of state governments must be attributed in part to their failure "to maintain an equitable system of representation.". . .

The basis of representation in state legislatures

. . . in the light of democratic principles, of history and of contemporary political theory, the only legitimate basis of representation in a state legislature is people. One man's vote must be worth the same as another's.

That is not a call for mathematical nicety. It is a statement of the fundamental principle upon which any proper system of legislative apportionment must be constructed. The purpose of legislative representation in a democratic system of government is just that — to represent. The legislature acts on behalf of the voters. The proper goal of the system of apportionment must, therefore, be to provide effective representation for the body politic. . . .

. . . . There is talk, for example, of "area representation." But acres do not vote; nor do trees. When a sparsely settled area is given as many representatives as one much more populous, it simply means that the *people* in the sparse area have more representation. No matter how stated, it is people who choose the representatives.

And so any forthright statement of a non-population theory of representation must rest on one of two propositions: Either there must be an implication that the residents of sparsely populated areas are more virtuous than other Americans and hence deserve more representation in legislatures, or else a contention that they have special needs which can only be met by giving them greater representation than that afforded others.

Belief in rural virtue does exist, but that is not likely to be advanced seriously as a reason for non-population apportionments. Not many legislators would stand up and argue openly that their constituents are so much more honest and intelligent than others that each should have two or three or ten votes. In any case, it is impermissible in a mature

democracy to start comparing the merits of different population groups for purposes of weighting their votes.

The principal reliance, then, of those who advance something other than population as a basis for representation must be on the argument that certain classes of citizens have special problems that justify giving them more than proportionate power in the legislature. This contention is indeed made in behalf of the rural areas which are now so generally over-represented in state legislatures; it is often said that the rural population is a minority with special needs that would be neglected in a legislature faithfully representing the state's population as a whole. But surely the problems of cities and suburbs, and their need for government aid, have been as great as those of rural areas in recent decades; yet no one has been heard to argue that city and suburban voters should therefore have been given disproportionate weight in legislatures. As for the argument that rural citizens are a minority needing special protection, would anyone contend that in the states still predominantly rural — North Dakota, for example, or Mississippi — the urban minorities should be given extra legislative seats?

Our constitutional system protects minorities by other means than giving them majority control of legislatures (as rural minorities now have in many states); and the claim that such legislative control is needed by the rural minority leads to some absurd results. In Maryland rural counties containing less than 15 per cent of the state's population elect a majority of the members of the state senate. This apportionment has been defended against legal attack on the ground that the rural counties must have such control for protection of their minority interests. But Negroes are a slightly larger minority in Maryland than the population of those rural counties; they make up almost 17 per cent of the state's population. Logically it should follow that Negroes are entitled to elect a majority in one house of the Maryland legislature — if legislative control were the American method of protecting minority rights. But of course it is not and logically cannot be.

Some other, less important arguments are also made in favor of "area representation" — i.e., a system that gives residents of sparsely populated areas extra weight at the polls. One is that campaigning is more difficult in a large, unpopulous district. But many politicians feel the contrary is true: It is easier to make news and get one's name known in country districts than in cities. Another argument heard is that non-rural voters indulge in "bloc voting," which is bad, and are under the control of political machines. Actually, "bloc voting" — or, at least, predictable voting on certain issues — seems about as prevalent in rural areas as in cities. At all events, this argument seems at heart simply a variant of the belief in the rural voter's superior virtue.

Regionalism remains a factor within states, but regional interests can be recognized without distortion of voting power. It is desirable to consider regional characteristics when drawing up districts for a state legislature, but it is neither necessary nor proper to give any one regional population group greater voting power than some other group. It is good for dairy farmers in New York, for example, to have a voice in the legislature through one or more members from dairy areas; it does not follow that the votes of dairy farmers should carry greater weight than those of business men or union members.

The central fact is that any basis of representation other than population gives one citizen's vote greater value than another's. There is no justification in our democratic heritage, in logic or in the practical requirements of government for choosing such a course. . . .

The second house

. . . . the principle of apportionment on the basis of population is equally applicable in both houses of a state legislature. The fact that all voters have an equal voice in the choice of one house would be no reason to give some voters more weight than others in electing the second chamber.

The arguments for basing representation in one state legislative chamber on something other than people are the familiar ones: principally, that the rural population has special interests requiring protection by disproportionate voting power. Two further arguments are made.

First, it is pointed out that in Congress the House represents people and the Senate states. This is said to provide precedent and justification for a similar "Federal plan" in the state legislature, with one house representing people and the other counties or some similar geographic unit. But the analogy is false. The United States was created by thirteen sovereign states, and the Constitution embodies a theory of federalism which divides sovereign power between the nation and the states. A key device for protecting their residual sovereignty was the equal state voice in the Senate. Thus the Senate was a condition of union among a group of states which the Federal Government created by that union has no power to destroy. Counties, by contrast, were never independent or sovereign. They did not create the states but were created by them. They are wholly creatures of the states and may at any time be merged, divided or abolished by state governments. . . .

Second, it is contended that a bicameral legislature would have no purpose if both houses were representative of population. This argument assumes two propositions: that the only function of bicameralism is to provide contrasting bases of representation in the two houses (i.e., one people and the other "area"), and that making both houses representative of population would make the second house a mirror of the first and hence redundant. Neither proposition can be supported.

The second house has a function quite apart from giving preferred political status to one population group — the function of providing checks and balances in the legislative process, of assuring more mature and deliberate consideration before a law is enacted. That was in fact the reasoning that underlay the adoption by many states during the nineteenth century of a population basis for both houses of their legislatures.

Later in that century, and in this, factors other than population were often introduced by constitutional amendment or by failure to reapportion. Those who held political power abandoned population representation in order to retain their control in the face of population changes that they saw coming. Such philosophical justifications as the so-called "Federal plan" were designed to obscure the real motivation, just as today most of the elaborate arguments against representation on the basis of people are simply covers for a naked struggle to retain political power.

The justification for bicameralism remains the provision of checks and balances. Bicameralism may also serve to further the very objective of representing the people equitably in a legislature. In any districting, geographic features are bound to cause some inequalities of population among districts. When there are two houses, an area that is somewhat underrepresented in one may be given a compensating advantage in the other and minor inequities in apportionment thus be balanced off.

Nor is it true that two houses based on population will be mirror images of each other. They will, rather, present different reflections or combinations of the various elements that make up the population. For one thing, one house will have more members than the other, representing smaller districts. The length of terms will differ. In addition, members of one house may be elected from single-member districts, while multi-member constituencies are used in the other house. And, not least, politicians are human beings whose differing personalities produce institutions of differing qualities.

A number of states offer contemporary evidence that two houses based on population are by no means duplicates of one another. . . .

The role of the courts

. . . it would be desirable if the problems of legislative apportionment could be resolved without the help of the courts, but . . . in the United States this ideal is evidently unattainable at present. That judicial intervention was essential to break the political deadlock on apportionment had become increasingly obvious before the Supreme Court recognized as much in *Baker* v. *Carr*. The astonishingly swift response of the lower courts in following up that decision indicates a general understanding by the judges of the need for judicial action, and a willingness to assume the heavy responsibility. The great question is how the courts can be most effective in bringing about reform. . . .

. . . in determining the Federal constitutionality of an apportionment . . . it should make no difference whether the apportionment is embodied in a state constitution or in a statute. That a past generation (as long as 150 years ago, in some states) froze into the constitution a basis of representation that the state's citizens have no political means of changing today cannot enhance the standing of the districts before the Federal Constitution.

Nor would it seem to matter if a state permits its people to legislate through initiative and referendum, or even if the people by such method have chosen a basis of apportionment other than population. The Constitution protects minorities as well as majorities. A Protestant majority could not lawfully adopt an initiative measure prohibiting Catholics from voting. If the Fourteenth Amendment protects the worth of the individual vote, no political majority may constitutionally deprive any protesting citizen of that right.

Another aspect of the legal problem still being explored by the courts is the question of judicial remedies for invalid apportionments. Courts, and especially the Federal courts, wisely shy away from getting into the actual business of drawing district lines. The function of the court is rather to goad the political process into action on apportionment. There are a number of possible remedies consistent with that purpose:

1. One remedy is to order an election at large unless the legislature reapportions. That is a drastic course which could have some ill effects. However, many political experts believe that most legislators probably would rather accept reapportionment than face the prospect of running state-wide.

2. A second remedy is for a court to cure the most egregious inequalities by consolidating a few of the least populous districts and awarding the seats to underrepresented areas, as Justice Clark suggested in *Baker* v. *Carr*.

3. Again, a master or masters may be appointed to draft a new apportionment.

4. Alternatively, a court may simply declare the existing districts invalid and give the legislature a fixed time to reapportion, leaving the question of further relief open.

5. Or finally, as an interim measure, the court could weight the votes of the existing members of the legislature to reflect the population each member represents — giving the member with the smallest district one vote, members with districts approximately twice as populous two votes, etc. The legislature so weighted would draft a permanent new apportionment. This course would have the advantage of leaving the existing districts undisturbed for the moment, avoiding the political pain of actually costing incumbents their seats. . . .

CHAPTER SEVEN

State Legislatures

THE LEGISLATURES OF THE VARIOUS STATES differ greatly from each other in a multitude of respects, despite the obvious things they have in common. Among the matters held in common, unfortunately, most find themselves the target for a steady stream of criticism relative to their effectiveness, their alleged subservience to special interests, their antiquated procedures, and so on. For some of the shortcomings the legislators may properly be held to blame, but for others the attitudes of the public are clearly responsible. In a few states significant forward strides are being made, but taking the nation as a whole the pace is slow. In this article Mr. Miller provides a composite picture, based on personal investigation from coast to coast, and suggests or implies the kinds of reforms which seem called for if these bodies are to play their proper role in the complex society of the present day.

30

Hamstrung Legislatures

By James Nathan Miller

THOUGH VISITORS TO THE MASSACHUSETTS STATE House on the Boston Common invariably come away impressed by the beauty of this fine piece of Bulfinch architecture, the more observant among them also make note of a strange and significant architectural omission: In the building's 170 years of existence — from the cornerstone-laying by Governor Samuel Adams, assisted by Paul Revere, through the five subsequent additions that make the building today over ten times its original size — nobody thought to provide offices for the 280 legislators who are its major tenants.

With the exception of a few rooms for legislative

leaders, the law-makers' only "offices" are their mahogany desks in the Senate and Assembly chambers, which during legislative sessions rapidly disappear under piles of documents.

As a result, working conditions for the law-makers — who are supposed to act as efficient overseers of a $750 million annual budget and the operations of 50,000 state employees — are squalid in the extreme. The secretarial pool for the 240-man Assembly consists of five stenographers. Their message center is a honeycomb of little alphabetical pigeonholes reminiscent of a fraternity house mailbox. Their private discussions are held on green-leather couches in the public corridors. "My real office is a telephone booth," says Thomas McGee, representative from Lynn — and sometimes he has to wait in line fifteen minutes to reach this office during a recess.

Conditions such as these, duplicated in state capitols from coast to coast, are merely visible symptoms of a deep and dangerous paralysis that is sapping the strength of state legislatures — and in the process weakening the very basis of state government in the United States today. For though one hears much about the federal government's push to take over state functions, there is also a tremendous pull: the mechanical inability of state legislatures to keep up with the racing demands of the twentieth century.

Recently, I toured the country from Massachusetts

James Nathan Miller, "Hamstrung Legislatures," *National Civic Review*, April, 1965, pp. 178–187, 219. Reprinted by permission of the publisher.

to Oregon to watch legislatures in action. I visited a cross-section sample of a dozen of them, running from the best to the worst, from the most honest and efficient to the most corrupt and incompetent. I read a foot-high stack of reports on suggested reform, talked to scores of legislators, students of government, legislative clerks and secretaries, lobbyists, and members of taxpayer groups.

In Washington, Charles S. Rhyne, a close observer of state government, summed up the size of the problem. Rhyne, a past president of the American Bar Association, has long been involved in efforts to modernize state laws. It was he who argued the historic *Baker* v. *Carr* case before the Supreme Court, bringing the "one man, one vote" decision that is revolutionizing the makeup of legislatures. I asked him whether this revolution would make them more effective. *"Baker* v. *Carr,"* he said, "affects only the way we select our law-makers. Internally, the legislatures remain as archaic as before. They continue to try to solve jet-age problems with horse-and-buggy methods and, in their failure to do it, they're digging their own graves and inviting federal intervention."

These horse-and-buggy methods are clearly identifiable and can be remedied. Ironically, the remedy involves divorcing ourselves from the theories of one of our greatest political philosophers, Thomas Jefferson. For it is Jefferson's dream of a simple agrarian society that today haunts operations of state legislatures. Jesse Unruh, speaker of the California Assembly and a leading legislative reformer, describes it thus: "Jefferson's model American would till the fields by day, improve his mind by study and learned discourse in the evening, and, for a few weeks during the winter when it was too cold to plow, he would travel to the seat of government, there to meet with his peers from other parts and enact just laws."

After 150 years, it is incredible how closely legislatures are still modeled after this image. For one thing, it is the reason they nearly all convene right after New Year's Day, in the dead of winter. But far deeper, it is the reason for their worst internal mechanical inefficiencies. To appreciate how serious these inefficiencies are, first observe the massiveness of the demands that modern society puts on state law-makers.

In size alone these responsibilities have been transformed in just the last generation. In voting on California's projected $4-billion 1965–1966 budget, its 120 legislators are responsible for more money than was spent by all 48 states in 1938. New York's current budget is larger than Australia's. Even tiny Maryland, which spent $67 million in 1946, has budgeted some $800 million for the coming year. Indeed, this year, for the first time in our history,

states may spend more for goods and services (an estimated $70 billion) than the federal government.

One sees the signs of this growth all over the country. Twenty years ago, Louisiana had about 25 state agencies; now it has 240. In 1954, Illinois built a ten-story office building in Springfield to provide office space for its employees; since then, they have spilled out and are now once again housed in temporary quarters all over town. Says Thomas Graham, speaker of the Missouri House, "When I came to the legislature in 1951, the state university had one campus; now it has four."

But the problems are not only far bigger; they are also incredibly more complex. William Nelson, director of research for the Missouri legislature, explains: "When I was elected a representative in 1943, the legislature had no interest in the mentally retarded, in civil rights, in the growth problems of the cities, in air or river pollution. Pesticides were relatively harmless and atomic energy wasn't even heard of; our only concern about radiation control was with X-ray machines in dentists' offices."

Industrial safety laws used to involve simple problems like provision of fire escapes and installation of safety guards on machines. Now (as was the case recently in Bodega Bay, California) legislators must weigh the problem of whether a whole community may be endangered by an atomic plant. Conservation problems used to be as simple as cops and robbers: how to curb predatory interests that were destroying the wilderness. Now, increasingly, we the people have become the predatory interests as we blanket the land with houses and lace it with highways — while at the same time demanding more green space in which to enjoy increasing leisure time.

Hugh Sandlin, a representative in the Oklahoma legislature, sums it up: "I'm supposed to be an expert on everything."

Yet the basic fact is that most of our legislators are not experts. For, while we have become a complicated and urban society, legislatures remain geared to face the problems of Jefferson's simple agrarian day. There are three key areas in which their failure to make adjustment is causing basic damage to state government.

1. *Not enough pay.* The very basis of Jefferson's citizen-legislator concept was that a law-maker should not earn his living making laws. Edward Staples, executive director of the Missouri Public Expenditure Survey, is an exponent of the modern version of this view: "You don't want to develop a staff of professional governmentalists; you want the broad viewpoint of the farmers, the lawyers, the teachers, the doctors, the businessmen. A good farmer gives the flavor of the general citizenry to the legislature. Raise the pay too high and someone who values the job

for the salary alone will run against him. It would be a sorry day."

Agrees Carl Dodge, a senator in the Nevada legislature: "We don't want to attract a lot of bums."

The voters, too, seem to concur. For years, in state after state, blue-ribbon commissions have been recommending more pay; when it has been put to the voters, however, in more cases than not, raises have been refused. The result is simple: By conservative estimate, at least 75 per cent of our population that would otherwise be qualified to serve cannot possibly afford to.

How many people, for instance, do you know who could afford to devote most of their weekends and evenings to campaigning and sitting at the phone "servicing the electorate," quit their jobs for an average of two to four months a year, support themselves during these months in a hotel in the capital city, spend anywhere from $1,000 to $15,000 every couple of years for campaign expenses — and do all this on a salary and expense allowance of $4,000 or $5,000 a year? This is what state legislators, whose annual pay ranges from a high of $10,000 in New York to a low of $100 in New Hampshire, must do.

The result? Take Connecticut, for instance. Says Rhyne, "Perhaps the most shocking and unbelievable discovery for me was the fact that, to augment their salaries, some Connecticut legislators have collected unemployment compensation insurance during the regular session of the Assembly."

In every state I visited, I asked the following question of a wide range of legislative observers: Have you lost any good men recently because of the low salary scale? Invariably the answer was the same — a ticking off of a half-dozen names that had dropped out in the last few sessions.

Jerome Waldie, majority leader of the California Assembly, cited a typical case: "Bill Biddick from San Joaquin County was as able a legislator as California ever had. He served two terms in the Assembly and rose to chairman of the Judiciary Committee. But, after the 1959–1960 session, the money problem caught up with him. He was in his late 30s, had five kids, didn't have the kind of law practice that would permit long absences in Sacramento and he just couldn't keep it up on a salary of $6,000. So he left and now he's a judge in a county court earning $24,000 — when we need him badly here to do the really important work of California. It's a tragic loss to the people of the state."

Who can afford to run? Study the makeup of any legislature and you'll find it to be mainly three groups: retired people, men with independent incomes and professional people. The last group is the largest — lawyers, insurance men, real estate agents, well-to-do farmers, all of them with partners or families back home to keep the business running while they are gone. Many of them are fine people (in fact, the level of integrity and industriousness in our state capitols is far higher than the public appreciates), but they represent a very thin slice of America. Says John Driscoll, director of legislative relations for the Massachusetts Federation of Taxpayers Associations, Inc., "What the legislature doesn't get is the 35- to 40-year-old family man; we're short on the backbone of the community."

Agrees William Swackhamer, a well-to-do businessman who is speaker of the Nevada House: "There are many fine people operating one-man ranches and one-man law firms in the cow counties who'd like to run but can't afford to." In Oklahoma, Representative Sandlin says his tax man figures that his income drops by $3,000 to $5,000 every year the legislature is in session. He adds, "If I didn't have a law partner, I couldn't afford to serve."

The solution is obvious. Pay must be raised to the point where it will not cost a man money to serve in the legislature. The amount might vary from state to state — since the amount of legislative activity required would tend to be bigger in the big industrial states — but common-sense reasons for it are the same in all states: First, we want good men. Second, good men can earn good money in their own businesses. Third, though they should not get rich making laws, neither should they have to pay for the privilege.

What about the danger of creating "professional legislators?" Says Robert Crown, chairman of California's Assembly Ways and Means Committee, "Look. This is the twentieth century. The California legislature is the board of directors for a $4 billion corporation. The average assemblyman services an electorate of 200,000 people. Serving and getting elected is a full-time job. We need professionals. In fact, I like to think I am a professional. Yet I'm paid less than my secretary." He might have added that he is also paid less than a member of California's Board of Barber Examiners — which is a part-time job, at that.

2. *Not enough time.* In simple agrarian days, the idea of requiring the part-time legislator to get on his horse and travel to the state capitol every year seemed absurd. Problems didn't change that fast. Every other year was plenty.

Moreover, in order to guarantee that the legislatures would get work done expeditiously, various constitutional or statutory requirements placed strict limits on the time they could stay in session. In Louisiana, for instance, the constitution forbids sessions longer than 60 calendar days; in Alabama, no longer than 36 legislative days. The Texas legislature can meet for as long as it wants but it collects no pay after 75 days; in Nevada, pay ceases after 60 days.

Today, in most states, regular legislative sessions, still held every other year, consist of three to six months of short Monday-through-Thursday work-weeks that give law-makers long weekends for handling their personal affairs back home. Though a stopgap patchwork of off-year "special" and "fiscal" sessions has developed in an attempt to handle growing business volume, the overwhelming bulk of the work — from 500 bills to upwards of 17,000 — is still concentrated at the alternate-year regular sessions. This attempt to meet twentieth-century needs on a nineteenth-century timetable results in pure chaos.

In many states, legislators vote literally thousands of times during the brief session. In California, Waldie estimates he averages 30 to 40 floor votes daily, plus many more in committee.

The result? A Louisiana law-maker cites a typical instance: "Not long ago an ex-legislator complained to me that he'd been arrested for speeding and had his license taken away because he couldn't post a bond. He was mad as hell. Said anyone who'd voted for a law like that must have been nuts. When I told him he voted for it, he swore I must be nuts. So we looked it up and, sure enough, he had."

In West Virginia, a lobbyist cited his rule of thumb for gauging the quality of a legislature: "If they understand 20 per cent of the bills they vote on, they're a damn fine bunch."

To see what all this adds up to in legislative conduct, listen to Rhyne's account of the 1963 spasm of the Connecticut legislature. It met for five months. At the end of the first two months, only five bills had been passed. Then they began to come through in increasing numbers — 4,000 of them in all, droning through so fast and furiously during the final few days that many members had no idea what they were voting on, and the legislature actually adjourned while forgetting to pass an essential $6.4 million education bill. A special session had to be called to remedy the oversight. Said the *New Haven Register* of this comic-opera performance, the legislature "seemed to make more errors than the New York Mets do on one of their worst days."

The solution, again, is simple: Legislatures should meet every year and stay in session for as long as is necessary to get the work done. This requirement goes hand-in-hand with the need for higher salaries.

3. *Not enough help.* At each Oregon legislator's desk are two chairs, one a swivel chair for the law-maker, the other a straight-backed model for his secretary. As in Massachusetts, Oregon law-makers have no offices, no privacy. "It can be extremely embarrassing," says Daniel Thiel, president *pro tempore* of the Oregon Senate, "to have to discuss private matters with a constituent — a drunken driving conviction, say, or a veteran's loan — and to know that a couple of other legislators at their desks a few feet away can hear every word. Sometimes I have to scribble a note telling the man to talk softer."

The same shortage applies to space for official deliberations. With 37 legislative committees, the Oregon legislature has only eighteen committee rooms and often a hearing must be cut short to make way for another committee. "It's like a bunch of people sharing the same bed in shifts," says a Senate official.

But it goes much deeper than mere shortage of space. In fact, probably the sickest aspect of our sick legislatures is their failure to provide themselves with adequate staffs and facilities to keep themselves informed. For, though laws can be no better than the information on which they are based ("We're really a great big jury," says Thiel), most legislatures are miserably equipped to gather information. Though most of them have permanent staffs of so-called "legislative councils" that are supposed to dig up facts, in all but a few states these are woefully understaffed and provide little help beyond the actual technical drafting of bills.

In Massachusetts, for instance, which has one of the country's largest insurance businesses, the House Committee on Insurance has neither secretary nor researcher. No transcripts are kept of committee meetings. How does the committee function? Says John F. Donovan, Jr., representative from Chelsea, "For each legislative session, we elect one of our members as clerk but we all take notes."

(In fact, probably 90 per cent of the debate and discussion in legislatures is never recorded, and one result is that courts have no so-called "legislative history" of state laws. Says Nelson in Missouri, "I get calls about once a month from attorneys asking for transcripts of committee hearings that would show legislative intent, but I have none.")

So woefully understaffed is the Massachusetts legislature that the Republican and Democratic clubs of Harvard Law School operate a kind of charity program of volunteer research assistance for the law-makers. Similarly, in Oregon, the state bar association provides 21 volunteer lawyers in two-week stints to help out with bill-drafting.

Says Bryce Baggett, an Oklahoma senator, "I'd rather have a research assistant than a raise."

This lack of research leads directly to the two worst weaknesses of our state legislatures. First is their domination by the governor and the huge machinery of his executive departments. In Oklahoma, a legislator put it this way: "The governor of this state has people working for him who are experts in anything you can name and we legislators are the people who are supposed to be checking on them for the taxpayer. But much of the time we don't even know what questions to ask them." Agrees Waldie in California, "Bureaucrats don't like to admit their mistakes and they can run rings around an uninformed legislature."

"It's a perfect example," says Unruh, "of the old truism that knowledge is power."

Where can the legislature go? "We are forced to depend primarily upon the lobbyists for necessary information," says Thomas Graham, speaker of the Missouri House. This leads into their second weakness: domination by lobbies and pressure groups.

Winton Hunt, chief clerk of the Oregon House and a former legislator, cites a typical example: "When I was in the legislature, a highway was being built through my district, and I started getting complaints from farmers that they weren't being adequately paid for damage to their land. To get a law correcting the situation, I first needed a lot more evidence but I had no way of getting it myself. So I asked the Farm Bureau, a lobby group, to go out and interview farmers along the route. It came up with a fine report and the law got passed, but I never did feel comfortable about having to depend on a farmers' lobby for the facts in this kind of bill."

In the last session of the Oregon legislature, one lobbyist contributed several days to interviewing highway department officials in order to help the Senate Highway Committee evaluate the merits of concrete versus asphalt. Some years ago, in an investigation of the alleged misuse of road money in Oklahoma, the Senate investigating committee's entire staff consisted of a researcher loaned to it by the Oklahoma Public Expenditures Council, a lobby group.

Such help is perfectly legitimate. Indeed, most lobbyists work publicly and straightforwardly, the way a lawyer presents his case. "Of course, a lobbyist gives you a prejudiced point of view," says F. F. Montgomery, speaker of the Oregon House. "You wouldn't respect him if he didn't."

For a legislature equipped to evaluate these prejudices, the lobbyist's role is honorable and constructive. But few legislatures are so equipped. As a result, in a majority of states the lobbyist — well paid, well staffed, well informed and working at his job full time — has become the tail that wags the dog of the under-paid, overworked, under-informed, part-time legislator. The lobbyists' collective title — "the third house" — is no fiction.

In the *New York Times* last year, reporter Charles Grutzner cited an incident that gave a revealing insight into third-house power: At two o'clock one morning, after an evening of nightclubbing, a lobbyist told a companion that he wanted to show him proof of popular opposition to a bill that was then being opposed by a lobby group. Thereupon the lobbyist drove with his companion to the deserted capitol building, produced a key that admitted them to an important senator's office and handed his companion a report. He then went on to boast that he had written the report, had the keys to nine other lawmakers' offices and had earned the right to such access by providing facts and research assistance to these law-makers.

Senate Majority Leader Walter Mahoney's outrage over the incident was equally revealing. "I condemn the slime of the lobbyist," he thundered, "who in his boastful way would tell what he did to the reporter."

Report-writing is just the first step in the exercise of third-house power. Recently, a person very close to the workings of a state legislature described an example of the next step: law-writing. In the last legislative session, when a bill was put into the hopper that would have transferred the weighing of trucks from the Highway Department to the Department of Public Safety, a labor lobbyist recognized that it would cost the jobs of a number of union weighers. Investigating, he found that the bill was the creature of the truck lobby, which felt the fines on overloaded trucks would be lower under Public Safety than under Highways. The bill would also mean, however, that local townships would lose their share of the fines. So the labor lobbyist contacted the one for townships, and with the truck lobbyist they worked out a compromise that kept the weighers under the Highway Department but reduced fines. The compromise bill was passed.

In West Virginia, a lobbyist, after giving me his version of how the legislature really worked, added: "If you're going to use any of this stuff, don't quote me. These bozos [the legislators] like to think they make the law."

This subservience to outside forces can be licked. California's legislature — a dozen years ago infamous for its domination by lobbies — shows how. During the 1950's, following a national magazine exposé of lobby influence, the legislature intensified its fight for independence, using as a major weapon the development of its own fact-gathering facilities.

Today, it is superbly staffed and informed. Every legislator has his own office and secretary, plus an office and administrative assistant in his home district. A six-man reference service headed by a former political science instructor digs into questions submitted by individual assemblymen. A legislative counsel bureau of some twenty attorneys drafts all bills. All important committees are staffed with full-time researchers, who spend months gathering background on important bills. For special studies the legislature raids universities for experts, sometimes hires outside consulting firms.

The result is that rarest and most essential of legislative qualities: intellectual independence. For a recent legislative study on the care of mentally retarded children, for instance, committee researcher Arthur

Bolton spent a year investigating Californian hospitals, interviewing hundreds of professionals in the field, as well as parents of children. Says Waldie, who headed the committee: "Bolton was able to do what no legislator would have had the time to do: become a true expert and ask truly penetrating questions. Just one part of his investigation — preparation of a 40-page questionnaire that was submitted to the hospital directors — would have been far too much to expect of any of the committee members. On the basis of Bolton's investigation, the committee is recommending a total change of direction in the program, something we could never have had the confidence to do without this kind of research behind us."

The result is that, though lobbyists have by no means died on the California vine (there are over 500 of them, outnumbering legislators four to one), their power has distinctly shrunk. Bert Clinkston, political editor of the *Sacramento Union,* calls the legislature's research facilities "the fourth house"; one lobbyist commented to me, only half jokingly, that the fourth house was some day going to cost him his job.

The vicious circle. The failure of legislatures to reform themselves works 'round and 'round in a self-perpetuating cycle. It goes like this.

First, underpaid legislators begin to find it easy to accept entertainment and minor favors — office space, secretarial help, etc. — from lobbyists. No specific favors are asked in return and it seems innocent enough. Even more elaborate favors — use of an oil company's private plane by a legislative official in California, a Caribbean cruise for New York legislators paid for by a savings bank association — can be explained away as deserved perquisites for overworked and underpaid officials.

Last winter I got to feel how nice these perquisites can be when I was guest at a party given by Harrah's Lake Tahoe gambling casino to welcome the Nevada legislature into session. I was treated — along with about 250 legislators, their wives, secretaries and secretaries' boyfriends — to an all-expenses-paid evening on the house, complete with dinner, champagne and entertainment by Robert Goulet. Nobody seemed to question the extending of such hospitality by a regulated industry to its regulators. Indeed, another such affair was scheduled for the following evening at The Nugget in Carson City. Said a member of the legislature's staff: "I'm just a flunky around here and I can't possibly do any favors for these gamblers. But if I ever go into a casino and they know where I work, I have to fight with the headwaiter to pay the bill."

Second, such relatively minor favors blend imperceptibly into the vast, grey area known as conflict of interest. Though every year brings to light a few cases of outright bribery, by far the most per-

vasive method of "getting to" a law-maker is far subtler and less easily combated. Bryce Baggett in Oklahoma, himself scrupulously honest, describes what happens: "You start getting indirect approaches — offers to retain you as a lawyer, hints that the members of a trade association would like to place their insurance through your firm. Nothing criminal, nothing you can really put your finger on. It's there but I'd hate to be the district attorney who had to prove any bribery was involved."

For some, it is easy to rationalize such offers as being totally divorced from legislative activities. In a recent article in *Harper's Magazine,* Illinois State Senator Paul Simon estimated that a third of the Illinois legislators accepted payoffs in the form of legal fees, public relations retainers or campaign contributions.

In Massachusetts, a commonly accepted method of helping a law-maker make ends meet is to "run a time" for him: throw a party at which local interests — the electronics plant, teachers' association, railroad brotherhoods — kick in for "campaign expenses." Says a Massachusetts legislator, "on $5,200 a year, how else can I possibly support a family decently? Sure it means my vote gets tied down in some areas, but . . ." — and here comes the rationalization — "after all, these are legitimate local-interest groups."

The only cure lies in the honor and integrity of the men we select. Which brings us back to the vicious circle. For, while it is undoubtedly true that in most states the great majority of legislators are honest, a constant cloud of suspicion created by continual conflict-of-interest revelations colors them all in the public mind. Thus the circle is complete: low salaries and poor facilities, causing low standards and poor performance, causing public disgust, causing refusal by the public to raise salaries and improve facilities — and around and around.

"Mediocrity," said the *New Republic* recently of state legislatures, "attracts mediocrity."

Enter, the federal government. Thus state legislatures, slow-moving and bewildered in a world they never made, create a vacuum that pulls hard at the federal government. The *Baker* v. *Carr* reapportionment decision is a case in point. In the words of William J. D. Boyd of the National Municipal League, "The state legislatures brought it on themselves." At the time the case was argued, twenty legislatures were violating their own state constitutions by refusing to reapportion. Tennessee, where the case was brought, had not reapportioned for 61 years. Yet, sixeen years before *Baker* v. *Carr,* the Supreme Court had said it did not want to get involved in the "political thicket" of reapportionment. If legislators had done the job themselves, it would never have had to change its mind.

The real tragedy of this premature senility of state governments is the contrast it provides with the bright promise of their youth. Wrote Supreme Court Justice Louis Brandeis in 1932: "It is one of the happy incidents of the federal system that a single courageous state may . . . serve as a laboratory and try novel social and economic experiments without risk to the rest of the country."

In the last century and the beginning of this one, it was the states that pioneered in such legislative fields as child labor, railroad and utility regulation, unemployment and old age compensation, and factory inspection. Fifteen states, starting with Wyoming in 1869, had voted female suffrage before the federal government got around to it in 1920.

But, today, states have become the citadels of status quo and the federal government, the laboratory of change. (There are a few honorable exceptions — such as California in higher education, New York in state support of the arts, Wisconsin in conservation — but they merely prove the rule.) Why, for instance, is President Johnson now requesting a federal law to clean the junkyards from our highways? For the simple reason that the states, which could have long since abolished them, have allowed them to fester and grow. Why does the Interstate Highway Act contain a bonus provision to reward states that ban billboards from the interstate system? It is presented as a carrot to state legislatures to get them to stand up to the billboard lobbies.

Indeed, why is the federal government moving in across the board — in air and stream pollution, education, housing, mass transportation for cities, etc.? Though there can be honest disagreement about the rights and wrongs of this move, there is no question that a major cause is the failure of the states to do what needs doing.

In the words of Governor George Romney of Michigan, "People have needs and if state and local governments are unwilling or unable to meet those needs, we have only ourselves to blame."

That, in its simplest form, is why we must drag our state legislatures out of the age of Jefferson and into the twentieth century.

Persons interested in the reform of state government have frequently advocated the unicameral legislature, a development long accepted in the organization of city councils. Yet despite an apparent high degree of success in Nebraska, that state remains the only one to have made the experiment. In the following article the former director of research for the Nebraska Legislative Council reviews and evaluates nearly twenty years of experience with unicameralism in the cornhusker state. Mr. Horack follows with a spirited defense of the bicameral principle, contend-

ing that a bicameral legislature acts with equal facility on issues where there is general public agreement, and that it provides a desirable brake on precipitous action when sentiment has not crystallized.

31

The Nebraska Unicameral Legislature

By Roger V. Shumate

. . . NEBRASKA enjoys some distinction in being the only state which has a unicameral legislature. This institution has become so much a part of our political life that we have converted the word "unicameral" from an adjective into a noun. Despite the protests of purists, we commonly hear that the *unicameral* — not the *legislature* — convened, or adjourned, or passed a law. The belief seems to prevail in some quarters that we abolished our *legislature* and established a *unicameral* in its place.

For the first seventy years after being admitted to the Union, Nebraska followed the traditional bicameral pattern in its legislative body. Its legislature, just prior to the change, consisted of a Senate of thirty-three members and a House of Representatives of one hundred members. In 1934, however, the voters of the state, by initiative petition, placed upon the ballot a constitutional amendment which proposed the substitution of a single chamber. Perhaps it is unnecessary to explain why this proposal was started by initiative petition. Bicameral legislatures have not been noted for their willingness to confess their own inadequacy by proposing that they be abolished and something else established in their place.

At the general election in 1934, the voters approved the constitutional amendment providing for a unicameral legislature by a vote of 286,086 to 193,152, or a majority of almost 60 per cent. Since similar proposals have been submitted to the electorate in several other states and have failed, it may be asked why the proposal was approved in Nebraska, and a number of more or less valid reasons have been suggested. Among them the following may be noted:

Roger V. Shumate, "The Nebraska Unicameral Legislature," *Western Political Quarterly*, September, 1952, pp. 504–512. Footnotes in original omitted. Reprinted by permission of the author and publisher.

1. The proposal was made at the lowest point of the depression when citizens were casting about desperately for means of securing more efficient and more economical government in the hope that a reduction in taxes would follow. During this period the voters showed more willingness than usual to break with tradition and try something new.

2. The proposal to establish a unicameral legislature was fortunate in attracting an able and effective type of leadership. For example, the late United States Senator George W. Norris was its most eminent advocate, and he was ably assisted by civic groups and by many persons in academic circles, though he encountered a great deal of opposition from the press and other influential sources.

3. The proposal was submitted at the same time as two other popular proposals, namely, the repeal of the state prohibition law and the legalization of pari mutuel betting at race tracks. Some observers have been unkind enough to allege that the popularity of these two amendments was sufficient to secure the adoption of all three, though friends of the unicameral legislature resent this implication, and point out that the proposal for the one-house body got a larger vote than did the one which legalized gambling on horse races.

The new amendment provided that "Commencing with the regular session of the legislature to be held in January, nineteen hundred and thirty-seven, the legislative authority of the state shall be vested in a legislature consisting of one chamber." It provided further that "The legislature shall consist of not more than fifty members and not less than thirty members." Incidentally, the body thus established is officially styled the Legislature — not the Senate, the House, or the Assembly — and the members have no constitutional title other than members of the Legislature, though they are given the courtesy title of Senator.

Members of the bicameral legislature which met in regular session in January, 1935, were chosen at the same election that approved the establishment of the unicameral legislature. It then became their duty to implement the amendment by determining the number of members within the prescribed constitutional limits, and by dividing the state into a suitable number of districts for purposes of election. Proposals for membership in the new body ranged from the minimum of 30 to the maximum of 50, but the legislature finally compromised on the number 43 and divided the state into 43 districts as nearly equal in population as was feasible. This action had the effect of determining the salaries of the individual members, since the constitutional amendment stipulated that "The aggregate salaries of all the members shall be $37,500 per annum, divided equally among the members and payable in such manner and at such times as shall be provided by law."

During the campaign, the proponents of the unicameral legislature argued that the small single chamber would cost the state less in salaries and general operating expense; that it would be able to handle the business of the legislature more expeditiously, thus reducing the length of legislative sessions with an additional reduction of costs; that it would concentrate responsibility for the enactment or defeat of laws, thus making the legislature more responsive to the public will; that it would work more efficiently in the scrutiny of proposed legislation, thus improving the legislative output through the elimination of duplicating, conflicting, and unconstitutional provisions; and that it would increase the prestige of the legislature, thus attracting a higher quality of members. The opponents, on the other hand, aside from pointing out that the measure was not in the "American Tradition" and that the state had grown and prospered under the bicameral system established by our forefathers, argued that removing the check provided by a second chamber would result in hasty and ill-considered legislation; that a small chamber would be more susceptible to influence by lobbyists and pressure groups; that a small single chamber would be less representative of the varied interests in the state; that the likelihood of electing a majority of "wild men" to a small single chamber would be greater than in the case of a more numerous bicameral legislature; and that the radical or extravagant legislation which might be expected would result in increased over-all costs of the state government far outweighing any savings that might be made in the cost of operating the legislature itself.

More than fifteen years have now elapsed since the unicameral legislature was established. During that time eight regular and three special sessions have been held. Some of the original arguments on both sides are still heard and it is impossible to prove or disprove all of them to the complete satisfaction of all citizens. We may, however, offer the following observations:

1. The unicameral legislature has clearly effected a saving in the matter of members' salaries. The present salary total is fixed at $75,000 per biennium, whereas that of the bicameral legislature was $106,400. Furthermore, each special session under the bicameral system meant additional salary payments, whereas no extra salary allowance is now made for special sessions. Thus the net savings in members' salaries has averaged about $35,000 a biennium. Because of the inflationary trend, the present salaries of legislators should undoubtedly be increased, but that would be just as true if the bicameral system had been retained.

2. Despite the increased cost of government generally, the unicameral legislature has effected a saving of some $8,000 to $10,000 a biennium in general legislative expense — mileage for members, clerk hire, printing, stationery, postage, etc. This is, of course, an insignificant amount when the total cost of the state government is considered.

3. The unicameral legislature may work more expeditiously but it has not reduced the length of legislative sessions. On the contrary, it seems to have had the opposite effect. The last five regular sessions under the bicameral system averaged 93 days in length, though the three special sessions totaling 46 legislative days brought the average number of days for sessions to 102 for each biennium. The eight regular sessions of the unicameral legislature have averaged 101 days in length and the 29 days in special session increased the average number of days in session during each biennium to 104½. It may be, of course, that the increasing functions and problems of the state government associated with the war years and the post-war period rather than the changed structure of the legislature caused this increase. In all probability, however, the increased length of regular sessions should be attributed to the more deliberate procedure adopted by the unicameral legislature as will be explained later.

4. It is impossible to prove whether or not the unicameral legislature has appropriated more money for the use of the state government than would have been appropriated had the bicameral legislature been retained. The present biennial budget is more than three times as great as it was at the end of the bicameral era, but obviously most, if not all, of this increase must be attributed to the general rise in the cost of living and the increased services demanded of government. At any rate, it is clear that the unicameral legislature has not been prodigal with the taxpayers' money. It has repeatedly defeated proposals for a state sales tax, a state income tax, and state aid for schools, which are common features in other states, and which tend to increase the cost of government. Nebraska consistently ranks almost at the very bottom of the list of states in the annual per capita cost of the state government. This may be regarded as favorable or unfavorable to the unicameral legislature, depending upon one's prejudices.

5. It is not possible to prove that the intellectual and moral caliber of the members of the unicameral legislature differs markedly from that of the members of the older system. Professor John P. Senning, who has made some very detailed studies of this question, concludes that the members of the unicameral legislature show up a little better in the average number of years spent in school, and in business, professional and civic experience. He has also shown that the biennial turnover is smaller, and hence that the proportion of experienced legislators in each session of the legislature is higher than it was under the preceding system.

6. The quality of legislation produced under the two systems can not be compared in a completely scientific manner. Again, however, Professor Senning argues on the basis of his analyses that fewer laws are declared unconstitutional under the unicameral system and that fewer statutes are found to have "bugs" or "jokers" in them as a result of faulty draftsmanship or as a result of bills being shunted back and forth between two houses, with each house amending freely and perhaps finally adopting a measure agreed upon in conference committee. Much of this improvement, if it is a real one, may be attributed to the improved research and information furnished by the Legislative Council, and to the improved bill-drafting service which is now correlated with statute revision and with the legal services provided for the Committee on Enrollment and Review. All this could have been accomplished under the bicameral system, but it was not accomplished.

7. Has the removal of the check provided by a second chamber resulted in hasty and ill-considered legislation? Apparently not. As indicated before, the technical product seems to have been improved. Also, as was pointed out before, the unicameral legislature has tended to be quite conservative in the enactment of tax laws and the extension of governmental services and responsibilities. Its history thus far furnishes no basis for the fear that it may become a body of "wild men."

8. Instead of giving less consideration to each bill, it may plausibly be argued that each bill now receives more consideration than it did under the bicameral system. For example, during the last five regular sessions of the bicameral legislature, the average number of bills introduced during each session was 908; during the eight regular sessions of the unicameral legislature the average number was only 517. This is approximately 57 per cent as many bills considered, yet the sessions of the unicameral legislature have been a little longer than under the old system. In other words, the legislature now spends more time in considering 517 bills than it formerly spent in considering 908 bills. The reason for this lies in the fact that the founders of the unicameral legislature purposely provided for a very deliberate procedure for the purpose of insuring more careful consideration of each bill. Every bill upon introduction must be printed and distributed to the members, must be referred to a committee, must be subjected to a public hearing announced five days in advance, and must be reported by the committee unless excused from reporting by motion of the legislature. Thus,

there is no steam roller, no suspension of the rules and bringing bills directly to the floor for vote without committee consideration, no committee report on a bill without a public hearing, and no bills smothered in committee without hearing or consideration. This undoubtedly accounts for the greater time consumed.

9. Although fewer bills are introduced in the unicameral legislature, a substantially greater number are passed. During the last five regular sessions of the bicameral legislature an average of 181 bills were passed each session, or slightly less than 20 per cent of those introduced. During the eight regular sessions of the unicameral legislature an average of 260 were passed each session, or slightly more than 50 per cent of those introduced. Thus, if the purpose of a legislature is to facilitate the enactment of laws, the unicameral system is better, but if, as many apparently believe, its excellence is to be judged by the success with which legislation is resisted, the awards must go to the bicameral plan.

10. The deliberate procedure described above, plus the fact that, with few exceptions, every committee clears its calendar and reports all bills either favorably or unfavorably before the legislature adjourns, has probably had one incidental effect not anticipated. It appears to have reduced somewhat the pressure for special sessions. For example, the bicameral legislature held three special sessions totaling forty-six days during the last five years of its existence, whereas the unicameral legislature has held only three special sessions totaling twenty-nine days during the fifteen years of its existence. It may be argued, of course, that these facts are not significant since special sessions are often called as a result of accidental or unforeseen circumstances. It is also true, however, that they are frequently called because legislatures in regular session adjourn without dealing with all of the important proposals before them. The Nebraska legislature at least takes some definite action on all bills introduced, thus eliminating one reason for calling special sessions.

11. The question as to whether the legislature is now subject to more or less influence by lobbyists or pressure groups cannot be answered with certainty. Lobbyists have been heard to criticize the unicameral legislature by saying that it is a "lobbyists' paradise." This criticism would be more impressive if it came from a source less likely to favor influence by lobbyists. On the basis of logic, it may be argued that lobbyists will be less influential in a small single body in which the responsibility of individual members for passing or defeating bills can be more definitely fixed than under a system in which responsibility can be shunted back and forth from one house to another, but neither argument is susceptible of easy proof. It has been shown that the unicameral legislature considers fewer bills than its predecessor but passes more. This suggests that the success or failure of pressure tactics may depend in part upon whether they are used to favor or oppose proposed legislation, but the evidence is not conclusive. Interest groups, of course, have a right to be heard, and there is no disposition here to argue the question as to whether or not their influence should be curtailed. . . .

Although the principle of unicameralism seems to be fairly well entrenched in Nebraska, there are some features of the present system which are often criticized. The two principal ones are as follows:

1. *Size.* As previously noted, the legislature consists of only forty-three members. Many critics allege that this number is too small to give adequate representation to the varied interests of the state, and allege further that the small number results in overworking the individual members because of heavy committee assignments. Consequently, suggestions have been made for increasing the membership to sixty, eighty, or one hundred. In reply, however, it is argued that the state is just as adequately represented now as it was when there were one hundred and thirty-three members, and that increasing the number of members would increase the number of bills introduced and the number and size of committees, thus imposing as much work on each individual member as at present. As one member put it, "My district could be better represented by electing a better man than I, but it could not be better represented just by electing two or three more like me."

2. *Non-partisan feature.* The members of the unicameral legislature are elected by non-partisan ballot and party lines do not appear in legislative organization. To the surprise of both political scientists and "practical politicians" the non-partisan feature is respected. Through the non-partisan ballot, Democratic members have been elected from Republican districts and vice versa. The party affiliation of most members is known but this is not always true. The speakership and important committee chairmanships have frequently gone to men who were known to be members of the minority party, and it is seldom possible to recognize party lines in the sponsorship of bills or in the votes thereon.

The non-partisan feature is frequently criticized on the ground that it does not provide adequate leadership in the legislature. It is argued, for example, that the majority party in the legislature, which will normally be the party of the governor, should assume responsibility for the formulation and adoption of a legislative program. Under the present system, it is sometimes said that there are merely forty-three would-be leaders, and that the influence of the governor is minimized by the fact that there are no recognized leaders of his party in the legislature upon whom he can rely to support his program or to sustain his vetoes.

Despite these criticisms, the non-partisan feature has thus far survived. It is defended by many members of the minority party who feel that their chances of influencing legislation are better under this system. It is also defended by many members of the majority party who like the feeling of independence from gubernatorial and party control. Those who favor retention of the non-partisan system argue somewhat as follows:

1. The problems of state government are generally non-partisan in character and should be solved on the basis of the independent judgment of the members rather than on the basis of their party affiliation.

2. The "party responsibility" and "political leadership" advocated by the opponents of the nonpartisan legislature may, in practice, mean the enthronement of a party "oligarchy" and facilitate "steam roller" tactics in legislation.

3. Partisan organization of the legislature might enhance the power of the governor but it is not clear that this would be desirable. The governor has a great deal of power through the appointment and removal of administrative officers, the preparation of the budget, the veto, and the political eminence of his office. He is always able to find individual members — quite often members of the minority party — who will give enthusiastic support to his proposals, though these proposals must then stand upon their own merits rather than upon party endorsement. It may be doubted, therefore, that the principle of representative government would be better served by giving the governor a greater degree of partisan control over the legislature.

It is not the purpose of this paper to argue that the unicameral legislature has completely revolutionized government in Nebraska, or that other states should immediately follow Nebraska's example. Political scientists, at least, should not be so naïve as to suppose that a mere change of legislative structure, whether from two houses to one, or vice versa, will solve all of the problems of government. Most of us, no doubt, would go at least part way with Edmund Burke's often quoted assertion that "Constitute government how you please, the greater part of it must depend upon the exercise of powers which are left at large to the prudence and uprightness of ministers of state. . . ." The mechanics of government are important, but no mere institutional device can be substituted for character and intelligence on the part of the body of citizens and of those whom they elect to public office.

In conclusion it may be said that the unicameral legislature has not fulfilled either the most optimistic hopes of its friends or the most pessimistic fears of its opponents. On the whole, however, it has given a good account of itself.

32

Bicameral Legislatures Are Effective

By Frank E. Horack, Jr.

THE PROPONENTS of unicameralism have catalogued its merits with a persuasive marshalling of virtues. They assert that the single bodied legislature:

1. Saves time and expense.

2. Guards against hastily enacted, and ill considered legislation.

3. Eliminates the evils of the committee system and the dictatorship of the conference or steering committee.

4. Reduces total legislative costs and permits increases in legislators' salaries so that more qualified legislators may be procured.

5. Facilitates the non-partisan election of legislators.

The worth of these assertions can be measured only in terms of the function of a legislature in our modern society. The choices involved relate not to the form of a particular system of legislative organization but rather to the capacities of any system to realize the social and economic objectives of democracy.

In brief, society expects of a legislative body:

First. An adequate and accurate representation of the electorate in matters legislative.

Second. A capacity to enact accurate and effective legislation based on reliable research and reflecting practical experience.

Third. A facility for the expeditious enactment into law of the wishes of the community when the desires of the community are crystallized and the community is ready for action.

Fourth. The ability to retard legislative enactments when community policy is not yet crystallized and when inaction is more protective of sound community growth than is premature legislative experimentation.

Frank E. Horack, Jr., "Bicameral Legislatures Are Effective," *State Government*, April, 1941, pp. 79–80, 96. Reprinted by permission of the publisher.

Bicameral assemblies have long been criticized for their "unrepresentative" character. It is true that the historic origins of bicameralism stem from a desire to give preference to propertied and titled classes. It is also true that this basis of representation has been discarded in American legislatures and legislators are selected by all electors without qualifications based upon economic status. The apparent irrational consequences of continuing a bicameral legislature with a unitary basis of representation is the foundation of the unicameralists' argument. But a system of representation founded on area will remain just as arbitrary in a unicameral legislature. And the practicality or desirability of formal interest group representation certainly is not now worthy of consideration.

Economic representation by lobbyists

Furthermore, the failure of the American legislature to secure adequate interest group representation is more apparent than real. Such representation, today, is informally achieved through lobbyists and representatives of farm bureaus, trade associations, labor unions, temperance organizations, and the multitude of interests that have found legislative representation desirable. The informality of this representation is its chief virtue. Within the framework of an orderly two party system, highly specialized interests may make their influences felt. And no matter what the popular superstition may be, legislators and lobbyists know that influence must come from integrity and ability.

With the growing formalization of legislative committee procedure, the lobbyist must work more and more, as the lawyer, in open court, relying on his special knowledge and skill. To be sure he represents his client — but that, indeed, is democracy.

In an ever increasing measure interest group representatives have demonstrated their capacity for these responsibilities. We have, in fact, today, a type of interest group representation which could be no more effectively achieved under the unicameral system.

The proponents of the unicameral system assert that it will attract more qualified men to the legislature. There is little assurance, however, that a change in legislative form will have more than temporary significance in improving the caliber of legislators. Nor indeed is there any certainty that the caliber of legislators should or need be improved. In spite of the over-emphasis on the deficiencies of legislative bodies the competence of legislators compares favorably with that of judicial and administrative officials. It is true that misfits find their way to legislatures as they do to positions of responsibility in other walks of life. But in a legislature these individuals seldom if ever have significant influence in the enactment or rejection of legislative proposals. Legislative leadership, in the main, is on a high level.

Legislative procedure

Even with competent legislative personnel many critics assert that the bicameral procedure prevents fair and expeditious consideration of legislation. This argument is unconvincing. On the one hand unicameralists contend that existing procedure clogs and delays the efficient consideration of legislation and on the other hand they assert that legislation may be rushed through the legislature and enacted without the safeguards of deliberation. Even if true these are not exclusively the consequence of the bicameral system. Procedure must rely on human integrity and judgment.

Criticisms directed at clumsy procedure frequently overlook the cause and justification for such procedure. Without desiring to defend some of the archaic constitutional limitations such as the three reading rule and certain voting procedures, justification of many deterrents to action may well be defended on the grounds of their deliberative effect. In other words when legislatures are unable to agree on proposals they frequently reflect the uncertainty of the society which they represent and the resulting inaction may best accord with the wishes of the electorate. On the other hand when controversies over policy have been settled in a given community the obstacles to rapid legislative enactment frequently are dissipated. Many informal devices promote this result.

With a single party in control of the legislature, the party caucus provides ready means for agreement on procedure and on enactment. The governor likewise in many instances provides the legislative leadership. He may sponsor specific legislation, submit administration bills, and through his office, insure their adoption. The legislature itself, by joint committees or by the joint meeting of the committees of the two houses, can and often does reduce the time for committee hearings and irons out the minor controversies so that final enactment is a speedy and formal process. Where solid public interest supports a particular legislative program, the bicameral system accomplishes the expedition of unicameral procedure so that *de facto* unicameralism is achieved.

The unicameralist will still respond that although the bicameral system can achieve the efficiency of the unicameral system its legislative product is still unconsidered, unsupported by reliable data, and poorly drafted. Often these charges are true, but the question remains whether the creation of a unicameral legislature will improve the product. Improvement can be achieved only through adequate legislative research and competent draftsmanship. These requirements are unaffected by the form of legislative organizational structure.

Within the framework of the bicameral system great improvement has already been made. The active and able research organizations maintained by the Kansas and Illinois Legislative Councils and the code revision commissions of several States have made outstanding contributions to the improvement of the content and form of legislation. The continuation of this improvement will depend, however, not so much on the change of legislative form as it will upon the increase in funds and personnel for those legislative agencies which have already demonstrated their capacity in improving the legislative process.

Legislative costs insignificant

Perhaps the reader will feel that if the unicameral and bicameral systems are so similar in operation, that on the ground of expense alone the unicameral method should be adopted. An analysis of state budgets provides the answer. Legislators' salaries or even legislators' salaries plus the legislative perquisites are so small a proportion of the total state budget that an elimination of fifty per cent of the elected representatives would not change the proportion of state expenditures for the legislative department a single percentage point.

Though generally considered a controversy of form the unicameral-bicameral debate involves a fundamental issue of political phisiology. It raises a question of the flexibility of legislative action in terms of legislative responsibility to the electorate.

The streamlining of deliberation is obviously attractive in a world which places high value upon action. It is not accidental that the democratic influences of the early Greek civilization and the democratic movements of the later 18th and 19th centuries paralleled philosophical movements which found importance in idealism rather than in realism, which placed greater value in contemplation than in action. Conversely the pragmatic and realistic schools of the early 20th century consciously abandoned much of the moral and ethical nature of man for pure mechanism or Watsonian psychology.

The challenge of actionism

In the realm of politics, although the forms remain unchanged, innumerable straws in the wind indicate the effect of a machine age on the thinking and acting habits of the people. Even the bitterness of a politi-cal campaign has not produced great editorial writers or outstanding commentators; news print moves to larger type and shorter stories, from word to picture, and from printed word to radio voice. The forum fights an uphill battle to regain the position of the town meeting. Men have become accustomed to delegate tasks to others, to institutions, to machines. They want their answers ready made and so a philosophy of action challenges, in the realm of ethics and politics, the philosophy of deliberation. And it challenges a double-bodied legislature as an extravagance and a monstrosity. Indeed, the philosophies of those we consider not quite respectable challenge even the existence of any legislative or deliberative body. Action is the password. *Blitz* is the fashion.

The usefulness of joint legislative committees and the party caucus have already been elaborated as a means of unicameral action within the framework of the bicameral system. Unicameral action is necessarily the result of single leadership. It occurs in the American legislative scene only when there is a general unification of political and social objectives which have insured a political party a dominant position on the political scene. It seems to me that this is the outstanding advantage of a *de facto* unicameralism — it is not a permanent or fixed way of life for the State and its people. When there is uncertainty and doubt, the additional brakes that a second house of a legislature can provide is both necessary and desirable in order that legislative action does not run ahead of popular acceptance. When popular demand has unified on a particular social program so that whatever opposition develops cannot be described in terms of general uncertainty, machinery is then available in the framework of our present bicameral organization to speed the achievement of the objectives without an application of brakes by the second house. This ability to accelerate or brake the speed of government should not be abandoned quickly for a vehicle built on horsepower and without brakes.

To a great many persons a legislature is a rather remote body "passing laws" by means of some formalized procedures about which they have involuntarily read at some time in the past. In the next selection Richard L. Neuberger, late United State Senator from Oregon and a former member of the Oregon state senate, brings a legislature to life for us with his highly readable first-term impressions of legislators, constituents, and the legislative process.

33

I Go To The Legislature

By Richard L. Neuberger

IF, IN THIS HOUR of crisis for democracy throughout the world, you seek direct contact with democracy in action I recommend service in the legislature of your home state. There you will become acquainted with the problems and aspirations and pet schemes of your neighbors, and you will find out all you want to know about their virtues and their peculiarities. You will be told their intimate opinions on the ridiculous and the sublime — what they think haircuts should cost and how we can avoid inflation.

In the six months I have been a member of Oregon's House of Representatives, I have learned more about the people and government of my native state than in four years at its university. I am taking a practical course in American democracy. A meeting of the Utilities Committee, at which we stormily try to arbitrate the conflicting proposals of power companies and public ownership groups, offers a perspective on democracy never gained from textbooks.

Charles A. Beard and James Truslow Adams cannot tell me as much about representative government as a delegation of angry taxpayers from my district, demanding to know why I have introduced a bill providing pensions for firemen. And after I have defended the bill and listened to their rebuttals, some of the taxpayers still indignant, a few halfway mollified, I somehow feel that I have acquired additional knowledge about my fellow citizens and what makes them tick.

At the desk ahead of mine in the fir-paneled legislative chamber sits a piano salesman. Next to him is a haberdasher. To my right is a prominent lawyer, to my left a longshoreman. I can turn around and talk to a Ford dealer who was born in the Scottish highlands. We are a cross-section of our state, and the issues we decide upon, ranging from the length of passenger trains to the test for pure milk, touch the personal lives of every man, woman, and child in Oregon.

Any American who is free and twenty-one may do what we are doing. Without fiat or permission from high authority he can submit to other Americans like

himself his candidacy for public office. In these troubled times we hold this privilege in common with the people of few other lands. Cattle rancher or accountant, banker or freight brakeman, any citizen of the United States may put his name on the ballot. In our ranks we have all four of these occupations and many more besides.

It is part of the American tradition for political careers, whether destined for fame or obscurity, to begin in state legislatures. . . . This training ground of American politics is open also to those marked for the commonplace, and one of the pastimes of the public is to wonder who among us will become United States Senators and who will fade into oblivion.

I ran for the Legislature as an amateur. It was an end in itself rather than a means to higher position. I wanted to see at first hand what made the wheels of government go around. Yet I am afraid there is something contagious about the ambitions which hang like clouds in our chamber. I am going to exert all my will power in an effort to retain my non-professional political status. I have no desire to straighten up pompously and think I am confronting a future governor each time I look in the bathroom mirror.

West Point trains our generals and Annapolis prepares men to command the fleet. For half a century Americans have proposed an academy which would equip citizens for careers in public life. To date membership in the various legislatures has been most nearly the equivalent of this. There takes place the sifting and winnowing that matches the weeding-out process at our military institutions; there men discover whether they are temperamentally suited to the great game of politics. A few win their epaulets and go on to Congress or the governorship, and the rest gradually fall by the wayside.

What is membership like in one of these forty-eight academies that offer embryo American politicians their first practical experience?

I arrived at our new marble Capitol expecting to spend most of my time considering momentous issues — social security, taxes, conservation, civil liberties. Instead we have devoted long hours to the discussion of regulations for the labeling of eggs. We have argued about the alignment of irrigation ditches, the speed of motorboats on mountain lakes, the salaries of justices of the peace, and whether or not barbers and beauty parlor attendants should be high school graduates. For two days we wrangled about a bill specifying the proper scales for weighing logs and lumber.

None of these questions concerns large numbers of people. Yet each question concerns a few people vitally. Two or three poultry raisers told me that a change in the labeling of fresh and cold-storage eggs would put them out of business. I have received several dozen letters from merchants in my district

Richard L. Neuberger, "I Go To The Legislature," *Survey Graphic*, July, 1941, pp. 373–376, 410–412. Reprinted by permission of the publisher.

complaining that parking meters along the curb are destroying their trade. More mail has come to my desk about what high-powered speedboats would do to the tranquility of Diamond Lake than about a series of anti-sabotage bills in which the issue of free speech is said to be involved. The solitary "old grad" letter from a fellow alumnus of the State University has asked not for lower taxes or improved law enforcement, but for action to control Bang's disease which afflicts goats and cattle.

In common with most other states Oregon has antiquated county governments. The state must undertake innumerable functions that are purely local. These things may be fundamentally unimportant, but the people directly concerned do not think so. A farmer cares whether his livestock can cross a state highway. Jewelers are deeply interested in regulations governing the sale of watches. Residents quickly protest an unreasonable speed limit in their suburb. After five months in the legislature I am convinced that the position taken on these many questions of comparatively high significance has a lasting effect on a political career.

A few doors from me lives a prominent manufacturer. Going home on the streetcar we have argued violently about free trade *vs.* tariffs, Roosevelt *vs.* Willkie, the New Deal *vs.* rugged individualism. Not long ago I received a letter from him. Looking at the envelope I was sure another clash of political philosophies was impending. But he was writing me, as his representative in the legislature, seeking support of a bill to prevent canneries from gutting Oregon's streams of trout and salmon. If I voted for the bill my neighbor's devotion to fishing would overcome his Republicanism and "all would be forgiven."

Here my neighbor and I were in ready agreement. I not only voted for the bill but made a speech for it. My anti-New Deal neighbor is one of my backers now.

A member of the legislature, I think, assumes reality in the eyes of a constituent when he does something which touches that constituent personally. In preparation for my political debut I diligently read Marquis James' *Andrew Jackson,* Beard's *Rise of American Civilization,* White's *The Changing West* and *History of the Pacific Northwest* by Fuller. Into debates on the general conduct of the state government I have injected facts and quotations from these books. My colleagues, I fear, grow a little weary of hearing me tell what Old Hickory or the founding fathers of Oregon would say and do were they in our places.

To these oratorical efforts I have had no reaction whatsoever — no mail, no approval, no condemnation. I have drawn a blank. As far as I can determine, my best speech [*sic*] has not won me as much political support as my mailing copies of the official legislative calendar each day to schools, labor unions, and commercial clubs in my district. Nor do I believe that my worst speech has cost me as many votes as endorsement of a "no-first-bite" bill which has offended some of the dog owners in my part of the city of Portland. "Many small make a great," said Chaucer and in that light our constituents seem to appraise our performance.

I received a letter from an elderly man, obviously in difficult circumstances. He was confronted with loss of his small house. For some reason he had been denied an old age pension. He recited the details of his problem. Did I know his rights in the case? I spent a few minutes looking up the Social Security law. Then I wrote the old man about his legal claim to a pension. I also wrote state relief officials in his behalf.

The old man gratefully showed the letter to several of his neighbors. It was read at a pension club. Speakers commented on it at the meetings of other pension clubs. Members of these groups began thanking me for taking a personal interest in the old man's troubles. People seem to feel more intently about an episode such as this, with its human aspects, than about broad general principles which apparently have no direct application to their own problems. I came to the legislature expecting to be judged exclusively by my attitude on a few basic questions. This, however, is only about a dozen inches on the yardstick by which the voters measure their officials.

Mail is highly important. Letters unanswered are votes thrown away. This is particularly true of personal mail which some man or woman has taken the bother to write in longhand. There are stock letters sent to every member of the legislature; these we disregard or reply to with a perfunctory "I will give your views all possible consideration." But a personal letter from a constituent, a letter which has come to us alone — that is a totally different proposition. A citizen interested enough to write his legislator is also interested enough to tell his neighbors and friends and relatives his estimate of that legislator. This is why, if necessary, we miss a session of the House to turn out the morning mail.

I am a newspaper man. Before going to the Legislature I heard my fellow newspapermen criticizing the trades and compromises customary in lawmaking. I resolved to have no part of this. Through thick and thin I would stick to every original promise. I would not yield an inch. My strength would be as the strength of ten because my heart was pure.

I am older and wiser now. My newspaper friends were partially correct, but they also were downright wrong. The legislature is as full of compromises as the Pacific Ocean is of water. Yet I wonder how else laws could be enacted at all. There are 60 of us in the House of Representatives. Thirty-eight are

Republicans, 22 are Democrats. Some of us think Franklin D. Roosevelt is the greatest President since Lincoln; others are sure he is the worst. A few blame the world crisis on labor; a few others attribute it to big business. Some of us are from metropolitan Portland; others are from the wilderness of the Cascade Mountains. On a multitude of issues the area of disagreement among us seems as vast as the universe.

We include many professions and occupations. Among us are lawyers, real estate agents, editors, prune growers, school teachers, storekeepers, mechanics, and men who are out of jobs. Each of us has prejudices and predilections which others consider unreasonable. Some members hate and fear doctors. Two members are doctors. Three or four legislators belong to the Associated Farmers, an organization bitterly fighting labor unions. One legislator is president of the largest labor union in the state. A member from Portland is proud of his pet police dogs, which he rents to movie companies. A member from a woodland district forty miles from Portland insists that police dogs have been killing his sheep.

Yet all of us represent the people of Oregon. They have sent us to their Capitol to make laws regarding medicine, agriculture, roads, taxation, schools, and a huge variety of other subjects. We have to agree somewhere, or government will break down. We must be able to give and take. This was impressed upon me early in the session. I sponsored a bill proposing a State Resources Council. I wanted to provide for an appropriation of $60,000. The Ways and Means Committee informed me that unless the appropriation were half that, the bill would not even be considered. I swallowed hard — and asked for an appropriation of $30,000.

Democracy is the fusing together of many ideas and that is what we are doing in the legislature. I introduced a measure making it mandatory for Public Power Districts to recognize the collective bargaining rights of their employees. The bill also gave the state commissioner of labor the right to fix the wages paid by those districts. Republicans on the Utilities Committee were against the bill entirely. They wanted to table it. The Democrats sought its passage unchanged. At last both sides gave in. The Republicans agreed to allow the bill to come out on the floor. We agreed to eliminate the provision permitting the labor commissioner to stipulate wages.

Was this a compromise with principle? I do not think so. The wage clause in the bill was important, to be sure. Yet insistence on it would have meant adoption of no bill at all. Now, at least, an act is on the statute books calling for the recognition of collective bargaining. Perhaps a future session of the legislature will add the clause which we had to

abandon. After the settlement one of the Republicans wryly said to me, "Well, neither of us seems very satisfied. I guess that means we've got a pretty fair bill, huh?"

"Politicians are as compromised as a kept woman," say my cynical friends. Yet the concessions we have made in the legislatures typify the way democracy works, and by and large they have done considerably more good than harm. Representative Herman Chindgren, a farmer from Clackamas County, will support my bill to guarantee school teachers adequate notice of reemployment or dismissal, provided I reduce the required time from nine weeks to six weeks. I will vote for the bill of Representative Jim Rodman, a real estate man from Lane County, to waive the penalties on delinquent property taxes if he will limit the tenure of the bill to two years. . . . I am sure that in this fashion laws were passed in Thomas Jefferson's time — and in this fashion will be passed one hundred years from now, if only we can hang on to democracy.

Our angriest battle so far has been over unemployment insurance. The lumber industry, dominant among businesses in Oregon, contended that any increase in the payroll tax would push it into bankruptcy. With equal emphasis both AFL and CIO maintained that a boost in the tax was absolutely essential to the security of the unemployment compensation fund. I entered the legislature a confirmed champion of labor's viewpoint. The controversy bogged into a stalemate. Neither side would budge. After weeks of pulling and hauling the question finally was compromised midway between the demands of each group.

That night the head of one of the state's biggest sawmills told me in a Capitol building elevator, "Well, you fellows didn't do so bad. That agreement is pretty good. I think it will work out all right." And the next morning over coffee and butterhorns at breakfast the secretary of the Oregon Federation of Labor observed, "We've got no kick coming. Labor will get along O.K. under the new arrangement. The compromise bill is fair to everyone concerned."

That democracy in Oregon — and very likely in other states — has been operating like this for a long time is demonstrated by the fact that at least half the bills we consider are amendments to earlier laws. Some of the acts thus amended are extremely old, going back to the days before the railroads were thrust into the Northwest. Quite conceivably the frontiersmen who carved Oregon out of the forest fastnesses were of the same mortal clay as ourselves. Probably they had to make concessions to the other fellow and the other fellow had to make concessions to them, and all the time they hoped that the legislators who came along in the future would patch things up.

Despite the chasms of disagreement there is a certain comradery among us which not the most savage debate can stifle or discourage. I think this stems largely from the fact that we in the legislature are not responsible to each other. Our only masters are those unseen folks back home, those folks whose letters are piled on our desks in neat stacks every morning. If Representative French assails my resolution for the construction of the Umatilla reclamation project, I tell myself that irrigation farmers in the 22nd district will take care of him at the next election. He, I am sure, is equally positive that taxpayers in the 5th district will deal sternly with me.

No matter how contentiously we may argue, we invariably refer to each other as "My illustrious colleague from the picturesque Willamette Valley" or as "The worthy and honored member whose historic district occupies so warm a spot in the hearts of our people." We can be locked in desperate verbal combat one hour, and then eat lunch at the same table in the Capitol restaurant the next. Not only are we independent of our fellow members but also of the executive department officials and functionaries who swarm through the Statehouse. We have only to make our peace with God and the voters back home who elect us.

Many of my acquaintances speak of "politicians" with amused contempt. The word to them connotes venality, bribes and a fat man in a checked suit doling out payment contracts. Perhaps I need stronger spectacles, but I have seen no more evidence of corruption or dishonor among my colleagues than among any other similar group of citizens. The majority of the legislators work hard. They want to do a good job. One of the reasons for this is not without its humor. We are addressed as "Honorable." Lobbyists flatter us like prima donnas. We are provided with imposing stationery. Suppliants seek favors and audiences. Pages fetch and carry at our bidding. As a result of all this we probably harbor certain modified Napoleonic tendencies.

Yet I think the very fact that we are overly impressed with our own importance assures the state zealous and conscientious service. No man shirks a task he considers vitally essential. We take ourselves seriously. Almost half of us are just getting started in politics. We have none of the sophistication of men who have been to the political wars many times. And always lurking in subconscious minds is the lingering hope of outdistancing the crowd and reaching the governor's chair.

The outstanding human shortcoming in the legislature is timidity. In front of most of the members, tantalizingly near, is the will-o'-the-wisp lure of higher office. The temptation is strong to avoid taking a position on red-hot issues. Why court disaster? One particular legislator can be depended upon to develop a stomach attack the night before a bristling question is scheduled for debate. We never learned the truth of the report that on the evening of one of these convenient "attacks" a well-tipped bellboy smuggled a sirloin steak and hashed-browns into his hotel room.

Men who are neither venal nor dishonest will try to dodge a controversial vote. Bills which arouse both bitter opposition and strong backing give these members some difficult moments. Caught in a pincer movement, they do not know where to turn.

Along with a Republican colleague, I put in a measure to raise the shamefully low minimum salary paid school teachers in Oregon. . . . A number of legislators moved Heaven and earth to have the bill smothered in the Education Committee. They hesitated to antagonize powerful economy groups, yet at the same time feared the displeasure of the teachers. I may have whittled a few years off these gentlemen's lives when I introduced a motion to discharge the committee from consideration of the bill and then demanded a roll call vote upon the motion.

But despite these examples of pusillanimity, I am not convinced that politicians as a whole are more timid or spineless than anyone else. I remember an article which appeared some years ago in *Harper's* by Charles Willis Thompson. Its title was "Wanted: Political Courage." He mourned the lack of valor in public life. Politicians, he claimed, were straddlers and trimmers. At the time of reading I heartily concurred in these accusations. I am not so sure now. I am sure, however, that Mr. Thompson himself never occupied any political position.

Among us are men from every possible level and class of Oregon's people — owners of dairies, a former president of the State Bar Association, the leader of the CIO loggers and lumberjacks. Are these men any less valiant as legislators than in their other capacities? I think not. What I do think is that no chance ever is overlooked to embarrass politicians or box them in tight places. Pressure groups demand commitments and will take nothing short of Yes or No for an answer. Newspapers seek statements on all conceivable issues. The privilege of inconsistency, vouchsafed to others at will, is rigidly denied us.

What would anyone else — your butcher, your seamstress, your dentist, yourself — do if projected into similar circumstances? "Politicians are just people," William Allen White once remarked. I am afraid that the voters occasionally forget this. Frailties allowed us at home are taboo at the Capitol. We can change our minds about how to run our business or which house to buy, but if we switch on a political question we are cowards and trimmers.

Pressure groups alternately cater to our fears and hopes, threatening us with political doom one minute and promising us unlimited support for the United States Senate the next. We are constantly besieged for jobs and favors. If we cannot deliver a clerkship or a state police sergeancy, we are regarded as political washouts. Even our personal effects and habits are subject to goldfish-bowl scrutiny. I was severely criticized during the campaign for attending a luncheon wearing a sweater. And, conversely, a suspicious farmer said he would not vote for me because I drove to a meeting in a large Buick sedan.

Yet despite all this — and it may be heresy to say so — I believe politics frequently brings forth the best rather than the worst characteristics of an individual. Our colleague who had been a rather drab president of the Bar excited our admiration when he led a long fight to obtain representation on County Welfare Boards for the men and women on relief. "I am successful financially now," he said, "yet who knows what tomorrow will bring? For the first time I fully realize the problems confronting people who must rely on public charity for food and shelter."

Later this legislator told me that his efforts in behalf of the reliefers had given him greater satisfaction than a dozen legal victories. Here, I submit, is one of the real reasons Americans seek political office. In all of us the crusader spark flickers. We no longer can be Sir Launcelot or Robin Hood pursuing the wicked Sheriff of Nottingham, but public service presents a chance to express these suppressed tendencies. Listless indeed the member among us who has not some underprivileged group he is forever championing.

Near me sits a dull and asthmatic insurance agent. His political views antedate the McKinley era. Little or nothing stirs his interest. Yet he has a cause. He has struggled for many years to get state appropriations for crippled and handicapped children. Inert and lackadaisical though he may be when any other question is under discussion, let the Ways and Means Committee fail to do something for crippled youngsters and he can leap to his feet in wrath and hold the attention of the chamber. In this, I am sure, all his long-distant boyhood desires to be a Canadian Mountie or a U.S. Marine and save the weak and lowly find bold expression.

A group of elderly women, advocating beautification of Oregon's highways and roadsides, came to the Statehouse with a bill to regulate and control signboards. By giving free billboard space to commercial groups and patriotic societies, the sign companies had built up a powerful lobby. The discouraged ladies finally came to me with tears in their eyes. They were ready to go home — beaten. I took the bill, gulped as I thought of the possible political consequences, scrawled my name on it and shoved it into the hopper. As they poured out their gratitude I could not have felt more heroic had I rescued Loretta Young or held the Tiber bridge.

The fate of this anti-signboard bill demonstrated vividly just how clever lobbies can gang up on politicians. The sign companies first got the Signpainters' Union to denounce the measure in general and me in particular. Then people renting their land to the companies wrote tearful letters implying that passage of the bill might put them in the poorhouse. I am convinced that a vast majority of Oregon's citizens, proud of the state's scenery and anxious to tear away the billboards in front of it, favored the measure. Yet to the legislature it seemed as if the public was in arms against the bill and it failed decisively.

In the time I have been a member of the Oregon House of Representatives I have not enjoyed conspicuous success in sponsoring proposals. I am a New Deal Democrat in a chamber where Republicans hold a tenuous but working majority. Although they have dealt me some hard blows my faith in democracy is undiminished. In most instances my colleagues either in their personalities or attitudes, pretty much symbolize the districts from which they come. "If you send a rogue to Albany to represent you," Henry Ward Beecher once told the voters of New York, "then indeed he represents you." That applies to every state. Whomever the men and women of Oregon want as their legislators they can have.

If the other members do not share my views, my disagreement is not primarily with them. It is with the voters in their districts. I am certain that indiscriminate logging imperils the economic security of Douglas County. Yet if the people of that great fir belt want to be spoken for in the legislature by Representatives Gile and Hill, who are deadset against my resolution for selective cutting of timber under the supervision of the Forest Service, that is their inalienable right. Patriots died at Valley Forge to enable the electorate of Douglas County to make that mistake, if mistake it be.

Some men and women despair of democracy because it is cumbersome and works slowly. In the legislature I have had the experience of sitting with men of many faiths, of many political creeds. Somehow, out of all our quarrels and differences, we have produced the laws under which the people of a great Pacific Coast state will live. Some of those laws I voted against; others I supported. Yet only a few of them are very bad and a lot of them are pretty good. Whatever failure there has been in the legislature has been the failure of the human machine, and that failure, I suppose, occurs in armies, factories, chancelleries, and everywhere else on earth.

Skulduggery has not gotten very far. A bill before us exempted parsonages from taxation. In committee a utility lobbyist sneaked into the bill an extra sentence. The sentence would have lightened the tax load of power companies. Leaders of the public ownership forces rose and pointed out what had been attempted, how the companies were using the clergy for protective coloration. The legislators hooted the contraband sentence out of the bill, although had it been presented to the House in bona fide fashion I am sure that many members would have favored it. So even though democracy may not be a perfect method of government, at least it is basically a decent one.

For the next century to come legislators may improve and revise the laws we are now enacting, just as we are patching and remodeling the laws which those early settlers adopted long ago. This is the legislative system, the democratic way of shaping policy. Faults and defects the system assuredly has, and yet after six months of active participation in it I am more convinced than ever that it is a system worth defending.

Another important and well-publicized phase of the legislative process involves the activities of lobbyists, representing almost every organized interest and employing a multitude of varied tactics. These "legislative advocates" are stereotyped in the public mind as evil manipulators, though such a designation fits only a few. In a sense they provide a kind of functional representation in the legislature, and they "carry" their bills through the legislative channels in much the same manner as will the individual legislator. On occasion one will come to wield tremendous power in a legislature under certain circumstances, the classic account of such a situation being Lester Velie's widely read article, "The Secret Boss of California." The reader should bear in mind that the article describes conditions in the 1940's, which have not prevailed for many years. As indicated in a previous article in this chapter, the California legislature is now considered one of the outstanding ones in the nation. The power of Artie Samish in the California legislature was broken shortly after publication of this article (and partly as a result of this publicity). Samish himself served a prison sentence for income tax evasion. The State Board of Equalization in 1956 was divested of its control over alcoholic beverage licenses, and elections placed new members on the Board. Legislative salaries have been improved and a number of procedural improvements instituted. The political parties are notably stronger. The 1959 legislature abolished California's curious system of primary "cross-filing," partially defunct since 1954. Read in this context, the article is still instructive.

Hardly anyone can have escaped some contact with the many criticisms. sometimes well justified, of lobbyists and lobbying, but little is usually heard of the more favorable side, presented in the concluding article by a lobbyist for a state League of Women Voters.

34

The Secret Boss of California

By Lester Velie

"IT SAYS IN THE BOOK," said the college professor, "that we elect a legislature in California to make our laws for us. It says the legislature is responsible to the people. It says also that we elect delegates to political conventions, that we elect attorney generals and mayors and district attorneys.

"Well, let's see. . . . There's a man in California today who holds no public office and is responsible only to the interests who hire him. Yet this man can push laws through the legislature or stop them cold. He named our attorney general. He elected the mayor of San Francisco and he told him whom to name for police commissioner. He has the power to make or break governors.

"This man once delivered California's delegates to a Presidential candidate — Wendell Willkie. He is the most powerful non-officeholder in California."

The professor studied the alert, upturned faces of the 50-odd University of California seniors before him.

"Who is this man?" he asked.

None in the class of fifty knew.

This was not surprising. Few in California knew. Had the professor queried the faculty or stopped people on Los Angeles' or San Francisco's streets, maybe one in 100 could have named the state's most powerful man.

But the politically sophisticated know.

When Preston Tucker sought permission to sell Tucker Corporation stock in California, his lawyers unerringly led him to a six-foot two-inch, 300-pound mountain of a man with the sensitive face of a great actor and the forthright mouth of a stevedore.

"I want to get permission to sell stock in this state," Tucker said. "Can you get it for me?"

The outsized man with the shrewd eyes studied the promoter's boyish face, seeking in it a clue to his character and his proposition. Deciding against what he found, the big man said:

"No. I'm not for you, I'm against you. I'm against any lovin' stock pushers going to people's mothers to

Lester Velie, "The Secret Boss of California," *Colliers*, August 13, 1949, pp. 12–13, 71–73; August 20, 1949, pp. 12–13, 60–64. Reprinted by permission of the author and publisher.

sell stock. Why, you might sell some of that lovin' stock to my own mother!"

The California Division of Corporations turned Tucker down, labeling his promotion, "a fraud upon the purchasers."

When Paul Smith, editor of the San Francisco Chronicle, sought to get a pro-One World resolution through the California legislature and made no headway, he telephoned Room 428 of the Senator Hotel in Sacramento and asked for "Mr. Arthur H. Samish."

"Artie," said Editor Paul Smith, "can you help me get a resolution through, supporting One World and a world federalist union? We're stymied."

"What's One World?" Artie asked.

When the editor explained, Artie said, "Sure, right away."

The resolution was whipped through the legislature promptly. California became the first state to back a national convention favoring American entrance into a world federalist union.

What promoter Tucker and editor Paul Smith knew of Arthur Samish's political power, the governor of California also had reason to know. Once, when Governor Earl Warren vetoed a bill backed by Samish, the big man lumbered over to the chief executive's office.

"What's wrong with the bill, Governor?" he asked.

When the governor explained, Samish — who holds no political office — said, "All right, Governor, I'll give you another one."

Soon he tossed another version up to the governor, in his stride.

Attorney General Frederick Napoleon Howser, too, had reason to know Samish's political heft. When Howser got into political hot water because some of his aides tried to muscle in on the statewide gambling rackets, he went to Samish, the man who put him in office. Samish, alone, could save his political life. But Howser was in such bad odor politically that Artie thought he was better rid of him.

For two hours the attorney general of the sovereign state of California cooled his heels outside Samish's hotel rooms. Allowed in, the attorney general found Samish entertaining some 30 assemblymen and senators at lunch.

"What are you doing here, you lovin' ———!" Samish thundered at Howser. "Don't ever let me see your lovin' face again!"

Howser slunk out, knowing that failure to heal the breach meant he was living on borrowed political time.

Movie tycoons, too, the "yessed" lords of their own domain, acknowledge Samish's higher authority at Sacramento.

When movie producer Cecil B. de Mille, feuding with labor, sought to curb unions with a restrictive law, his lawyer rightly telephoned Samish. But wrongly the lawyer said:

"We'll hold you responsible if this bill doesn't pass."

"No one gives ultimatums to Art Samish," roared Art Samish. "Now, just try and get that lovin' bill through."

Labor had despaired of blocking the measure. But suddenly in an assembly dominated by conservative Republicans 54 votes (out of a possible 80) materialized mysteriously against the anti-union bill. Never in the history of the California legislature had labor mustered such strength. With a grateful bow toward Samish, an A.F. of L. vice-president said:

"This ought to show who controls the state of California!"

The man who "controls the state of California" falls into no easy identifying niche. He is neither labor boss, oil king, press lord, financial nabob, nor rabble rouser of the Huey Long type. You can't even neatly tag him as the Boss Pendergast or Crump or Hague of California.

A superspecial kind of boss

Not for Artie Samish are the mildewed methods of these political Neanderthalers. He is *sui generis* — the only one of his kind. An original, both as a human being and a political operator. He is a political boss without a party. He bosses both Republicans and Democrats with equal impartiality. One "Samish man," the head of a key legislative committee, derives support from leftist unions. Artie is a political boss without political clubhouses. He has no precinct organizations.

What does he have?

He has what he himself describes as "an endless chain of political strength" whose strongest links are "the little fellows" of the industries that hire him: the 44,000 license holders who sell wine, liquor and beer; the growers of barley and hops; the truckers who haul the stuff; the culinary workers, musicians and other employees of many spots where liquor is served.

"A nucleus of 500,000 people protecting their investment and the livelihood of their kiddies," says Artie. "I weld them together into the damnedest political machine you ever saw. Boy, we can exploit it when we need it!"

But Samish has other strong links in the "chain of strength" with which he has girdled a great state.

He has campaign money, barrels of it, supplied by clients who ask no accounting. He has — when he marches to the political wars — the use of practically every billboard in California. These again are supplied by obliging clients.

Artie has a political espionage system at the state's

capital and beyond, which he describes as "the damnedest Gestapo you ever saw."

Samish has the eye of Mind Detective Polgar for ferreting out human character. He will know "quick" (as he puts it) what a man wants.

"I can tell if a man wants a baked potato, a girl, or money," says Artie.

He has a master's grasp of the inner workings of the legislature, knows its lawmaking machinery as intimately as, say, Toscanini knows the pieces in his symphony orchestra.

To this chain of strength Samish has forged another link. It is California's Board of Equalization, a key state agency which, his close friends as well as critics will tell you, "is in the palm of Artie's hand" because Artie, the political powerhouse, can see to the election of its four members.

The Board of Equalization administers the state liquor laws, and grants and revokes licenses. It has important discretionary powers over a wide range of taxes, and over assessments affecting vast corporations as well as sales taxes affecting small merchants. Its potentialities as a political pork barrel are second only to the state legislature. Samish can deliver both the board and the legislature.

All this came about because Samish is a practical man. Starting out as a lobbyist he found an easier way to persuade legislators than the method ordinarily employed.

Lobbyists usually perform the legitimate function of bringing their clients' interest to the attention of the lawmakers. Representatives of farmers' groups, teachers, labor and business interests have a recognized place in the state capitals and Washington. They appear before legislative committees and legitimately try to affect the shaping of legislation.

But Samish, a forthright and logical man, went right to the heart of his lobbyist's problem. The problem: to deliver legislation beneficial to his clients. Why bother with such chancy and indirect methods as marshaling arguments before legislative committees? Why not control the committees themselves?

Although he never got beyond the seventh grade in school and so never took geometry, Artie well knows the shortest distance between two points. The shortest distance to the control of committees and legislation is the control of legislators. Surest way to control a legislator: elect him.

Artie Samish's system worked.

Candid reply to a blunt question

This writer asked Governor Earl Warren, elected by the majority vote among California's nine millions:

"Who has more influence with the legislature, you or Artie Samish?"

The governor replied:

"On matters that affect his clients, Artie unquestionably has more power than the governor."

Matters that affect Artie's clients include legislation on beer, liquor, motor buses, railroads, cigarettes — and have included banks, building and loan companies, race tracks, chemicals. These are the clients Artie admits to.

When someone hires Artie, that customer can expect solid returns.

To his liquor clients Artie simply turned over the lawmaking facilities of an entire state.

"Meet the man who's written every liquor law in the state, good or bad," Artie told this writer, introducing, "one of my lawyers, Emil Hoerchner. He's counsel for the California State Brewers' Institute."

The lawyer blushed his acknowledgment, protesting modestly:

"But the ideas were all yours, Artie."

For his beer clients Artie built, as he himself puts it, "a granite wall." In other states, brewers pay an average of $2.03 per barrel in excise taxes. In California, they pay 62 cents. License fees are nominal there.

"Even when the state was running $70,000,000 deficits and they were hitting up other industries we held our rates at the present level," Artie says. "What more could I do for my clients?"

For a race track client, the famed Santa Anita course near Los Angeles, Samish built a similar wall. It shuts out the state from higher parimutuel takes and barred new, competing race tracks. Then, because he was miffed, Artie started to pull that wall down. A client scorned gets the works in reverse.

"When I worked for him (Dr. Charles Strub, Santa Anita's executive vice-president) I let nothing go through," Artie told me. "Then when Artie quit, everything began to break."

All of a sudden bills materialized to let the state tap additional millions from the track's pari-mutuel machines, to allow the building of competing tracks, to force Santa Anita to drop nonracing investments.

"The fellow wields unlimited power," Santa Anita's bewildered Dr. Strub said of his erstwhile champion, Artie. "If you don't think I'm in trouble!" he exclaimed. "Why, I may have to close the track."

But for a banker client Artie once was instrumental in changing the state's banking laws.

To get a bill through under normal procedure usually takes hearings, arguments, public debates, sponsors who are out in the open. Artie openly sponsors nothing. His is the power, *not* the glory.

"Samish never fronts for anything or anyone," says Samish.

Unlike a Hague or a Crump, against whom voters can occasionally rebel, Artie provides no visible target. How can you beat a man when you don't even know that he's there?

Mastermind in the shadows

Operating in the shadows, he is so well hidden that it is only by patient and diligent sleuthing that an investigator can find that Samish is the man behind a candidate, the man who is master-minding a drive in the legislature, the man who's backing a referendum that means millions to some private interest, or boosting a spate of laws that will work against a former employer.

Only by cloak-and-dagger detective work, involving the careful tracing of printers' identity marks on campaign literature, could the San Francisco News identify Samish recently as the chief backer of an Assembly candidate. Artie, who had spent thousands secretly in the campaign, was indignant at this invasion of his privacy. Besides, it brought about one of those rare events: a Samish defeat — by a hairbreadth 134 votes.

Only the motor bus companies that hire him knew that Artie was the genius who got behind a successful referendum that saves them millions of dollars in taxes yearly. In California — thanks to reforms by the revered Hiram Johnson — the people can vote their own laws directly by approving them . . . in a general election. Here's how Artie turned this reform to the uses of his clients:

He plastered the state's billboards with pictures of a giant hog. With the hog went a slogan:

"Drive the hog from the road. Vote Yes, on proposition No. 2 (the busses' tax proposal).

"Neither the hog nor the slogan had nothin' to do with the tax measure," Artie told this writer. "But nobody likes a road hog. So, of course, the people voted *yes* to drive him off the road. Yes, for my tax proposition.

"Who but an S.O.B. like Art Samish would think of a thing like that?" he chuckled, his nose puckering happily in the center of his expressive round face.

Who would? Not the people who read the billboards and thought they were voting to drive a road hog off the road but were really voting low taxes for the bus companies.

Samish rarely makes a political speech (although he can "stimulate 'em, bring 'em to white heat" when he tries). Even more rarely does he get into the papers.

And yet here is what three lifelong friends of Artie's, men whom I saw on Samish's own, earnest request, said of him:

One, a distinguished corporation lawyer — "Artie is a one-man Tammany Hall."

Another, a great California political strategist — "Is Artie a political boss? Absolutely — he's more. More than any man in California, he can deliver the legislature."

A third, a successful corporation lawyer and the author of a best-seller — "Artie's the real governor of California. The governor's only the Mikado. But Artie is the Great Shogun."

The man who is all these things will only describe himself as:

"Who, me? I represent industry. I'm a lobbyist, a public relations man."

This lobbyist label, like the stripe on a zebra, gives Artie protective coloration. It is the secret as to why he remains California's secret boss. The zebra blends and disappears into a jungle backdrop. Artie blends into and loses his true identity as a political boss against a similarly lush growth — the lobbying at California's state capital at Sacramento.

So numerous are the lobbyists that they outnumber California's 120 state Senators and assemblymen four to one. So influential are they that they are known as the Third House. The name Third House is no exaggeration. In actual power it could be called the *First* House.

Under the dominance of the Third House, California's legislature has become the grab bag of pressure groups. Two governors, Culbert L. Olson, Democrat, and Earl Warren, Republican, told this writer that the Third House had made a shambles of their administration. (Olson preceded Warren as California's chief executive.)

Socially, the lobbyists are the elite of Sacramento, ranking with state senators. When Assembly speakers leave public office they graduate into the Third House. Three have already done so, one of them, Walter Little, resigning his speakership to become the lobbyist for the railroads.

In the Third House are many lobbies. They range from oil, railroads, utilities, liquor to cemeteries (there are four cemetery lobbyists), dog defender leagues, race tracks and slot machines. The slot-machine gambling lobby is clandestine but well heeled and powerful.

Against this lobbying background Samish has flourished for more than two decades. The public outcries that were raised against Tweed and Murphy for delivering the legislatures of their day to special interests have remained unuttered in Samish's case.

Modestly, the man who delivers the California legislature, who has helped name every Assembly Speaker save one in the last dozen years — who elects mayors, judges, attorney generals — registers himself simply as the "legislative representative of the California State Brewers' Institute." Even the informed San Francisco Chronicle, in a recent profile, was satisfied to describe Samish as "the kingpin California lobbyist," and let it go at that.

But when Artie is in the mood, he can give you a better picture of himself than that. A Collier's photographer was taking routine shots of him to illustrate this article. Patiently, Artie posed this way and that.

Then he burst out:

"You want the real picture? I'll give you something that tells the whole story."

The big man disappeared into his bedroom and soon emerged with a dummy, togged out as a bum, its wooden toes poking from tattered hobo's shoes.

Artie Samish then lowered his round bulk into a chair and fought to control the great good humor that rolled in waves over his billowing belly and up over his jolly, convulsed face. In an elephantine imitation of Edgar Bergen, he plunked the dummy on his lap.

"That's the way I lobby," he said, pointing to the dummy. "That's my legislature. That's Mr. Legislature. How are you today, Mr. Legislature?" he inquired of the dummy.

Artie had another idea.

"If you get a long enough ladder and put it up against the Capitol dome, you can take a picture of me unscrewing the gold cupola!"

Artie was clowning. But the picture he gave of himself and "Mr. Legislature" is a true one. Ten years before, legislative investigators and a grand jury painted the same picture. Only they weren't so happy over the whole thing.

The investigators described Samish as "California's archlobbyist" and quote him as saying, "I'm the governor of the legislature. To hell with the governor of the state!"

What is he like, this "governor of the legislature," whom nobody elected?

He is an outsized 300-pounder. (Artie, as bashful about his bulk as a spinster about her age, admits to being "over 250".) He has a warm engaging face which, reminiscent of Victor McLaglen or Wallace Beery, reveals its owner's great gifts for making friends.

"I'm not a bad kid," Artie will say. Or: "You've just got to love me for this," he will declare as he tells of one of his exploits. Or: "We never stop doing nice things for people."

Artie has a filing system for remembering birthdays, anniversaries, a clipping system for learning of illnesses and accidents. This makes him a more redoubtable dispenser of remembrances than Jim Farley at his political zenith.

In one of his warm, outgoing moods, Artie will utter your first name with a rumbling caress. From a grand jury witness stand he almost drove the prosecutor frantic by addressing him continually as, "My dear man!" Over old friends, particularly objects of his benefactions like Tony the Newsboy in downtown Sacramento, Artie will purr:

"How are you, doll, how are you, baby?"

In Artie, "the not bad kid," there is a vein of sentiment as broad as he is.

"If you were nice to me when I was a kid, or were nice to my mother, I love you and will do things for you," he says. . . .

Artie, the man of sentiment, is also a figure of Falstaffian fun — a lumbering Puck with an agile brain whose barbs reveal the unfettered inner man.

He sometimes reserves his merriest pranks for the voters. When California's Drys succeeded in getting a local option proposal on the ballot last year, Samish countered with a confusing Wet amendment. Voters could vote for both. The trick was that, if they did, one would cancel out the other.

"Never in the history of American politics did two propositions on the same ballot cancel themselves out," chuckled Artie.

Then he told how he turned to his billboards and decorated them with a mother wielding a broom — "the most wonderful mother God ever made."

"Oh, what a mother we had!" Artie relates, mimicking with elephantine grace a mother sweeping out the kitchen. The slogan read:

"Mother says, 'Let's clean them out. Vote Yes, No. 2.'"

"The slogan had nothing to do with the amendment — but who won't vote for Mother?" Artie said.

"That's my mob psychology, my mass element," Samish explains.

Fun with a grand jury

When a Sacramento grand jury investigated Samish, looking for evidence of legislative corruption, the proceedings became an occasion for more of Artie's fun.

First, he had the law of the state changed so that his grand jury hearings should be open to the public. Then, arraigned on a contempt charge arising out of the public proceedings, Artie reached into his pocket and posted bail — with a $1,000 bill.

On the stand, he noticed something was missing.

"I'm on the witness stand," Artie relates. "The investigators got all sort of books and records and lawyers. I got nothing. No records. All I got is Art Samish, that's all. I decide I got to have records. Everybody has records, so I got to have records too."

Back in his hotel rooms Artie dug out two big suitcases, filled them with newspapers and a brick or two and locked them with giant padlocks.

"Now, I've got records," he said.

"I had a piano player carry the two suitcases into the grand jury room every day. Now we all had records.

"I put the suitcases in front of me, one on top of the other and drew doodles on a piece of paper. Just like the lawyers taking notes," said Artie, aping with his pudgy fingers elegant Spencerian scrolls. He laughed so hard at this happy reminiscence that tears came to his eyes.

In the middle of the grand jury probe, the district attorney had to run for re-election.

As a final gesture, Artie found a young man just out of law school and backed him for the prosecutor's job — as usual, secretly.

The young man, Alan McDougal by name, walked out of his home one morning and was startled to see the town's billboards placarded with posters urging:

"Honest McDougal for District Attorney!"

Asked on the grand jury witness stand later whether he had backed young McDougal, Artie told the district attorney (who had beaten McDougal by a fistful of votes):

"If I had had 24 more hours to devote to you personally, you wouldn't be sitting there now as district attorney."

As political autocrat and connoisseur of human frailties, Artie Samish has been accused of doing more to destroy human dignity than any other man in the state.

When a group of tobacco distributors called on him recently to seek his help in passing a law, Samish pointed to one delegate and said:

"I'll have nothing to do with this, unless *you* get out of here."

"Why, Artie, what have I done?" asked the embarrassed delegate.

"Listen, you," boomed Samish, "I heard what you said about me in Chicago. Now you get out."

The delegate got out. Alone. The rest, impressed by the long arm of Artie's Gestapo and his contempt for human feelings, stayed meekly and made their deal.

They take what he dishes out

Sometimes, as an unsparing debunker, Artie dishes it out with fierce zest. State senators, assemblymen, officials and industry leaders take it. . . .

His scorn for the men who do his bidding is near the surface. At dinner with this writer, Artie, in a gust of humor, motioned to a waiter:

"Hey, Senator!" he called.

But his scorn for the men whose bidding *he* does, the men he calls bosses, is even fiercer.

"I hate bosses," Artie says. "Put that down. Love those lovin' bosses," he repeats for emphasis.

Not wanted at swanky clubs

A middleman in the business of selling privilege, Artie has enriched important interests in California. But the very men who hire him and accept his favors, who make millions from his labors at Sacramento, do not invite Samish to join their exclusive San Francisco clubs. Although Artie's protective intervention

at Sacramento has meant millions to the Santa Anita Race Track, Artie could gain admittance to the track's exclusive boxes only through the use of a friend's ticket. Artie, operating in the political shadows, is socially unacceptable.

But he has become as rich as he is powerful. His wealth is estimated by friends to "run into many millions" — some of it acquired, as Artie says, "by people doing things for me, because they like me." His lucrative oil wells in Indiana, according to Artie, were acquired in this friendly fashion. Mostly, in the money way, Artie can do things very well on his own. He made his first million by age thirty-two.

"When I was still a baby," says Artie.

He got off to this start by shrewdly buying up a bus route which turned out to be the needed link in a subsequent merger. With his native business sense he might well have become an industrial giant had he set his cap in that direction.

During the war Artie struck a blow for the servicemen, and made a buck besides. Noting that servicemen had to pay black market prices for scarce wartime liquor, he conceived a chain of "military bottle shops" which sold to the military only.

The special allocation of liquor that Artie was able to obtain on patriotic grounds netted a tidy penny and raised anguished cries from competing, shortrationed liquor merchants. Artie explained the stores weren't his anyway. He had given one to "Frances the maid," who cares for his room at the Senator Hotel, another to "a piano player," another to Tony the Newsboy.

Artie's lieutenants said he gave away only "5 to 10 per cent" pieces of the stores.

Besides Artie's business interests, there are his lobbying fees.

The market value of the lobbying services Artie sells? The Santa Anita Race Track paid him $50,000 a year until he quit three years ago. To get him back the race track offered $200,000 yearly, but Artie said no.

Artie owns some palatial establishments in San Francisco and at Los Gatos. . . .

"I can't spend all I've made."

But for all that, he lives, as he himself says, "A Jekyll and Hyde existence."

"More than anything else, Artie hungers for respectability," two close friends of his told this writer. . . .

A mecca for favor-seekers

. . . To his hotel rooms, the open-sesame to power in Sacramento, flow the favor seekers, the lawgivers, the law enforcers. Along with their wants and needs each brings to Artie bits of information. For Samish must know in intimate detail what goes on.

"I want to know everything. I want to know what the sons of guns are doing," Artie says.

And so with a professional's devoted regard for detail, he has woven a net of espionage about Sacramento, and California, and beyond, which he describes as "my Gestapo." . . .

In New York City this writer experienced how far the Samish eye can see and how far the Samish ears can hear. As routine briefing for this assignment, I had lunch with a friend who knows about Samish's power. He spoke of him in awed tones.

"Why, I'll bet Samish already knows you're going to California to write about him," he said.

Before I left New York I learned that Samish did know I was California-bound. But how?

At Sacramento, Artie resolved the mystery.

"I had a telephone call from New York that you were coming," he said straight out, showing no ill feeling. "You've read the Philbrick (legislative investigation) report about my lobbying. You've read about my grand jury investigation," he continued.

Then he said, "I hear you've come out to chew me up."

There were other things the 300-pound Artie had been hearing.

"Here's what you've done since you've been here," he said. One by one he confronted me mischievously with conversations with California assemblymen, senators and state officials — conversations which I had thought were private.

"Why do you want to ask of the Equalization Board whether I take the state liquor administrator to Florida and to the World Series?" Artie asked with good humor.

The man Artie named, one of the four elected members of the important Equalization Board, which administers the state liquor laws and has wide tax powers, had relayed my questions to Artie the moment my back was turned, I learned from Artie himself.

"This tells a lot about your hold on that board," I told Samish.

"You've got it," Artie agreed affably.

Artie's hold on legislators was just as apparent.

"What made you think you could learn anything from Senator S——or Assemblyman D——?" Artie asked.

With a glint in his eye he repeated snatches of conversations, including interviews of mine in Los Angeles.

"As a matter of fact," he said, leaning over confidentially, "there's a man waiting to see me outside. Says you wanted to see him about me. Says he's willing to swear he hasn't seen me for two years.

"You've got to love me for telling you this," said Artie. "You know, I'm not such a bad kid."

How undercover workers operate

Artie introduced me to an intelligence system which has turned a state capital into a private goldfish bowl.

"I have about 25 people spotted around the capital," he said.

Most of these operate "undercover," unknown to outsiders and often unknown to one another. Artie told of a girl and a youth who, each a private Samish informer, were reporting to Artie everything that was going on. The girl really did report everything.

"The guy tried to date the girl. She puts it down in her report," Artie related. "I tell you, they tell me everything. I surprised the hell out of the guy by confronting him with it. He didn't know she was working for me too. Ain't nothing going on we don't know about."

Members of his corps of informal reporters sit in on legislative hearings which Artie never attends. According to a Samish lieutenant, they report on casual conversations in hotel lobbies and in the Capitol's halls. Hotel bellboys and Assembly and Senate pages use their eyes and ears for Artie.

"Let me put it together," Samish says of the bits and pieces of information brought to him. "If I have enough kids (tipsters) I'll know what's going on."

No competent intelligence system could be without its dossiers on people, and Artie's is a competent system.

"You'd be amazed at the detail I have on the people in office," Artie said. "Legislators? We have the damnedest file on them in the world. We really make a business of this thing. Believe me. What lodges the man belongs to, how many votes he won by. I know all their weaknesses. Every lovin' move they make. That's a record!"

This "record" is supplemented by Artie's shrewd and sure ability to probe character quickly, a native talent sharpened by 33 years' battle of wits and personality in California's political jungles.

"You ask me about a legislator. I'll tell you quick, just what he is," says Samish.

So good is Artie at telling character that the president of a great Eastern corporation asks Artie to appraise men for him when he is in doubt about his own judgment.

California had a chance to learn in detail, more than a decade ago, about the Samish political operation of which the intelligence system is only one part.

First to challenge Samish after years of undisputed bossism was a Sacramento grand jury. After a charge of attempted bribery was made on the floor of the State Senate, the grand jury was called into special session in 1938 to sift charges of corruption in the legislature. The grand jury questioned members of the Third House, as California's lobbyists are called — including Samish, who soon became the chief target.

The district attorney and the special prosecutor underestimated Artie's talents. They sized him up first as a lobbyist, then as a political boss of the traditional type, say like the former state czar, Abe Ruef. The prosecutors didn't realize they had, in Artie, a creative political genius who had fashioned something new in American politics — an original political machine without a party, without clubhouses, without precinct organizations.

Artie didn't use Ruef's methods to whip legislators into line. All he had to do was to use money and advertising to elect them. He didn't even have to have an understanding with them. But if they failed to go along they faced a fight for their political lives. It was as simple as that.

The grand jury was disappointed

Obligingly and in some detail Artie told all this to prosecutors and grand jury. To his unique dissertation — a blueprint for making legislators and influencing the policies of a whole state — the grand jury listened in sullen boredom. That wasn't what they wanted. They were looking for bribes. The hunt was in vain, for Artie's operations are legal. No indictments materialized.

Here is what Artie revealed to the grand jury:

"When there is a candidate for office, many times . . . I go in and help conduct his campaign. We very definitely do our best in the personal conduct of campaigns.

"The industries I represent have approximately 44,000 outlets. We have allied interests. We advise (them) to uphold you or support you. . . . We really think we have quite a setup so far as an organization throughout the state is concerned. . . . (It) . . . is a pretty good network of strength around the state.

"We believe . . . (We) . . . have some real effect upon the election or defeat of various candidates."

All this Samish told the grand jury openly.

About some other things he was more reticent. Only after resisting up through the State Supreme Court did Samish produce his income-tax records. From these, investigators traced "a total of $496,000 during the years 1935–38, provided (according to a summary report) by individuals, businesses and organizations directly interested in legislation."

Samish was equally reticent about his concern with the powerful State Board of Equalization which administers liquor laws and handles a wide range of taxes. Samish is credited with having strong influence over this board because he plays a key role in the naming of its four elected members. Before the

grand jury was spread the story of how Artie's chief lieutenant, Frank X. (Porky) Flynn, sought to dissuade one John F. Dondero from running for the board.

"Run for the State Senate instead," Porky urged Dondero, promising to raise $12,000 to $15,000 for the Senate race.

Porky offered a clincher which told much about lobbying methods in California. To Dondero he said:

"It isn't the $100 a month (salary of a state legislator). It's the money you make being there. Look at Assemblyman Hornblower. He's attorney for Bay Meadows Race Track, doesn't do anything, gets $5,000 a year."

When Artie told the grand jury of his "effect upon the election of candidates," he spoke truthfully.

Faces on the barroom wall

For years, perceptive observers in California have been able to predict winning candidates by noting which had their pictures in the bars. Another sure-fire way of picking political winning in California is to see whose pictures dominate the billboards.

Most of the billboards in the state — there are about 4,000 of them — are leased by Artie's clients. In the political season they are turned over to Artie to use in backing his candidates.

The clients who obligingly relinquish billboards also provide other and more substantial sinews of political war.

Samish told the grand jury that California brewers, with some exceptions, tax themselves five cents per barrel to raise a yearly $150,000 "Educational Fund." Samish has such unquestioned control over this fund that (as the grand jury found) he is permitted to destroy the canceled checks drawn against it. This fund pays Samish's salary and is also used normally to support candidates for the legislature. For special crises, such as the Drys' attempt to bring local option to California last year, Samish can muster much more.

"The fight against the Drys cost $750,000. Put that down," Samish told this writer. "The big boys paid the bills; the little fellows (the licensees, the workers in liquor-serving establishments) did the work."

Samish can tap other sources. The Motor Carriers Association, which he formed, "is Art Samish" he told the grand jury. Presumably, its funds are available for campaigns, too.

Artie explained his campaign methods to me.

"If you're my candidate you become everybody's (i.e., the bartender's, the teamster's, the musician's, the liquor clerk's) problem day and night. I may put a man in charge of you or send in a whole team of workers.

"I'm not interested in giving you contributions. We don't do it that way. What do I care about contributions? I'll spend ten times as much as the other fellow if necessary. I'm interested in electing you. What good are you to me unless you're elected?"

What Artie meant by "You become everybody's problem day and night" was illustrated by his successful drive to elect Judge Elmer E. Robinson, San Francisco's mayor. Literature that he spread through the liquor trade urged:

"You must vote. Your employees must vote. Your families must vote. Your friends and their friends must vote. Vote for Judge Robinson for mayor."

When, in addition, Robinson posters overnight appeared on downtown San Francisco billboards and Robinson signs sprouted in saloons, the wise money knew Samish was behind Robinson, and that Robinson — one of four candidates — was in.

Samish campaign funds go for no frills. He rents no headquarters, provides no personal campaign expenses to candidates.

The money goes into advertising, billboards, radio and newspapers.

Samish usually concentrates his activities on the races for the legislature.

"Give me an Assemblyman, and you can have all the mayors in California," he says.

At Sacramento, the California capital, it is estimated he controls a hard core of 30 Assemblymen (out of a possible 80). Dominating the biggest block of votes, Samish is able to trade. He makes defensive and offensive alliances with lesser lobbyists. These alliances permit him to deliver the legislature on any matter that concerns his clients or is of special interest to him.

So firm is his grip on the legislature that other lobbyists, to be successful, follow a simple rule: They lobby Samish.

Artie takes a hand in organizing the legislature. The object: to capture those committees that can speed or kill the laws he's interested in. Here California's reforms help him. The majority party does not organize the Assembly and name the Speaker and the committees as in most other states. At Sacramento the Speaker is elected by all parties and then *he* names the committees.

To win the Speaker's job, the successful candidate must make promises in advance to give important committee assignments to those who will support him. In the hectic trading that precedes the opening of every legislative session, a Samish favorite usually captures the speakership and with it the important committee posts that are at the Speaker's disposal.

One day Assemblyman Sam Collins and the district attorney of Los Angeles, Frederick Napoleon Howser, came to Artie. Both were "Samish men." Howser had got his start in politics when Samish had him elected Assemblyman, as Artie says, "at the request of one of my bosses."

Both wanted to be attorney general.

"I analyze the situation; it's a cinch," Artie recalls. "There's a lieutenant governor by the name of Fred Houser, and people are likely to be confused between the familiar *Fred Houser* and my *Fred N. Howser.*"

California voters (with no parties to guide them) usually vote for the familiar name on the ballot and re-elect incumbents. So Artie advised Howser to run for attorney general — "It would be a cinch."

To Sam Collins he gave a consolation prize.

"You be the Speaker of the Assembly," he said.

In California, Artie proposes and Artie disposes. Sure enough, Howser (what's in the spelling of a name?) became attorney general, and Collins became Speaker. . . .

Speakers usually are on good speaking terms with Artie. One spoke so often to him that he had a direct phone from his office in the Capitol to Artie's rooms in the Senator Hotel. They don't rack their brains about suitable timber for committees in which Artie is interested. Artie always has suggestions.

By coincidence — as even casual investigation will reveal — the two committees in which he has the greatest stake are outfitted with almost identical sets of lawmakers, most of them known in Sacramento as stout Samish men.

One important Samish committee is the Committee on Public Morals, which handles all bills affecting liquor, gambling, and race tracks. The way it handles them is to kill most antigambling measures and throw its weight on the side of sporting life in California. (Sometimes Public Morals lets an antigambling measure through. When it does, a Senate committee "takes care" of it.) . . .

Armed with a commanding block of votes, a friendly Speaker and key committees Artie is ready for all eventualities in the state legislature. But to deliver laws or kill them, Artie needs one more thing: insight into and mastery of the obscure twists and turns, the detailed legal protocol by which a bill moves from the idea stage through the legislative hopper to become a law. This is known as *procedure.*

Listen to Artie:

"Procedure," he says, "is the secret of success around here. It's the one lovin' thing I know. There isn't a short cut around the place I don't know."

No one in California knows them as well.

When a banker once asked Artie to help him cope with an onerous provision in the state banking laws, Artie said, "You've come to the doctor."

The banker's dilemma: The law allowed him to hold foreclosed real estate for only five years. He might have to sell at depressed prices.

How to amend banking laws

Here's what Doctor Artie ordered: a change in the state's banking laws to permit the banker to hold his real estate for *ten* years instead of *five*. And here's how Doctor Artie delivered:

"I had the whole banking law printed up," he relates. "It was this thick (using thumb and index finger to illustrate a document several inches in bulk). Only one word was changed. The word *five* was changed to *ten*."

Here's where Artie's knowledge of procedure came in.

When a law is amended, the amended portion is italicized to aid legislators in spotting it. The changed single word in the bulky law would be a needle in a haystack, even if italicized. But Artie made doubly sure that prying eyes wouldn't find it. He was instrumental in having the law quietly amended a second time (on a minor matter) thus removing — in the final printing — the italics from the crucial word *ten*. Now, there seemed to be no change at all in the old banking law.

"It passed unanimous," Artie recalls happily. His grasp of legislative procedure saved his banker client more than $20,000,000.

"I know a million tricks," says Artie.

Other men devote a lifetime to studying the law or medicine. Artie, who never got beyond the seventh grade because he had to support his mother, has devoted 33 years to studying the legislature. Starting as a page boy, the teenage Artie absorbed everything and he forgot nothing.

"He'd learn more in a minute than I'd pick up in a week," Al McCabe, Hiram Johnson's secretary, recalls.

One of the useful things that Artie learned was the strategic importance of a seemingly innocuous legislative functionary known as the "engrossing and enrolling clerk." Artie once had this job and learned its duties: to check the spelling, punctuation and wording of a measure after it passes both houses. If a comma is misplaced, if a word is misspelled, the measure can't move on to the governor for his signature. Thus, late in the session, a bill can be expedited, and live — or delayed, and die.

This job has possibilities

"The engrossing and enrolling clerk is the key figure in the Assembly," says Artie. "How can the governor act on a measure if it doesn't get to him —

or if the bill has to go back to the printer?" he asks with a ponderous air of innocence.

Many a measure has died because of a misspelled word. The timing of the bill's appearance on the clerk's desk had to be calculated carefully.

So slick was the strategy with which an anti-slot-machine rackets bill was maneuvered to death recently that frustrated law enforcement officers blamed it on the fine (but hidden) hand of the legislative master, Artie. The slot-machine racket is like sin: everybody is against it. So it was a brilliant political feat to have the anti-slots bill defeated without even forcing Senators or Assemblymen to go on record *for* the gambling rackets.

Samish vigorously denies any interest in slot-machine matters. But in any case, here is what happened: Passed by the Assembly and safely voted out of committee in the Senate, the anti-slot-machine bill nevertheless did not become law. Artie's closest friend in the Senate, onetime Lieutenant Governor George Hatfield, openly took over the fight against the anti-racket bills. So close is Senator Hatfield to Samish that nothing is ever allowed to interfere with their Friday-night dinners together. There they often discuss items of mutual interest.

It was Senator Hatfield who miraculously produced an obscure rule to show the anti-rackets bill had been reported out improperly by the Senate committee. . . .

In the legislature, Artie uses his power with reserve. He usually confines himself to matters that concern his clients. Here he exerts his greatest power. By sticking to these he doesn't risk getting into fights he might lose. In this way he shrewdly strengthens the legend of his juggernaut power. But occasionally he will stray into extracurricular matters through whimsy, or to do a favor, or to indulge a growing bent toward liberal causes.

Although Samish, at a client's behest, once helped kill a bill to set up a "Little Wagner Act" for California, he has at times helped labor lobbyists at Sacramento, and they swear by him. It was Artie who apparently cooled off State Senator Jack B. Tenney, chairman of California's famous Un-American Activities Committee — whose burning crusade against subversives was beginning to run wild.

"Meet Tenney on the street and say 'hello' to him. He calls you a Red," Artie mocked.

And so in mid-June, seemingly at the apex of his career, Tenney resigned as Un-American Activities Committee chairman, and his chief "loyalty" proposals landed in the legislative quick freeze.

"Who'd you like to see next as Un-American Activities Committee chairman?" Artie affably asked this writer on the eve of Tenney's eclipse.

Tenney's rise and fall illuminates the whimsical side of the Samish operation. Artie came upon young

Tenney while he was looking for an Assembly candidate to run in a Los Angeles district.

"What's your background? What have you done?" asked Artie.

"I've written the song Mexicali Rose," said Tenney.

"Mexicali Rose?" said Artie, a lover of music. "That's good enough for me."

A crusader in the doghouse

Samish saw that Tenney got elected to the Assembly where the future crusader against un-American activities promptly got into hot water by co-authoring a bill backed by leftist elements. The measure would have repealed California's criminal syndicalism law which provides punishment for advocating violent overthrow of the government. Later Tenney changed his mind, and lived this down to become chairman of the Public Morals Committee. Then he was promoted to the Senate. . . .

Paradoxically, no state in the Union has as many reforms aimed at overcoming political bossism as has California. State and city jobs are almost all civil service, so that there's little patronage for party machines and bosses to thrive on. Most local elections are nonpartisan. Candidates can thumb their noses at political parties and machines by running in both Republican and Democratic primaries at the same time. Cross filing — as it is known in California — has killed off party bosses. But it has also weakened the two-party system, and with it, party responsibility.

In a state like New York, where parties designate candidates, Samish would have to capture a whole party to control the state Legislature. In California all he has to do is capture individuals. In a state like New York the voter can rebel against both party and party boss by occasionally "throwing the rascals out." In California, where legislators are elected either as Democrats or Republicans or both, which party are you going to hold responsible for a do-nothing legislative session? Whom will you throw out?

Another point: In other states, a candidate receives a party designation and party campaign funds. In California he is largely on his own. Any Californian with $30 in his pocket can get on the ballot and run, say for Assembly or State Senate. But it costs as much as $5,000 to win such a race. With no party to put up $5,000 to win a $1,200 Senator's or Assemblyman's job who will put up the money?

The answer: The new-type lobbyist-bosses who collect stables of legislators. Chief of these is Samish.

Bob Kenney, a former attorney general — who has a talent for picturesque phrases — summed it up:

"We have reformed ourselves right into the hands of our executioners."

So powerful is California's so-called Third House

that at the recent session it spelled out the budget policy to the two legislative houses.

Scene in a lobbyist's hotel

When the legislature hacked Governor Earl Warren's budget bill, it was using a cleaver that had already been swung in Sacramento's Senator Hotel — in the rooms of Monroe Butler, lobbyist for independent oil companies in California.

"I had five or six Assemblymen up here at a time for lunch until about 50 had come," Butler told me. "I explained the budget to them, and we laid out the strategy for slashing it. Elmer Bromley (utility lobbyist) and Vincent Kennedy (retailers' lobbyist) helped. And Charlie Stevens (lobbyist for major oil firms) worked the Senate."

What has made the Third House so persuasive?

Obligingly, Mr. Butler (the independent oil company lobbyist) explains:

"These people (the legislators) don't get elected by accident simply on their own steam," he told this writer. "Hell, we give them contributions. We give them checks.

"The contributions," added Butler, "are made on the basis of a man's record."

When legislative investigators summed up their own and a grand jury's findings back in 1938, they said:

"Corruption is not necessarily bribery. The term is a general one suggesting loss of integrity — a taint. Instances of bribery encountered in the investigation were relatively few. . . . The principal source of corruption has been 'money pressure.' The principal methods of applying such pressure: fees paid to lawyer legislators and expenditures of lobbyists. The principal offender has been Arthur H. Samish. . . .

"As long as lobbying of the type and on the scale practiced by Mr. Samish is countenanced there will be corruption in the legislature. For he seeks to establish . . . a secretive 'fourth branch' of government — in effect a supergovernment overriding the legislative, executive and judicial branches."

How can California's people get their government back? Here are some ways to do it, say the political experts:

First, restore the two-party system and reestablish party responsibility by abolishing cross filing. Running as a party designee, a candidate will get his campaign funds from the party and be responsible to a party caucus. Even if this brings back the party boss, an admitted evil, at least he's in the open where you can get at him and turn him out on occasion.

Make candidates disclose the source of all campaign funds. (In California, lobbyists can contribute to a candidate's campaign "without his knowledge" and so, under existing law, he doesn't have to report it.)

Increase the legislators' salaries. When $5,000 has to be spent to win a $1,200-a-year job, that money is usually put up by someone who wants something. Once elected, on $1,200 a year, it's hard for a legislator to resist offers of legal fees, insurance and other business patronage with which lobbyists wheedle favors....

"How can the people get rid of you and others like you in California, Artie?" this writer asked Samish.

"There is one way," Artie replied. "The people must take more interest in the men they elect."

35

Lobbies and Pressure Groups: A Lobbyist's Point of View

By Gertrude L. Schermerhorn

MR. AVERAGE CITIZEN goes to the polls and votes for the person to whom he wishes to intrust the business of legislating for him in matters which affect almost every phase of his life. Mr. A. C. then goes on about his own business, and Mr. Legislator goes to the capital city to make the laws. It is left to the so-called "lobbyists" to follow that elected legislator to the legislative halls, watch his behavior, and report to the voter.

The voter sees his representative as a single individual in the home environment, or he sees him, especially in our larger cities, as part of a local political machine which operates like clock-work along a traditional line. The lobbyist sees him in an entirely different light. To her, he is, to be sure, an individual bringing with him all his traditions, prejudices, and personal ambitions; but he is to a greater extent a part of an organization almost entirely isolated from the outside world.

Gertrude L. Schermerhorn, "Lobbies and Pressure Groups: A Lobbyist's Point of View," *Annals of the American Academy of Political and Social Science*, January, 1938, pp. 88–94. Reprinted by permission of the publisher.

Party pressure

If the legislator is newly elected, he has no way of knowing what is ahead of him in actual experiences. He may make ever so many promises and have ever so many preconceived ideas about what he intends to do, but when he once steps into the legislative chambers, he is no longer a free agent. First of all, he becomes part of a political group by being seated on the side of the house designed for his party. This goes a long way toward making it easy for him to conform to the wishes of the party, and difficult and embarrassing for him to be independent. On his side of the house and in his midst sits the so-called "party whip," and the lash curls around the whole "pack" on that side of the room when a real party battle is on. He cannot hide; he is never overlooked when his vote is needed. If he is not in his seat, there is a vacant place in the party ranks and someone is sent to look for him.

Then there is the party caucus. That is where the legislator gets a real workout. It takes the courage of a Daniel to be independent in a caucus, and even more courage to be independent on a vote on which the caucus has agreed to take a party stand. If the legislator does not agree to go along in the caucus, his influence with his fellow party members is nil and he is handicapped in every piece of legislation in which he is personally interested. If, under pressure of the meeting and the influence of hearing only the one side presented, he agrees to go along, he has little chance of escaping when arguments presented to him afterwards are sufficiently convincing to make him want to change his mind. He is a traitor of the worst kind if he does not "go along" on a thing agreed to in caucus, although occasionally a legislator is excused from voting with the party if his vote is not needed and his political strength back home is involved.

The one consideration that has real weight with the party bosses in the legislature is the effect of the vote on chances for reëlection. If the legislator can show that there is mass demand for his vote in a certain direction, even though the party stand is in the opposite direction, he is usually permitted to vote according to the demands of his constituents.

This would be extremely encouraging to those interested in the democratic conduct of government if it were not equally possible for that same influence to come from one individual or one minority interest which holds the purse strings to the campaign funds back home. However, it is the former possibility that encourages citizens to be informed on legislative matters and to keep constantly in touch with their representatives on these matters, provided they have access to the necessary information. It is here that the lobbyist who has followed the man to the legislative halls and knows what is going on there becomes useful and necessary to Mr. Average Citizen.

Party responsibility

Usually it is this pressure from home that accounts for various degrees of liberalism and conservatism in the ranks of the same political party, though all have been elected on the same platform. Party platforms are vague and misleading as guarantees of what legislators will do. A governor is more conspicuous in his responsibilities as an individual, and he and his people are more conscious of the platform pledges; but a legislator can get lost in the mesh of some three thousand bills and can hide behind almost as many excuses, because of the intricacies of the legislative process and the ignorance of Mr. Average Citizen concerning them.

A few years ago when the trend started toward liberal legislation in my state, the party whose power was being challenged for the first time in many years came out on a liberal platform in the state and promised to pass most of the legislation which its leaders had been opposing for the last fifteen years. In the first two weeks of the session those senators introduced about a dozen bills identically the same as the ones they had defeated in previous sessions. Those bills then became known as the bills of that party introduced in fulfillment of party pledges.

One of the least controversial of those bills was the one to raise the age for the employment of children to sixteen and decrease the working hours of those under eighteen to an eight-hour day and a forty-four hour week. This bill was introduced on January 14 by a senator who could be relied on to follow party orders. It was reported on January 29 from the committee controlled by the same party, but was sent back to committee on February 4 by agreement by the action of senators of the same party. On April 30, fourteen weeks later, this bill was included in a long list of labor bills on which a public hearing was held, and finally, on May 15, with the end of the session in sight, the bill came out of the Senate Committee. On May 27 the same party leaders, with the consent of the sponsor, attempted to send the bill back again to committee, where it would have died. But through the efforts of the minority party and two or three independent liberals in the majority party, the bill was passed in the last week of the session, against the protests of the party leaders who helped write the platform which included that bill.

Pressure from constituents

This story illustrates what happened to the platform pledges of that party in so far as the conduct of the state legislators was concerned. It also serves to demonstrate how necessary it is that citizens do not drop their responsibility after election day is over, regardless of what issues may appear to have been decided at the polls. Issues are decided in the legislative halls, and the direct influence of the voter is needed there every minute of every day. By keeping in touch with constituents the lobbyist gives the public, through correspondence, speeches, and written articles to the local press, the information which it would not otherwise have. It is for this reason that a lobbyist should have back of her a well-organized group for contacts in as much of the state as possible, and effective channels for receiving news and getting action.

At one time we were interested in the passage of a bill for shorter hours for working women. The chairman of the committee considering the bill was favorable to it and wanted his committee to report it out for a vote. But he came to me in real concern. "I've had hundreds of letters against this bill and only these two in favor of it," he said, showing me what he had in his hands. "You'll have to get me letters from the women who want this legislation, especially those who will be affected by it, or I can't get it out."

There were thousands who wanted that bill and expected it to pass. They had voted the best way they knew at the polls, but they did not know in what way they could help their own cause at the legislature. We knew their leader and we told them that this was the moment when their letters and their visits to the legislators would do the most good. The letters came, and the bill was passed in the House. The chairman had the support he needed, and the legislators voted for the bill because there was a demand for it from the people.

Legislative blocs

When the legislator has passed through the fire of the party caucus and the party whip and felt the pressure of his constituents by personal contact when he is home over the week-end or between sessions, or by letters and telegrams and personal visits to him at the capitol, he has still other hurdles to jump. He may belong to a so-called "bloc" composed of members of like occupations or interests, such as a rural or farm bloc, an American Legion or other ultra patriotic influence, a religious or racial group, a labor or employer or special interest group, any of which will cut across party lines.

Lawyers will be expected to stand together on certain legislation affecting the legal profession; doctors are a unit on questions of health insurance when it is opposed by the organized medical profession; the rural vote goes against child labor legislation, joining with the manufacturers for fear that children on the farms will be affected, while it can usually be counted on to support laws prohibiting commercial or amusement enterprises on Sunday or prohibiting the sale and use of alcoholic beverages.

These last-named matters often put the city vote on the defensive and thus serve to consolidate the city vote as opposed to the rural vote, not necessarily because the rural legislators have better morals, but because the city depends on these activities for its business. On such questions as loyalty oaths and bills intended to curb the activities of radical groups, the wearers of buttons and emblems of patriotic organizations have their minds made up for them.

Of course, the best known of these blocs are the labor vote and the big business vote, which are sure to cut across lines of the two major parties, though at times one party or the other may find it politically expedient to take sides over a period of years.

How the machine works

During my first few years as a lobbyist, the majority party was closely allied with the organized employer and big business interests. The President of the Manufacturers Association was also one of the political bosses in the state where one party had held an exaggerated majority in both houses for many years. When the legislature was organized at the beginning of the session, it was the political bosses who sat around a table — not at the capitol, but in the city where the party machine was intrenched — and picked the chairmen of all important committees. These chairmen were naturally chosen on their record — sometimes their record for leadership in the interest of big business and the political machine, and sometimes for their lack of leadership, which made them dependable in their obedience to orders.

When all bargains were over and the committees were announced, the line-up held no surprises for the political observer. Those committees likely to handle labor bills were packed with members who followed the wishes of the Manufacturers Association and the State Chamber of Commerce, the former being more interested in labor legislation, and the latter in utilities and tax questions. Those committees likely to handle election law reform and local government reorganization bills were given to the party machine bosses.

The result was that, while the political boss who depended on the labor vote and the support of the common people in the congested city areas was naturally a good fellow who would gladly have supported "humanitarian" legislation, he was bound to oppose such legislation, because he needed the support of the big business bosses to defeat legislation designed to interfere with machine politics on elec-

tion day, such as bills for voting machines, for abolishing the poll tax for voters, and for permanent registration.

Therefore, when the doors opened on the session and the public was admitted and the daily record was published for the people to read, everything was set for operation of the machine behind the scenes.

The "invisible government"

This worked smoothly, because of the committee system. All bills are sent to an appropriate committee, upon introduction. Committee meetings are open to members only. Occasionally the chairman will permit a visitor when a particular bill is being discussed, or will hold a public hearing, but all final decisions are made in executive sessions held behind closed doors, and no public records are printed and no roll calls recorded.

The subcommittee is still further in the dark. While the names of the chairmen of all committees are on public record, subcommittees are appointed behind closed doors. A subcommittee seldom holds scheduled meetings. The chairman carries the bill around with him and he alone can report it for action, either in the committee as a whole or to the floor for vote. Constituents who are interested in such bills have no way of knowing about this subcommittee unless they can get their own legislator to find out for them, or a lobbyist informs them. The lobbyist must know when a bill is referred to a subcommittee and who are its members, and she must report this information to the districts represented by those members.

Penetrating the committee system

My early experience was almost exclusively with child labor bills. No improvements had been made in the state child labor law in fifteen years, in spite of the facts that more children were employed in industry in that state than in any other in the Union, and that all neighboring states had far higher standards. Other laws for the welfare of workers were in the same backward status, but the fight at first centered around child labor legislation. Progressive citizens were more easily aroused where children were concerned, and when public opinion really began to clamor for improvement and some gains seemed inevitable, the big business interests regarded child labor legislation as a symbol of the bigger enemy, labor legislation of all kinds.

Bills to improve the employment conditions for children were introduced and sent to some one of the controlled committees, and they never came out for a vote. Legislators were powerless to get their own bills out of committees controlled by the so-called "invisible government"; public hearings on bills were merely gestures. Friends of the bills spoke before committees which had previously made up their minds. The opponents seldom appeared, for they had been "back stage." A lobbyist was helpless to get information, and public opinion was not considered. There was a public opinion however, on this child labor question. There must be a way for it to penetrate the committee system!

It was then that we started to use the rule which was the key to locked committee doors. This rule provided for the discharge of committees from further consideration of bills. At first the motion to discharge was invariably lost, but that gave us a record vote on a motion which meant the life or death of a bill, and that vote was used by constituents at election time. Legislators who had always escaped doing any voting on child labor bills could campaign in the interests of "women and children"; but on the basis of their votes on discharging committees, they began to get a reputation in their districts for opposing good bills. This soon reduced the number of votes they received at the polls. Public opinion was beginning to work!

Over a period of about five years there was a complete change in the House, the legislative body closest to the people. The party in power, the party allied with the Manufacturers Association and the State Chamber of Commerce, lost its majority there, and the other major party came into power on a platform favoring all the social and labor legislation which the previous party had opposed. It was another two years before those interests lost their grip on the Senate, but finally the party which became increasingly callous to the popular public demand and increasingly brazen in its use of tricks to keep the control behind the scenes, entirely lost its grip on the state.

Working in the dark

In their final effort to defeat social legislation in the Senate, the leaders of the reactionary party used the subcommittee method to keep the public in the dark.

When the House passed the labor bills and they reached the Senate, they accumulated in great numbers in the appropriate Senate committee. We observed that no meetings were ever scheduled for this committee and that its chairman was continually absent. One day he was seen walking out of the capitol when a meeting was scheduled on the very bills for which we were holding him responsible. Finally we discovered that there was a subcommittee to which all those bills had been referred, and the chairman of the subcommittee was having everything

his own way. With this information we could tell the people who needed most to know that it was their senator who was responsible for what was happening to those bills. It so happened that the second man came from a district where he had no organized opposition, and very little could be done by the democratic process of influencing him through his constituents; but we let him know that we and the great public who wanted that legislation were holding him responsible.

In the case of the bill to shorten the working hours for women, this same senator, realizing the great public demand for something better than the fifty-four-hour week and ten-hour day which the state had, made a pretense of giving consideration to the measure by reporting it out of committee and then sending it back for amendments on four different occasions, until the end of the session was reached.

At the next election these reactionary senators were defeated on their own record.

Promoting legislation

A lobbyist occasionally plays as important a part in the passage of legislation as the members of the legislature. When the ratification of the so-called "lame duck" amendment to the United States Constitution was before our State legislature, neither party was interested in the measure, and it brought no particular advantage or disadvantage to any member or his constituents; but its passage meant a step forward in good government, and the League of Women Voters was interested in it.

The bill passed the Senate without opposition, and we expected easy passage in the House; but a week went by and nothing was heard of the bill. We investigated and found that the chairman of the committee to which the bill had been referred had been absent during the entire session, this being a short special session in the summer. This might have been the only bill referred to that committee, and the session would undoubtedly have adjourned without action on the "lame duck" amendment if we had not brought the matter to the attention of the Speaker. The Speaker quickly asked the next ranking member of the committee to call a meeting to act on the bill; it was reported immediately and passed without opposition, and the "lame duck" amendment was ratified in one more state.

Will democracy work?

The longer I worked in the legislative halls the more I was convinced that lobbyists of the right sort were needed. I felt a great responsibility, not so much for a single victory through having a particular bill passed, but for the whole democratic process which works only when constituents are informed on legislative matters and representatives of the people are responsive to the will of the majority.

Therein lies what I believe to be the twofold advantage of lobbying: by being constantly on the scene one can follow the course of a bill, watch the behavior of the legislators, record their votes and one's own conclusions, and report to the constituents; and by being oneself informed on the subject matter of the proposed legislation, and employing the simplest possible methods to instruct one's public as well as the legislators themselves, one can make it possible for constituents to let their representatives know what they want, and can assist those representatives at the capitol who want to follow the wishes of their constituents.

This is a work which requires lobbyists, at least in our present stage of the democratic process, for the average citizen either does not find time to be informed on those measures in which he is really vitally interested, or finds the legislative process too involved and the task of reading bills too burdensome for one inexperienced in legislative procedure. So let us keep our lobbyists when their methods are democratic, and let the public cease to blame legislators for all the failures in the legislative process. Let the people share this important responsibility of citizenship by performing their duties as constituents. We in the United States are engaged in a serious business — the business of making democracy work.

CHAPTER EIGHT

State Executives

GOVERNORS are acutely conscious of the discrepancy between what the public generally expects them to be able to do, as implied by the title of the office itself, and what is actually possible for a chief executive with quite circumscribed powers, surrounded by a number of other independently elected executive officers rather than by a cabinet. The potentialities and the limitations of the office are here discussed by Senator Desmond, with a plea for steps necessary to make the office that of a true chief executive. Professor Gove argues, however, that we have accepted ritualistically the demand of the reformers for strengthening the governor, without the case being proved. At least, he says, it should be evident that no single formula is equally applicable in all the states.

36

To Help Governors Govern

By Thomas C. Desmond

THE RISE of a growing crop of able young governors across the country has been a striking political phenomenon of recent years. They are in some cases ambitious, independent and better equipped for their offices than their predecessors — and a good thing, for their problems are bigger, too. Depression, wars and zooming population have combined to multiply the responsibilities of state governments.

Lord Bryce found in the Eighteen Eighties that our governors had little money to spend, little dignity, little power, and little to do. Today, however, governors preside over a middle layer of government that spends nearly $20 billion a year, helps support more than a million indigent elderly, operates huge mental hospitals, a vast system of prisons and bulg-

Thomas C. Desmond, "To Help Governors Govern," *New York Times Magazine,* June 2, 1957, pp. 14, 20, 22. Reprinted by permission of author and publisher.

ing universities, employs a million persons, including armies of inspectors and state troopers, minutely regulates big utilities and the corner grocer, constructs thousands of miles of highways, tollways and speedways, and pokes a well-meaning if often heavy hand into most social, economic, and psychological dislocations in the country.

The governor is expected to be a court of last resort for any one wronged in his state, referee between conflicting economic forces and chief social worker. He must be (or at least appear to be) a sage financial expert, and at the same time a kind of Roy Rogers chasing "the bad guys," whether they be "the insurance lobby" or "the public utilities" or "the corrupt opposition" or any other convenient scapegoat of the moment.

He is the symbol and conscience of the state. As such he must fulfill a role that calls upon him to visit the sick, the lonely, the aged, and to pat on the back an underpaid mental hospital attendant. He must be the state's chief tub-thumper, a one-man chamber of commerce, heralding the glories of his state's valleys, mountains, rivers, farmers, laborers, women, manufactures, and agricultural products. The Governor of Oregon, for example, last fall bet a native salmon against a hog wagered by the Governor of Iowa as to whose state university would win a football game. It's all in a chief executive's workday.

The heart of a governor's job lies in legislation. "More than half of my work as governor," said

Theodore Roosevelt, "was in the direction of getting needed and important legislation." Governors, through their power to approve or veto legislation and to call special sessions to deal with specific problems, are an integral part of the lawmaking process.

A governor must understand our check-and-balance system of government. A study has shown that one governor was able to get only 17 per cent of his bills through a hostile legislature, while in another state the governor was able to get 75 per cent of his program enacted by a friendly legislature.

Even for politically shrewd, veteran chief executives the task of dealing with traditionally balky, unpredictable, and sensitive legislatures and their politically wise legislative leaders is a critical challenge that can plunge a governor into political oblivion — or, sometimes, propel him into the national spotlight.

The governor also finds he must serve as party fund-raiser and patronage dispenser. He must buoy the morale of party committeemen in Squidunk and bring peace to warring intraparty factions in Squeedunk. More fundamentally, he learns that if he is truly to be effective as governor it is not enough to be governor. He must capture his own party's political machine . . . or else be forced to dicker, scrap, or submit to a party boss who is the real source of power and leadership.

While, up to recent times, many governors were boss-selected, boss-elected and boss-run, today more of them are running their parties and either openly or covertly are the "bosses". . . .

All this would seem to make the office of governor a potent — and, in some respects, a pleasurable — one. Certainly there is never any dearth of candidates for election and re-election. But once in office the winner quickly finds that our outdated state structure is perversely designed to make it harder, not easier, for him to play his many roles.

The problem is as acute for the people of each state as for their governor. Their first concern clearly is that he serve them well while he is in the State House. And they must ask themselves whether the office itself is equipped to handle the massive problems that confront our commonwealths today — problems like segregation, air and river pollution, port development, water shortages, and the need for huge school and hospital outlays.

At the eighth American Assembly, meeting at Harriman, New York, in 1955, outstanding students of state government agreed that we need governors "empowered to lead." Today, as the Kestnbaum Commission on Intergovernmental Relations, appointed by President Eisenhower and congressional leaders, has said: "Few states have an adequate executive branch headed by a governor who can be held accountable generally for executing and administering the laws of the states." Our chief executives are shackled with ancient but effective managerial handcuffs that would be intolerable in most private businesses.

For example, the typical governor is confronted with hordes of state commissions, boards and departments, although modern management principles decree that no executive should have more than eight to ten officials reporting directly to him. The Council of State Governments found in 1950 that the governor's "span of control" in Texas covered 124 agencies; in Ohio, 122; in Colorado, 140. The result is that most governors cannot keep a controlling finger on what is going on in their own state. The Council of State Governments concluded: "Most governors have a more difficult job than that of the President of the United States in giving effective managerial direction from the top."

The typical governor, however, receives for this massive task a take-home pay that would be sneered at by a Madison Avenue account executive — or even by some of the school superintendents in his own state. Salaries scale down sharply from the $50,000 a year, plus tax-free expense, paid New York's governor to a median take-home pay of about $10,000 for other chief executives. One recent governor, blessed with five children, complained to his fellow chief executives that his wife, in addition to her duties as First Lady, had to do the family cooking and washing.

To add to the chief executive's difficulties, many state agencies are headed by boards appointed to terms overlapping his own, or are designated by the legislature and are, therefore, quite independent of him. Thomas E. Dewey, when governor, summed up the feeling of many of his fellow governors, when he frankly said, "I get ten to twenty letters a day complaining about state boards and commissions over which I have no authority. I don't mind writing back that I have no control over them, but what galls me is that people don't believe me."

Al Smith, one of the really great practicing political scientists of the twentieth century, said in an age when problems were far simpler than those which confront our modern governors: "The man doesn't live who can understand the job in his first two years." Yet twenty-two states today restrict the governor to a two-year term and in many states he cannot succeed himself. What stockholder would invest in a private concern that limited its chief executive to a two-year, or even a four-year, hitch?

In some states, the people still elect not only their governor and lieutenant governor, but also the secretary of state, the attorney general, treasurer, auditor, tax commissioner, highway commissioner — and even the state printer in Kansas and Nevada, and collector of oyster revenues in Delaware! Many such elective officials, although nominally on the governor's "team," spend most of their time plotting to unseat him. "Seventy per cent of the governor's time," one chief executive has candidly confessed, "is spent picking the daggers out of his back each morning thrust there overnight by other ambitious elected state officials."

In many states the rivalry between the governor and lieutenant governor has become notorious. One governor in recent years did not dare leave his own state because he could not trust his lieutenant governor not to pardon a corps of prisoners; another was a virtual prisoner within his own state lines because he feared, if he took a trip outside, the acting governor would raid the treasury.

State constitutions commonly affirm that the "executive power" shall be vested in the governor, and then proceed to strip him of effective executive power over state agencies. Some measure of the frail powers of the governor is seen in the complaint of Frank Lausche, until recently governor of Ohio, about the inadequate power of governors to remove local officials. "The tragic situation exists," he says, "where lawless people in the community, working in consort with duly elected local officials, are able to laugh at the governor in his helplessness."

At the same time laggard laws give our governors petty pen-pushing jobs and clerical assignments. . . .

The modern governor is by no means helpless. He has three powerful tools with which he can sometimes overcome the handicaps thrust in the way of being a real chief executive: the force of public opinion, the executive budget and political patronage. He can go over the heads of opposing officials and reach the public through press, radio and TV; by marshaling public opinion he may be able to lead state agencies. He can use the power of assembling the state budget to keep warring departments in line. He can use his political patronage and influence to build up support.

But the need to resort to such methods merely emphasizes the central fact: election to a governorship does not earn a man the right to govern, only the right to struggle to govern.

Today we need to meet the challenges of our times with sufficient authority vested in our chief executives to enable them to serve us effectively. And we can do this without losing our liberties. We need to give our governors a sufficient administrative staff to relieve them of many of their minor duties. We need to finish the "short-ballot" campaign, begun so valiantly years ago, by chopping down the list of state-wide elective offices to two or three at most. The term of office should be long enough to enable the governor to learn his job well and serve the public expertly and earn the right to reelection. All boards and commissions need to be consolidated into a dozen agencies headed by appointees of the chief executive. We cannot rid the governors of all their problems, nor should we. But at least we can mold the office into a post better suited to the ever-increasing demands of modern times.

37

Why Strong Governors?

By Samuel K. Gove

THE IDEA THAT OUR GOVERNORS need to be strengthened, or at least that the office does, is hardly new. It has been an accepted tenet of "reformers" for many years.

It has been said that term limitations, the long ballot, earmarked funds, inadequate appointive powers, as well as other factors have operated to "shackle" the governor. The "nonreformers" might well argue that the civil service system, local government home rule and removing some governmental services (such as education) from politics have all worked to hinder the governor as head of state.

In trying to determine if our "weak" governors should be made "strong" we need to consider many hard questions. One of the first is, what are the consequences of strengthening the role of the governor? Will this mean that our unshackled governor will behave properly and use his newly won powers for the "public" good rather than for his own advantage or, worse still, for political advantage? Will the newly freed governor stay within bounds and not stray to such off-limit places as the university gates?

There are many other important questions with far reaching implications that we should consider before creating our new "strong" governor. Does the establishment of a strong governor suggest that we then must have a weak legislature? How can we have a strong legislature without impeding our strong governor? What assurance do we have that the individual who is elected to our reformed strong governor's office will be capable of governing? Does the establishment of a strong governor automatically assure that capable people will be elected to the office? In this connection, will the political system of a state

Samuel K. Gove, "Why Strong Governors?" *National Civic Review,* March, 1964, pp. 131–136. Reprinted by permission of the publisher.

automatically reform itself with the advent of the strong governor? Will the lobbies in the reformed state lie down and die as soon as they know they will have a strong governor to contend with?

We cannot, as has been the tendency in many circles, talk of a strong governor concept in the abstract, or in a vacuum. Maybe it would be easier if we could but unfortunately we have to contend with the real political world.

It is an obvious truism to say that the several states vary greatly and the greatest variations are found in the political systems of the states. As a result, for example, on a political basis we can hardly equate the governor of New York with the governor of Florida. Changing the structure of the governor's office in New York will not change the image of the New York governor as a potent force on the national political scene. The governor in New York, no matter who he is, what party he belongs to, or under what governmental structure he serves, will undoubtedly continue to speak out, and will be expected to, on national and international affairs. The governor of Florida, on the other hand, is not expected to play such a political role, and if he did speak out on national issues he probably would receive little attention outside his own state.

The Florida governor is handicapped, according to many observers in that state, by the unusual organization structure of that state's government, which includes a unique cabinet system. The Florida governor also is restricted by a one-term limit. But it is debatable whether a change from the cabinet system and one-term limitation would greatly change the Florida governor's role.

Many other examples as diverse as Florida and New York could be cited that raise questions about the wisdom of trying to implant a uniform governmental structure on all states and that indicate the great variations among states, especially in the political patterns or political cultures. Likewise, it is obvious that the role, and even the image, of the governor in each of the 50 states varies considerably. Should we then be aiming toward strengthening the office of governor in all states and making these offices identical in power and scope? Obviously this is unrealistic, and was well understood by the authors of the new *Model State Constitution*. In the first sentence of the introduction to the revised *Model,* the authors state that "strictly speaking there can be no such thing as a 'Model State Constitution' because there is no model state." If there is no model state, we can hardly talk about a model state governor. Each governor operates, and will continue to operate, in a distinct political world and, even within one of these worlds, governors, who after all are human beings, will operate quite differently.

We should not be trying to establish a strong governor in each state, for the case has not been made that the office of governor needs to be strengthened in each state. Perhaps, if we knew more in depth about the real world in which the governors of the fifty states live, we would be talking about weakening the office of governor in some states. This raises the point that, when we talk about the real world of state government in each of the 50 states, we are talking on the basis of some thin evidence, indeed. We can count the states which limit the term of governor, or the states with a statewide civil service system, but we know little more on a state-by-state basis. Even in regard to civil service systems, the existence of a statewide system is no assurance that the letter of the law or general intent of the law is being followed.

Let us now turn our attention to some of the organizational difficulties that have been said to hinder the development of strong governors. Probably the most obvious is the limitation found in several states of not permitting the governor to succeed himself in office. This limitation, it would seem, should make it difficult for a governor to get favorable responses for his programs from the legislature and the bureaucracy. Is this, in fact, the case? Are the governors under this limitation able to accomplish their programs by the development of public opinion or otherwise? If the legislature is not responsive, is this due to the one-term limitation or are there other causes? There are many other states, such as Massachusetts, where governors have trouble getting their legislative programs adopted. Massachusetts has no one-term limitation and one would guess that the governor's failures there have something to do with the political climate and the political divisions found in that state. In other states with a term limitation might the reason for a nonreceptive legislature be based on other factors such as a malapportioned legislature? All we can say is that we do not know much about the consequences of the term limitation. We do know that it makes it impossible for an incumbent to run on his record and to establish a record for that purpose. Probably most of us, using our intuition, would say the term limitation is undesirable, but are we on really tenable ground?

Another claimed handicap to effective gubernatorial control in some states, such as Massachusetts, is the existence of dominating legislatures. It is said that in these states the legislature in many ways ties the governor's hands and is unresponsive to his programs. Some of the states where there are remnants of a legislative budget illustrate this. Is the answer to this situation the strengthening of the office of governor while at the same time weakening the legislature? If we do make this change in balance of power, will there be adequate review of the governor's program? And is there an underlying assumption that "good" men will be elected to the office of governor? And, more realistically, are we having a semantic argument with ourselves when we talk about strong or weak governors and strong or weak legislatures?

The practice of earmarking tax revenue by either constitutional or statutory authority for specialized purposes has been said to be in some states a severe handicap to the effective administration of a state government. Is this valid? Probably in some states it is; in others it is not. In my own state, the legislature has somewhat reluctantly in recent years diverted road funds for other purposes. Earmarking is probably a more significant hindrance where there is a constitutional basis rather than a statutory basis, as is the Illinois case.

What about the long ballot? Does the existence of these separately elected officials tie the hands of the governor? We are told that these other elective officials diffuse responsibility. But in reality are these other officials so minor as to be only a slight hindrance? In some states the incumbents to these elective offices are returned to office without opposition year after year and, when a vacancy occurs, it is filled by appointment. In these states, the voter is not seriously inconvenienced by the long ballot at the state level. But for our purposes does the multiplicity of offices hinder the establishment of a strong governor? In Florida, the existence of the elected officials serving together as a cabinet, and with the governor having only one vote, establishes the potential for an intrusion on the executive power. Again, nationwide, there is a great deal we do not know about the consequences of the long ballot at the state level.

Another suggested hindrance to our strong governor is his limited appointive power. In some cases he faces a state government organization with agencies administered by departments with multi-headed bodies. Sometimes a majority of the members of these boards and commissions have been appointed by a predecessor and may be members of the party opposite to that of the governor. The single-headed agency is the ideal of most reformers but, when it comes to certain functions, they argue that this function needs to be kept out of politics and therefore the multi-member board or commission is justified. The reformers are in a dilemma, however, on which functions should be put "outside of politics" and which should not. Generally the regulatory agencies are under a multi-member commission but here there are many inconsistencies. In my own state, we feel that one man can regulate the banks and another the insurance companies but we need five to regulate public

utilities. In other states, the conservation people have "avoided" politics by creating commissions as their cover; elsewhere it is the public assistance programs which are cleansed in this manner.

Probably the functional area that has caused the most consternation in this regard is education, both secondary and higher. Almost unanimously we hear that this is one area that certainly must be outside politics — the intrusion of politics here will mean the "downfall" of our civilization. But, try as hard as we do, politics does seep into education and occasionally governors exert much influence in this costly and vital area. But should our conscientious governor whom we want to make stronger be excluded from participating in this vital budget consuming area? It seems a little inconsistent to argue that the governor should be strong, a real chief executive, but on the other hand he is not to stick his finger into this function or that.

If there is some inconsistency in prohibiting our strong governor from getting into nonpolitical affairs, the nonreformers would argue that the reformers have further weakened the governor's potential power by insisting on strong civil service systems and home rule for local government. Given the nature of civil service systems and the way they have been administered, it is not unexpected that governors feel that civil service generally ties their hands. The governors feel, sometimes justifiably and other times not, that they are unable to get rid of incompetents and that they are not able to hire persons loyal to them. These criticisms would, of course, vary depending on the details of a particular state's civil service system.

Home rule theoretically would mean that all functions of local governments are beyond the power and authority of the state government. If we really wanted to make a governor "strong," shouldn't we give him authority over these local bodies that in many cases spend state money and in other cases enforce state laws or at least state administrative regulations? Does not a governor have the right and the duty to see that state public health standards are met?

We simply do not know enough about the real world of state government. We know little pieces here and there but political scientists have not given us enough information on which to base our conclusions. In fact, the urging for a strong governor seems to be based on "these are the findings on which I base my facts." . . .

. . . what is needed is a major effort by political scientists across the country to learn about their office of governor and their state and local governments. When the evidence is in and they can accurately tell us how it is in the real political world of their state, this information can be turned over to the decision-makers—the legislators, the governors, public minded citizens, or others — and these decision-makers should be able to make more defensible recommendations than in the past.

Finally, we should declare a moratorium on suggestions for uniformly strengthening the governors until this evidence is in. We must keep an open mind until such evidence is in and realize that in some states we may even want to weaken the governor. In the meantime, perhaps we should stop concerning ourselves with structures of state government and start paying more attention to the substantive state problems.

CHAPTER NINE

State and Local Judicial Systems

IT IS AN UNFORTUNATE FACT that the weakest element in our judicial structure is the minor courts with which the average citizen is most likely to come in contact. On the basis of nation-wide personal investigations, Morton Sontheimer paints a dramatic picture, fortunately not universal, of the gross shortcomings of many of our local courts. A good number of states now boast local court systems with competent judges and adequate facilities, and there is steady, if slow, improvement. Progress demands an active citizen concern.

38

Our Reeking Halls of Justice

By Morton Sontheimer

THEY ARE CALLED — with more significance than intended — the inferior courts. To them, in each community, comes the ordinary citizen to seek protection, to look for justice.

In one of these municipal courts stands a man accused of assaulting his wife. This man is of doubtful mental condition and the court is considering a recommendation that he be sent to the Psychiatric Clinic for examination.

The defendant speaks: "I'm good to my wife and kids when I'm sober, Judge. I just can't seem to stop drinking. I want to, but I can't seem to."

"Do you know what I'm going to do to you?" asks the judge. The defendant lowers his head.

"I'm not just going to send you to the workhouse," His Honor resumes. "Over there they have a snake pit, deep and with slimy sides that you can't climb.

Morton Sontheimer, "Our Reeking Halls of Justice," *Collier's,* April 2, 1949, pp. 19, 75–77; April 9, 1949, pp. 28, 74–75. Reprinted by permission of the author and publisher.

I'm going to have them throw you in that snake pit!" The judge stands up and leans over the bench toward the defendant, then he runs wriggling fingers towards his own nostrils and over his face, and sneers:

"Those snakes will crawl in and out your nose! And your eyes! And ears! And mouth! I'm going to keep you there for six years! Bailiff, take him away! And be sure to mark 'Snake Pit' all over his papers!"

As the bailiff leads the prisoner out, the judge laughs. He turns to reporters and a social worker standing beside his bench and in open court, he says, "My God! Ain't that a hot one?"

This occurred in a domestic relations court, that keystone of social importance where disintegrating families first turn for help in a society that holds the family to be of sacred value. When I witnessed this scene in a Chicago court I couldn't comprehend how much of the judge's graphic oration on the defendant's fate might have resulted from his having seen too many movies or how much of it was actually true, although I knew that he had no power to sentence to six years.

After court, I asked a bailiff about this "snake pit" at the county jail.

"Aw, there's no such thing," the bailiff explained. "The judge was just having fun with that guy. What was actually written on his papers was 'Psychiatric Clinic,' that's all. The judge is always pulling stunts like that. You oughta hear him when he's got a non-support case before him. He tells 'em: 'I'm going to sentence you to the prison bakery to work and have them sew your lips shut so you'll know what it's like to be hungry.' And if they got no money for support he says: 'Take 'im down to the police pistol range. The police will use you for a target, then they can sell your body for $1,000 and give the money to your family.' These ignorant jerks believe him."

"Yeah," chimed in the bailiff who had led away the prisoner. "This last one almost collapsed on me before I could put him away for the Psychiatric."

When I told Chief Justice Edward S. Scheffler of Chicago Municipal Court of my findings, he deplored the fact that some unfit judges could discredit the whole municipal bench. Not long ago he was forced to admit that the Chicago municipal courts were a "legal cesspool."

Chief Justice Scheffler is a sincere official with a city-wide reputation for honesty, and he feels that the Chicago municipal courts generally have improved since he made that statement. That appears to be true. In fact, many cities have claimed an improvement in their lower courts of late years. This report is simply an attempt to show you what many of the courts are like today, after improvement. In doing so, it cannot dwell upon the few excellent lower courts and judges who need no criticism.

Hard as the good courts may strive, in cities like Chicago, their accomplishments are offset by incidents like that of the twenty-three-year-old girl who appeared in court with her four-year-old child. She told the judge that she had been engaged to a youth who had been drafted into the Army five years ago. A week before his final induction they became intimate, and the child holding her hand was the result. Now the youth was out of the Army and refused to marry her, she said.

During the hearing of her complaint, the judge sat with his feet on the bench, reading his morning mail. At this point, the child carefully scrubbed and neatly dressed, began to fidget in the strange surroundings and talk in a high piping voice. The judge put down his feet, leaned across the bench and shouted: "Tell the little b—— to shut up!"

The girl broke down. The case had to be continued.

Vile language from the bench is not exceptional. In women's court, particularly, some judges seem to revel in gutter talk, especially (as one of them put it) "talking to prostitutes in their own language."

One metropolitan judge used to take the names, addresses *and phone numbers* of pretty defendants who appeared before him. For "official reasons," of course.

From coast to coast, from the Canadian border to below the Mason and Dixon's line, I have sat in these courts and have come away feeling that, by and large, Justice needs not only a blindfold on her eyes but a clothespin on her nose to survive in their atmosphere. Yet, as Chief Justice Fred W. Vinson of the United States Supreme Court told me, these are the courts where the great mass of our people are likely to form their ideas of justice and democracy. For most people, the inferior courts are in actual practice the courts of last appeal — and last impression.

Let me describe a typical court. You approach it down a street lined with blatant signs advertising bail-bond brokers, attorneys, notaries public. You enter a battered building, pass a police booking desk, and a barred door, through which escapes the fetid odor of a city jail. As you climb creaking stairs to the second floor, you hear a babble of voices. It comes from a corridor teeming with people through whom you must thread your way to get to the court-room. Linger a while under the "No Loitering" signs. Push your hat on the back of your head and light a cigar so you don't look conspicuous.

Snatches of conversation will reveal the professional complexion of these busily conferring men — bail-bond runners, lawyers, a man who "just came from the Boss's office," another who "ain't worried — Jim says it's all taken care of." Occasionally, a pay-station phone bell pierces the clamor and a policeman answers it and bellows a name. Some of the lawyers use this corridor as their offices. Down the hall a steady stream of confident-looking men pass in and out of a door marked "Judge's Chambers. Private." There is much handshaking down the length of the corridor — and not all hands come away empty.

It is 10:00 A.M., the time that all the summonses, writs and subpoenas say people must be in court. The scene inside duplicates the animated scene in the corridors: hatted men, smoking and talking. Adorning the grimy plastered walls are three calendars, advertising respectively, a tailor, an insurance company and a funeral home. Behind the empty judge's seat is a dusty American flag.

The spectators' benches are filling up and the rear aisle is already crowded, so you slip into a seat. As time passes, the policemen, sitting in a row awaiting to appear as prosecuting witnesses, make loud jokes.

"What're you beefing about?" one of them says. "Can'tcha see the judge is too busy to open court?"

"I ain't beefing," is the reply. "I love to work all night and sit around here all day!"

The spectators join in the laughter at this.

Sometime between 10:20 and 10:40 a short-sleeved man with a badge on his vest, a bailiff, yells something unintelligible. Hats come off, cigarettes rain to the floor, and for a moment there is silence. The judge whisks out of his private door to the bench.

"Hey, you!" the bailiff growls at a laggard. "Take yer hat off!"

The first 30 cases are all drunkenness charges. Most of the defendants are "repeaters." The judge greets several by their first names. They are disposed of in 15 minutes — all guilty, some freed on suspended sentences, some sent to the workhouse. It is justice at the rate of two cases per minute.

Conversation and the milling about in the courtroom have picked up. The judge calls for order. "Tell those guys to shut up!" he shouts. Most of the noise, though, is being made by the bailiffs hollering for "order in court!" and by court attachés conferring with privileged characters who walk through the rail separating court officials and public.

Quiet is of little consequence, however. Even if there were complete silence, you could hear little of what is going on because most of the cases are conducted in the form of a football huddle around the judge's bench and disposed of inaudibly. The clerk and the prosecutor seem to be running the show. The judge frequently holds back-of-the-hand conferences with them, and every now and then an important-looking character walks around behind the bench, shakes hands with the judge and holds a long private conversation. But court business goes right on and the judge occasionally interrupts his conversation to pass sentence.

There is an attitude of vast impatience in the judge and all the court officials. The bailiff shoves defendants up to the bar, pulls witnesses into place. The clerk administers the oath as if it were a single word: "YousolomsweartelltruthholtruthnothbutruthselpyaGod?" The prosecutor continually interrupts witnesses and defendants, snarling, grimacing in disbelief, showing that he is human only in flashes of sarcastic humor: "Oh, so all you did was say 'yessir' to the lovely policeman?" If anyone besides court attachés snigger after such sallies, the bailiff growls for order.

A list of female names is called, and seven girls and two older women step up to the bar.

"This is that big call-house raid last night," the knowing fellow alongside you says.

Everyone strains forward. Even the judge pays attention. The vice-squad officer introduces a little black book in evidence, "names and addresses of the customers." The judge takes it, leafs through it noncommittally, announces, "Court recessed for 10 minutes," and strides into his chambers with the book. When he returns there is no book in evidence.

Invariably, in prostitution raids, there is "a little black book" entered as evidence, and almost as invariably it never appears in the record. One of the things "expected" of a police judge is to protect the names of "our better citizens" in prostitution cases. As a vote-getting device it's a sure thing.

The next case is a wizened little man and a young man with delicate features — homosexuals. Psychiatrists would tell you that these people, a growing problem in our courts, can often be cured or adjusted to society, but that they are likely to become a menace under the stigma of shame and ostracism. Penologists know jails are hotbeds of homosexuality.

But in city court, scorn is written over the face of every official, and the prosecutor cannot resist a small-boy urge to mimic the affected voice of the young prisoner. The judge gives them each a stiff jail sentence.

Gradually, the crowd has been thinning. The last case is an acquittal, but the judge does not seem satisfied with his own finding of "not guilty." He dismisses the defendant with the words: "Get out of here now, and stay out!"

It is five minutes to twelve. "Court adjourned!"

The fresh air outside makes you aware of the foulness you have breathed.

I have given a composite description — about average. I have witnessed worse courts, and better. Every character and every incident in this court is a repetition of what I have seen in others.

That a spectator cannot tell what is going on during these proceedings is obvious. Far worse is the fact that the average defendant, his freedom in jeopardy, is equally confused. He is hauled before the bar, addressed in legalistic jabberwocky, accused of a statute violation by number, interrupted when he tries to speak, seldom appraised of his rights, then sentenced, often without his understanding even the charge against him.

In Detroit, a Negro brought to court on a writ (not even a warrant) in an assault case, paid a shyster $250 to defend him. The writ was promptly dismissed, but the Negro understood so little of the proceedings that he did not know he was free, and was preparing to pay the lawyer's demand of another $250 for a "trial" that would never take place, when a reporter discovered the despicable swindle and intervened.

His Honor is usually tardy

Only twice during my two-and-a-half months' investigation did I see a court which opened on time. At the convenience of a tardy judge, I found witnesses, defendants, lawyers, police and the public sometimes kept waiting as long as four and a half hours before court convenes — then they must wait for their cases to be called.

Generally, though, city courts are only 20 to 30 minutes late in opening. They rush through their calendars, trying to finish by lunchtime. This gives the judge, who in most big cities is paid as a full-time public servant, the afternoon off to golf, fish, or mend his political fences. A study of St. Louis magistrates courts revealed that one "full-time" judge spent an average of from one to two hours a day in the Courts Building.

Small-town lower courts are frequently presided over by a justice of the peace who holds court only when it's necessary or convenient, often in a barbershop, business office or the judge's parlor. A California defendant in a traffic case discovered in the course of conversation with a justice of the peace that he had been tried, convicted and fined without realizing his trial had commenced.

Some municipalities demand that their judges inflict heavy fines, especially on out-of-towners — it swells the treasury, keeps taxes down. One Western town fired three judges in a year until it got one who handed out fines severe enough to balance the budget.

Fee system enriches J.P.'s

Instead of paying local justices of the peace a salary, some states permit them to pocket the court costs they assess. Not only does this encourage the notorious speed traps that swell the incomes of the justices of the peace, but it makes it next to impossible for a defendant to win a small-claims suit in these courts. For if the justice were to rule against the plaintiff, that gentleman might take his future "business" to some other justice.

"What our fellow citizens see and hear (and in some instances smell) in our police courts, our traffic courts and in proceedings before our justices of the peace quite naturally determines their idea of American Justice," says Chief Justice Arthur T. Vanderbilt of the New Jersey Supreme Court.

In our traffic courts the average citizen is more likely to see and hear bedlam compounded than the majesty of the law: smothered humanity spilling into the halls, the din of a political convention, bailiffs crying for order, clerks bawling out fines.

Much of this chaos and delay in the big-city traffic courts is the result of maladministration and inefficiency. What it amounts to is that the average person is judged, tried and sentenced by the traffic cop, because it is cheaper for him to pay his fine automatically to the Traffic Bureau than to plead not guilty and lose a day's income waiting around traffic court for a trial. Either that, or he gets his traffic summons fixed!

Recognizing these conditions, Justice Vanderbilt has written: "In many places traffic courts are in fact integral parts of the political rather than of the judicial system."

I sat in open traffic court in San Francisco for 30 minutes during which not a single case was called. The judge was too occupied with a procession of people whispering to him across the bench, turning in their summonses and walking away.

Of 45,000 traffic summonses handed out in Newark, New Jersey, in 1947, 15,000 were said to have been fixed.

New York City discovered that in a number of traffic cases marked "five dollars' fine" on the court records the defendants had actually paid much higher

sums — in most cases, to avoid waiting hours in court. Court attachés were suspected of pocketing the difference.

A questionnaire was sent to 1,000 Philadelphians whose cases were marked "dismissed" in traffic court. Of the 900 who answered, many blatantly replied, "I saw my committeeman." But 248 of them said they had paid. The only logical conclusion was that they had paid some fixer, probably a ward leader, who pocketed the money and arranged the dismissal.

Publicity-loving show-offs on the bench have become such a menace that in many courts, such as one I visited in Missouri, smart defense attorneys plead with reporters to leave the room during the hearing of their cases "so the judge won't throw the book at the prisoner to get his name in the papers." A Cincinnati judge justified this practice with the explanation: "It's like any other selling job. If people keep seeing your name in the paper, they recognize it on the ballot."

In every big city there seems to be at least one judge whose opinions from the bench have given him the reputation of "Jew hater" or "Negro hater" or both. Many times this latter prejudice takes an odd turn, as expressed by a municipal judge in a Western city to a Negro defendant in a knifing case: "I don't care how much you people cut each other up. There'll be fewer of you and that's okay with me!" So saying, he freed the prisoner.

Negro leaders are fighting this attitude because it turns dangerous criminals back on the Negro communities.

These are the courts where you may have to look for justice someday, where your liberty or your property may be at stake, where you could be sentenced to as long as three years in jail.

Oh, yes, *you*.

The fact that you are a respectable citizen and have never been in trouble carries no immunity. Fifty per cent of the people arrested each year are in custody for the first time. The average person becomes involved with the lower courts at least once in his lifetime.

Anyone may be a criminal

Don R. Sanson, Chief Adult Probation Officer of Los Angeles, says, "I don't know anybody who at sometime or other couldn't be convicted of what is generally considered a serious crime. The 11,000 adults handled by our department annually are a perfect cross section of the community, weighted only by the more congested areas."

At the same time, we must depend upon the lower courts for our protection against real criminals. Some of the gravest crimes in the statute books come before the lower courts first, and the lower courts can whitewash them or eliminate them.

Every mistake and misconduct of the lower courts may not mean a criminal's bullet in somebody's body, but at best it means money out of your pocket. The prostitutes routinely sentenced in these courts go back to prostitution, the alcoholics go back to alcohol, the gamblers never close shop even while paying their fines, and it all helps to pile up the cost of law enforcement which is already taxing Americans $6,000,000,000 a year.

The inferior courts are the people's perimeter in the battle against crime. The psychopath made sport of here may become a dangerous maniac, the sex offender treated with scorn instead of understanding may become the "fiend" of tomorrow's headlines, the petty thief introduced to this summary justice may become Public Enemy No. 1. In fact, they do.

Dillinger, Floyd, Bailey, the most dangerous killers of our times, were "graduated" from our lower courts.

In one of our big city police courts, an old Negro eccentric, a neighborhood character, circulates among the people, interrupting the proceedings now and then with a cry for order in the court. It amuses the judge, who has deputized him as a "special bailiff."

What struck me about this farce was not the bewilderment it caused people expecting serious-minded justice, but the fact that the poor addle-brained old Negro, in his broad dialect, was actually blurting out at ill-timed intervals:

Odor in the court!"

There was something in that idiotic cry that was symbolic of many of the lower courts I had visited across the nation. I don't mean the offensive smells I described, . . . that could be wiped out with a good scrubbing and ventilation. I mean the kind that are not so easy to obliterate, the sort of justice that is common fare in these courtrooms. In that same tribunal where the old zany held sway as unofficial court jester, for instance, a man with a bandage on his head and a charge of attempted burglary against him received a hearing. A hearing is supposed to be an examination of both sides of the story to determine whether an accused person should be held for trial and to inform him of his rights.

A plain-clothes policeman testified, "I saw this man acting suspiciously around ten o'clock at night and I chased him. I finally caught up with him and subdued him by hitting him over the head with my pistol." The charge was attempted burglary! The judge ordered the prisoner held without bail! As the officer started to lead him to jail, the man spoke for the first time:

"May I say something, Your Honor?"

"What?"

"I wasn't breaking any law, Your Honor. I have a good job. I don't have to steal. I was on my way home from a movie —"

The judge looked bored. The officer pulled the prisoner away to a cell.

"Odor in the court!" came the cry, once again, from the old eccentric, only by this time I wasn't sure either that he was eccentric or speaking in dialect. Even to his clouded wits must have come the realization that this man could have been innocent. But what may not have occurred to a mind that couldn't think straight was: This man, held without bail for "acting suspiciously at ten o'clock at night," could have been you or me!

That's one kind of odor in the court. The case we'll call Tommy Starcke's is another.

Tommy does break the law. He admits it. Nothing serious, you understand, but it's a nice racket and a fellow's gotta make a buck. Occasionally, though, Tommy gets arrested. When he does, the cops don't bother to put him in a cell, because a bondsman always appears to release him on bail within a few minutes.

Next day, outside court, a man with a brief case comes up to him and says, "You Tommy Starcke? I'm your lawyer. Just plead guilty and shut up." So when they call his name and read off a charge about violating Section Two-Oh-Something-or-Other, Tommy says, "Guilty," and shuts up. The judge, without even looking up, mumbles a fine, and maybe he adds "fine and costs suspended." If he doesn't add that, the lawyer says, "The defendant has a friend in court who has offered to pay his fine." A big man in a camel's-hair polo coat, who appears to be a friend of several people like Tommy, counts off the money to the clerk and says to Tommy, "Go on, scram back to the job now." And Tommy goes back to his illegal job.

That little scene, with different names or some slight variations, you could have witnessed for yourself in Cleveland, Cincinnati, Chicago, Philadelphia and many other large cities in America. But don't get the idea that that, too, could happen to you or me, unless, like Tommy, we should find ourselves working for a gambling syndicate.

There is a very strong odor in the court from gambling cases. According to the Chicago Crime Commission nine out of every ten cases that came to court in that city resulted in no punishment or penalty. No one in Cincinnati, not even the detective in charge of the gambling squad, could recall an instance of a bookmaker being sent to jail (although the law provides for it, of course). Checkups in several other cities revealed a similar pattern.

In the handling of gambling cases some judges find themselves caught up in a system reminiscent of the prohibition era, which demonstrated that it is difficult if not impossible to enforce an unpopular law. There are big profits in catering to a forbidden pastime and a large chunk of these profits is used to buy immunity from the law.

Gambling finances politics

Authorities generally agree that gambling is the foulest odor in our inferior courts and the greatest force for corrupting local law enforcement today. Gamblers have worked out a smooth system. In most of the cities, large and small, that I visited, the lower court judges are endorsed by the ward leaders. So when a gambler wants to open up, he takes care of the ward leader. In some cities, the gambling interests are the financial drive wheel of the whole political machine. Where this system works — and it's working in a lot of towns — the judge isn't likely to get tough with gambling cases, if he wants to remain in office.

"If the lower courts are corrupt or susceptible to partisan influence," writes William Bennett Munro in his book *Municipal Government and Administration,* "the underworld is quick to find it out; and by its whisperings carry to thousands of minds the impression that all tribunals of justice are purchasable or partisan. That is what has happened, with or without good reason, in many of the larger American cities."

How does the underworld find it out? One tip-off is a seemingly innocuous device called the "continuance." A continuance is simply a delay, holding a prisoner for further hearing. The prisoner is brought in and the judge says, quite officiously, "Case continued, one week." Nobody asked for the delay, neither the police nor the defendant; it just seems to be a matter of court routine. But the Pennsylvania Supreme Court has found that when a magistrate thus delays a case, for no good reason, it allows time for " 'the fixing' of cases between hearings, for the practice of extortion by police officers and others, and for the operation of sinister political influences."

When the whisperings issue from the corners of underworld mouths and the wise offender gets a continuance like that, he knows enough to hang around the corridor outside the courtroom until he finds out whom to see about a pay-off. The one to see is often a hanger-on, one of those mysterious fellows who holds no official position in the court but is frequently seen with the judge.

And what is the purchase price of justice in a corrupt court? It varies. Some idea may be gained, though, from the records of a recent grand jury. A man charged with shooting another man testified that a hanger-on had told him the case could be fixed up for $750, but, when the defendant didn't have that

much, the "fixer" finally accepted $250. And the gunman was freed in court.

Some of the odors in the lower courts are subtle and hard to detect because they are covered over with this perfume of legal jabberwocky, like "continuances," and "changes of disposition." In a change of disposition a magistrate may hand out a stiff sentence in open court and secretly change it to a lighter one later. This is not always done for the benefit of the defendant. The practice once brought a neat profit to somebody in a Chicago Court. Hundreds of dollars in fines were remitted, or canceled, after they had been paid. But investigators reported that the people who had paid the fines were never notified of the "change of disposition" and didn't get their money back. The city never got it either. Who did? That remains a question to this day.

Many judges find it convenient to dispose of certain cases in their chambers, before court officially opens. In a Middle Western city I visited, police waited in court all morning to testify against a prisoner, only to find that the judge had "taken care of" the case before he came on the bench.

These star chamber sessions don't always work to the advantage of the defendant, either. The American Civil Liberties Union reported that in a California town a man was tried in the secrecy of his jail cell and sentenced to 180 days for "disturbing the peace," a sentence that turned out to be 90 days beyond the maximum permitted by law. Court records failed to show that the man had been arraigned first or informed of his rights; they showed only that he had pleaded innocent.

The rights of the accused

"Disturbing the peace" is a loose charge. Almost anybody could be arrested for it at some time or other. Against such a possibility, it pays to know your rights. The Constitution and our state laws give you the right:

To get word to the outside when you are arrested.

To a prompt appearance in court, usually within 24 hours at most.

To know the charge against you, in language you can understand.

To engage an attorney and see him.

To a public hearing.

To be heard in court, and to plead not guilty or guilty.

To demand a jury trial.

To get another judge if the one hearing your case is prejudiced.

To be freed on bail while awaiting trial, except in the rarest instances.

Besides your rights, there are some practical tips not contained in the Constitution that every person who might be accused of a traffic violation, or "disturbing the peace" or "acting suspiciously" ought to know:

If you are innocent, don't let policemen grown suddenly friendly talk you into pleading guilty with promises that "you'll get off easier and avoid trouble." Some policemen have a habit of doing this. It improves their conviction record and saves them time in court.

Wear your best clothes to court. Appearance and financial status are not supposed to make any difference to a judge, but compare the treatment generally given the shabby defendant and the affluent-looking one!

Beware of lawyers who pick up cases around the courts and police stations. One citizen, charged with disorderly conduct, paid such a lawyer a $500 fee before he found out that the maximum fine with costs for that charge was only $110.

Investigating committees have recommended that defendants' rights be printed, posted and given to every prisoner. Although there may be some jails or lower courts where this is done, I have yet to see one.

However, in Los Angeles municipal courts, I did see judges and prosecutors carefully explaining to all defendants the charges against them, and informing them clearly of their rights. It was in keeping with the whole atmosphere of that city's municipal courts. Throughout the country there are good lower courts, conscientiously run and decently conducted, and Los Angeles is an outstanding example. Here the people themselves have provided that prerequisite of respected justice — decent courtrooms. They are clean and well kept. There is little complaint that the judges do not spend enough time in court.

In Cleveland, a municipal judge who had been criticized for not spending enough time in court waved his arm around his chambers, almost touching the four walls as he did so, and said to me, "Would you spend time here if you were a judge?" The dingy cubicle contained a tiny overflowing desk and two extra chairs, one a rickety rocker. The sun spotlighted in through a single unshaded window, itself in such disrepair that cold air blasted over the desk. The voters of Cleveland had just defeated a bond issue for new courthouse facilities.

Criminal code is inadequate

Los Angeles municipal judges are paid $12,500 a year. In some cities, like Philadelphia, the magistrates get $5,500 and are supposed to have no outside business. Yet Los Angeles is not satisfied with its municipal courts. Even the court officers admit that the courts are not giving the public the protection it deserves, because good courtrooms, good procedure and good judges are not the sole solution.

The best of judges must work within the framework of a criminal code so inadequate it led to the late Supreme Court Justice Oliver Wendell Holmes to question whether "half the criminal law does not do more harm than good?"

"Most of our sex laws, our treatment of prostitutes and of narcotic addicts, and certainly our handling of the problem of alcoholism, are examples of this," declares Edwin J. Lukas of the Society for the Prevention of Crime. "Our criminal code is 50 years behind science."

Los Angeles averages about 100,000 arrests a year for drunkenness. But records show that 37 per cent of these are repeaters. One had been arrested 280 times and spent most of the last 10 years in jail.

Don R. Sanson, Chief Adult Probation Officer of Los Angeles County, told me, "If we could just remove from our dockets the 500 most frequently arrested alcoholics, it would do more than anything else to clear the court calendars and allow time for fair justice for other cases."

New York City has taken a first step toward doing that with Bridge House, an institution to which the magistrates can send alcoholics to be cured rather than futilely punished. The courts of that city have also set up a specialized council to treat intelligently the growing problem of homosexuality.

In all the lower courts, time is the enemy of justice. Though approximately six per cent of our population passes through them every year, judges have little time for the individual. Modern courts are learning to use probation officers and the social agencies to help with this job. But even in the progressive courts of Los Angeles, Detroit and New York, the probation departments are understaffed or inadequately equipped.

Untrained probation workers

Good probation departments can cut down crime by scientifically sifting the hopefuls from the hopeless in the court line-ups and salvaging those who can be restored to decent citizenship. This is highly skilled work, calling for special training and social-work experience. And in most of our cities, probation officers, like clerks, bailiffs and other employees of the courts, are outright political appointees, their only qualification being "pull."

Even the ranking employer of the court, the judge himself, is not required to have any scientific training in the field of crime. Professor Sheldon Glueck, Harvard's noted criminologist, recommends special courses for all criminal courts justices.

Standing outside the courtroom of a notoriously incapable, semi-illiterate judge, I heard a reporter say, "If the people who elected him would only take the trouble to visit this court once, he'd never hold office another term."

When I asked Chief Justice Edward S. Scheffler of the Chicago municipal courts how the people could elect, and re-elect judges who degrade the lower courts, he replied, "I don't think the people do. I don't think the people, as a whole, bother to vote for judges."

That is the key to the ward leaders' control of the lower courts. That is why, in many cities, the judges they endorse are automatically elected or appointed, regardless of honesty or ability. But it works both ways. Asked how he accounted for the higher quality of justice in Los Angeles courts, Presiding Judge Leo Freund said, "Our people take a great interest in our municipal courts."

There is very little wrong with the lower courts that a few thousand interested voters couldn't cure in each community. But municipal judges' names trail at the end of the ballot, and the average voter doesn't know anything about them. Few public organizations try to inform him, and when they do, he often disregards it as too trivial. One municipal judge was re-elected after he was openly charged with having business connections with a notorious mobster.

In the last election in Missouri, an election board forgot to include the judges' names on the ballot, and none of the voters noticed it until the election was half over. In California the voters elected as justice of the peace a man who had died before the election.

Various schemes have been tried to break the corrupt politicians' grip on the lower courts — the non-partisan ballot, appointment of judges, and a combination of appointment with voters' approval. Wherever there has been public apathy, all of them have failed.

Every authority and every observer, every honest judge and every grafter I talked to in this investigation came around to the same statement:

"The people usually get just what they want in the way of justice."

Is your city's court giving the sort of justice you'd want?

Trial by a jury of one's peers in criminal cases is a traditional right in English and American law, a right highly prized in the days of the founding of this country. In recent years the operation of the jury system in practice has given rise to a great deal of sharp criticism, coupled with varied recommendations for reform and even occasional suggestions of outright abolition of the system. In the following two selections the merits and demerits are expertly aired through the pens of two well qualified observers, Jerome Frank, late judge of the U.S. Circuit Court of Appeals for the Second Circuit, and Louis E. Goodman, judge of the Federal District Court for the Northern District of California.

39

Something's Wrong With Our Jury System

By Jerome Frank

IF A SURGEON were to call in 12 men untrained in surgery, give them an hour's talk on the instruments "used in appendectomies, and then let them remove a patient's appendix, we would be appalled." Yet similar operations on men's legal rights are performed every day by juries, amateurs entrusted with the use of legal rules which lawyers and judges understand only after long special training.

No sensible business outfit would decide on the competence and honesty of a prospective executive by seeking the judgment of 12 men and women, taken from a group selected almost at random — and from which all those had been weeded out who might have special qualifications for deciding the question. Yet juries chosen in this way are given the job of ascertaining facts on which depend a man's property, his reputation, his very life.

That man may be you, for no one is immune from lawsuits. Your landlord may sue you on your lease. Someone may assert in court that you broke your contract to sell him your house. The driver whose car you bumped one Sunday afternoon may bring an action against you for a broken leg. You may be charged with falsifying your income-tax return or violating the antitrust laws. If any such case is tried before a jury, the decision will depend on that jury's verdict. The way jury trials are conducted is, then, pretty serious business for every one of us.

Thomas Jefferson described juries as "the best of all safeguards for the person, the property and the reputation of every individual." His words have been so often repeated that the man in the street regards it as gospel that no better form of trial could be imagined. Many of our lawyers and judges feel the same way.

Increasingly, however, in recent years, eminent members of the bench and bar have expressed a contrary opinion. One of our wisest judges, Learned Hand of the United States Court of Appeals, said he was "by no means enamored of jury trials, at

Jerome Frank, "Something's Wrong With Our Jury System," *Collier's*, December 9, 1950, pp. 28–29, 64, 66. Reprinted by permission of the author and publisher.

least in civil cases." He also said of such trials: "As a litigant, I should dread a lawsuit beyond almost anything short of sickness and death." The late Supreme Court Justice Oliver Wendell Holmes said he had "not found juries especially inspired for the discovery of truth," and the late Chief Justice William Howard Taft believed that civil-jury trials should be abolished.

A well-known jurist warned me that if I published such views I would expose myself to severe criticism. But I think those views are justified and that the public should learn that the jury system is by no means all it's cracked up to be.

This conclusion stems from reflection on the methods jurors often use to arrive at their verdicts. For there is a world of difference between the theory and practice of jury trials.

At the beginning of a trial every juror takes an oath, as a public official, that he will "well and truly try the matters in issue and a true verdict render according to the law and the evidence." After the evidence and the lawyers' arguments have been heard, the judge addresses — or "charges" — the jurors. He describes the "law" — the legal rules — which, he says, must govern their verdict. He instructs them that it is their sworn duty to apply those legal rules, whether or not they like them, to the facts they "find"; that their "finding" of the facts must be based entirely on the evidence they have heard during the trial, and not on any personal knowledge; and that they must dismiss from their minds all bias for or against either party to the suit, and act fairly and impartially.

Inside story of verdict isn't told

The jurors then retire to the jury room for secret deliberations. If they agree on the result, they come back to the courtroom and report their verdict. They are not required to, nor do they, give any explanation whatever of this verdict. What went on in their secret session, whether they acted in accordance with their oaths and with the judge's instructions — this the judge very seldom learns.

But it is known, through later interviews with jurors, that juries frequently pay no heed to what the judge tells them to do. In many a civil trial the jurors decided for one side or another on the flip of a coin. In one instance the jurors agreed to draw a number between 1 and 100, the decision to be that of the juror whose age came closest to the number he drew. Then, too, there are cases in which one of the jurors who disagreed with the others surrendered his honest judgment because he mistakenly thought he had to go along with the majority, or because the other jurors threatened him, or because he was anxious to go home.

Of course not all juries behave this way. But there is reason to believe that if full reports were made on all jury deliberations, public confidence in jury trials would be badly shaken.

In his 1932 book, *Convicting the Innocent,* Edwin Borchard, Yale law professor, revealed an alarming number of cases in which innocent men were convicted in jury trials — several of them for murdering persons who were later found to be still alive. He noted that when a sensational crime occurs the jury often succumbs to the public demand for a scapegoat.

Since Borchard's book there have been many other such demonstrated tragedies. In 1938, a New York jury found Bertram Campbell guilty of passing forged checks. In 1946, after Campbell had spent eight years in jail, another man confessed to the crime. The court then vacated Campbell's conviction. The state of New York awarded him $115,000 for the wrong it had done him. But he died three months later. In Colorado, Loren Hanby, after serving six years of a life sentence for murder, was found innocent and pardoned in 1946. Only last June, in New Jersey, Clifford T. Shephard received the governor's pardon as an innocent man after he had already completed his sentence of 18 months for forgery.

If there have been such mistaken verdicts in criminal cases, it is most unlikely that similar mistakes have not often happened in civil cases. A wrong decision in a civil case may also spell tragedy. When, through a jury's mistake, a man loses his savings, his business or his job, then his life may also be ruined.

In some criminal cases, like Campbell's, the mistakes were subsequently uncovered, and the innocent victims released from jail. But we can by no means be sure that all such blunders have been uncovered and rectified. Maybe — although I doubt it — all those mistakes would have been made just the same by judges deciding in juryless cases. Maybe they were made by jurors who acted conscientiously. But no one knows. Some of these tragedies may well have resulted from dicebox verdicts or from other irrational and improper methods used by jurors. On the other hand, similar cases may have led to the acquittal of many guilty men.

You may ask: Won't judges do their best to discover whether the jurors have decided by lot or flipping a coin, or by otherwise disregarding the trial evidence or the legal rules? Won't most such verdicts be overturned? The answer, unfortunately, is no.

What courts prefer not to know

For the truth is that, in general, the courts don't want to know, and won't permit themselves to learn, how juries reach their verdicts. Most courts have this amazing rule: After a jury has reported its verdict and been discharged, the judge is ordinarily not allowed to listen to jurors who offer to swear that in the jury room the members of the panel had not complied with their oaths — although usually only by such testimony can jury-room misconduct be learned. In one typical case, after a Negro had been convicted of a crime, a Negro juror wanted to testify that he had voted for conviction because the 11 white jurors had intimidated him. The court said that, were this true, of course the conviction would be vacated. But it also said that this fact could not be proved by his testimony — the only method of proof available.

The courts give this reason for this rule: If a judge were allowed to consider such revelations by jurors after a case was over, then jurors might be subjected to improper pressures by the losing party to upset the verdict — and, under those pressures, the jurors might lie about what had occurred during their deliberations. That is an unconvincing reason: Jurors are not more likely than other men to testify falsely.

Some judges have given a different reason. If, said Judge Learned Hand, the courts were actually to apply the test "that every juror has been entirely without bias, and has based his vote solely upon evidence he has heard in court," it "is doubtful whether more than one in a hundred verdicts would stand such a test." No one knows, of course, whether that percentage is precisely correct. But it does seem that many courts are unwilling to inquire closely into this skeleton in our legal closet because of an apprehension that the disclosures would cause the collapse of the jury system — as it now operates.

We ought, however, not to blame jurors if they do not always behave as they are supposed to, since the duties imposed upon them are often impossible to discharge. For one thing, jurors are supposed to discard all sympathy, passion or prejudice. But do trial lawyers generally aim to pick jurors capable of acting impartially? Look at any one of a large number of books by reputable trial lawyers, books designed to be read by other lawyers, not nonlawyers. There you will find the lawyer advised that in many types of cases, he should seek the sort of juror who "will most naturally respond to an emotional appeal," and that, as the jurors' "judgment is more easily deceived" when their "passions are aroused," the lawyer has an obligation to make the best use of that weakness in his client's interest.

Lawyers misuse acting talent

Prominent trial lawyers boast of "hypnotizing" juries. They regard themselves as master actors before audiences of 12 each. Since such are the acknowledged aims and beliefs of lawyers who daily deal with juries, it is folly to think that most jurors

will be able to decide solely on the basis of the evidence. The jury lawyers, however, should not be censured for the methods they use. Most of those methods are the natural accompaniments of trial by jury.

Some lawyers maintain that since jurymen in their own daily out-of-court affairs, reach many decisions about facts after listening to other persons, they are admirably equipped similarly to find facts in the courtroom. This is a slimsy argument. Not only are the issues of fact in some trials of an unusually complicated character — involving intricate details of engineering, chemistry, physics, medicine or accounting — but the surroundings in any jury trial differ greatly from those in which the jurors conduct their own affairs.

No juror is able to withdraw to his own room or office for individual reflection. After the judge instructs them, the jurors are cooped up in the jury room and urged to come to a joint decision in a few hours — scarcely a good atmosphere for conscientious deliberation. It is well known that sheer fatigue often plays its part in coercing a reluctant minority, or the desire to escape bickering and to get home. Even 12 able judges, conferring together in such circumstances, could not function effectively.

Another large obstacle with which jurors have to contend takes the form of "exclusionary" rules of evidence. Those rules bar the jury from hearing an immense amount of important testimony without which, often, no one — no matter how competent — could possibly get near the true facts of the case.

One such rule is that which, in jury trials, excludes "hearsay" — so-called "secondhand" evidence, based not on a witness' own direct observation but on what someone else saw and told him.

Hearsay, to be sure, should always be cautiously used. But on its use depends 90 per cent of the world's work out of court. Much of the data utilized in making decisions by businessmen, government officials, legislatures and commanders of armies consists of such secondhand evidence. Yet we cut juries off from it — because we don't trust them to handle it wisely. And since, frequently, hearsay constitutes the sole available evidence of a crucial fact, the hearsay rule may leave a litigant without any proof of that fact.

A third well-nigh impossible task we ask of jurors is to perform prodigious feats of memory. Often the judge and the lawyers, trained listeners, forget just what a witness had said on the stand a day or two earlier; and when a judge tries a long nonjury case, before rendering his decision, he reads over a typewritten record of the testimony he has heard. But we pretend that jurors, given no transcript, and usually not allowed to take notes, will recall the evidence even in a trial lasting several weeks.

To make matters worse, not until all the evidence has been heard does the judge (by his instructions) let the jurors know the issues; that is, just what facts they are to look for.

In a trial there are many dull but significant stretches, with little lively interest for the jury. With no training in listening to testimony, the jurors' minds wander. I've often seen jurors actually asleep when some important witness was testifying. All lawyers know that a witness' demeanor — his tone of voice, gestures, use of his eyes — may furnish the most valuable clues to the reliability of his testimony. An inattentive juror will miss many such clues.

The legal rules with which jurors are entrusted as they go into their jury-room deliberations are yet another factor in making a juror's lot a difficult one. Do we or don't we want jurors to apply these rules which the judge's instructions and the jurors' oaths say they must apply? Some legal minds say yes, others no.

A Bar Association report

Even a committee of the American Bar Association took a yes-and-no attitude on the issue. In a 1946 report it argued on the one hand that jurors should be told that, as "sworn officers of a court" they must "let the law prevail" without regard to their "likes or dislikes." Yet that same committee report also said that "the jury often stands as a bulwark between an individual . . . and an unreasonable law." Many distinguished lawyers have proclaimed it the glory of the jury system that, thanks to jury-room secrecy, juries can and do defy any law they deem undesirable and, instead, apply secret laws the jurors choose to make.

Yet you can't possibly square this notion of juries as secret lawmakers with the idea that, in the courts, a law should not mean one thing for one man on one day and something wholly different for another man the next. If each jury may apply different rules from those on the books, then each jury is a small, ephemeral legislature which may make an unpublished law for each particular case — surely a most undemocratic method of lawmaking.

In truth, jurors often fail to apply a rule enunciated by the judge not because they dislike it but because they pay no attention to it. They don't dislike the rule, which may be an excellent one. They dislike the defendant's lawyer, or they are sorry for the plaintiff — a poor widow or a beautiful brunette with soulful eyes. Or they are prejudiced against the defendant's chief witness, an old man who speaks broken English. I know of one case where a woman juror voted for the plaintiff because his lawyer kept his papers in a "nice neat stack."

Even more often, a jury disregards a legal rule because it just can't understand its niceties. For most legal rules contain legal words and phrases that through decades have acquired subtle shades of meaning. Even the relatively uncomplicated rules include such terms as "proximate cause," "willfully," "malicious," "good faith" — and about the legal significance of those, and other legal terms, hundreds of lawyers' treatises and court opinions have been written.

The judge's law lecture

Since, as law-school examinations show, many second-year law students cannot fully comprehend the legal subtleties, it is ridiculous to suppose that they will be intelligible to jurors through the judge's brief law lecture to them. So the judge's charge to the jury about those rules is frequently a futile ritual.

The rise and fall of the jury's reputation is an interesting story. England was the home of the modern jury trial. Thence it was imported into the American colonies. With the colonists, juries became immensely popular because they resisted the Royalist judges who were regarded as oppressors. As a result, our state constitutions required jury trials in all cases which had been so tried at English common law.

From England, jury trials in criminal cases spread to almost all civilized countries. But in the twentieth century the jury's popularity markedly declined. Pre-Hitler Germany gave it up; so did some Swiss cantons; France grew increasingly critical. Most significant, England — before the advent of the . . . Socialist regime — virtually abandoned the jury except in major criminal suits, and of such suits relatively few are now tried by jury. More and more English litigants, dissatisfied with the incompetence of juries, came to prefer trials by judges. Canada has seen much the same development.

Since in none of the democracies, other than ours, today the jury is held in high esteem, it cannot be considered as an essential part of democratic government.

Every year in our own country thousands of civil cases are tried in which trial by jury is neither required nor permitted. For example, if John Doe sues a private company because he was injured by one of the firm's trucks, he may have a jury trial. But he may not have one if the truck was owned and operated by the United States government. So, also, there can be no jury trials in many suits in admiralty (as, for instance, suits for heavy property losses when ships collide), and in many other types of cases, such as those seeking accountings by trustees, or injunctions, or usually when the suit is against the estate of a dead man or of a bankrupt.

If the jury is an indispensable bulwark of legal rights, as its admirers claim it is, then surely it is absurd and unjust to deny such a trial in the above-mentioned cases, for ordinarily they are fully as important as — often more important than — the civil cases where a jury can be demanded. Nevertheless, even the most devout jury worshipers do not suggest that we should cut out most of those judge trials; and they never explain why the judges should be trusted in those cases and not in all others.

Any visitor to the courts can see for himself the striking difference between a jury trial and a judge trial. A trial by jury is full of melodrama. The lawyers put on an act. In a juryless trial, the histrionics, the stagy tensions, the constant appeals to the emotions and the aroma of the prize ring vanish. The judge and the lawyers speak the same language; the judge, unlike the jury, is accustomed to court-room ways.

Any able, well-trained trial judge understands the legal rules better than the wisest juror; he also has far more experience and skill in getting at the facts, in seeing through the lawyers' tricks of the trade, in detecting the lies of a "coached" witness, and in perceiving that an honest but timid witness, heckled by a lawyer, may give the appearance of speaking falsely.

Judges are human, therefore, fallible. No judge trial will ever be perfect. A skilled judge, however, has learned to discount and control his worst prejudices.

A few judges may perhaps be biased, bigoted or stupid; a very few may be, alas, corrupt. Indeed, I think that escape from decisions by unfit trial judges is the only good reason for trial by jury. But making all allowances for unfit judges, still no one would think of saying of decisions in judge trials the equivalent of what Judge Learned Hand said of jury verdicts — that probably not more than one per cent would stand up if tested by whether the jurors fully discharged their supposed duties.

Moreover, reformation of the bench is possible. We can get rid of the very few dishonest judges, and we can see to it that virtually all trial judges have a high degree of competence — by special training for trial judging and by providing that no lawyer may be eligible for the post of trial judge who has not passed stiff oral and written examinations. Nothing can be done to provide jurors possessed of anything like the same competence. For jurors are amateurs, and adequate judging is a job for professionals.

An increasing number of American lawyers and judges wish that we would abandon all jury trials in civil cases. If we do, it might be well to have suits tried before a bench of three judges, so that the possible biases of each judge will tend to be modified.

Because of our traditions, almost no American lawyer would deprive a man accused of a crime — particularly a major crime — of the right to be tried by a jury if he so wishes. Some lawyers, however — I am one of them — do not share the belief that a jury will invariably be more merciful than a judge to a defendant in such a plight.

At any rate, the accused should be told that, if he so desires, he need not go to trial before a jury, but may "waive" the right, as he is permitted to do in many states. He should always know — as today he often does not know because ordinarily his lawyer doesn't tell him — what he may be up against if he chooses a jury trial: that the jury may ignore the evidence, may be dominated by passion, or may decide the case by drawing lots.

Two states lead the way

In the federal courts the country over, juries still try more than 50 per cent of criminal cases; much the same is true in many states. But in Maryland, for more than 30 years, criminal trials by jury very often have been waived; in 1949, only 118 out of a total of 7,754 criminal cases in Baltimore were tried by jury. The story in Connecticut is much the same. Apparently in those states the lawyers and their clients have come to trust their judges. Perhaps before long the rest of the country will catch up with Maryland and Connecticut.

In civil suits, everywhere in America, "waiver" of jury trials is on the increase. But many such suits are still jury-tried (in the federal courts, about one third). And inasmuch as our constitutions require such trials, if requested in certain types of cases, and since many years will certainly elapse before those constitutional provisions could be wiped out by amendments, we must count on the continued use of juries for a long period. We ought, therefore, to consider reforms of the jury system to purge it of its greatest evils; the worst of these evils stems from verdicts which cover up what the jurors did and tell nothing of what facts — if any — the jurors found. Sometimes, however, some courts use another less opaque kind of verdict, a fact verdict, called a "special verdict": The judge requires the jury merely to report for instance, whether Jones phoned Smith on June 5, 1948, or whether the signature on Brown's deed to his house is genuine. To facts thus specifically found the judge, not the jury, then applies the appropriate legal rules; the jurors need neither understand nor apply them. And because the jury may be unable to figure out whether its answers will favor one side or the other, the appeal to the jurors' prejudices sometimes may be far less effective. But the special verdict, at best, is no panacea, for it still leaves to the jury the difficult task of getting at the facts.

Whether or not the judge uses a special verdict, he ought to be obliged at the trial's opening to give the jurors a tentative rough outline of the issues, so that, while listening to the evidence, they may know what facts to look for. There also is every reason why, to aid their memory, the jurors should be permitted to take with them into the jury room a written transcript of the evidence and of the judge's charge.

One helpful device is now too rarely employed: When some of the facts of a case are complex, the judge refers them to an expert; the expert's report is presented to the jury — although they are not obliged to accept it.

At one time, in England and in some of our own states, jurors were selected because of their peculiar knowledge of the customs of a particular trade in which the parties to the suit were engaged. "Special juries" of that kind, often far more skillful in finding facts than the usual jury, might well again be employed.

Reforms in selection of prospective jurors have thus far been rather feeble. Certainly, we should test each juror's eyesight and hearing before he enters the jury box. In some cities no one can obtain a license to drive a car who hasn't passed a psychiatric test; because deciding court cases is at least as serious as driving through traffic, we ought similarly to screen prospective jurymen.

Aptitude tests for jurors

In a widely approved statement, the late Merrill Otis, federal district judge in Missouri, said a few years ago that serious injustices are bound to happen unless all jurors have the "capacity quickly to comprehend the applicable law and intelligently to apply it." He also said that no more than one man in ten possesses that capacity. To restrict juries to such unusual men, he proposed this method: Enact some very generally worded high standards for jury service, and take care of choosing the officials who select those citizens eligible to become jurors. Some states have adopted that method and have obtained somewhat more competent juries. But it's unbelievable that any such simple expedient will give us jurymen able quickly to understand and to apply complicated legal rules. A Los Angeles practice has more merit: A prospective juror must meet oral and written aptitude tests.

But those tests can hit the high spots only. A more helpful proposal is that of barring from jury service any person who has not attended and passed a detailed course, to be given in the public high schools, on the function of the jury and the nature of jury trials. (I won't guarantee the constitutionality of such a plan.) With better-equipped jurors, we could well afford to eliminate most of the "exclusionary"

evidence rules, especially the rule which bars "hearsay."

Everyone knows it's wrong for an outsider to talk to a juror about a case while it is on trial. Yet, during an important criminal trial, newsmen and radio commentators in effect insinuate themselves into each juror's home to comment on the defendant's guilt or innocence.

Another source of prejudice

Since it is all but impossible to suppose that jurors won't read the papers and listen to the radio, such discussions, which may gravely prejudice the jury for or against the defendant, add seriously to the difficulties of trial by jury, as United States Supreme Court Justice Robert Jackson said in a speech some months ago. The English courts forbid and punish such publications. (The English press did not comment on the . . . case of Klaus Fuchs, the atomic-secrets spy, until it ended.)

The United States Supreme Court has held that almost no such publications during a judge trial may be punished, but has left open the question as it applies to jury trials. Some lawyers, who think that a judge should know how to and have the courage to withstand pressures, hope the Supreme Court will recognize that jurors are more susceptible. Perhaps, as an alternative, our editors and news commentators, if made aware of the gravity of the problem, will exercise self-restraint.

To sum up, here are the reforms I think would improve our jury system:

(1) Use "special" or "fact" verdicts in most cases.

(2) Have the judge, at the trial's beginning, roughly outline the issues for the jurors.

(3) Let the jurors take with them to the jury room a transcript of the evidence and of the judge's charge.

(4) Supply the jury with an expert's report of complicated facts.

(5) Employ, in many cases, "special juries" composed of jurors having knowledge of the customs of the trade involved.

(6) Strictly enforce the ban against jurors who have defective hearing or eyesight or who are physically or mentally ill.

(7) Require all prospective jurors to take a detailed course of study dealing with the function of juries.

(8) Eliminate many of the "exclusionary" evidence rules.

(9) Discourage publication, in the press or on the air, of anything but straight reporting of the courtroom evidence in a jury trial, until the case ends.

Although trial by jury can be improved, in my opinion it will remain the weakest spot in our judicial system — reform it as we may. But the judges (like me) who want to see the civil jury abolished and the use of the criminal jury limited, will, of course, as long as the jury system endures, comply with their oaths of office and strive to make the jury system work as best it can.

40

In Defense of Our Jury System

By Louis E. Goodman

A NEW PLAGUE is upon us here in America. The "efficiency expert" wants experts to take the place of juries in our administration of justice. He wants motorists to decide accident cases, physicians to decide malpractice cases, accountants to decide tax cases, engineers to decide engineering cases, chemists to decide chemical cases, real-estate experts to decide lease cases, and so on.

One of the exponents of this dismal philosophy is no less eminent a figure than Federal Appellate Judge Jerome Frank of New York. In *Collier's* on December 9, 1950, in an article entitled "Something's Wrong With Our Jury System," he asserts in effect that jurors are incompetent, moronic, corrupt and sleepy, that they are no longer an essential part of our democratic government, and should be abolished in most cases.

The appellate judge usually has the last word. This is a most fortuitous opportunity for a trial judge to reverse the process.

Critics of our jury system, like Judge Frank, cite or write books or scenarios about cases of mistake or misfeasances committed by jurors, and then conclude that juries are not competent and should be done away with. It is true that some highly placed judges have or have had this view. But I have not heard of a competent trial judge of experience who has expressed such a belief. It is not too difficult to understand this difference of viewpoint. High appellate judges mostly see only the written record of appealed cases. These records are cold and inanimate. From them it is almost impossible to see the picture and the story of what happens in the trial courtroom. This view is confirmed by my own experience in

Louis E. Goodman, "In Defense of Our Jury System," *Collier's,* April 21, 1951, pp. 24–25, 45, 48. Reprinted by permission of the author and publisher.

sitting, by assignment, in many sessions of the Court of Appeals.

The actual practical functioning of trial jurors cannot be adequately learned from appellate records or legal articles, or hearsay or from plays or moving pictures. In my opinion, it takes long-continued contact with juries in the trial court to qualify a jury critic.

It must be remembered that juries sit in trial courts and not in appellate courts. Practically, what does a lawyer or trial judge learn about juries? A trial judge sits in most courtrooms within 10 feet of the jury. The lawyers sit almost as close. What happens in a courtroom in the selection and functioning of a jury?

The judge questions those who are not excused from serving, as do the lawyers in many courts, concerning their qualifications to serve in a particular case. Day in and day out, year in and year out, the trial judge hears the views jurors may have on social or economic problems, what they think about law-enforcement officers or taxes or insurance companies, and even judges and lawyers. And so as time passes, the judge begins to get a firsthand knowledge and understanding of the people who make up the jury panels, their likes, their dislikes, their weaknesses, their strong points, their capacity to be fair.

The judge observes the impact, upon the 12 people who sit as jurors, of the testimony of witnesses, of the attitudes and habits of lawyers. He observes that some jurors are nervous or restless and others are calm and relaxed, that some are comfortable and others uncomfortable. He learns to perceive the effect of the atmosphere of the courtroom on the jurors. The judge learns that recesses should be declared often so the jurors may not become overtired.

Questions for the trial judge

Even after the case has been submitted to the jury and they have retired to deliberate, the judge's contact with the jury does not end. The jurors frequently call on the judge during their deliberations. They want to know about the exhibits. They want clarification of some instruction. They want advice on the materiality or immateriality of evidence or documents or exhibits. These queries in themselves are illuminating indices of the kind of people who are on the jury. Thirty-six years of continuous jury experience, as lawyer and trial judge, have taught me and other judges like me many things about the workings of trial juries.

I wonder whether critics like Judge Frank, either as lawyers or judges, have had this kind of experience.

I hope that my friends on appellate courts, like Judge Frank, will not consider me impudent if I say that no one is truly qualified to speak in generalities about juries unless he has actually had day-by-day contact with juries.

The critics seem to be of the opinion that jurors are not experts or specialists and that an untrained mind has no business rendering decisions. If we take Judge Frank's argument seriously, we must accept his analogy that the mind of the juror is similar to the untrained mind of a layman who might be called upon to perform a complicated surgical operation. But this analogy is fallacious. It is predicated upon the false premise that 12 people taken at random from different walks of life have no sense at all.

We use about 1,200 jurors a year in our court. Perhaps well over a million citizens serve on juries in all the courts of the United States each year. If we accept Judge Frank's premise, we must assume that a million American citizens doing jury service each year have no sense at all. The fact that a layman cannot perform a surgical operation does not mean he cannot decide a question of fact, that he cannot use his common sense and decide who is telling the truth.

Judge Frank makes the bald statement that in "many" civil trials the jury decides for one side or the other on the flip of a coin. I am curious as to how and where such evidence was obtained. In 36 years, no such case has come to my attention. Judges and lawyers to whom I have talked have had no such knowledge. I have read or heard of such cases, though no proof has to my knowledge been offered, and there may well have been such instances, but the sweeping statement that this happens in "many" cases does not appear to be justified without having the kind of evidence upon which both trial and appellate judges should act.

Judge Frank also says that juries "frequently" pay no heed to what the judge tells them to do. I believe that this does happen in a few cases, but I venture to be skeptical as to whether or not there is any basis in fact for the flat statement that juries frequently follow such a course.

Of course, as Judge Frank says, it sometimes happens that juries have convicted innocent people. Books like *Convicting the Innocent* makes good popular reading. They have great human interest. *Causes célèbres* result in great crusades. The dramas involved reach the playhouse and the screen. But such cases do not prove we are engaged in the daily enterprise of convicting innocent people.

Bad decisions can be corrected

All this sort of argument, and the citing of picturesque instances, proves is that human beings make mistakes. In equally important issues of life and death and in civil and property-right matters, judges make mistakes. If the trial judge makes a mistake, the appellate judges can correct the mistake and reverse the judgment. Sometimes, if the question is important enough, the Supreme Court may intercede and make its own decision.

It must not be overlooked that the verdict of the jury is not final. It may be reviewed by the trial judge; it can be set aside by him. In like manner it can be reviewed and set aside by the higher court. This is part and parcel of the system of checks and balances which is inherent in our constitutional form of government. It applies to jurors just as much as it applies to the executive, administrative or legislative departments. No judge of integrity or conscience will let an unjust verdict stand.

The mistakes the jurors may make are in no different category than mistakes that may be made by the legislators, executives or administrators or professional men or organizations which equally with juries, may vitally affect the life and security of the individual citizen.

Thousands of criminal jury cases are tried every year in the United States. Since they are decided by human beings, we should expect some mistakes.

Judge Frank makes the comment, "I've often seen jurors actually sleep when some important witness was testifying." That means, I take it, that it was almost a regular event in whatever cases Judge Frank participated, in a trial court, for a juryman to fall asleep while important witnesses were testifying. I have never seen this occur. I have observed, on rare occasions, some juror fall asleep during the course of a long routine presentation or because of a hot, humid courtroom atmosphere.

Again, I wonder whether this statement is based upon actual investigation or whether it was made for dramatic value. I seem to remember that on one or two occasions, when I was practicing, an appellate judge nodded and appeared to be in the arms of Morpheus during a long and extended argument. It would hardly follow from this that the institution of appellate judges should be abolished.

The critics, like Judge Frank, say that only experts in a particular field can do justice.

Is there any reasonable certainty of accomplishing justice by having experts rather than juries pass judgment in the ordinary civil disputes? My experience leads me to the conclusion that we would get much less justice.

M.D.'s disagreed on X-ray plate

I have seen experts disputing with one another on the witness stand in innumerable cases. In one case, an X-ray plate was submitted in evidence. There was a line on it. One expert doctor said emphatically it was a fracture. On the other side, a doctor said with equal emphasis that it was a blemish in the film.

Picture the chaos if such experts, each with perhaps a different background, experience and viewpoint, were to pass judgment! At least a jury has the opportunity of determining which doctor's testimony is the more credible.

Medical experts are influenced by partisanship, just as are litigants. Not so long ago a physician appeared in several cases on behalf of employees who had been injured in railroad accidents. His testimony was always most favorable to the employees. Some six months later, I was astonished to find this same physician testifying on behalf of a railroad and on this occasion his testimony was most unfavorable to the employees.

I recall a case in which the government was condemning some land which the owner claimed to be very valuable because of alleged oil and gas deposits. An expert testified the property had a fabulous value. In my opinion he was grossly and fraudulently overvaluing the property, and I so told the jury. Individual members of the jury told me later that they had the same opinion. Is it wise to allow experts, who may have preconceived notions, by reason of prior associations and affiliations, to pass final judgment?

In one case, the court was called upon to determine the value of legal services rendered by an attorney for a client who had sued a corporation. Another attorney, whose background was that of counsel for big corporations, testified as an expert and he greatly minimized the value of the legal services rendered. Would he have given the same kind of testimony if it were the attorney for the corporation who was seeking to have his fee fixed?

There are experts willing to say that almost every defendant charged with crime is suffering from some kind of psychosis or mental infirmity which should relieve him of responsibility for his crimes. What would happen if these experts were the judges?

The examining staff of the United States Patent Office is a highly trained group of experts with continuous daily experience in deciding questions of fact. They have passed upon and issued millions of patents. They have scientific library of over 37,000 books and 44,000 bound volumes of scientific periodicals; they have the official journals of the Patent Office and over 6,000,000 copies of foreign patents. Yet their decisions as patent experts are constantly being reversed by courts of the United States!

Too many experts on one jury

What of the cases in which questions of medicine and engineering and traffic are all present in one case? I suppose in such cases (and there are thousands of them) there should be four doctors, four engineers and four traffic experts on the jury. What a terrifying scheme for administering justice!

A real-estate agent suing for his commission, who would be content to rest his cause in the hands of 12 real-estate brokers, should consult a psychiatrist. I have never heard of a lawyer who would be willing to submit the cause of his client to a jury of 12 lawyers.

It is not unfair to say as to experts — whether judges, doctors or engineers — that their interests, their ambitions, their pleasures, their passions and their frailties influence them sufficiently to make them, as has been aptly said, ". . . idols with eyes, ears and mouths."

I do not mean that experts should be eliminated or that they do not have a proper function to perform. I do not mean to say that they do not perform a proper function as witnesses. But, in the long run, it is better to have the truth determined not by experts, but by juries made up of a cross section of the citizens.

We have a legal test which we apply in determining whether a person is guilty of negligence. We say that a person is negligent if he fails to do what an *ordinarily* prudent person would do under the same circumstances. Our standard is based on the precautions which ordinary people take. It is not a standard fixed by scientific experts. And that is fair and just, for people do not perform their daily tasks with experts at their side. And so it is right that ordinary people should be the judges as to whether such standards have been observed.

My years of experience have increased my faith in my fellow men who serve as jurors. They have not increased my faith in experts. I say this even though I might be labeled by the jury critics as a "devout jury worshiper."

The instinct of our democratic society is wise in providing that into our judgments in our system of justice, as Chesterton has said, "there shall upon every occasion be infused fresh blood and fresh thoughts from the streets."

Judge Peter Shields, now retired, was the dean of trial judges in the West, having served almost 50 years on the trial bench in Sacramento, California. This beloved jurist, out of the wisdom of his experience, told me that the common sense of citizen juries accomplishes more just results than all the cold scientific intellects combined could bring about. You cannot, in seeking justice, he said, apply the expert's slide rule to run-of-the-mill human controversies.

I have had occasion to talk with many trial judges and trial lawyers of long experience. They, as well as I, have a firm conviction that juries in 90 to 95 per cent of cases come to just conclusions. Of course in some cases, jurors may reach the wrong result or be too generous or too niggardly in money awards. But those of us who have daily contact with juries rarely see a case where jurors are indifferent to their responsibilities or are corrupt.

Who would do the job better?

Certainly no more so than judges. And indeed certainly no more so than executives or administrators or legislators. They have no more than their share of the frailties or prejudices or indifferences that human beings on the average have in America. These averages may vary in different parts of the United States; they may vary in different states; they may vary between urban and rural communities. But, in the over-all picture, jurors have no more infirmities as jurors than any other class or group which may be entrusted with the power of making decisions.

It has been my experience, in an overwhelming number of cases in which jury verdicts have been set aside or reversed, that the errors have been the errors of the judge and not the jury. The number of cases in which a verdict is set aside by the trial judge or reversed by the appellate court for mistakes on the part of the jurors is nothing in comparison to the cases in which decisions are reversed because of mistakes by the judge in instructing the jurors or in ruling on evidence during the trial.

The records of the Ninth Circuit Court of Appeals, which has jurisdiction in the Western states, Alaska and Hawaii, do not, in the years since I have been on the bench, record a single case in which the court of appeals has reversed a lower court-trial verdict because of any actual misfeasance or misconduct on the part of a trial jury.

Placing the blame for errors

The mistakes that occur are not due to the fact that 12 laymen are jurors, but lie in the manner in which the jury system is administered by those who have it in charge or review its functions. It is completely erroneous to place the blame for mistakes in jury trials upon the doorsteps of the 12 people who make up the panel.

During my years as a lawyer and trial judge I have been much more concerned about the errors of judges who stray from the facts than I have been appalled by unfairness of jurors.

It is not fair to charge the jurors with inconsistency when judges themselves are most guilty in that regard. How frequently judges reverse themselves! Recently Mr. Justice Jackson of the United States Supreme Court repudiated an opinion which he himself had signed when he was Attorney General. It was a magnificent confession of error by the Justice when he said, "Precedent, however, is not lacking for ways by which a judge may secede from a prior opinion that has proven untenable and perhaps misled others."

Do we not almost monthly see the spectacle of the Justices of the United States Supreme Court disagreeing with one another and with their predecessors and changing the very law which they or their predecessors have laid down?

To say that 12 laymen are unfit to sit in most cases and resolve issues of fact is to say that a cross section of the American people is in the main made up of morons and weaklings. I know of no better statement on the subject than that made by the late Merrill Otis, United States District Judge of the Western District of Missouri: "In the last 12 years I have worked with a thousand juries and out of that experience I say to you tonight, and I mean it every word, that he who says or intimates or contends for that which necessarily implies that American juries, intelligently constituted, are made up of moral and mental weaklings, that man greatly slanders better men than himself."

Judge Frank's conclusion that the jury system is no longer an essential part of democratic government is most astonishing. Because pre-Hitler Germany, or France or Switzerland, and, more latterly, England, has abandoned, in whole or in part, jury trials, is no reason at all to assume that it should no longer be considered an essential part of our democratic government. The fact that democracy may have become weaker in those countries is no reason for us supinely to throw in the sponge and quit.

Judge Frank says that Maryland and Connecticut lead the way as states which have very few juries in criminal cases. In Baltimore, he says, only 118 out of 7,754 criminal cases in 1949 were tried by jury. This, he implies, means that juries are being abandoned. These figures mean very little. For in a huge percentage of criminal cases, defendants plead guilty and many minor offenses are tried by the judge. In our court, in 1950, out of 617 criminal defendants, only 21 were tried by jury. But 570 *pleaded guilty* and 26 were tried by a judge! Statistics are often a trap for the unwary. The important thing about such statistics is now *how many* cases are involved, but *what kind* of cases they are.

To say that 12 citizens are not competent to decide questions of fact in court is tantamount to saying that they are not competent to vote for sheriff, or mayor or governor or legislative representative.

What does a citizen decide when he has to choose between two candidates for President? He has to decide a question of fact. It bears upon the safety, security, health, well-being and prosperity of all the people of the country. Is not that just as important a question of fact as whether or not Smith is liable to Jones because he ran into him in his automobile? If these arguments are carried to their logical conclusions, perhaps the President of the United States should be elected by experts!

Thomas Jefferson, when he wrote the Declaration of Independence, and in it declared that life, liberty and happiness were God-given rights, certainly did not have in mind that the protection and preservation of these rights should be left solely to the decision of any so-called experts.

It should be the citizens' decision as to whether the life, liberty or happiness of any other individual should be abrogated or curtailed. Therein lies the core of democracy.

The critics of the jury system are unmindful of its historic basis. Jury trial did not come into being because of the desire to have an efficient scientific system of adjudicating controversies between men. The institution of the jury came into existence, as has been said, as a "living bulwark of the laws."

The jury can be an effective weapon against government efforts to restrict the liberties of the people. A classic case occurred when the press was given new freedom in 1735 by the jury which acquitted the newspaper editor John Peter Zenger of the charge of libeling the governor of the colony of New York. That jury refused to follow the instructions of the English judges that truth was no defense for a person who had published criticisms of the government.

Respect for law increased

The citizen's participation as a juror in the administration of justice has unquestionably spread among all classes a respect for decisions of the law. "Each man in judging his neighbor thinks that he may be also judged in his turn," said William Forsyth, the renowned English man of letters. Even in Athens of old, the virtue of jury decision lay in the fact that jury service made the citizen in a degree responsible for the purity of court proceedings. Alexis de Tocqueville very aptly has said that the jury is a political institution because it actually places the direction of society in the hands of the people. It is truly a political institution grafted into the process of justice because the jury is a segment of the community. As such it represents the people.

Today, as in the past, the jury system may be criticized for its lack of sureness. It has not been a perfect instrumentality for justice. No more so is the administration of the government of the country as entrusted to the administrative or executive or legislative departments of the government. We might attain, of course, greater efficiency if one man, without restriction, were to make all orders and decrees affecting our lives. But we would have to sacrifice liberty.

It is true that many improvements are needed in the administration of the jury system. Better techniques in selecting jury panels are necessary. We need better methods of training jurors and in the procedure of instructing jurors. More careful screening of potential jurors to eliminate the unfit is undoubtedly needed. Progress is being made in these

directions. We aim to have much more. But reformations are also needed in other phases of our administration of justice. Before us always is the warning that to make justice work, eternal vigilance and constant and intelligent effort are essential.

I say: Hold fast to the jury system. It is of the essence of democracy. It is a symbol of freedom. To abolish it is a step toward totalitarianism.

One of the most serious problems in the achievement of the American ideal of equal justice is the financial one. The length and complexity of many cases today may easily put them beyond the financial ability of most persons, yet without the expenditure they will be unlikely to have adequate defense. The situation is dramatically portrayed in an article by Allen Murray Myers, a member of the New York Bar, who makes a vigorous plea for the widespread adoption of the public defender system, with the facilities of the public defender's office available to defendants who are able to hire their own attorneys but unable to handle the costs of extensive investigations, transcripts, witness expenses, etc.

Still another crucial issue involves the role of the press in criminal trials and the extent to which extensive publicity and prejudicial comment may make a fair trial impossible. This problem of reconciling freedom of the press and the rights of persons accused of crime is discussed here by the chief London correspondent and former Washington correspondent of the New York Times.

41

Could You Afford a Fair Trial?

*By Allen Murray Myers
as told to A. E. Hotchner*

I AM A LAWYER with an average practice. Ordinary citizens — like you who are reading this article — come to me for help when they get into trouble.

Allen Murray Myers (as told to A. E. Hotchner), "Could You Afford a Fair Trial?", reprinted from *This Week* Magazine, Nov. 28, 1954, pp. 7, 27, 29. Copyright 1954 by the United Newspapers Magazine Corporation. Reprinted by permission of the authors and publisher.

Some of these people are accused of committing crimes. You may think that being accused of a crime is something that could never happen to you — but it can. Crimes that range from not reporting all your income to manslaughter and murder are charged against ordinary citizens every day. In some cases, I become convinced that these people are innocent; but innocent or not, this is the point I want to make:

If you are accused of a crime in the U.S. today, you probably could not afford adequately to defend yourself. Even though you can hire the best of lawyers, this may be a minor financial item in a trial that often requires detectives, experts, out-of-town witnesses and other expensive participants. We must all of us face this staggering truth: criminal justice in the United States today has priced itself beyond the reach of the average man.

Now I know that this is a serious charge to make, but in the seventeen years I have practiced law I have watched, with growing concern, the unbalancing of the scales of justice. Federal Judge Harold Medina said recently:

"There are few defendants who can afford today's criminal trials. Even though a defendant is found not guilty he may be ruined financially by the cost of a trial. And his reputation may be so impaired that he can't retrieve his fortune. The Constitution guarantees every one the right to counsel, but that's not enough without providing transcript of the trial, witness fees, fees for experts and all other expenses."

Nothing for defense

My point then, is this: through our taxes, we have set up vast, expensive machinery for getting convictions — prosecuting attorneys with large staffs, entire police and detective forces, the FBI and other federal investigative agencies, costly crime laboratories — and this is as it should be, for crime detection is difficult. But while we have been steadily strengthening the prosecutor's office, most places do not provide one cent to help the poor accused persons.

What help they do provide is limited to penniless persons for whom the court's Legal Aid Society provides a free lawyer. For example, in 1953 Manhattan spent $1,165,287 of its taxpayers' money to operate the District Attorney's office, but no money at all is provided for the defense of those who are accused, except in the case of first-degree murder. In the course of this article I am going to tell you how taxpayers can purchase "criminal accusation insurance" for less than 25 cents a year.

Not many people know how difficult and expensive it is to defend yourself. Let's say you are suddenly arrested on a charge of having left the scene of an accident after you have struck a pedestrian. Your defense is that you were not aware that you had struck any one, or perhaps you maintain that it was not your car at all — mistaken identity. I would estimate that a proper defense in a trial of this nature, plus attorney fees, would run between $2,000 and $5,000 depending on the circumstances. You can see what this would do to your finances. When murder is the charge involved, the cost of a defendant's trial can run as high as $10,000.

Perhaps you can recall the recent case of the man who was indicted for the murder of his wife. His trial cost him $10,000; he was found guilty. It cost him $5,000 to appeal that verdict; a new trial was granted. The new trial cost another $10,000; again he was found guilty and again he appealed — for another $5,000. This time on appeal he was set free. Total cost of proving himself innocent — $30,000.

To illustrate why a defense is often so costly, I can cite a case I tried very recently that involved a woman who was accused of murdering her husband. Her alibi was that she was on a bus going from New York to her home town at the time her husband was murdered. But how to prove this at the trial?

Her bus ticket had been surrendered. It would be necessary to hire detectives who would go out of the state and locate the bus driver, other passengers, taxi drivers, ticket sellers, redcaps or any one else who might remember the woman. And then, if located, they would have to be brought to New York and put up in a hotel with all expenses paid, including whatever salary they were losing for missing work.

I estimated that $1,640 was needed for this phase of the defense alone. The woman could not possibly afford such expense so the search was never made.

But if the prosecutor, with his vast resources, wanted to locate such witnesses, how quickly it could be accomplished!

The Pfeffer case

One of the most dramatic of recent cases is the one that involved the fate of a young man named Paul Pfeffer. Penniless, and with a previous prison record, Pfeffer had been quickly convicted of the murder of a sailor named Edward Bates. He had protested his innocence, claimed that he had been with his girl at the time the murder was committed and maintained that a confession he had given police had been beaten out of him. However, he had no funds with which to hire detectives to substantiate his alibi, and as a result he got twenty years to life.

Ten months later a murderer-rapist named John Roche stated that he had killed the sailor, and he gave details to the police on how he had beat him with a length of pipe and then thrown the pipe in a clump of bushes. The most amazing aspect of the case was that at this juncture the District Attorney who had convicted Pfeffer announced that he was not satisfied that Roche's statement was true. As far as he was concerned, Pfeffer would stay in prison. It took a newspaper to break the case open by locating the pipe and pressuring for justice until Pfeffer was finally released. . . .

Examiner's error

In another recent case, a young man discovered the nude, strangled body of his girl friend when he went to her apartment on a Sunday night. In panic, he fled the apartment and the body was not discovered until Monday noon.

He had an ironclad alibi for Friday, Saturday and most of Sunday — he had been on a hunting trip with friends — but the medical examiner was inexperienced and estimated the time of death as Sunday night instead of Friday night when it actually occurred. The accused had a lawyer but he could not afford to hire medico-legal experts who could have examined the body and proved that the death had occurred on Friday night.

He was convicted and it was only a fluke development, after he had spent four years in prison, that led to the discovery that the girl had in fact been killed on Friday night.

And how many prisoners there are in this country who have never been able to appeal the verdict against them because they did not have the relatively large amount of money which a defendant must pay in order to get a transcript of the trial. Every man supposedly has the Constitutional right to appeal to a higher court, but a higher court cannot consider the appeal unless it has an official record of all the testimony of the trial. Such a transcript usually costs between $750 and $1,000.

Although the police supposedly undertake an impartial investigation of the facts in each case, they actually only look for that evidence which will convict. We are now duty bound to create machinery that will help those who are accused. On the basis of my own experience and that of many other attorneys and jurists, this solution is offered:

1. Establish in every major city in the United States, which does not now have one, the office of Public Defender to provide legal counsel for the completely indigent. This office would parallel that of the Prosecuting Attorney, but it must be emphasized that its *legal* services would be made available only to those defendants who can prove they have no money with which to employ an attorney.

2. But what about the average citizen like yourself who can afford to pay a lawyer, but cannot afford to hire detectives, take depositions in distant cities, bring witnesses to the trial from out of state and pay their expenses, pay for transcripts, hire experts, and all the rest of the expensive items that constitute the heart of a good defense? (Or even if he could afford them, the expenses would exhaust all of his resources and put him in debt.)

This citizen, who, let me emphasize, pays for his own lawyer, should be entitled to use, without charge, the machinery of the Public Defender's office. Investigators, experts, crime lab technicians, etc., would be available to devote as much attention to proving his innocence, as the State devotes toward convicting him.

"Justice insurance"

The cost of such a system — less than 25 cents a head tax money — is certainly small when you consider it as insurance against the day — however remote the possibility — when you might be accused of a crime. You regularly pay burglary insurance but chances are you will never be robbed. Why not "justice insurance"?

No city in the United States has such a Public Defender's office whose facilities are available to all defendant lawyers, regardless of the financial status of their clients.

To illustrate how this system would work, let's go back to that case of mine that involved the woman accused of murdering her husband. I must prove she was on a Greyhound bus when the murder was committed. As her lawyer, I go to the Public Defender and ask that detectives be assigned to locate the bus on which she rode, the bus driver and the woman who sat next to her.

The Public Defender also sends a man to the bus terminal where my client bought her ticket, and this man takes the deposition (sworn statement) of the ticket agent who remembers selling her a ticket.

Under such an arrangement, when it is time for trial, my client can be assured she has had full and equal justice under the law.

Unprepared, unaware

As matters stand now, there is virtually nothing I can do to produce this kind of evidence for a client who is not wealthy. Even if I personally could afford to do so, legal ethics will not allow me to pay the expenses of a client's litigation. So I must often go to trial partially unprepared, unaware and unprotected.

Claude B. Cross, a distinguished Massachusetts attorney, writes in the "American Bar Association Journal," "The Sixth Amendment to the Constitution of the U.S. states that in all criminal prosecutions the accused shall enjoy the right to have the assistance of counsel for his defense. Today the issues in a criminal prosecution may involve so extended a hearing that the costs of a stenographic transcript and of a modest per diem to counsel will ruin the ordinary man."

As for the necessity for Public Defenders, this is what James V. Bennett, Director of the Federal Bureau of Prisons, has to say:

"A prison director sees many strange things, hears many a weird and tragic story, and now and then comes into contact with genuine miscarriages of justice. Here's a letter from a prisoner I know who impressed me as being sincere and honest:

" 'I have been sentenced for two years and three years' probation. When I was judged I was asked by my attorney to plead guilty. He was an attorney who happened to be in court. Please believe me I didn't know nor did anyone explain to me the meaning of pleading guilty. I have never in my whole life committed any crime. Since I am serving this sentence I have learned that by pleading guilty, I have committed myself to something I was not aware of. I have had but four years' schooling and the ways of the court were foreign to me."

Good results

"There is nothing unusual or extraordinary about this case," Director Bennett says. "Many letters similar to this pass over my desk every month. There should be a local Public Defender to whom these cases could be referred. He has experience and facilities for investigation at his disposal. Where there are such Defenders — Los Angeles, Oakland, Sacramento, Columbus, Indianapolis, Chicago, Memphis, St. Paul, Minneapolis, and the States of Nebraska, Connecticut, Oklahoma, Rhode Island and Virginia — the results have been extraordinarily good."

But remember that the facilities of these P.D. offices are available only to the penniless. Why not, for a few cents tax money, open their doors to the average citizen who has no chance of adequately defending himself if he is left on his own?

The plight of the accused in the courts today is a situation which, most lawyers agree, lacks justice. It is our duty — the duty of all of us — to put it morally right. A Public Defender's office, with adequate facilities for all accused defendants, would certainly put us on the right track.

42

The Case of "Trial by Press"

By Anthony Lewis

A QUESTION THAT HAS LONG NAGGED at the conscience of Americans concerned about justice is posed most acutely by the report of the Warren Commission on the assassination of President Kennedy: Does this country's practice of unbridled liberty for the press, radio and television to report on pending criminal cases permit any man charged with a notorious crime to get a fair trial?

Chief Justice Earl Warren and his six colleagues on the commission were highly critical of what happened after the arrest of Lee Harvey Oswald. In the corridors of the Dallas Police Headquarters reporters and cameramen were so numerous and unruly that witnesses could hardly get through. Under the pressures of the press, officials repeatedly disclosed damaging evidence and said Oswald's guilt was certain. A desire to please the press was one reason for the ill-handled transfer that led to Oswald's murder. If he had lived, the commission said, his "opportunity for a trial by 12 jurors free of preconception as to his guilt or innocence would have been seriously jeopardized by the premature disclosure and weighing of the evidence against him."

What happened in Dallas last November was an extreme case. But the American Bar Association was stating the obvious when it observed, in a comment condemning conditions in Dallas, that "excessive and prejudicial publicity with respect to criminal cases is not unusual in America."

Everyone knows, as Justice Arthur J. Goldberg said recently, that the American press commonly uses "labels such as 'killer,' 'robber,' 'hoodlum' . . . to describe the accused weeks before and even on the eve of the trial." Thirteen years ago, a predecessor of his on the Court, Justice Robert H. Jackson, said that "trial by newspaper" was "one of the worst menaces to American justice."

Since Justice Jackson's day, television has emerged as a potentially even more searching intruder into the criminal process. The bar and most courts have stead-

Anthony Lewis, "The Case of 'Trial By Press,' " *The New York Times Magazine,* October 18, 1964, pp. 31, 94, 96, 98–100. Copyright 1964 by The New York Times Company. Reprinted by permission.

fastly resisted demands for admission of TV cameras to trials because they believe such broadcasting would make the process of determining guilt still more a public spectacle and less the quiet inquiry the law intended it to be. Even without entry into the courtroom, television can outdo the newspaper in pretrial comment on criminal cases.

Even before the tragedy in Dallas, concern about the conflict between free press and fair trial had been growing. A number of newspapers were criticizing excesses on the part of their profession or by broadcasters. As for the bar, its prevailing sentiment was probably expressed by Federal District Judge Hubert L. Will of Illinois in this 1963 comment:

"The press, even when it reports crimes and criminal trials with reasonable thoroughness and accuracy — which is seldom — too often in the very process encroaches upon and subverts the constitutional right to a fair trial by an impartial jury."

The argument on the other side has also been vigorously pressed. A major contention is that the press helps to prevent official abuses by its close watch on criminal cases. J. Russell Wiggins, editor of The Washington Post, mentioning such police practices as the third degree, said:

"These conditions much more menace the right of accused persons than pretrial disclosures in the press. . . . Newspaper publicity is the best way of treating these abuses."

As for the performance in Dallas specifically, it has been defended by numerous editors, among them Mr. Wiggins's colleague on The Post, Alfred Friendly. He made the point that the press is fiercely competitive and that when some reporters moved in aggressively on the Dallas police, the others could hardly afford to be gentlemen. He seemed to be saying that there is a kind of Gresham's Law of the press, with the tawdry and sensational driving out the responsible.

Mr. Friendly argued also, as many others have, that it was basically up to the authorities in Dallas to lay down the rules — not up to the press. He said: "The press was not pretty in Dallas. But it may not be fair to accuse it for failure to embrace a system that was not its to prescribe."

The Warren Commission was not insensitive to the point. It said that "primary responsibility for having failed to control the press and to check the flow of undigested evidence to the public must be borne by the [Dallas] Police Department."

But the commission also said that the disorder in Police Headquarters disclosed "a regrettable lack of self-discipline by the newsmen." Looking past the immediate incidents to a broader moral, the commission concluded:

"The experience in Dallas during Nov. 22–24 is a dramatic affirmation of the need for steps to bring about a proper balance between the right of the public to be kept informed and the right of the individual to a fair and impartial trial."

In considering how to balance these sometimes conflicting interests, it is well to put to one side first a slogan often shouted by press zealots: "The right to know." The phrase is used as if there were something in the Constitution, or in logic, that gave the press a right to demand the facts about anything.

There is no such abstract "right to know." The freedom of the press guaranteed in the Constitution, most students of the subject have agreed, is a freedom to publish — not a compulsion for everyone else to tell all to the press. Common sense supports that view. Surely reporters and television cameras have no "right" to be present at meetings of the National Security Council or conferences of the Supreme Court.

There is a *public* interest, as the Warren Commission phrased it, in being kept informed about criminal proceedings. This high interest is often cited by the press, but the desire to provide titillation and entertainment is usually the real motive for lofty demands to get the facts and admit the cameras. The honest argument for press entry in each case is that a useful social function will be served in the particular circumstances, not that the press has some "right."

The constitutional right that is involved here is the one guaranteed by the Sixth Amendment: "In all criminal prosecutions, the accused shall enjoy the right to a speedy and public trial, by an impartial jury. . . ."

The public trial, it should be noted, is for the benefit of "the accused," not of the press. Its purpose, in the minds of the Constitution's framers, was to prevent the former English practice — made infamous by the Star Chamber — of trying men *in camera,* without access to friends or public opinion.

"The public trial exists," Justice William O. Douglas explained a few years ago, "because of the aversion which liberty-loving people had toward secret trials and proceedings. That is the reason our courts are open to the public, not because the framers wanted to provide the public with recreation."

It is the defendant who can demand a public trial, not the press. That was the holding of the New York courts in the case of Mickey Jelke, whose trial for sex offenses was held with the press excluded. Newspapers' demands to be admitted were rejected, but Jelke's own claim that he had a right to a trial in the open was sustained and his conviction reversed.

The Sixth Amendment's guarantee of "an impartial jury" is what gives concern about the performance of the American press. How can an impartial jury be found when the press and television and radio have been trumpeting for weeks ahead their certainty that a defendant is guilty?

The British deal with the problem in a clean-cut way. They punish for contempt of court virtually any publication about the defendant in a criminal case before trial except the bare fact of his arrest. And they punish severely. The editor of The Daily Mirror of London was sent to jail for three months in 1949 for publishing details of alleged murders by a man just arrested. In 1961, The Daily Express was fined £5,000 ($14,000) for describing a suspect before his arrest.

The British are also severe on criticism of judges. Ronald Goldfarb, an American expert in this area, describes cases in which British publications were severely fined for having suggested that judges were less than wholly impartial — although their comments came after decision, when they could not possibly have affected the course of justice.

Such restrictions on the press cannot be squared with our written Constitution's broad assurance of the right to speak and write freely. Thus the Supreme Court, applying the First Amendment, has severely limited the power of courts to punish, as contempt, comments on pending criminal matters.

The leading case was decided in 1941. It involved public pressures applied to the courts from two contrasting sources — Harry Bridges, the cantankerous left-wing labor leader, and an editorial in The Los Angeles Times, a conservative newspaper.

Bridges had published a telegram denouncing a California court's decision in a labor case as "outrageous" and threatening a strike over it. The Times editorial dealt with the assault conviction of two union leaders — it called them "gorillas" — and demanded that they be sent to prison rather than put on probation. Both Bridges and The Times were held in contempt of court.

The Supreme Court, by a vote of 5 to 4, set aside the contempt findings. Justice Hugo L. Black said the Constitution did not allow such punishment for comment on judicial proceedings unless the publication presented a "clear and present danger" of obstructing justice.

Under that difficult standard there is almost no chance of using contempt proceedings to discourage sensational pretrial publicity about criminal cases, no matter how severely the defendant's right to a fair trial may be hurt. Nor is there any sign that the Supreme Court may relax the standard, for Americans are wary of putting vaguely defined power in judges' hands to punish speech and writing.

Since the Bridges case, the damaging effects of publicity on criminal proceedings have become much more widely recognized. Justice Douglas, a strong believer in the Bridges rule, praised it in a 1960 speech, but then added:

"This is not to say that the influence of newspapers on trials should go unnoticed. At times the papers can arouse passions in a community so that no trial can be a fair one."

In the absence of direct control over press comment, the courts have been forced to other remedies. These are to delay a trial if a community has been saturated with adverse publicity about the defendant, or move the trial to another city.

Appellate courts are finding more and more often that convicted defendants could not have had a fair trial in the circumstances of publicity and that there should have been a change of venue. When this is decided at the appellate level, the result is to require a new trial, often long after the event.

The Supreme Court first reversed a conviction because of newspaper influence on a jury in 1959. That was a relatively narrow decision, involving a Federal trial in which jurors were shown to have read in the press material specifically excluded from evidence in the trial.

In 1961, the Supreme Court found an Indiana conviction unconstitutional because the jury had read numerous articles describing the defendant as a "mad-dog killer." This was followed in 1963 by a decision throwing out a Louisiana trial held after the defendant's alleged confession to the sheriff had been filmed and shown to the community on television three times. Justice Potter Stewart used the term "kangaroo-court proceedings" for that episode.

The lower courts have got the message from the Supreme Court and are bearing down harder on trial by newspaper. Last summer, a Federal district judge in Ohio issued a writ of habeas corpus releasing Dr. Samuel Sheppard after 10 years in prison for the murder of his wife, on the ground — among others — that newspaper and broadcast intimations of his guilt before trial had fatally infected the proceedings with unfairness.

This technique — the setting aside of past convictions because of the influence of publicity — has obvious and serious deficiencies. If an innocent man really was railroaded to jail by public passion, it is not much cheer to him to have a new trial 10 years later. And the public may suffer as well as defendants. Years after a crime, at a new trial, it may be difficult or impossible for prosecutors to reassemble the evidence needed for conviction of even the guiltiest man.

For these reasons, there has been more and more thought about ways to stop the evil, not after it has had its effect, but before — to curtail indiscriminate, unfair publicity before criminal trials.

One course would be to move closer to the British system and curb irresponsible press or broadcast comments by contempt proceedings against those who make them. Retired Supreme Court Justice Felix Frankfurter, who dissented in the Bridges case, would have preferred this approach. He objected to the idea that, as he put it once, "while convictions must be reversed and miscarriages of justice result because the minds of jurors or potential jurors were poisoned, the prisoner is constitutionally protected in plying his trade."

But that does not seem a practical solution, for there is no discernible trend in the Supreme Court toward lessening the protections of freedom for the press. Some abuse goes along with freedom, the Court might say, but it must be handled in ways that do not lead to restriction and timidity.

The idea endorsed by the Warren Commission was "the promulgation of a code of professional conduct governing representatives of all news media" in reporting on pending criminal cases. This idea has had a good deal of attention in newspaper and broadcast circles, too.

With all deference, the proposal for a self-promulgated code is not very promising. It is likely to be ignored by those who sin most. H. L. Mencken disposed of the idea a generation ago when he wrote:

"Journalistic codes of ethics are all moonshine. . . . If American journalism is to be purged of its present swinishness and brought up to a decent level of repute — and God knows that such an improvement is needed — it must be accomplished by the devices of morals, not by those of honor. That is to say, it must be accomplished by external forces, and through the medium of penalties exteriorly afflicted."

Another course, which has attracted growing support, is for the courts to crack down on those more clearly within their disciplinary jurisdiction than the press — the prosecutors and defense lawyers and police who are the sources of the material printed or broadcast.

Senator Wayne Morse of Oregon and 10 other Senators introduced in the last Congress a bill along that line. It would punish as contempt, in Federal criminal cases, any disclosure by a Federal employee or defense attorney except of material already admitted as evidence. There would be a fine of $500 for violations.

A more sweeping proposal for legislation, state or Federal, has been put forward by Justice Bernard S. Meyer of the Supreme Court of Nassau County, N.Y. It would apply to newspapermen and broadcasters as well as lawyers and others involved in criminal trials. It would go into effect only when a defendant was to be tried by jury, the theory being that judges are less susceptible than laymen to influence by external forces.

The Meyer proposal would flatly prohibit any disclosure of the existence of a confession, of the defendant's prior record and of similar damaging matters unless they were brought out at the trial. It would also ban any expression of opinion on the defendant's guilt or the credibility of evidence or witnesses.

Justice Meyer would go even further in a second section listing other practices which would not be automatically condemned but would be violations if a jury found that they threatened substantial prejudice to justice. Among these are interviews with victims of a crime, appeals to racial bias and publication of the names and addresses of jurors.

The theory is that such a statute would be constitutional because it would not put the press at the hazard of a judge's virtually undefined contempt power. Instead, there would be specific legislative findings that certain activities threaten the right to a fair trial, and all would be on notice to steer clear of these. The first, or mandatory, part of the statute would be more easily sustainable on this reasoning than the second section.

It can readily be seen that the Meyer proposal is a severe one. Yet it has attracted wide attention and support as worthy of consideration in light of the serious threat to fair trial in this country.

The truth is that excessive pretrial publicity does flaw our generally civilized standards of criminal procedure. More of the press should recognize its responsibility and consider effective measures to prevent abuses instead of talking about "the right to know." Otherwise, there may come the external retribution of which Mencken spoke.

Judge Emory H. Niles — like Mencken a civilized Baltimorean — said recently:

"I believe that in the end there will be a popular revulsion as well as a judicial revulsion, a sharpening of the public conscience that will condemn the practice of entertainment and amusement through uncontrolled publication of gossip and scandal."

One of the long-standing controversies in the judicial field still rages over the question of whether judges should be elected or appointed. Both systems are widespread, though in a few states a kind of compromise has been adopted in which a judge initially appointed to office periodically "runs against his own record," the voter merely being asked "Shall Judge Blank be retained in office for another term?" As a matter of actual practice even in a state with an elective system it is often true that most judges are appointed. This is accomplished by means of a gentlemen's understanding that a judge planning to retire should resign prior to the end of his term so that the governor may appoint to fill the vacancy. Barring major scandal, incumbent judges are rarely defeated for re-election. Under either system the Bar Association is likely to play a dominant role by recommending appointees or publicizing their support of certain candidates. The relative merits of election versus a system of modified gubernatorial appointment are debated by the U.S. District Judge for the Western District of Missouri and a Chicago attorney who holds a number of professional honors.

The third article deals with the related and equally difficult problem of removing unqualified judges, emphasizing the value of commissions on judicial qualifications recently inaugurated in a few states.

43

There's a Better Way to Select Our Judges

By Elmo B. Hunter

THE INCREASING COMPLEXITY of contemporary life and the increasing rapidity of social change require higher qualifications for the personnel who operate our government. This is not only true for the executive and legislative branches, it is particularly pressing with regard to the third, the judicial branch of government.

In recent months, I have participated in citizens' conferences on the courts in ten different states. In the course of these conferences, I have met and discussed this problem of securing and retaining qualified judicial personnel with over a thousand non-lawyers representing all segments of state life. Their response to the merit selection and tenure plan advocated by the American Judicature Society since 1913, approved by the American Bar Association in 1937, and first adopted in Missouri in 1940, has been consistently enthusiastic after they had an understanding of the basic elements of the plan and how it has worked for almost 25 years in Missouri. It is this demonstrated interest, particularly in how the plan has worked, which has prompted this attempt to set forth our experience in Missouri. What follows is not theoretical — it is cold and hard fact. It is not hearsay — it is first-hand experience. . . .

In 1940, judges for our trial courts, our three intermediate appellate courts, and our supreme court were elected under a partisan political system. At times the results flowing from this system ranged from the ludicrous to the near chaotic. No man aspiring to the bench and who had to give up his law practice to do so could be at all sure of his tenure in office, irrespective of his merit, ability or fine record. He could not control national or state landslides nor

the whim of the current political power or boss who might knife him in his party's primary if his judicial decisions did not suit. The result? In the twenty years between World Wars I and II, 1919–1939, only twice was a judge of the Supreme Court of Missouri who had served a full term re-elected.

In our two large cities, St. Louis and Kansas City, the situation was even worse. The tenure and selection of the judges was controlled by certain politicians and political machines. The dockets were congested as the judges had to spend much time keeping their political fences mended and campaigning. Many lawyers believed that some judges might be influenced by political considerations and hesitated to go to court unless they co-employed an influential political attorney who might be favored in that particular court. Their worry was that the other side might co-employ an attorney who had more political influence than theirs.

The judges themselves were beset with problems and influences which they did not relish and which had no proper place. Many of those who had made money or time contributions to a judge's political campaign did not hesitate to remind the judge of that in any case where, they, their friends or political associates had a personal, political or financial interest.

In such a climate precinct captains and political faction leaders not only did not hesitate to put in a good word for a friend or faction associate involved as a party in litigation — but some were even bold enough to convey the message that the judge would "get his" at the polls at the next election unless he "did right" by a certain side. In some instances grand juries, the heart and soul of adequate law enforcement, were indirectly selected by certain politicians through the method of having the judge calling the grand jury first submit to the politician the list of names he intended to use, to be sure none were personally obnoxious to that politician or to his group. The judges themselves, in the face of larger dockets and increasing backlogs of cases, lost valuable working time as they "took off" from three to six months before every election in order to campaign.

Committee investigates problem

Not all of these things were publicly known, but there was a sufficient awareness of these problems to occasion the formation in Missouri of a citizen-lawyer committee to study the problems. This committee publicly set out certain fundamentals, so well known as to be almost trite, yet possessed of a new meaning:

(1) The judicial, as contrasted with the legislative and executive branches of government, has no political purpose or political function to serve. Hence, politics has no proper place in the courts, and, if present, serves only to distract from justice.

Elmo B. Hunter, *A Missouri Judge Views Judicial Selection and Tenure* (Chicago: The American Judicature Society, n.d.) (Pamphlet). Reprinted by permission of the author and the publisher.

(2) The judges of the courts should come from the ranks of our most able and most talented lawyers — from men chosen on the basis of personal integrity, impartiality, judicial temperament, ability, legal training, and physical and mental vigor for the arduous work of the position.

(3) These judges, after their selection, must be assured freedom from political influence and threat, and provided with reasonable security of tenure so long as they perform properly.

(4) The system of selection and tenure must be such as to free them from having to conduct campaigns or engage in time consuming activities for their retention, and leave them free to do the one thing they are supposed to do — devote their full time to doing the work of a judge.

Man is a creature of habit and he shies away from a thing that is new and different. Then there are always some who for one reason or another desire no improvements. This means that judicial reform is not for the short-winded.

It was difficult to be the first to try a substantial change of judicial selection and tenure. It took a tremendous citizens' effort to put over the plan in Missouri. The 1940 constitutional amendment carried by 80,000 votes. Those against the plan did not rest. Just 60 days later they endeavored to have it repealed, saying our people did not understand it when they first voted on it. The repealer was defeated by twice the earlier vote — 160,000 plus.

Two years later when our state constitution was being redrawn these opponents endeavored to have our court plan omitted from that constitution but without success, for our people had experienced some of the fine results of the plan. A weak, scattered and utterly futile effort in 1955 was made in our legislature to abolish the plan. There have been no further public attacks. . . .

Criticism of court plan

There are some who continue to be critics of our court plan, and understandably so. Some of these are sincere and well motivated and others are not. I will try to classify most of them as I view their thinking, so you may understand the basis, or lack of basis, for their criticism.

Since I am one, I will commence with lawyers. In Missouri, and elsewhere, lawyers as a class are notorious for their lack of unanimity on almost any subject, and for their inclination to seek out the opposite side of any matter. We lawyers thrive on controversy and enjoy withholding a complete endorsement of any idea or thing. We think we can say it better, and we usually differ on details. We laughingly say of ourselves that if at a typical bar meeting someone would propose a resolution commending

the 23rd Psalm as written, at least a dozen or more would jump up and offer amendments to improve the Psalm. So to expect complete unanimity among lawyers on any serious subject is to expect what seems seldom to occur. Much of the criticism in Missouri from lawyers is not with the basic plan, but rather it is no more than the individual lawyer's idea of some comparatively minor change that he would suggest or prefer or his wish that it would be administered a little differently.

However, there have been and still are some few, but highly vocal, lawyers who deem their pocketbook or other personal interest involved, who put that consideration first, and who deliberately want a court that will give them some "in," some break, some advantage, some special influence; or a court that is "friendly" or "sympathetic" to them or their clients' interests to the corresponding disadvantage of the other party who may be involved. Sometimes they talk in terms of "conservative" or "liberal," but what they really mean is "friendly" or "unfriendly" to their clients' or their particular type of business or interest. They refuse to recognize that it is not a proper function of a court to be either "friendly" or "unfriendly" to any particular group. These persons do not want an impartial court where all may come on equal terms and receive justice based solely on the merits of their cause. They do not like the merit court plan and probably never will, at least as long as they openly or secretly seek a special advantage, for under this plan where the judiciary is selected and retained on merit and merit alone no group or interest is likely to acquire any special "in" or advantage over any other.

Another group is composed of those who think — but mistakenly — that their group will get less than a fair deal from a judge selected under this plan. Some of these are claimants' attorneys who erroneously have concluded that such selection brings to the bench only "conservative" lawyers from large law firms. Studies conducted in Missouri over the past 24 years show this simply is not true. Many of the nominees have been individual practitioners. Of those who were in law firms, the majority came from offices of three or less lawyers. . . .

Another small group are those lawyers who mistakenly think any system other than the 100 per cent political elective system for judges is undemocratic. Those in this group just have not studied their history. None of the 13 original states at the beginning of our republic obtained their judges by election at the polls. They all used an appointive system. Three, New York, Maryland and Massachusetts obtained judges through appointment by the governor subject to consent by the council. In New Hampshire and Pennsylvania appointments were made by the governor and the council. In the remaining eight states the power was vested in one or both houses of the legislature. To repeat, no state in 1789 obtained its judges through the election process.

Historical perspective

Our forefathers, to avoid weakening our democracy, did not provide for judges to be obtained at the polls by a partisan ballot. It was not until seventy years later, in 1846, that any state elected judges by political party ballot and, of course, our federal judiciary has always been obtained by appointment by the president with the consent of the senate. As a final history lesson, let me point out that of all the countries existing in this world today only Russia plus a very few small cantons of Switzerland and Argentina obtain judges by election at the polls.

The merit plan, which combines the best features of the three historical methods of choosing judges — selection, appointment, and election — is thoroughly democratic. . . .

I am a judicial product of this plan. I was a practicing attorney in Kansas City in one of the general practice law firms and was teaching in the evening at our local university law school. At the age of 36 in 1952, I went on our trial court under this plan. I was retained in office for a six-year term by our electorate in 1953. In 1956, I went on the bench of our intermediate appellate court under this plan and in 1958 was retained by our electorate for a twelve-year term. As the immediate past presiding judge of my court, I have been the chairman of the five-member judicial commission that selects a panel of three from which our governor must fill any vacancy in our trial courts in the Kansas City, Missouri, metropolitan area.

Missouri plan in action

While the process is essentially the same as to appellate and trial courts under the plan, it may be best to give a concrete and recent example of how a trial court vacancy is filled in Missouri. Just a few months ago two of our trial judges retired because of a combination of age and illness. This created two judicial vacancies. Our judicial nominating commission issued a public statement carried by our press and other news media that the nominating commission would soon meet to consider two panels of three names each to be sent to the governor for him to select one from each panel to fill the vacancy, and that the nominating commission was open to suggestions and recommendations of names of those members of our bar best qualified to be circuit judges.

It received the names of many outstanding and highly qualified lawyers who were willing to be considered by the commission because of the nonpolitical merit type of selection involved. The commission on its own surveyed all eligible lawyers in the circuit to see if it had before it the names of all those who ought to be considered. From all sources the commission ended up with fifty-seven names.

After several weeks of careful study by the commission, the list of eligibles was cut to twelve then to nine and finally to those six who the members of the commission sincerely believed to be the six best qualified of all. Those six names, three on each of the two panels, were sent to the governor who, after his own independent consideration of them, made his selection of one from each panel. His selections were widely acclaimed by the press and the public as excellent choices from two very outstanding panels. The commission was glad to see the governor get this accolade, but its members knew that no matter which one of the three on each panel he selected, the people of Missouri would have been assured an outstanding judge.

It might be noted in passing that each of the two panels of three names submitted to the governor happened to contain the names of two Democrats and one Republican. The governor was a Democrat. He appointed a Democrat from one panel and a Republican from the other. I do not think this was deliberate. I am convinced that our plan has so proven its merit that our governor, who is oath bound to follow the constitution, shares its spirit as well as its letter. He selected the two he thought best qualified, irrespective of political party.

This is not an isolated instance. Another rather dramatic example occurred just a few years ago when our legislature created three new judgeships for the Kansas City area to meet the increasing cases resulting principally from population growth. The judicial selection commission sent three panels of three names each to another Democratic governor. On each panel there were two Democrats and one Republican. The governor appointed two Republicans and one Democrat.

We, in Missouri, do not claim our plan results in an equal mathematical division of Democrats and Republicans, for that is not its purpose. The constitutional duty of the members of the judicial selection commission is to select the three best names available, regardless of political party or other such irrelevant considerations, and the constitutional duty of the governor is to make an independent study of those three nominees and appoint that one he believes to be the best qualified of all.

Let me hasten to add that certain things are necessary if a system such as we have in Missouri is to work properly. I cannot stress too strongly that it is the nominating commission which is the important factor. If it selects a highly qualified panel, it is immaterial which one of the nominees a governor might appoint. To assure such a selection, the membership of the nominating panel must be composed of persons who will sincerely and faithfully carry out both the letter and the spirit of the plan. They must be men and women who will approach their task objectively, striving only to find the highest and best qualified men as nominees for appointment. They must disregard political and personal attachments and look only for those qualities which produce an outstanding judge.

In Missouri, the lawyers of the circuit elect the two lawyer members of the five-man nominating commission for filling vacancies on the circuit (trial) bench. Our bar has fully recognized the need to elect to commission membership lawyers who will carry out both the letter and the spirit of our plan. The governor appoints two laymen from within the circuit and their terms are staggered so that no one governor gets to appoint both of them. Fortunately, our governors have recognized the need to appoint objective, high-class civic leaders to the nominating commissions.

Additionally, our bar, our newspapers, radio, television, and other news media help acquaint our public with the plan and work toward its success.

Value of lay commissioners

In our state from time to time the question has been raised, usually by lawyers, as to why laymen should be included as members of a judicial commission whose purpose is to select those from whom judges are to be appointed. The discussion usually runs along the line that laymen are not personally acquainted with the bar generally and are not in position to know the individual qualifications of the members of the bar. I confess to having shared that type of thinking until I became a member of a judicial nominating commission. Then the experience of seeing first hand how the commission actually worked quickly demonstrated to me the real need and great value of having laymen on the nominating commission.

Usually, the laymen on the judicial commission have had some previous experience in panel selections, but whether they have or not, it is true that as the nominating commission first commences to study potential nominees, the laymen tend to be listeners. As the list of names begins to narrow and the discussions become more detailed, the laymen find themselves somewhat in the position of jurors. They carefully listen to how each lawyer member evaluates the potential selectees and, in turn, they evaluate what the lawyer members are saying. If a lawyer member, in discussing the relative merits of one potential nominee over another, puts forth weak, immaterial, ill-formed, or prejudiced views, the lay-

men quickly discern this. They ask quite pertinent questions. They make some independent investigations. They are determined that the lay public get the best judges possible and they quickly cast aside improper or detracting considerations. They avoid the purely personal antipathies that occasionally arise among lawyers. By the time the vote is taken, the laymen members are as well informed as the lawyer members.

The laymen keep the entire selection process objective. They help remind the other commission members that the courts are not just to serve lawyers and their interests, but truly and ultimately belong to the people who are entitled to the best. They are concerned, not only about legal skills but also about character. I am convinced that laymen do have a very important function to serve in the work of a judicial selection commission and that their very participation promotes objectivity and care in selection and, finally, instills public confidence in the results reached.

"A better way to select judges"

The merit selection plan in Missouri is not perfect. Through the years we have had our problems and have noted where improvements could be made. Proper provisions for retirement and judicial compensation are two areas where changes are desirable. An effective and fair method of disciplining and removing judges from office would enhance our system. A more realistic method of exercising local option provisions of the plan is needed. In spite of these limitations, however, the plan has stood strong under the numerous tests and strains placed upon it. Many who opposed it originally are now its staunchest supporters after having observed its many years of successful operation. It has substantially met the expectations of our citizens. It has grown in favor among lawyers and the public as the years have passed.

Our lawyers and citizens have seen first hand how a system of merit selection of judges results not only in attracting to the bench those who are best qualified, but also assures security of tenure and the preservation of the experienced services of those who ably serve the administration of justice.

After more than a dozen years of experience, I personally know we now have a truly independent judiciary in Missouri. Our litigants are receiving a higher quality of justice and our people have a growing confidence in our courts. Excellent lawyers now agree to serve on our bench who would not submit themselves to the ordeals of the old political system. We have been successful in attracting to the bench some very outstanding and able young men who desired to make the judiciary their career and whose vigor and energy are needed for, contrary to popular conception, judicial work and particularly trial court work is physically demanding. The courts have been completely freed in every respect from party politics.

Today our judges devote their time to their courts and its business, free of political pressures or loss of time. The administration of justice has been speeded up. This merit plan, admittedly not perfect, admittedly not a panacea for every judicial problem, has fully demonstrated to the citizens of Missouri that it is the best yet devised and that it is a tremendous improvement over the old system of partisan political election.

Today, features of this merit plan of judicial selection and tenure are being used for some or all judges in ten states. It has been approved by citizen groups or bar associations in another ten states. After almost a quarter of a century of experience, the bench, the bar and the citizenry of Missouri commend it to our sister states. It is, in Judge Rosenman's words, "a better way to select judges."

44

Don't Destroy the People's Right to Choose Their Judges

By John J. Kennelly

RECENT "AUTHORITATIVE" VIEWS on this question voiced by some members of the bar may be reduced to three basic goals which they allege are wanting in the elective system — namely, how to select the best qualified men for the position of judge, how to get them on the bench, and how to keep them there. These authorities simply beg the question when they gratuitously *conclude* and *assume* that the first goal — the selection of qualified men — cannot possibly be attained through the elective method, and thus, inferentially and without proof, sanctimoniously attack the integrity and fidelity to their trust of the leaders of both political parties who nominate judicial candidates.

The proponents of the appointive system generally support the American Bar Association plan

John J. Kennelly, "Elect Judges? — Yes," *The Rotarian*, June, 1961, pp. 40, 54, 56. (This article was published as one-half of a debate in this issue of *The Rotarian*.) Reprinted by permission of the publisher.

which has been adopted in Missouri. Essentially, this is an appointive-elective plan which is claimed to have the best attributes of both methods. However, the following objections have been noted:

(a) It renders practically meaningless the electorate's right intelligently to exercise discretion. Its provision for the appointee to run unopposed in the election following his appointment with a "Yes-No" question asked of the voters is pretty much of a farce. In almost 20 years under the Missouri appointive plan, only one man has failed to be reappointed. Proponents of the plan point out that the electorate knows little or nothing about the judicial nominee, and yet they would use the electorate as the only effective method of discharging an appointee without the traditional method of information and comparison, criticism from an opposing candidate. A political axiom is that it is virtually impossible to beat an incumbent with no one. The original appointment therefore is virtually for life.

(b) The Selection Commission is or can be partisan. Under the Missouri Plan, the Commission consists of three members elected by the State bar association, three laymen appointed by the Governor, and the Chief Justice of the Supreme Court. The contingent from the bar association does not reflect the sentiment of the lawyers in the State, let alone the people. Most bar associations are controlled by powerful minorities, usually aligned with large firms and vested interests, who guide the policy of the association in conformity with their respective philosophies. Secondly, the vast majority of lawyers are informed of the qualifications of judges purely through hearsay, similar to the layman, for the reason that comparatively very few members of the bar are ever involved in courtroom litigation. Also, the "values of the bar . . . are not necessarily identical with the values of the people whom courts must serve. This is only to suggest that what lawyers value in each other and in judges may not be the same as what laymen value in judges." In Chicago, Illinois, approximately 20 per cent of the lawyers vote in the Bar Association polls, and probably less than 10 per cent of these have firsthand knowledge of the candidate judges. The independent, self-employed lawyers generally take little, if any, part in bar-association activities. This is not to say that bar associations do not serve the legal profession, the courts, and the communities in many other areas; but just as students should not have the right to vote concerning the selection or retention of their teachers, so also the lawyers should not have the right to turn the selection or retention of judges into a popularity contest.

The members of the Selection Commission appointed by the Governor ordinarily can be expected to be loyal to the Governor's political party, or at least a "safe" choice. Realism compels the conclusion that the Governor would actually participate in the selection of judicial candidates through his nominees to the Selection Commission.

(c) Governor appointments will be partisan. Under the plan, the Governor appoints one of three candidates nominated by the Selection Commission. Realistically, for example, a Republican Governor would be inclined to appoint a Republican judge in a Democratic county, thus depriving the majority of the local electorate of their choice of judicial candidates. Experience has proved that prior to 1953 in Missouri, all judicial appointments were made along party lines except in one instance, when all three candidates were of the opposite party. To the present time only one Governor willingly selected candidates from the opposite party, a truly remarkable and unusual occurrence in American history. Not only Governors but Presidents are notorious for their partisan appointments; and why not, as long as the men are competent? President Roosevelt appointed 217 Democrats and 8 Republicans. President Truman appointed 118 Democrats and 12 Republicans. President Eisenhower appointed 175 Republicans and 11 Democrats. The composite box score of the two Democratic Administrations as compared with the recent Republican Administration reveals a virtual tie percentage-wise.

Thus, when the Missouri, American Bar Association, California, and similar appointive-elective plans are tested "in the light of human experience," they not only suffer from the same criticisms attributed to the elective system, but indicate weaknesses which could be much more dangerous.

The basic premise of the critics of the elective system is that judges are not and should not be treated as political officers. Yet it is obvious that judges formulate public policy as much as — and in certain areas, greater than — the legislature. This is a traditional and distinctive phase of American democracy; and, further, the only feasible and practical method by which the people can control the judges and their philosophy is through elections. Until relatively recent times, the decisions of most courts reflected an adherence to reactionary concepts concerning property, with little regard for the basic rights and liberties of mankind. Judge Talbot Smith stated only recently: "The bloodless bookkeeping imposed upon our juries by the savage exploitations of the last century must no longer be perpetuated by our courts."

We have a two-party system in the U.S.A. Each party endorses a distinct philosophy. With this in mind, it is little wonder that the electorate in the majority of States have refused to give up their right to elect State court judges, and subject themselves to judges designated by an elite group, deceptively styled as an "impartial commission."

In the elective system, the political party which nominates a judge is responsible to the public for his performance. Inescapable sanctions are imposed upon a political party which nominates candidates for judicial office who are incompetent. In the Chicago area (Cook County), vivid examples of the imposition by the electorate of these sanctions have been evident. In one fairly recent election, virtually an entire county ticket was defeated because of unsavory disclosures concerning a judge whom the party leaders refused to drop from the slate. The political parties are well aware of their responsibility to the public.

James C. Worthy, formerly a vice-president of Sears, Roebuck and Company, warned in his book, *Big Business and Free Men,* that nonpartisan politics is a contradiction in terms and offers no chance for effective action. "Freedom includes freedom to make a wrong or fatal choice; but it also includes freedom to make perhaps a better choice than has ever been made before."

The "reformers" who glibly postulate that elected judges are subject to party domination are unable to answer why it is that, for instance, in Cook County, more than 90 per cent of the elected judges are consistently determined qualified even by the Chicago Bar Association poll.

There seldom has been a truly "nonpartisan, nonpolitical" judge at the time of his appointment. This is not to say that judges, once elected or appointed, let their rulings be guided by any partisan feelings. The contrary is the fact; and except for a few cynics, most trial lawyers believe that elected judges are fair and honorable. It is hypocritical and merely lip service to label judges who may be selected by appointment as "nonpolitical" or "nonpartisan." Take away from the people their inherent right to elect State court judges, and the judiciary will be subjected to multiple pressures to rule expediently rather than upon principle. Furthermore, and perhaps worse, we shall return to the abhorrent control of the bench by the aristocratic, sanctimonious lawyers, often the products of and dominated by the vested interests, who are noteworthy for their haughty criticism of "politicians." Judges need apologize to no one for their participation in politics. Many outstanding judges were great lawyers and advocates and yet were not above serving their communities in political office. These judges often have a deep love for their fellowman and a sense of justice acquirable only in the school of hard knocks, and not in the insulated sanctuaries of ivy halls.

Those who would take away the right of the people to elect State court judges cite early American history to show that the appointive system is an "American tradition." It might better be described as a holdover from colonial days, when the American colonies preferred to have judges selected by their own Governors rather than by the Crown. . . .

. . . between 1830 and 1861, 15 of the older States changed to the elective system. Among the explanations given for this "Jacksonian Revolt" were the growth of the West and the desire to break judicial monopoly by the aristocratic groups in the older States; the wave of democratic fervor which swept the world, bringing about universal manhood suffrage throughout America, and resulting in the Revolutions of 1830 and 1848 in Europe; recollections of judicial persecutions in the British Isles, which were partly responsible for waves of immigration to America; the unpopularity of many reactionary and inhuman rules of the common law which the courts followed and which the new State legislatures believed should be remedied by statutes; and the exercise by the courts of their power to declare laws unconstitutional, which thereby nullified liberal, remedial legislation.

It is significant that *every* State admitted after 1846, with the exception of Alaska and Hawaii, adopted the elective system. Presently, judges are popularly elected in three-fourths of the States. In Delaware, New Jersey, Maine, Massachusetts, New Hampshire, and Hawaii, the Governor appoints with the advice and consent of the Senate or the Governor's council. In Missouri, California, and Alaska there are composite appointive-elective plans; and in South Carolina, Virginia, Rhode Island, Connecticut, and Vermont the judges are elected by the legislature.

Those who say that no other country in the free world employs the elective system forget that the local judges in Switzerland, generally conceded to be a model of excellent government, historically have been selected by popular vote. . . .

Concededly, there are many defects in the elective system. A familiar criticism is that the mass of the people know little or nothing about the courts or judges. The same criticism of the elective system as to judges could, with equal plausibility, be applied to the many Federal, State, and municipal executive and legislative officeholders. In most instances, voters follow their political party's recommendations, on the basis that its nominees will so conduct themselves as to reflect the philosophy and tenets of their party. To cut into the right of the people to elect judges is a long step toward fascism. Soon, the vested interests, having acquired control of the judiciary, would, with equally plausible, if unsound, reasoning, seek domination of the executive and perhaps eventually the legislative branch of municipal, State, and Federal governments, by setting up self-perpetuating "commissions" and "committees" to select "qualified men." The people, they say now, are not capable of electing good judges. Next they will say the people are equally incapable of electing other government officials. . . .

Virtually all lawyers are unanimously in favor of reform of the court system in the sense of streamlining procedural rules, eliminating delays in the administration of justice, and in general the modernizing of judicial procedure. Some "reform groups" seek to obstruct this reform of the courts unless they can also acquire the appointive system of judges. Reform of the courts can be accomplished without taking away from the people their right to elect judges.

45

Unseating Unfit Judges

By Murray Teigh Bloom

IT IS RARE that a judge goes wrong. But, with 6,700 judges in the country, inevitably a few turn out incompetent or incapable of administering justice. And when it happens it is, in most states, a near impossibility to get them off the bench.

For example, in March 1961, the complaint of Mrs. Sylvia Goszkowski of Detroit came before the Michigan attorney general. Henderson Graham, the 43-year old probate judge of Tuscola County who had handled the settlement of her parents' will, was pressuring her to give him an unsecured loan of $20,000. If she didn't give it to him, he threatened, he would increase her bond as guardian of her younger sister's estate.

The Michigan attorney general's office started an investigation. Twice more Judge Graham visited the two sisters, who told him their answer was "No." He then warned them that the guardianship bond of $3,000 would have to be increased.

The attorney general's office presented evidence to the State Supreme Court, which held hearings and heard Judge Graham's explanations of his conduct: a non-lawyer, he said he was not familiar with judicial ethics. (Michigan is one of many states which do not require probate judges to be lawyers.) The court then unanimously recommended that the state legislature remove him from office. "Such conduct on the part of a judge is both intolerable and unpardonable," the court found.

In Michigan, as in most other states, the only effective way of removing a judge from office is through legislative removal proceedings. Two-thirds of the

Murray Teigh Bloom, "Unseating Unfit Judges," *National Civic Review,* February, 1963, pp. 70–72, 119. Reprinted by permission of the publisher.

House and Senate must approve the resolution ordering a judge's removal before the governor can take action. In April 1962 the Michigan House of Representatives met to consider the Judge Graham case and voted 100–3 to *turn down* the Supreme Court's recommendation to remove the judge.

The State Supreme Court promptly stripped Judge Graham of the power to act in any probate cases, but it was not able to stop his salary of $9,500 a year which he . . . [drew] until the end of his term in 1964.

Contrast this with what happened in April 1961 when a California woman wrote to her state's newly established and unique Commission on Judicial Qualifications about a local judge. He was often drunk on the bench and had recently been arrested in another county for drunken driving. "Please check on this situation so that we may have decent justice in here," she pleaded.

Within a week a state investigator was assigned to look into the accusation. Ten days later the investigator's carefully detailed report was studied by the full commission meeting in its permanent offices in San Francisco. The nine members agreed the judge was guilty of "habitual intemperance" and wrote him they would recommend his removal by the State Supreme Court. Late in May 1961 the judge resigned rather than face public charges.

The Graham case is typical of the great difficulty most other states encounter. In 1960 George E. Brand, former president of the Michigan Bar Association, checked court records as far back as possible and found that, out of 40 states, legislative attempts to invoke impeachment proceedings against judges had been made in only seventeen states. As a result nineteen judges were removed and three resigned — out of 52 impeachments.

The judicial salary Henderson Graham . . . [continued] to draw . . . [is] only a tiny part of the billion dollars we spend every year to pay our 6,700 judges and run the courts in which they sit. In most states once a judge assumes the bench his re-election as an incumbent is little more than a formality, and he can serve indefinitely with almost no danger of being unseated.

This almost certain job security plus the traditional deference for a judge is too heady a mixture for some. In a detailed analysis of the Los Angeles trial courts made for the American Bar Association in 1956, James G. Holbrook, professor of law at the University of Southern California, described what happens to a lawyer who is suddenly elevated to a judgeship:

"He finds himself surrounded by an almost fawning group. It is 'Yes, your honor, this' and 'Yes, your honor, that' from morning until night. Court attachés

are dependent upon him for what at his whim can be a pleasant or unpleasant task. Lawyers are dependent upon his pleasure as to the time of trial, conduct of trial and result of trial. Citizens have their property, their independence and even their lives dependent upon his judgment. There is no real control over his hours, his industriousness or his thoroughness. It must be a breath-taking sensation when all this finally dawns upon a judge. It takes both humility and untold strength of character to emerge unscathed."

Clearly, not all judges have the requisite qualities to emerge unscathed. During the American Bar Association convention last August an informal poll of ten trial judges and court administrative officers from different states revealed that each knew of at least one judge in his state who was unfit because of unjudicial conduct, senility or downright incompetence.

The problem also exists in federal courts where judges are appointed for life. It has happened even on the U.S. Supreme Court, as was disclosed only recently by Walter F. Murphy, associate professor of politics at Princeton University, after he was given access to the private papers of former Chief Justice William Howard Taft. In 1924 Taft was in poor health but was afraid to take any time away from court work because the senior associate justice, Joseph McKenna, 81, was no longer capable of sustained mental effort and had shown gross signs of senility for several years. In desperation the other justices agreed not to hand down decisions in cases where McKenna's vote was the deciding one. Finally after a reluctant showdown meeting in 1925 McKenna was persuaded to resign.

The court administrative officer of an eastern state told me of a judge, apparently mentally disturbed, now sitting on the bench in his state. "Sooner or later his antics are going to make headlines," the official said. "But under our state constitution only the legislature can remove a judge and so far they never have."

Sometimes, in desperation, harassed lawyers will try to unseat an unfit judge by political methods. The county bar association president in one western state told me how he and several other lawyers bucked a senile but politically powerful judge: "We got a good lawyer to run for the nomination and we had to raise a war chest to finance his campaign. Well, our man squeaked through — but if the old man had won, a lot of us could just as well have started building a law practice elsewhere."

In 1959 the American Bar Association, the American Judicature Society and the Institute of Judicial Administration, meeting in Chicago, unanimously concluded that we needed "a less cumbersome method to bring about the discipline or removal of a judge whose conduct has subjected or is likely to subject the court to public censure or reproach, or is prejudicial to the administration of justice."

That same year a California state legislative committee on the administration of justice found that certain judges "delayed decisions for months or even years." Some of the state's 898 judges took long vacations and worked short hours despite backlogs of cases awaiting trial. Some refused to accept assignment to cases they found unpleasant or dull. Some tolerated petty rackets involving "kickbacks" to court attachés. Some failed to appear for scheduled trials or took the bench while obviously under the influence of liquor. Some clung doggedly to their positions and salaries for years after they had been disabled by sickness or age. In one case a 68-year-old judge who continually pleaded ill-health was found to have received more than $33,000 in salary for nine mornings of work in two years. Yet in nearly a century California had had only two impeachment trials, one at the time of the Civil War when a conviction was changed by a later legislature. The second resulted in acquittal.

In November 1960 California voters overwhelmingly approved a constitutional amendment creating a state Commission on Judicial Qualifications empowered to recommend to the State Supreme Court the removal of a judge for cause, and granting the State Supreme Court power to act on the recommendation. The commission has nine members: five judges appointed by the Supreme Court, two experienced attorneys selected by the State Bar, two citizens named by the governor.

In its first two years the commission received 163 complaints, all carefully looked into even though many obviously came from disgruntled litigants who were simply bad losers. Of the 163 complaints, 46 merited further investigation. In ten cases the judges involved resigned or retired because of the commission's inquiry. In three of these cases, drinking was the problem. In three it was absenteeism. In three other cases it was emotional disturbance: one judge made improper comments to jurors, went out of his way to embarrass witnesses, had fits of rage at counsel; another was admitted by his psychiatrist to be "very disturbed" and emotionally unsuited to making judicial decisions. In only one instance was there intentional mishandling of court proceedings.

"Just the fact the commission is around has made many of our short-day judges sit much longer," says Justice A. Frank Bray, chairman of the commission. Also, there has been an improvement in the conduct of some judges. One complaint was about a judge who wouldn't permit the plaintiff to speak and told her if she didn't get out of the courtroom she would be arrested. Another was about a judge whose only reply to an attorney's lengthy, earnest argument was, "Horse feathers." These judges have been warned that no judge has a right to be crusty, arbitrary or short-tempered in his dealings with lawyers, litigants or witnesses.

Jack E. Frankel, executive secretary for the commission, is an attorney who for five years handled major disciplinary matters for the State Bar. One of the commission's most useful accomplishments, he says, is that at last it gives people an effective place to lodge complaints against judges. "Right now there are, I'm certain, hundreds of such complaints floating around in the other 49 states. The great majority of these are unmerited. But as long as a state doesn't have an agency to run down the grievances against judges and take action, these criticisms remain unchecked and dangerous rumors. In this way the few misfits on the bench can help accumulate a reservoir of distrust that tends in time to discredit the entire judiciary in the eyes of the public."

In the concluding selection Judge Vanderbilt, late Chief Justice of the New Jersey Supreme Court and one of the nation's most distinguished jurists, discusses the features which should characterize a good judicial system, with particular reference to ways in which common public complaints against the courts may be met.

46

The Essentials of a Sound Judicial System

By Arthur T. Vanderbilt

MEN INEVITABLY have disputes, and it is one of the great functions of the courts to adjudicate these according to law. This is termed the administration of civil justice. Men also commit offenses against the laws provided for the protection of all of us, and at the suit of the state the courts pass on the question of their guilt and enforce the law against any

Arthur T. Vanderbilt, "The Essentials of a Sound Judicial System," *Northwestern University Law Review,* March-April, 1953. Footnotes in original omitted. Reprinted by permission of the author and publisher.

wrongdoers in an effort to protect society. This we call the administration of criminal justice. Of the two, although most people, including many lawyers who should know better, do not seem to realize it, the administration of criminal law is by far the more important. Of what value is a civil right under a contract or to a piece of property, or even the right to life itself, if its owner cannot enjoy it because of some breakdown in the enforcement of the criminal law? Going a step further and looking at both the civil and criminal law, of what real worth are the fundamental rights guaranteed by our federal and state constitutions if they cannot be enforced in a fair trial? In the last analysis, then, the right to a fair trial is the most fundamental of all rights, for without it all other rights are mere words, empty and meaningless.

From this point of view the judiciary, though the weakest of the three great departments of government — "It has no influence over either the sword or the purse," to quote the *Federalist* — is the most important of all to the citizen in distress and looking for a fair trial, either civil or criminal. Everything that is necessary to accord him a fair trial is an essential of a sound judicial system. Here at least is one point where there is no conflict between the needs of the individual and of the public.

Fortunately for us all the essentials of a sound judicial system are relatively few in number and are well known to the legal profession from centuries of experience (both good and bad, I hasten to add). All we have to do to attain a sound judicial establishment is to overcome our professional inertia and selfishness and adopt the standards of judicial administration that every intelligent and public-spirited lawyer (my adjectives, you will note, limit the class considerably) knows should long since have been adopted. . . . Nothing else . . . would contribute so much to restoring the faith in government and the respect for law so essential to the preservation of democratic, representative government.

Let me enumerate and comment briefly on the several essentials of a sound judicial system as I see them:

1. The first essential of a sound judicial establishment is a simple system of courts, for the work of the best bench and bar may be greatly handicapped by a multiplicity of courts with overlapping jurisdictions. Lord Coke lists 74 courts in his *Fourth Institute,* but three are all that are needed in a modern judicial establishment: (1) a local court of limited civil and criminal jurisdiction, (2) a trial court of general statewide jurisdiction, and (3) an appellate court or courts, depending on the needs of the particular state. Although only three courts are called for, instead of the many courts with special jurisdictions as we now have in many states, there may well be — indeed there should be — considerable specialization by judges in the trial courts. Without limiting the general jurisdiction of each trial judge, he should be assigned to a division of his court specializing in the kind of work for which he is best qualified — criminal, civil (generally with a jury), equity, probate, juvenile, traffic, and the like. Some very good equity judges shrink from jury work and some very good law judges dislike equity. For sound judicial administration, therefore, someone should have the power to assign the judges where they are needed and to the work for which they are best fitted. Because this power of assignment is a delicate one to be exercised only on mature reflection for the best interest of the judicial establishment as a whole, it may best be committed to the chief judicial officer in the state and he, in turn, would do well to seek the advice of his colleagues, even though the ultimate responsibility for assignments must be solely his.

2. The second essential of a sound judicial system is, of course, a corps of judges, each of them utterly independent and beholden only to the law and to the Constitution, thoroughly grounded in his knowledge of the law and of human nature including its political manifestations, experienced at the bar in either trial or appellate work and preferably in both, of such a temperament that he can hear both sides of a case before making up his mind, devoted to the law and justice, industrious, and, above all, honest and believed to be honest. These standards necessarily exclude all judges who are not members of the bar and all part-time judges who are judges one minute and practicing lawyers the next. Relatively few judges have all these qualifications and yet are there any of them that you would dare to term superfluous? Of course, some good judges have learned their law after ascending the bench, and more have acquired courtroom experience as judges rather than as lawyers, but either process is an expensive and unsatisfactory one both for the litigants and the public and would not be tolerated in business. Some may question my insistence on a knowledge of man as a political animal, but politics plays so large a part in American life that a judge to be competent must know what it is all about. Understanding politics, however, is one thing; playing politics from the bench is something far different. It is utterly reprehensible.

How are we to recruit judges such as I have been describing? There is, it must be frankly admitted, no entirely foolproof way of selecting judges. The practice of executive appointment from among the leaders of the trial and appellate bar pursued in all common-law countries except our own produces the best results, but even so every now and then a distinguished barrister proves to be a mediocre judge. No system of selection could be worse, however, than popular elections on party tickets along with a host of other national, state, and local party candidates running for a wide variety of offices. . . .

The plain truth is that popular, partisan judicial elections would have failed long since were it not for the fact that in state after state about one-third of the judges in office die or resign, giving the governor an opportunity to make ad interim appointments. . . .

There is much to be said for requiring . . . the appointment of all judges on a bipartisan basis. Justice, on principle, should be bipartisan. Its administration should not be vested in a single party. Bipartisan appointments are the best way of proving to the public that one party does not control the courts and that the courts are not in politics. The matter is of especial importance in the decision of highly controversial political issues. If all the judges in a bipartisan court, regardless of party affiliations, concur in the decision of such an issue, as they frequently do, their decision carries a weight with the public that an opinion from a partisan bench could not possibly do. I am speaking from experience because in New Jersey, without any constitutional or statutory requirement, we have had a bipartisan judiciary for nearly a hundred years.

3. Honest and intelligent juries, representing a cross-section of the honest and intelligent citizenry of a county, are as essential to the administration of justice as upright and learned judges. It is a mockery of justice to go through the form of a trial with a dishonest or unintelligent juror in the jury box. The jury is an integral part of the administration of justice and the selection of the panel from which juries are drawn should therefore be entrusted to the courts or to commissioners appointed by the courts. This has been done in thirty-three states, but in the remaining fifteen states the selection of the jury panel is in political hands, with the inevitable resultant dangers to the administration of justice.

4. In addition to good judges and good jurors, we must have honorable, well educated lawyers, and an effective organization of the bar. It is too much to expect that the work of judges or of juries will often rise much above the level of the work of the lawyers appearing in the cases the judges and juries decide. . . .

The complexities of our age call for more than individually good lawyers. We need a good organized bar. And how may we recognize a good bar? Without attempting a definition, I venture to say that a good bar will feel a very real sense of responsibility for the administration of justice, for the selection of judges and jurors, for legal aid to all in the state who need it, both in civil and criminal litigation (I am very proud that the bar of my state was the first to realize this), for legal education both before and after admission, for enforcing the canons of judicial

and professional ethics, for eliminating the unauthorized practice of the law, for improving the substantive law, and for encouraging good government. A large order, you will say, but what may we omit without loss to both the profession and the public?

5. A simple court structure, good judges, jurors, and lawyers — what more do we need? We must have competent court clerks, stenographic reporters, and bailiffs, but above all we need an administrative judge and his *alter ego,* an administrative director of the courts working under him, to supervise the judicial system and to see that it functions effectively as a business organization. The Constitution of New Jersey was the first to declare that "The Chief Justice of the Supreme Court shall be the administrative head of all the courts in the state" and that "He shall appoint an administrative director of the courts to serve at his pleasure." I have found that my administrative work takes from a third to a half of my time and all the time, of course, of the administrative director and his staff. What other statewide business do you know of that attempts to operate without management, without supervision, without operating statistics, without periodic conferences of its key personnel, or without administrative rules? When you think of the lack of all these factors in most of our court systems, the wonder is that the judicial branch of our government has worked as well as it has.

With the right kind of courts, judges, jurors, lawyers, court officers, and administrative organization available, what else is needed for a sound judicial system suited to the needs of these troublesome times? Manifestly the next thing that is needed is a realization by all concerned of the defects of the judicial establishment, especially those defects which are so obvious that the people are complaining of them. These defects may be grouped under three heads, inexcusable delays, the lack of a fair trial on the merits of each case, and bad judicial manners. I will next discuss these defects in the order named.

6. Subordinate only to the complaint against dishonest judges is the popular resentment of the law's delays. The grievance is an ancient one. We find it mentioned in Magna Carta. Hamlet comments on it. Every step in the process of litigation, of course, takes time, but that is not what the public is complaining of. What the people object to is unnecessary delays. Often delays that are attributed to the courts should really be ascribed to the lawyers. I know of one New England state where the judges are unusually prompt in their decisions, but in which cases are often delayed by the bad habits of lawyers. The judges there owe the public and themselves the duty of placing the blame where it belongs.

Most of the delays of which complaint is made are quite avoidable. They fall into three classes:

First of all, litigants, witnesses, and jurors alike get very much annoyed when the judge fails to open court at the appointed hour. No single judicial fault, save lack of integrity, can do so much to create a bad impression. The failure of a judge to appear in court on time indicates to laymen his lack of interest in his judicial work and his unwillingness to conform to the rules of court, while insisting that others conform, as well as a failure to appreciate the value of other's time. It irritates the laymen's sense of equality, for with all their respect for the law and for judicial office as symbolizing the law, people regard a judge as a man. They have been taught, have they not, that all men are equal, and a judge should be wise enough to recognize their teaching. I have discovered that this bad judicial habit could be cured only by a positive rule requiring the opening of court at a fixed hour throughout the state. Here again a strong example has proved helpful; if the seven justices of our supreme court can get to the state house from all over the state in time to open court at ten o'clock, surely any judge can manage to get to his nearby county seat by the same hour. To some of you this may seem a small matter and unworthy even of mention here, but in actual practice it is an essential rule of judicial administration.

The second cause of complaint about the law's delays is the failure to get on to trial after all the necessary preliminaries of pleading and pretrial procedures have been disposed of. Here let me observe that a judge can never do his best work when he is asked to tackle a task which he knows is impossible of accomplishment, when he sees that for every case he tries two are being added to the list. Where arrearages have accumulated, the number of judges must be increased, either temporarily or permanently. It is a curious but nevertheless demonstrable judicial fact that two judges working on the same calendar can dispose of twice as many cases as they could working separately in different courthouses. The extent to which this principle may be applied depends upon the number of available courtrooms, the number of available trial judges, and the number of available trial lawyers. But subject to these limitations, an increase in the number of judges, either permanently or temporarily, at the congested spot is the first step in eliminating delays in bringing cases on to trial. This requires giving to someone, preferably to the chief justice, the power to assign the trial judges to those counties where they are most needed. Whatever success we have had in New Jersey in clearing our calendars — some cases in Chancery as much as ten or twenty years old — I think must be attributed in large measure to the power given by our Constitution to the chief justice to assign judges. In Chancery matters we cleared the decks within six months. On the law side within two years we disposed of all arrearages in sixteen of our twenty-one counties so that cases could be tried within three or four months after they were started, and in the remaining five counties we obtained a similar state of currency within the third court year — a striking contrast to the delays of the old system, in which one not infrequently had to wait two or three years for a jury trial.

In the work of clearing the dockets compulsory pretrial conferences, in all court cases except divorce cases, have also played a large part, for we have discovered that in county after county numerous cases have been settled before trial as a result of what has developed at the pretrial conference. The pretrial conference is an invaluable feature of adequate judicial administration and I shall refer to it again in dealing with trials on the merits where I deem it even more important. . . .

The final cause of delay is the failure of the judge to promptly decide a case after he has heard the testimony, read the briefs (in advance of the arguments, of course), and heard the arguments of counsel. These delays in deciding matters are largely a matter of bad judicial habit. A judge can only decide one case at a time. No judge, moreover, will ever know more about a given case than he does when the testimony is fresh in his mind and while the arguments of counsel are still ringing in his ears. We in New Jersey have suffered much in the past from this bad judicial habit of delaying decisions. Some of our vice chancellors were truly judicial descendants of Lord Eldon. For them to delay a decision six, eight, ten, or even twelve years was not unknown. Four years ago when our new system started I had to assign three judges to work for several weeks on the arrears of one distinguished vice chancellor who had retired leaving a large number of cases undecided, some dating back more than six years. This bad habit of delaying decisions is not an easy one to break, but our administrative rule requiring all motions to be decided as a matter of routine within ten days, all cases to be disposed of within four weeks after trial, and all motions and cases heard but undecided to be reported in the judge's weekly report has completely eliminated the public's justifiable criticism of this phase of the law's delays. Most judges would rather decide a case than report it as undecided. The judge's weekly report is therefore an indispensable aid to sound judicial administration, and I shall have more to say of it in another connection.

7. The next great popular grievance against the courts is a failure in too many cases to get a decision on the merits. All too often the tendency is for a trial to become a battle between opposing counsel rather than an orderly, rational search for the truth on the merits of the controversy. There can be no doubt of the justice of this complaint. It is a com-

plaint that is more difficult to overcome than the dishonesty — or the reputation therefor — of some judges or the law's delays. Three factors in particular contribute to this great evil. The first is the popular notion that a trial, and especially a criminal trial, is a sporting event rather than an orderly search for truth with justice as its great objective. In all too many communities counsel are still rated primarily for their histrionic ability. Secondly, this improper attitude toward litigation has been heightened by the fact that in the second quarter of the nineteenth century in many of the states the chief powers of the common-law trial judge were taken away from him by legislation as part of the equalitarian and anti-professional revolt that culminated in the triumph of Jacksonian democracy. In many states the trial judge was deprived of the right to put questions to the witnesses even when they were necessary to bring out the truth. He was stripped of the right to organize the evidence into a systematic whole in his charge to the jury and to comment in his charge on the testimony of the witnesses. He was even shorn of his right to charge the jury in his own language, being obliged to charge in the technical language of the requests to charge submitted to him by counsel. Moreover, his charge so-called, but really his selection between the plaintiff's or the defendant's requests to charge, came before the summation to the jury by the defendant's and the plaintiff's counsel, so that whatever the judge said was quite forgotten by the jury after it had listened to the lawyers' barrage and counterbarrage of eloquence. The third cause of difficulty in the trial courts is the fact that the rules of pleading, practice, and procedure were prescribed by the legislature and in many states became increasingly complicated as a result of continuous legislative tinkering, with the result that the trial judge was often forced by statute to do things in the course of the trial that were obviously unjust and contrary to common sense. The trial judge was thus reduced to the position of an umpire all but gagged and blindfolded.

The situation I am portraying is by no means fanciful. In this age of scientific inquiry, there are still twenty states in which the judge is not allowed to sum up the evidence, thirty-six states in which he is not allowed to comment on the evidence, twenty states where the instructions precede the final argument of counsel, and three states in which, believe it or not, the court must instruct the jury that his statements of the law are purely advisory and that it has the right in criminal cases to find the law as well as the facts! And yet with these odd notions of trial procedure we still expect judges and juries to do justice.

The first step in remedying the situation is, of course, to restore to the trial judge his common-law power to preside effectively at the trial. This is easier said than done. Many counsel cling tenaciously to their prerogative of surprise in the courtroom, to their concept of a trial as a battle of wits between two lawyers rather than a search for the truth, to the notion that the judge should be seen but not heard. Until these false notions are banished, justice will often be but a sham and a mockery.

The next step is to give the rule-making power to the highest court in each state. After what has been accomplished in the federal courts through the judicial exercise of the rule-making power, there should be no need of any argument to establish its advantage over legislative codes. The results of judicial rule-making speak for themselves. I doubt very much that strict judicial rule-making — and by that I mean the making of rules by the judges alone — would have been a great improvement on codes and statutes had not the methods pursued by the United States Supreme Court in drafting the Rules of Civil and Criminal Procedure insured the workability of its rules. Not only were the rules drafted by advisory committees of experts appointed by the court, but they were submitted and resubmitted to the criticism of the bench and bar throughout the country. After ten years of use the Civil Rules have again been reworked by the same process and over half of them have been amended. This method gives the court the benefit of the experience of both trial judges and practicing lawyers. The process of rule-making should be continuous. Judicial conferences or judicial councils in the several states should annually call for suggestions from the bench and bar and these suggestions should be carefully debated each year for the benefit of the supreme court in its rule-making capacity. Through such a continuous process, and through this process only, may we hope for a system of procedure that will be at all times adapted to its purpose and that will be at all times subordinate to establishing the substantive rights of the litigants.

A third step in obtaining a trial on the merits rather than a theatrical performance is the full use of modern pretrial procedures, such as interrogatories, depositions, examinations before trial, inspections and the like, culminating in a pretrial conference at which the pleadings are reviewed to see how they can be simplified and the issues are restated as preliminaries to seeing what facts may be stipulated and what documents may be admitted so as to shorten the trial. The pretrial conference gives counsel an opportunity, if they so desire, to canvass the possibilities of settlement, but the judge, of course, must never attempt to force a settlement. The most important aspect of pretrial conferences is not that many cases are customarily settled as a result of each party facing the facts on both sides for the first time under expert guidance, nor is it that the trial time of each case is greatly reduced. The great advantage of pretrial conferences is that the judge has a pre-view of what will be coming at the trial, and he can, if he thinks it necessary in an unusual case, direct the filing of briefs in advance of the trial. No longer does he have to fumble through the pleadings to find out what the case is all about, while endeavoring to listen to the opening statements of counsel. No longer need he guess the answer to novel questions of law. He has a complete outline of the trial before him in the form of the pretrial conference order and he is master of the situation from the outset.

8. The third significant cause of public discon-tent with the courts springs from an occasional ex-hibition of judicial bad manners. There is less of it in the appellate courts than in the trial courts for the reason, among others, that the process of legal argu-ment does not so often lead to the clashes that char-acterize the presentation of testimony. Judging from the number of complaints that come my way, judicial discourtesy is very much more prevalent in the crimi-nal courts of limited jurisdiction than in either the general trial courts or the local civil courts. This may be accounted for in part by the fact that a large number of municipal magistrates are still laymen, in part by the difference in the mental attitude of the attorneys appearing in the local criminal courts, and in part by the volume of work in some of these courts. But whatever the cause there can be no ex-cuse whatsoever for judicial discourtesy. A judge's bad manners can only serve to bring the administra-tion of justice into disrepute. Establishing conditions under which a judge may work honestly and keep his self-respect will go a long way toward reducing com-plaints on this score. A judge who is not beholden to anyone and who is up to date with his work is less likely to be irritable than one who is under obli-gations and fears that others know it, or who is be-hind with his work. But whatever the cause, an irritable judge cannot be justified or tolerated in view of the disrespect for law which he inevitably creates. Requiring a judge, even of a local court, to wear a judicial robe has a marked tendency to increase decorum in the courtroom. It helps to keep court officers in their place. Every witness should stand and everyone in the room should remain silent while the oath is being administered to the witness by the judge himself. Applying to the local criminal courts the same rules of conduct as are applied in other courts is equally essential. But the affirmative way of meeting any charges of discourtesy in the local criminal courts is for the judge to take the necessary minute or two to explain to each defendant just why he is being found guilty and why the particular sen-tence is being imposed on him. This can be done in a friendly manner so as to make clear the purpose of the sentence, whether it be intended as punishment for a violation of the law or as a deterrent for the

purpose of saving life and limb. I know of one judge who by doing just this had eighty per cent of his "customers" thank him publicly for his courtesy, while at the same time he had increased the amount of his fines over sixty per cent. There is much to be said for the practice of the English chancellor who, when asked his formula for selecting judges, replied, "I pick a gentleman and if he knows a little law so much the better." We need gentlemen in our local courts quite as much as in our courts of general jurisdiction.

While we are awaiting the judicial millennium, perhaps the most effective way of counselling cour-tesy is for the chief justice to bring to the attention of the individual judge every charge of discourtesy by sending him a copy of any complaint against him and asking for his version of the facts. Sometimes the judicial alibis are so thin as to be almost trans-parent and they are often accompanied by a consid-erable show of indignation, but it is noticeable that following such correspondence complaints cease to come from the particular community again. More-over, the news of such correspondence travels fast throughout a county by what is commonly known as "the grapevine" and serves as a deterrent to other judges. From my experience I arrive at another principle of judicial administration. Every complaint should promptly receive the chief justice's personal attention and should be pursued to a conclusion both with the complainant and with the judge against whom the complaint is made. . . .

9. Judges as well as litigants have their complaints. A principle of judicial administration, rarely dis-cussed publicly but never out of the minds of the judges, is the fair division of work. Some judges are much more effective in their work than others; some judges are reversed less than others; some judges give more satisfaction to the bar and to the public than others; and some judges are more conscientious, more devoted to their work than others. These individual differences cannot be changed administratively, but there should and can be equality in the number of hours each judge of the same court spends in the courtroom. This may be accomplished by having each judge make a weekly report of the number of hours he has spent on the bench each court day, the number of cases and motions he has heard and dis-posed of, and the number of cases and motions he has heard but has not disposed of, with the reasons therefor. With this information available in sum-marized form, the chief justice is in a position not only to make assignments of the judges to meet emergencies at the time they arise without waiting until a heavy list has been allowed to accumulate in a particular county, but also to prevent inequalities in work. You may ask, how will the making of a weekly report make an indolent judge work? The chief jus-tice and his administrative director cannot hope to

make a lazy judge work, and neither of them should be expected to be a policeman, but if summaries of these weekly reports are circularized among the judges in each court, it is truly remarkable how the relatively few laggards will mend their ways rather than incur the silent or occasionally vocal censure of their brother judges.

10. Statistics from the judges' weekly reports and from other data supplied by the court clerks are compiled in weekly and monthly reports by the administrative director, and these in turn are combined into quarterly and annual reports. In these reports there are comparative summaries of the work of the individual judges which disclose to every judge and to the public, whether his record is above or below the average for his court. In the relatively few states where any judicial statistics at all are gathered, they have all too generally been compiled long after the event. I call these "dead" or historical statistics, because for the most part they are useless in affecting the work of the judicial establishment currently. After working with "live" statistics for four years, I am so impressed with their importance that I do not see how a judicial system can function effectively without them any more than a business could be run without current reports from its accounting department. By using "live" statistics and by assigning our judges on the basis of such statistics where they were most needed and to the kind of work they could best do, we not only increased the output of our general courts ninety-eight per cent in the first year and an additional twenty per cent in the second year — with twenty per cent fewer judges — but we have also improved the judges' working conditions and the quality of their work immeasurably. I am therefore rather emphatic in asserting that "live" statistics assembled into weekly, monthly, quarterly, and annual reports, both for the use of the chief justice and the judges themselves and for information of the public, are an essential of orderly judicial administration.

11. The examination of these weekly, monthly, quarterly, and annual reports, the assignment of judges and the general supervision of their work, the investigation of complaints from individuals or bar associations, conferences with individual judges concerning their work, attendance every few months at informal meetings of the judges of each court and each division thereof (I would list such meetings, which generally are dinner meetings with their friendly personal contacts, as indispensable to sound judicial administration) all put a heavy burden on the chief justice of a state who is given broad powers of administration, even though he has the aid of a competent administrative director of the courts and staff. I am convinced from my experience, however, that all of these things are as indispensable to the functioning of an effective judicial establishment as they are to a business organization. Yet strangely enough those powers are rarely granted. Indeed, in twelve states the chief justice shifts every year or so and in two of these states, believe it or not, every six months. It is not without political significance that these short terms are so arranged that the title goes to a judge who is about to run for reelection. Clearly, it is essential for the proper administration of justice that there be a chief justice with a substantial term of office and with the power to call for reports, to collect "live" statistics, to assign the judges, to supervise the work of all the courts including the local criminal courts, to hold informal conferences with the judges, and to call judicial conferences in which the bar and the public are liberally represented to discuss the work of the judicial establishment.

12. The burden of this work necessitates giving the chief justice an administrative director of the courts to act as his *alter ego* in attending to the multitudinous details of running a great state-wide business with branches in every county and in every community of the state. Time will not permit me to detail the wide variety of his activities. Such an officer must not only be a good lawyer and a diplomat versed in the ways of judges, but he must have executive ability and be skilled in the dispatch of business. Such an administrative director is, it goes almost without saying, a *sine qua non* of successful judicial administration.

13. The final essential of a sound judicial system is an abiding conviction, consistently acted upon by everyone in the judicial establishment, that the law and the courts exist not for the benefit of judges or lawyers or court officers who are merely the servants of the law, but for the benefit of the litigants and of the state.

There is nothing esoteric about these essentials of a sound judicial system. They are all quite obvious. They are not difficult to put into effect once there is the will to do so. They must be achieved in every state if we are to have an administration of justice worthy of the name. There can be no doubt as to the importance to us all of attaining such a goal if our kind of government is to function as it should. The only question is whether the judges and lawyers in each state will take the leadership in fulfilling the foremost obligation of the profession to society or whether they will abdicate to laymen. Once we become convinced of this self-evident truth, the law becomes our mission in the sense so eloquently described by Holmes:

"Law is the business to which my life is devoted, and I should show less than devotion if I did not do what in me lies to improve it, and when I perceive what seems to me the ideal of its future, if I hesitated to point it out and to press toward it with all my heart."

CHAPTER TEN

Forms of City Government

NO PATTERN OF GOVERNMENTAL ORGANIZATION or machinery will guarantee good government, but it is nevertheless true that certain forms at least may make good government easier to achieve. Experience with the four major types prevalent in the United States has been sufficiently extensive to permit worth-while comparisons. In the first article the indictment against weak-mayor and commission government (with faint praise for the strong-mayor form) is read by the National Municipal League, for many years the principal national organization devoting itself to the cause of local government reform. As the leading crusader in its behalf, the League then presents the case for the council-manager plan.

While generally successful and until rather recently rarely criticized, council-manager government has naturally had varying results in different cities. It is most vulnerable on the point of the providing of adequate political leadership, particularly in the larger cities, and the apparent assumption of some of its proponents that "good government" means simply efficient municipal housekeeping. The working of the plan in practice is vigorously criticized by a Madison, Wisconsin, newspaper publisher. Professor Sayre then advocates the strong-mayor plan with a mayor-appointed chief administrator, in the process suggesting that the council-manager system is inadequate for the larger communities. The reply, assailing both his logic and the validity of his criticisms, is by a prominent research scholar and consultant to constitution and charter commissions.

47

Weak-Mayor, Commission, and Strong-Mayor Government

WHAT FORMS of municipal government are there in the United States and how have they worked? . . .

Experience with the several forms has been ample

Forms of Municipal Government — How Have They Worked? (New York: National Municipal League, 1953), pp. 1–12. Footnotes in original omitted. Reprinted by permission of the publisher.

to enable qualified observers to assemble overwhelming evidence of their relative usefulness and effectiveness. The discussion in these pages may be considered not simply the judgment of the [National Municipal] League but as representing the findings of hundreds of recognized authorities.

Local government exists to perform functions and render services which the people of the community demand and which can be performed more cheaply and satisfactorily by government.

The gross cost of government in taxes cannot alone determine how good government is. Rather, the citizen's questions should be: (1) Am I receiving all the services which government should, by reason of economy and convenience, rightfully perform? (2) Are those services being efficiently rendered? (3) Is government sufficiently subject to democratic control, sufficiently responsive to public opinion, in performing those services? . . .

WEAK-MAYOR FORM

The weak-mayor form . . . has shown itself to be a thoroughly inadequate type of municipal structure. In recent years this form has been discarded by city after city and virtually no new adoptions are being recorded. Its early extinction should be welcomed. It was most in vogue during the nineteenth century, when a theory was current that democracy was best served by directly electing as many officials as possible, dividing responsibility and relying on elaborate checks and balances to prevent abuse of power. . . .

The weak-mayor form of government has been found undesirable because it lends itself easily to political manipulation, does not provide successfully for competent department heads or other personnel, lacks a unifying, responsible, single executive head, and is so diffused as to make effective voter control at the polls almost impossible.

COMMISSION FORM

The commission form of government . . . is little if any more successful than the weak-mayor form. . . . Its apparent simplicity gave the plan a quick vogue but later, after trial, many cities discarded it. More are doing so each year. Des Moines, Iowa, rated with Galveston as co-author of the commission plan, abandoned it in favor of the council-manager plan in 1949. . . .

While the plan sounds simple, it has been found to have most of the defects of the weak-mayor form and some others peculiar to itself. Government under this form lends itself to political manipulation, does not provide successfully for competent department heads or other personnel, lacks a single unifying responsible executive, and provides no adequate brakes on government spending. It is so conducive to buck-passing that although the voter needs to make only five choices at the polls he does not know whom to blame for bad government or to praise for good government.

Policy and administration fused

The chief fault of the commission form is that it makes no organization distinction between the policy-making function of government and the administrative function. This is not only unworkable from the practical point of view but it is also contrary to firmly established American governmental tradition, which from the beginning distinguished between the executive and legislative branches of government and attempted to keep them separate.

An even more important objection to fusing in a commission both administrative and policy-making functions is that successful administrators and successful legislators need very different qualifications. Administration of a city department, especially in a large city, is a job which takes considerable executive ability plus knowledge of the particular specialized subject matter with which the department is concerned. A policy-maker, on the other hand, must be the kind of person who *represents* others and knows what they want government to do.

Commissioners are very likely to be unfit for administrative jobs. The process of election can seldom carry to office men who have the talent for administration. Personality, connections, backing, a political organization, are the factors which produce votes. A good administator may not — and frequently does not — have these attributes. Moreover, those men who have the qualities necessary to successful public administration are rarely willing to run for office under the conditions of the commission plan. A professional man is likely to refuse to face the uncertainty of tenure and possible loss of his job after two or four years for reasons which may be entirely unconnected with his ability to do his job well.

Elected commissioners inevitably have political debts to individuals or machines that help elect them. This means that they make appointments within the departments they administer, not because of the fitness of appointees for the job, but because of their political qualifications or relationships. The number of votes a job applicant controls becomes more important than his training. Since most commissioners look forward to reelection, after past political debts are paid they must maintain their political bridges by continuing to administer their departments on a spoils basis. Sometimes political obligations may carry even further than appointments. In awarding city contracts, in the thousands of transactions connected with any city department, a commissioner can easily throw business or favors in the direction of political advantage.

A frequent result of the commissioners' free access to spoils is that one commissioner eventually succeeds in building up a personal political machine so powerful that he can dominate all the other commissioners. Some notorious commissioner-bosses have been produced in American commission-governed cities and their names have frequently been associated with scandal and corruption.

No executive

One of the most serious shortcomings of the commission form as an instrument of practical, democratic local government is its failure to provide an executive head for the government. History shows an impressive record of failure with the multiple executive form. Even parliamentary forms of government give one of the ministers the title and powers of an executive. But, while under the commission plan one official is designated mayor, he is legally no more than a chairman for the commission while it is exercising its legislative role. The mayor has no authority at all over his fellow-commissioners in their administrative roles. Whatever influence he may have is moral, not legal.

The result of the lack of an executive head can be a catalogue of governmental failure. There is no brake on the activities of each department. There is no way of coordinating the activities of the departments. There is no one with an over-all, balanced view of the financial needs of each department. In case of some serious governmental error or misdeed, there is no one on whom the legislative body or the voters can fix blame. There is no one source of authority to whom citizens and government employees can go with problems or complaints. There is no agent competent to devise and execute a plan for the work of the government. In short, under the commission form there is not one government but five little governments, all of which may be riding off in different directions.

A spending machine

One of the most serious faults of commission government is its failure to provide any check on governmental spending. Because the men who vote the funds are the same men who spend them, there is little chance of governmental appropriations being cut down, whereas the tendency for them to rise is almost irresistible. Each commissioner is characteristically near-sighted in estimating the needs of his own department. It is inevitable that he should always ask for as much as he can possibly get. If the commissioner is trying to advance politically, he will fight for more jobs to fill and more contracts to award, in order to build up his sphere of influence. Even a politically unambitious commissioner will inevitably see the needs of his own department more clearly than those of other departments and will fight for the aggrandizement of his division of the government. Executives everywhere recognize this characteristic short-sightedness on the part of a department head and commonly scrutinize departmental budget estimates, for instance, with an eye to paring down some in order to make them more nearly comparable to the others. But the commission form provides no one to pare down, adjust or coordinate. Spending is the commissioner's job and there is no executive whose job is saving. The old principle of the pork barrel is always in operation. From the financial standpoint, the *commission form is a motor car with an accelerator but no brake.* . . .

STRONG-MAYOR FORM

The strong-mayor form has been more successful than either the weak-mayor plan or the commission form. . . .

Many cities, finding it impossible to obtain satisfactory results from their weak-mayor charters, sought relief by simplifying structure, strengthening the mayor and eliminating some or all of the separately elected administrative officers. Some of these cities have thus come to possess fairly clean-cut strong-mayor charters, but a great many others retain enough of the characteristic features of their old charters to make it difficult to classify them. The fact is that mayor-council cities range all along the scale from those where the mayor is little more than a figurehead to those like Detroit, Cleveland and Pittsburgh, where the mayor is the responsible head of the whole city administration. This explains why there are no comprehensive lists of weak-mayor and strong-mayor charters. . . .

The strong-mayor form automatically corrects one of the most serious defects of both the commission form and the weak-mayor form — lack of a single responsible executive. It also eliminates the commission plan's dangerous union of administrative and policymaking functions. The council is responsible for legislation and policymaking, while the mayor's job is administrative except in his power to recommend measures and veto acts of council.

But the strong-mayor form does not eliminate other defects.

A politician-administrator

First of these is the lack of administrative expertness. For the same reason that trained municipal executives are not normally elected to a city commission, only by chance would a qualified administrator be elected mayor. The experience of cities operating under the strong-mayor form is that *occasionally* a mayor is elected who is competent to direct the complicated business of the city. When this happens, the strong-mayor form of government is at its best. But such mayors are rare. There are few men who are both good enough executives to run a huge city organization and good enough politicians to be elected.

Even when a strong executive does happen to be elected mayor, there are serious obstacles in the way of successful government. The tremendous political effort which must be expended to achieve election inevitably carries with it strong political obligations. The mayor's comprehensive power to make appointments to and direct the workings of city departments provides a convenient avenue for the discharge of those obligations and for the maintenance of the political machine which is necessary to reelection. In other words, almost any mayor is forced to play politics with the city administration. Only a man of exceptional personality, capacity, determination and ideals could avoid this necessity. So rare is this combination that it might be called the exception that proves the rule. The extent to which the American people have taken spoils politics for granted in their local governments is sad evidence of this fact.

Another hazard inherent in the strong-mayor form is the possibility of a deadlock between the mayor and the council. Since council controls the purse strings, it may stop the mayor at any point. But the mayor may block the council with his veto power. Therefore, political differences between mayor and council sometimes seriously impede the day-to-day governmental functions which are so essential to the ordinary progress of city life. Even where there is little or no open antagonism between mayor and council, there has generally been a marked disinclination on the part of council to provide an able mayor with the expert staff needed for effective management.

In the cities where the strong-mayor form is in use, it has provided good government only spasmodically. . . .

Mayor-administrator plan

To correct some of its defects, a variation of the strong mayor form is sometimes proposed which involves the employment of a chief administrative officer by the mayor. Experience with it is meager, since only a few cities have tried variants of this plan. It is an attempt to combine professional administration with an executive who is elected.

The plan provides that the mayor shall appoint an administrative officer who is charged with supervising the work of city departments while the mayor concerns himself only with broad questions of administrative policy. This officer in theory would be a professionally qualified non-political executive. It is the intention of the plan thus to make up for the mayor's shortcomings as an executive while continuing to elect the one man who would be responsible for administration of the city's affairs.

That the appointed administrative officer is likely to become a glorified secretary of the mayor, who has the power to hire and fire him, is indicated by experience in some places, but experience is too limited to generalize it. It is, of course, impossible to have *two* responsible executives. The administrator or manager or deputy mayor — whatever his title —

is likely to be deprived by this arrangement of the independence of action which is necessary to keep administration expert and free of political influence. At any rate, the success of the plan in any city will depend entirely on the inclination and ability of successive mayors to appoint the right kind of man and give him the necessary freedom to act.

In effect, then, this plan would appear to have advantages and disadvantages somewhat similar to those that attend the strong-mayor form. It may have other benefits and defects as well, which are yet unknown because the plan has been so little tried. It is probably one step ahead of the strong-mayor form since it provides at least the *possibility* of professional administration. . . .

48

The Case for Council-Manager Government

How the plan works

The essential features of the plan are:

1. A short ballot with few elective offices and all of them important enough to attract full public scrutiny.

2. A small council which holds all the city's powers.

3. A single-headed administration under a professional city manager chosen by the council. . . .

A big reason for the success of the manager plan is its simplicity. The voters elect councilmen. The council appoints and may remove the city manager, a trained administrator. The manager appoints and may remove all department heads. Subject to civil service provisions he is responsible for selection of other administrative employees.

Although the council may fire the manager at any time, it may not interfere with his appointments or dismissals. Neither may the council go over his head to give orders direct to employees.

. . . Responsibility is centralized so that both credit and blame may be fairly placed. Here is a

The Story of the Council-Manager Plan (New York: National Municipal League, 1952). A few excerpts are from the 1949 edition of this pamphlet. Footnotes in original omitted. Reprinted by permission of the publisher.

governmental organization that any voter can understand.

The manager plan surpasses other systems because it remedies their inherent defects. Here's how:

1. The plan provides better executives. Appointment on the basis of experience and ability pays off far better than election on the basis of hand-shaking and baby-kissing.

2. The plan tends to eliminate the spoils system. To protect his own record and to advance in his profession, the manager must hire on merit instead of because an applicant was sent around by Fred or Mike.

3. The plan is understood by the voter. Other forms of government compel the voter to choose executives as well as policy-makers. Under the manager plan the voters elect only the five, seven or nine councilmen. That's easy, since the voter picks the councilmen whose policies he agrees with.

4. The plan centralizes responsibility in the council. The voter knows whom to blame for bad government and what to do about it at the polls.

5. The plan gives a coordinated administration headed by an experienced man who is not dependent on politics. The old forms usually divide administrative responsibility among untrained executives whose political interests tempt them to act like prima donnas rather than as a team. On the other hand most public school systems (which were designed to keep the schools clear of politics), most business corporations, labor unions and other enterprises have exactly the same setup as the manager plan. The voters, stockholders or members choose a board to determine policy and to hire a competent executive to do the work. If the executive makes good, he keeps his job and gets a raise. If he fails, he is out. . . .

The plan was impartially surveyed over a 3-year period (1937–1940) by the Committee on Public Administration of the Social Science Research Council. The committee found that the plan "by comparison with the preceding forms of government . . . brought a diminution of partisan or factional influence over the government . . . furthered long-range planning . . . raising the standards of public employment . . . improving the methods of financial management. . . . The great contribution of the new form of government was to make a single small governing body collectively responsible to the voters for all aspects of the city government."

The form is important

A form of government is like a workman's tools. The best mechanic cannot do good work with defective tools but a mediocre workman can do better with good tools than with poor ones.

American cities have generally used two forms of government other than the manager plan: (1) the mayor-council type and (2) the commission type. Neither has consistently provided good government. Both have produced poor executives and furthered the spoils system.

Why?

Because both these forms attempt to *elect* administrators to manage the city's business in denial of the sound principle: to get qualified administrators, *appoint:* to get representative policy-makers, *elect*.

For many years the trend has been away from the old long ballot listing countless officers from mayor to dogcatcher. A popularity contest is a bad way to pick a school superintendent, a health officer, a water system engineer or anyone else for a job that requires technical training. Hence it is all the more important to appoint on the basis of training and ability the administrator who must direct the work of all these technicians.

Voters have no way of measuring a candidate's administrative ability, if any. They can determine whether they agree with his policies and politics and whether they want him as a representative. But they can hardly check on the details of his career to decide whether he would make a good executive. . . .

No one-man power

In this country we rightly fear anything that smacks of dictatorship no matter how efficient it may seem. There is no trace of dictatorship in the manager plan. The plan's greatest strength is derived from its sensitivity and obedience to informed public opinion — and informed public opinion is always in favor of good government.

Democracy consists in *controlling* public officials, not in *electing* all of them. There is nothing undemocratic about appointing the top administrator. Our experience in electing administrators has been a disappointment. This system has tended to produce distinctly anti-democratic political machines and a record of graft and waste that adds no laurels to the democratic tradition.

The most effective way for the people to get a firm grip on the governmental organization is by putting in the city hall a policy-making council of citizens who will appoint a professional administrator to carry out their policies. Democracy cannot work unless the administrators do the people's work. In some cities inefficient administration defeats the voters' wishes more effectively than outright defiance.

Council holds the reins

The council is very important under the council-manager plan. It is the board of directors of the municipal corporation, with power to hire and fire the city manager and to direct policy. Councilmen usually meet with the manager every week, find the business well prepared for their consideration, review his proposals, put him to the proof and take responsibility for whatever they authorize him to do. By its importance, coupled with relief from technical detail, the position of councilman attracts high-caliber candidates and makes service acceptable to men who value their time. . . .

The mayor's role

Paradoxically, the manager plan gives the mayor a chance for a better role than he can fill under the strong-mayor plan (next best to the manager plan). The mayor is freed from technical administration which he may not be fitted for and may not desire. Above all, he is freed from the daily procession of job and favor seekers. Hence the mayor can concentrate on leadership of the council while it shapes policies.

It is the mayor's job also to preside over council meetings, to act in emergencies, to interpret to the voters the work of the city, to take the spotlight at official functions and to get himself and his colleagues reelected on their record. The mayor is, in the finest sense of the term, the city's political leader. . . .

The manager's reward

The city manager is a professional. He should not be expected to have divine wisdom but he generally possesses talent, experience, the ability to work hard and a desire to get ahead in his career. Good city managers are rewarded with higher pay and bigger jobs. . . .

City councils demand experienced men and they can and do get them. In 1950 they selected out-of-town managers in 76% of the cases — proof of their freedom from political and patronage considerations, especially when it is remembered that the manager-ship is always the top-salaried job.

There have now been hundreds of promotions from city to city. Twenty-nine managers in office each have more than 25 years of manager experience. The pool of experience is vast. Since 1912 there have been more than three thousand managers. . . .

The citizen's responsibility

Some people object that the manager plan does not guarantee good government. Of course it doesn't. No system can. But former Governor Charles Edison of New Jersey, president of the National Municipal League, has pointed out that a good council-manager charter makes "good government easy and natural, boss-ridden government difficult and unnatural."

That is the story of the plan in a nutshell. It opens wide the door to good government whenever the good citizens are ready to move in and take over.

49

The City-Manager Plan Is
Not the Answer

By William T. Evjue
as told to Ray Josephs

HAVE YOU EVER planned some activity or project, imagined it through to perfection, then gone from paper to practice — only to discover that ideas which sound great in theory don't always work out in action?

That's one of the major reasons I am so strongly opposed to the city-manager system. Again and again I've listened to the persuasive arguments from its advocates:

"If your community needs better government, try our neatly prepackaged, all-purpose solution."

But take it from one who has lived through the plan in operation — the practicalities don't equal the suppositions.

The basis of the manager plan is that *you,* the voters, elect a city council to set policy and that *they* hire a manager to administer the decisions. What you usually get, I'm afraid, is a distant executive, far removed from and neither responsive nor responsible to you and me, the average citizen.

I think I can best explain how it works by the very personal experience of our community — largest city to have tried and then abandoned the plan in the last ten years.

As a civic booster, I bow to no one in calling Madison, Wisconsin, a wonderful town. Yet I've never been blind to its shortcomings. Like most Madisonites, I'm naturally anxious to see it run better.

As the state capital, and home of the progressive University of Wisconsin, our population of 100,000 has always had standards far above many communi-

"Is the City-Manager Plan the Answer? No," William T. Evjue; Reprinted from *Better Homes and Gardens* magazine, June, 1957, pp. 14–18, 21–22, 191, by permission of the publisher.

ties — or so we like to believe. That, I'll agree, is as it should be. High standards improve any town. Simultaneously, however, they result in a more critical demand for superior performance from all public officials.

For 90 years we had an elected mayor and council. Of course, there were problems and dissatisfactions. That's inevitable in any government. In 1946, manager-plan proponents campaigned that not only would their scheme overcome all our difficulties but give us an era of progress. The task wasn't easy. We had neither rascals to throw out nor political scandals to provide ammunition. The city-manager plan won.

First result — we got a council of seven members elected at large, replacing our twenty aldermen, each representing a ward. In theory, a small, nonpartisan council sounds good. In practice, it proved neither representative nor democratic. Let me explain.

Madison occupies a long, narrow area between lakes. They enhance our civic beauty but also spread our population. Capital Square divides the eastern and western sections. Five of our seven councilmen came from the west side. This is our better-income area. It has the smallest population density, the largest homes, the best recreation facilities.

One of the two new council members lived three blocks east of the square. But the big part of town, where most of our working people reside, got only one representative.

Second result of the new manager-council system was that with councilmen-at-large, most of our citizens lacked any sense of direct contact with government. Under the old ward-alderman setup, you usually knew the man from your area, in many cases by first name. He lived nearby; you saw and talked to him like a friend. Whether you had a blocked sewer or hazardous crossing, a street needing repairs or a vacant lot threatening to become an eyesore, you could quickly and easily reach your alderman. And you got action with a minimum of delay or red tape.

The system worked because *your* alderman made himself responsible for the welfare of *your* area. Citizens could, and did, make their viewpoints, aims, and desires felt — quickly, forcefully, and accurately. Most aldermen felt the best government was one that governed least — and was most responsive to all classes and areas.

Under the manager system, you had to take problems up with an official in City Hall downtown. Most citizens found they didn't know a single councilman, much less the outside expert brought in as a manager. In effect, the manager plan seemed designed to prove that the farther government could be taken from the people, the more efficient it might be.

Additionally, when we eliminated neighborhood representation, we lost our most effective training ground for citizen entry into civic affairs — a vital need as city growth weakens that contact between government and the governed.

Third result of managership was that instead of open debate on new and important policies and developments, with all areas represented, there were frequently secret discussions. With two alert, vigorous newspapers, our citizens counted on the press to keep them fully informed on local affairs. Under the new regime, though, everybody's welfare was threatened. Our own paper and the Wisconsin State Journal — a strong manager-plan supporter, incidentally — were often barred. Editorial protests were unavailing.

Even councilmen experienced great difficulty finding out what was to be on the council's agenda until the matter was tossed on the table. Not infrequently, as some manager proponents admitted, real decisions were made by the manager in conference with private individuals who were better informed than the council.

Some insist that such procedures vary with the manager's personality. Under the ideal operation, they tell you, all business is supposed to be conducted openly. But managers concede that letting the public in on policymaking is up to council. Whatever the "buck pass," however, my point is that what is supposed to be true in theory isn't always observed in action.

Fourth result of the manager plan was a series of steps designed to improve municipal efficiency. Our manager first tackled city finances, sought to reorganize various departments, expanded the planning program, and reformed our civil service procedure.

The effectiveness — or lack of effectiveness — of these changes is debatable. They certainly didn't get the backing of a majority when the test of the next election came around, one good measuring rod. Our reassessment of property for tax purposes is a good example. We needed a change after 22 years. Under the manager plan, a board of five citizens was established to hear the inevitable complaints. However well-intentioned, it didn't work out half as well as our older system of a review board of three elected officials whose very election was a voter demonstration of belief in their impartial judgment.

Business efficiency was also imposed in other departments — some good, some completely valueless — and dropped as soon as our manager departed. Our voters' decision on this point, it seems to me, was based on something manager proponents often overlook: that *mere efficiency isn't necessarily municipal government's primary aim.* Running a community is not a private business. If a poor neighborhood requires more recreational facilities than one with large homes and lovely gardens, they can't be denied just because the poorer area doesn't contribute the same percentage of taxes.

If a dangerous grade crossing must be eliminated or fire hazards corrected, elected officials must take a vigorous lead and enlist public support as well as find the best corrective engineering. Public welfare can't always be measured in terms of the dollars-and-cents profit and loss which guide private business. It must, of necessity, be judged in the light of what's accomplished to help everybody.

Moreover, when you have a flood, epidemic, or any unusual activity, you can't stop to argue the cost of helping victims or the possible budget deficit. You have to get the job done quickly and effectively — and handle the memos and documents later.

Point five turned out to be the vital difference between policy and administration. The manager plan lays great stress on the fact that a manager is supposed to serve as administrator and the council as policymaker. In action, however, you find managers often forcibly inject their own views and personalities into policy matters, frequently becoming storm centers. Realistically, most managers can't be effective administrators of controversial policies without sacrificing their professional managerial status. Thus, in effect, they lose their purported advantages of purely administrative impartiality.

Conflicts between managers and councils are, as a result, far from infrequent. They are the hidden reason for more abandonments than generally believed.

In other cases, since council meets only irregularly to "advise" on policy, while the manager works full time, managers in practice frequently dominate their councils. Councils are too often put in the position of going along with a strong manager's policies and acts — or passively accepting his recommendations simply because he's the only top official to guide the follow-through. Thus, managers often become the very political bosses they so vehemently decry with one personal advantage — they aren't as responsive to, or aware of, local customs, traditions, personalities, and priorities as the political leader who derives his strength from the people.

Ofttimes, proponents feel that once the manager plan has been adopted, all their problems are solved. This turns out to be anything but the case. In fact, under the mayor-council plan, citizens are much more alert day-by-day to the various aspects of their government and, hence, are likely to be more concerned, interested in, and anxious to support it.

A mayor who must, as in our community, go to the voters for re-election after two years — and who can also be recalled by the voters themselves — is far more likely to be in tune with his community than any outside official appointed to his post by council, no matter how highly experienced.

Of course, council has the right to fire a manager when dissatisfied with his performance. But here again, theory and practice are often worlds apart.

Once someone gets into a post where you can't see him as clearly as a mayor, dismissal usually is no easy matter.

On the other hand, there are many cases where a manager "ups and quits" just when he may be needed most. Many managers, especially in smaller communities, seek to make names for themselves to get better jobs. To gain reputations as doers and accomplishers, they frequently advocate unrealistic spending, increasing local tax rates or indebtedness beyond the community's real needs and abilities. When they've made a record at your community's expense, they may be hired away. Many towns have lost to a higher bidder the man in whom they have placed an investment of both time and effort. Mayors who are residents of a community don't switch around in this fashion.

As an elected chief executive, the mayor working with a representative council is the center of energy and public leadership, as well as a focus of responsibility for both policy and performance. And he does his job according to an American tradition known and understood by most citizens.

The proof, I think, lies in the figures. Advocates of the manager plan are fond of pointing out how many new communities adopt it yearly. But they conveniently forget their plan has *not* found acceptance in far more, particularly our largest cities. There's good reason.

Cincinnati, largest managed city, has a population of 500,000. Of the 17 other communities of that size or larger, only one, Cleveland, has gone manager. And Cleveland turned thumbs down more than 20 years ago after a 7-year trial. Other large communities who have abandoned the system include Houston which gave it a 4-year try; Akron, Ohio; Trenton, New Jersey; and Waltham, Massachusetts; each after 3 years; Fall River, Massachusetts, and Tampa, Florida. In my own state, the city of Rhinelander abandoned the plan after 23 years; Stevens' Point after 8. Ashtabula, Ohio, decided it had enough after 32 years; Mason City, Iowa, after 17; Albion, Michigan; Cape May, New Jersey; King's Mountain, North Carolina; and St. Albans, Vermont, each after 13 years. Official statistics of the 52 abandonments give no idea of the number of towns which have considered the plan and then voted no.

In the last decade, and perhaps even longer, not one of our largest and most progressive cities has given the manager plan serious consideration. This includes Philadelphia, Pittsburgh, and St. Louis which have done outstanding jobs of municipal rejuvenation, as well as others where, despite the demand for reform, the manager idea failed to convince a majority of voters.

City manager advocates rarely point out that half of all council-manager cities are concentrated in six states — California, Florida, Maine, Michigan, Texas, and Virginia. Nor do they usually mention that a majority of local governments still operate under other systems.

In my opinion, no professional manager is a match for the sincerity and genuine interest in the people of a community held by elected officials. For too often, the manager — perhaps because of the very nature of his professional training — lacks the human touch, the warmth and the appreciation of the subtleties, nuances, and give-and-take of the man who's come up the elective way. (Copyright 1957, Meredith Publishing Co., Des Moines, Iowa.)

50

The General Manager Idea
for Large Cities

By Wallace S. Sayre

A NEW MANAGERIAL IDEA is taking hold in the large cities of the United States. This idea is that the administration of large city governments requires general managerial direction and that this requirement can best be met by establishing under the mayor a general manager who will, in greater or less degree, be the city government's second in administrative command. The general manager plan thus builds upon the strong-mayor tradition as the most widespread form of city government in the United States. By marrying the manager idea with the idea of the elected chief executive, the general manager plan preserves the office of mayor as the center of political leadership and responsibility. In large cities this center is widely regarded as indispensable to effective government.

The general manager plan may be regarded either as a competitor of the council manager idea or as a more mature form of the manager idea, reflecting the judgment in the larger cities that the council manager plan represents an unnecessary surrender of the values of leadership and accountability found in the institution of the elected chief executive. The general manager or mayor manager plan, its proponents

Wallace S. Sayre, "The General Manager Idea For Large Cities," *Public Administration Review,* Autumn, 1954, pp. 253–258. Reprinted by permission of the publisher, the American Society for Public Administration. Footnotes in original omitted.

emphasize, captures the advantages of the council manager plan without the risks of abandoning the elected chief executive. An effective manager, they believe, is no less likely to be chosen by a mayor than by a city council.

The council manager plan has not found acceptance in the large cities of the United States. Cincinnati, the largest city using the plan, has a population of a half million. Of the seventeen other cities having a population of a half million or more, only one city — Cleveland — has ever adopted the plan, and it was abandoned there more than twenty years ago. In the last decade (perhaps even longer), no large city has given serious consideration to the adoption of the council manager plan.

The literature of the council manager movement does not provide an answer to the question: why has the plan failed to find support in large cities? In fact, the literature does not tell us much about the ecology of the council manager plan in adoptions and operations. Why, for example, are half of all the council manager cities to be found in six states (California, Florida, Maine, Michigan, Texas, and Virginia)? Does the council manager plan find acceptance primarily in particular social, economic, and political environments? Does it, for example, find greatest acceptance and operate most successfully in one-party or in "non-partisan" constituencies? Is the affinity between the council manager plan and small and middle-sized cities the result of the plan's suitability for the management of the particular governmental problems to be found in cities of such size? Is the council manager plan particularly attractive to cities which are growing rapidly in size or to those which are declining in population and resources? To these and other questions about the council manager plan we do not yet have the answers.

The large cities turn toward the
mayor manager plan

Eight large cities (Boston, Los Angeles, Louisville, Newark, New Orleans, New York City, Philadelphia, and San Francisco) have now established some kind of general managerial assistance for the mayor. In two others (Chicago and Detroit) proposals for such general managerial arrangements have been made.

This new managerial trend in large cities has not resulted from an organized effort by municipal reformers with a symmetrical design for the improvement of city government. In fact, this new form of the manager idea in city government has not yet acquired a distinctive label. Some observers call it the mayor manager plan, to emphasize its contrast with the council manager plan; others call it the mayor administrator plan; and still others name it the general manager plan.

The general manager idea for cities began its governmental history in San Francisco in 1932, when charter revision movement established the office of chief administrative officer. This office represented a compromise solution between those who urged a council manager form and those who supported the retention of the strong mayor form. The plan was not widely noticed, but it has prevailed to the general satisfaction of the electorate. In 1938 New York City's new charter established the office of deputy mayor, an office which developed more as a center of legislative and political assistance to the mayor than as a center of managerial aid. In 1941, Lent D. Upson proposed a general manager under the mayor for the city of Detroit, but the proposal was not accepted. In 1948, Louisville began a related experiment with the appointment of a city consultant-administrator who serves as general managerial assistant to the mayor. In 1951, Los Angeles established a city administrative officer. In the same year, Philadelphia's new charter took a long step forward in developing the general manager idea by establishing the office of managing director with substantial powers. In 1953, New Orleans adopted a new charter which established the office of chief administrative officer, with powers similar to but greater than those of Philadelphia's managing director. In the same year, Boston established a director of administrative services and Newark adopted a new charter which established the office of business administrator under the mayor, the option under the New Jersey statutes closest to the general manager idea. In 1954, New York City established the office of city administrator, with Luther Gulick the first incumbent. And in September, 1954, the staff report to the Chicago Charter Revision Commission recommended the adoption of the general manager plan for that city.

Thus the experiment begun in San Francisco over twenty years ago has captured civic interest and has led to official action in an impressive portion of the large cities. Why has this happened? Several explanations may be suggested:

1. The council manager plan had proved to be unacceptable in large city environments, but the values of the managerial idea were still sought in some more attractive structural form.

2. The office of mayor — an elected chief executive who is the center of energy and of public leadership and the focus of responsibility for policy and performance — had become too important an asset in large cities to be exchanged for the speculative values of legislative supremacy and a city manager as represented in the council manager plan.

3. The mayor manager plan fits comfortably and easily into the American political system: it preserves the elected chief executive; it keeps the mayoralty as the focus of the party battle; it emphasizes the values of integration, hierarchy, and professional management, all made familiar doctrine by a half-century of administrative reorganizations in national, state, and municipal governments and by the doctrine of the council manager movement itself.

Emerging elements of the general manager idea

The idea of a general manager serving under the mayor has not been a pre-packaged solution developed as finished doctrine by municipal reformers. Rather, its evolution has been experimental, each application being worked out in relation to local experience and governmental conditions, and varying with the boldness or caution of local leadership. There are several discernible trends in the successive adoptions, however. These can be briefly stated as follows:

1. The general manager is increasingly made more clearly the managerial agent of the mayor, "the mayor's man." In San Francisco in 1932 the manager was made virtually irremovable, but under 1953–54 provisions in New Orleans and New York City the manager holds office at the pleasure of the mayor.

2. As the manager is made more responsible to the mayor, he tends to be given more power — to approach more nearly the status of second in administrative command. In New Orleans and Philadelphia, the cities which represent the most full-bodied application of the general manager idea, the manager is given, for example, the power to appoint and remove the heads of most of the city departments with the approval of the mayor.

3. There is a continued ambivalence in deciding whether the general manager's authority and responsibility should center upon the "staff" or upon the "line" agencies and activities of the city government.

In almost every instance the manager is given primary responsibility for administrative planning and for other organization and methods work. In Los Angeles and New Orleans he has responsibility for budget preparation and execution; in Philadelphia and New York these activities are not under the manager's jurisdiction. In no city does the manager directly supervise the personnel agency. In New Orleans, New York, and Philadelphia the "line" agencies are the manager's major responsibility. The two extremes are represented by Los Angeles, where the manager's responsibilities are focused upon the management functions (except personnel), and by Philadelphia, where the manager's powers are centered upon the "line" agencies.

4. There is some tendency to create a new and smaller cabinet institution under the mayor, consisting of the general manager and the heads of the "staff" agencies. This is particularly the case in Philadelphia and New York. The heads of the "line" agencies, when they function as a cabinet (as they

do in Philadelphia), do so in a meeting presided over by the manager.

Variations in the office and powers of the general manager in five large cities

The variety as well as the trends in the development of the general manager idea in the large cities of the United States may perhaps best be seen through a more specific description of the office and the powers conferred upon it in Los Angeles, New Orleans, New York City, Philadelphia, and San Francisco.

Title: In San Francisco and New Orleans the manager is called chief administrative officer; in Philadelphia, managing director; in New York, city administrator.

Appointment: In every instance, the manager is appointed by the mayor. Only in Los Angeles is council approval required.

Term: In San Francisco, Los Angeles, New Orleans, and New York, no term is specified. In Philadelphia the term of the manager is four years, corresponding to the term of the mayor appointing him.

Removal: In New Orleans and New York the mayor may remove the manager. In Los Angeles, the mayor may remove the manager, but the approval of the council is required. In Philadelphia the mayor must prefer charges; the manager may appeal his removal to the Civil Service Commission which may award him compensation but may not restore him. In San Francisco the mayor may not remove; the manager is subject to recall in an election, or the legislative body may remove him by a two-thirds vote. In Los Angeles and New Orleans the council may also remove the manager — in Los Angeles by a two-thirds vote and in New Orleans by a majority vote of all members.

Powers of the manager: The powers of the managers may be described in three categories: (1) the power to appoint and remove heads of city agencies; (2) the power to supervise city administrative operations; (3) the power to provide general advice and assistance to the mayor.

1. *To appoint and remove heads of agencies:* In Philadelphia, New Orleans, and San Francisco, the managers appoint and remove the heads of specified city departments and agencies. In San Francisco the manager does not need the mayor's approval for such appointments or removals; in Philadelphia and New Orleans the mayor's approval is required. In New Orleans the manager's power to appoint and remove extends to the heads of all but two city departments (law and civil service); in Philadelphia it includes all but finance, law, and personnel. In neither of these two cities does the power to appoint and remove include members of boards or commissions.

In San Francisco, the power extends to departments specified by name in the charter; such departments constitute about half of the city agencies.

In neither Los Angeles nor New York does the manager have the power to appoint or remove heads of departments.

2. *To supervise city administration operations:* In San Francisco the power of the manager to supervise is confined to the departments specifically assigned to him by the charter. In Los Angeles the manager's opportunities for supervision flow solely from his role as city budget officer. In Philadelphia the manager's power to supervise is largely confined to the departments whose heads he appoints, but some more general supervision flows from his powers to perform the administrative analysis function in all city agencies.

In New Orleans the manager has more general supervisory authority. He supervises not only his own subordinate agencies (which include most of the city agencies), but he also gives "general oversight" to law, civil service, and the City Planning Commission (which are outside his appointing and removal authority), prescribes standards of administrative practice to be followed by all agencies and boards, prepares and supervises the operating and capital budgets, surveys the organization and procedures of all agencies and boards, and may require reports from any or all of them.

In New York City the city administrator, although lacking any power to appoint or remove, has a broad supervisory assignment. Under the direction of the mayor, he "shall supervise and coordinate the work of all agencies under the jurisdiction of the mayor" except law, investigation, budget, the construction coordinator, and boards, commissions (which include personnel), and authorities. He may convene heads of agencies singly or collectively, procure information and reports, require the keeping of management records, conduct work studies, and establish management standards for most, if not all city agencies.

3. *The power to provide general advice and assistance to the mayor:* In Philadelphia and New York the manager is under a special obligation to serve as general management adviser to the mayor. In Philadelphia the managing director is required to report periodically to the mayor concerning the affairs of the city government (not merely the affairs of his own departments), and he is authorized to make recommendations on matters concerning the affairs of the whole city government. In New York the city administrator is required to "prepare annual and all such other reports as the mayor shall require," and to "analyze and report to the mayor concerning impending policy decisions affecting the management of the city and the agencies." He is also directed to "maintain liaison with civic and community groups on matters of governmental management."

In both Philadelphia and New York the manager derives special status from cabinet arrangements, established by the charter in Philadelphia and by the mayor's action in New York. In each city there is a small top-level cabinet group meeting weekly with the mayor, in which the manager plays a central role.

The managers in the other three cities have no explicit responsibility to serve as the general adviser to the mayor on management matters. In these cities, the manager's role in this respect is implicit, if it exists at all. In San Francisco it would seem difficult to join such a role with that of an almost autonomous manager. In New Orleans it would seem to be a logical and natural development. In Los Angeles, it would appear to be a more confined but possible development.

The future course of the mayor manager plan

The invention and recent growth of the general manager idea in large cities is a product of many influences. Some of these influences would seem to be of reasonably permanent rather than transient character. The larger cities of the United States have developed complex administrative establishments which require strengthened central managerial leadership, direction, and coordination. These cities have also, almost without exception, developed an increasing reliance upon the elected chief executive — a mayor with extensive powers to appoint, to remove, and to direct the heads of administrative agencies — as the main institution of governmental leadership and accountability. The electoral contest for this office has become the primary instrument of popular control of the city government and the main occasion for public education and participation in city affairs. The office of mayor in large cities has, in addition, become more important as a prize in the party battle, its possession one of the significant keys to state and even national party power. It would seem unlikely that any large city would abandon such a governmental and political asset.

But if the institution of the "strong" mayor in large cities has come to stay, then it would also seem that such mayors, no less than the President, need managerial help. The mayor manager idea is a response to this felt need in the large cities. In this sense, the mayor manager plan is in the mainstream of the administrative doctrine heralded by the President's Committee on Administrative Management in 1937, and reaffirmed by the Hoover Commission's later studies of the national government. The central idea of these studies, and dozens of their counterparts in the states, has been to strengthen the position of the elected chief executive in his political and administrative leadership.

The mayor manager plan is likely to dominate the course of large city administrative reorganizations for the next several years. The council manager plan is not likely to break into the large city league, because this plan does not represent an accommodation to either the political or the managerial requirements of the large cities. The emergence of the mayor manager plan has breached the monopolistic claim of the council manager plan to the managerial virtues by presenting the new and strong competition of an alternative manager plan.

Not only is the mayor manager plan likely to hold its own and to extend its scope to most of the largest cities, but it is also probable that it will become an attractive solution for many (perhaps most) of the one hundred and five cities with 100,000 population or more. In contrast with the council manager plan, the mayor manager plan is elastic in its formal arrangements, and it can thus respond more easily to local priorities, customs, and personalities. To the strong mayor cities, it offers an evolutionary transition, buttressing rather than discarding the values which have been built up around the leadership of the elected chief executive. To these cities, the mayor manager plan offers the same managerial gains as does the council manager plan, but at much less risk. The strategic and tactical advantages of such an offer in the political world can hardly be exaggerated.

The mayor manager plan will, as it evolves toward its own institutionalization, be confronted with dilemmas which can now be only partially anticipated. The plan may ultimately acquire its own protective guild of practitioners and advocates, transforming it into an inelastic plan unresponsive to the changing needs of the cities. It may be drowned in a few dramatic "failures."

The mayor manager idea will probably encounter its severest test in the effort to give the manager sufficient power to provide him with adequate leverage to infuse the values of professional management into the administration of a large city government. Philadelphia and New Orleans have made the clearest and strongest effort to insure this result. The Devereux Josephs Commission, in the most complete formulation of the mayor manager plan (*Four Steps to Better Government of New York City,* 1953–54), proposed still greater strength for the manager while making him also more clearly the mayor's administrative agent. The range of variation in managerial power is wide among the cities using the mayor manager idea. The trend in official action and civic opinion — particularly on the manager's appointing power — is not conclusive, but it seems to run toward the grant of greater managerial leverage.

The mayor manager plan will also encounter, perhaps early in its development, the politics-administration dilemma which increasingly bedevils the council manager plan in operation. Can the general manager be at once both a professional administrator and the mayor's second in administrative command? That is, can he be (with the mayor) the effective maker and protagonist of policy proposals which are certain to be controversial without sacrificing his professional managerial status? This dilemma plagues the council manager plan even more deeply (because council manager doctrine emphasizes council monopoly over policy while practice underscores the necessity for policy leadership by the manager), but this fact provides merely an advantage rather than a solution for the mayor manager advocates. The trend in mayor manager cities is not yet clear, but the general manager in a large city seems at this stage no more likely to become a career manager in that city than has the city manager in this.

Some observers profess to see in the mayor manager plan merely a compromise step toward the council manager plan. The reverse would seem to be the more likely development, if any such transference is to occur. The essential ingredient of the mayor manager plan is the appointment and removal of the manager by the mayor as the elected chief executive. The distinctive contrasting feature of the council manager plan — the selection of the chief administrator by the city council — was not only something of an historical accident in the United States; it was also a striking anomaly in a country in which the most distinctive political institution is the elected chief executive as the keystone of political, governmental, and managerial progress. The mayor manager idea has the great and lasting value that it brings the reorganization of our city governments back into a familiar focus, consistent with our efforts in the national and state governments. In this respect it is an indigenous political idea.

51

Management for Large Cities — A Rejoinder to Wallace Sayre

By John E. Bebout

WHILE MR. SAYRE'S ARTICLE purports to deal simply with the problem of management in "large cities," whatever they are, many of the author's reflections

John E. Bebout, "Management for Large Cities," *Public Administration Review,* Summer, 1955, pp. 188–195. Footnotes in original omitted. Reprinted by permission of the publisher, the American Society for Public Administration.

on the council-manager plan raise serious questions about the validity and permanence of the place it has already won in the American municipal scene. Consequently, the article amounts to an oblique attack on the foundations of a system that has been generally hailed both here and abroad as one of the most important American contributions to the science and art of government. It is, therefore, necessary to review the Sayre thesis in a somewhat broader context than would be called for if it actually applied only to the few giant cities.

In developing the case for the "new managerial idea" Mr. Sayre asserts that it is built "upon the strong-mayor tradition as the most widespread form of city government in the United States." He puts great stress upon the office of the elected chief executive "as the center of political leadership and responsibility." An underlying idea running through the article is that the mayor-manager or mayor-administrator plan is more consistent with the history and tradition of the American political system than the council-manager plan with its reliance upon legislative supremacy. The plan, he asserts, "is in the mainstream of the administrative doctrine heralded by the President's Committee on Administrative Management in 1937, and reaffirmed by the Hoover Commission's later studies of the national government. The central idea of these studies, and dozens of their counterparts in the states, has been to strengthen the position of the elected chief executive in his political and administrative leadership."

This is an interesting interpretation of American political and administrative history as it relates to city government. It fits neatly the theory that government, like all Gaul, is or should be divided into three parts, executive, legislative, and judicial. It also accords with the popular notion that, despite the fact that local and state government came first, the pattern hammered out in the Constitutional Convention of 1787 should be the inspiration and guide for all our governments. Unfortunately, it strikes the present writer as about as historical as Parson Weems' story of the cherry tree.

There are no statistics that support the notion that the strong mayor plan is or ever has been "the most widespread form of city government in the United States." On the contrary, the tradition of American city government is one of government by commissions and committees. To be sure, there are more so-called mayor-council cities than there are commission or manager cities. According to the 1955 *Municipal Year Book,* 52 per cent of all cities over 5,000 have the mayor-council plan, whereas 14.1 per cent have the commission, 30.3 per cent have the council-manager plan, and 3.6 per cent operate with town meeting or representative town meeting. However, a substantial majority of the mayor-council cities have what any textbook would rate as the weak mayor rather than the strong mayor plan. Since one of the common characteristics of weak mayor governments is supervision of departments by council committees, which often means the chairmen thereof, many so-called weak mayor governments are much closer in operation to the commission than to the strong mayor plan.

If we go back some years we discover that since 1917 the mayor-council plan has lost a good deal of ground percentagewise, especially in larger cities. Of cities over 30,000, the percentage with the mayor-council plan (weak and strong) dropped from 59 in 1917 to 43 in 1952. During the same period the percentage of council-manager places rose from 5 to 36.

Cincinnati, with council-manager government, is the only city over 500,000 that does not have some variation of the mayor-council plan. It is certainly not without significance, however, that the council-manager plan is the most popular in the next lower population group — 250,000 to 500,000 — as well as in the 50,000 to 100,000 and 25,000 to 50,000 population groups. Except for the small group of very large cities, it is in the distinctly small-city class — 5,000 to 10,000 — that the mayor-council plan has a wide margin over all others. Of these 1,181 cities, 62.2 per cent have the mayor-council plan, 23.7 per cent the council-manager plan.

To say the least, these trends cast doubt on the thesis that the strong mayor-administrator plan is better tuned to American tradition than the council-manager plan.

At the end of his article Mr. Sayre complains that a "distinctive . . . feature of the council-manager plan — the selection of the chief administrator by the city council — was not only something of an historical accident in the United States; it was also a striking anomaly in a country in which the most distinctive political institution is the elected chief executive as the keystone of political, governmental, and managerial progress. The mayor manager idea," he continues, "has the great and lasting value that it brings the reorganization of our city governments back into a familiar focus, consistent with our efforts in the national and state governments. In this respect it is an indigenous political idea."

Despite the fine dash of patriotic fervor in this peroration, perhaps one may be permitted to ask certain questions. How old does a political idea have to be in order to be "indigenous"? If the council-manager idea of the twentieth century was an historical accident, was not the elected Presidency of the late eighteenth century equally an historical accident — especially since the makers of the Constitution did their best to protect the Presidency from the evils presumed to be inherent in popular election of the chief magistrate? Or, having once made the accidental but unquestionably happy discovery, must we

stigmatize all future and variant avenues toward "political, governmental, and managerial progress" at whatever level of government as nongenuine?

These questions begin to have more focus when one reflects on the failure of most states to develop the office of governor in the image of that of President. The recent report of the Commission on Intergovernmental Relations points out that "today, few States have an adequate executive branch headed by a governor who can be held generally accountable for executing and administering the laws of the State." In other words, very few *states* have anything analogous to the strong mayor plan that Mr. Sayre finds so natural to the American scene. As already suggested, an examination of the charters of mayor-council cities would also show that there is only a relatively small number of cities that have as yet been prepared to entrust their elected chief executive with the powers necessary to justify holding him "generally accountable for executing and administering" the affairs of the city. The truth is that the strong mayor plan is largely a myth, or at best an objective.

Of course, it is true that state Little Hoover and economy and efficiency commissions going back almost half a century have been urging the strengthening of the office of governor. Some progress has been made in this direction. In like manner there has been a tendency in some mayor-council cities that have not gone over to the council-manager plan to add, bit by bit, new strength to the office of mayor. This is all to the good for the states and cities concerned, but one wonders why the generally more substantial and spectacular progress resulting from the adoption of the council-manager plan in approximately 1,300 communities should not be regarded as at least an equally characteristic American achievement.

Mr. Sayre is careful to avoid referring specifically to the American doctrine of the separation of powers as a justification for the strong mayor plan. Yet what he is saying in effect is that the separation of powers between independently elected legislative and executive branches, which is one of the prime characteristics of the United States government and a theoretical characteristic of all our state governments, should be embraced at the municipal level. This justification, naturally enough, has not escaped the attention of persons advocating adoption of strong mayor-administrator charters.

For example, the final report of the Newark Charter Commission, dated September 3, 1953, lists "a *clear separation of powers* between the council as the legislative body, and the mayor as the head of the city administration" as the first of "six basic principles deemed essential to efficient and responsive local government." The second principle is that the mayor "be the chief policy maker" and the third calls for "unified administration of all local services" under its mayor. The council is, however, supposed to "serve as an independent critic of the exercise" of the mayor's executive power and checks and balances between the mayor and council are stressed. The commission's own words reveal the dilemma that is inherent in the separation of powers system. In the policy area, for example, the commission declares that the council "will legislate on matters of public policy," but "the mayor, who will be directly accountable to the people, . . . will be the chief policy maker." Although the record of the first year of Newark city government under its new strong mayor-administrator charter is generally a good one, the check and balance system has already produced some unfortunate conflicts between the mayor and council and the council has succeeded in preventing the mayor from appointing certain well qualified persons of his choice to important posts.

But the deadlocks, the buck-passing, and the evasions of responsibility that are common occurrences in governments organized on the basis of the separation of powers are too well known to need recounting here. Nor is this the occasion to argue the ultimate merits of the separation of powers principle for the higher levels of American government. It may be appropriate to observe, however, that the circumstances that led to incorporation of the separation of powers into the United States Constitution were of such a special character that they do not necessarily indicate it as a principle of universal or even of wide application. It probably was and still is the most practical solution of the complex problem of organizing government at the federal level. It may be the best solution for most states despite the fact that few of them have followed the national model closely enough to give it a good try.

A basic reason for resort to the separation of powers is to compensate through the elected chief executive for deficiencies in representativeness and leadership in the legislature. Such deficiencies are perhaps unavoidable both in the Congress and in many state legislatures. The bicameral system is an almost insuperable obstacle to responsible government based upon legislative supremacy. Fortunately all but eight American cities have found that they can get along very well with a one-house municipal legislature and the overwhelming majority of them have discovered that it is not necessary to have a large and unwieldy body in order to achieve representativeness. The improvement in the quality and effectiveness in city councils has assuredly been a major element in the general improvement in the quality of city government which has occurred since James Bryce pronounced the government of cities to be the American people's "one conspicuous failure." While much of

the improvement of city councils has been associated with the spread of the council-manager plan, it has also occurred in many mayor-council cities.

It seems hard to believe that if Mr. Sayre had taken full account of this phase of municipal history, he would have embraced the conclusion that the most promising if not the only road to municipal progress lies in maximizing the office of the elected mayor both as chief executive and as chief policy maker.

Let us now turn specifically to the problems involved in strengthening the governments of our largest cities. First, it is clear that the choice of means for improving management must depend heavily upon the kind of city council it is deemed desirable and possible to have. No one, for example, would suggest trying to make an appointed manager responsible to the present bicameral New York City Council. If the council-manager plan were ever to be considered seriously for the city of New York, it would have to be on the assumption that the present City Council would be replaced by a reasonably wieldy and representative one-house body. It would also be hopeless to try to base a council-manager operation on the present 50-member, completely ward-elected, Chicago City Council. It is almost equally impossible to imagine a sound council-manager government with the 35-member council, composed of 25 ward representatives and 10 aldermen selected at large, proposed by the recent report of the Chicago Home Rule Commission.

Large cities are complex entities. If there is any representative pattern or formula that will work best in all cases it has not yet been discovered or generally agreed upon. The tailoring of a city council to the needs and political realities in such a city is, therefore, one of the most difficult problems in representative government and one which calls for a certain amount of boldness and willingness to experiment. It is well worth the effort, however, because a sound city council is the surest first step toward good management, as it is toward wise policy making.

Mr. Sayre seems to suggest that there is something inherent in the nature of large cities that requires the leadership of an elected mayor who holds the principal prerogatives of a chief executive — "extensive powers to appoint, to remove, and to direct the heads of administrative agencies."

Of course policy leadership is necessary in large cities. It is also necessary or at least highly desirable in medium-sized and small cities. Fortunately, out of the richness of American municipal experience, we have learned that there is more than one way of providing for it. There are, for example, some pretty big council-manager cities that have not suffered for lack of policy leadership. In Cincinnati a number of vigorous personalities, beginning with Murray Seasongood, elected by their council colleagues to serve as mayor, have been more effective policy leaders than many a separately elected mayor enjoying substantial prerogatives of the traditional chief executive. Since the fall of Pendergast the same thing has been true of Kansas City where the mayor is elected separately from his colleagues on the council and has proved to be a political leader in the best sense of the word.

Before comparing the relative leadership potentialities in the strong-mayor and council-manager plans more closely, we should, perhaps, pause to consider just what we mean by leadership in city government. Much that passes for leadership in politics is strangely reminiscent of the sound and fury that accompanies a battle between two bulls. It is a matter of great importance to the contestants and may be to their more ardent partisans, but it has very little to do with the public interest.

Admittedly, this personalized counterfeit of public-oriented leadership may appear in connection with any form of government. But surely no sophisticated student of politics or administration now doubts that form has something to do with selecting the people who choose or qualify to play the game, and even more to do with the rules by which the game is played. This unstated assumption, indeed, underlies Mr. Sayre's whole thesis.

Our common objective must be to find the formal or structural framework that will be most conducive to municipal progress. This means that we should seek a structure that will be as favorable as possible to the rise of elected leaders who are more concerned with municipal objectives than with their own future, more anxious to achieve substantive results than to wield power.

Experience indicates that, on the whole, the council-manager plan has certain positive advantages over the mayor-council plan as a vehicle for such constructive leadership. The basic reason for this is that the design of council-manager government is essentially functional. It is the simplest available structural arrangement for obtaining representative decisions on policy and competent execution of those decisions.

The structure of the strong-mayor, separation-of-powers plan, however, reflects the preoccupation of its designers with power and the struggle for power. In the endeavor to control the lust for power, it actually diverts attention from the public objectives to the private or personal perquisites and incidents of politics and limits participation by those who are unwilling or unable to compete on these terms. Even in the absence of strong personal or partisan rivalry, the normal interaction of the parts of the system tends to generate unnecessary friction and conflict. These tendencies adversely affect both short- and long-term policy planning and continuous, skilled administration.

The mayor in council-manager cities is usually chosen by his colleagues on the council because they deem him their most effective spokesman. If he is separately elected, he is likely to have been nominated to lead the winning slate of council candidates. In either case, there is no built-in invitation to bickering between the mayor and the majority of council. Moreover, the fact that the mayor has no personal appointments of consequence to make and no orders to issue to administrative personnel eliminates patronage as a potential source of discord between him and his associates. And since the mayor is the leader only as long as he speaks for the majority, he can be replaced or by-passed by a new mayor or *de facto* leader if he gets hopelessly out of line. All of this helps to account for the fact that issues of policy, including the basic issue of maintaining or of raising the quality of administration, tend to loom larger in comparison with mere questions of personality in elections in council-manager cities than they do in others.

Another advantage of council-manager government is that it does not put all its leadership eggs in one basket. Neither the city charter nor the fact of popular election can be counted on to endow a legally strong mayor with the skill and wisdom to be the kind of leader in policy and administration that a city should have. But, if a "strong" mayor fails to provide proper leadership, there is generally no one who can fill the breach. Members of the council are in no position, legally or politically, to compensate for his deficiencies. They are on the other side of a wall and their natural bent is to throw bricks at the mayor and make political capital out of his weaknesses, not to bolster him. An ambitious councilman or a leader in a rival faction or party may be grooming to succeed the mayor, but until he has the office his efforts are likely to be disruptive rather than constructive in terms of their effect on both policy and administration. This tendency of the separation of powers system has been demonstrated repeatedly at all levels of government.

In a council-manager city, however, the mayor is simply the first among equals. He is presumed to be the chief policy spokesman of the majority in council, but leadership can be and often is shared by several council members in a manner that would be difficult or impossible in a mayor-council city. Deficiencies on the part of the mayor can thus be made up by, literally, putting leadership in commission.

In addition the council-manager plan has the manager, a leadership asset of no mean importance. There are no people more firm in their determination to keep managers out of politics in the ordinary sense of the word than the managers themselves. On the other hand, the manager is recognized not only as the council's agent for executing policy but also as the council's servant in developing plans and proposals for its consideration. While responsibility for public advocacy of proposed policies is vested in the council and in the mayor as its chief spokesman, the manager is responsible for maintaining a continuous flow of public information of the kind that provides a basis for public understanding and evaluation of policy proposals. . . .

It is now clear, if there was ever any doubt about it, that when a city hires a manager it should expect to hire not only a good generalist in municipal administration but also a sensitive civic and public relations consultant to the city council. Thus the manager is to the city government something like what an efficient executive secretary is to a large voluntary civic, welfare, or other community agency.

It was suggested earlier that leadership in council-manager government could be and often is shared by the mayor and other members of the city council. Actually, it is also shared between them and the manager. The mayor and council members handle the conventionally political aspects of the task and the manager plays a role in the area of public information, the visible dimensions of which will depend to a considerable extent on how much of the limelight the mayor and council want to reserve for themselves.

It is sometimes true, as managers themselves have complained, that mayors and councilmen are too ready to let the manager carry the ball. Whether or not this is a special weakness of the council-manager plan as some have suggested is open to question, for many a "strong mayor" has failed equally to give effective attention to the constructive aspects of political leadership. In any event, in a council-manager government inadequate leadership on the part of the people's elected representatives can at least to some degree be compensated for by an articulate and effective manager speaking with the knowledge and consent of the council which may fire him at any time it feels he is not representing it properly. It is safe to say that many a city has been saved from civic or governmental stagnation because of the professional civic leadership that the manager has been able to bring to bear in the making and explanation of public policy.

This brings us to consideration of the "politics-administration dilemma which," according to Mr. Sayre, "increasingly bedevils the council-manager plan in operation" and also is a problem for the mayor-administrator plan. Mr. Sayre is able to comfort himself with the thought that the mayor-administrator plan may have the advantage in the ultimate resolution of this dilemma by imagining that "council-manager doctrine emphasizes council monopoly over policy while practice underscores the necessity for policy leadership by the manager. . . ." The council-manager plan is today a going operation of some 40-odd years' standing. Many theories, appropriate and inappropriate, have been propounded in connection with it. The plan continues to gain ground, however, on the basis of practice, and the practice is essentially that described in the preceding paragraphs. This practice, more naturally and efficiently than that of any other plan, reflects that "unity of the governmental process," which the Temporary State Commission to Study the Organizational Structure of the Government of the City of New York accepted as fundamental to a sound system of government. In developing its concept of this essential unity the commission asserted that "politics and administration are not airtight departments separated from each other by clearly identifiable walls. They are merely phases in the continuous process of government, which, in itself, is a phase in the process of social organization." Splendid! No better justification for the council-manager plan in practice has ever been written. The commission was able to fall into the trap of using this as an argument for preferring the strong mayor plan to the council-manager plan because it saw the council-manager plan through the haze of the curious notion about council-manager doctrine or theory that Mr. Sayre later expounded in his article.

The foregoing observations on the practice as distinct from more or less gratuitous theories of council-manager and mayor-council governments do not, of course, tell us what form of government most of the country's dozen or so giant cities will or should have in the future. The purpose of this article has been primarily to try to keep the record straight and see to it that the claims of America's distinctive contribution to municipal government, government based upon the marriage of legislative supremacy with professional competence, shall not be sold down the river.

The present writer is inclined to believe that most of these largest cities will continue to operate with some variation of the mayor-council form. In some cases the great unlikelihood of reorganizing the city council so that it would provide a safe basis for administration by a manager solely responsible to it is reason enough for this prediction, though it may be hoped that political ingenuity will not cease to work with the problem of giving our largest cities, as well as our states, more effective and more representative legislatures. In other cases, tradition and entrenched political interests would make a break to the council-manager plan pretty difficult to achieve.

Mr. Sayre points out that in some large cities the office of mayor is very "important as a prize in the party battle, its possession one of the significant keys to state and even national party power." He adds that "it would seem unlikely that any large city would abandon such a governmental and political asset." Maybe so, but it should not be imagined that mayors and council members in council-manager cities, whether elected on party or on nonpartisan ballots, have no influence in behalf of their cities in Washington or the state capitol. The recent past president of the American Municipal Association, for example, was Mayor William E. Kemp of Kansas City who, though elected mayor on a nonpartisan ballot, has been a highly effective leader in the dominant national party in his city and state.

Assuredly there will continue to be mayor-council cities. Let us hope that more and more of them will give their mayors the prerogatives necessary to be effective chief executives and policy leaders. This writer shares with Mr. Sayre the hope that those cities will learn how to make the maximum use of professional managerial talent. Mr. Sayre believes he sees a trend toward appointment by the mayor of a single general administrator to be his second in command with respect to the entire city administration. Actually, the number of cases that it is yet possible to analyze is so inconclusive on this point that it is far from certain that the single top administrator is necessarily better for every large city than some variation on the Philadelphia plan of providing the mayor with several high-level administrative aides. The problem of providing the mayor with an adequate professional staff is not altogether different from that of staffing the office of governor or of President, or even that of manager. What is needed is continuing experimentation and objective analysis of experience with various methods of staffing the chief executives in our larger governments. Mr. Sayre disclaims any wish to develop a new cult interested in promoting the mayor-manager or mayor-administrator plan. Premature identification of a "trend" in that direction might conceivably tend to discourage further progress by making it appear that "the way" had already been found.

There are, of course, many matters in connection with the government of our cities that cry out for further research, as Mr. Sayre himself has suggested. Some of these have to do primarily with the best ways to organize professional assistance for elected political and citizen officials. Some of them have to do with the relation between form and structure, on the one hand, and political organization and leadership, on the other. Some of them have to do with the ways and means by which citizens may best organize and conduct themselves through voluntary political and civic organizations to get and maintain good government. Some of them have to do with the relations between local and state and national politics.

There is special need for increased attention to research on many problems of political and civic leadership, organization, and action. In the long run no government will remain permanently far above the level of the capacity of a fairly good cross section of the citizens to work together through political and civic agencies for sound, common objectives.

CHAPTER ELEVEN

City Councils and City Executives

CITY COUNCILS are often not greatly different in organization and formal procedures from other legislative bodies, but as a rule councilmen do perforce operate in closer continuous contact with their constituents. The opening selection, a first-hand account of a councilman's political brokerage for the citizens of his ward, is by a prominent professor of political science who combined academic duties with service as a member of a city council.

Although most council elections in the United States continue to be based on simple majority or plurality decisions, many civic reformers have advocated proportional representation elections as a significant improvement. Successfully used in a few cities, they have not been widely adopted in the United States. No one seriously contends that P.R. will not accomplish what it claims in terms of mirroring quite accurately on the council the actual voting strength of the various groups in the community — the argument is largely over the desirability of the results. The second selection presents the viewpoint of the proponents in the words of one of P.R.'s most ardent advocates, George H. Hallett, Jr., proportional representation editor for the *National Civic Review*.

52

The Councilman as a Political Broker

By Arthur W. Bromage

MANY OF US HAVE READ with extreme interest the analysis by H. F. Gosnell of the "benevolent services" performed by precinct captains in Chicago. These services included: (1) goods, (2) advice, (3) brokerage agency, and (4) deference. Goods related to the providing of food, coal, rent, and Christmas baskets. Advice referred to juvenile guidance and

Arthur W. Bromage, *On The City Council* (Ann Arbor, Michigan: George Wahr Publishing Co., 1950), pp. 51–57. Footnotes in original omitted. Reprinted by permission of the publisher.

domestic difficulties. Brokerage service at the local level comprised jobs, streets and alleys, tax adjustments, permits, building and zoning regulations, contacts with social and relief agencies. Deference required attendance at weddings and funerals. In Philadelphia, J. T. Salter found that precinct leaders also handled a wide variety of services.

The literature of political science dealing with machines and bosses is replete with emphasis on brokerage service. Machines survive because they do favors, sometimes legal, other times questionable, for those who only vote and for Very Important Persons. Serving the precincts and the wards means the delivery of tangible things which people need. In return for services, votes are demanded and secured. No one should condone graft and brokerage in illegal tangibles. But my experiences as an alderman have revised my notions of "brokerage." In a democracy it seems inevitable and appropriate, provided the players keep the great game of politics clean.

Politics and public administration

It is often difficult to draw a sharp line between politics (or policy) and public administration. Politics reach downward to influence administration, and administration spirals upward to make an impact on politics. The two-package theory of politics (or policy) and scientific administration just doesn't work out neatly in practice. The public apparently isn't too interested whether the service is delivered in one or two packages. Administration can be scientific, only until it impinges upon political forces. Then scientific administration will be either bent or broken to politics. In so many operations, politics and administration, rather than being separately packaged, are one and indivisible. At least, this is a fact in my home community of Ann Arbor, Michigan.

I have been serving the people of Ward 6 as one of their two aldermen on the Common Council of Ann Arbor. The ward has currently only one voting precinct and about 2200 registered voters. The precinct captain appears as an active force just before elections and shortly disappears. Meanwhile, 365 days of the year, the alderman acts as a combination of representative and precinct captain. Ward 6 is a silk-stocking district and predominantly Republican.

To take Gosnell's categories of (1) goods, (2) advice, (3) brokerage agency, and (4) deference, I would classify my activities under the heading of legitimate brokerage. Ward 6 does not require food, coal, rent and Christmas baskets. Advice, in terms of juvenile guidance or domestic difficulty, is likewise uncalled for. I have never had a telephone call about this kind of problem. Deference is apparently not expected of me, for I am not invited to weddings. Brokerage, however, is a different matter. Let us start with a few simple illustrations.

Examples of brokerage

On Street V in Ward 6, there are two sharp curves, relatively blind to drivers who are intent on getting somewhere too fast. Between the two curves is a short straight-away. On this straight-away, there are about a dozen homes. Small children from these homes and from the adjacent neighborhood have a habit of playing beside the curb of the straight-away. There is no sidewalk and children must ride tricycles and bicycles somewhere, pull carts, and leap through piles of grass! I had sometimes observed the flutter, when a fast car bypassed these gay youngsters. Several parents wanted something done about it, and I was their alderman. I had to be their broker, because I knew how wheels turned at City Hall. After conferences with the chairman of the traffic committee and a police captain, I submitted a resolution to council, and backed it with a simple explanation of the problem. Now there are warning signs before each curve: SLOW, Children on Curb. Some of the parents called me and expressed their appreciation! They had only received something they had long been entitled to, under normal city operations.

One voter was incensed because residential Avenue G flowed into main-traffic Avenue W without a STOP sign. He was in the habit of motoring down Avenue W to work, and he was tired of near collisions with heedless drivers darting out of Avenue G. Now there is one of the biggest STOP signs at the foot of Avenue G, and it costs a traffic ticket to drive into W from G without stopping.

In the summer of 1949, brokerage service demanded attention to three advertising signs. Ward 6 is allergic to signs, and aldermen are the last in the chain of authority. These signs were respectively: (1) an old lighted sign advertising tourist rooms; (2) a new small 8″ × 11″ illuminated sign advertising tourist rooms; and (3) a rather large unlighted sign advertising room and board. It was Sign No. 3 which touched off the wrath of some constituents, because it was new, large, and fastened to two poles close to the sidewalk. Moreover, No. 3 interfered with driver's vision in coming out of Boulevard U onto Avenue W. I observed these signs by day and night, and I read up on the zoning ordinance and sign restrictions. I came to the tentative conclusion that No. 1 was a long-existing, non-conforming use, antedating restrictions; that No. 2 was legal; and that No. 3 was illegal. I checked with the Building Inspector. When Sign No. 3 was shortly removed, my telephone temporarily lapsed into silence.

In the late spring of 1949, Circle N needed a curb and gutter job. It had a considerable grade, and new construction plus rains had led to erosion and silting. Property-owners at the foot of the Circle were encountering damage to their lawns from rain-water and silt. The property-owners on the Circle had filed a petition for curb and gutter, to be paid by special assessment. Unfortunately, their action was too late for the annual contract award for construction of curb and gutter throughout the city. Good brokerage demanded that curb and gutter be installed on Circle N before snow fell. When supplementary bids for curb and gutter work were advertised, Circle N was one of the projects. In early November, the workers arrived, and in a few days, Circle N was outlined in new curb and gutter. Erosion ceased and the area began to look like a street worthy of our "fair city." The voters were then informed how and when to apply for a "blacktop" paving job by special assessment, so they would be certain to be included in the 1950 program. A little push on the wheel of scientific administration satisfied the property-owners.

In the fall of 1949, a potentially bad fire broke out in a house which rented rooms to students at the University. When I got there, the firemen were already inside the rear of the house fighting fire with high-pressure fog. It was a stubborn blaze, and this made it necessary to use a 750 g.p.m. pumper to replenish the water tank in the high-pressure fog vehicle. It was an uphill haul from pumper to fog vehicle, and 2½ hose is heavy, in case you have never pulled any. My fellow alderman was ahead of me. He was helping, I discovered, with the flood lights. Whether you call this brokerage, or just being a fire buff, is immaterial. When the fire was over, the property-owner energetically set in motion a contractor. The damage was repaired in one week, so that these students, in our crowded University city, could return to their rooms.

Complex brokerage

Other issues of brokerage are not so simple. When someone calls about a traffic ticket and fine, there isn't anything I can or should do about it. The tickets are numbered, they are in triplicate, and they are of the uniform type with standardized fines for common offenses. All I can do is explain the system, its merits, and its inevitable, end results. Usually, this type of telephone conversation ends with the laconic voter's remark: "Well, I didn't really expect you to do anything about it, but I had to blow off to some one, so I called MY alderman." This phrase MY alderman intrigues me, for it is a homey, down-to-earth expression, like MY butcher, MY baker, or MY broker.

Soon after I became a councilman, I was appointed to the Zoning Board of Appeals, and to other appeal boards dealing with the building code and the housing law. I am now familiar with the type of telephone call by which some one wishes to explain to me informally, and, in advance, about an appeal which is due on the agenda next Monday night. It may be an appeal to remodel from single-family house to duplex in a single-family zone, or to build on an odd-shape lot without the minimum, legal set-back of 25 feet, or to do any number of "reasonable" things contrary to zoning, building, and housing regulations.

All that brokerage amounts to in such cases is to explain procedure, and make NO commitment. Has the proper petition been filed? Has the necessary fee been paid? Does the petitioner know that such a variance requires a public hearing and legal notice to all property-owners within 300 feet of the proposed structure or structural alteration? Does the petitioner realize that the Zoning Board of Appeals cannot possibly hand down a decision for or against, until the second Monday in the month of blank? Has a proper plot plan been submitted? Has the architect submitted drawings to the Building Inspector? Legitimate brokerage on such questions extends only to procedural guidance, and there the line must be drawn.

Not all "voters," sovereign as they may be, leave a session of any board of appeals with gaiety. Sometimes a negative decision lingers on like a black cloud. It can and does, on occasion, amount almost to a severance of diplomatic relations. In serving on quasi-judicial bodies, an alderman has to take a scientific position in administration, although he may feel the hot breath of politics at his neck.

Since zoning has been mentioned, attention must be given to larger issues of brokerage. Ward 6 is adamant against amendments to the zoning districts on Avenue W. It is zoned throughout as single-family, duplex, or multiple residential. Early in 1950, one voter petitioned to have his residential corner rezoned from B to B1. Zone B is multiple family, plus doctors' and dentists' offices. B1 permits, in addition, offices for architects, executives, realtors, and radio studios. The petitioner had to have his day in council. The opponents accumulated 250 signatures against the change, and many of these came from Ward 6. The opponents really did call their alderman. They couldn't possibly wait for the scheduled public hearing to express their views. At the public hearing, they turned out in force, headed by an attorney. This particular episode involved a number of technical procedural matters pertaining to protest petitions, public hearings, and special majorities in the common council. An alderman is expected to know about these matters, and this is "brokerage." In this case, it was probably important to vote right, or suffer the political consequences. Zoning is an art as well as a science.

More brokerage

Even the budget sometimes involves brokerage. In the spring of 1949, various organized groups of women learned that the budget director had denied a request of the health department for an additional public health nurse. This caused a mild revolution, and aldermen were faced with many statistics about standard ratios of public health nurses to population. Other groups were incensed because the police chief asked for eleven additional rookies, and found zero new rookies in the budget director's column. By the time the budget committee of the council was through with budget hearings, there was a revision of figures. The health department got that additional nurse; the police chief had two new rookies; and the contingent fund was shaved downward. Political brokerage, as practiced by aldermen in response to administrative and citizen reaction, had compromised the hard-and-fast logic of the budget director. Politics came to the aid of a budget director who had gone down the line as he saw it. Administration may run in straight lines, but politics tend to take on the appearance of the battle of the bulge.

Sometimes, brokerage extends to broad policy matters. For years, advanced citizen groups in Ann Arbor have urged that the city health department be abolished in favor of an integrated county health unit. . . . Political brokerage brought about a solution in favor of city-county health coordination.

It is a far cry from city-county health coordination to the telephone call of a dear old lady, too old to rake the leaves out of the street gutter. Cars parked on her side of the street all day, and the leaf-sucking machine never got to clean up in front of her house. She called the police and got nowhere. So she called her alderman. A cooperative city engineer turned out the crew and the leaf-sucking machine early in the morning, too early for all-day parkers. The whole neighborhood got an unexpected clean-up.

An alderman, in my town, becomes an intimate friend and servant of the people, or else ———. Some experts will say that this is wrong, that streamlined administrative structures and scientific management will solve these small matters, and councilmen can then retreat to the higher ground of high policy. I laud this as a principle, and congratulate council-manager cities which have achieved this desirable end result. But, Ann Arbor is a weak-mayor, strong-council community without an integrated executive. So the answer is — call your alderman. Politics and administration come in one package in small and large matters. Every alderman has a constituency, and voters have their demands. In theory, it may be wrong, in practice, it appears to keep the voters reasonably well-satisfied. I suspect that in many cities, the impact of politics on administration is very profound, whenever one probes beneath the surface of charts, reports, and statistics.

53

Does P. R. Provide Better City Councils?

By George H. Hallett, Jr.

ALL POPULAR GOVERNMENT is founded on elections. It is of the utmost importance that the rules of elections shall make it easy for the people to get what they really want.

For achieving this result the modern machinery is proportional representation. Experience with it has brought heartening evidence that people want something very much better than they usually get. It appears actually true that the cure for the ills of democ-

George H. Hallett, Jr., *Proportional Representation: The Key to Democracy* (New York: National Municipal League, 1940), pp. 2–6, 58–100, 176–177. Reprinted by permission of the author and publisher.

racy is more democracy, a system of election which makes representative government a reality instead of a sham. . . . We try to carry over to more complicated situations a method which is only suitable in deciding the simplest sort of issue, that is, whether a question with only two possible answers shall be answered "yes" or "no." For such an issue a simple majority election is, of course, sufficient.

An essentially similar situation is presented when only two candidates are running for a single office. Here also there are only two possible answers, and the best that can be done is to hold a majority election to let the voters divide into two groups and to give the prize to the larger.

As soon as three candidates present themselves for a single office (or three answers to a single question) the situation becomes more complicated and a simple majority election is no longer suitable. To illustrate, let us consider the three leading candidates for city comptroller in the New York City election of 1934 and the votes cast for them:

Taylor, Democrat	831,390
McGoldrick, Republican and Fusion	815,561
Laidler, Socialist	77,695

Under the simple relative majority system which was in use Taylor was elected by a plurality of only 15,829 votes, while the 77,695 who voted for Laidler had no share in the decision. If the Laidler votes had been consulted in the real contest between Taylor and McGoldrick, it is quite possible that the outcome would have been something like this:

	McGoldrick	Taylor
Votes actually received	815,561	831,390
Preferences of the Laidler voters	60,000	17,695
Totals	875,561	849,085

Obviously an election method which can elect one candidate when a majority of the voters prefer another is not a suitable method to use. . . . When what we want is not a single officer or a *decision* among alternatives, but *a body fit to make decisions* on behalf of the voters, something quite different is required. As Ernest Naville, the eminent Swiss publicist, wrote in 1865, "In a democratic government the right of decision belongs to the majority, but the right of representation belongs to all." . . .

Advantages of P. R.

It is surprising how many advantages flow from this change in election methods . . . [to proportional representation].

Effective voting. First of all, it makes nearly every vote count. . . .

In the first seven P. R. elections in Cincinnati nine out of ten who cast valid ballots each time helped elect councilmen. In plurality elections nearly half the ballots are usually wasted, sometimes more than half.

Even that is not the whole story as to the relative effectiveness of the two systems. . . . While a larger number of candidates would of course decrease the proportion that see their first choices elected, a good majority usually do so and a large part of those that are left see a second or third choice elected. Such is the variety of representation always secured that even a large part of those whose ballots are technically "exhausted" are sure to have marked early choices for candidates elected by others.

An examination of the ballots cast in the 1919 election in Ashtabula, the only American P. R. election in which the ballots have been made available for complete analysis, showed that many more voters were actually represented by early choices than were recorded on the result sheet as having helped elect candidates. The voters who themselves helped elect candidates numbered 83 per cent of the total, but 86 per cent saw a first or second choice elected, 91 per cent saw one of their first three choices elected, and only 7 per cent failed to see someone elected for whom they had voted.

In contrast to this nearly or quite half of the voters in a plurality election frequently see no one elected for whom they have voted, and great numbers of those who do vote for successful candidates vote for what they regard as a mere choice of evils after their real wishes have been thwarted at a primary.

Unanimous constituencies. Under P. R. each member elected represents a separate equal part of the voters, as he is supposed to under the ward or district plan. But under the district plan the constituents of a member have nothing more in common than sleeping in the same part of the city. As they don't agree on policies, it is impossible for one person to represent them all. Under P. R., on the other hand, each member represents a part of the voters who agree. He has been voted for, and wanted, by them all. He can represent them all without straddling.

Minority representation. The most obvious advantage of P. R. is that it gives representation to minorities. This may be of very great importance. Who can doubt that everyone would gain from some degree of opposition representation in the "solid South" — or, for that matter, in parts of the North where it has often been absent? . . .

P. R. gives representation to various sorts of minorities. Sometimes it is to minority parties, as when it gave representation to the Conservative and Liberal minorities in Edmonton and Calgary in the Social Credit landslide in Alberta in 1936 and to the Labor Party in every national election in the Irish Free State. Sometimes it is to groups within parties, as when it gave representation to the Democratic,

independent Republican, and labor elements on the ticket of the municipal party known as the City Charter Committee in the first P. R. election in Cincinnati. Sometimes it is to unattached independents, as when it elected one outstanding citizen without the support of either party in each of the four districts in the first P. R. election in Cleveland. P. R. lets the voters make their own groupings, on whatever basis happens to appeal to them, and gives them all fair treatment. The groupings may not always be wise or fortunate, but experience shows that they are usually far better than the artificial political groupings forced on the voters by defective methods of election.

Majority rule. P. R. assures majority rule to an extent that no other system of election approaches. Under other systems, as we have seen, a majority of the votes gives no assurance of electing a majority of the members. Under P. R. any majority of the voters can in general be sure of electing such a majority. . . . In Cincinnati five more than half of the votes can always be sure of electing five out of nine, for that number will fill up five full quotas of one more than a tenth of the votes each.

In order to do this it is not necessary to stick to any given number of candidates or agree on any given order of choice or division of votes among them. The City Charter Committee of Cincinnati, which elected a majority of the council the first five times under P. R. always nominated nine candidates — three more than it ever elected or expected to elect — and simply urged the voters to support all of its candidates with their first nine choices in any order. The votes of its supporters then piled up by transfer on as many of its most popular candidates as its votes deserved to elect.

If there is a split in the majority the advantage of P. R. is still more obvious. Under a plurality system such a split is almost sure to be fatal. Under P. R. the two parts of the majority can elect their representatives separately, and together they can retain their proper majority of the members. . . .

Whenever there is no single group with a clear majority, the maintenance of majority rule depends on the proper representation of minorities. Even when one party has an absolute majority, the proper decision on questions which do not follow regular party lines depends on the proper representation of minorities within the parties. Under P. R. any majority of the members is practically sure to represent a majority of the voters. . . .

There can never be a situation such as is usual under plurality systems of election, in which all the members represent only about half the voters and a majority of the members may therefore represent only about a quarter of them.

A new freedom in voting. Just as important,

perhaps, as the fair treatment of groups of voters is the new freedom that P. R. gives to the individual. He can nominate and vote for the candidates he really wants whether he thinks they are likely to be elected or not. . . . This new freedom to nominate and vote makes startling differences in the calibre of candidates and the votes actually cast.

A check to machine rule. In particular it often makes startling differences in the support given to political machines. Many a machine which has polled large actual majorities for its candidates under the limited choice of plurality elections has gone down to ignominious defeat under the new freedom of P. R. Machine rule usually exists not because a majority of the people want it but because they do not know how to escape it. Under P. R. a way of escape is provided. Under it a political machine cannot rule unless, with every voter free to vote effectively against it, it can get a willing majority for its candidates. . . . However, it must not be thought that P. R. does away with the need of eternal vigilance. Nothing does that. But it does make vigilance effective.

The transformation of machines. Under P. R. a political organization has its choice of breaking or of bending to the popular will. Instead of fighting the changes that the people want, it can, if it is wise, promote them and take the credit for them. It can nominate candidates who are genuinely popular and trustworthy or give them its blessing when they are nominated by others. Thus it can share in the victory which will usually come to such candidates under P. R. whether they have organization support or not. With the help of such representatives an organization may continue to rule, but not in the ways that have normally characterized organization rule hitherto. . . .

Under P. R. the voters control their party organizations instead of being controlled by them.

The gerrymander killed. One of the incidental benefits of P. R. is its effect on the fine art of gerrymandering. The purpose of a gerrymander is to draw district lines so that most of one party's votes will count and most of the others will not. You cannot do this, of course, when nearly all votes will count in each district. . . .

Continuity. P. R. assures a wholesome continuity of personnel. There is no case on record, so far as we know, certainly none in this country, in which, after P. R. once has been established, some of the members have not been re-elected at every election. . . .

P. R. avoids landslides. When a minority becomes a majority, it merely increases the representation it had before as a minority. It does not have to train in a whole new group of inexperienced legislators. And as for the former majority, it retains a part of its representation when it becomes a minority. The leaders of both sides remain, and only the less important and less popular members come and go.

The development of leadership. This continuity in office is assured not merely to party leaders but to any member who takes a sufficiently positive and appealing stand on big issues to hold the support of a quota of the voters. . . .

This new situation also makes the position of legislator more appealing to men and women of outstanding ability and independent character. Such people do not usually come out of their own accord and beg to be elected. They have made a place for themselves elsewhere. They need persuading. If the persuader can offer only a career subservient to a machine or a hope of success against it which is manifestly forlorn, they are not attracted. But if they can run without entangling alliances and with a good chance of election, the case is different. Many a person has been elected under P. R. who would not have considered running before P. R. was adopted. . . .

Development of interest. The chance to vote for and actually elect such candidates gives a new interest to intelligent voters. Men and women who stay at home in disgust under the old plan, either because they see no one on the ballot that they know or want or because they think no candidate that they want has a chance of election, find voting under P. R. worth while. . . .

Reduction of fraud. In plurality elections a slight shift in votes in close districts may make a great difference in the result. In close elections the temptations to fraud may therefore be tremendous. In P. R. elections stolen or bought votes have only their proportionate effect on the result. The cost and risk, therefore, of stealing more than one seat, perhaps any seat at all, become prohibitive. Furthermore the supervised central count and the checks in counting that go with a P. R. election make even a small amount of fraud very difficult. Repeatedly, defeated candidates have come forward at the end of P. R. elections and said that for the first time they felt sure they had had a square deal.

Elimination of primaries. One of the greatest practical advantages of P. R. is that it does away with all need for primaries. Primaries are a trouble and expense, and they often allow a mere fraction of the voters to decide the all-important question of which particular candidates shall represent the dominant party. P. R. requires only one trip to the polls and lets all the voters who support a party's candidates decide which ones are to be elected to represent it. It does everything that a primary can do, and much more, without its disadvantages. . . .

Co-operation and good feeling. Not the least of the advantages of P. R. is that it promotes decency and good feeling in elections and afterward. Instead of trying to beat a particular person, with the temptation to belittle his ability and blacken his character, each candidate is trying to win a group of supporters for himself out of the whole field. He knows that he cannot defeat the leaders of the opposition, and he knows further that unfairness to any candidate may alienate second choices that he might otherwise receive from that candidate's friends. He dare not be colorless in his desire not to offend, for then he will surely be over-looked in the stiff competition, but it does not pay to throw mud. His best course is to make a vigorous statement of what he himself stands for, without gratuitous attack on anyone else. . . .

Objections to P. R.

. . . We shall [now] consider briefly the objections to P. R. which are most often heard.

Does P. R. promote racial and religious blocs? The most frequent objections to P. R. are not to the principle itself but to the real or supposed effects of applying it. "Your arithmetic is good," some objectors say, "but we can put up with bad arithmetic better than with some of the evils its correction would bring."

The most usual objection of this kind, particularly in cosmopolitan cities, is based on the fear that P. R., in offering representation to minorities, will divide the people into national, racial, and religious blocs, that the representatives of these blocs will trade with each other for their selfish advantage, and that the general interests of the public will suffer.

In meeting this objection it would be foolish to deny that some of the voters will vote along these lines under P. R., as they do under other methods of election, or that they will elect some of the representatives on this basis. It would be a mistake, however, to concede that such votes are always unintelligent or that their representation is unfortunate.

Could anyone seriously contend, for example, that the Negroes of Harlem, with special and difficult community problems of their own, should not try to elect one of their own leaders to represent them? . . .

Even in Cleveland, which is one of the most cosmopolitan of our cities, a majority of the councilmen were never elected on racial and national lines under P. R. There were certain parts of the city, however, where people with a common national ancestry were congregated and where, quite nautrally and properly, the nebulous differences between national party affiliations in city elections were subordinated in the voting to the voters' desire to elect one of their own people. The representation they secured on this basis was in many cases better than they had secured under the ward plan. Such representation did not emphasize sectional feeling, but rather the reverse. With each element fairly treated, with no group feeling the sting of discrimination, they were all free to work together as fellow-Americans in solving the common problems of the city. . . .

While P. R. gives to any sort of community of interest among groups of voters such prominence as the voters themselves wish to give it, it does not *create* a division of any kind and it does not enforce a division arbitrarily as the ward or district system often does. As a practical matter a person living in Harlem, whether colored or white, *must* be represented in the state Assembly by a Negro, and a person living elsewhere in New York City *must* be represented by a white man. . . .

Does P. R. deprive localities of representation? Strangely enough, persons who object to P. R. because it even allows one sort of sectional representation often object to it also because it does not require another kind. Representation by place of residence may have as little to do with big governmental issues as representation by race, nationality, or religion. Yet one of the most frequent objections to P. R. is that it does not require representation by localities.

Here again the objection is highly theoretical and has practically no basis in fact. A city electing its council at large by P. R. *could* elect all the councilmen from one neighborhood, but no city has ever done so. For to get this result under P. R. it would be necessary for nearly *all* the voters to vote for candidates from one neighborhood in preference to the candidates who live elsewhere, and that never happens.

If a quota of a man's neighbors want to elect him under P. R., all the other voters together cannot prevent it.

Parties and civic groups, in nominating their tickets, take geographical as well as other sectional divisions into account so as to give those voters who think geographically a chance to vote that way without going outside their tickets. That makes it easy in most cases to vote for the policy you want and for a neighbor at the same time. . . .

Does it help extremists and faddists? P. R. is often objected to on the ground that it will help extreme parties or groups with particular fads that might not otherwise have had a chance of electing anyone.

That P. R. may give representation to such groups is not to be denied. But it will not do so unless they have a substantial part of the votes. . . .

If an extremist group does have a substantial part of the votes, denying it representation is as silly as an ostrich's sticking his head in the sand. There is always the danger, under the old plan of elections, that such a group will suddenly sweep in with more than its share of the members and with no minority experience to prepare it for the responsibilities of control. . . .

It is said that "the best way to discredit a fool is to hire him a hall." And if, as sometimes happens, a "faddist" or "extremist" turns out to be not a fool but a wise man ahead of his time, then too the best thing to do is hire him a hall.

Does P. R. increase the bargaining power of minorities? Under proportional representation as under the old system of election, a minority may hold the balance of power. And it may use this advantage to bargain effectively for what it wants. . . .

Those who make this objection are straining at a gnat and swallowing a camel. For the sake of avoiding an occasional bargain, which may indeed give a minority something that it wants but only with the consent of a majority, they are willing to substitute downright minority control. . . .

Whenever there are two or more people to be considered, there is no way of avoiding bargaining and compromise. There has always been plenty of it in the old New England town meeting. If there must be bargaining, let us see that it is such as a majority of the people would probably approve. This is much more likely if it is done by representatives of a real majority after an election in which the people have had a chance to vote freely on the issues, as under P. R., than it is if the issues never come before the people at all.

Does P. R. make legislation harder? People sometimes fear that a body with all elements in it will be strong in oratory but weak in accomplishment.

This fear has little basis in experience. Because of the superior quality and public spirit of a majority of the members elected by P. R., the records of P. R. bodies have almost always far surpassed those of bodies elected by the old methods. . . .

Is P. R. hard to understand? Admittedly very few of the people in P. R. cities could conduct a P. R. count. But the people can readily understand everything about P. R. which really concerns them. They can understand how to vote; that is as simple as 1, 2, 3. They can understand that the system gives them a chance to have their vote count, if not always for a first choice, then for a second or a third. They can understand that it gives representation to minorities and assures majority rule. And they can look upon the results and see that they are good.

The voters do not have to count the ballots, though anyone of average intelligence can easily learn how if he wants to take the trouble. The rules are simpler than those of baseball, and incomparably simpler than those of bridge.

But, except that a thorough understanding will keep them from accepting the false statements about P. R. which machine politicians often circulate, it is not important whether the voters master the succession of simple steps in the P. R. count or not. When you post a letter in New York to a village in Scotland, you do not know by what route it will go. And you do not need to. All you need to know is that the system of transmission is one that will stand investigation and carry the letter.

Does the P. R. count take too much time? People used to getting unofficial results on election night often object to the time taken for a P. R. count.

In Cincinnati the results have usually taken about a week. The time was longer than necessary, but no great harm was done. As the people had to live under the results for two years, it was worth a week's waiting to get the right ones. In the meantime the transfers made an exciting continued story which the people followed in the papers from day to day. A good idea of the general nature of the result was given, of course, by the count of first choices within the first few hours.

In Cleveland, the last two P. R. counts took three days each after a few hours of preliminary work in passing on disputed ballots. . . .

Does P. R. lend itself to manipulation? It often occurs to those who have not given the matter much thought that the handling and rehandling of paper ballots in a P. R. central count gives excellent opportunities for juggling and manipulation not afforded by the usual election methods.

The truth is just the opposite. The rehandling of ballots provides a check by different persons. Two or three counters may be dishonest, but a whole force is not likely to be. When a team of Bronx counters in the first New York P. R. election changed some of the ballots, their operations were promptly brought to the directors' attention from several different directions by clerks who were given these ballots to record. The offenders were dismissed and indicted and immediate steps were taken to give effect to the voters' original intentions by court action. In contrast, recent judicial recounts in New York City have given evidence of startling irregularities in ordinary paper ballot primaries. Such irregularities are usually not discovered except in the rare instances where the courts reopen the ballot boxes.

The balancing of totals after every transfer is a further safeguard in the P. R. count. Finally, a central public count is much easier to supervise than a count in scattered precincts. If, as in most P. R. communities, the precinct count is eliminated entirely and the candidates' agents are given adequate facilities for watching the general count, P. R. furnishes as fraud-proof a count of paper ballots as can well be devised. . . .

Does P. R. make campaigning harder? Candidates and their friends sometimes complain that P. R. makes them cover a larger area and thus gives an advantage to those with money or newspaper support.

Of course money and newspaper support always

help. But those who make this objection overlook the fact that it is not necessary to reach all the voters, but merely to convince a quota of them. A quota may be cultivated in one part of the city or in one group of citizens. To convince a quota anywhere in the sort of competition that P. R. provides is a formidable task for one who starts unknown. But for a candidate with an established reputation, the sort of candidate whose election is likely to be of most value to the city, it may require no campaign at all. . . .

Does P. R. leave elections to chance? The part that chance plays in a P. R. election is very small. Most of the ballots are not affected by it at all. But when a candidate has more ballots than he needs, there is an element of chance — though no possibility of deliberate selection — in the usual methods of deciding which of his supporters shall make up his constituency and which shall help their later choices instead.

In New York City the ballots will be taken for counting in a prescribed order of polling places which scatters the ballots taken in any one part of the count as evenly as practicable over the entire borough; and the last ballots counted for a candidate, sure to be a fairly representative sample of all of them, are the ones passed on to second choices. In Toledo the same plan is followed except that the order of precincts is arranged by lot. In Hamilton an equal number, as nearly as possible, is taken from each precinct to make up the surplus. In Cincinnati, if one fourth of a candidate's ballots are to be transferred, every fourth ballot that has been given to him is taken. In Boulder and in British, Irish, and Canadian, P. R. elections all of an elected candidate's first-choice ballots are sorted according to second choices and the same proportion is taken for transfer from each second-choice pile, the particular ballots from each pile being taken at random.

Any one of these methods is incomparably fairer than the procedure to which it corresponds for separating constituencies under the single-member district or ward system. Ward lines can be deliberately drawn so as to deprive some voters of all opportunity to be represented, whereas the chance selection of surplus ballots under P. R. cannot be made with deliberate intent without a violation of law and in any case cannot deprive anyone of a representative.

It has been demonstrated mathematically that in a large election the chance of getting different results with the same ballots under the usual P. R. rules is so small as to be negligible. . . .

Conclusion

To sum up, P. R. can be applied with great profit to all elected bodies whose business it is to make decisions on behalf of the voters. . . .

Proportional representation is not to be dismissed

as a passing fad. It is not even to be classed with other important reforms. It is the greatest single need in government today. It clears the way for all other needed changes, for it makes government responsive to what the people want.

As the next article points out, stereotypes die hard and few are more tenacious than those surrounding the institution of "city hall." The editors of Fortune, *as a part of their study of the modern metropolis, contribute to dispelling some myths as they evaluate contemporary big city mayors and the significant leadership they are providing. Stephen K. Bailey, a well-known political scientist and former mayor of Middletown, Connecticut, lends a touch of humorous realism to the day-to-day problems of "His Honor."*

54

New Strength in City Hall

AT THE TROUBLED CORE of the big city stands City Hall, a block-square, granite citadel heavily encrusted with myth. It was a half-century ago that Lincoln Steffens described the "shame of the cities" — the bosses, the boodlers, the job sellers, and the hopeless inefficiency of the city's housekeeping. The image persists. Most people are aware that the machines have fallen on parlous times — but they're not sure that what's left is much better. The dramatic corruption may have gone but the belief that the big city's government is a mess remains. When people look for models of municipal efficiency, it is outward, to the hinterland, that they are apt to turn; here, where "grass roots" are more visible, are the slumless smaller cities and the towns with city managers, and it is to them that most of the accolades for municipal success are directed.

The emphasis is misplaced. Where the problems are the toughest — in the big, crowded, noisy city — government has vitally transformed itself. Today the big city must rank as one of the most skillfully managed of American organizations — indeed, considering the problems it has to face, it is better managed than many United States corporations. . . .

. . . the suburbanization of the countryside has

Reprinted from the November 1957 issue of *Fortune* Magazine by special permission; © 1957 Times Inc. Pp. 156–158, 251, 264.

plunged America's big cities — specifically the twenty-three cities with population of 500,000 and over — into a time of crisis. Hemmed in by their hostile, booming suburbs, worried about the flight of their middle class, and hard pressed to maintain essential services for their own populations, they need, if they are to hold their own, let alone grow, top-notch leadership.

They have it. Since the 1930's, and at an accelerating rate after the second world war, the electorate in city after city has put into office as competent, hard-driving, and skillful a chief executive as ever sat in the high-backed chair behind the broad mahogany desk. At the same time they have strengthened the power of the office.

This has not been a victory for "good government." To most people, good government is primarily honest and efficient administration, and they believe that the sure way for the city to get it is to tighten civil service, eliminate patronage, and accept all the other artifacts of "scientific" government, including the council-city-manager plan. But today's big-city mayor is not a good-government man, at least in these terms, and if he ever was, he got over it a long time ago. He is a tough-minded, soft-spoken politician who often outrages good-government people, or, as the politicians have called them, the Goo-Goos.

One of the biggest threats to his leadership, indeed, is too much "good government." The big problem at City Hall is no longer honesty, or even simple efficiency. The fight for these virtues is a continuous one, of course, and Lucifer is always lurking in the hall, but most big-city governments have become reasonably honest and efficient. Today, the big problem is not good housekeeping: it is whether the mayor can provide the aggressive leadership and the positive programs without which no big city has a prayer. What is to get priority? Industrial redevelopment? More housing? (And for whom?) There is only so much money, and if hard policy decisions are not made, the city's energies will be diffused in programs "broad" but not bold.

The mayor is hemmed in. As he strives to exercise policy leadership, his power is challenged on all sides. In his own house the staff experts and the civil-service bureaucrats threaten to nibble him to death in their efforts to increase their own authority. Then there are the public "authorities." Some are single-purpose authorities — like the city housing authorities, and the sewer districts; some, like the Port of New York Authority, handle a whole range of functions. They are eminently useful institutions, but however efficient they may be, they are virtually laws unto themselves and they have severely limited the mayor's ability to rule in his own house and, more important, his ability to plan for long-range development.

The power struggle also goes on between the mayor and the state legislature, which has a controlling voice in the city's fiscal affairs, but whose membership is apportioned in favor of the rural areas. It is the rare mayor who need not make frequent trips to the state capital for additional funds, and the legislature is usually unsympathetic. . . .

There is the continuing struggle between the mayor and the suburbs, whose people, the big city firmly believes, are welshing on their obligations to the city. The mayor must win the cooperation of his suburban counterparts if he is to do anything at all about the city's most pressing problems — e.g., the traffic mess — and the going is grim. No one is against "saving our cities," but in this seemingly antiseptic cause there are fierce conflicts of interests and the power struggle is getting more intense.

What citizens want: More

There has been a change in City Hall because there has been a change in the city itself. For the better part of a century, the core of big-city life was its immigrants — waves and waves of them, many illiterate, few English-speaking, all poor. Their grinding misery kept the machine in power at the hall. The machine fed on the immigrants, but it also helped them — with jobs, with welfare services and personal favors, with Christmas baskets and dippers of coal — and the immigrants, in turn, were generous with their votes. The 1924 Immigration Act put an end to this cycle. Reduced immigration gave the city time to absorb the earlier newcomers, reduce the language barriers, educate them and their children, and raise many of them into the middle class. This, along with federal social security and unemployment insurance, reduced the dependence of the big-city masses on the political machines. After World War II came the huge influx of southern Negroes and Puerto Ricans, but by this time the machine was beyond a real comeback.

A half-century's work by the National Municipal League, the Institute of Public Administration, and other government research groups was a big factor. They fought and in many places won the hard fight for the short ballot, which eliminates "blind" voting, and for better city charters, better budgeting, and more efficient management methods.

Better-qualified people came into government. During the unemployment of the 1930's governments could recruit talent they couldn't before. Most of the bright young men went off to Washington, but many of them went into city government too. Some now man its top administrative posts, and they have done much to raise civil-service standards.

Most important, the public began asking for more. It now demands as a natural right better-administered services — police and fire protection, water, sewerage, and all the rest — and it judges its public officials on how well they are able to satisfy this demand. It also demands services — psychiatric clinics, youth boards, air-pollution control — it never had before. City government, as a result, has been transformed into an enormous service machine, infinitely complicated to run.

The management men

To many an aspirant who wouldn't have thought of city politics a generation ago, the mayoralty is now eminently worth his mettle. This has been particularly true in cities where long-standing sloth and corruption had created the possibility of a dramatic reversal; in these places an able and ambitious man might well conclude that his opportunities for spectacular, visible achievement outran those of a governor or senator. But the new mayors are more than opportunists. They come from widely different social and economic backgrounds, and they differ as widely in temperament, but all share a sense of mission: while it also happens to be good politics, they feel deeply that they should make their decisions in terms of the community-wide interest rather than the interest of any one group.

The profile of today's big-city mayor — with one difference — is quite similar to that of the chief executive of a large corporation. Typically, the mayor is a college graduate, usually with a legal or business background, and is now in his late fifties. He puts in hard, grinding hours at his desk, sometimes six or seven days a week, and his wife suffers as much as his golf game. The difference is in salary: he usually makes $20,000 to $25,000. There is also a chauffeur-driven limousine and, in some cities, an expense allowance, ranging from $2,000 (Milwaukee) to $55,000 (Chicago).

"Public relations" take a big chunk of his time. He is aggressively press-conscious, holds frequent news conferences, often appears on TV-radio with his "Report to the People"; and from his office flows a flood of releases on civic improvements. About five nights a week there are civic receptions, banquets, policy meetings, and visits with neighborhood civic groups. In between he may serve as a labor negotiator, or a member of the Civil Defense Board.

The mayor is also seeing a lot more of the city's business leaders, whose interest in urban renewal is growing steadily. Despite the fact that His Honor is likely to be a Democrat, he gets along very well with the businessmen, though he is apt to feel that they have a lot to learn about political decision-making. A City Hall man recently summed up the feelings of his fellows: "These businessmen like everything to be nice and orderly — and non-political. They're getting hot now on metropolitan planning. They think it's not political! Throw them into shifting situations where there are a lot of conflicts and no firm leadership and they're completely buffaloed. It's painful to watch them trying to operate. But once there's a firm program lined up and they've bought it, they're very effective."

Above all the mayor is a politician. True, he may have risen to office on the back of a reform movement. But he is not, as happened too often in the past, a "nonpolitical" civic leader who rallies the do-gooders, drives the rascals out of City Hall, serves for an undistinguished term or two, and then withdraws — or gets driven out — leaving the city to another cycle of corruption. Instead, he fits the qualifications of the mayors whom Lincoln Steffens called on the public to elect: "politicians working for the reform of the city with the methods of politics." His main interest is in government, not abstract virtue, and he knows that the art of government is politics.

De Lesseps Morrison of New Orleans is a notable example of a political leader who leaped into office on a reform ticket, then used the methods of politics to put his programs across. In the eleven years since insurgents elected Mayor Morrison over opposition from the long-entrenched regulars who had run the town wide open, he has done more than demonstrate that hard-working and efficient management can change the face of a city. Morrison has consolidated the gains — in large part by his ability to turn the loose organization that first supported him into a thoroughly professional political organization, which regularly helps elect friendly councilmen. The Morrison organization, not surprisingly, is anathema to the old Democratic machine.

In Philadelphia, Richardson Dilworth and his predecesor, Mayor (now Senator) Joseph Clark, have followed the Morrison pattern up to a point. Six years ago Philadelphia civic groups wrested control of City Hall from a corrupt and contented Republican machine, and the Clark and Dilworth administrations have given the city vigorous and honest government ever since. Mayor Dilworth, in office since 1956, is making considerable headway with his programs; unlike Morrison, however, he has not yet chosen to organize followers into a political organization that can regularly get out the vote on election day. The old-line Democrats and Republicans, as a result, have been increasingly successful in electing their own men to the council.

The new mayor, of course, does not need a dragon to fight. Indeed, some of today's best mayors are in cities that have enjoyed reasonably honest government for quite some time. Detroit's aggressive Mayor Albert Cobo . . . was one of these. He believed that government should be run like a business: during his eight years in office he overhauled the city's government, department by department, replacing the old, wasteful ways of doing things with machines and management systems that would do credit to any corporation.

St. Louis, Cincinnati, and Milwaukee, all with long traditions of honest government, have a remarkable trio of mayors: each wears a distinctively scholarly air, and is a pretty good politician to boot. St. Louis, once an ailing city, has found one of the ablest leaders in its history in an engineering professor, Raymond Tucker. Enthusiastically backed by the city's business leaders and the St. Louis press, Mayor Tucker has persuaded the voters to approve new taxes and public-improvement bond issues with which he has pulled the city out of the red and away from the blight. Milwaukee, a well-governed city since 1910, now has professorial, mild-mannered Frank P. Zeidler as its mayor. He too has stimulated a conservative, frugal citizenry into approving needed physical improvements. Cincinnati, under council-city-manager government since 1926, has Charles Taft, a top mayor who has given the city's urban-renewal and highway programs a powerful boost.

Bridging the gap

The mayors of Pittsburgh and Chicago bridge the gap between the traditional machine-boss mayor and today's management-man mayor. Pittsburgh's David Lawrence and Chicago's Richard Daley are both powerful Democratic organization leaders as well as strong mayors: each has given his city increasingly good government — and a big push forward in meeting its problems — while at the same time maintaining his organizations in viable if declining power. Of the two, Daley has been the biggest surprise. When he was elected . . . many people believed he would sell City Hall to Cicero without a qualm. Instead, Daley went along to a remarkable extent in putting into effect reform legislation that tightened and improved the structure of Chicago's city government. Chicago, Senator Paul Douglas once observed, is a city with a Queen Anne front and a Mary Ann rear. That may still be the case with its government: it undoubtedly has much to do before its rear is as respectable as its front. But Daley, a man who has been known to do odd things with the queen's English, seems determined to close the gap. "We will go on," he once announced at a town-and-gown dinner of the city and the University of Chicago, "to a new high platitude of success."

The strong mayor

In his drive for more power, the big-city mayor is in direct conflict with a strong trend in municipal government. This is the council-city-manager plan, which is the fastest spreading form of government among cities of 25,000 to 100,000. To many do-gooders, it is the ideal form of government for the

American city, big or small. Basically, it is government by a board of directors: an elected committee decides on city politics, and the hired manager and his experts carry them out.

The system has been most successful in smaller cities — e.g., Watertown, New York (population, 35,000), whose inhabitants are for the most part homogeneous and native born, where ethnic and economic tensions are low, and where the future holds no big threats. Cities like Watertown may thrive under such government; most big cities cannot.

Their electorates seem to sense this. When asked to vote on a new city charter, they have usually settled on one providing for a strong mayor rather than committee leadership. As a result, the trend to the strong chief executive, long evident in the federal government and the urban state capitals, is now running high in the cities. Of the twenty-three largest, fourteen have adopted some kind of "strong-mayor" charter, five still vest most power in the council, and four use the council-manager plan. . . .

Tactics vs. strategy

In dealing with the how-to problems of government, the mayor is making considerable progress. At another task, however, he is failing. In his preoccupation with means, he is in danger of neglecting ends. He is not doing a good job of planning the city's future. When he is asked for his ideas on what the city should be like in twenty years, he is apt to reel off a long list of particular improvements — a new expressway here, a new superblock of housing there. Sometimes he will point to a spanking marble-and-glass civic center built in the downtown business district to increase property values and to act as "a center of decision making."

But the projects, however worthy, are too often unconnected: the mayor doesn't really seem to have a general plan for the city's development. His pragmatism, of course, is not to be scorned, and a static, all-embracing master plan would never really work. But while any plan must be revised time and again, without a continuing effort to look ahead — far ahead — many basic policy questions will be left unasked. . . .

Expert as professional planners may be, planning is ultimately a line rather than a staff function. To be effective, it requires the mayor's active support and coordination. It is here more than anywhere else that he is required to serve as a center of leadership and responsibility: if he is unwilling to mesh planning and execution, no one else can. In too many cities the mayor has abdicated this responsibility, and when he has, planning becomes an exercise in futility. . . .

Pittsburgh's Lawrence, who countenances both planning and fragmentation, may have been speaking for the middle ground when he said recently: "My effort must go not into architectural and planning critiques, but into the limited, tedious, persevering work of making things happen."

The mayors, indeed, have made things happen — and this is prerequisite. But it is not enough. Long-range strategy for *what* is to happen is as badly needed. If the city is to reassert itself as a vital center in American life and, not so incidentally, if it is to help the federal and state governments prevent the rest of the country from turning into a suburban mess — the mayors must take the lead. The omens are promising.

55

A Structured Interaction Pattern
for Harpsichord and Kazoo

By Stephen K. Bailey

"AND SO, GENTLEMEN, I would conclude that proper delegation, a reasonable span of control, an executive budget, a well organized personnel system, a clear division between line and staff, and a properly structured interaction pattern for decision-making are the necessary ingredients of good administration. Next hour we shall discuss headquarters-field relationships."

The well-trained bell rings. I gather up my notes, drop them on my cluttered desk, grab my hat, trot down the stone steps in front of Fisk Hall, and slide into the front seat of a waiting police cruiser.

"Good morning, Mayor. City Hall?"

"Hi, Al. Yes, City Hall."

The cruiser burps and purrs and turns down College Street.

"Say, Mayor."

"Yes, Al?"

"We gonna get a raise this year?"

"Gee, Al, I dunno. Depends. . . ."

"On what, Mayor?"

"Well, Al, it depends on the chief — and on the

Stephen K. Bailey, "A Structured Interaction Pattern for Harpsichord and Kazoo," *Public Administration Review,* Summer, 1954, pp. 202–204. Reprinted by permission of the publisher, the American Society for Public Administration.

Police Commission. And, of course, I don't know what the Board of Finance will say — or the Merit Rating Board — or the Council. And, of course, if you fellows get a raise, what will the firemen and the boys in Public Works say. And the School Board. To say nothing of the party."

"Election year, huh, Mayor?"

"Yuh."

"Guess things are tough all over, huh, Mayor?"

"You can say that again, Al."

"Yuh."

"I'll do what I can for the boys, Al. But you know that I'm only the mayor. And in Centerville, here, we have no scalar system and damn little posdcorb."

"How's that, Mayor?"

"Skip it, Al. Thanks for the ride."

"O.K., Mayor."

. . . .

As the elevator creeps toward the fourth floor, I turn to the elevator operator.

"Anyone waiting, Fred?"

"I think the comptroller wants to see you, Mayor. He's down in Bill Blake's office."

"O.K., Fred. Thanks."

I find Harry as directed.

"Oh, Mayor. Bill and I want to talk to you about the sewer bond."

"Sewer thing, Harry. Shoot." (I always pun when I know I'm in trouble.)

"Mayor, do you want these on short terms or 20-year reinvested?"

(With serious tone) "Well, Harry, there is of course a great deal to be said on both sides. Incidentally, how's the market?" (This last question I'd overheard Harry asking a banker on the phone the previous week, and it sounded dandy.)

"It's good, Mayor. It's good."

"Well, in that case, Harry, why not?"

"Why not *what,* Mayor?"

"Er — ah — why not follow the market?"

"You mean 20-year bonds, Mayor?"

"If that's what you and Bill think best, Harry, go right ahead."

"O.K., Mayor, we ought to get them for one-ninety or two."

"Yeah, Mayor," Bill breaks in, "It was up to two-forty last August."

Me, horrified, "You mean it's gone *down?*"

(Bill and Harry together) "But that's *good,* Mayor."

(Me, laughingly) "Oh, is it — I mean — well, ain't I the old card, boys?"

(Harry and Bill, shaking their heads good naturedly) "You sure are, Mayor."

. . . .

Ellen has been avoiding my glances for about a week. She's a good secretary, but her morale is obviously not high. (What *was* it Elton Mayo said to do in cases like this?)

(Jovially) "Good morning, Ellen!"

(Matter of factly) "Good morning, Mayor."

(Ebulliently) Quite a day, Ellen, huh?"

(Glumly) "I guess some people might think so, Mayor."

It is quite obvious that something has to be done about Ellen's attitude.

"Ellen."

"Yes, Mayor."

"Is something wrong?"

"Nope."

"Ellen. Look at me. There *is* something wrong, isn't there?"

(Avoiding my penetrating eyes) "Is there?"

"Yes, Ellen, there is. For a week now you've been treating me like a discontinuous continuum."

"A what, Mayor?"

"A — oh, never mind. Now what is it, Ellen?"

(Pause. Then with a burst) "You know as well as I do what the trouble is, Mayor. You gave that — that — that *woman* on the third floor a raise. She's now in *my* classification, and she — she — she — OH!"

"But, Ellen, she . . ."

"She doesn't deserve a clerk-typist rating, that's what. It's all politics, and I could just die."

"But, Ellen, the Merit Rating Board upon recommendation of the Ernst and Ernst study changed that one. She's been working for the city for twenty-eight years. You've only been here six."

"I do six times the work *she* does, that's what."

"But, Ellen, everyone knows that. Everyone knows you're the best, most hardworking, most efficient girl in the building. You know I'd be lost without you. And you realize of course that the whole city would grind to a halt if you were not at the helm."

"There no sense talking about it, Mayor. I've been hurt and you know it."

(Lamely) "I'm sorry, Ellen."

.   .   .   .

The telephone buzzer buzzes.

"Yes, Ellen."

"Mr. Dugan on two, Mayor."

I push the button.

"Hello, Jack? How the heck are you? . . . You're what Jack? . . . But, Jack, I never said that. I must have been misquoted. . . . The *Bridgeport Herald* said what? . . . Jack, that's ridiculous. Why would I call one of my own councilmen, and one of my own party, a 'pinhead'? . . . No, I did *not* say that. I simply told the reporter you had one of the sharpest heads on the Council. . . . Jack. . . . Jack. . . . Hello? Hello?"

.   .   .   .

"Mayor."

"Yes, Joe."

"You asked me the other day about, what did you call it, central purchasing or something? Would you spell that out again please?"

"Sure, Joe. It's just this. I figure you in Public Works buy tires, and the Second District Highway buys tires, and Police buys tires, and the Fire Department buys tires. Instead of each one of you going down to a local filling station and buying retail, why don't you pool your orders and buy wholesale?"

"And go *outside* the city, Mayor?"

"Well, not necessarily. Can't you buy wholesale inside the city?"

"Not if you got to bid. The big distributors in Hartford and New Haven would cream the locals."

"They would?"

"Sure. And what'll the local filling stations say if you start buying out of town?"

"Why, they'll say — they'll say that I'm saving the taxpayers' money. That's what they'll say."

"Oh, Mayor — you slay me! You slay me, Mayor."

.   .   .   .

"Charter Revision Committee will come to order. Minutes of the previous meeting? What is the pleasure of the committee?"

"I move they be approved and placed on file."

"Without objection, so ordered. Well, gentlemen, this evening the first item on the agenda is what to do about the councilmanic committee system. It's my own feeling that councilmanic committees should not have administrative control over departments. We must not fuzz up responsibility."

"Well, Mayor, who *should* the department heads be responsible to?"

"Well, I should say — and I don't want you to feel that I want power for *myself* here — this is a matter of administrative principle — I should say they should be responsible to the chief executive."

(Vehemently) "We don't want any dictators in Centerville."

"No, no. You don't understand. For instance, who runs a big industry?"

"A board of directors."

"Well, yes, in one sense. But you have a general manager *under* the board of directors. Now the Common Council is like the . . ."

"Who's going to control the Mayor?"

"The people."

"Yeah, like stockholders control G.E."

"No, it's not quite the same. You see, in industry,

management is not in a goldfish bowl. In government, I suffer, the city suffers, from lateral pressures on the hierarchy."

"Pepto-bismol will fix that up in a jiffy, Mayor."

. . . .

(6:30 a.m. My wife, sleepily) "Hello? You want to speak to the Mayor? Well, it's awfully early in the. . . . All right, just a minute. (Poking me) Hey! Psst! It's for you, Highness."

(Early morning bass) "This is the Mayor speaking."

"Mayor?"

"Yes. Who is this?"

"This is a taaaaxpayer."

"What can I do for you?"

"Mayor. I seen that big pitchur in the paper last night about redoin' the whole East Side — tearin' down all those tenements and puttin' up a new civic center. That your idea?"

(A little proudly) "Why, yes."

"Mayor."

"Yes."

"Why the hell don't you stop tryin' to build Radio City and come down here and collect my garbage. It *stinks!*" (Click!)

. . . .

"And I give you a man who needs no introduction to the Civitans — a man who, though young in years, has certainly done a great deal for — well, that is, has certainly caused much comment during his tour of duty at City Hall. Your Mayor and mine. . . ." (Polite applause)

"Mr. Chairman, distinguished guests, members of Rotary — I mean Civitans — I'm not very good at telling stories, and you have probably all heard this one about the politician and the kangaroo. Well, it seems there was a politician and he went to the zoo one day and he went over to the kangaroo cage. Well, sir, that old kangaroo backed away and said, 'Here's *one* pocket you don't get your hands into,' and the politician said. . . ."

. . . .

"Mayor."

"Yes, Ellen."

"You look tired."

"A little weary, Ellen. What have I got on tonight?"

"Tonight isn't bad. Sports banquet and Park Board. But tomorrow there's Zoning Board of Appeals at 9:00; Red Cross proclamation over WCNX at 10:00; lunch at Rotary; Planning and Development at 2:00; party caucus at 5:30; dinner with the Parking Authority; and a long session with the Board

of Finance on the Town School budget in the evening."

"At least I have no classes tomorrow, Ellen."

"Day *after* tomorrow, Mayor."

. . . .

"Gentlemen. As I was saying last time, a pyramidal structure with proper staff-line relationships, emphasis upon a proper organizational theory, with a functional decision-making interaction pattern — these make up what might be called the administrative way of life.' " ·

. . . .

The wise city manager cannot become publicly embroiled in council elections or other direct partisan activity. The council-manager plan presumes to make a distinct separation between policy making and execution, yet in practice a manager can and must play a major role in the development and recommending of policy. Whether he should scrupulously remain in the background as the agent of the council or step forth as a leader in the community is still a point of controversy. The resolution of the dilemma proposed here is the view of two well-known managers. The concluding comment, by a former city manager, argues the need for putting politics back into council-manager government and suggests some points of desirable changed thinking on the part of supporters of the plan.

56

The City Manager and the
Policy Process

By C. A. Harrell
and D. G. Weiford

WHEN THE NATION's city managers assembled in Dallas last October for their annual conference, the atmosphere was one of enthusiasm and optimism. The conference theme was the commemoration of

C. A. Harrell and D. G. Weiford, "The City Manager and the Policy Process," *Public Administration Review,* Spring, 1959, pp. 101–107. Footnotes in original omitted. Reprinted by permission of the publisher, the American Society for Public Administration.

the fiftieth anniversary of the appointment of the first manager, and the delegates who gathered for the occasion could justifiably look back over the years with a feeling of pride and accomplishment.

The facts could not be disputed. In the short span of half a century, the council-manager plan had spread so rapidly that it was on the verge of becoming the most prevalent form of municipal government in the United States. In the past twelve years alone it had displaced nearly a thousand mayor-council and commission governments, and the widespread trend of public acceptance showed no signs of abating.

Increasing steadily at the rate of seventy to eighty cities each year, council-manager government was already firmly implanted in nearly half of all cities over 25,000 population. To the managers and to thoughtful observers of public administration alike, it seemed abundantly clear that the next few decades would see council-manager government become the rule and other local governmental forms the exception.

Considering the slowness with which traditional governmental institutions give way to substantive changes, the rapid growth of council-manager government seemed little short of phenomenal. Of even greater significance was the fact that the old battle cry of an outraged populace, "Throw the rascals out," had in recent decades subsided to a whisper. The great growth of council-manager government was taking place in an era of generally honest government, where the major issues had long since ceased to be crime and corruption but rather were centered around the more staid objective of getting the same job done more efficiently and with less confusion and disorder.

Perhaps it was inevitable that such success could not go unquestioned even at a birthday celebration. The Dallas conference was primarily one of soul-searching. Speaker after speaker rose to point out the pitfalls of success and to caution against the real or imagined problems of the future. The familiar, never-answered questions concerning the philosophy of professional city management, the proper role of the council and manager, and the dearth of "political" leadership were discussed time and again.

It was easy to review the achievements of the past, and this was ably done. But the future, although rosy from the standpoint of anticipated growth, nevertheless seemed clouded in mystery. The managers and their political scientist friends knew very well where they had been and what they had done, but no one stepped forward to define the intangibles of the future.

What role would be served by the city manager of tomorrow? What would be the relation between elected council and appointed administrator in matters of community leadership? What position would the manager occupy in the mainstream of democratic life?

Though these and similar questions went unanswered, there seemed to be an underlying feeling among the delegates that there had been a sufficient degree of experience with council-manager government so that some rather definitive conclusions on the various evolutionary stages of the plan could be developed, and that a reasonably accurate forecast of the future could indeed be drawn.

A project of such a nature, involving as it does an analysis of the dynamic social order of a swiftly changing world, is quite an undertaking. We will, however, attempt to set forth our own views on the subject, hoping only that more able and comprehensive analyses will follow.

Criticisms of the manager plan

Throughout the history of council-manager government, critics of the plan have lodged various charges against it. The criticisms have ranged from denunciations of the "foreigner" who was imported to administer the affairs of the city in preference to a local man "who has a better understanding of the problems of the community," to charges that the manager was a dictator whose mere existence was a threat to the priceless heritage of democracy.

Most of these charges were made in the heat of local campaigns centering around the form of government to be adopted by a particular community. Time and again the electorate listened patiently and then voted in the council-manager system with little apparent fear that any basic principles of democracy were at stake. Criticisms of this type have had little significance except for the purposes of campaign oratory.

On the other hand, the more thoughtful apprehensions expressed by a few political scientists in recent years do merit consideration. Centering on the difficulties of separating policy and administration in council-manager government, their primary arguments are: that the city manager has assumed duties of policy and community leadership which were not contemplated in the original concepts of the plan, that the mayor and council seldom assert political or community leadership or initiate policy, and that the attempts they make to sell policy to the public are both infrequent and ineffectual. The manager fills this apparent void by initiating policy recommendations, and, after adoption by a seemingly acquiescent council, he proceeds as a matter of "good public relations" to debate and defend the policy before the general public.

Therefore, goes the argument, the inherent difficulty lies with the nonpartisan council which has defaulted on its proper role of policy leadership. The city manager meanwhile, posing as a professional who knows the answers, has stepped in and taken over both policy and administration.

This undue dominance over local affairs by an appointed officer is held to be improper in a democratic society and to contain the seeds of danger to representative local government. The only solution offered is to de-emphasize the manager and to re-elevate the mayor and council to a position of unquestioned eminence in policy-making and in community leadership.

The changing role of the manager

One must immediately concede that the role of the city manager has changed considerably through the years, and that the manager of today participates to a far greater degree in the total processes of government than was originally contemplated. The city managers have not pretended that their role has remained unchanged. On the contrary, they have been acutely aware for many years that circumstances flowing from the near revolutionary changes in American life were putting them squarely within the policy-making processes of government.

Beginning with the first conference of the International City Managers' Association, much of the discussion centered around the question of whether the manager could be a relatively anonymous and colorless administrator even if he tried to be. The events of the years and the experiences of thousands of managers answered this question decisively in the negative. Indeed, the city managers' original code of ethics, adopted by ICMA in 1924, apparently recognized the fact that the manager — simply by virtue of his position — was inevitably caught up in the policy-making process: "It is the council, the elected representatives of the people, who *primarily* determine municipal policies and are entitled to credit for their fulfillment." In calling for the council "primarily" to determine policies, this official statement implied that the manager should assist in their determination.

In the years that followed, the managers gave official recognition to their evolving role through amendments to their code of ethics. In 1938, the code was amended to read that "the city manager keeps the community informed on municipal affairs. . . ." The earlier code had stated that the manager should keep the community informed only on "the plans and purposes of the administration."

The 1938 code went on to say that the manager "leaves to the council the defense of policies which may be criticized." In 1952, however, an amendment was adopted which eliminated this provision and provided instead that "the city manager defends

municipal policies publicly" but "only after consideration and adoption of such policies by the council." The 1952 code frankly referred to the manager as a "community leader."

It hardly need be pointed out that changes in such documents almost always lag considerably behind the general acceptance of change by practitioners. The amendments to the code of ethics thus came many years after the institution of these practices by most city managers. But the question still must be posed: Is the assumption of community leadership by city managers desirable?

A new concept of administration

At the same time as the manager's view of his responsibilities was changing, observations of scholars concerning the political role of the administrator at all levels of government also changed. The pre-World War II view of public administration as a neat well-ordered world clearly divided from politics has been replaced in most postwar writing by a definition of public administration as an integral part of the political process, with all administrative agencies and their staffs engaged in politics.

Of course the word "politics" no longer has the evil connotations that it once was forced to bear. When modern political scientists state that administration is part of the political process and that administrative agencies are engaged in politics, they mean that administrative officials and their staffs are inescapably a part of the total process of government which includes the determination of policy. This new definition seems to the city manager perfectly evident and arguments to the contrary uninformed.

A sweeping conclusion of this kind with respect to public administration in general goes far beyond a determination of the proper role of the city manager in American life. If such a conclusion is correct, then it follows that there must now begin a wholesale re-examination of political theory and of the relationship which public administration as a political process bears to the fundamental elements of democracy. An undertaking of this magnitude is, of course, far beyond the limits of this paper. But within the smaller framework of council-manager relationships, it is possible for specific observations to be made and tentative conclusions drawn.

The changing nature of "political" issues

Some of the critics of council-manager government have prefaced their remarks with wistful recollections of the "good old days" and have deplored the fact that color and bombast seem to be disappearing from the municipal scene. Related but perhaps more important, it is charged that popular participation in local decision-making and public debate of local issues has declined. Professionalization of the public service is presented as the principal villain in this unhappy story. The city manager is particularly at fault, the critics continue, for the unnatural quiet that has descended. The solution, say these people, is to re-establish in some fashion the control of municipal governments by political parties or by politically aggressive mayors. The results will be exciting, stimulating, and earthy, and cities will once again face up to their problems with confidence and vigor.

It is our belief that these critics have underestimated the profound changes which have been taking place in the American political process and in the American people themselves. In such dramatic glorifications of an era which fortunately no longer exists to any great extent in American cities, the point is completely overlooked that almost revolutionary social and political changes have taken place during the past few generations.

The lusty type of local government political leadership which emerged in the United States during the transition from frontier towns to urban centers is rapidly becoming a thing of the past. Patronage — the life blood of a local political party power — is dead in most cities and is not likely to be resurrected. Political parties have evolved to where the control of only the largest city administrations is still an important goal and a steady withdrawal of partisan influence is underway even here.

It is quite true that the old-fashioned variety of political issues are not so actively debated locally as they once were. But it is also true that such issues appear today with less frequency than was once the case.

There is no magic in this. As the body of knowledge on municipal affairs continues to grow, as leagues of municipalities and university bureaus of public administration continue to develop research data on municipal problems, the alternative courses of action to be considered by a city council dwindle. As the exchange of knowledge among city officials continues to flourish and as the details of successful municipal experiments are passed from city to city, the solutions inevitably narrow in scope.

What were once flaming municipal issues, subject to the oratory of candidates for public office, have in many instances become routine elements of city administration. In other words, where both fact and value once were debated politically because fact was a matter of conjecture, now mainly value questions are debated because we have a far wider knowledge of fact.

Nor is the public of twenty-five or fifty years ago the same public as today. The public today is better educated and more alert to governmental progress or the lack of it than ever before. The demands and

desires of the public have undergone a drastic change. There must now be unquestioned morality in government, there must be effective work performed by city employees, there must be no nepotism, and there must be no important policy determinations unless they are supported by thoughtful analysis and research. If there is a cardinal sin which will not be forgiven by the public of today, it is to hand out governmental favors which others cannot receive. Modern local government thus is held in check by public standards which are higher and more exacting than those of any earlier time.

The body of municipal knowledge has grown to the point that an increasing number of problems is resolved factually, and this has been accepted and even demanded by the public. The nostalgic belief that the reintroduction of partisan politics into local government would stimulate a more widespread discussion of issues than is now the case thus appears to be erroneous.

The impact of a changing society

The vast changes occurring in our society have been enumerated so often that little space will be given to them here. The impact that such changes are having and will continue to have on the habits, traditions, and institutions of the American people is difficult to measure. But the fact that the impact is substantial is hardly subject to debate. Old patterns of life are being uprooted by newer modes of thought. The country is caught up in a restless, dynamic age in which large masses of people are constantly on the move and in which many heretofore isolated problems of cities no longer can be solved within the city boundaries but only on an areawide basis.

A large majority of the people in the United States have suddenly found themselves compressed into a tiny percentage of the country's land area. Great masses of people whose needs can be met only on an economic-area basis find satisfaction of these needs bottled up by a multitude of independent, jealously competing political subdivisions. Local government institutions designed for an earlier time have proven archaic; the slow-moving machinery of checks and balances, long ballots and nineteenth century organization structure are perverting democracy rather than nourishing it. The cherished principle of local home rule no longer is sacred but must be re-examined in relation to the broader needs of metropolitan areas.

The country is moving swiftly from Jacksonian democracy to a democracy which is simply more workable in the modern climate. It must be a democracy with clear lines of responsibility and authority, one which encourages rather than weakens direct action to cope with the complex problems of the times.

It is this new concept of democracy coupled with the growing number of questions solved with factual rather than value answers, that has brought the professional city manager to the fore. In the years to come these same factors will result in a continued institutional remodeling with a heavy emphasis on professional administrative leadership.

While this trend is considered on the whole to be both inevitable and desirable, it nevertheless causes serious questions to be raised concerning the role of the professional city administrator.

In a time when great change is the order of the day and when governmental processes are becoming increasingly technical, does the elected council tend to rely too heavily on the city manager for leadership in policy matters? Does this reliance sometimes develop so strongly that the manager can correctly be accused of dominating the city council? Does the manager's involvement in policy questions mean that he should consider resigning if and when a policy he favored is rejected by a new council or by the electorate in a referendum? Is it desirable to lessen the influence of the manager in policy matters?

The question of managerial dominance

Clarence Ridley in his study of municipal policy formulation found that 75 to 90 per cent of all policies adopted by city councils originate outside of the council, and that many of the policy proposals are actually initiated by the city manager and his staff.

The typical city council thus relies heavily on the manager for advice on policy matters. There are sound reasons for this. In his relationship to the council, the manager's key role is that of fact finder. It is his duty to assemble all of the pertinent facts on any policy matter which involves the operation of the city as a municipal corporation and to submit them to the council for review. Stated another way, it is the duty of the manager to assimilate the growing body of municipal knowledge as it relates to policy matters and to pass on to the council the results of his analysis and research. It is necessary for this to be done for the simple reason that the city council as a lay body is unable to obtain much of this information in any other way.

Occasionally the charge is made in local campaigns that the manager really runs things and that the council is little more than a "rubber stamp" agency. The charge is fictitious. In the years in which we have served as city managers we have never seen a city council which could be led around at will or which meekly acquiesced in policies proposed by the manager. However, if a council is interested in seeking out the best solution, heavy re-

liance will be placed on the accumulation of factual background data and on the judgment of the city manager. What is the local history of the policy proposal? What have other cities in the state done with the same problem? What has been the national experience? What is the current nature of the problem? Finally, what alternative solutions appear to be available, and how will they affect the operation of the city as a municipal operation?

Once these questions have been subjected to staff analysis the typical city council customarily debates the matter, pursues lines of inquiry which may not have been fully developed, and makes a final decision. The better the staff work on these questions the more frequently a reasonable legislative body will adopt the staff recommendations. There is no hidden evil lurking in this procedure. On the contrary, it is the act of intelligent legislators to require that a complete job of analysis be submitted before final determinations are made, and it is likewise the act of a conscientious legislative body — at whatever level of government — to give considerable weight to thorough staff analyses.

The council is expert in matters of community desires and on questions of timing, and in such areas the elected representatives impose their judgment in terms of rejecting, changing, or withholding the policy proposals to a later time. The city manager is expert in fact-finding and in technical knowledge concerning the impact of alternative policies on the administrative organization. The result is policy formulation based on teamwork, with the council and the manager contributing according to their special abilities.

In our opinion the evidence overwhelmingly indicates that the typical city council which operates with a city manager is better informed on alternative areas of decision-making than is the case in any other system of local government. The accumulation by legislative bodies of full information on the problems which lie before them is a positive affirmation of democratic principle. It is the contrary approach which is open to condemnation.

As Ridley puts it, "The council's importance [in council-manager cities] has increased substantially in reviewing proposals, judging what the community wants and needs, and representing the policy after adoption. The research and fact-finding has been assumed by the city manager so that the council has more time to study, review, revise, and promote policy. Basically, the manager's knowledge and experience combined with the council's political sense and judgment will result in the best policies."

The question is sometimes raised as to whether the manager should resign when a policy he has advocated is rejected, or when a policy he has discouraged is adopted. The question apparently centers around the idea that a city manager might sabotage through poor administration a policy he does not believe in.

In actual practice such cases appear to have arisen rarely. The manager profession is steeped in the tradition that the city council is the policy-determining agency and that the manager is clearly a subordinate figure. If a proposed policy were supported by the manager and approved by the council and then were overturned in a subsequent council election, the manager's duty would be to accept the new policy without question and to administer it to the best of his ability.

The proof of the pudding is in the eating. If the manager does not administer policy in a manner satisfactory to the city council he should be dismissed. The council is the judge of managerial performance and summary action is readily available.

The manager does not become involved in partisan political questions. On other policy issues he customarily sets forth in writing his analysis of the problem and the solution which to him seems preferable. If this is not acceptable to the present council or to a subsequent council, he devises an alternative policy proposal or simply does what the council tells him to do.

Except on questions involving the attempted control of purely administrative matters by the council or where a policy is enacted by the council which is unethical or lacking in morality the manager has no cause for voluntary resignation.

The city manager understands that policy flows from many sources, that his duty is to give the council all of the information he can compile, and that the council must then make the final decision and bear full responsibility for it. Unless he is content to accept the decision of the council and to implement it as best he can, he does not properly belong to the manager profession.

The great need for leadership

The evidence indicates that the once-political, now-routine problems of local government are often resolved more promptly and efficiently in council-manager cities than in those which maintain other structural forms. The time has come, however, when we must turn from these relatively simple matters to larger questions which as yet have received little effective attention.

The minds of men can no longer be stirred by the simple problems of local streets and sewers. These have become matters of routine policy and governments are expected to resolve them easily and quickly. The truly important political issues lie on a different level altogether and constitute a host of problems unlike those of any earlier time.

The great issues of the immediate future lie in the dilemma of the metropolitan areas, sprawling across thousands of overlapping political boundary lines. Here, the American public desperately needs effective political leadership but is not receiving it. No single city, village, or town in a metropolitan section can hope to solve its ills alone. Yet the existing governmental machinery in many of these areas remains as outmoded as a horse and buggy in a jet age.

The leadership job which lies ahead is truly staggering. Functions of government must be redefined on an economic area basis rather than upon the existing political boundary line basis, human value goals must be realistically established, work must be redistributed, and staffs made more professional.

Here, then, is the great need for political leadership. Such leadership, however, must be intertwined with that of the professional administrator if solutions are to be found and implemented. Both are essential and neither can be effective without the other.

If political leaders are to appear who can rise to the challenge it will be both necessary and proper for them to work closely with their leader counterparts in administration. It seems evident that in the difficult years that lie ahead it will prove neither practicable nor desirable to lessen the influence of the professional city administrator on broad policy matters.

Conclusion

When measured against the problems of the present and the anticipated greater problems of the future, it is difficult to conceive of a better-balanced, more effective system of local government than the one which has found expression in the elected council and the appointed city manager. The primary strength of the plan is the unification of powers in the elective body rather than the spreading of powers piecemeal among various segments of the legislative and executive branches as is done in mayor-council cities. It is this unity of powers which has enabled the council and the city manager to enter into a successful teamwork relationship in the development of policy.

As a result of this relationship, the council under council-manager government is able to devote its time to the truly important areas of municipal government: the weighing of proposals against the needs and wants of the community, and the expression of final determinations through the adoption of specific programs.

It is probable that the large-scale remodeling of local governmental machinery which must now be undertaken will be drawn along these same lines.

There is no danger to representative government

from the council-manager system. The elected representatives alone make the final decisions and in the true American spirit stand or fall on their decisions. As for the city manager, he continues to occupy the uneasy role of serving solely at the pleasure of the council. This is as it should be. So long as the elected representatives finally determine policy, take full responsibility for it, and retain the power of dismissal over the professional administrator, the cause of representative government is adequately secure.

It is our belief that the role of the city manager has been altered and shaped by the complex forces of the times, evolving over a span of fifty years to the point where the manager properly participates in the policy-making process.

In an age where great change is commonplace, governmental institutions — reflecting as they do the fabric of American life — must also undergo change. The professional city manager is but a single example of this new era, and nostalgic references to the past will be to no avail.

57

Democracy in Council-Manager Government

By Kent Mathewson

FOR MANY YEARS city managers and their form of government have been the darlings of the political science professors from coast to coast. In *Public Administration Review* of last summer, a Rackham postdoctoral fellow at the University of Michigan with wide experience in municipal research raised grave questions about the future for council-manager government. It was charged that the plan often creates a political vacuum and that if the manager allows himself to be drawn in, he becomes an autocrat. If he stays out, the city flounders from a lack of leadership. The article charges that the manager's preoccupation with efficiency makes him sterile to political considerations and — in the absence of a

Kent Mathewson, "Democracy in Council-Manager Government," *Public Administration Review,* Summer, 1959, pp. 183–185. Reprinted by permission of the publisher, the American Society for Public Administration.

strong political mayor — democracy goes down the drain. Also, warnings of growing criticism of council-manager governments by political scientists were voiced at last year's International City Managers' Association conference.

Some of these views were partially confirmed last year by a report by Clarence E. Ridley who retired in 1956 after serving twenty-seven years as executive director of the International City Managers' Association. Ridley, a strong advocate of council-manager government, received questionnaire replies from eighty-eight city managers from coast to coast as to the importance they placed on their annual budget as a means of formulation of municipal policy. While in council-manager government, the city manager has sole responsibility for recommending the coming year's city plan through an executive budget, few managers gave it the place of importance that the budget customarily receives from elected chief executives. In fact the majority of managers reported that they work up their budgets as a "team" effort through informal meetings with their mayor and councilmen. While this assures a minimum of friction in municipal affairs, it strikes a severe blow at the democratic process. By developing the budget at "informal" meetings with the council, officials present a cut and dried budget to the public. If the citizens don't like the budget when it finally becomes public, they have an uphill job of trying for a change because the mayor, council, and manager are largely wedded to it through their informal meetings. Likewise this procedure almost completely nullifies the considerable public interest that could and should be developed in the budget.

Some council-manager cities see the matter in a different light, with the manager presenting his budget (without prior councilmanic review of the budget document) to the council and public simultaneously so that the council may feel free to change it as it sees fit in the light of public opinion. This is the democratic process that is followed at other levels of American government. The chief executive's budget is his plan, to be debated and changed in any way desired.

A key to understanding public response to council-manager government in these days of increasing complexity (in everything from home appliances to government operations), may be found in the persistent lack of enthusiasm for manager government in our large metropolitan centers. It may be that the larger the city the smaller the fraction of population that can personally know its city hall leaders, and therefore leadership at the city hall must be realized by the masses through a symbol. A strong mayor makes a much better symbol than the mayor who is part of a council-manager government. The mayor of the council-manager city cannot and does not have the opportunity or responsibility for the total operation of the city and therefore does not become the full symbol of city government as does the mayor of the mayor-council government. In the smaller city, the symbolism is not nearly so important because people see their city manager or their mayor or their councilmen or their department heads at civic club meetings, in church, and on the street, and they can deal with their city government through personal contacts rather than through symbolism expressed periodically at election time. The need for symbolism in the large city is not entirely compatible with council-manager government and undoubtedly will continue to present a problem to advocates of manager government in the larger cities.

Friends of good government everywhere should be concerned about questions being raised about council-manager government because supporters and detractors alike agree that this innovation, now fifty years old, worked the most significant advance in government in the twentieth century. Mayors, councilmen, and managers should carefully review their thinking on these eight points:

1. The people of this country in choosing between democracy and efficiency have always chosen democracy. They will revolt against slide rule solutions or recommendations by "experts" when such action becomes oppressive or devoid of the common touch. For every pound of "expertise" there should be a counter portion of Jacksonian democracy.

2. The larger the city the greater the need for a personality to symbolize the municipality's government — "the mayor of our town." The leadership position of the mayor in council-manager cities is usually stronger when he is elected by the public than when he is elected by his fellow councilmen.

3. The cause of democracy will not be served by the city manager ducking responsibility, refusing to take a stand, or assuming a "milk toast" personality because of a mistaken belief that making important policy recommendations will place him in an inappropriate role. He is the municipality's chief executive — while the mayor is the chief political and policy leader.

4. Every city deserves bold thinking, research, and reporting to the public on the major municipal issues of today, such as urban sprawl, downtown blight, urban renewal, and mass transit. Fulltime, paid, and elected mayors in noncouncil-manager cities face removal if they fail to use their talents on these issues. Part-time, nonpaid mayors in council-manager cities often cannot devote sufficient time to these affairs. Recommendations on these and other vital matters, then, should be made by the fulltime, paid city manager and his researchers. This should be done in the manager's annual budget message or other major "white papers" that will receive legislative and public debate. These policy recommendations should be presented simultaneously to the council and public without the deadening effect of cut and dried solutions arrived at through informal conferences with council.

5. Matters of street locations, sewer needs, and other "routine" municipal housekeeping affairs need not be finally decided by technicians. The public usually has a keen interest and opinion about these matters, and there are elements in these decisions on which the public, not the technician, is expert. While the public's desire may not always represent the "technical solution," it represents nevertheless the *right* answer.

6. Mayors and councilmen in council-manager cities have a pressing obligation to exert political and policy leadership to the fullest. The public and city manager should insist on their fulfillment of that role.

7. In council-manager cities the term "ward" should no longer be considered a dirty word and instead should be considered synonymous with "representative." In many council-manager cities the democratic process could be strengthened by electing councilmen from wards rather than at large.

8. Finally, caution should be exercised in embracing metropolitan or "super" government as a solution to our problems created by the multiplicity of local jurisdictions in the urban regions because "metro" can only lead to a weakening of the democratic process in local affairs. Instead, greater research and effort should first be expended on the development of intergovernmental cooperation among elected officials on a formal but voluntary basis, for meeting overlapping, uncoordinated, or undeveloped urban matters.

The academes at the first of the century who developed the council-manager plan may have succeeded too well in taking politics out of city government. Their counterparts of today are saying let's put politics back in. The trick is to get the good back without the bad. To the observers at the ICMA conference this would seem far from hopeless. The key is the American city manager with a code of ethics and principles as high as the ministerial profession, expertly trained, serious, dedicated, but with an inexhaustible enthusiasm for public service and the common touch that comes from daily and intimate contact with the hometown citizens. If the city managers of the next fifty years will develop a devotion to the democratic process that outstrips their desire for job security and sterile efficiency, the trick will be turned. The first fifty years proved council-manager's efficiency; the next fifty will prove its democracy.

CHAPTER TWELVE

The County

WHILE THE STRUCTURE OF COUNTY GOVERNMENT in the United States has remained little changed for generations, the functions performed have been increasing and the problems faced have been becoming steadily more complex. Most recommendations for strengthening the counties involve proposals for internal administrative integration and for some type of area or functional consolidation. (In connection with the former, the proposals for county manager or chief administrative officer plans are essentially similar to those for council-manager city government, discussed in Chapters 10 and 11.) In the opening article the executive director of the National Association of County Officials presents a rather optimistic view of both the present and the future of county government, while giving some attention to typical problems being faced. He argues that counties are destined to play a much larger role in the America of the next few decades.

Mr. Millspaugh then examines the claims of "consolidationists," seriously questions their validity, and suggests that from the standpoint of practicality the whole idea may as well be forgotten.

The most striking changes in county government involve developments in several highly urban counties across the country, where in differing ways the county is becoming an instrument for greater metropolitan coordination. The leading examples are described and tentatively evaluated by Professor Kammerer in the concluding selection.

58

County Government Is Reborn

By Bernard F. Hillenbrand

MANY PEOPLE HAVE MISTAKEN IDEAS about county government. They have a mental picture of fat politicians sitting around a pot bellied stove, spraying tobacco juice into a copper spittoon, and plotting how to grease the political machine. Actually, have you been in a courthouse lately? One is more likely to find that it is a modern, air-conditioned building with automatic data-processing machines in the basement; an ultra efficient, two-way sheriff's radio on the roof; and everything in between just as modern — symbols of 20th Century progress.

County government will be the dominant unit of local government in the United States in the next decade. The following facts offer support for this belief:

1. In the six-year period from October 1951–October 1957, county government (as reflected by the number of full-time employees) increased an incredible 36 per cent — an average increase of 6 per cent per year, while municipal government and the general population increased only 3 per cent per year.

2. Virtually every state in the union reports that its county governments have been authorized to undertake a host of new governmental responsibilities.

3. Our 3,047 county governments now employ 668,000 full-time people and spend about $6.5 billion per year.

Bernard F. Hillenbrand, "County Government Is Reborn," *Public Administration Survey*, May, 1960, pp. 1–8. Reprinted by permission of the publisher.

4. One county (Los Angeles County), for example, employs 37,000 persons and has a payroll larger than 41 of the states. In these terms, many counties are larger than one or more states.

5. Some 133,360,000 Americans are served by county governments.

These facts seem to indicate that counties are growing like adolescents. A portion of the increase in the importance of county government is reflected in the expansion of traditional county government services, due both to the population increase and the traditional American demand for improvement and expansion of existing services. These demands have brought spectacular county improvements in election administration (automatic ballot-counting); penal administration (honor farms); administration of justice (streamlined court procedure and use of special service personnel, psychiatrists, etc.); roads and highways (use of modern earthmoving equipment); record keeping (up-to-the-minute machines and techniques); education (student aptitude testing, special counseling, etc.); health and welfare (out-patient clinics for the mentally ill and spotless hospitals).

The really tremendous growth of county government, however, has come in urban areas where the existing units of government have demonstrated that they are not capable of solving area-wide problems. Here one finds counties assuming responsibility for police and fire protection, planning and zoning, water supply, sewage disposal, civil defense, industrial development, air pollution control, airports, traffic control, parks and recreation, urban renewal, and finance administration.

Rural and urban counties today

Today, the life and needs of the rural citizen have changed. He drives an automobile and probably shops as often in the downtown area of the city as does the suburbanite. He sees the same programs on television and his general standard of living is not in any way inferior to that of his city cousin.

From the county government, this rural citizen demands very high and efficient levels of services. He wants good roads, the best of educational and recreational facilities, modern fire and police protection, public health and welfare facilities, and a host of other services.

County governments, moreover, have expanded to provide these services but this expansion has caused many problems, particularly the problem of how these services are to be financed. Counties to a very large extent depend upon the property tax for revenue. The inadequacy of property taxes in our present economy is well known and, as a result, our counties have been experimenting with sales taxes and state-collected, locally-shared taxes to aug-

ment the property tax. As long as counties are dependent upon the property tax as their principal source of revenue, county officials must appeal to both state and national governments for financial assistance, even though there is strong resistance on the part of these officials to increased state and Federal control.

The population shift from rural to urban areas is compounding rural problems. A county road, for example, is just about as expensive to maintain as a city road, even though there are fewer citizens to use it. In fact, most services increase greatly in cost per-citizen-serviced when there is a decrease in population. Many counties in Mississippi and in other parts of the South are struggling with areas that are depopulating, which has stimulated these counties to pursue vigorously new industry. Those familiar with the property tax know that in most cases residential property alone cannot support a high level of education and other services. A community, therefore, must have new or expanded business and industry. In a county that is depopulating, the need to attract new industry is more urgent than ever.

Here again we see the particular value of the county as a unit of government. A municipality usually cannot serve effectively as a unit to promote new industry. It is a costly activity; and after a great deal of effort, the industry sought may locate in the vicinity but outside the very municipality which attracted it in the first place. Since the industry is outside the municipal taxing jurisdiction, it would derive no immediate tax advantage. A county, by contrast, serves the entire area; and the business is taxable by the county no matter where it locates in its boundaries. Since all citizens in the area bear the cost of county government, a new industry eventually helps reduce the total tax liability of all the individual citizens of the county.

County government in the rural areas, by and large, seems to have satisfied its constituents. That the county is the most promising and virile unit of rural government is attested to by the tendency of rural citizens to dissolve their township governments, where they exist, and transfer their functions to the county.

In the urban areas, on the other hand, "the fat is in the fire." Substantially, there are two different arguments advocated as solutions to urban problems: one group argues that the only real solution is the creation of more municipalities or independent authorities while an opposing group argues that all existing units of government are ineffective and should be abolished, giving way to new "super governments." But county officials find that neither position is a realistic solution to immediate problems. Instead, the county is being called upon to assume those responsibilities (one by one) that are of an area-wide nature, such functions as transportation, civil defense, water and sewerage, planning and zoning, and others.

In a typical urban area we find these conditions. The central city is declining in population and the more well-to-do are moving to the suburbs. The central city is being populated by the less well-to-do; gradually it contains more older people and fewer business and professional people and those whom college professors like to call the "leader group." The tax base no longer is able to provide sufficiently high levels of services because new business and industry continues to locate outside the city. Traffic congestion and deterioration of the downtown business district set in.

The core city tries annexation as a means of increasing its tax base. Surrounding the core city are a host of smaller cities that do not want to lose their identity. In unincorporated areas there is equal resistance to annexation because the suburbanites would be required to pay city taxes but could not, in most cases, obtain the same level of services as those in the core city. Often when the core city taxpayer realizes how much it is going to cost initially to provide city services to annexed areas, he balks too!

The crisis usually comes in a single functional area. The airport, for example, needs to expand its runways to provide jet service, but airports are (contrary to fancy bookkeeping) usually money losing propositions. Usually this airport is located physically outside the city. Always it serves the people of an entire area but is supported usually by city taxpayers only. The city fathers realize this fact, and the county is asked to take over their responsibility. Thus one finds that two of the most modern airports in the nation — Miami in Dade County, Florida, and Detroit, in Wayne County, Michigan — draw upon the total resources of the county area.

Here it is important to burst the bubble of a popular fairy tale. County officials are not trying to take over anything. The reverse is true. Most county officials have plenty of problems to occupy their minds and are reluctant to seek new ones. Usually the idea starts with some study group or with municipal officials themselves. County officials have, of course, urged legislation to allow them to provide municipal-type services (at a fair price) to county residents not in incorporated areas, which is something quite different.

It might be well to dispel another fiction. The day of rip-roaring city-county fights is just about over. Cooperation is the new watchword. For every case of real or imagined city-county tension, there are a dozen cases of city-county cooperation. These range from something as simple as informal exchanges of equipment or services to something as complex as formal contracts for services. Sometimes the city provides services to the county and sometimes the county provides services to the city. In either event both sets of officials are working together far better than most people realize.

Advantages of county government

As a solution to local problems, county governments offer many innate advantages that theoreticians sometimes overlook. In the first place, counties have a long and honorable history of service, dating from the earliest times in America and before that in Great Britain. Henrico County, Virginia, for example, was established in 1611. It will not be until 1967 that this county will have served the United States of America as long as it served as a unit of local government of the Virginia Colony. This county is, today, one of the most progressive in the nation; its advance in the area of automation is the envy of many larger communities.

Second, counties provide the territorial limits for the organization of many non-governmental as well as governmental activities. Medical Societies are nearly always countywide, as are Bar Associations. Nearly all of the nation's agricultural and rural service programs are based upon the county as the primary unit. A large part of our educational systems are county-oriented. The national census uses the county as the basic accounting unit. Virtually all of the country's systems of courts and administration of justice are county-oriented. Conservation and soil conservation districts are usually coterminous with a single county.

Perhaps the greatest advantage of a county is that everyone in the state is served by a county government. Whether a voter lives in a city or in the rural portion of the county, he is represented on the county governing body. The notion that county functions are beyond the control of the city resident is, of course, false since the city resident is required to contribute to the financial support of the county [and] since he participates in the election of representatives to the county governing body just as the rural resident does. It is true, however, that very often a rural resident has a stronger voice in county affairs because he has only one unit of government to keep an eye upon and therefore is more vigilant in county affairs. The city person has both his city and county governments to watch; and because his attention is divided, he may be less knowledgeable about his county government. This problem, however, can be remedied. In a democracy every citizen has the positive obligation to participate fully and intelligently in the affairs of his governments no matter how many there are. We certainly concede that actual participation in local affairs is increasingly difficult—particularly for that poor citizen who is served by a city, school district, multiple-service-district or authority, and by his state and Federal governments as well.

Finally, the county serves as the political base upon which our two-party system is built. The county is the fundamental organizational unit of both major parties and is their basic strength both state-wide and nationally. Because the parties are based on the county, they are controllable by the electorate. This political arena is the one place where all of the interests of the community are represented. Many decisions about local affairs are and should be made at this level because all interests are represented. The decision as to whether limited community funds are to be used to build a school or a bridge is, in this sense, political; and typically it is debated (or mutually endorsed) by the two parties in two-party areas and by opposing factions of the same party in one-party areas.

County problems

To say that counties have a bright present and an even brighter future is not to say that they do not have problems. Chief among these is the absence of home rule (the right of local people to decide local affairs for themselves). Originally (and presently, for that matter) counties were established as local administrative districts of the state. Their responsibilities were quite simple in the beginning, enabling the state to establish a uniform system of county organization and to spell out in precise detail, in statute or constitution, exactly how the counties were to discharge these responsibilities. Most counties, however, are still forced to operate under these same rules in spite of changed circumstances which have brought on new responsibilities. As a result, counties now find themselves in a veritable strait jacket of state control.

The problems created by this rigid control are numerous. Most county officials are severely restricted in establishing local salary scales for county employees. In Massachusetts, for example, the state legislature has complete control over local county budgets, personnel and all. In order for a county official to purchase a typewriter, the item and the specific cost must be included in the county's budget and approved by the state legislature.

Increasingly the functions that counties are called upon to assume require endless special state statutes, and yet all but a handful of state legislatures meet only once every two years to consider substantive legislation. Many of the restrictions that are most disruptive of orderly, sensible local determination, moreover, are spelled out in the state constitution — an extremely difficult document to amend.

The need for executive leadership

Of all the difficulties facing counties, perhaps the most complicated is the absence of an executive comparable to a municipal mayor, a state governor, or the President of the United States. As a matter of fact, in some states there is no real separation of legislative, judicial, and executive functions at the county level. Instead, we find single, elected officials discharging all three functions.

Opposition to a single chief executive runs very strong at the county level and apparently lies deep in the American concept of government — stemming from a fear of placing too much power in the hands of a single individual.

Two trends in the practices of American counties appear to be running contrary to this attitude, however. In some states—California, for example—the elected county supervisors (composing the county governing body) are turning to the professionally-trained, appointed county executive to discharge the mountains of detail incident to conducting the public business. Approximately 36 of the 57 counties in California have reported the creation of a position of this nature (under various names). Once adopted, the elected supervisors appear to have become the strongest supporters of the concept.

The other trend is in the direction of an elected county executive, undistinguishable from a strong mayor at the municipal level. The city and county of San Francisco and the city and county of Denver both have an elected mayor who also is, in varying degrees, responsible for county affairs. This is also true of the mayors of New Orleans and Baton Rouge and their parishes (counties) in Louisiana. Baltimore County in Maryland; Westchester, Erie, Nassau and Suffolk Counties, all in New York; and Milwaukee County in Wisconsin also have recently adopted the county-wide elected chief executive plan.

One of the most strenuous criticisms of county government has come from those who argue that there are too many elected executive positions at the county level, and indeed the list is long. Some 68,000 county positions are filled today by election. Chief among those attacked is the position of coroner. Lately, many statistics have indicated that there is a trend away from the election of many of these officials, but the National Association of County Officials has always taken the position that every community, in accord with home rule standards, should have the right to elect or appoint their officials as they see fit. If they want to elect the coroner, then they should have that right. It could very well be, as many of the defenders of the long ballot argue, that most of the officials who are elected to these positions now would probably be the ones who would hold them as appointees if the system were changed. Compared to the county problems caused by the crippling effect of almost exclusive reliance on the property tax, the election-appointment controversy pales into insignificance. This is not the problem over which to draw the battleline.

Relations between governments

Nowhere is the philosophy that "no man is an isle unto himself" more true than in county government. At no time in history have the relationships between the Federal, state, and local governments been more complex; and, to quote an old infantry maxim, "they are bound to get worse before they get better." Take a single function — highways. The Federal government imposes a tax upon gasoline and other highway-user products and uses a portion of these funds to help finance certain highways that have been determined according to national defense or national economic need. The states in turn build and maintain all Federal-aid roads (with minor exceptions) and in addition levy gasoline and other highway-user taxes to finance a portion of the Federal-aid roads and all state highways. Counties, in turn, do not generally have access to highway-user fees (unless shared with them by the states) but do build and maintain an overwhelming proportion of the roads in the United States — largely with property taxes.

Why not, then, give one level of government the responsibility for all roads? Could the Federal government abandon the roads and the Federal gasoline taxes to the states and leave it to them to build all roads? No! States are all in competition one with the other for business and industry. Some would not levy the gasoline tax; many roads of national import would not be built in individual states. The same arguments would apply if the county were to build all roads. The opposition to having the Federal government build them is obvious.

This one case, therefore, illustrates why, for the foreseeable future, most governmental functions must be on a partnership basis (including private enterprise) and why these interrelationships are so complex.

County and metropolitan problems

Metropolitan problems of today have grown so numerous and important to the welfare of our society that a whole new profession dedicated to their study has sprung up; but from the nearly 200 major studies produced by these professionals, less than half a dozen have realized the adoption of a substantial number of their recommendations. Because metropolitan problems often spill over the bounds of a single county, these studies have ne-

glected the county as the potential core around which their solutions might have been built. But those studies which have shunted aside the county have done so in the face of evidence in practice of the adaptability of this unit of government to new conditions.

Counties have met metropolitan problems through the use of multi-county arrangements. . . .

If the county is proving that it can be placed in combination like building blocks, it is also showing that it is divisible, too! Counties everywhere are reporting great success in creating special districts to provide special services to selected parts of the county. All residents of the county pay a basic tax for county-wide services such as welfare, education and administration of justice. In addition any area that wants water and sewerage, for example, can have it provided by the county and can pay separately for the service. Thus the special service district under the control of the county governing body can provide municipal services to those that need them and who will pay for them without interfering with the farm resident who does not need them. Thus we have the farmer and the city dweller living happily side by side and serviced by the same county, and once again the county has shown its adaptability to the needs of its residents and their circumstances.

Is the county obsolete?

Critics of county government have taken heart from the fact that the Connecticut Legislature, under Governor Abraham Ribicoff's leadership, has voted to abolish the state's eight counties on October 1, 1960. Does not this refute much of what has been said here? No. County government in Connecticut was not typical of county government in other parts of the United States. The county commissioners were not elected; they were appointed by the state legislature upon recommendation of the county representatives and senators elected to the General Assembly. Through years of centralization of power at the state level in Connecticut, the counties had been gradually stripped of all important functions and were left pretty much with the single major function of maintaining jails. . . .

In only a few other areas of the United States are there no counties to be found. Rhode Island is so small that it has never needed county political subdivisions and Alaska has created local units called Boroughs. There is now some consideration being given to creating counties. Hawaii, of course, has no separately organized cities. Honolulu is a city-county like San Francisco. With these few exceptions, therefore, county government can rightly claim to be the one universal and all-encompassing unit of local government. County government is not dead. Instead, it has just begun to live. It has proved that it is flexible, adjustable, resilient, and full of potential for meeting the needs of a new America. County government is, indeed, reborn.

59

Is County Consolidation Feasible?

By Arthur C. Millspaugh

REDRAWING COUNTY BOUNDARIES has become a popular pseudo-scientific pastime. A political map is as fascinating as any other puzzle and in some respects more so. Its lines and colors sketch the paths taken by social movements, and mark their momentary hesitations and resting places. The political map, too, in spite of its quaint relics, is alive with real issues. It is a puzzle which is all the more absorbing because it seems to present various interesting possibilities. Academically none of the solutions are beyond the powers of a patient mind; but practically it is difficult to select the best solution and, when a selection has been made, it is almost impossible to put it into effect. . . .

Consolidation and financial savings. It is usually found that total county expenditure in two adjacent small counties is greater than in some other county similar in area, population, and taxable resources to the two counties in combination. In other words, as we have already noted, per capita county expenditures are likely to be larger in the small counties. From these facts it is inferred that savings will be made by transforming two, three, or four small counties into one large one. This inference may or may not be justified. In the first place, county expenditures rarely constitute the whole of public expenditure within a county. Accurately to compare public expenditures in two different areas would require the summing up of federal, state, county, city, township, town, and village expenditures within each area. When this is done, it is sometimes discovered that the lower county expenditure in a large county is due to the fact that, in that county, the state

Arthur C. Millspaugh, *Local Democracy and Crime Control* (Washington: The Brookings Institution, 1936), pp. 104–119. Footnotes in original omitted. Reprinted by permission of The Brookings Institution.

or a city is bearing a relatively large share of governmental costs. In fact, as a rule it appears that governmental costs per capita are greater in urban than in rural areas; although county expenditures, taken alone, may decrease as population increases.

Even though it can be shown that, in two comparable counties, per capita public expenditures are less in the more populous county, it is still difficult to prove that the quantity and quality of public services per capita is the same. As a general rule, however, public service tends to improve as population increases. . . .

Governmental costs may be reduced by consolidation in two ways: (1) by eliminating duplications in overhead expense; and (2) by concentrating in one organization a volume of work now apportioned among two, three, or four organizations.

With consolidations, one county board would take the place of two or of several; and one set of county buildings would supposedly serve for both or all of the combined counties.

. . . A governing board in a large county is likely to cost more than in a small one. In many regions, too, the buildings erected for the use of one county are not sufficient for the needs of two or more counties. Not infrequently, courthouses are already overcrowded, and consolidation would necessitate new construction or additions. At the same time, it would mean the scrapping, in abandoned county seats, of buildings which may be comparatively new and which can not be dedicated overnight to other useful purposes.

It is just as difficult to calculate what may be saved by concentrating in one administrative organization a volume of work that is now subdivided among two, three, or four organizations.

Some of the recent discussions of the subject assume that consolidation will automatically reduce county costs. Such an assumption seems to be unwarranted. The costs of consolidation may in part offset its economies; and an enlargement of the county may set in motion forces which make for increased rather than decreased expenditure.

Consolidation and better public service. A helpful method of studying the possible effects of county consolidation is to examine particular public services. While such an examination may fail to indicate any substantial and direct savings from consolidation, it will demonstrate in most cases that in a consolidated county more effective service can be rendered at the same cost than in two or more separate small counties. The administrative benefits are due to the fact that consolidation, by increasing the population served, increases volume of work and permits a departmental form of organization and the employment of full-time specialized workers under competent direction. When counties are too small separately to satisfy the requirements of a service unit or administrative district they are more likely, when consolidated, to meet those requirements. . . .

Consolidation and the problems of area. In the preceding chapter the conclusion was reached that, as a general rule, a local unit performing and financing major functions should have a population of not less than 20,000 and an area not exceeding 6,400 square miles. Since a county with the minimum population and the maximum area would have a density of 3.1 per square miles, it is evident that the full advantages of consolidation are doubtful within any region of extremely low population density. In 1930, about 200 counties in the United States had a density of less than 3 per square mile; and 333, or more than 10 per cent of the total, had fewer than 5 per square mile. . . .

Moreover, in the far western states a considerable number of these low-density counties are adjacent to each other. . . . In certain regions in the West, therefore, it is not possible to create counties having the minimum population without exceeding the maximum area. . . .

When we pass eastward from the wide open spaces where counties are counties, opportunities for consolidation of local units grow more alluring. Here the units are smaller in area and more densely populated; and, theoretically, they can be drastically reduced in number without making any of the new units unduly extensive. . . .

Nevertheless, consolidation is less necessary in these states, because of the greater density of population and more substantial property valuations. . . .

Consolidation and the problem of equalization. The system of county self-government and self-financing, operating in units of different size and different property valuations, produces striking inequalities in the tax burden and in the quality and quantity of public service. If a county of low per capita wealth were merged with a more opulent taxing unit, not only would a portion of the fixed overhead presumably disappear, but also the tax rates throughout the area of consolidation would be the same. Consolidation would thus bring about equalization of the tax burden within the consolidated area, a laudable purpose for which consolidation has been frequently advocated. . . .

In such a case, consolidation might reduce the taxes of the underprivileged county without increasing the burden of its favored partner. In a majority of cases, however, county consolidation is likely to effect equalization by lowering taxes in one area and raising them in the other. . . .

Some county consolidations . . . seem to be chiefly concerned with creating a unit that shall be financially and administratively adequate. In pursuing this aim, however, they appear to forget the "natural" community or to assume that financial and administrative adequacy is sufficient alone to re-create community consciousness and restore the psychological ingredients necessary for self-government. . . .

If democracy depends exclusively on financial and administrative adequacy, it would seem that a state would be considerably more democratic than any of its subdivisions. On the other hand, if local self-government depends on its being really local, there must be a limit somewhere to the size of counties. If local self-government depends on a common cultural or economic focus or on personal contacts and acquaintanceships can these desiderata be obtained simply by annexing one county to another? Can communities be created by a combination of things that are not communities? Is there some chemical magic in county consolidation? If local self-government depends on *feelings,* what would be more likely to kill it than the statistical juggling of county boundaries?

Practical obstacles to consolidation. Using purely theoretical tests, county consolidation is a hard enough nut to crack; but, in those cases where it may be found theoretically desirable, its practical accomplishment would be extremely difficult, if not impossible. Serious obstacles are presented by popular habit and popular inertia, by the selfish interests of office holders and politicians, by sectional jealousy and distrust, by considerations of partisan advantage or disadvantage, by the unwillingness of towns to abdicate as county seats, by the situation with respect to county buildings, by the requirements of the courts, by differences in the indebtedness of adjacent counties, by reluctance on the part of one county to assume the excess burden of another, and by other difficulties real or imaginary.

County consolidation demands regional planning under state control; for if the movement is allowed to proceed along lines of least resistance, the consolidation of certain counties may prevent the union of others in greater need. Furthermore, a long-term program of county recasting requires that new county buildings should be suitable in location and size for the new and larger units of local government. New construction must be discouraged in obsolescent county seats. But what hope is there that county consolidation can be logically planned and consistently controlled? The problem is too complex and in appearance too academic for planned control. . . .

60

The Changing Urban County

By Gladys M. Kammerer

THE COUNTY, hedged in by constitutional restrictions and judicial strict constructionism in the majority of states, has been the unit of local government most severely strained by population growth in recent years. The remarkable increase in urban population since World War II is in sharp contrast to the fact that nearly half of all counties lost population. The failure of rural counties to grow has obscured the strains on the growing urban counties for state legislators hitherto under rural domination.

County responses to pressures for more services and authority have varied across the country and follow no fixed rule. However, there are certain discernible trends. . . .

If we were to try to plot all significant adjustments of function and structure of county government along a continuum from the most thoroughgoing changes to the least extensive alterations, we could locate both the polarizations of change and gradations between such polarizations. Thus, at one end we can locate the Metropolitan Government of Nashville and Davidson County. At the other end is the Lakewood Plan of Los Angeles County. Nearer to the Nashville-Davidson County plan is the Metropolitan Dade County system of government. The various county manager governments under charter plans would be somewhere in the middle. More toward the Lakewood end would be the various functional consolidations under separate county-wide authority. However, categorization may also be made on the extensiveness of legal changes required to effect a restructuring of government into a single unit. In other words, classification rests upon the distance from one measuring point: a single consolidated county unit for all local government.

Unitary consolidation of city and county into a single government — Nashville-Davidson County

By constitutional amendment in 1953 Tennessee authorized cities and the counties in which they are

Gladys M. Kammerer, *The Changing Urban County* (University of Florida Public Administration Clearing Service, 1963). Four footnotes in original omitted. Reprinted by permission of the author and publisher (reduced by about one-fourth).

located to draft charters for a consolidation of their governments, subject to Nashville and Davidson County referenda approval in all units concerned. In June 1962, the charter for a single consolidated government was adopted by Nashville and Davidson County voters. Although decades before this time various consolidations of cities and counties had elsewhere been voted into effect, these earlier consolidations had always been engineered under city dominance. For the first time, the county superseded the city in the single unit created by consolidation of Nashville and Davidson County.

Nashville and Davidson County groped their way over an eleven year period to this consolidation. . . .

. . . [It] brought into a single metropolitan county unit the city of Nashville and Davidson County. This is a simple, uncluttered, and apparently uncomplicated union, in contrast to other more involved and, at the same time, less thoroughgoing recent Metropolitan reorganization attempts.

Davidson County had in 1960 a total population of 399,743, with 253,386 living in Nashville and 16,283 in six small suburban towns. There were also five utility districts. Nashville became under the Metropolitan charter an Urban Services District, which receives a greater number of services from the county than the outlying rural areas.

The old structures of city and county government were swept away, and instead a county mayor and a much enlarged Metropolitan council of forty members were established. Because of Tennessee constitutional restrictions that county millage voted by the county governing body must be uniform, a subcouncil of three members from the Metropolitan Council meets as a separate Urban Council to vote the additional millage in this district required to cover the particular additional services desired by the Urban District over and above general county-wide services. These Urban Councilmen are the three at-large who reside in the Urban District and received the highest votes. Setting the millage for the Urban Services District is the sole function of the Urban Council. Although all officials of all units in the county and the cities were included in the reorganization and city offices were abolished, nevertheless, constitutionally created county officers could not be abolished. However, their duties were lessened in number and moderated in importance. For example, the sheriff was left in charge of the jail, but metropolitan county police took over the policing of the county.

Metropolitan Davidson County provides all services and administers both Urban District and general county-wide functions. County-wide functions are rendered through a General Services District over the entire county and include police, courts, jails, property assessment, health, welfare, hospitals, streets and roads, traffic, schools, parks and recreation, library, airport, auditorium, public housing, urban renewal, planning, codes, transit, and general administration. The Urban Services District receives, in addition, added police protection, fire protection, water, sanitary sewers, storm sewers, street lighting, and refuse collection.

Executive power, including administrative direction, was lodged by the Charter in the county mayor who is popularly elected. The term of the mayor is four years, and a maximum of three successive terms is fixed as a limit. The Charter sets his salary at $25,000 per year. All departments of government, including that of law, are responsible to him and their heads are appointed by him. Members of twenty boards or commissions are also appointed by the county mayor. Significantly, one of these boards appointed by the mayor is the consolidated board of education of nine members superseding the separate city and county boards of education. These members are appointed from nine districts. . . .

The large, forty-member Metropolitan Council exercises all legislative authority. Thirty-five of its members are elected from that number of individual districts. Five members are elected at large. All members have a four year term. The presiding officer of the Council is the vice-mayor who is elected at large for a four year term.

The first Metropolitan Government election of officers was held in November 1962. On April 1, 1963, the new mayor and council took office, and the new government went into effect. As a tailor-made structure of government, the new Charter carried on certain local traditions and preferences. For example, a preference for large legislative councils and a tradition of administration of many functions through boards and commissions were maintained. There is no provision for either a county manager or a chief administrative officer, as neither Nashville nor Davidson County had developed any pattern of professionalized career top level management.

Partial city-county consolidation — Baton Rouge

Prior to the successful merger of Nashville and Davidson County in 1962, Baton Rouge and East Baton Rouge Parish had been the only city and county to consummate a consolidation in this century. But this was actually only a partial consolidation for the reason that the city of Baton Rouge, in effect, continued its separate existence through the continuance of the city council. City functions fall under the jurisdiction of the city council of seven members. Two additional council members elected from the rural area outside the city of Baton Rouge sit with the city members when the council meets as the parish council. A mayor-president who is popu-

larly elected from the entire parish directs the administration of most functions, both city and county.

To cite examples of how this consolidation works, the entire parish is zoned, and parish zoning is regulated by the entire council. On city zoning, however, the two rural council members do not vote. Street maintenance and drainage are considered parish-wide functions subject to vote by the entire parish council and financed from the four mill parish tax.

Three taxing districts were created to provide that number of levels of taxes to correspond to as many levels of services. One level of taxes is the urban services level, one with fewer services and lower taxes is the rural district, and the third, with no services provided is the industrial level.

Despite population changes since 1949 when the Baton Rouge consolidation took place, no adjustment has been made in the representation allocated to the area outside Baton Rouge in the Parish Council. At the time the consolidation took effect, the city of Baton Rouge was expanded in area from five square miles to thirty-two square miles to bring all urban people within its jurisdiction. But suburban development since 1949 has created a need for urban-type services in the rural tax area where the tax rate is inadequate to support such services. Therefore, special service districts have had to be formed with special taxing powers to furnish such services at quite expensive cost. At present, 90,000 people live outside the city limits of Baton Rouge and 157,000 live inside the city. It is easy, therefore, to understand the reason for some dissatisfaction by those outside the city as to the basis of representation, and it is not surprising to discover that the rural representatives advocate a more complete consolidation, with only one council for all matters in the parish.

Miami-Dade Metropolitan Government
Federal type county-city reorganization —

Occupying a midposition between a consolidation of county government into a unitary form of organization and no reorganization of structure, the Dade County Metropolitan government is a federal plan. This means that the county government is granted by home rule charter a separate sphere of powers from those left in the hands of individual cities. Each city is left undisturbed as a governmental entity. In other words, the Dade County Metropolitan government is modeled upon the same principle of division of powers prevailing between our national government and the states. The major difference is that residual powers are in the hands of the county rather than the cities, the reverse of the presumption stated in the Tenth Amendment to the U.S. Constitution, as between national government and state powers.

Twelve years elapsed from the first serious effort to effect consolidation of Miami and all other cities within Dade County into a single unit in 1945. . . .

From a political standpoint, the most significant change wrought by the establishment of Dade County Metropolitan government has been the transfer of control of internal affairs of the county from its legislative delegation to its electorate and elected local officials through home rule. No new municipalities could be created and no existing ones abolished by special legislative act. On the legal side, the most important charter provision is not the delegation of specific powers to the county government but the conferring on the county of all residual powers that have not been delegated to the cities.

As to the specific powers delegated to the county government, control over certain municipal-type functions was granted. These are to provide for arterial roads, bridges, tunnels, related facilities, parking facilities, and regulate all of them, and develop master plans for central traffic and parking controls. Also authority is granted to provide and operate public transportation systems, air, water, rail, and bus terminals and port facilities, hospitals, health and welfare programs, housing, slum clearance, urban renewal, flood, beach erosion, air pollution, conservation control and drainage programs, water supply, waste and sewage collection and disposal, fire stations, jails, central records and training for fire and police protection, parks, playgrounds, libraries, museums, recreation, traffic control, central crime investigation, zoning, and comprehensive plans for county development. The metropolitan county government may also adopt and enforce building and related codes and regulations for the entire county; it may regulate, grant, and take over franchises for public utilities under certain restrictions, sewage, water supply, transportation; and finally it may appropriate public funds for advertising the area. A metropolitan court is created by the Charter itself, but its size is under the power of the County Commission to determine.

Over the unincorporated areas the Metropolitan County government has power to create new municipalities, license and regulate vehicles for hire, regulate the sale of alcoholic beverages, exercise municipal taxing power, and receive municipal revenue allocations from the state. Creation of new municipalities must be preceded by a recommendation from the Planning Advisory Board, a public hearing, and an affirmative vote in a referendum to be held in the area proposed as a municipal corporation.

Minimum standards of performance for any service or function performed by any other governmental unit in the county may be established by the Metropolitan County government. Services may be turned over to the county government by a municipality if a majority of voters in a referendum vote to do so or the governing body of the municipality votes to do so by a two-thirds majority.

Cities are guaranteed their separate existence so long as their voters prefer this. An important corollary of this is that all cities are guaranteed home rule as to the nature and substance of their charters.

The council-manager government in virtually its pure classic form, adhering to the outlines established in the Model City Charter, was chosen for the structure of the new Metropolitan county government. The Board of Commissioners consists of five commissioners, each elected from a district only, five commissioners, each of whom represents a district but is elected at large; and one commissioner elected by each city of at least 60,000 population. Now there are three commissioners of the latter category representing Miami, Miami Beach, and Hialeah. The county manager is, of course, selected by the county commissioners and subject to a dismissal by them. The chairman of the commission is selected by the majority vote of the commissioners, as, indeed, a popularly elected chairman was apparently not considered. . . .

Professor Edward Sofen in his comprehensive study of the Dade County Metropolitan government* points out that residents of the smaller cities of that county are not former Miamians, but came directly from other parts of the country. Hence they have little feeling of loyalty to the municipalities in which they now reside. In contrast, the officialdom of these cities has a built-in vested interest in the maintenance of municipal separatism to protect its own jobs and status and has spearheaded the almost incessant attacks on the Charter.

Almost from its inception in 1957, the charter has been under municipal attack. The Dade County League of Municipalities, the institutional political arm of the local officials, forced a referendum on a charter amendment that would have guaranteed municipal autonomy. Through various local countervailing pressures and court action the referendum was postponed until September 1958, when the autonomy amendment was defeated by 24,527, in contrast to the narrow margin of victory of 1,784 for the charter adoption in 1957. The cities and the Dade County League of Municipalities had spent public funds generously and marshalled municipal employees quite openly in their campaign for auton-

---

* Edward Sofen, *The Miami Metropolitan Experiment* (Bloomington: Indiana University Press, 1963), p. 7.

only. The county government in contrast spent no money for a campaign against the proposal. Again, in 1959 five charter amendments for charter changes were on the ballot and were defeated. The most sweeping set of proposals to strip down county powers and change the form of government back to the old commission type was the McLeod amendment of 1961. McLeod had been a county commissioner prior to the adoption of the Metropolitan charter, with his term carrying over to 1960, and he had resented the change in structure of government and the enlarged size of the commission. This attack on Metro was defeated only after the county manager reduced county property assessments by 20 per cent after a blanket raise had been effected through a charter requirement for a county-wide reassessment by January 1961. The manager further got a charter amendment introduced to abolish the reassessment requirement, and the reassessment issue was finally resolved by voters in August 1961. Thereby the McLeod amendment was defeated in October 1961.

At the height of the McLeod amendment campaign the county commission created a Charter Review Board under the chairmanship of a former county commissioner, Charles Crandon. In 1962, five charter amendments proposed by the Board that had been turned down by the County Commissioners were forced into a referendum by petition. Their major purpose was to reduce the county manager's power, especially over appointments and administrative orders. These amendments for the two purposes indicated passed, but others were defeated in the August 1962 referendum. The mere recounting of the story of these referenda indicates the continuity of the warfare within Dade County that has raged over the Metropolitan County Charter.

Because the Dade County Charter represents in actuality a compromise and not a consolidation of government, no reforms were made in the county tax structure. No additional taxation powers were added. Indeed, the sources of taxation open to cities were not made available to the new county. Lack of added fiscal power is handicapping the county in planning future programs.

The local outcries against the Metropolitan Charter by officials of most of the twenty-six municipalities* in Dade County are understandable to a sophisticated outsider who realizes that nothing pains a government official or bureaucrat more acutely than a reorganization that threatens his position, paycheck, or perquisites of office. The ferocity of the anti-Metro attack by the radical right-wing propagandists from other parts of the country on the ground that it is dictatorial and un-American is a little more difficult to explain, however, because the Metropolitan Charter did *not* abolish the cities, it did *not* confer crucial new taxation powers on the Metropolitan County Commission, and it most certainly did not consolidate local government as the advocates of reform had originally aspired to do. The right-wing propagandists' attack must, therefore, be attributed to ignorance of the true state of affairs.

Knowledgeable observers of Dade Metropolitan government, like Professor Sofen, have pointed to quite a different set of shortcomings. One of the most serious is the lack of well-structured political support because there are no real parties of a local nature or organizations analogous to parties that can clarify issues, slate candidates, or focus politics in any way to reach and appeal to the average voter. Consequently, there is no effective political leadership. The way in which the chairman of the county commission is selected — by the other commissioners — softpedals his opportunities for leadership. The only institution which serves to counteract this fragmentation and blurring of influence in the community is the *Miami Herald*. But a newspaper is not a political party, and regardless of its influence, it cannot play the various roles that valid political parties would play.

By the same token, the lack of an elected leader places an exceptionally heavy set of demands for political leadership on the appointed county manager. He is expected to propose major policies and has campaigned for adoption of particular policies up before the electorate in referenda. The first manager who followed the traditional council-manager doctrine and tried to avoid open advocacy of policy was criticized for "lack of leadership," among other points of criticism by a number of Dade Countians. A conflict in role expectations as to political leadership responsibility appears to prevail among county commissioners, prominent businessmen, newspaper editors, political activists, and the manager himself. The very critics who condemned the first manager for lack of leadership, praised the "nonpolitical" character of the county manager's position, apparently totally unaware of the paradox implicit in their judgments.

The more the county manager is compelled to enter the vacuum created by lack of Board of Commissioners' leadership on policy, the more the Commissioners themselves seem to avoid the hazards of leadership. In other words, there is a "feedback" effect accentuating the vacuum of elected leadership. Commissioners do not seem to realize or care, if they do realize, that the county manager, by serving as the dominant policy originator, is building up a following of his own in a county where no group has yet constructed anything resembling a solid political base.

---

* Now twenty-seven, but the latest municipal corporation is virtually uninhabited and cannot be considered of significance as a participant in the anti-Metro fights.

However, the overall success of Dade County Metropolitan government in providing a viable set of solutions to the variety of problems of a complex metropolitan area is attested by Professor Sofen in a detailed study of the first five years of this experiment. So although the federal form of county organization may in itself be complex and not eliminate any of the numerous units of local government, nevertheless political scientists who have had a chance to study it believe that it has been a success. They point to the preservation of the strong civic identifications connected with some of the individual municipalities and the cooperative arrangements developed to work out solutions to a number of pressing local problems. Finally, Sofen states, "The Miami metropolitan experiment has contributed to the maturity of the public and its officials. Municipal officials, in general, had had their fears of Metro quieted because of the experience of the past five years. They also feel they can work with County Manager McNayr, who holds no dogmatic views regarding the division of powers between Metro and the municipalities. . . . Indeed, Mr. McNayr represents the spirit of compromise that led to the successful creation of the nation's first metropolitan government."

The Lakewood Plan
County administration by contract —

A bilateral contractual system for county administration of services for particular municipalities has developed in Los Angeles County as one way of coping with the growth of urban service demands in a vastly enlarging county. . . .

Council-city contracts are not new as a feature of local government and have been permitted in California since 1915. But the Lakewood Plan provides in one single general services contract an entire range of municipal services, the exact number and scope of each to be determined annually in city-county negotiations. The county has had to develop real unit cost accounting in order to establish unit costs for all the services it sells to small cities. Each city can, therefore, determine at the time of negotiating a contract how much it can afford to buy in services. The contracts all include fire and police functions and may include a number of other services. Some cities contract for only a few municipal services. . . .

Los Angeles County had not had a municipal incorporation from 1939 until that of Lakewood in 1954, but from 1954 to 1961 twenty-eight municipal incorporations occurred. Almost all of the cities involved were deemed to be "contract cities" like Lakewood. But only one older city went over to the Lakewood Plan. All told, there are 69 cities in the county. Therefore, it is reasonable to conclude that the contract system arranged for Lakewood ushered in a new type of county-small city relationship in one of the fastest-growing urban complexes in the nation and the largest county in the nation. . . .

Inasmuch as Los Angeles County has enjoyed home rule since 1913 and has long performed many municipal type services, especially in unincorporated areas, it was natural for Lakewood to seek to retain county services after it became incorporated. This is particularly understandable in view of the fact that Los Angeles County is known for the rather high level qualitatively of its administrative management. The general services contract seemed to be the answer.

Administratively, the consequences for the county of all these contract-based services to smaller cities is the growth of its staff to 37,000 employees and its budget to over $500,000,000. The county is already performing municipal services and exercising authority that elsewhere require the kinds of constitutional and charter changes characterizing Dade and Davidson Counties. Los Angeles County has long had a county merit system and rather highly professionalized cadres of civil servants. . . . county administration heads up to a professional administrator, called the chief administrative officer. Most of the municipalities in Los Angeles County are either council-manager in type or utilize a chief administrative officer. As Dr. Samuel K. Gove of the University of Illinois has cited, "The emphasis on professionalization has also aided in communication between local officials,"* and to this ability of all major city and county officials to maintain the same level of discourse, he attributes a part of the smooth functioning of the contracting plan.

One might well ask why cities continue to incorporate in Los Angeles County if the same county employees perform the same services as before incorporation and the citizen requires the intervention of local municipal officials to procure the services for him. Would he not be better off remaining unincorporated? However much this view may appeal to those who deplore the burgeoning of suburban cities, it ignores the "sharp cutting edge" of local politics — control over local planning and zoning. Protection of one's property through public policy — a zoning ordinance — by banding together with like-minded fellow citizens is a goal not to be ignored by political realists. In addition, incorporation of an area protects against annexation by adjoining cities, especially significant if such cities are dominated by "undesirable" people. Another major consideration is the availability to an incorporated city of certain earmarked state revenue sources. . . . Finally, two

---

* Samuel K. Gove, *The Lakewood Plan* (Urbana, Ill.; University of Illinois Institute of Government and Public Affairs, Commission Papers, 1961), p. 4.

other factors may be persuasive: 1) difficulty in reaching and influencing of county policy making, and 2) dissatisfaction with the level and quality of county services. Through a services contract both the quality and quantity of county services purchased by a city may be raised above those rendered to residents of an unincorporated area. At the same time small cities need not try to establish a credit rating and enter the bond market to acquire expensive equipment, such as fire engines, fire houses, police cruisers and ambulances, street cleaning and garbage trucks, incinerators, water mains, sewage disposal plants, and similar facilities. The small city resident can easily reach his local council, and they have "access" to county officials to make service demands.

County-city contracts may be cancelled on sixty days' advance notice just before the beginning of each fiscal year. Not all knowledgeable observers of local government in Los Angeles County agree that the Lakewood Plan is a step in the right direction. For example, one larger city, Long Beach, has considered this plan a tool to help thwart its expansion by assisting in the birth of small fringe cities, and Los Angeles itself considers that certain municipal functions should properly be carried on by a city itself and the city be held responsible for the way they are exercised and they should not be contracted for with the county. Certainly it would seem to add almost infinite complexities of administration to an already large county organizational structure. It is also always more difficult to hold government responsible when an additional layer must be penetrated to reach those charged with rendering services. The matter of "access" to those so charged is one of significance. Certainly it is possible to view this problem in two ways, as the proponents and opponents of the Lakewood Plan attest.

A survey of Lakewood Plan contracts prevailing in Los Angeles County does not reveal the true scope of county-city contracting. Actually forty-five cities were already engaged in contracting for services with the county up to 1954, and the number of contracts doubled between 1954 and 1960. A listing by Dr. Gove shows 887 contracts in effect in 1959. Lakewood itself has undertaken to supply its water and to operate a public recreational program since incorporation. The fact that smaller cities may provide their own services or contract with private suppliers has created a competitive bargaining system for the making of contracts and, in the opinion of some observers, a responsiveness by the county to city demands for services. Both cities and the county are said to be very much aware of cost factors in the rendering of services and of the need for highly detailed, accurate cost analyses on the most modern accounting and budgetary principles.

The major organizational consequence of the Lakewood Plan on the structure of county government has been the creation by the county in the office of the Chief Administrative Officer of the position of County-City Coordinator to direct all business relating to the contracts. Each department of the county also has a county-city coordinator to work with the overall county coordinator and with the contracting cities. These latter positions are essentially liaison and expediting positions for two-way communication and improvement of service. The over-all county coordinator keeps the county board informed of city reactions and spends as much time on contracts with older cities as on Lakewood Plan contracts. Additional regional offices have been constructed by the county to supervise contract services and handle local complaints quickly. Closer political ties are claimed to have been forged between city council members and county board members as a result of the need to coordinate policies between the two units of local government. Differences between the two units of government tend to be pushed into the area of negotiation, with differences worked out.

Thus, an unanticipated consequence of the whole system appears to be the blunting of the sharp edges of policy differences among local units of government in the metropolitan area and the political protection of incumbents. This system, particularly in the California setting of political nonpartisanship, could be expected to blur issues and personalities so much that it would become almost impossible for political rivals to upset incumbents. The ambivalent position in which the city manager of a "contract city" is placed is worthy of separate study and analysis. What is he other than an expediter or "errand boy" or a mere record keeper of contracts? Also what are the basic loyalties of county employees assigned to certain cities? One observer quoted by Dr. Gove alludes to the "emergence of a 'county-city employee' with no visible symptoms of the classic schizophrenic personality." Does the so-called "adjustment" of these employees also fit into the blunting and blurring process that is inevitable in the local political process produced by the whole system?

The Lakewood Plan obviously needs to be analyzed as a political system as well as an administrative device. Important political consequences flow from any major management arrangements in the field of public administration, and these consequences may bring about a new kind of politics not originally consciously sought.

In addition, it would appear that such a contractual system can operate successfully only in a region that has advanced to a rather high level of administrative management, with skilled technicians and professional administrators in plentiful supply, able to cope with the complexities of budgetary and fiscal administration, contract negotiation, liaison and supervision of a great variety of diverse operations in many jurisdictions, and the integration of policies emerging from a complex mass of units and elements. Many urban counties have not enjoyed the long tradition of professionally trained administrators that prevails so widely in California and do not have the large scale local training programs available in Los Angeles County for technicians as well as administrators. The entire California educational system, including higher educational facilities, is geared to produce the kinds of employees required to operate the whole system successfully.

CHAPTER THIRTEEN

Town, Township and Village

IN THE SMALLER New England towns (and a few of the Swiss cantons) are the last vestiges in the modern world of governmental units governed by direct democracy, the whole body of citizens convened in annual meeting constituting the governing body of the community. There is in this perhaps an air of unreality for most of us; here is a flashback to an America of a bygone day, an America of the hot stove and the cracker barrel in the general store, whose problems extended little beyond the creek that bounded Wilbur Smith's north 40. Yet those town meetings which have remained effective have actually kept pace with the times in terms of the kinds of problems faced, even though their procedures may have changed but little for generations. L. H. Robbins in this article has captured for us some of the spirit and flavor of the New England town meeting; of "Democracy, Town Meeting Style."

61

Democracy, Town Meeting Style

By L. H. Robbins

DEMOCRACY IS CHALLENGED today, and in the sudden need to defend its principles even its best friends have difficulty in defining it clearly. Those who are in doubt as to just what democracy is and wish to see it in full and lively action close up could hardly do better than to study it here in snowy Wolfeboro [N.H.] or in any one of 1,300 other little towns of rural New England in the spring town meeting season.

In these smallest units of American government, these "cells" of pure democracy, the citizens rule directly. Here the lowliest inhabitant has a personal part in his town government, and if he has a good

L. H. Robbins, "Democracy, Town Meeting Style," *New York Times Magazine,* March 23, 1947, pp. 24, 35, 38. Reprinted by permission of the author and publisher.

cause and a good speaking voice to go with it, his part is a leading one. For his will may become the will of the town meeting, and the will of the meeting regarding town affairs is the law within the town's boundaries — at least until the next meeting rolls around. Here the citizen is sovereign, and well he knows it, and so do the town officers whom he elects to perform the town chores for him.

Wolfeboro held its spring town meeting the other day. The citizens had been talking about it since the first hearing of the town budget committee early in the year. For a week before the meeting they turned Main Street into a forum. There were debating groups at the postoffice, the bank corner, the paper store, the barber shops, the diners. They met in argument even in the middle of the icy, sanded street, slowing up the buses to Sanbornville and the trucks hauling logs to the sawmill.

People for ten miles around left their farms and their woodlots to come to the village and have their say. They left even their ice fishing, and for once since January the stove-warmed bobhouses of "Fisherville," out there on frozen Lake Winnipesaukee, were deserted.

Much of the talk was about taxes. As if they weren't high enough already, somebody had put an article in the town meeting warrant to see if the town would invite the State Tax Commission to come in and re-assess everybody's property — and the town budget going up and up, clear up to $150,000 this trip! Some of the noisier debaters were for firing the budget committee and giving its job to the selectmen, whose job it used to be. The budget committee, they said, was getting too big for its pants.

But most of the talk had to do with the choosing of a selectman, and all phones between Tumbledown Dick Mountain and Upper Beach Pond were buzzing with that same subject. There are three selectmen, chosen one each year to serve for three years. They have the most to do with carrying out the mandates of the town meeting. Mighty important public servants they are — though heaven help them if they get to feeling their importance! The town meeting is the only boss tolerated around here.

They must be shrewd, thrifty, practical. (Time was in Yankeeland when the local clergyman ran his town's secular affairs, but that was a couple of hundred years ago.) They must be solid men and businesslike. The three present selectmen here are all of that. Wayne Parkhurst is in real estate and insurance. Earl Willand manages a summer estate. Noyes Moore is a farmer. They give a lot of their time to the town. They look after roads, bridges, sewers, wharves, parks, street lighting. They supervise expenditures, okay bills and check on a hundred other details of town housekeeping. They are the people you complain to if you don't like your tax bill or your neighbor's carelessness with brush fires. It takes an able man and a fair and patient one to be a selectman. For his services he gets $500 a year and an equal amount for expenses.

The citizens entrust the nominating of town officers to the party caucuses, reserving the right to criticize the men chosen, particularly the men the Democrats put up. Three out of four of the voters still shudder at the sight of the names of New Dealers Morgenthau and Farley on the cornerstone of the PWA postoffice; yet, as a rule, they allow the Democrats to have a selectman and one or two other town officers every third year. This spring, however, a Democratic nominee stirred up so much conversation and excitement that the town meeting proved to be one of the biggest in the town's 177 years.

"Hank," the philosopher of *The Granite State News,* tries to explain the surge of civic passion in the annual town election and gives it up. Says he: "Sumtimes I wonder why Town Meeting Day ain't called Town Scalping Day. There is something cussed in human nature which makes folks fight and wrangle on Town Meeting Day when they get along awful good the rest of the year. Why," he asks, "should a man with a good business, a nice home, several clubs and lodges and everything he can tend to want to be a town officer anyways and get himself cooked over a slow fire on Town Meeting Day?"

The only answer is that it is just a way Americans have in parts where direct democracy prevails.

Ordinary days the town hall is devoted to motion pictures, but on Town Meeting Day it puts away childish things, as happened this month. When the clock in the tower struck noon and Moderator Robert Thurrell rose to read the warrant, thirty voters were waiting to mount to the platform and enter the polling booths at the back of the stage.

All afternoon the citizens poured in — old folks whom Constable Harold Thompson had to help up the steps; sturdy young people, some of them in uniform; women in afternoon dress, on their way to a pre-spring meeting of the garden club, and men in the many-colored garb of wilderness guides, which most sensible men wear in northern New England between October and May.

By 3 o'clock John Clow, Republican town chairman, watching the check list, reported that 300 had voted. By the end of the day the total was 822 — this in a town with a population of 2,646. Name, if you can, a big city that does better than that, proportionately, even in a Presidential year.

At 7 o'clock, when the town meeting proper began, every seat in the hall was occupied. That meant that 488 people had cut their supper short in order to do their duty by the town. Those who had lingered at table didn't get in; the stairs and the entry were full of them. If you were reared on the traditional kind of information about town meetings, you might have been astonished at the urbanity of this crowd. No fists were lifted, no taunts — or hardly any — were hurled about, nobody chewed tobacco and nobody said "By gosh!" The meeting was a little disappointing in that way.

It liked its moderator; he was forthright, courteous, competent, and he and the meeting were in perfect tune. When he gave his interpretation of a vague rule of procedure a voice shouted, "I think you're right, Rob," and the audience nodded.

Item by item, the budget committee's recommendations: "For moth extermination, blister rust and tree care, $1,200." "For town libraries, $1,350." "To the Public Health Nursing Association, $2,000." A woman citizen moved acceptance of that one. Another asked: "If we vote $5,000 toward the Legion hall, will the hall be open to meetings of the Veterans of Foreign Wars?" She was assured by a Legion spokesman that it would certainly be open. On a question regarding the Australian ballot system a third woman reminded the meeting, "Ossipee has been using it for years."

There was debate whether the town ski slope should receive $30 more than its allotted $300. A voter settled it with, "If we need it, let's have it and get on." Should a sum be given for insurance of town firemen? "Yop!" spoke a big voice, and that was that. When the State Tax Commission matter came up, a shout of "Let's pass over that article" killed it dead. So, too, with the article aimed at scrapping the budget committee. One aggrieved citizen got in his licks first, however. Said he, "They've been promising to reduce our taxes ever since they've been in business, and look at the taxes now!"

On the surface the meeting seemed cut and dried, for it needed only an hour to settle its long list of questions. But those questions had been discussed throughout the town for weeks and the voters had come with minds made up. Everybody's business may be nobody's business in some places, but not in a town-meeting town.

The counting of the votes on the stage consumed another hour, and most of the people waited and watched. They heard the results and they witnessed the swearing in of the new town officers. Then they went home amid a great peace that had suddenly fallen upon Main Street, a peace that remains at this writing. Today a stranger would never guess that a town so placid had ever been so stirred up.

And that's how one little town held its town meeting. . . .

But the story has barely begun. You'll find more of it every weekday of the year in the dingy old office where the selectmen meet, where the tax collector works at his books, where Town Judge Leaman Cunningham presides over his court and other town agents and officers come in to consult.

You will find still more of the story in the town's 100-page annual report. There you may learn that the salaries of all town officers, meaning selectmen, town clerk, tax collector, treasurer, moderator, auditors, constable and overseer of the poor come to the grand total of $2,876 — this in a day of billion-dollar governmental payrolls!

Officers like these are fond enough of their town, and proud enough of it, to give it such of their time as it needs. All of them have private responsibilities; shop to keep, fields to plow, the everyday jobs of earning a living. Constable Thompson, for example, must in the summer supply the bass fishermen with tender young crawfish and appetizing hellgrammites. Still these citizens find time for public duty.

Some of them give the town years of devotion. Chester Abbott, at the bank, served as town clerk for twenty-six years. Abel Haley has collected the town's taxes for two decades, following in the footsteps of some of his ancestors. The town honors its servants, thought it may be sharp with them. When one of them comes to the end of his life, as Selectman George Britton did a few weeks ago, the whole town closes its doors and suspends business at the hour of his funeral service.

John Clow puts the spirit of the leaders of such a town into words. "After all," says he, "it's our town,

and it's up to us to see that things go right with it."

The plain citizens feel that way, too. Between town meetings they keep their eyes on everything done in their name, from the laying of a sidewalk to the buying of a fire engine, just as they watched the counting of the ballots on town-meeting night. They look over the shoulders of the selectmen around the council tables. As a committee of the whole, a democratic-action committee, they see that Highway Agent Leslie Chamberlain keeps the roads snow-plowed to suit them, and that Water Superintendent Charlie Lucas maintains sufficient pressure in the mains.

They are proud of their town's institutions; of the smart little hospital, the academy, library, the town-owned electric plant, the miles of town-paved country roads, the town's water-supply pond, spring-fed, forest-girt, 500 feet up in the hills. You feel that with these riches which years of toil and careful management have brought, the people have good right to be proud.

Thomas Jefferson called the town meeting "the wisest invention ever devised by the wit of man for the perfect exercise of self-government and for its preservation." And town-meeting government is a native product of American democracy. It was not imposed upon the first-comers to these shores. It had no pattern to follow. It just grew.

The lordly proprietors of colonial days sent little companies of settlers into the lonely wilderness and bade them get along somehow. And this is how those pioneers did it. Needing order and organization, they banded together in the town meeting, developed the system by rule of thumb, and found strength in it with which to establish a nation.

Is democracy hard to define in these days of challenge? Well, the town-meeting towns like Wolfeboro are practicing it 365 days a year for anybody to see. And in such places it seems to be doing right well, as it has done in this part of America for close to three centuries.

That the highly idealized picture of town meeting government presented by many writers in the last few years is not completely in accord with the facts is attested by the authors of the next selection, though their conclusions are based on studies of larger population towns. It seems clear that when a community grows beyond a few hundred population town meeting government gradually loses ground. Most of the larger New England cities have moved in the direction of representative government, in a few instances the device being that of a representative town meeting.

The attempt of the early settlers in the trans-Appalachian West to transplant the familiar institutions of town government to the 6 by 6 land areas known as Congressional townships was never a huge success. In some areas during the days of very limited transportation township governments were reasonably satisfactory for minor services, but their boundaries were artificial, most lacked a real sense of community, and before long villages began separating themselves from the townships, thus withdrawing the focal point of community sentiment. In the next article Paul W. Wager discusses the gradual elimination of the township, an eventuality recommended for years by virtually all students of the subject. Despite the fact that the obituary has been read repeatedly, there are a number of states in which the corpse shows remarkable tenacity if not vitality.

62

Is the Town Meeting Finished?

*By John W. Alexander
and Morroe Berger*

ON OCTOBER 4, 1948, a New England town which we shall call Winston celebrated its annual political holiday. The townspeople voted for local officials, participated in a parade, and some of them looked forward to the town meeting in the evening. About 2,300 of Winston's 2,600 registered voters cast their ballots, but fewer than 200 citizens were interested enough to attest to the vitality of "pure democracy" by going to the town meeting.

It wasn't that the meeting wouldn't take up important local matters. There was the town budget to be voted upon, a decision on new street lights to be made, a report on sewage and water supply to be presented, and finally, the results of the day's election were to be announced. Not many Winston townsfolk considered this agenda worth their personal attention. It is hard to estimate how many persons attended the town meeting merely out of reverence for this ancient New England institution. A few were caught up in the general but moderate excitement of the holiday. Some close friends of the candidates for first selectman were anxious to learn who'd won the election. A handful of people felt especially peeved or elated about the items in the budget and wanted to state their views or to needle

the budget committee. But the meeting produced fewer than half a dozen questions and no hot arguments; it proceeded rather perfunctorily to its close an hour and fifteen minutes after it had begun.

This was the New England town meeting. It is an institution which we, perhaps like many others, had come to venerate as the last stronghold of pure democracy because we had read so many laudatory accounts of it. But we had no first-hand knowledge until we examined it recently during a survey of three New England towns which we conducted for the Columbia University School of Engineering. Many writers contributed to the shaping of our admiration for the town meeting. Two years ago one writer stated: "In these smallest units of American government, these 'cells' of pure democracy, the citizens rule directly." Another asserted in a book published at the height of the Nazi-Communist challenge to democracy in 1940: "In a world where democracy perishes . . . it is startling and refreshing to find the New England Town Meeting alive and able and in the hands of a tight-fisted people who keep their heritage well." Campaign oratory produces its share of plaudits for the town meeting. Speaking in Massachusetts last fall, Governor Earl Warren proclaimed: "It is neither necessary nor desirable for the national government to depart from the spirit of the old town meeting of New England."

To our surprise we found these praises mainly folklore, a sentimental devotion to a past misunderstood and a present vastly exaggerated. The town meeting may be alive in some places, but it was dead in the three contrasting towns we studied. In Winston, a highly industrialized town of 5,000 which is dominated by two big plants employing the great majority of the wage earners, the regular annual meetings generally draw a couple of hundred persons, while special town meetings often draw as few as thirteen and never more than about forty participants. In "Richfield," a residential-commercial town of 5,000 that is a showplace of colonial New England architecture and tradition, only twenty or twenty-five persons have attended the town meetings. In very recent years attendance in Richfield has been greater because there is a hotly-contested zoning issue now under discussion. In "Barrington," an industrial town of 30,000, town meetings play an even less important rôle, since Barrington is also a city and is governed by a mayor and a council. The town meeting as we found it is perfectly described in a Richfield citizens' club report of a few years ago. On one side of the town hall the artist drew a town crier in a colonial costume, ringing his bell and announcing, "Town Meeting Tonight." On the other side of the hall a Richfield citizen was fleeing in the opposite direction.

How are we to interpret New Englanders' lack of interest in an institution which has won the deep (if

John W. Alexander and Morroe Berger, "Is the Town Meeting Finished?" *American Mercury*, August, 1949, pp. 144–151. Reprinted by permission of the publisher.

ritualistic and uninformed) respect of Americans from other sections of the land? An easy answer is to say that the political apathy supposedly characteristic of the large urban centers has now developed in smaller communities as well. But it must then be pointed out that in Winston, Richfield and Barrington the percentage of adult citizens who register and vote is certainly not smaller than the proportion for the United States as a whole. It is difficult to compare voting participation in these three towns with that of the rest of the nation because this New England state has continuous registration — that is, a voter registers once and that registration permits him to vote year after year. In Winston voting has usually been high. Last October's local election, for example, brought out the votes of nearly 90 per cent of the registered voters, and a like percentage took part in the national elections the following month. Yet for the United States as a whole, only about 50 per cent of the adult citizens actually voted last November.

The real answer, we think, lies elsewhere. Bigness has come to the American small town. This, in its economic aspect, is nothing new. Thorstein Veblen, the great American social thinker, a quarter-century ago pointed to the influence of Big Business in the rural community: "It has been falling into the position of a way-station in the distributive system, instead of a local habitation where a man of initiative and principle might reasonably hope to . . . bear his share in the control of affairs without being accountable to any master-concern 'higher-up' in the hierarchy of business."

What we are now witnessing in the decline of the town meeting as an effective instrument of self-government is the political side of the economic process to which Veblen referred. Business has become national in organization, market, and general focus of interest; the economic unit is no longer a small area, a town or region — it is the entire stretch of country to the West and the South. And government has followed this broadening and centralizing tendency too. The result is that the reach of the town meeting has become relatively smaller, while the reach of state and Federal power has extended farther and farther. The great business organizations and centralized government profoundly affect life in the small town.

II

The issues that touch our lives intimately today are the issues that are grappled with and settled at the level of the state and Federal government, and by economic forces beyond the ken, much less the control, of the small community. Such issues are jobs, wages, social security, union organization, prices, hours of work, war and peace, the allocation of manpower and materials for the production of all kinds of goods, entertainment and even education. Big Government and Big Business and Big Labor deal with these problems. The town meeting is powerless to affect their solution. We think, then, that the New Englander who goes to a movie or listens to the radio while the town meeting drones on is not necessarily remiss in fulfilling his obligation or in exercising his rights as a citizen. For all he can do at a town meeting to make his influence felt in the significant affairs of political and economic life he might as well be enjoying himself at the Bijou or in his favorite easy chair.

Thus far we have been discussing the people who stay away from town meetings. But what about those who attend them — what motivates them? "Folks around here come to a meeting only when an issue touches their pocketbooks," the first selectman of one town told us. "What I mean is," he went on, "people won't bother to come around unless some particular matter interests them — say, snow removal, or zoning, or something like that." Even in matters of purely local concern, however, we found that a citizen doesn't always have to attend the town meeting. He can get the first selectman on the phone and tell him, "Say, Walt, when do you think you'll be able to get the road gang up here? You know, last spring's thaw left some mighty bad holes in the road, and it wasn't too good to begin with." And Walt does what he can to oblige — but the town meeting is nowhere in this picture.

The town meeting, we have said, does not affect the solution of the basic problems of living which most of us face. But even those questions which it does examine and vote upon are already structured before they reach the town meeting. Take, for example, the main business of most town meetings, the consideration of the budget presented by the board of finance. This budget, like that of the Federal government, represents a statement of policy since it allocates the town's resources and sets the tax rate. The board holds public hearings on its budget suggestions, but these special meetings attract even fewer townsfolk than the annual town meetings in the fall. The board's budget is not effective until the regular town meeting has ratified it, but by that time its general character has already been settled and the town meeting has little freedom of choice in settling this most significant of all the issues placed before it. For the assembled citizens may neither increase the appropriations made by the board of finance, nor may they add new ones. This limitation upon pure democracy has been imposed by the state government, and it makes of the town meeting little more than the occasion for a referendum on the budget presented by the powerful board of finance. Here is no "pure democracy" in the sense meant by the enthusiastic admirers of the town meeting — it is simply representative democracy (which, incidentally, is a pretty good brand too).

Other matters which come up at town meetings relate to the schools, roads and welfare. All of these functions are no longer left exclusively to the town meeting, since the local agencies and officials for many years responsible for these activities must also answer to state boards. Sewage and water supply problems, too, are handled by outside professional engineers whose expert testimony is then considered by the appropriate town agencies before the alternatives are placed before the town meeting.

It is clear what has happened. The old powers of town meetings, themselves of only limited significance for most persons, have passed to local elective and appointive officials. Representative democracy has displaced the "pure democracy" of the town meetings as the effective means of local self-government. The issues remaining for the town to settle become fewer and fewer, but broader and broader, just as in the government of our states and the nation. Today only the very broadest policy control is exercised by the voting citizen.

Despite the town meeting's loss of political relevance, it has continued to function in many places as an expression of the townspeople's community spirit, a reaffirmation of their solidarity. This kind of vitality, however, appears to characterize mainly the meetings in small towns, where there is a high proportion of self-employed persons or jobholders in small business units, a high proportion of residents whose families have lived in the town for generations, and a small proportion of persons of recent foreign descent. The three towns we studied, with the partial exception of one, do not have these traits. They have populations of 5,000 and over, a high proportion of their workers are employed by large manufacturing companies, relatively few belong to families that have lived in the towns for generations, and there is a very high proportion of foreign-born and second-generation residents, especially in Winston and Barrington. In the urban areas the town meeting is weak. What matters is not size or population, but rather the nature of the town's economic life and the ethnic and regional origin of its people.

The extent to which the myth of the town meeting has spread outside of New England was brought home to us in a talk we had with one of Richfield's leading citizens. Upon his retirement twenty years ago from a highly successful business career in New York, he chose to live in Richfield because of its long and famous tradition, and because he was anxious to participate in the local self-government for which New England was famous. "At first," he told us, "I attended town meetings regularly, but eventually I had to admit to myself that they mean little either as a legislature or a public forum. Their values, I found out, are mythical ones. I hardly ever go any more." But he did not withdraw from Richfield's community life. Finding that he could participate in local affairs without going to town meetings, he has become Richfield's elder statesman and its presiding authority on local history.

III

Governmental functions of the town meeting were transferred to town agencies soon after the town meeting itself developed in the colonial period. Very early, therefore, the town meeting took on a non-governmental rôle as an expression of community solidarity, and town meeting time became a day of festivity and reunion among friends and acquaintances who might not often see each other throughout the year. Perhaps its main function was similar to that of a local fair.

Today, however, fewer and fewer New England town meetings serve even this social function. Towns are too big, for one thing, and everyone knows that the meeting-place won't hold more than a small percentage of those eligible to attend. The growth of transportation facilities has made it easier for people to get to town meetings, but they haven't used these facilities for that purpose. The penetration of urban patterns of living into rural areas and small towns has, too, stripped the town meeting of some of its significance. People nowadays don't come into contact very often with persons who belong to different social groups except in a fleeting way; we live segmented lives, with but infrequent overlapping of the separate parts of our existence. George Wilson, for example, is a church-going Protestant, a Republican, a clerk in the Winston branch of a large nationwide corporation, a Mason and so on. George is a member of one group for his recreation, another for his religious worship, another for the purpose of earning a living, and still another for going out for a good time. In none of these rôles and activities is he likely to meet or to feel that he has much in common with Stanley Wisniewski, a church-going Catholic, a Democrat, a member of the Polish-American Society, and a semi-skilled worker in the same branch factory in Winston. Community activities, then, have become specialized and departmentalized: we join special groups for special purposes, and we no longer tend to belong to generalized community groups, such as the town meeting.

We can, of course, say that all this is too bad, that a town meeting at which the Winston manufacturer and the lathe operator can discuss local problems in a spirit of cooperation is a good thing. But the manufacturer's political and economic interests are focused on the state or the national capital, and the chances are that he doesn't live in Winston but in some nearby residential town. As for the lathe operator, the decisions that affect the basis of his existence are certainly not made at town meetings, and the prospect of talking over town meetings with the industrial and political leaders probably scares more than it attracts him. What can he gain, he reasons, by sitting alongside his boss at a discussion of the need for new street lights? Such a meeting has no relevance to the things he sees as important in his life, for this sort of equality is neither an index of, nor a means to, any other equality which he values more highly. We may deplore this situation, or we may choose to ignore it, but we can't deny that it exists.

Those who extol the town meeting frequently quote Jefferson's well known tribute to the towns of New England: "They have proved themselves the wisest invention ever devised by the wit of man for the perfect exercise of self-goverment and for its preservation." Because journalists, intellectuals and politicians who want to "get down to the grass roots" sentimentally overestimate the rôle of the town meeting (and because one good quote deserves another), we should like to repeat what John Dewey, another great American democrat, has said of the machinery of democratic government. "It is a form of idolatry to erect means into the end which they serve. Democratic political forms are simply the best means that human wit has devised up to a special time in history."

What are these democratic forms? Perhaps up to Jefferson's "time in history" the town meeting was the best means for the practice and maintenance of local self-government. Today, at least, the best means is no longer the town meeting but the representative system. We think that the people of New England, who have actually shifted from reliance upon the town meeting to reliance upon representative democracy, are far more realistic than those misled admirers of the town meeting who are oriented toward a past that cannot be recovered. Does the fact that the town meeting's direct form of democracy is obsolete mean that democracy is out-moded too? This question was answered long ago by the development of the newer democratic form, representation. As representative governments, the small communities now face the same major problem that the nation faces with respect to the Federal government: how can we secure expert handling of the technical, complex affairs of our welfare state, and yet leave the control of policy in the hands of an electorate that has neither the training nor the time to comprehend these affairs in detail?

All of us are in the process of working out the answer to this question on every level of government, but the crucial, the decisive answer is being worked out in our relation to the Federal government. Our focus of political interest is upon the government at Washington, and less than ever on the local community. It is this change in focus, we believe, that explains the fact that in Winston, Richfield and Barrington only scores attend the town meetings, whereas over 90 per cent of all the registered voters went to the polls in the national election last November.

We must always be ready to examine anew the forms we consider to be the means of democratic government. The social basis for the direct form of democracy known as the town meeting has disappeared even from the local scene; that basis was the small, autonomous, homogeneous and somewhat isolated community. Are we developing new techniques appropriate to the kind of society we live in now? — with extreme interdependence of widely-separated areas, social and class differences of which we are becoming ever more conscious, specialization in economic and political affairs, and the departmentalization of our group life which we have already mentioned. What part can local government play in such a fundamental revaluation? It is probably not too much to say that we shall be unable to make the necessary adjustments on the national level if we find ourselves unable to make them on the local level.

It is self-deception to pride ourselves on the town meeting when it apparently doesn't function where it is supposed to, and when its rôle is misunderstood. The evidence we have found about the town meeting certainly demands serious reflection on some assumptions that we have been accepting without much thought. The town meeting is a sacred cow that deserves to be laid to rest.

63

Townships on Way Out

By Paul W. Wager

POLITICAL INSTITUTIONS, particularly at the grass roots, change slowly. In 1934 the Committee on County Government of the National Municipal

Paul W. Wager, "Townships on Way Out," *National Municipal Review*, October, 1957, pp. 456–460, 475. Footnotes in original omitted. Reprinted by permission of the publisher.

League issued a report, *Recommendations on Township Government*. It was written by Arthur W. Bromage, chairman of a subcommittee set up to look into the need and effectiveness of this unit of local government then existent in 22 states. The recommendation was that, except in New England, the unit be gradually abolished.

At that time there were 18,725 organized townships (or towns) outside New England. They existed in sixteen states excluding Washington, which had townships in only two counties. Now, in 1957, according to the U.S. Bureau of the Census, the number has decreased to 15,692 in fourteen states, again excluding Washington and also South Carolina, which has two organized townships. In two states, Oklahoma and Iowa, township government either has been completely liquidated or has been reduced to such a shadowy existence as to warrant exclusion from the enumeration.

In Oklahoma townships were abolished, for all practical purposes, by a constitutional amendment of 1933 which deprived them of the power to levy taxes. The Oklahoma legislature then transferred to the county those functions which had been performed by the township, the most important of which was highway construction and maintenance.

In Iowa, the townships lost jurisdiction over local roads by act of the legislature in 1929. They continued for some years to enjoy a few other functions — oversight of the poor, provision of minimal health services, control of noxious weeds, care of cemeteries and the assessment of property. A few years ago the county was given jurisdiction over the assessment function and also the appointment of the weed commissioner. While townships there still have a certain amount of vestigial status, Iowa townships are now treated in census statistics as adjuncts of the county governments and are no longer counted as governmental units.

The net reduction in the other states is only 389 units. This reduction has been due to the liquidation of township government in individual counties, notably in Minnesota and the two Dakotas. The change in two decades is shown in the . . . tabulation [below].

The decline in the importance of township government may be measured also in the loss of functions by those still in business.

Administration of justice: Justices of the peace and constables are still elected in a majority of the states but in steadily declining numbers. Also from all over the country there comes the report that in few townships are there any candidates, and some who are elected do not bother to qualify. The explanation for the rapid disappearance of the ancient office of justice of the peace is, of course, the absence of a need for a neighborhood magistrate in

	1933	1957
Illinois	1481	1433
Indiana	1016	1008
Iowa	1602	—
Kansas	1550	1540
Michigan	1268	1262
Minnesota	1973	1828
Missouri	345	328
Nebraska	506	478
New Jersey	236	233
New York	932	934
North Dakota	1470	1392
Ohio	1337	1335
Oklahoma	969	—
Pennsylvania	1574	1565
South Dakota	1177	1080
Wisconsin	1289	1276
Total	18,725	15,692

these days of automobiles and good roads and the widespread establishment of county or district courts with a somewhat broader jurisdiction.

The constable is even more of an anachronism in a modern high speed age and has almost disappeared from the scene. The evidence multiplies that the township is no longer needed or much used either for law enforcement or the administration of justice.

Welfare and health: The many faceted social security program, supported in large part from federal and state funds, has pretty generally relieved the townships of such residual welfare functions as they had twenty years ago. In New York State the last vestiges of poor relief were transferred to the county in 1947. Today only in Illinois, Indiana, Ohio and in some counties in Minnesota do the townships play any rôle in welfare administration and only in Illinois is their contribution to its support more than nominal.

Twenty-five years ago the township was still being utilized quite widely as an area for a rudimentary health service. As of 1952, there were 1,333 full-time local health departments of one sort or another serving 1,637 counties, including 279 cities and covering areas with a combined population of approximately 120 million people. The picture throughout the nation is by no means uniform, however. In 1950 there were only two county units in South Dakota and one in Pennsylvania; on the other hand, New York had 100 per cent county-wide coverage and Michigan 89 per cent.

The availability of federal funds under the Hill-Burton Act to assist with the cost of hospital construction has given further stimulus to the adoption of the county as the unit of support of hospitals and the hospitalization of indigents.

Assessment and collection of taxes: The property tax has always been the mainstay of local government, and in earlier days the practice developed of having real and personal property assessed or listed by assessors representing jurisdictions smaller than the county. In the states which had townships, these were used as assessment districts with the assessor almost always popularly elected as a township officer. The values placed on property by these local assessors were used not only as the basis for township levies but for county and state levies as well. To overcome competitive undervaluation, it was usually necessary to provide some method of equalization at the county level.

This system has been perpetuated and assessment of property remains one of the two most common functions of township government. It is a township function in all or many of the counties in twelve of the fourteen states covered in this report. It is a county function in Ohio and, since 1950, has been in Nebraska. In Indiana it is a township function in townships with 5,000 or more population but in South Dakota in the rural areas only. It was the loss of this function to the county that completed the liquidation of township government in Iowa and in several other states there is now a county assessor who gives general supervision to the work. This is true in Indiana, Missouri, Kansas, Nebraska and in a number of counties in Minnesota. The trend is unmistakably in the direction of county assumption of the assessment function, usually over the vigorous protest of the state associations of township officials.

The collection of taxes has not so generally been a township function though it is, at least prior to delinquency, in New York, Pennsylvania, Michigan and in a few populous counties in Illinois.

Highway administration: The principal function of township government, far outweighing all others combined, is the maintenance of local roads. Though all township roads were transferred to the counties over twenty years ago in three states — Iowa in 1930, Indiana in 1932 and in Michigan gradually from 1931 to 1936 — the movement thereafter slowed down. There have been additional shifts from the township to the county-unit plan but only county by county and by local option rather than by legislative fiat.

Under such a county option plan, more than half the Kansas counties have abandoned township highway management. As of January 1955, there were 53 counties which had adopted the county unit plan and 52 which cling to the township system. The townships which have lost the road function have little to do and this is reflected in the fact that in these townships 40 per cent of their budgeted expenditures are for administrative overhead.

A similar optional law for the transfer of township roads to county-wide road districts is in effect in Illinois, but little advantage has been taken of it.

Still another method is being used to overcome the handicaps inherent in the conduct of road work on the township scale. This is for the officials of a township, of their own volition, to enter into an agreement to have the township's road work done with county forces and equipment. Widespread use is made of this contract plan in Minnesota and Wisconsin. A study made of 545 Wisconsin towns in 1952 showed that county forces were maintaining town roads in more than half the towns.

Pennsylvania has no county roads in rural areas — only state roads and township roads. In the 1930s the State Department of Highways absorbed into the state system a large mileage of township roads, but the effort some years later to transfer responsibility for the rest of the local roads to the counties was defeated. Today Pennsylvania has many small and poorly managed township highway units. It has been estimated that only 263 of the state's 1,513 second class townships could meet the minimum qualifications for an effective highway unit.

In Illinois in 1953 local rural roads were administered by 1,408 townships in 85 counties which have organized townships and 107 road units in non-township counties. In four of the latter counties the road unit was the entire county. The average road unit was comprised of 48 miles of rural roads. The State Division of Highways, in a detailed study to determine the effect of size of road unit on cost per mile of road concluded, "there appears to be ample justification for the belief that costs per mile decrease as the miles maintained by the administering unit increase."

In New York, as of 1950, the town highway system accounted for more than 52 per cent of the total mileage of rural highways and urban streets. The bulk of the mileage had a traffic count of less than 50 vehicles a day and some of the town mileage had fewer than five vehicles. About 36 per cent of it did not even have a gravel surface. One-third of the town highway mileage was serving land abandoned or unlikely to remain permanently in agriculture.

The state legislature of 1950 set up a ten-year town highway program which called for the improvement of about one-half of the town highway mileage, or more than 26,000 miles, at a total cost of $146,-400,000, with the state providing about half the over-all cost. The act was designed (1) to limit improvement to those roads that would serve communities of economic stability and (2) to require each township to contribute to the cost in proportion to its ability.

A decreasing role

These illustrations of the decreasing role played by the townships in the four fields in which they once played important roles are evidence enough that in the rural areas they have outlived their usefulness. Further evidence is the lack of interest in township meetings in states providing for such meetings, and the dearth of qualified candidates for township office in the township states generally. Every argument advanced twenty-odd years ago for their elimination has become even more cogent with the passage of time.

Tradition, the alleged values of local self-government, and political advantage are the main reasons why townships remain. The last of these factors is probably the principal one. Threatened with the loss of their jobs and political influence, township officials have united into powerful state associations — as, for example, in New York, Pennsylvania, Michigan and Ohio.

Township government has shown greater signs of weakening in those states that do not use the township as the basis of representation on the county governing body. For example, Minnesota and Missouri both reduced the number of townships during the 1940s, but Wisconsin, Michigan, New York and Illinois townships remain relatively powerful because they are units for representation on the county board of supervisors and thus can offer another reason for continuing their existence. But this is an insufficient reason for retaining an outmoded unit. Town government is no more needed in the rural parts of New York State than it is in North Dakota for the very good reason that it has nothing particular to do.

Costs go up

Surprisingly, despite shrinking functions, the cost of township government does not show a decline. Township revenues in the fourteen township states increased from $197 million in 1942 to $422 million in 1953, 114 per cent. Expenditure figures for these two years are not available but presumably they do not differ greatly from the revenue figures. The comparative figures for the two years by states follow.

It will be noted that the only state which showed an actual decrease in township revenue was Indiana and this appears to have been due to a reduction in township taxes for schools. The state which showed the sharpest increase was Michigan due no doubt to the generous allocations to the townships from the proceeds of the state sales tax. Indeed in the township states as a whole the upsurge in spending has

Township Revenue
(*in thousands of dollars*)

	1942	1953
New York	$53,487	$132,615
New Jersey	20,027	58,174
Pennsylvania	23,408	43,125
Ohio	8,305	24,492
Indiana	30,696	10,790
Illinois	22,928	32,780
Michigan	4,138	26,670
Wisconsin	19,500	59,613
Missouri	1,658	3,836
Kansas	4,687	9,083
Nebraska	722	2,937
South Dakota	1,204	3,616
North Dakota	1,268	4,364
Minnesota	5,257	10,138
Total	197,285	422,233

been stimulated by aid from other governments. In the eleven-year period revenues from local sources increased 104 per cent, whereas grants from other governments increased 163 per cent. Increased spending does not necessarily signify rejuvenation if somebody else is furnishing the money.

A closer analysis of contemporary township government would almost certainly show that most of the increased activity is in a relatively few populous townships which are providing a number of urban-type services. This suggests that in recommending the dissolution of townships a distinction needs to be made between townships in rural areas and densely populated townships, often but not necessarily within metropolitan areas. Here there is often a demand for services not demanded or needed on a county-wide basis and which cannot always be supplied by a nearby city.

Several states have already recognized the need for some diversity in township organization and powers. New York distinguishes between first and second class townships — those with a population of 10,000 or more being designated first class and vested with somewhat greater police power.

Townships in Pennsylvania are likewise divided into two classes. Townships of the first class are those having a population density of 300 or more per square mile; all others are townships of the second class. However, change from second to first class is subjected to referendum. First class townships are urban in nature and frequently perform functions similar to cities and boroughs.

Townships in New Jersey are given a wide range of power and frequently perform functions associated elsewhere with municipal governments.

Termination overdue

There is no threat to local self-government when the enlargement of the service area is no greater than the new modes of transportation and communication warrant. The radius of a county is no greater in travel time today than was the radius of a township in 1900. The average citizen in his business and social activities is offering testimony every day to this fact, yet he will often let himself be persuaded that a larger political unit is a denial of local self-government.

Local government needs to be preserved and strengthened but it needs to be defined in twentieth century terms. It has been amply demonstrated that in most areas there is no longer a need for township government. There may be a need to develop in the densely populated townships a kind of township government that approximates the town government of New England. Where town government can evolve into a useful vehicle of community service it certainly has a place in contemporary America; elsewhere its termination is already overdue.

While the New England town usually combines urban and rural areas, the Midwestern township is normally strictly rural, even small concentrations of population tending to incorporate as villages. Large villages become essentially indistinguishable from cities, but the small rural village is more likely to resemble the township organizationally. The most significant difference is in the substitution of a representative council for the town meeting, and one of the most striking characteristics of village government is in its high degree of informality. It is this aspect which the editor of the Goshen *(N.Y.) Independent-Republican pictures for us here.*

64

Local Democracy Gets a Workout

By George L. Seese

ANY SUBJECT WITHIN the extensible limits of public interest or good taste is open for discussion at Goshen Village Board meetings. When they gather, Board

George L. Seese, "Local Democracy Gets a Workout," *American City,* April, 1949, pp. 81–82. Reprinted by permission of the publisher.

members know there is a certain amount of public business to transact, but when the Mayor looks around to size up the gallery, and asks, "Any new business?" they don't know what will come next.

Sometimes what follows is mild and pleasant, as when the lady managers of the library reported that Roland Harriman, eminent patron of harness racing, had suggested the founding of a Hall of Fame to celebrate Goshen as "The Cradle of the Trotter." Sometimes it is amusing, as when a lady asked the Board to reprove another lady, next door, whose dog had bad garden manners, or when a group of television-set owners asked to have an interfering "ham" radio operator declared a public nuisance. But there are occasions on which shirt-sleeved indignation boots fancy-pants decorum out the window.

"Spirited exchanges"

"That's a hell of a way to treat a hero!" roared Phil Pines, an exasperated Erie track supervisor, when the Board recently expressed a doubt of its power to piece out or supplement the slender pension of a disabled cop. It sounded as if Pines were addressing negligent section hands. The policeman, John Golemboski, had suffered a cerebral stroke some time after he had fought, hand to hand, with a robber cornered in a village hotel, and was retired on $33 a month.

"Peanuts!" shouted Pines in disgust. "It won't pay the rent of a roof over his head!"

"Damn!" is another expletive perhaps not in frequent, but still not uncommon use. Board members generally manage to maintain their dignity, and especially when women are present, some restraint is practiced by vehement advocates of this or that. Yet four-letters words do slip out in the course of what *The Independent-Republican* weekly calls "spirited exchanges" — and the women never seem to mind.

There was a woman in the audience during the Board's January meeting, when an ordinance was discussed to prohibit car parking in the path of snowplows clearing streets after winter storms, and she heard a lot of four-letter words. *The Independent-Republican* reported the session as the most tempestuous of the year. The ordinance was enacted, and immediately dissidents who wanted the village kept "as comfortable as an old pair of bedroom slippers" announced organization of a Taxpayer League to make the village election this month something of a trial for trustees who want another term.

Orange is one of the original New York counties, and Goshen one of the original (though not the first) Orange settlements. The village was built around a church, the Presbyterian, which three years ago observed its 225th anniversary. Many of its structures, including dwellings, were built a century or more ago. The building in which the Board meets is Town Hall, which originated as the Farmers' Academy, embodying a smaller school where Noah Webster taught before the Revolution, and where he is said to have prepared the first drafts of the Blue-Black Speller.

Besides Mayor Luft, a bank president, the Board comprises four trustees: Charles Fitzpatrick, a real-estate broker and insurance agent who once was an iron molder; Dr. Roy Lippincott, a physician often summoned on sick call in the midst of meetings; Robert Walsh, a robust boss truckman high in the lay councils of the Presbyterians, and Frank McBride, one of two brothers who first established milk-truck transportation on the highways of the state.

Popular participation invited

. . . Until a few years ago, the Goshen trustees operated in the privacy cherished by the average small-town government in the United States. Seldom did anyone but officials show up for Board meetings. But Mayor Luft, saying public business was not a private affair, invited popular participation. Goshen responded with the bright-eyed alacrity of an old lady bidden to a tea at which she could hear the gossip of the town. The Board of Trade detailed members regularly to attend, and every citizen feels free to come in and get a weight off his chest.

Somebody appears with a complaint that the buses running to and from the million-dollar Central School go through the village at dangerous speed. "We don't" reply a deputation of bus drivers. "We can't; every bus has a governor limiting speed to thirty-five miles an hour."

"Too fast," says the Board. "Slow down to twenty in town." And the Board of Education issues the necessary orders.

Sewer and water-line problems aired

Bruce Schoonmaker has built half a dozen dwellings on a new street extension to relieve the housing shortage, and needs official cooperation. "Where the hell is that sewer pipe the Board is supposed to have ordered more than a year ago? Anybody think he can sell houses to houseless families without sewer and water connections?"

"O.K. Just keep your shirt on," says the Board in soothing effect. "Get the street graded. No ungraded street can be accepted, and we can't lay sewer lines on a street we haven't accepted."

Mrs. George Gregg, widow of a newspaper editor, has terraced a village hilltop, and marked it off in spacious building lots. Her engineer, Van Duzer Wallace, makes a formal offer to cede a street if the Board will extend sewer and water lines there also.

This poses a question. Joe Fix-It comes in steaming. Joe (last name Dunlevy) is a young Navy veteran of the last war who advertises — sometimes in rhyme — that he can make anything go that was made to go. In the development of the sewer system, Dunlevy's neighborhood was somehow overlooked. What the heck! His tax bills show assessments for sewers he and his neighbors have yet to get. Now somebody wants the village to put in new lines absolutely free. It can't do that!

As Clerk John Connelly, the chuckling MC of nearly every Legion or KC show, reaches the end of the routine, the Mayor's query, "Any new business?" is the signal for the gallery to become vocal. Frequently Board members start something themselves. Not long ago members severely criticized the police force, of which, counting the Chief, there are five members in a village of 3,000 inhabitants. "Damned rotten," was a term used in momentary abandonment of official dignity. "Not as good as two men in the neighboring village of Walden or Warwick. Especially on traffic regulations!"

To the next meeting came Chief Robert Bruce, a ponderous figure of a man, now past retirement age, but under special dispensation still in uniform after more than thirty years of service. "Look," he said, "we caught thirty-seven speeders last month. If you want us to do better than that, give us a new prowl car." He added that the car in use (a gift, by the way, ten or twelve years ago) was about to fall apart, a menace to the life of any patrolman trying to chase speeders over thoroughfares that in horse-and-buggy days were the scene of thrilling sleigh races whenever there was snow on the ground.

Thereupon, the Board asked Village Treasurer Harold Parker to report on whether, under current budget limitations, he could provide money for a new car. He couldn't.

Not all of the Board sessions are exciting. Patients in the doctor's office next door may await their turn for consultation without hearing the slightest commotion in Town Hall. Sometimes county-seat reporters despair of getting a headline out of the proceedings. On such an occasion the Mayor and his colleagues are capable of creating a diversion. They gave a recent demonstration. Mrs. Frank Beane, a young matron interested in civic affairs, joined the gallery around the council table, with nothing special in mind except a desire to see the Board in action.

Sparks fly over railroad service

"Sorry," said the Mayor. "We don't seem to have anything particularly important tonight." But a moment later he remarked, "Before we adjourn I think the Board should consider something that has been in the air for a year. Erie commuter service. . . ."

The session was interesting from there on. Mrs.
Beane heard a debate liberally larded with words of
body and spirit. Everybody talked, and at times
all at once.

The Erie, though not without its apologists and
defenders, seemed to be suspected of trying to bargain over something the village ought to have. Trains
taken off during the war might — might — be restored if communities all along the line into New
York City were kinder in the matter of taxes. There
was a snort from one end of the table. As men personally interested in highway transportation, neither
McBride nor Walsh seemed to think much of rail-
road-tax reduction.

"The Erie's got smooth tax agents," observed a
fellow trustee. "But," somebody in the gallery inter-
jected, "trucks and buses didn't have to build their
own roads, and then pay taxes on the values thus
created."

"You can't expect the Erie to give something for
nothing." This from Trustee Fitzpatrick.

"Right," came from the gallery again. "And if you
keep on calling Erie trains filthy, and the service

terrible, as somebody did in the last conference with
Erie officials, you'll damn well be without more trains
until Kingdom Come."

"Goshen," muttered an elderly galleryite as he rose
to go, "don't want more population."

"There'll be more buses and trucks anyway when
there's more business for them," comforted a companion.

"Nope; I remember years ago when a delegation
of prominent citizens went to Albany to protest granting a suburban trolley line franchise. Said the trolley
would bring in a lot of undesirables, and spoil the
beauty and charm of the village."

"Move to adjourn," said Fitzpatrick.

"Good night, gentlemen," said young Mrs. Beane.
"I've had a most interesting evening."

Everybody sauntered out smiling.

"No hard feelings," said the Mayor complacently.

He was right then. But after the winter parking
ordinance was passed, there remained some exacer-
bation of spirit, though Carlisle Neithold, a hotel
keeper vigorously opposed to the measure, said as he
left the hall, "after all, it was democracy in action."

CHAPTER FOURTEEN

Special Districts

SPECIAL OR AD HOC districts constitute the most numerous and probably the least known units of American local government. Multiplying rapidly under the authority of frequently liberal permissive state legislation, and often disappearing with even greater facility, the actual number of such districts existing at any one time can only be estimated. While the use of special districts state by state varies tremendously, they have become a generally commonplace feature of the political landscape. The following discussion of the varied nature of these districts, their advantages and disadvantages, and prospects for the future is from the only comprehensive study of special districts published to date.

65

The Significance of Special Districts in American Local Government

By John C. Bollens

SPECIAL DISTRICTS, a varied class of governmental units, have without much notice and concern become a significant part of the governmental pattern of the United States. They are furthermore becoming increasingly important despite a widespread lack of general understanding and knowledge about them. Only one kind of special district, the school district, is reasonably well known, although subject to frequent misconceptions, and many nonschool districts are erroneously regarded as parts of other governments. Special districts, particularly those in the nonschool categories, constitute the "new dark continent of American politics," a phrase applied earlier in the century to counties. . . .

John C. Bollens, *Special District Governments in the United States* (Berkeley: University of California Press, 1957), pp. 1–3, 5, 247–263. Footnotes in original omitted. Reprinted by permission of the publisher.

GENERAL EVIDENCE OF SIGNIFICANCE

Numbers and geographical extensiveness

One test of the significance of special districts is their number in relation to the over-all total for all governmental units. There are more than 79,000 of them, constituting about two-thirds of the approximately 116,000 governmental units in the United States. This means that about thirteen of every twenty governments are special districts — eleven in the school category and two in the nonschool category. In addition, they are not only very numerous but also geographically widespread. These two characteristics are both evident in the fact that in thirty-five states special districts are more numerous than any other class of government. Even the school and nonschool categories separately often outrank numerically each of the other governmental classes. School districts alone in twenty-nine states, and nonschool districts alone in fourteen states, are more numerous than any one class of other governments. Tens to thousands of special districts exist in every one of the states, and at least one such district is found in a large majority of the 3,049 counties in the country.

The large number, relative proportion, and geographical dispersion of special districts are not the only criteria for demonstrating their significance. Numerically they have been very much in flux, most noticeably since 1942. Unlike other governments in

243

the United States which, with the minor exception of townships, remained virtually unchanged in total number, special districts declined by almost one-third in the period from 1942 to 1952. A closer look at this development indicates that it actually consists of two countertrends, each of consequence in itself. While one group of special districts, the school district, was decreasing by almost two-fifths (38.0 per cent), nonschool districts were increasing by almost one-half (48.4 per cent). The number of school districts has been decreasing faster and the number of nonschool districts has been growing faster than any other class of governmental units. Then, too, the number of kinds of nonschool districts has substantially increased since the early 1940's. The highly significant changes in numbers and types of governments in the United States have been occurring in the special district category. Rapid growth in particular is evidence of increasing significance. In this instance, rapid decrease has been important, too, for it generally involves territorial enlargement of the remaining districts and further strengthening and reinforcement of the district concept in the field of public education.

Finances and personnel

Special districts are also consequential because of the extensiveness of their collective activity. In the fiscal year ending in 1955, school and nonschool districts spent $8.2 billion and $1.6 billion, respectively. This combined total of approximately $9.8 billion easily outranked the collective expenses of counties, townships, and towns, and stood close to the $10.5 billion figure for cities. At the same time the outstanding debt of all special districts was more than $13 billion, more than two-fifths of which was owed by nonschool districts. The indebtedness of the school and nonschool groups of special districts each exceeded that of counties, townships, and towns combined, and the total district debt was more than that of all state governments together. Payrolls further illustrate the large amount of activity. The monthly payrolls for October, 1955, totaled $486 million for all special districts, more than nine-tenths of which went to school districts. The total for all district payrolls was thus larger than that for any other class of state and local governments. In the same month special districts also stood first among state and local governments in the number of persons employed. Slightly more than 1,570,000 people were professionally engaged in district activities. To state it in another way, about two of every five employees working for a local government were paid by some type of special district. More than nine-tenths of the district figure related to school districts. . . .

Status and prospects

Special districts are consequential. They are also different. Deviating in many ways from most kinds of governments, they present a number of extraordinary patterns. Some of their features are completely unusual and others are different in the sense that they are present more commonly in special districts than in any other class of governments. The differences between special districts and other governments are demonstrable through a consideration of representative characteristics.

Conspicuous among the unusual aspects of special districts is the limited scope of the functions they may individually perform. Here are governmental units originally designed to be public agencies individually restricted to one or a very few activities. No other class of governments, including townships which have been experiencing a decline in functions, was similarly conceived. Furthermore, special districts render services to the virtual exclusion of enforcing regulations, much more so than other governments. Although each is of narrow functional scope, together they embrace an extremely broad range of matters of public concern.

Outstanding, too, is the frequency of their area flexibility. They can usually overlap one another, a permission not granted to other classes of governments, and they overlie other units to an extensive degree. They often initially contain and subsequently add territory without regard to other existing boundaries covering part or all of the same land. They usually have exceptional latitude as to locale and areal extent. Most of the pyramiding of governments at a specific location is caused by special districts. Unlike other state and local governments, some districts are interstate. Some are international. Many are coterminous with a general or special district unit, a practice otherwise in use in only a few cities and counties which are consolidated. Some have noncompact territory and a few lack an explicitly defined area. Some must include another government within their boundaries, which are at times determined by the population and legal limits of the included unit. An area practice of school districts is unparalleled. Through numerous mergers, the most comprehensive area reorganization ever to occur in the history of the United States has been under way for some time. The long tradition of increasing the number of governmental units is being broken by substantial subtractions.

District organization is often extraordinary. A skeletal structure exists in practice in many instances, and frequently the governing body is granted complete power to shape the operational framework according to its own desires. Whether the organization is large or small, it is more often fully integrated under the governing body than in other classes of government. The contrast is most distinct in comparison with counties, an overwhelming number of which feature numerous officials chosen independently of the governing board. Furthermore, there is seldom a division of responsibilities among two or more basic parts. For example, special districts have no elected executive resembling a governor or a mayor. Few district officials are elected. Most often only the members of the governing body have elective status, and much more frequently than in other governments the incumbents run without opposition. In many districts no official is chosen by the electorate.

The extensive utilization of appointment in selecting governing body members is a particularly prominent differentiation in organization. Sometimes the appointing authority, such as the governor or a judge, functions in a larger jurisdiction than the area of the district. In other districts the directors are selected by combinations of appointing authorities from different branches or levels of government, each generally choosing a certain number separately. Both of these selection procedures are expressions of a theory of accountability to the people most directly concerned, which can in operation be very remote from them and extremely difficult for them to use effectively. Also unknown elsewhere is the requirement in some districts that part of the governing body select the remainder of its membership.

Other structural and operational district arrangements are highly uncommon among governments. A governing body characteristic unique to certain districts is the absence of a specific term of office, and in several district types the electorate has the extremely rare opportunity of deciding at the organizational election whether the governing board shall be elected or appointed. One operational process unfamiliar to governments in general is the stipulation of unit or bloc voting by governing body members who represent specific areas within the district. Although unit voting is not unknown in legislative actions of other governments, it is mandatory only in these special districts. Another unusual technique is to apportion voting strength among the members on the basis of assessed property valuation represented, instead of following the traditional standard of equal individual voting power.

An especially odd feature of some district governments is their theory of representation, which bases participation in important matters on property ownership. This means that the voting power of adult residents is not the same. The criterion is used with some frequency, especially by rural districts. It may be a standard of eligibility to sign petitions and vote

to create a district, to select governing body members, to serve on the governing board, and to participate in decisions authorizing particular district activities. Sometimes the property ownership requirement is extended to permit nonresidents who possess property within the district to vote, or to authorize plural voting, which makes the number of votes per person dependent upon the amount of district land he owns. In some districts, therefore, a few individuals may have a majority of the votes and control the operations. . . .

Special districts are out of the ordinary in other fundamental ways. Financing is an excellent case in point. Taxation is a common corollary of governmental operations, but nonschool districts place much greater reliance upon other financing means, such as service charges, and constitute the only group of governments not depending heavily upon direct taxation. School districts, too, are exceptional in obtaining an unusually large proportion of their money through transfers from other governments. There is also variation in such fundamentals as formation proceedings, activeness, and dissolution. . . .

Not all of their deviations from widely known governmental molds and practices are beneficial, and in total their characteristics are a mixed blessing. Although they have features of government which are not generally considered governmental, special districts are much more than governmental curiosities. Their greatest contribution is that, in responding to demands for action under the name and powers of government, they reveal much about the operation of the over-all governmental system of which they are an established part.

What are some of these matters that they reveal? Three of them are particularly indicative. First, many districts are the product of the unresponsiveness, whether voluntary or involuntary, of other local governments, and are symptomatic of weaknesses in them. Special districts therefore frequently result from the unsuitability of existing governments, especially in area and financing characteristics and in the lack of sufficient ingenuity and compatibility to work out intergovernmental agreements. Second, special districts may develop from the actions of other governments and private organizations which are making an increasingly specialized approach to public problems. This is most graphically revealed by functional specialists who, although not deliberately trying to undermine general local governments, want to see a service provided but are unconcerned about its best governmental location. Sometimes their advocacy of special districts is directly related to the inadequacy of general units. At other times it is rooted in a desire, also held by interested laymen, to keep or take a function "out of politics."

Keeping or taking a function "out of politics" is a phrase which is often employed very loosely. If by "politics" is meant extreme partisanship or personal patronage, its existence in some nondistrict governments as well as in some special districts is undeniable. If by "politics" is meant the formulation of policies, a special district does not take a function "out of politics," but it may change the policy-making or political emphasis since the group in control of a district may differ from the group in control of a general government where the function could be located. In both circumstances a special brand of politics (partisanship or policy-making) is utilized instead of a general variety. Significantly, too, policy-making activities are not carried on by special districts in isolation. Policies are not made without influencing the policies of other governments, particularly those functioning in the immediate area, because such policies require decisions on social and economic matters, and such decisions directly affect other governments and the people they serve and are in turn affected by comparable political actions of the other governments.

The creation of some special districts also reveals a third feature of the governmental system of the United States, the desire of some residents and property owners for local autonomy or home rule. At times related to functional specialization, this desire may be a genuine feeling for a small government whose people are intimately acquainted with one another and with the locale. On the other hand it may be only a camouflage for individuals and groups seeking to derive a special advantage. Whatever the motive, the feeling for autonomy is frequently an element in the governmental process. These three aspects of the general governmental pattern — unresponsiveness, activity of a specialized nature, and the home-rule objective — aid considerably in understanding the rapid development of special districts.

Many special districts can be validly criticized. One serious argument against them is the inability of the public to exert adequate control over them. Special districts have multiplied so rapidly that citizens no longer keep themselves well informed on this aspect of governmental affairs. At the same time, general multipurpose governments have been expanding their functions. Although conscientious citizens might conceivably have exercised effective control over a few governmental units, it was unreasonable to expect them to watch and regulate a multi-ring circus. The fragmentation of governmental activities while governments were growing in functional importance has greatly increased the difficulty of citizen control and, in fact, has been made even more remote and superficial by the theory of representation based on property ownership and the theory of accountability, under which the appointing agent operates in an area larger than the district, performs his selection duty as part of a complicated arrangement, or lacks the power to remove appointees without substantiating serious charges. Whatever the details, appointed governing body members are at best twice removed from the voters, and residents can seldom legally bring a direct recall action against any of them.

The basic problem would not be resolved, however, by making all district directors elective. Although such a change could make public control more direct, the lengthening of an already long ballot would immediately dissipate any advantage that might emanate from the alteration. Simply stated, there are too many separate governments, and special districts are largely responsible. If "grass roots government" means broadly based public control, it is frequently an illusion in special districts. A very important way to improve citizen control and to solve the problem is to have fewer special districts.

The lack of popular control in special districts leads to a further important charge against many of them. Citizens have too little interest and consequently too little participation in the affairs of most districts. The fragmentation of governmental functions, particularly when coupled with extraordinary area overlapping, creates confusion, misunderstanding, and indifference. For example, many people living in metropolitan areas believe that some types of special districts are actually parts of general local governments. The aim of substantial citizen interest in a democratic political process is vulnerable to extreme fractionization. Citizen disinterest is not wholly unknown in other classes of governments (where it is partly attributed to the scattering of public attention among different governments through the rise of districts), but it is especially marked in respect to special districts. There is usually a low level of public concern about rural districts, and an upsurge of interest is often temporary and very emotional. Very seldom is there much interest in coterminous, urban fringe, or metropolitan districts. Among special districts, school districts receive the most citizen attention, chiefly because of parent-teacher groups and because of the contact and research work of taxpayers' organizations, which realize the extent of school financial outlays. Such interest has recently been further stimulated, in various sections of the country, by controversies over curriculum content and teaching methods. Nevertheless, public participation in electing school board members is proportionately lower than in electing city officials and is at times scarcely perceptible, in part because of fewer contested elections.

The underlying reason for the low level of public interest and participation in many districts is not difficult to diagnose. Few citizens feel that they can afford to spend much time on governmental affairs, and responsibility is now so widely shared by many independent governments that thorough comprehension is not easy. In fact, it is hardly an exaggeration to say that a citizen, especially one living in a highly urbanized area, who took part in only the important activities of all the local governments affecting his welfare would not have enough time left to earn the money he has to pay those governments. Lack of sufficient knowledge, and the competing demands made on personal time by numerous independent governments, force citizens to concentrate rather than disperse their attention. . . .

What is the principal detrimental result of the lack of citizen interest? It is that many districts function largely unnoticed and uncontrolled by the public.

In addition, strong disapproval of the super-abundance of special districts is justifiable because their uncoordinated, splintered efforts disperse activities among many independent governmental entities. This piecemeal, unintelligent attack on the problems of government, and the lack of over-all administrative and policy planning which grows out of the proliferation of governmental units, hinder the orderly development and sound utilization of the resources of an area. The approaches of different governments to a common problem often conflict and work at cross purposes, thus dissipating needed energies. A special district that handles only one aspect of a many-sided problem may do so with harmful results. Far too often has a special district tried to alleviate one difficulty and has simply succeeded in creating another. Interference with natural drainage by flood control work performed independently is a prominent example. Also, the functions of some special districts, such as housing authorities, may impinge upon related programs of general governments, which are powerless to require a coordinated attack on basic problems.

Another outcome of the lack of coordination among governments in the irrational competition for public monies, for which many special districts can be condemned. The only legal restrictions on this practice is the existence of tax limits. Heedless of the needs of other special districts and of general governments in the area, each district has its own fiscal policy and makes its own demands upon the total financial resources of the area. There is no over-all financial planning and no method of intelligently weighing the relative merits of competing demands. Emotional competitiveness frequently prevails instead of rational comparative consideration.

Furthermore, special districts are often indefensible because, as a result of being too small, they are uneconomic. They do not benefit from the financial advantages that accrue to larger governments through the widely accepted administrative devices of personnel pooling and central purchasing, maintenance, and repair. . . .

The expanding use of special districts has also been detrimental to general local governments. It has reduced their effectiveness through by-passing them or stripping them of particular functions. . . . Because special districts are too numerous, and because they are only palliatives offering no long-range solution, they weaken general local governments and lessen the possibility of attaining a governmental system that is both responsive and responsible.

These criticisms of special districts should not be interpreted to mean that general local governments are nearly perfect and that special districts are alone accountable for deficiencies at the local governmental level. They do indicate that districts constitute an important problem of local government and that they are excessive in number and type. Reform is very much in order, but it is irrational to proclaim simply that all special districts should be abolished immediately or that a moratorium should be declared on the creation of new ones. The mere advocacy of elimination or diminution does not remove the causes that created special districts.

A reform program should therefore be related to the possibility of improving general local governments, whose deficiencies have greatly contributed to the rapid expansion of special districts. Again the problem must be viewed realistically. The history of general local units is one of additions rather than mergers, and during the present century the number of such governments has increased rather than decreased. The number of townships has been somewhat reduced, but the total number of county consolidations and city mergers has been negligible indeed. Except for the continuing downward trend in townships and the possible realization of some proposals for metropolitan area governmental simplification, it seems highly unlikely that thoroughgoing area consolidations of general units will occur in the foreseeable future. If this is an accurate forecast (and unforeseen technological factors sometimes make predictions about government unreliable), proposals for changes in the realm of special districts should be made within this framework. To strive for more general changes is one thing, but to expect that in the near future such changes will be widespread and will lead to special district alterations seems fanciful. . . .

School districts that have long been independent governments in many states are likely to continue so for some time to come, and recommendations for reform of special districts should be made in the light of this reality. But some immediately applicable suggestions can be made without necessarily precluding the long-range objective of integrating school districts into general local governments.

The current trend of merging school districts into larger district areas should continue and accelerate. The area reorganization problem was so immense, when attacked on a broad geographical basis in recent years, that some people have been overwhelmed by the results. The record is impressive and much has been done. But much remains to be done. Furthermore, reforms sometimes need to be redone. . . . Fulfillment of these two objectives will in itself constitute a major special district reform, providing a strong contrast to the chaos of more than 100,000 separate school districts existing as late as the early 1940's, and will contribute greatly to broader, more efficient educational services. . . .

There should be closer intergovernmental planning and coordination between school districts and other governments operating in the immediate vicinity. . . .

It is also an appropriate time for state governments to authorize comprehensive interstate studies to be undertaken jointly by social scientists and professional educators on the relative merits of independent school districts and dependent school operations. . . .

. . . the basic recommendation about nonschool districts is that many of them should be absorbed into other types of governments. Nonschool districts that are coterminous with or smaller in area than general local governments should be made parts of those governments and stripped of all governmental autonomy. This can almost always be accomplished through state legislative action. To be effective such changes must be preceded by certain alterations in general local governments which should be more widely attainable than extensive area mergers. These governments must be granted authorization to establish service and financing differentials, instead of being required to give reasonably uniform service uniformly financed throughout an entire jurisdiction. They can then provide more intensive services in some portions to meet increased needs, and collect additional taxes or assessments from the people receiving them. In some states general local governments must also be freed of rigid tax and debt limitations. It is advisable in some situations to furnish the legal means for internal administrative reorganization. Districts that are coterminous with general units can be transformed without utilizing the service and financing differentials, since they cover exactly the same area. Districts that are smaller than general units can become areas within them, serviced by the regular departments and financed by special taxes or assessments determined by the governing body of the general unit. All of them (as well as all comparable dependent districts currently possessing a degree of separateness) will be fully integrated into general governments. Thus the district idea of additional service will be maintained, but within the framework of general governments. . . .

This reform will substantially reduce the number of special districts, but more vitally it will eliminate one of their principal causes and will strengthen local government.

On the assumption that extensive area mergers of counties and other general units will not soon materialize, it is obvious that the recommendation just made will not eliminate all nonschool districts. Even if consolidations of general units do unexpectedly develop on a broad basis, special districts will still be needed for areas which are extremely large or which involve difficult jurisdictional questions. Some rural types are illustrative of the former and some metropolitan ones, especially those embracing land in two states, are examples of the latter. Although the broader use of intergovernmental contracts should be encouraged in some of these situations, a supplementary reform proposal is also to the point.

The suggestion is that many of the remaining single-purpose districts be brought within multipurpose district operations. This would require the elimination by state legislatures of much of the remaining district enabling legislation and its replacement by legislation possessing a multipurpose base. . . .

This recommendation for multipurpose legislation would reduce the overlapping of districts and the diffusion of authority and responsibility. In effect, it would establish another class of general governments which would be limited in number.

A number of less important and less meaningful suggestions can be made. One is to increase state supervision and reporting. A second is to broaden county governmental control over budget preparation and execution when districts are smaller than counties. Another is to revise the state laws to effect a greater uniformity in the basic characteristics and procedures of special districts. Still another is to require that the state or county government investigate requests for creating new districts. All of these moderate recommendations would improve the situation, but none of them would really come to grips with the basic difficulty. It appears, therefore, that the two major reform proposals — to make many nonschool districts parts of general local units and to convert many others to a multipurpose form — are needed to alleviate the growing special district problem. Each can be applied alone, but in combination they will be much more effective. . . .

Although at present regarded as detrimental, the growth of special districts may sooner or later serve as the impetus necessary to bring about needed and long overdue changes across the whole fabric of local government. In the future, therefore, special districts may be evaluated as having been a necessary and vital evolutionary step toward a general advance in the adequacy and quality of government in the United States.

The most familiar of the special districts are of course the school districts, which comprise almost half of all the governmental units in the United States. It is here, however, as Professor Bollens pointed out, that by far the greatest success has been achieved in area reorganization of government. The reduction since World War II in the total number of school districts has been remarkable. A long-standing controversy between many educators and political scientists deals with the question of whether school systems should be a part of the government of the cities and counties in which they exist, or separate and independent units of government despite their serving the same area and population and being supported by the same taxpayers. The following article summarizes the contentions of both sides and argues a case for semi-integration as a possible practical resolution of this controversy.

66

Toward City-School District Rapprochement

By Robert L. Morlan

IN TERMS of the size of the public served, the importance of the service, the number of public employees involved, and the magnitude of total budgets,

Robert L. Morlan, "Toward City-School District Rapprochement," *Public Administration Review*, Spring, 1958, pp. 113–117. Footnotes in original omitted. Reprinted by permission of the publisher, the American Society for Public Administration.

the administration of public education in the United States is truly a major segment of governmental activity. Yet it has functioned in relative isolation from other public services and almost completely out of touch with the rest of the public administration profession. Public education is in large measure administered through more than 50,000 separate, independent units of government. Its practitioners rarely take academic training in the broad field of public administration, and they are brought up through a system of intellectual inbreeding within the collegiate departments and schools of education. Professional contacts tend to be limited to the education field; only occasionally does a representative from the public schools participate in an association of public administrators. Not uncommonly there is a measure of guarded verbal sniping across the very real boundary between the two fields.

This verbal battle of separation versus integration has been waged in a desultory fashion for a great many years without much visible success for either side. There have been few if any notable conversions, perhaps in part because of the rather dogmatic and unbending nature of the arguments expressed by spokesmen for each point of view. Is it not time to consider seriously the possibility that there may be certain merits in both sets of arguments, and to discard the uncompromising "all or nothing" approach in favor of attempting to develop more significant avenues of intergovernmental cooperation in this area?

The separation-integration argument

Every profession quite naturally develops not only its own jargon but also certain creeds of orthodoxy. The desirability of operating schools through independent districts has traditionally constituted one such creed among the educational administrators, something to which each neophyte must subscribe in order to be a respectable member of the fraternity. While hardly a burning issue in other areas of public service, the mere suggestion of possible advantages in the integration of public educational and general units of local government can raise blood pressures rapidly within this group. On the other hand, most students of public administration have been conditioned to believe in the benefits of integrated organization as a virtually unvarying principle, almost regardless of special circumstances.

The educators have contended that education should be separate because it is so big, because it is not like other functions of government, because independence insures better financial support for the schools, because it keeps the schools "out of politics," and because it focuses public attention upon the schools and thus guarantees greater interest and support.

In turn, the "political scientist-general administrator clan" has replied that education from an administrative point of view is no more different from other functional services, such as social welfare and fire protection, than they are different from each other, and that the logical extension of the principle of independence would be the chaos of a separate unit of government for every major governmental service. Experience, they say, does not indicate that the schools suffer financially in the integrated ("dependent") systems that exist, nor does it appear that school districts have been unusually immune from corrupt politics. In the proper sense of the term "politics," moreover, school systems ought to be *in* politics — actively responsive to the people they serve — a theme vigorously supported by the education profession. Further, extensive public interest is hardly apparent at present in the notoriously small voting turnout in the average school board election or in the attentiveness of the public to the board's actions once elected.

In a more positive vein, the general administrator would contend that the citizen-taxpayer would benefit from a more comprehensively planned budget and tax program which included education with other local government services, that a great deal of costly duplicating activity could be eliminated, and that responsibility to the public would be enhanced by ending the confusion caused by the existence of these separate governmental units and focusing attention upon a single one.

A special problem area of current significance, to which very little systematic attention has been given, is that of direct conflicts between governments arising where separate city and school governments serve essentially the same community. While a certain amount of intergovernmental cooperation normally exists, there are an increasing number of friction points — particularly in areas of rapid growth. When the school district builds a new building can the city require it, like any other developer of property, to put in street improvements and sidewalks and to plant trees as a condition of permission for development? If not, is the city responsible for a condition it did not create? If facilities are constructed in a previously undeveloped area, is the city obliged suddenly to distort its engineering budget to construct access roads and water mains? How much of the summer recreation program can the city expect the school district to handle? Is it the city's or the school district's responsibility to hire crossing guards on city streets adjacent to school buildings? And the list goes on.

Each government has a limited budget; as a rule neither is eager to assume any tasks that are not clearly its responsibility. Complete separation of school districts either creates or intensifies such difficulties; a single authority contributes to the planned and orderly solution of the various problems.

How different is education?

While the functions and problems of administrators in different governmental activities may be fundamentally similar, they tend to have their own peculiar characteristics. Is it true that education is a basically distinctive function? What are some of the features which may make educational administration look "different"? Certainly the sheer magnitude of the job being accomplished is in itself impressive — some 30 million children in the schools, involving the work of over 1.25 million teachers and a total annual expenditure of more than $8 billion. School systems are faced not only with burgeoning enrollments but also with steadily increasing demands as to what they should be doing for this multitude of children.

In the second place, school administration commonly operates in a comparatively favorable public relations environment. With only occasional exceptions the press tends to handle school matters relatively sympathetically and with a minimum of sensationalism. There is rarely a continuous focus of attention upon them. Moreover, the American public is conditioned to a belief in the desirability of public education and is inclined to accept rather readily proposals which are said to be for the good of the schools. The public is also less likely to think of the school system as "government," and it thus escapes some of the effects of the basic American antagonism toward government and politics.

In this connection, educational administration benefits tremendously from the solid backing of a "built-in" pressure group, the National Congress of Parents and Teachers. Here is a large body of citizens, feeling an obligation to be a part of the organization while their children are in school, who by the very nature of the relationship are easily influenced by the school administration. It in no way detracts from the very real importance of the PTA to note its usefulness to the administrator as a sounding board and a base of support on policy questions. While many administrative agencies have a special clientele group which is similarly useful, few are blessed with one of such size and malleability, which, at the same time, represents such a complete cross-section of the population.

Differences in personnel and budget matters are essentially differences in degree. The educational administrator is no less concerned with personnel management than is the general administrator, but the problems tend to be more narrowly channelized. The majority of the personnel are professional people, a situation which provides its own headaches, but the process of recruitment is simplified and no really elaborate classification system is necessary. While it is difficult at present to secure adequate numbers of qualified teachers, eligibility is determined through a procedure of state certification based primarily upon academic training. The common practice of providing a formal system of "tenure" for the professional group injects an added complication. For so-called "noncertificated" personnel, principally clerical, service, and maintenance, a more familiar pattern of recruitment, testing, and classification is prevalent.

Stretching a limited budget in the attempt to cover all needs is of course a universal administrative challenge, but it may be true that tax increases and bond issues are often a bit easier to secure for schools than for other purposes. At least the school district finds fewer problems of allocation than does a multipurpose unit of government. It performs a single function, and the bulk of its current funds goes into salaries. There is normally very little variety in revenue sources, dependence in most communities being almost exclusively upon the general property tax and state aids.

Since school districts are ordinarily able to concentrate upon the sole function of education, they need not be concerned with functions incidental to the main task, such as assessment and collection of taxes, which are necessarily major activities of the general unit of government. Such services are usually performed for them by county governments. Indeed, it is a striking fact that although school districts are so often independent of the cities which share much the same area and population, they are commonly more dependent than other units upon both the county and the state.

While the states, of course, exercise authority over all local governmental units, they have tended to subject school district activities to unusually detailed regulation. For example, the state legislature may fix the minimum length of the school term, provide that a certain percentage of school funds must be used for teacher salaries, and prohibit paying a salary to any teacher who is not certified by the state. The state department of education not uncommonly has power to approve or reject proposed building plans, to prescribe the use of certain texts, and to require specific physical equipment. Its influence is greatly extended through the issuance of various manuals and curriculum guides, the sponsorship of conferences and other training programs, and through inspections, audits, and report requirements. A considerable amount of this state control is exercised through the mechanisms of the ordinarily extensive state grant-in-aid programs.

The case for partial integration

While it would seem to be apparent that administrative differences provide no significant grounds for separation, yet size, tradition, and other considerations may nevertheless justify for education a relationship different from that which prevails for other local functions. Not only is opposition to integration strong among most public school administrators, but the volume of business and number of difficult problems already facing the average city council will not lead many councils to seek the addition of school responsibilities.

The logical development seems to lie in the direction of a type of semi-integration of the schools and general government whereby most of the advantages of an integrated organization might be accomplished while retaining areas of independence for the schools. Under such a proposal the school system might become a part of city (or in certain cases county) government, but continue to have its own board for certain policy determinations and the selection of the "superintendent." Such an arrangement might, incidentally, tend to keep the schools from being embroiled in controversies involving other departments, and vice versa.

In view of the immensity of their expenditures, it is probably desirable to retain a separately designated tax levy for the schools. This is useful from a public information point of view, and the public also is perhaps better able to swallow two tax bites than one all-inclusive one.

Despite these features of separation or independence, the significant advantages of cooperative budget and tax planning, centralized assessment and collection, a single treasury management, centralized purchasing, and so on could be realized through partial integration. Bond issues may often be sold by such a joint unit at a more favorable rate than a school district alone could hope to secure, and the shifting of temporary fund surpluses may not uncommonly reduce or eliminate costly tax anticipation borrowing. There is no good reason why the city attorney's office cannot serve as legal counsel for the school system, why the services of the city engineer's office should not be made available, or why the central personnel office should not handle personnel matters involving noncertificated school employees. Much needless conflict and confusion in the field of physical planning could be avoided. Integration in some of these areas already exists in certain places, but frequently it is haphazard and at best it includes only a minority of districts.

As city administration continues to become more and more professionalized, some of the existing barriers to city-school integration may be broken down. It is undoubtedly true that little advantage could be gained by integrating the schools with a city government which is itself unintegrated, and there is interesting evidence of a more favorable attitude on the part of some educators toward a degree of integration with council-manager-type city governments.

Much could be achieved by a sincere effort on the part of those in the public administration profession and their counterparts in the education field to improve their understanding of one another's problems, methods, and accomplishments, especially through the informal contacts possible in the local and regional professional associations. In the colleges and universities there is an obligation on the part of the departments and schools of education and of political science and public administration to consider ways in which the traditional chasm may be bridged through better mutual understanding. This may take the form of cooperatively taught seminars and the wider acceptance of credits toward "majors" for courses given in the other departments; but at least it should involve the inclusion of relevant materials and discussion in courses in the respective fields. There are also numerous untapped opportunities for significant cooperative research.

Educational administrators and those of the generalist point of view have traded rather fruitless arguments at arm's length for long enough. Can they not turn now to a cooperative approach toward coordination and integration that will enable the citizen to benefit from better and more economical local government services?

CHAPTER FIFTEEN

The Metropolitan Area Problem

PERHAPS THE MOST ACUTE set of problems in the whole field of local government today arises in our steadily mushrooming metropolitan areas — problems for which a number of possible solutions have been proposed but few adopted. There is a great deal of current research on the subject, and a vast amount of writing in recent years. The nature of the "disease" is first diagnosed by a distinguished scholar and public administrator, Luther Gulick, former city administrator for New York City, who suggests a series of broad courses of required action. Professor Smallwood then provides a careful evaluation of the first ten years of experience in Toronto under the North American continent's principal experiment with "metropolitan federalism." Proposals for metropolitan areas take many forms, some broad gauge and others constituting perhaps only an indirect or tangential approach. In the next article Chester Bain explains Virginia's unique system of city-county separation by judicial process. The reader is also referred to article 60 in Chapter 12, where the various techniques of the "metropolitan county" are discussed.

67

Design for the Future

By Luther Gulick

How CAN the metropolitan areas of America get the governmental services and powers they now need to deal effectively with their new metropolitan problems? This is now the toughest domestic governmental problem of the United States, in the opinion of many.

The metropolitan age is now upon us. Well over 60 per cent of the American people now live in and around what the United States Census Bureau calls

Luther Gulick, "Design for the Future," *National Municipal Review,* January, 1957, pp. 6–13. Footnotes in original omitted. Reprinted by permission of the publisher.

standard metropolitan areas. With an expanding national population, the only areas of marked growth now are these 174 standard metropolitan areas. In fact, in the years 1950 to 1955, 97 per cent of the national growth, made up of 11.5 million people, took place in metropolitan areas, while rural areas were losing almost 2 per cent of their population.

In 1950, even before these changes, the standard metropolitan areas, with a land area of 7 per cent of the nation, contained 69.8 per cent of the manufacturing employees of the United States, 63.8 per cent of business and professional workers and 65.9 per cent of those in wholesale and retail trade, and were responsible for 77.1 per cent of the total national value added by manufacture. These metropolitan workers have over twice the median income of the farm workers and, interestingly enough, a more equal distribution of income over their whole populations. The greater the center, the greater the average income and the less the index of inequality.

The resulting agglomerations of population are not evenly spaced over the continent. They are heavily concentrated in three zones: first, a wedge which runs along the northeast coast for 600 miles and across the country to the Mississippi River; second, a narrower strip along the Pacific coast; and, third, an area along the lower Mississippi and west into Texas.

As the result of these dramatic population developments we now have great patches of urbanized population, with interwoven cities, suburbs, ribbon developments, homes, factories and shopping centers, and then more cities, suburbs, factories and shops, each within easy commuting and shopping distance of the next, stretching over the country often for hundreds of miles.

This is a new pattern of life.

The people who live in this new pattern of industrial, commercial and cultural life, even in the "country," are no longer rural folks, tied to the soil and to a distinct local culture and economy. They are urbanites, with all the tastes, demands and education of city people. They want and must have all the special services, amenities and governmental controls which in the recent past we thought were required only in the cities and the geographically restricted territories of isolated dense settlement.

This new pattern of life in America is not temporary. It will not recede. It is just at its beginning and is destined to advance vigorously unless, of course, our whole society is wiped out in some nuclear holocaust. The proof of this statement is obvious to all: our national population is growing rapidly again. Within 50 years, we will be a nation of not less than 300 million souls. Where is this great added population going? Can it go onto the farms? Into the rural areas? Certainly not. It will go where there is high income and where there are "city standards." Not less than 120 million people will go right into and around the metropolitan areas even if we build a few sparkling "new towns" in fulfillment of the dreams of the planners. But even these new towns must be within the metropolitan complexes we already have, because they too must have high standards and high wages.

Another proof of the permanence of metropolitanism is the way factories and industrial expansions are now located. What determines their location today? Not power, not rail connections, not raw materials. Nine out of ten new plants are located to reach the market, the mass metropolitan market, and to draw on its labor reserve and facilities.

Another proof that what we have started will expand rather than shrink is the continued growth of privately owned cheap transportation, the automobile and truck now and the aircraft tomorrow. This revolutionary private, flexible transportation rests on three factors: (1) mass production of low priced automobiles; (2) fast and hard roads; and (3) high wages and short hours for industrial and other workers, which bring the ownership and the extensive use of the auto within reach of at least 80 per cent of our

families. Is this development going to slow down? Not with all the new expressways we are building, toll free, with federal and local subsidies.

From these facts, there is only one deduction: this new great, metropolitan regionalism, these extensive patches of contiguous urban settlement, are not only here to stay, they will be broader and thicker, more intermeshed, with each decade.

This fact creates new problems for government.

Breakdown of government

Already we are painfully conscious of the breakdown of our governmental services and institutions in handling the governmental problems of these new metropolitan areas. Everywhere traffic and mass movement is strangling urban life. Each new traffic "improvement" is immediately swallowed up with oversaturation while streets designed for movement have been turned into car storage and freight yards. Even with the heroic efforts to end bad housing, most cities are faced with spreading slums and increased decay. Water is short in many great cities and sewage disposal and air pollution control fall far behind our needs. And what a sad situation exists in the schools, even more overcrowded in the new suburbs than in the old cities! The crime rate, rising sharply since 1944, is not a bad indicator of many other strains and shortages.

The breakdown of services and controls in the new metropolitan concentrations is bad in itself. But the catastrophic factor is that we have as yet no adequate institutions, governmental or nongovernmental, capable of doing anything effective about this rising tide of human need.

As a result, individual cities strive to "solve" their own water problem, pushing others into a shortage position. Parents migrate to uncongested areas and soon the schools, water systems, sewers and other services are overwhelmed. Each new superhighway we build draws factories and homes and shopping centers and restaurants into "the open country," where there is no planning and zoning, and soon the beauty and convenience are lost or pushed further and further into inaccessibility and congestion becomes even more intolerable at the old centers.

We rush to tackle the modernization of the cities with "urban renewal," and find that the urban center itself is frequently too restricted to deal even with its own housing, its total traffic and mass transportation pattern, its need for recreation, to say nothing of water and wastes and the suitable location of future industrial developments. And even within the central city the governmental structure is confused and chaotic. Speaking of urban renewal efforts, the *Baltimore Sun* of September 23, 1956, says editorially:

We have plenty of cheer leaders, public and private. We have a housing authority, a planning commission and a planning department, a zoning board, a redevelopment commission. The health department is busy enforcing a housing code and the police department and fire department enforce the building code. There is a special housing court. There is the Citizens Planning and Housing Association, the Downtown Committee, the Greater Baltimore Committee and other private groups too numerous to mention. All are useful. Yet the place keeps going to pot.

As the Council of State Governments points out in its recent report to the Governors' Conference, the metropolitan problem is a series of unsolved problems characterized by inadequate governmental structure, service and regulatory defects, financial inequalities and weaknesses, and deficiencies in citizen control.

This breakdown of governmental and nongovernmental social institutions in the face of the new metropolitan spread comes, I am convinced, primarily from ignoring three clear social laws. These are: the law of continuity, Gresham's Law applied to land use, and the law of the whole.

Fundamental causes

The law of continuity is a law of land use in urban areas. It is also a law of economics and of human behavior, because "use" means use by human beings. The law of continuity says that the free use of each piece of urban land tends to be controlled by the surrounding land. This is the law, which even without zoning puts shopping districts together, which centers business and financial activities and groups amusements. This is the law which accumulates racial and economic residential districts be they rich or poor, black, yellow or white. This is the law which explains why the front foot value of neighboring lots is approximately the same while, in the country, neighboring farms vary not by propinquity but by their soil and natural resource factors.

Now we come to Gresham's Law. We all recognize that most improvements to urban land tend to become obsolete. This is certainly true of housing, factories, business edifices, street patterns and such services as water, sewers, pavements, etc. You notice I leave out cathedrals, great parks, true monuments and noble vistas! They do not depreciate with age. Gresham's Law applied to this situation says that "the bad tends to drive out the good." That is, the slums tend to spread as if by contagion. Rooming houses tend to take over the old residential areas and force respectability out; run-down factories run down the factory sections; cheap shops depreciate the better shops next door; low-grade amusements tend to

honky-tonk their neighbors; and shabby business establishments drive out the up-and-coming.

The individual owner is almost helpless in this situation. If you own a good apartment house in a neighborhood that is being taken over by blight on both sides of you, there is almost nothing you can afford to do alone to save your investment except to "go along with destiny." A vicious element in this picture comes from the fact that the new "bad" uses are not always productive economically, as when overcrowded rooming houses take the place of depreciated private homes.

Another sad fact is that depreciation marches inexorably piece by piece, without organized effort, and spreads by contagion; while regeneration can come only in large composite units, with extensive organized effort, because of the law of continuity.

The law of continuity, and especially Gresham's Law, are important not only for the land but also for the buildings. Unlike most other goods which are manufactured and sold for human use, buildings once located cannot be moved except at great cost. They are fixed in a given location and tied by that location to their neighbors. This profoundly alters their status and the economic laws which govern. Houses and factories are bought and sold like other things; but always in their context, tied to their neighbors and to the land ownership pattern established by the past. For this reason, the second-hand market which gives us such a good solution for supplying automobiles and furniture, for example, even to the lowest income levels, does not give us an equally good solution for furnishing second-hand housing even to the middle-income levels. An entirely different set of economic and social factors is apparently involved because of the law of continuity.

The third law we must recognize is the law of the whole. This is a law of administration. It says that the chances of dealing satisfactorily with any complicated situation or problem increase when you have before you all the significant elements and decrease when any of these elements are missing. To do the whole job, you need the whole problem, not one or two of the interdependent parts. You cannot solve a chess problem with half the board and pieces hidden; nor build across a river half of a suspension bridge; nor let two architects work independently and at the same time on one building. The law of the whole applies even to a good dinner or a good conference program not only because too many cooks spoil the broth but also because you need one guiding genius from "soup to nuts."

The laws applied

I dare say that no one disagrees violently with what I have written so far. Now let me apply the law of continuity, of which Gresham's Law is an element, and the law of the whole to the governmental problems of the metropolitan regions.

With the new pattern of settlement and work in the already dominant but still expanding metropolitan regions of this continent, the law of continuity is already binding together, as in a single social, economic and cultural web, great patches of population and great masses of land. This growing human continuity over vast stretches of industrialized and urbanized geography is lifting more and more of our urban services and controls out of discreet localized patterns and weaving them together in larger and larger wholes. Continuity does this by natural law.

But how are we trying to deal with these new problems? We are trying to deal with them initially through the desperate efforts of each little local government, no one of which can reach more than small pieces of each situation. Thus we violate the law of the whole and wonder why we fail. How can any one small sector of a great metropolitan region solve its water supply problem alone? How can one segment solve its general traffic or mass transportation problems alone? Or its housing problem? Or its waste disposal problem? Or its health or crime or air pollution problems, in isolation? There is a law of the whole which stands squarely in the path of fractionated administration, fractionated plans, fractionated decisions.

Yes indeed "we have plenty of cheer leaders, public and private. . . . Yet the place keeps going to pot."

And from this I draw the rather obvious conclusion that our present governmental and social institutions in the metropolitan areas are just as obsolete as are the old city centers themselves with their inadequate street patterns, traffic congestions, spreading slums and decadent business, shopping and recreational facilities. Our local governments are not solving the basic urban problems, and they cannot, however hard they try, each working alone. The new problems cannot be faced the old way. They can only be tackled in accordance with the law of continuity and the law of the whole.

While the application of these two laws constructively and in detail will call for a great deal of hard thinking, particularly the idea of unifying the end product of administration while separating the "aspects of functions," we can be sure that solutions which ignore these laws will get us nowhere.

Next steps

And this brings me to nine suggestions for action.

1. The major responsibility for governmental action now passes to the state governments under the American constitutional system. As says the *Model State Constitution* of the National Municipal League in Article VIII, "Provision shall be made by general law for the incorporation of counties, cities and other civil divisions," and the constitutions of most states, like that of New York, running back to 1846, say in so many words, "It shall be the duty of the legislature to provide for the organization of cities and incorporated villages" and for counties and all the other institutions of local and regional government (Article IX).

This state responsibility for the machinery of local government and the needs of the metropolitan areas can be approached through several major lines of action:

a. The creation of state commissions of inquiry to find out what the metropolitan areas of each state will look like over the next generation and to design the appropriate new governmental structures to meet the requirements. They may be governor's commissions, legislative commissions or joint commissions designed to meet the needs and the possibilities of each situation.

b. The development of existing state services in such ways as to be of particular value in meeting the governmental service and control needs of the state's metropolitan regions. The state can be especially useful in dealing with water supply, and over-all traffic, health, educational, housing, recreational and planning matters.

c. The passage of enabling legislation designed to permit local governments to work together on their local problems more effectively.

d. The drafting of appropriate interstate compacts through interstate cooperation for those of the 23 interstate metropolitan districts which have problems that cannot be solved by unilateral state action; and

e. The creation of special purpose local authorities and agencies to deal on a regional basis with one or more identifiable services.

However, I am inclined to think that we should now emphasize the creation of exploratory commissions and the extension of state services, particularly as to planning, and should go slow on enabling legislation and the creation of new authorities or compacts until we have a clearer answer to our problems.

2. There is a further task for the states which cannot longer be postponed. This is the task of starting now to hold back from intensive development and urban settlement large tracts of carefully and scientifically selected land for three long purposes: first, to serve as the rights of way for future communication sytems; second, to become the recreation areas of the future; and third, to aid in maintaining man's

ecological equilibrium. These are extremely important matters, the significance of which is not measured by the space I am giving them here. The thing that makes them vitally significant now is partly the new federal aid throughway program but even more the rapid pace of uncontrolled metropolitan spread and its progressive destruction of the human habitat.

3. While it is clearly the state government, under our constitutional system, which must step up now and begin to think and act, this in no way lessens the responsibility or the opportunity of the local communities within the metropolitan areas. Perhaps competitive localities cannot settle these problems, but they can do a lot of exploring, a lot of imaginative thinking, and they can "put on the heat." Part of this action can be taken by official governmental officers, as has been done by Mayor Robert E. Wagner in the tri-state New York region, but nongovernmental local action is also essential as has been demonstrated by the Allegheny Conference in Pittsburgh, the Greater Baltimore Committee, the Municipal League of Seattle and King County, the Cleveland "Metro" and in St. Louis by Civic Progress Inc. The local drive for action may well be the starting point. In any case it is indispensable.

4. The federal government has a responsibility too. This involves the management of federal programs so that they will not make matters worse but will contribute to solutions and to the mutual integration of federal activities as they touch the metropolitan regions. Fortunately this is now beginning to be recognized in Washington with the appointment on the White House staff of a special assistant to the president on intergovernmental affairs and the assignment of the Bureau of the Budget to assist him in a staff capacity for this work, particularly in the metropolitan areas. Surely the federal programs on urban renewal, mortgage insurance, hospitals, schools and interurban highways must be tied into each other and into the needs of the urban areas more directly and consciously.

Finance requirements

5. The financing requirements of governmental activities and services in the metropolitan areas now call for an entirely fresh attack on the theory and practice of local taxation, debts, prices and tolls, and fiscal and revenue administration. We cannot rely on the local tax systems we now have nor on the simple extension of tolls and charges to carry the budgets of the revised structures which are clearly in the offing. We must have new fundamental and comprehensive thinking before we move aimlessly and precipitately into the taxes, charges and debts of the future.

In this area we need fundamental research most of all. . . .

6. Another area of required fundamental research relates to the realities of political leadership and action in the changing metropolitan areas and the impact of these factors on the design of appropriate political institutions. . . .

. . . .

8. The time has come for inventive thinking and action as inventive as were our forefathers when, in the face of great need, they brought the squabbling colonies together under the federal constitution of the United States in 1789. And it may well be that they set for us a pattern of federalism nationally which we now need to adopt locally in the metropolitan regions. Certain it is that annexation of suburbs to the great cities is seldom the answer for which we are seeking today in the metropolitan areas, and that nothing but chaos will follow the creation of a flock of single function state "authorities" each to handle one of the many new needs of the metropolis. It may even be appropriate in the largest cities we already have to experiment with smaller internal units of administrative and civic action, recognizing the danger of already unwieldy constituencies in big democracy.

Action by citizens

9. Finally the American people as a whole need to see themselves, from now on, in a different role. We are now, and are destined to be for the future, an urbanized and industrialized nation, in which most of the people do live and work, and want to live and work, in great metropolitan regions. This changes our whole outlook on the governmental needs of these areas and on the nature of the services and controls and political architecture we now require. We are not dealing with a temporary situation. This is now normal, natural and permanent. The sooner our business leaders, labor leaders, educators, newspaper editors, civic groups and governmental researchers, governmental officials at all levels, and planners begin to think and act on this new basis, the better off shall we be, and the sooner shall we redesign the physical and institutional trappings of the metropolitan region to meet the needs of our people.

There may be those who think that what is happening to America in the metropolitan areas is an unmitigated calamity. But this is not a calamity, it is a challenge, the response to which will carry us to new levels of effective democratic life.

68

Metro Toronto: A Decade Later

By Frank Smallwood

ON APRIL 15, 1953, when the Municipality of Metropolitan Toronto held its first council meeting in the red-carpeted chamber of Ontario's Provincial Parliament building, one crucial question monopolized its agenda: "Will it work: And can it be made to produce results that the previous system did not produce?" Some ten years later enough evidence has accumulated to subject this question to the acid realities of the test of time.

In making an appraisal of Metro's first decade, it is necessary to recognize that the original framework of this first, full-scale North American experiment in metropolitan integration was never regarded as providing the final answer to all of Toronto's pressing problems. Instead, Toronto's new government was an interim product of conflict and compromise, between the central city demanding full-scale amalgamation of all neighboring communities and its adjacent suburbs insisting upon retaining their local autonomy. The Metro organization, as finally conceived, represented an attempt to bridge the gap between these two extremes, with the "Cumming Report" (i.e. the report of the Ontario Municipal Board, under the chairmanship of Lorne R. Cumming, which recommended the creation of the new governmental body) displaying a pragmatic awareness of the art of the possible under the then-prevailing circumstances. The Ontario Municipal Board "quite frankly attempted to prepare a plan . . . acceptable and practicable and not too far in advance of the existing level of public opinion . . ."

The result was a federation of local municipalities, which particularly accommodated local demands in two areas: (1) the division of powers between the new Metropolitan Council and the existing local municipalities; and (2) the system of representation of these municipalities upon this new Council.

Frank Smallwood, *Metro Toronto: A Decade Later,* (Toronto: Bureau of Municipal Research, 1963), pp. 1–12, 16–19, 28–29, 32–33, 35, 38–39. Footnotes in original omitted. Reprinted by permission of the author and the publisher.

THE ORIGINAL SETTING

At the time of its inception, the Metropolitan Council was given exclusive jurisdiction over only a limited number of basic services, most notably assessment, borrowing and major arterial highways.

The thirteen local municipalities were also given exclusive jurisdiction over only a limited number of services such as police, licensing, fire protection, libraries and local tax collection.

The great majority of major services were shared between the Metropolitan Council and the local municipalities, or between a number of quasi-independent boards and the local municipalities. Services shared between Metro and the local municipalities included planning, parks and recreation, water supply, sewage disposal and welfare. Responsibility for public housing was divided between a number of special housing boards and the thirteen municipalities, while the educational services were shared between a new Metropolitan School Board and a group of locally elected school boards.

Finally, another new quasi-independent group, the Toronto Transit Commission, was given exclusive control over all forms of public transportation, exclusive of railroads and taxis.

The essence of this original scheme was that Metro was to perform a "wholesaler" role in such service fields as water supply, sewage disposal and the like, while the local municipalities were to perform a "retailer" role in these same fields. Above all else, through its exclusive control over borrowing for all local government agencies (i.e. itself, the thirteen local municipalities, the quasi-independent boards, and the Toronto Transit Commission), Metro was designated to serve as the central capital works agency for the entire Greater Toronto complex. In effect, it was expected to provide the means, both financially and jurisdictionally, to carry out the major public works projects which were so badly needed throughout the Toronto metropolitan area.

The basic allocation of powers has remained essentially intact during the past ten years, although three significant changes were made following a Provincial review of Metro's operations in 1957. At that time Metro was given exclusive jurisdiction over the police and air polution services, while licensing was moved up into the "shared" services category.

While the initial allocation of responsibilities between the two tiers of government involved some difficult problems of accommodation, the representative arrangements that went into the making of the new Metropolitan Council presented an issue of even more controversial political overtones.

The 240 square mile Toronto metropolitan area contains thirteen local municipalities that fan out from the north shore of Lake Ontario in three concentric rings. At the very center of the area is the City of Toronto, which although by far the largest of the thirteen local governments, was experiencing a slight population decline during the immediate post-war period.

A second "inner ring" consists of nine suburban municipalities adjacent to, and encircling, the central city. While each of these nine municipalities had experienced some population growth during the post-war period, this growth was relatively small in absolute numbers, since all nine were reasonably well developed by the time of Metro's inception.

Finally, there is a third, "outer ring" of three large suburban communities: Etobicoke to the west, North York to the north, and Scarborough to the east. These three units, which were largely undeveloped in 1953, occupy a huge land area, and as Table 1 illustrates, they were already experiencing a massive population boom:

Table 1
POPULATION GROWTH: 1945–53

	1945	1953	% Increase
City of Toronto 35.1 sq. mi.	681,802	665,502	− 2%
"Inner Ring" 23.0 sq. mi.			
York	81,652	100,463	+23%
East York	43,266	65,736	+51%
Forest Hill	13,960	17,719	+27%
Leaside	9,227	15,910	+72%
Mimico	8,785	12,301	+40%
New Toronto	8,498	11,190	+30%
Swansea	7,142	8,344	+17%
Weston	6,214	8,374	+35%
Long Branch	5,049	9,140	+81%
"Outer Ring" 182.0 sq. mi.			
North York	25,100	110,311	+339%
Scarborough	24,140	78,803	+226%
Etobicoke	21,274	70,209	+230%
Totals	936,109	1,174,002	25%

In devising a formula to provide for the representation of these thirteen municipalities on the new Metropolitan Council, the major problem related to the realization of an equitable balance between the central city and the twelve suburbs taken as a whole. Since the City of Toronto contained approximately half the metropolitan area population, the "Cumming Report" concluded that there should be an equal division of seats between (1) the city and (2) the twelve suburbs, and it recommended that each of

these two groups should have four representatives on a nine-member council (with the ninth member, the chairman, being appointed by the Province). In the words of the Report, "there is at the present time a serious cleavage of interest between the city . . . and the suburbs . . . and until a better spirit of metropolitan unity is achieved, this cleavage must be recognized by giving equal representation to the two major divisions of the metropolitan population, notwithstanding the theoretical advantages of representation by population." However, in "Bill 80" (the final legislation actually establishing Metro), the Ontario Provincial Legislature rejected this formula, and instead provided for a twenty-five man council: twelve representatives from the City; one representative from each of the twelve suburbs; and an independent chairman, to be designated for the first two years by the Province, and elected annually thereafter by the Metropolitan Council.

The effect of this new formula was not so much to distort the representative balance between the City and the twelve suburbs taken as a whole, as it was to produce gross inequalities in representation between individual suburban municipalities. Swansea, for example, with 8,300 population was given one Council member, while North York, with 110,000 population, also received one representative on the Council. These initial inequalities were destined to increase dramatically during the ensuing decade.

The above division of powers and representative arrangements were the major influences shaping the initial organization of Toronto's new metropolitan government. In appraising this government's performance during the past ten years, a certain degree of speculation is inevitable, due to the fact that while relevant comparisons can be made between the pre-Metro years before 1953 and the current Metro performance in 1963, it is impossible to make the most meaningful comparison of all. This is, of course, an analysis of Metro Toronto as it actually exists in 1963 with its established metropolitan government, and Toronto as it would be in 1963 if this government had never been created.

The lack of any such comparative data poses especially difficult problems when one attempts to compile the debit side of Metro's ledger. Some of the problems noted in the ensuing analysis are as much an outgrowth of the environmental pressures which have accompanied Toronto's growing pains during the past ten years as they are the result of any actions, or lack of actions, on the part of Metro itself. While objectivity requires repeated emphasis of this fact, enough data is now available to provide a meaningful base for an analysis of Metro's major achievements, and limitations, in an effort to determine how well this governmental organization has fulfilled its original expectations.

METRO'S MAJOR ACHIEVEMENTS

Although Toronto's Metropolitan Council can point to a wide variety of accomplishments since 1953, three particular achievements stand out as being especially significant in terms of the challenges that Metro was designed to meet, and the environmental considerations that surrounded its original creation. These are: the realization of a strong base of public and political support for the metropolitan government concept; the resolution of a series of specific service crises; and the provision of a capital financial capability that has helped the Toronto metropolitan area meet the demands of its burgeoning population growth.

1. Securing its political base

The first, and in many aspects the foremost, accomplishment of the Metropolitan Council has been the realization of a solid expression of support for the general concept of metropolitan government in the Toronto area.

This is not to assert that the current Metropolitan Council is without critics, nor that suggestions are not being advanced for the total amalgamation of all local municipalities into one metropolitan city or for other basic changes in the status quo. It is to assert, however, that six months of interviews failed to produce a single individual who argued that Toronto should drop the concept of metropolitan government entirely, and revert to the independent governmental arrangements that had existed prior to Metro's creation in 1953. While some might hold that mere self-perpetuation can hardly be classified as a major achievement, the political tensions that surrounded Metro's birth argue otherwise.

The first and most crucial difficulty the new Council had to face was the widespread suspicion, if not acrimony, with which the existing municipalities greeted its initial establishment. Neither the central city nor the twelve suburban communities had realized their basic objectives in the final Metro compromise, and in 1953 it was by no means certain that they would not attempt to gang up on the new metropolitan government in an attempt to undermine its very survival.

In addition, since the Toronto program represented the first major experiment in metropolitan federation on the North American continent, there was little in the way of precedent, and the Council faced the necessity of improvising, and proving itself in the harsh glare of widespread publicity.

Three factors have enabled Metro to meet this challenge — the force of personality; the political significance of the representative formula utilized in determining the Metro Council membership; and the specific nature of the program priorities that Metro has elected to push the hardest.

The first of these three factors — the force of personality — highlights the crucial role of Metro's original chairman (1953 to 1961), Frederick Goldwin Gardiner.

To say that Gardiner — a highly successful, tough and dynamic Toronto corporation lawyer — ran a taut ship during his crucial tenure as Metro's chairman would classify as the understatement of this, or any other, year. Locally known as "Big Daddy" after the domineering character in Tennessee Williams' "Cat On a Hot Tin Roof," Chairman Gardiner provided a number of key ingredients that went into the making of Metro's initial success.

First, as a former Reeve (i.e. Mayor) of wealthy, suburban Forest Hill Village and as a successful lawyer of considerable personal means, Gardiner provided the Metro program with a symbolic aura of prestige, integrity and honesty. In addition, he transferred to this program his tremendous sense of personal drive, self-confidence and determination to "get things done." Third, as the former Vice-President of the Ontario Conservative Association, he was on very close terms with the then-Provincial Premier, Leslie Frost, and the personal liaison he established between Metro and the Provincial government was so close as to be characterized as a "Family Compact." Finally, and of most telling significance, Gardiner possessed an understanding of, and a willingness to utilize, his personal prestige and power to keep his potentially explosive Council from flying apart.

All four of the above elements are evident in Gardiner's terse explanation as to why he accepted the Metro chairmanship at Premier Frost's personal urging: "Hell, I knew what it was all about. I didn't want the job, but I knew someone would have to head it up — someone with the qualifications and who could afford it."

Despite more than occasional grumblings within Metro that Gardiner ran the organization as a tyrant, he was re-elected Chairman by the Metro Councillors for seven successive years, from 1955 through 1961. His tough, abrasive, pragmatic approach to the Council's problems attracted widespread support throughout the Toronto area. He provided the dramatic flair, and the symbolic sense of "no-nonsense" accomplishment that created a favorable image for the Metro operation.

It is important to observe, however, that Metro has paid a price for Chairman Gardiner's forceful approach to leadership. In essence, Gardiner became so closely identified with the entire Metro operation that it was often difficult to determine where he left off and where Metro began. The perspective of hindsight now indicates quite conclusively that much of Metro's original sense of purpose was actually embodied in the dynamic personage of its first chairman, rather than in any independently-conceived central philosophy. This fact has become increasingly obvious in the past two years, now that Gardiner has left the Council. Paradoxically, Gardiner's forceful brand of leadership played a crucial role in the successful launching of the Metro enterprise during the Council's formative years, yet once he had stepped down from his chairmanship post, he left a void that has threatened to undermine the subsequent success of the Metro operation during more recent years.

The second consideration contributing to Metro's successful political inauguration was also another paradoxical mixture of strength and potential weakness. This was the representative formula that went into the formation of the new Metropolitan Council.

The advantages of this formula were to be found in the fact that the mayors and other local political leaders in the area were automatic members of this new Council by virtue of their constituency positions in their local municipalities. As Council "insiders," they helped to formulate the new Metro program. Such an arrangement had the practical effect of diverting potential political attacks away from a wide-open, external assault against the basic concept of the new metropolitan governmental program. Instead, Metro's initial controversies were limited to a more restricted display of political in-fighting within the confines of Metro's council chambers. While the area's local political leaders may not have been in agreement with all of the Council's policies, they were hesitant to undermine the entire Metro operation, and in the process, do themselves out of a new job which carried considerable prestige and importance.

The benefits that accrued to the new government from this representative arrangement can be seen most clearly if one contrasts the formative years of the Toronto Council with the more recent formative experience of the new Winnipeg Metropolitan Corpo-

ration. In Winnipeg, the local political leaders are not members of the metropolitan council, and many of them, most notably the central city spokesmen, have launched bitter attacks against the basic concept of the existing Winnipeg metropolitan organization. While controversy also surrounded the early years of the Toronto program, it never took on the guise of such a broad external attack, but rather confined itself to a more genteel interplay for forces inside the Metropolitan Council. . . .

Hence Metro has been relatively immune from external political attack largely due to the inclusion of local political leadership on its Council. However, it is important to recognize that, while this representative formula may have helped initially to solidify the new government's early political base, it has not been without some very definite liabilities which, again, have become more apparent during recent years.

The third factor that has influenced the realization of a strong base for support for Toronto's metropolitan government is to be found in the Council's emphasis on public works' priorities.

To a large extent, this has been an inevitable response to a number of very serious crises, coupled with the capital financing mandate that Metro was given at its inception. Yet the observation should be made that Metro's emphasis on large physical projects has not been totally divorced from its continued political well-being.

An analysis of gross* cumulative capital and current expenditures from 1953 through December 31, 1962 (exclusive of education which is handled as a special account by the Metropolitan School Board) reveals quite clearly the nature of Metro's programmatic priorities:

---

* The figures are gross expenditures, exclusive of Provincial grants, etc., in an effort to give the clearest picture of how Metro felt it should expend its total resources.

Table 2
METRO'S CUMULATIVE GROSS EXPENDITURES: 1953–1962

Program	Capital Expenditures	Current Expenditures (Excluding Debt Charges)	Total	% of Total
Roads	$159,311,362	$ 45,964,774	$205,276,136	26.3%
Adm. of Justice & Protection	8,257,919	136,784,068	145,041,987	18.6%
Welfare & Housing	24,488,228	91,711,586	116,199,814	14.9%
Sewage	80,179,880	23,360,202	103,540,082	13.3%
Waterworks (Self-Liq.)	59,822,745	41,970,482	101,793,227	13.0%
Misc. & Gen. Admin.	1,028,436	43,488,900	44,517,336	5.7%
Toronto Transit Comm. (Metro Share only)	37,835,783		37,835,783	4.9%
Parks, Rec. & Conservation	14,973,811	10,933,716	25,907,527	3.3%
Totals	$385,898,164	$394,213,728	$780,111,892	100%

It is significant to note that three services — transportation, water supply and sewage disposal — have take up over 50% of all Metro's cumulative expenditures (capital plus current) since the Council inception in 1953. While each of these three services required huge capital outlays to alleviate desperately inadequate conditions that were fast approaching a crisis stage, it is also worth noting that Metro's expenditure pattern had some very direct political consequences.

In large measure, this pattern reflects the philosophy that Frederick Gardiner brought to the job of Metro Chairman. In his 1961 inaugural speech to the Metropolitan Council, when he announced his pending retirement and attempted to outline Metro's major achievements under his leadership, Gardiner made the telling observation that Metro's early years represented "a time when imagination had to be translated into physical accomplishments to prove that the first metropolitan government on the North American continent would work."

Gardiner reiterated this philosophy when he visited Winnipeg later in 1961, and in commenting on the problems of the embattled Winnipeg government, he observed, "the main thing is to get your plans, work out a system of priorities, and then put the steam shovels into the ground."

The political pay-off that comes from putting "the steam shovels into the ground" is, of course, obvious. One needs look no further in the United States than to the power positions of Robert Moses and the Port of New York Authority to see the role that tangible physical achievements can play in solidifying a position of political strength. Today, the direct evidence of many of Metro's most important accomplishments can be found throughout the metropolitan area, and this evidence ranges from a now adequate water supply system to the massive Frederick G. Gardiner expressway project taking shape on the north shore of Lake Ontario.

When Metro faces the challenge of explaining what it has been able to accomplish, there is a literal display of concrete evidence to justify its continued existence. As Professor John Grumm has noted, the policy "has been to place emphasis on tangible public works and to attack those problems where results could be immediate, concrete and apparent."

Whether this aspect of the Metro success story has also contained corresponding elements of potential liability is a difficult question to answer. Obviously, any governmental organization is limited to a definite amount of resources, and it can emphasize one type of program only at the expense of others. Existing evidence, shown later, does indicate that Metro has tended to underplay certain key responsibilities. Yet the point remains that the nature of existing needs, and the nature of Metro's original capital financing

mandate, indicated that the large public works projects would receive priority attention in the Council's new program.

In essence, Metro has been able to consolidate its base of support through the triumvirate of personality, political accommodation (in its Council representation formula), and an emphasis on physical priorities. The fact that some or all of these factors have created subsequent problems for the new government should not detract from the magnitude of this very basic initial feat.

2. Resolving specific service crises

The significance of a second major Metro achievement can best be understood through reference to the widely quoted local adage that Toronto's new government was "the product of desperation, rather than inspiration."

While this desperation was becoming more obvious on a wide variety of fronts, it was particularly apparent in the water supply, water pollution control, and education services. By 1953 the rapid post-war expansion of Greater Toronto was producing unprecedented demands on all three of these services with the most extreme crisis conditions buffeting the "outer ring" communities of North York, Etobicoke and Scarborough. . . .

As was indicated in Table 2, the Metropolitan Council has thrown its major energies into these crisis situations with spectacular results. During the past ten years water supply capacity has increased by 45 per cent to 345 million gallons per day, while trunk distribution mains have jumped from 85 to 207 miles. A comparable record has been established in sewage disposal where total treatment capacity has risen to 192 million gallons per day, a 70 per cent increase over ten years ago. School construction represents a third area of equally impressive accomplishments. Under the guidance of the Metropolitan School Board, an ambitious building program has been able to handle a 46 per cent area increase in public elementary enrollment, and a 92 per cent increase in secondary enrollment. Since 1954, the metropolitan area has witnessed the construction of some 175 new schools and 293 additions, at a capital cost of nearly $225 million. The result has been an increase of 166,055 pupil spaces in school accommodations. . . .

3. Provisions of capital finances

Metro's third major achievement — the provision of the capital financing necessary to meet steadily expanding local demands within Greater Toronto — represented another crucial consideration that led to the original establishment of the new governmental program. The fact that the new Council was given exclusive jurisdiction for assessment and capital borrowing for itself, for the area's special boards and commissions, and for the thirteen local municipalities provides the most striking evidence of the high priority that Metro's creators placed upon this particular responsibility. . . .

In the field of capital financing, inequalities between the different municipalities may well have taken place during the past ten years, but these may have been primarily the result of factors external to Metro, rather than any major actions on the part of Metro itself. The significance of Metro's achievement derives from the fact that it has enabled the municipalities to continue to borrow for their growing needs despite such external pressures. It has done this first, by acting as the debenture agent for these municipalities; and secondly, by assuming a variety of capital costs that the various municipalities previously had to meet on an individual basis.

Metro was established originally to provide the capital financing necessary to meet exploding growth problems throughout metropolitan Toronto, and in the past decade it has done just this. The fact that certain inequities have resulted begs the question of whether the original metropolitan federation concept has perhaps been too weak, rather than too strong, to permit the discharge of such responsibilities in an equitable fashion.

METRO'S MAJOR DIFFICULTIES

The three most difficult problems Metro has faced during its first decade have been quite closely interrelated. The first problem has contributed to the second, and both the first and second have influenced the third. . . . The three major problems are: the development of a growing imbalance in the economic resources, and burdens, between Metro's member municipalities; the failure to achieve a cohesive spirit of metropolitan unity among these members; and the reluctance on the part of Metro and its members to deal decisively with a number of important commitments and responsibilities.

1. The problems of economic imbalance

Since Toronto's Metro organization represented a very deliberate attempt to preserve a considerable degree of local diversity within the general framework of a larger metropolitan unity, it never promised to balance out all of the financial inequalities that existed between the various municipalities in the metropolitan Toronto area. Certainly, for example, this scheme was not designated to produce a completely uniform tax rate for all thirteen local communities. To the contrary, at least two factors indicated that such would not be the case.

First, the "Cumming Report," in recommending the establishment of a new governmental federation, enunciated the "fundamental principle" of careful avoidance of "any unnecessary reduction of the existing power of the local authorities with the object of preserving the greatest possible degree of local autonomy." Implicit in this concept was the expectation that service performances could, and would, vary between the thirteen local authorities (in both the exclusively local, and the "shared" functional areas), depending upon the demands and expectations of their respective inhabitants. Metro was designed as a federal program, and the exercise of a certain degree of local autonomy represents an essential component of the federalist principle.

Second, there was an obvious economic imbalance between the resources of the local municipalities themselves. . . .

Two basic assumptions can serve as significant guidelines for any . . . evaluation. The first is that the financial inequities that existed between municipalities in 1953 should be less severe now than they were a decade ago. The second is that with the passage of time, this situation should be improving rather than deteriorating. The indications are, however, that neither assumption is being met at the present time. Instead, there is considerable evidence to indicate that the financial inequities between the local municipalities are more pronounced today than they were in 1953, and that this situation appears to be deteriorating with the passage of time.

A number of factors helps to explain this unforeseen development. First, the local performance of specific service responsibilities has tended to vary more widely than originally anticipated; second, in certain key areas, Metro's relative share of service costs has failed to keep pace with the increasing burdens that have been carried by the local municipalities themselves; and third, there has been no real equalization of the basic resources (i.e. assessment base) of the thirteen local municipalities. . . .

2. The problems of metropolitan unity

When the "Cumming Report" was issued in 1953, it noted the "serious cleavage of interest" that existed between the City of Toronto and the twelve other municipalities, and expressed the hope that a "better spirit of metropolitan unity" would be realized in future years.

Perhaps if one of the Report's major organizational recommendations had been followed, the development of this spirit of unity could have been expedited. As has already been noted, the Report proposed that

the City of Toronto should have four members on
the new Metropolitan Council, while the twelve suburbs should have an equal number of members drawn
from four suburban "divisions," each of which would
appoint one councillor. Although this arrangement
would not have alleviated any potential city-versus-
suburbs split, it at least represented a step in the
direction of breaking down narrow local identities
within the suburban community. When the Provincial Legislature rejected this proposal in favor of a
24-member constituency-unit system of representation (i.e. one representative for each of the twelve
suburban municipalities plus twelve for the City of
Toronto), it both helped and hindered the future development of the new metropolitan government.

As previously argued, the help came from the fact
that such an arrangement tended to minimize the potentialities of an external attack upon the new governmental body by local political leaders. Because
these leaders were involved in the formulation of
Metro policies, they understood what these policies
were all about, and they were in a position to translate
the significance of the policies to their local communities. In essence, the Toronto arrangement provided
the means for a close liaison between the new Metro
Council and the existing local municipalities. Yet
the price the Council has been forced to pay for such
potential liaison has been a very severe one.

In effect, the representative arrangements adopted
by the Province have tended to turn the new metropolitan government into a very real "Assembly of
Sovereign States." Since the Metro Council members
are the actual Mayors, Reeves or other local political
leaders of their constituent councils, it has been virtually impossible for these members to ignore parochial interests in approaching their Metro responsibilities. Under the circumstances, Council deliberations
can easily turn into bargaining sessions, in which
local representatives tend to place more emphasis
upon their respective constituencies than upon the
larger needs of the metropolitan community taken
as a whole.

The appearance of such a conflict is not a new
problem unique to the Toronto Council. Despite
Edmund Burke's historic plea for the broad exercise
of representative judgment, political man has always
experienced considerable difficulty reconciling the
tug of local demands with some larger concept of
community interest, even under the very best of
circumstances. Yet by placing local leaders (who
have been elected to oversee the interests of their individual communities) upon its Council, Toronto's
metropolitan government has tended to magnify this
already difficult problem to the breaking point. It is
hard enough to serve one master well, much less two,
and perhaps the best insight that can be gained into
the true nature of the Toronto Councillors' dilemma

is to visualize a Canadian Parliament made up solely
of Provincial Premiers, or a United States Congress
consisting of fifty State Governors. . . .

. . . . Whatever else it may or may not have been
able to accomplish in the past decade, the federation
approach has made very little headway towards the
realization of the "spirit of metropolitan unity" that
the "Cumming Report" so wistfully contemplated
some ten years ago. Indeed, the most alarming aspect of the whole situation is that the relations between Council members appear to be growing worse,
rather than better, with the passage of years.

3. The problems of indecisiveness

The parochial strains within Metro have tended to
inhibit the Council's program in a number of distinct
ways. First, there have been occasions when the
more affluent municipalities have demonstrated a
reluctance to share their wealth with the area's less
fortunate communities. . . .

Second, and on the opposite side of the coin, there
have also been cases where the less wealthy communities have balked against accepting increased
responsibilities on the grounds that it would further
jeopardize their already precarious financial positions.
The field of public housing provides a dramatic example of this problem. . . .

The third sphere where Metro has displayed considerable indecision is not solely economic in its
underlying origins. Instead, it appears to be the outgrowth of a highly pragmatic leadership philosophy
that has shaped the Metro operation from its very inception.

There is little doubt that Metro's great leadership
strength to date has been in its response to the more
dramatic physical service crises that have exerted
the loudest demands for immediate and sustained
attention. Metro has realized its greatest accomplishments in tackling such drastic situations as those that
were to be found in the water supply, sewage disposal,
school construction, and transportation services. Although this effort has required a massive organizational and financial capability, it has not placed too
many subtle, or even controversial, demands on the
Metro Council members because both the nature of
these problems and the nature of the actions necessary to realize their solution have been relatively obvious. During its formative years, Metro's basic
raison d'être has been reasonably apparent to all.
Faced with a staggering backlog of previous neglect in
a variety of public areas, the Metropolitan Council
has had little choice but to emphasize the "steam-
shovel approach" to its job in order to build the miles
of new sewers and the myriad of new schools necessary to preserve metropolitan Toronto as a going,
and growing, concern.

Largely as a result of the pragmatic nature of this initial mandate, the Council has tended to adopt a highly pragmatic approach to all spheres of its operations that has meshed very closely with the personal philosophical orientation of its first chairman, Frederick Gardiner. Stated quite simply, Metro has often been inclined to operate more as a business than as a governmental organization — the more as a gigantic construction company operating under a metropolitan-wide mandate, than as a political body responsible for a wide range of social, as well as physical obligations. Ten years' cumulative experience indicates that the Metropolitan Council has been consistently aggressive in tackling the so-called "hard core" problems where results are concrete and obvious, and considerably less assertive in meeting some of the "softer," more socially-oriented issue areas where results are usually less tangible and more controversial. . . .

Three such fields are public housing, planning and the publicity and information functions that are involved in carrying Metro's story to the public. . . .

. . . . During its formative years, one of the reasons Metro has been able to achieve a considerable degree of consensus among its member municipalities is due to the fact that the basic problems that have represented its primary fields of concern have been relatively obvious in their priorities and relatively noncontroversial in their implications. While these different member municipalities may have been subjected to widely divergent fluctuations in their own local resources, it was hardly difficult for them to agree that a modern metropolitan community must have an adequate water supply system if it is to survive. As Metro now places increasing emphasis on such fields as welfare, housing, recreation and the like, the considerably more contentious nature of these newer priorities (complete with all their implications of "unnecessary frills") promises to place increasing strains upon the original federation framework. In short, Metro has been suffering from a growing lack of resolution during its first decade in precisely those fields that will demand an increasing amount of its attention during the next decade. It is highly debatable whether the existing Metro municipalities will be able to achieve a degree of consensus on these newly emerging issues of social reform that will be comparable to the degree of consensus they have been able to achieve in the past when considering the more tangible, "hard core" problems that have monopolized Metro's first decade.

Such an observation argues that there may well be political as well as economic forces of fragmentation at work that justify the consideration of some basic changes in the original Toronto federation framework as it was first devised in 1953. As was noted at the outset, this original framework was never regarded

as providing the final answer to all of Metropolitan Toronto's problems, and the environmental changes which have taken place during the past decade indicate that a basic review of the entire Metro program is, indeed, highly desirable. . . . Much local press and central city political sentiment appears to favor a total amalgamation of all thirteen local municipalities into one large metropolitan city. A second alternative, and one worthy of thoughtful consideration, was proposed by the Gathercole Report in 1961. This group pointed out that it might well be feasible to preserve the essence of Toronto's original metropolitan federation concept by rationalizing the existing second-tier structure through consolidation of the thirteen existing local municipalities into four, or five, enlarged and more equalized boroughs. . . .

There is one alternative, however, that lies beyond the bounds of political feasibility. This is the complete abandonment of the basic metropolitan government approach in favour of a reversion to conditions as they existed prior to 1953. No significant group, either inside or outside of Metro, has come out in favor of such a course of action. This fact, in and of itself, serves as the most telling commentary on Metro's first decade. Despite any of its shortcomings, Toronto's metropolitan government, when evaluated in terms of the totality of its achievements, has compiled an exceedingly impressive record during its first ten years of existence. It is now the responsibility of its parent body, the Provincial Government, to make any adjustments that may be necessary to assure that this will again be true at the completion of Metro's second decade of operations.

69

Annexation: Virginia's Not-So-Judicial System

By Chester W. Bain

ONE OF THE MOST ACUTE problems facing most municipalities today is the need to accommodate the growth and development that has taken place outside

Chester W. Bain, "Annexation: Virginia's Not-So-Judicial System," *Public Administration Review,* Autumn, 1955, pp. 251–262. Reprinted by permission of the publisher, the American Society for Public Administration. Footnotes in original omitted.

their corporate limits. In the search for means to meet this too long neglected problem, the so-called "Virginia plan of annexation" has not remained unnoticed. For many, however, the virtue of the Virginia plan lies in a single explanation — it has worked for the cities! Factually this is correct. Out of a total of 66 proceedings to extend city boundaries that were heard on their merits between 1905 and the end of 1954, there were only four in which the city was denied all the territory it sought. This impressive success of the Virginia cities may have misled some into believing that using the judicial process for extending municipal boundaries is the magic key to the problem of metropolitan integration. Fifty years of experience with this procedure, however, indicates that the plan is not strictly judicial in nature and that a number of factors should be considered before the final blessings are conferred.

The extension of city boundaries in most states does not result in a general dislocation of the state's primary, political subdivisions. Following the extension of a city's boundaries, the county, or other primary subdivision, continues to perform within the area annexed the same services and functions that it provided prior to annexation. County officials have the same authority within the annexed territory, as well as in the whole of the annexing city, as they previously possessed. The county loses no area, population, or taxable values; the property annexed remains subject to county taxation for general county purposes. Where city-county separation is not observed, the extension of a city's boundaries results in the imposition of an additional layer of government upon the area annexed but does not cause a diminution of the basic functions the county is required to perform as a primary, political subdivision of the state.

An entirely different situation is presented when the boundaries of a Virginia city are extended. In Virginia, cities are independent of the jurisdiction of the county or counties in which they are geographically situated, and the extension of a city's boundaries legally transfers the territory affected from one political jurisdiction to another with the result that the county loses, at the city's gain, a portion of its area, population, and taxable values. Moreover, when the annexation becomes effective, responsibility for providing all governmental services and functions, including those formerly supplied by the county, falls to the city. County officials no longer have jurisdiction within the annexed area, but the city, through its own instrumentalities, serves as a distinct primary, political subdivision for carrying out the policies of the state at the local level in addition to providing those functions that are municipal in character. The Virginia independent city is, in effect, a "city-county," or, as it is classified in English local government, a "county borough."

It requires no considerable amount of imagination to realize that under the Virginia practice of city-county separation an attempt by a city to extend its boundaries may easily result in a conflict of interest among the city, the county, and the residents of the area proposed to be annexed. On the one hand is the city's desire to grow in area and to acquire the additional tax values located outside its boundaries. The officials of most cities take the position that the fringe area residents should be brought into the city and made to contribute directly to the cost of the municipal services they enjoy when they enter the city to work or to play. It is also asserted that services of an areawide nature should be planned and administered under a single governmental unit and that the city can best arrange and provide these services. The county, however, is bitterly opposed to losing its area, population, and taxable values, unless the territory to be annexed is such a financial burden that the county is willing to have the city take it over.

Caught between the interests of the city and the county are the residents of the fringe area. As fringe areas develop, the residents require new services and facilities that are not urgent or are even unnecessary in a rural environment. Although a county can, and frequently does, provide some of the services required by areas that are approaching urban concentration, it frequently is unable, or unwilling, to provide the additional services required or desired in thickly populated areas around a city but not on a countywide basis. If the adjacent city can be prevailed upon to furnish these services, few of the fringe area residents are interested in being brought into the city. But cities are usually unwilling, even if able, to furnish municipal services outside their corporate limits. In these circumstances, many fringe area residents may be willing, and may even actively seek, to be brought into the city.

The decision involved in the extension of a city's boundaries where city-county separation is practiced therefore involves a three-way conflict of interests that can present myriad combinations. In no two proceedings are the local conditions exactly the same. At times there may be substantial agreement among all parties as to the need for annexation. At other times a proposed extension of a city's boundaries will be opposed both by the county and by the residents of the area proposed to be annexed. Between these two extremes there can arise every conceivable combination of favorable and unfavorable opinions. This great diversity of situations focuses attention on the real issue in the annexation question — who should decide when a particular area should be under city government and when it should be under county government? The crux of the question is whether there should be a procedure whereby areas cannot be annexed without the assent of the parties to the proceeding or whether the final determination should rest with an impartial, outside party. For fifty years Virginia has utilized the second alternative. . . .

Proceedings to extend a city's boundaries may be initiated by a variety of methods. A city may not annex all or part of another city but may bring action to annex unincorporated territory or an incorporated town, which under the Virginia practice of city-county separation remains a part of the county, by passing an ordinance setting forth a description of the area to be annexed, the "necessity and expediency" of the proposed annexation, and the terms and conditions upon which annexation is to be made. Although initiation by the city has been the principal method used in the past, annexation proceedings may also be instigated by petition of 51 per cent of the voters of an area who desire to be annexed to an adjacent city; by a resolution passed by the governing body of a county requesting that certain areas be annexed to a city; or by a resolution passed by the governing body of a town which desires to be annexed to an adjacent city. Irrespective of which party takes the initiative, the action is filed with the circuit court of the county in which the largest portion of the territory to be annexed is located and is heard by a specially constituted annexation court, consisting of the judge of the county from which the territory is to be annexed and two judges of judicial circuits remote from the area designated by the Chief Justice of the Virginia Supreme Court of Appeals. In almost every proceeding, the major controversy is between the city and the county as official bodies, but any individual or groups of individuals who can show an interest in the action may come forward and be made parties defendant or plaintiff and be represented by counsel.

The great statutory guide for the annexation courts during the years that the extension of Virginia municipal boundaries has been determined by the judicial process has been the "necessity for and expediency of annexation." If a majority of the court is satisfied that the proposed extension is "necessary and expedient," it must grant the extension, although in so doing it may add to or deduct from the area requested and alter the terms and conditions upon which the city proposes to make the annexation. This guide was established by the General Assembly in the basic statute enacted in 1904; it remained substantially unchanged until 1948 when the highly unilluminating qualification was added that in determining annexation proceedings the courts must consider "the best interests of the county, the city and the best interests, services to be rendered and needs of the area proposed to be annexed and the best interests of the remaining portion of the county." While this phrase, which was repeated at four different points in the statute, may have been intended as an amplification of the general standards of neces-

sity and expediency, it has had no discernible effect on the annexation courts' determinations, and in all proceedings decided since the enactment the attitude has prevailed that the Legislature merely added to the statute what the courts had already been following as a judicial maxim.

In the exercise of the function vested in them, the annexation courts have consistently clung to the principle that it is incumbent upon the city to establish by a preponderance of the evidence the necessity for and expediency of extending its boundaries. Although both opposed and unopposed proceedings require extensive preparations, the degree of effort required at the hearing to meet this burden depends upon the intensity of the opposition presented by the county and any intervenors who are made parties to the proceeding. Where the proposed extension is unopposed, the city can quickly submit sufficient evidence to satisfy the court that its boundaries should be extended. If this evidence is uncontradicted, the court normally has little alternative except to grant at least part of the territory requested. Where a proposed extension is vigorously opposed, however, a different situation arises. Here the city will have a much more difficult task proving the necessity for and expediency of annexation, and, as a result, the length of the hearing, the number of exhibits, and the number of witnesses will be greatly increased. The significant point, however, is that the burden of proof rests on the city.

During the years annexation has been determined by the judicial process, the courts have never set forth exactly what is required to show the "necessity for and expediency of annexation." The closest thing to a statement of what is required was given by the Virginia Supreme Court of Appeals in *Henrico County v. City of Richmond,* the first case appealed under the 1904 statute. The primary question before the appellate court was the constitutionality of the statute, but the court in passing upon this point also stated:

The necessity for or expediency of enlargements [of the boundaries of a city] is determined by the health of the community, its size, its crowded conditions, its past growth, and the need in the reasonably near future for development and expansion. These are matters of fact, and when they do exist as to satisfy the judicial mind of the necessity for or expediency of annexation, then, in accordance with the provisions of the act, the same must be declared.

In only one other case has the Supreme Court of Appeals given what might be called a definition of "necessity" or "expediency." Here the court asked:

Is the annexation "expedient" within the meaning of the statute? That is — as we interpret the word — is it advantageous and in furtherance of the aforesaid policy of the State with respect to annexation? [namely], placing urban areas under city government and keeping rural areas under county government.

While the courts have never set forth exactly what constitutes the necessity for and expediency of a proposed extension, there has been built up through the years a very definite pattern of factors that are considered in all annexation proceedings, whether opposed or unopposed. It has involved an elaboration upon and a development of the factors specified in the above quoted statement from the majority opinion in *Henrico County v. City of Richmond.* . . .

One of the principal factors and usually the first to be stressed at the hearing on the necessity and expediency of a proposed annexation, is the city's claim for additional territory in order that it may grow and develop. The city introduces evidence to support its position that it lacks suitable industrial and residential building sites and that this lack has forced many residents to go beyond the city limits in order to meet their needs. The city further contends that these fringe area residents are really part of the city and that its boundaries should be extended to include the built-up areas in which they reside. Counsel for the county, if the proposed extension is opposed, introduces evidence designed to show that there is still vacant land within the limits of the city and that it is not necessary to take the county's territory. The argument is also made that the people in the fringe area went there to escape city taxes and regulations and to enjoy country living and the benefits of lower county tax rates. . . .

As might easily be imagined, a considerable portion of the hearing in any annexation proceeding is devoted to the presentation of evidence on the annexation area's need for services not being supplied by the county, the types and quality of services that the city would provide in the event of annexation, and a comparison of the services that will be provided by the city with those currently provided by the county. . . .

Another of the factors considered in all proceedings to extend a city's boundaries is referred to as "community of interest." The idea underlying this phrase is that there are very close economic, social, and cultural ties between the residents of the city and those of the fringe areas outside the city. From this premise it is contended that when a city's "natural boundaries" have extended beyond its "legal boundaries," there should be an adjustment in order to bring the two into proper alignment. Accordingly, at the hearing evidence is introduced to show that the city and the area sought to be annexed are actually one uninterrupted and homogeneous community. . . .

The fourth principal type of evidence that is con-

sidered in all annexation proceedings is financial in nature. Since under the Virginia practice of city-county separation any extension of a city's corporate limits necessarily results in a diminution of the county's tax resources and a corresponding gain on the part of the city, it might be presumed that a considerable amount of attention would be given by the county to showing the financial effect of the proposed annexation on the tax structure of the county. Although this factor is not completely ignored, the courts' consistent position that the gain or loss of tax revenue is not *in and of itself* sufficient basis for granting or denying annexation has lessened the attention that is given to this matter. Instead, the principal emphasis at the hearing is on whether the city is financially able to assume the obligations that must be incurred as a consequence of annexation. . . .

After all the evidence has been presented and everyone who so desires has been heard, the annexation court must decide whether to grant or to deny the extension requested. Under the statute, if a majority of the court is not satisfied that the proposed annexation is necessary or expedient, considering the best interests of all parties concerned, the petition must be dismissed. On the other hand, if the facts satisfy a majority of the court of the necessity for and expediency of annexation, the court has no alternative but to determine the area to be annexed and the terms and conditions upon which annexation is to be had. The crucial point here, then, is how an annexation court determines the necessity and expediency of annexation.

The approach of the annexation courts to their task of determining when an extension should be granted and when it should be denied has been quite different from what might have been expected. While the evidence that is presented before annexation courts through the years has followed a substantially consistent pattern of factors both in opposed and in unopposed proceedings, the annexation courts have not reduced the elements so considered to rigid formulas or standards against which the local conditions of each proceeding must be measured and not found wanting before annexation is to be granted. They have never set up a minimum population density, land use vacancy, or definite population growth that must be present before annexation can be permitted, nor have they developed a judicial statement of the services that are required by unincorporated urban areas or the techniques by which the deficiencies in the services provided by the city or county are to be measured. No standards have been established to indicate what conditions must be present to show homogeneity between the city and its fringe areas sufficient to require that they be governed by the same unit of local government. And, finally, annexation courts have never given judicial standards for determining exactly when a city can afford annexation.

Rather, the annexation courts have regarded each proceeding as a local problem and have maintained a high degree of flexibility in the standards by which annexation is determined. In some proceedings one or a few of the factors considered appears to have been the principal reason for granting annexation. . . .

In a great many of the proceedings, no one of the elements considered in the evidence introduced has been particularly indicative of a need for annexation. In these instances the determination appears to have rested on a composite of elements and it has not been possible to ascertain the degree of emphasis, if any, that the courts have placed upon any single factor. It is here that the refusal of the courts to reduce the factors considered to strict standards becomes particularly outstanding. The 1941 proceeding by the city of Richmond against Henrico County is an exceptionally good example. In this case the county based its defense primarily upon the contention that it had a modern, streamlined form of government that was providing a higher degree of local services to its residents than the city could provide with its "outmoded, fossilized, bicameral, councilmanic form." The annexation court, although over the dissent of the "local judge," refused to accept this position and, unquestionably following the judicial maxim that urban areas belong under city government, granted most of the territory asked for by the city. Although there is ample evidence from this and other proceedings that the judicial scales are tipped in favor of the city, the evidence also clearly shows that during the fifty years the Virginia procedure has been in operation, each annexation court has very carefully heard the evidence presented before it and has then proceeded to make its decision upon the basis of what appeared to it to be best for all parties concerned. . . .

The real merit of the Virginia system . . . is that it vests final determination of these matters in an independent, third party. If any one factor had to be singled out as the outstanding feature and advantage of the Virginia procedure, it would be the use of an outside party to determine each annexation proceeding. By vesting the final decision in someone other than one of the parties affected, there has been an orderly development that very probably could not have occurred had some other procedure been used. While the normal respect for the judicial system may have assured early acceptance and enhanced the operation of the procedure provided, it was not so much that it was the judicial branch that was used, but that an independent, third party is the final arbiter of the three-way conflict of interests involved in these proceedings. . . .

The chief shortcoming of the present Virginia procedure for meeting the problem of fringe area development . . . centers in the very limited sphere within which annexation courts are permitted to operate. Annexation courts, like other courts of law, cannot initiate action but must wait until a case or a controversy is brought before them for adjudication. In view of the variety of means by which annexation proceedings may be initiated, this is not a particularly serious deficiency. A much more serious problem, however, is that even when an annexation proceeding is brought before an annexation court, the court's authority is limited to the single issue of determining whether that particular city's boundaries should or should not be extended. Although the court has the authority to add to or to deduct from the territory requested by the city, it cannot make any adjustments in the boundaries of other local governmental units no matter how sorely such adjustments may be needed. . . .

The proponents of metropolitan integration have been notably unsuccessful in selling their proposals to the public, despite the tremendous number of impressive community studies undertaken. Here one of the leading students of metropolitan areas takes a careful look at the principal criticisms raised by the opposition, as well as at the apparent weaknesses of the proponents themselves, and suggests the need for a new and more flexible orientation. In the final selection Victor Jones provides an interesting analysis of the practical politics behind support for and opposition to movements for metropolitan integration. Written a number of years ago, it remains a most accurate appraisal.

70

There Are Many Roads

By Robert C. Wood

IT HAS BEEN OVER 30 YEARS since the National Municipal League first put the topic of metropolitan reform on its agenda and a committee of the League undertook the first serious national study of the problem.

Robert C. Wood, "There Are Many Roads," *National Civic Review*, March, 1962, pp. 129–134, 174. Reprinted by permission of the publisher.

It has been twenty years since Victor Jones published his authoritative study *Metropolitan Government* and launched the first serious probe into the politics of metropolitan reform. For the past ten years we have witnessed a steadily mounting tide of metropolitan research and reform which has reached every corner of the nation.

Today, there are special courses on metropolitan government in colleges and universities from coast to coast. There are well financed and comprehensive studies of the governmental pattern in one standard metropolitan area after another. There are quick seminars for business men and journalists given over to analyzing the character of metropolitan political problems. And there are panels for the conscientious citizens sponsored by the League of Women Voters and churches adding to the drum beat of discussion and conversation.

Yet, here we are today — quite appropriately but with more than a trace of irony — inquiring again as to the purpose of this massive commitment of energy, time, resources and careers.

Behind the topic discussed here must be the unspoken premise that in our devotion to the subject of metropolitan government we may have been following a will-of-the-wisp and trafficking in fantasies. At least to many of our colleagues in journalism and the academic world it seems possible we have been engaged in nothing more than a twentieth-century search for a utopian community which can never be. And the disinclination of the public to support us, in many votes in many places, adds substance to this suspicion.

So the question behind the question of the character of metropolitan government is perhaps the most relevant one on which to begin. Has a generation of civic leaders, reformers and scholars gone wrong? More bluntly, are we only a small band of agitators with values which the majority of Americans do not share?

We can perhaps combine both the explicit and the implicit issue in the simple query: What is it we are after? Is it a new set of institutions comparable to those we now find in Miami that we seek everywhere as urban concentrations spill over the boundaries of old central cities? Or is it rather new governmental powers and programs expressed in more comprehensive and active planning and economic development programs that we seek? Or is it something more subtle which we have yet to define and characterize accurately?

One way to answer these questions is to look at the definitions provided by particular observers and formulations by particular scholars over the last generation. More specifically, we can look at three types of definitions and formulations: (1) Those inherent in the indictment of our critics in recent years —

what it is they think we are after; (2) those definitions which arise from our earlier attempts to formulate government reform in metropolitan areas which largely failed — in short the partial formulations inherent in our mistakes; (3) the definitions which are embedded in the more fundamental goals we seek but which we have never made clear — to the public, to the "influentials" and perhaps even to ourselves. If we survey the record in these three respects perhaps we will emerge with a clearer understanding of what . . . we mean by metropolitan government.

Indictment of our critics

We can find one set of formulations by considering the criticisms which we face today — indictments which now seem especially harsh and which come at us from many sides. Most critics apparently believe that the only version of metropolitan government acceptable to the experts is the most simple and obvious one: the restructuring of the present local political systems into one great municipality which will assume all the powers and all the prerogatives of our present governments. From this starting point, the critics add three characteristics of metropolitan government which they believe we seek. Their collective judgment is that we propose new arrangements which are at one and the same time undemocratic, unrealistic and close to un-American.

The observation that we are engaged in essentially an undemocratic enterprise finds perhaps its most sophisticated formulation in scholarly analysis. Raymond Vernon, for example, after concluding his directorship of the New York Metropolitan Region Study, made his first explicit excursion into policy analysis in the Stafford Little Lectures at Princeton in the spring of 1961.

Arguing that the course of urban development over the last generation has substantially improved the lot of the middle class and the poor, Vernon concludes that the drive for governmental reform on a metropolitan basis is initiated primarily by "the elite." As the central city continues to decline, Vernon points out, the mansions of the rich are threatened or they are forced into long commuting schedules between downtown offices and exclusive suburban homes. The "elite's" real estate holdings in the central city decline in value; their cultural pursuits in the museums, the theaters and the symphonies of the central city are more difficult to maintain. So they protest. The dissatisfactions of the wealthy are shared by other types of influentials not rich but articulate. The opinion-makers of the press, the city politicians, the city clerics, museum curators and professors join the well-to-do in their agitations.

In Vernon's words these are the most dissatisfied of all because they compose "the elite who do not derive their status from wealth. Sometimes these are rich but often they are not. And when they are not, their bitterness against the spread of the urban areas is greatest of all. They do not have the ability of the rich to maintain propinquity to their interests in the city by buying 'luxury downtown space.' "

According to this kind of analysis metropolitan government is not a drive for more rational, better coordinated, better financed local government. Instead it is the product of a tiny willful minority pursuing their self-interests and seeking to impose a new government on a majority which is indifferent or opposed.

A second formulation of the true character of metropolitan government comes from quite a separate group of critics. These observers hold that our proposals are essentially unrealistic in the sense that we vastly overrate the capacity of the structures we propose to fashion effective public policy. In this indictment not only does the majority of the public not want metropolitan government, as indicated by the closeness of the vote in Miami, the defeats in Cleveland and St. Louis, but the majority senses the inherent unworkability of the new schemes.

Most local governments at present are mediocre in quality, so the argument runs, too weak in talent, and local politics is too fragmented and divided to solve problems on a grand scale. The present system can maintain a semblance of law and order and it can provide minimum community facilities and services. But to ask the present political system to reform itself, to master the metropolis, to "guide growth" as the Committee for Economic Development suggests, is to ignore the "nonsense" which the system continually spouts out in the form of meaningless public policy.

So a group of scholars, exploring how decisions are actually made in major central cities today, concludes that governments at the local level can do little or nothing that is rational because the strain of compromise and consensus building is now too great. Few local leaders can do much more than preside over volatile, weak and conflicting interest groups in a highly pluralistic urban society. And as the urban sprawl develops into an even larger megalopolis, the design of governmental structures sufficient to the day comes close to defying the imagination of political science. In this context then, metropolitan reform is little more than a vision of impractical idealists.

A third conclusion as to the real nature of metropolitan government is found in the opinions of a different kind of observer. The fringe group of extremists and superpatriots at the local scene conclude that our plans are fundamentally alien to American political philosophy. Their rallying cry is that what we are really after is a form of "super-government,' a spectacular local version of some kind of totalitarian

dogma. This criticism is perhaps not the most sophisticated of the negative formulations we face but it is close now to ubiquitous. It appears in the small town press, public opinion rallies, political meetings and it is perhaps more influential than the indictment of the scholars.

Are these definitions of metropolitan governments valid ones? At rock bottom they are not. Though they increase our understanding of how straightforward proposals may be distorted and grossly oversimplified, they burlesque our principal aims.

So far as an interpretation of metropolitan government as an antidemocratic enterprise is concerned, a careful reading of this argument establishes it as a simplistic version of how the American political process operates. Elites have always been catalysts for providing substantial political change on the local level as much as on the state and national. In the twentieth century a text book version of a rational or wise citizenry arriving through sweet reason at universal consensus is not an approximation of reality — and no scholar should present it as such. To say that a small part of the body politic seeks to persuade the majority to adopt a new mechanism for policy-making is simply to identify the stage at which a reform movement has arrived. Like the leaders of any major American political change in its formative years, clearly we have not persuaded the majority to endorse our proposals. But just as clearly, our procedures in seeking such endorsements have been in the best democratic tradition.

As for the charge that metropolitan reform is unrealistic, there is more than a grain of truth in this analysis. But it is an open question as to whether the incapacities of the present systems of local government to make meaningful decisions stem from their innate incapacity as from their present structure and situation. Perhaps the "nonsense" of local public policy today is a reflection of the fragmented structure which we seek to correct and of a decade in which talent has systematically been discouraged from entering the public arena. Perhaps mediocre performance of many local governments stems from their incapacities in their present divided circumstances to formulate major goals and programs which will challenge able men. Given new governments with new powers and new promise we have no reason for supposing that present conditions will forever apply.

Finally, the anti-American doctrine represents the worst kind of illogic. It is rooted in the myth that the only truly democratic governments are those which allow a one-to-one correlation to electoral participation and policy formulation. What is missing from these charges is any recognition that representative government in America has been a going concern on a larger areal basis than the metropolitan region throughout the history of the United States. The national and state governments are of course not close to the people in the sense of direct democracy and universal participation. They are representative governments. But they work and have worked in the interests of America since the Revolution.

Mistaken images from our own analysis

If we can reject the definitions of metropolitan government provided by our critics, we need to re-examine earlier definitions which we ourselves have advanced. Although we have developed a whole battery of different forms which metropolitan government may take — from annexation and federation through the California contract device — it is not at all clear that we have identified all the critical aspects of the problem of governing modern metropolitan areas. And it is certain we have not informed the public at large of the complexity of the job ahead. Specifically, three mistakes now need to be recognized as contributing to our present quandary.

First, with the advantage of hindsight, it seems certain that we have seriously underestimated the size of the task of metropolitan reform. The pace of growth in urban areas has been too rapid for us to keep pace with complementary political concepts. We began, for example, with the belief that our chief obligation was to refurbish the central city, to restore it to the form we remembered in our childhood and consequently to extend its boundaries to include new residential development and new land values as rapidly as possible. We failed to specify the differences in urban development which occur in different regions in the country, the important qualifications which different sizes of standard metropolitan areas implied. In short, we did not have enough research and development inputs in our analyses to allow for flexibility and variety in devising new patterns of institutions.

The use of the urban county, new types of confederation and consolidation — all the other later versions which add sophistication and detail to our plans — have appeared only slowly on the scene. Especially we have not been prepared to take, as James A. Norton now suggests, the existing units of government as "givens" in the situation.

Second, we failed to specify all the kinds of changes which are required as governments undertake to adjust to the new urban complexes. We have not often emphasized, for example, that our aim is not only the more unified extension of local government, over larger and larger areas, but the extension of those governments with new powers and with new responsibilities. Not until the renewal program got fully under way in the mid-1950s did we come to recognize that local government today needs positively and actively to guide growth. Not until

the first suggestions of workable programs for entire metropolitan regions were born in the early '60s have we been able to articulate a new dimension of public policy at the local level which views the form of the new urban community as something more than the product of the private market place.

Third, as we worked toward these new formulations we failed badly to communicate the nature of our proposals to the electorate. It was not, as our critics have charged, that our objectives were undemocratic, unrealistic or un-American but that they were misunderstood. We have never given sufficient attention to the misconceptions, the fears and the resistance to change which voters naturally exhibit. Instead, we have assumed too often that "politics" is beneath us and that once our proposals are written down there is an easy and automatic process by which the voters could come to see their benefits. Thus we have failed to disseminate the new facts we were learning, to interpret the new duties and philosophies of local government. Instead we have allowed our definitions to appear as abstract, dry, unimportant, inconsequential proposals, discovered by scholars and accepted by small civic reform groups out of the main stream of American thought and culture.

Goals of metropolitan government

The distortions which critical interpretations have made of our basic proposals, our incapacity to keep abreast of the changes going on about us, our reluctance to communicate clearly enough the character of the new political institutions we seek now, make it appropriate and urgent that today we try again. I suggest that if we specify the underlying goals which a generation of reformers have been after we will come close to a better definition of metropolitan government than we have had before and that we will increase our prospects of public acceptance and support. This specification comes in two parts: Saying clearly and distinctly what metropolitan government is not today and then saying what it is.

It is imperative in mid-20th century with new urban forms scarcely dreamed of in the 1920s and 1930s to indicate to both supporters and detracters alike that our primary purpose is not the simple re-establishment on a broader territorial basis of the traditional city. It is not just annexation, not wider areas for administrative convenience and efficiency, not public budget savings, not more bureaucracy, not better principles of public administration that are our essential objectives. These we think in many instances will appear; and we do not discount them. But we do not rest our case today on the simple magnification in size of the present local political and governmental system.

Our real goal today and for the foreseeable future is a commitment to the proposition that urban growth and urban sprawl are matters of public interest and public concern. What we seek are forms and institutions of government which take their place in partnership with the private economy to build better urban regions. Bound up in this goal is a clear recognition that the private market place alone will not produce the kind of city or the kind of region which the public — given real policy alternatives — would prefer. What is involved, too, is the assumption that purposeful political participation by the public on a broad area base can make possible orderly beneficial development which the same public in the present structure of traditional local government cannot provide.

If these basic facts are understood, then metropolitan government is released from the chains of a single one-shot structural reform. It partakes of three qualities:

(1) Metropolitan government is "policy-oriented" government at the local level, a willingness and capacity to exercise planning and developmental powers across the entire metropolitan region.

(2) Metropolitan government is the infusion of talent at the research level, in the development stage of planning, in the exercise of top level executive power, in the recruitment of new career specialists at a rate and in a volume which we have not had for at least two generations.

(3) Finally, it is the coordination of these policy efforts through channels which maintain a metropolitan perspective. This may be one single government; it may be a federation; it may be the new semipublic, semiprivate councils which Victor Jones has emphasized. It may even come about more subtly. Economic studies which bring together public and private decision-makers, civic assemblies which could move toward formal legislative action — these are channels and institutions. The important thing to recognize is that there are many ways to advance a metropolitan strategy once a strategy is clearly identified.

In short there are many roads to achieve metropolitan government defined as the new and broader use of government as an instrument for shaping the urban environment. But underlying each of these approaches is one common denominator: The conviction that in the end we do not have to drift; that we can rationally and reasonably direct the course of action; that we can use our affluence and technology to build better urban communities than our forefathers did; that we can make local government responsible and effective once again.

These were the convictions of course that the earlier reformers held when they worked to combat the then prevalent deficiencies of corruption and mismanagement in local governments. They remain our convictions today as we tackle the more complicated and subtle task of local public policy-making: How to master the metropolis in the public interest.

71

The Politics of Integration in Metropolitan Areas

By Victor Jones

THE POLITICS OF INTEGRATION are the most important aspect of the problem. Experts can suggest any number of devices for complete or partial integration. Technicians can draft statutes or charters and are prepared to supervise their installation. The difficulty, or the dilemma if the term is preferred, lies in securing legislative or electoral approval. Venerable and accepted symbols are present on all sides to serve as material for the rationalization of opposition, sincere or otherwise, to integration. There has been little success up to now in transforming the unfavorable stereotypes held by a large number of suburban dwellers, rural and small-town folk outside metropolitan areas, legislators from these groups, and jurists who construe constitutions, statutes, and charters.

The configuration of attitudes in a metropolitan area toward a proposal to integrate local government is both static and dynamic. It tends to be static in that attitudes are rationalized around traditional conceptions of local self-government. Migrants to the metropolitan area hold on to their conception of the local government pattern of their home village or small city. On the other hand, the heterogeneity of the metropolis presents a variety of stimuli to cause the voter to react in several possible ways to an integration proposal.

DIVERSE INTERESTS

Proponents of integration have failed to recognize the diversity of interests which might be used as

Victor Jones, "Politics of Integration in Metropolitan Areas," *Annals of the American Academy of Political and Social Science,* January, 1940, pp. 161–167. Footnotes in original omitted. Reprinted by permission of the publisher.

bases of appeals for affirmative votes on integration proposals. They usually divide the electorate into voters of the central city, the suburbs and, where constitutional amendments or statutes are required, the rural and village districts of the remainder of the state. These groups are treated as if they were homogeneous, although supplementary appeals are sometimes directed to the electors as businessmen, professional men, laborers, or farmers. It is an error, however, to plan a campaign on the assumption that all residents of metropolitan areas outside the central city are of one mind.

There are many kinds of suburbs, even within the broad classifications of industrial and residential. The residential suburbs may be predominantly composed of laborers, middle-class commuters, or wealthy families; industrial suburbs may be under the influence of a single large corporation or they may contain many small and medium-sized plants. Suburbs differ from one another according to their relative social and economic coalescence with the central city. Historical traditions are thick in suburbs which were originally founded as isolated towns or villages, only later to be overwhelmed by the movement of population from the big city. Other suburbs have never enjoyed a distinct communal existence, having been created as real estate promotion schemes.

In addition to distinctions which may be used to characterize municipalities as a whole, innumerable groupings of the residents representing wide differences in economic status and power, religious affiliations and attitudes, cultural contacts and background, party affiliations, occupational interests, and racial and national loyalties, work within and across the boundaries of counties and municipalities. The politics of a large city and its metropolitan area are, it has been well said, "as much of a tangle and as full of movement as a canful of angleworms."

What groups in the metropolis have a special interest in the integration of local governments? What groups are opposed to integration? What support have the advocates or the opponents of integration secured from groups "downstate" or "upstate"? How have these groups rationalized their interests and around what symbols have they built their rationalizations? And finally, what techniques of appeal or persuasion have they resorted to, and how successfully have they employed these techniques?

BUSINESS AND PROFESSIONAL GROUPS

In many instances, agitation for a metropolitan government or for annexation to another municipality is provoked by objections to specific situations such as unpopular officials, objectionable tax rates, or embezzlement of funds. With the passage of time or a change in the situation, the movement is exhausted. Many people feel that these proponents of integration are attempting to grind their axes.

Although chambers of commerce are not primarily concerned with the organization and administration of local government, movements for integration are most frequently initiated by businessmen's organizations or by civic groups dominated by business and professional men. They have initiated and sponsored integration movements in several metropolitan areas, such as Pittsburgh, Cleveland, St. Louis, and Philadelphia. . . .

There are many associations besides chambers of commerce which draw their membership from business and professional men and women. . . .

The activity of most of these associations has likewise been sporadic and their interest in integration specialized. Taxpayers' leagues are obviously concerned with tax reductions, and they support consolidation schemes when they think economies can thereby be effected. They also tend to use every opportunity to attack the integrity of officeholders, and they often find such an opportunity in a campaign for integration.

The Civic Club of Allegheny County, the Philadelphia Bureau of Municipal Research, the Cleveland Citizens' League and the Milwaukee Citizens' Bureau have, on the other hand, shown interest in all phases of the government of their respective metropolitan areas. These associations are largely responsible for the publicity given to the problem over long periods of time. In the heat of the campaign preceding an election other groups climb on the band wagon, but in the long months of preparation, both in the metropolis itself and at the state capital, these are the associations that have kept persistently at work.

Some businessmen, industrialists, and professional men are opposed to governmental change of any kind. . . .

LABOR GROUPS

Organized labor and unorganized workers, even in the central city, often are suspicious of movements to integrate local government in the metropolitan area. In the first place, they suspect on sight anything initiated by, or under the auspices of, a chamber of commerce. Under the general policy, by no means confined to organized labor, of rewarding one's friends and punishing one's enemies, labor leaders fail to see why they should support part of the chamber-of-commerce program when at the same time the chamber is espousing the open shop or opposing labor legislation at the state or national capital. In the second place, they fear that any movement designed to reduce taxes will result in a curtailment of governmental services desirable or necessary to the laboring class.

Another reason why organized labor is often opposed is that suggested schemes of metropolitan government frequently provide for a short ballot and the council-manager form of government. The ideology of labor — in and out of trades unions or labor parties — is still largely that of Jacksonian Democracy. It is believed that appointees in responsible positions are more likely to be controlled by business, industrial, and financial leaders than by labor. . . .

Another point of concern with labor is the possibility that certain employees will lose their positions as the result of integration. Here is a sharp clash of interest between labor and chambers of commerce and taxpayers' groups, for the latter hope that integration will reduce the total number of employees and lower the cost of government. In Milwaukee, on the other hand, organized labor did not oppose the transfer of city parks to the county, because they saw therein an opportunity to organize the county park employees. This they proceeded to do immediately after the transfer was effected.

Labor has not uniformly opposed the integration of local government. . . .

More assistance from organized labor might be secured if the proponents of integration would seek the views, advice, and participation of labor leaders during the early stages of preparing the proposal and drafting the legislation.

POLITICIANS IN THE WOODPILE

It is often said that politicians, from a desire to hold on to their offices and emoluments, present insuperable obstacles to integration. They prefer, moreover, to act as big frogs in small ponds rather than to be small frogs in a big pond. The fear that integration will result in a loss of deference is not, however, confined to public officeholders. Leaders in all kinds of suburban groups, such as boy scouts, chambers of commerce, leagues of women voters, and luncheon and service clubs, are motivated by the fear of being swallowed into the general membership of the respective groups of the metropolis.

Politicians will openly oppose integration only if they think it "good," or at least "safe," politics to do so. If the dominant political party is opposed to integration (and it can easily be brought around to this position by influential suburban party leaders, the natural reluctance of party men to touch the patronage machine, and the downstate or upstate leaders' distrust of integration), it can usually manage to approve the movement locally and yet kill it by maneuvers in the rest of the state. Most integration movements have to clear the hurdle of an amendment to the state constitution or the proposed scheme must originate in or be approved by the state legislature. . . .

. . . Politicians, like other men, look suspiciously upon any potential threat to their job-security and personal income, but they are deference-hungry. It is less difficult for politicians to support reorganization and integration movements when a sizable portion of their constituents, as in Nassau and Westchester counties, pay deference to the exponents and practitioners of economical, efficient, businesslike administration. One key, then, to secure genuine party support and leadership is to alter the unfavorable or indifferent attitudes of the electorate, or to create new attitudes that can be evoked by old or new symbols and transferred into votes.

Suburban politicians almost always strike a responsive chord when they accuse the "machine" politicians of the central city of designing to pull, directly or indirectly, the clean, graftless, orderly suburb into the social chaos of the big "boss-ridden" city. The central city is accused of attempting to ease its financial condition by "forcibly annexing" the taxable resources of the thrifty and graft-free suburbs. (To the suburban opponent of integration, any form or degree of integration is "forcible annexation.") The suburbanites know that many of the facilities of the central city may be used by them, making it unnecessary for the suburbs to be taxed to maintain similar facilities.

Suburban officialdom is, as a rule, well organized, and finds a ready ear at the state capital for its cries of Wolf! Wolf! It has succeeded in many states in freezing an undemocratic impediment to integration into constitutions and statutes. The assent of a majority, and in California of all, of existing units of local government is required to integrate municipalities into a metropolitan government. This is done upon the theory that the home-rule principle means that the corporate integrity of each and every unit of local government must be preserved — irrespective of its population or of the degree of its economic and social coalescence with other units in the metropolitan area. The theory as applied in this manner allows a very small part of the total population of an area to veto any scheme, even though it is acceptable to a large majority of the electorate of the whole metropolis. The device cannot be considered democratic which allows, for example, fewer than 15,000 people who live in the smaller thirty-one of the sixty units of Cuyahoga County (Cleveland) to veto a plan which is approved by a majority of the electors representing the 1,201,455 inhabitants of the entire county.

ATTITUDES OF PEOPLE OUTSIDE METROPOLITAN AREAS

People who live outside metropolitan areas distrust the big city even more, if possible, than does the most confirmed suburbanite. After all, the suburban resident is a daily or occasional commuter, and knows the city. Time and again, the rural and village voters have denied the right to a majority of voters in a metropolitan area to decide upon issues vitally affecting no one save the metropolitan resident. Unscrupulous opponents of integration (such as suburban politicians, county politicians, public-utility men, contractors, and supply dealers) have told the rural and village voters that a large number of farmers would be brought under an expensive and cumbersome form of city government if the local governments of metropolitan areas were integrated. City-county consolidation has been described to them as a subversive scheme to destroy the American constitutional system! Judging from the fate of several integration proposals, the majority of upstate voters believe such statements.

MAKING INTEGRATION MARKETABLE

The proponents of integration, then, must prepare a marketable article and undertake to sell it. Campaigns must be well planned, the details carefully executed by technicians, and the proposal systematically and persistently sold to the public and to politicians. This calls for the use of various propaganda techniques. They are used by the opposition — thus far with almost complete success. It is not proposed to replace debate and discussion with deception and demagoguery; but it is quite clear that insistence upon the administrative and fiscal need for integration, in however great detail it is presented, is not sufficient to change popular allegiance to old concepts of local government. An academic presentation of the case for integrated local government will have no effect upon them. Counterattacks must be made frontally and by flank upon the symbol-reinforcing propaganda of the opponents of integration.

To be successful, the proponents of integration will have to reorganize the attitudes which are now elicited and reinforced by appeal to such symbols as *local self-government, home rule, the little red schoolhouse, "Keep our government clean!" government close to the people,* and, negatively, *centralization, forcible annexation, autocratic and un-American fascism, dictatorship,* and *corrupt city.* Each of these symbols is charged with high emotional voltage, and, by comparison, many of the symbols used by the proponents of integration arouse only a flicker of response. Symbols such as *economy, efficiency,* or *Pittsburgh . . . 1,500,000 people* evoke in only a few people central and dominating attitudes which can be translated into affirmative votes.

CHAPTER SIXTEEN

State and Local Politics

IT WOULD OBVIOUSLY BE MOST UNREALISTIC to assume a total separation between national politics and the politics of the states and local units, but this chapter focuses attention upon certain aspects of American politics where the state and local interest is predominant. In the opening selection the director of the Joint Center for Urban Studies of Harvard and M.I.T. examines the varying types of contemporary big city political systems and the nature of the changes they have been undergoing. "Reform," he notes, has traditionally been a dominant theme in the study of local politics, but both reform movements and reformers have likewise been greatly altered. The old anti-political bias is at least gradually disappearing, and today's reformer is far more likely to work within and through the political parties. Yet the basic class distinctions between the reformers and the mass of voters remain untouched.

The next two articles are in effect case studies of quite opposite patterns of city politics, and though they deal in part with events of a few years ago the pictures presented are very real. In the first the tactics and mechanisms by means of which a well-oiled city machine may maintain itself in control of a party are graphically portrayed by a liberal Democratic attorney experienced in intra-party battles with Tammany Hall. While recognizing the continued existence of machines, it is contended in the second that this is no longer the universal, or perhaps even the most common, situation the country over. In a great many of our cities, to say nothing of rural areas, the presumably customary tight precinct and block organizations simply do not exist today, and political action has often become periodic and considerably more amateur.

72

Politics and Reform
in American Cities

By James Q. Wilson

AMERICAN POLITICAL PARTIES, it has been frequently observed, are national in name but local in fact.

James Q. Wilson, "Politics and Reform in American Cities." From *American Government Annual,* 1962–1963, Edited by I. Hinderaker, et al., copyright © 1962 by Holt, Rinehart and Winston, Inc. Used by permission of the publisher (reduced by about one-half).

Although the President, Senators, and Representatives are known by their national party affiliations, and even though the electorate as a whole is divided principally on the basis of traditional allegiances to the two major national parties, political parties as full-time organizations are scarcely to be found at the national level at all. The leaders, workers, interests, financing, and routine activities of our parties are found almost entirely at the local level. The focus of party activity is the city hall, the county courthouse, the state legislature, and the governor's mansion. The national chairmen of the two parties are men of little power, generally preoccupied with paying off the party's debt and negotiating among rival factions. These national chairmen supervise perhaps twenty or thirty — sometimes as many as a hundred — full-time workers. The mayor of Chicago, by contrast, can command an army of political workers by means of city patronage appointments that number between 6,000 and 10,000. The governor of

Illinois has some 14,000 patronage jobs with which he can attract workers, while the governor of Pennsylvania has perhaps 40,000.

Every two years, these local organizations — literally thousands in number — seek to elect Representatives to Congress, but there is practically no national organization that conducts this campaign in any systematic or coordinated fashion. When the victorious Congressmen arrive in Washington, they are there largely as the result of 437 separate local political "games" played in the nation's Congressional districts. Only in certain cities and states is there any single organization which is responsible for the campaigns in more than a handful of these districts at any one time.

Every four years, these local organizations are brought together into an uneasy coalition for the purpose of electing a President. But no one "orders" local party leaders to support this or that man or to follow some particular tactic, and there is no single hierarchy which connects the national with all the local campaign headquarters. In the campaign for President, the strategies of the local leaders are often dictated more by considerations of local party advantage than by any enthusiasm for the national ticket. It is typical rather than unusual for enthusiastic amateurs, lured into a national contest by the personality of the national candidates, to discover that the local, professional party leaders do not share their enthusiasm. After every such campaign, there are always volunteers who complain bitterly that their man was "sold out" by party "bosses" who "sat on their hands" in the election because they were more interested in the identity of the next sheriff, judge, or mayor than in the identity of the next President.

That party leaders are, in varying degree, less interested in the Presidency than in local offices is often regarded as a defect of our political system. It is a defect only if one believes that the choice of the President (or of members of Congress) should always be the result of effort undertaken out of a concern for the Presidency and the issues with which the President must deal — if, in short, one believes that the end of political action (in this case, the choice of a President) should be the motive for action directed toward that end. In fact, however, an equally persuasive case can be made for the proposition that there are advantages in having the President chosen as the unanticipated consequence of action undertaken out of entirely different motives. If party leaders are preoccupied with the county courthouse, their support can be purchased by a President who is willing to help them retain control of that courthouse. If, on the other hand, party leaders are preoccupied with the personality and issues of the Presidency, their support and loyalty can only be purchased by making concessions on

matters of national policy. In the first case, the President can preserve a certain measure of discretion and freedom of action on matters which concern him *because* the "party" is decentralized and interested primarily in (to the President) trivial local affairs. In the second case, the President's freedom of action would have to be adjusted in a fundamental way to the demands of a national party organization deeply concerned with his conduct in office.

This issue is a familiar one in political science and it is common for scholars to take sides on it. But it is also largely a moot question, for we know very little about the actual effect that our decentralized, locally oriented party system has on the operation of the national government. Indeed, we know very little about local party organization generally. The purpose of this article is to sketch some of the major types of big-city, local party systems and to indicate some of the challenges with which they have been faced in recent years. It should be understood at the outset that there is very little systematic research on which one can draw for this purpose. Many of the comments made below are based on only the most superficial observations. Others are fairly well supported by studies of some aspects of a certain local party organization. But the student should regard most of the assertions below as hypotheses, not established generalizations.

TYPES OF BIG-CITY POLITICAL SYSTEMS

We shall speak of three kinds of big-city political organizations: machines, factional alliances, and nonpolitical elites. We shall look only at large cities (say, 250,000 population and over); the politics of smaller cities and towns are often different, not only in degree but in kind, from that found in the major metropolitan areas.

Machines

By a machine is meant a political organization which attracts and holds the loyalties of its workers primarily (although not entirely) through the distribution of tangible rewards. These tangible rewards will loosely be called patronage, and they include not only jobs on the city (or private) payrolls, but favors at city hall, contracts, and opportunities for personal gain. These workers canvass for votes, sometimes using material inducements but just as often relying on personal friendships and the indifference of certain voters to the identity of the candidate.

At one time, big-city machines flourished, and many (such as those in Philadelphia, Chicago, Cincinnati, and elsewhere) were Republican, not Democratic. Since the 1930s, however, the number of effective, city-wide machines has been declining and those which remain are almost all Democratic. To qualify as a machine system, the party must have control of the city as a whole (by electing the mayor and most of the legislators and judges); to qualify as a strong machine, it must also be able to control the selection of party leaders and the nomination of candidates for public office.

Machine cities, thus defined, include Chicago, Pittsburgh, New York, Philadelphia, Albany, Buffalo, Gary (Indiana), and a few others. Of the larger of these cities, only two have had strong machines in recent years — Chicago and Pittsburgh. In both cases, the party has been able to control nominations for office (which usually means controlling primary elections) and the party leadership has been able to enforce discipline on the rank and file. New York and Philadelphia are weak machine cities. In both instances, the machine leaders have not been able to control the nominations for all public offices, nor (particularly in the case of New York) have they been able to control the selection of party officials, such as district or county leaders.

Certain structural features tend to favor the machine system. The use of small districts or wards to choose city councilmen or aldermen permits these legislators to have direct contact with a small number of voters, often from a homogeneous ethnic or religious group. A large number of elective offices increases the number of rewards the machine can offer its followers, multiplies the points at which the machine has access to the formal government, and reduces the likelihood that more than a few voters will know the identity or personal characteristics of any but a small fraction of the public officials. The presence of a large, polyglot, lower-income population in the central city provides a reservoir of voters who are more susceptible to material rewards than are affluent middle-class citizens.

A machine can exist without these features, however. In Kansas City, Missouri, in the 1930s, for example, the Pendergast organization was able to exercise control over the city even after the number of councilmen had been reduced, some elected at large rather than from neighborhood districts, and a city manager appointed. Further, Kansas City was not a "port of entry" for large masses of immigrants; it was a heavily middle-class city, with little ethnic tension. Nonetheless, Kansas City (and a few other cities) are atypical in this regard; for the most part, the prospects for a machine are enhanced by any circumstances which make it easier for the party to mobilize racial, religious, and ethnic blocs by giving them "recognition" on a city-wide ticket and direct representation in the city's legislature.

The literature on machines is, of course, vast, and the major features of this political system are too well-known to require restatement here. The changes over time in the machine, however, deserve comment. It has been widely believed that the days of the machine are numbered because of the operation of certain factors hostile to it. The spread of the civil service merit system, the increased newspaper scrutiny of civic affairs, the growing American urban middle class and the assimilation of older ethnic groups have all been cited as reasons why machine politics is on the wane. Added to these changes were the federal welfare programs begun in the 1930s which, in effect, nationalized and impersonalized the distribution of those benefits which, formerly, the machine had made available on a local and individual basis. Edwin O'Connor in his popular novel, *The Last Hurrah,* explained the fall of his fictional boss of Boston (who many believe was patterned after James M. Curley) essentially in these terms.

Although there is a great deal of truth in all of these observations, they fall short of being a full account of the recent history of the machine. The organizations in New York, Pittsburgh and Chicago have survived the New Deal and the affluent society; indeed, the Chicago Democratic machine was founded in the early 1930s. The Republican machine in Philadelphia persisted into the 1940s and has now been replaced by a new Democratic organization which was, for all practical purposes, created in the 1950s. In Kansas City, the Pendergast machine collapsed, not so much from population or political changes, as from the federal prosecution of its leader on income tax charges.

Indeed, there are now forces at work which, in certain places, may partially offset the effect of assimilation and the New Deal. The exodus to the suburbs in such places as Chicago, Philadelphia, New York, Cincinnati, and Cleveland is leaving the central city more and more to Negro, Southern white, and Puerto Rican immigrants. Such people can benefit from machine services and be mobilized by machine appeals. Racial barriers and cultural limitations, which confine most Negroes and Puerto Ricans to the central cities, may provide new sources of manpower for machine politics.

The significance of the machine for national political parties is that its support can be acquired with a minimum commitment on issues. The boss of the local machine must acquire a steady stream of material incentives to sustain his organization; such incentives come primarily from patronage and opportunities to hold minor elective offices; these resources, in turn, are dependent simply on electoral victory, and not on victory in behalf of some particular cause, issue, or candidate. The boss is interested in picking winners; if he is a secure boss — i.e., if his machine is strong and he is its undisputed leader —he will be able to negotiate with national party leaders with great tactical flexibility. He can make commitments and he can, within certain limits, deliver on those commitments. His support is cheap in terms of the concessions on issues the national party leaders must make; it may be expensive in terms of demands for jobs and a reluctance to go all-out on behalf of a presidential candidate when more lucrative (in terms of patronage) local offices are at stake.

Factional alliances

By factional alliance is meant a big-city political party which is a coalition of groups, none of which can impose its will on the other members of the coalition. A faction is a party within a party, and may consist of a personal following, an interest group, a small ward or district machine, or a political club. A machine — a political organization based on material incentives — may exist for areas smaller than the city as a whole. In one ward of Boston, for example, a small Negro machine has been run by a local druggist who has dispensed favors and organized voters. A similar "submachine" can be found in Memphis. Parts of Baltimore and New Orleans have partial, or submachines. In such cases, the party of the city as a whole is not a machine — often because there are either insufficient resources, such as patronage, to extend the machine throughout the city, or because there are too few people living in the city receptive to the minor forms of patronage available. In such cases, these partial machines must enter into coalitions with other groups.

These other groups are organizations — usually rather informal ones — based on other kinds of inducements. A personal following is based on the value some people attach to the friendship and perhaps the charismatic qualities of some individual or family. An interest group is based on the value some persons attach to certain material rewards other than patronage (such as pay increases sought by teachers or civil servants) or ideological rewards (such as extensions in the merit system sought by good-government groups). A political club is based on the value some people attach to the camaraderie or social functions of an organization which is interested in contesting elections. The political club differs from the local machine in that, although both groups participate in politics for reasons other than matters of principle, in the club they are induced to work simply by the satisfactions of being a member of the club, rather than by the prospect of a job. In the actual case, of course, people may participate for both reasons.

There are probably more big cities which display a politics of faction than any other kind of local party organization. Factional politics generally occurs when a city-wide machine has been destroyed or seriously weakened, but not replaced with a wholly new set of institutions (such as nonpolitical elites, discussed below). Factional politics is found in Kansas City (Missouri), Boston, Cleveland, St. Louis, Jersey City, and Cincinnati, to name but a few. Such weak machine cities as New York and Philadelphia may be headed in the direction of factional politics.

The crucial problem in factional politics is the terms on which a coalition can be arranged. Although a single party (usually the Democratic) will win the general election and most of all officeholders will thus bear the same party label, they will have no common allegiance to any single party leadership nor will they be motivated by any single set of interests or principles. Such a local party system in big Northern cities is more similar to the kind of one-party factionalism which V. O. Key, Jr., described in his book, *Southern Politics,* than it is to national two-party politics. Allegiances to family names, the "friends and neighbors" effect, and the bloc votes of independent political clubs are all important factors. . . .

The significance of factional politics for national party leaders is that acquiring the support of such groups is often extremely costly. An alliance with one faction almost precludes an alliance with certain others. Some groups can be attracted by the promise of patronage, others with assurances of financial aid for local campaigns, others by endorsing their programs and ideologies. Building such alliances is a risky and difficult enterprise, however, for an outsider can never know the intricacies of local politics as well as do those involved. Massachusetts Democratic politics, for example, is often referred to as "the swamp" in which the light is poor, the stench unbearable, the quicksand everywhere, and progress impossible. In such circumstances, the national leader often abandons any hope of getting all factions to work together but relies instead on whomever he thinks is strongest and least expensive — in either money, jobs, or commitments on program.

Nonpolitical elites

By nonpolitical elites we refer to persons wielding substantial influence over the selection of public officials and the determination of public policy who are themselves not occupants of political posts or leaders of political (i.e., vote-getting) organizations. Newspaper publishers and editors, big businessmen, labor leaders, the executives and presidents of civic associations, bankers, lawyers, and public relations men are examples of such persons. Such people, of course, often play important political roles in machine cities, and commonly their aid is sought in factional cities; but, in the cities to which we refer here, they are the dominant, not the secondary, political actors and wield crucial, not partial, influence. In smaller American cities and towns, such nonpolitical elites often dominate public affairs entirely, even though parties exist. But in big American cities, it is typically the case that nonpolitical elites are most powerful in nonpartisan cities.

Some cities, of course, are nonpartisan in name only. . . . But there are big cities which are genuinely nonpartisan — not only is there no party label on the ballot, but the party does not nominate candidates or campaign for them as organizations. Detroit, Los Angeles, and Houston are examples of nonpartisan cities where the outcome of the electoral contest is not significantly the result of efforts made by partisan organizations but rather of efforts made by nonpolitical elites. Of course . . . such elites are not always successful nor do they always work in concert.

The genuinely nonpartisan city will have political parties within its borders, but customarily they are more interested — as organizations — in county, state, and national politics. The nature of city politics forbids them from drawing strength from participation in city affairs. In most nonpartisan cities, there is practically no patronage available for distribution to parties. In genuinely nonpartisan communities, it appears that the voters resent the open intrusion of party organizations in local elections and favor a method which they feel permits them to vote "for the man, not the party." Elective officials usually find it to their advantage to remain aloof from party affairs, even to the extent of concealing or playing down their own party affiliations. They prefer to cultivate support on a personal basis, appealing to broad segments of the population through the mass media of communication and contacts with voluntary associations.

Nonpartisanship usually tends to favor Republican — or, more correctly, business-oriented — political leaders. . . .

The nonpolitical elites carry weight in the absence of a party organization absorbed in city elections because they can provide alternative forms of political support to local candidates: money and personal endorsements. The money is used to hire public relations firms and campaign workers and to buy advertising space. The endorsements — by newspapers, civic associations, labor unions, and business leaders — are intended to distinguish one candidate from the other in the voter's mind on the basis, not of party identity (which cannot appear on the ballot), but of personal prestige and associational respectability. . . . [but] money and endorsements, while powerful, do not always bring success.

The significance of nonpolitical elites to national party leaders varies. In cities such as Los Angeles, nonpartisanship contributes to (although it is not the sole cause of) a situation in which there is no political party within the city upon which the national candidate can rely. If the national leader is a Democrat, it usually means that there is not much of an elite on which he can rely either, for Republicans are far more likely to have those resources (money, prestige, and business and newspaper connections) necessary for the operation of a nonpartisan campaign. In other cities, such as Detroit, the UAW-CIO and the Democratic Party have maintained a fairly effective precinct organization, normally used to wage statewide contests, which can be made available to national candidates. But whatever the situation, the national leader is deprived of the resources of city hall in a nonpartisan community: its influence, stature, patronage, and favors are not available for assisting the national party coalition.

TYPES OF REFORM MOVEMENTS

The principal theme in the study of local politics has always been the checkered history of reform in the major American cities. Long before Lincoln Steffens wrote *The Shame of the Cities,* the fundamental problem of local government was viewed in terms of a contest between rascals and reformers. Our federal government has only occasionally been seen from this perspective; usually, the national administration has been evaluated in terms of the substance of the policies it has carried out. Corruption and conflict of interest have always been discovered in Washington, but these unsavory incidents have rarely provided the leitmotif for the study of national politics.

It is by no means obvious why this discrimination against local government should persist. It is not enough to say that local affairs are seen in terms of corruption simply because there is more corruption to be found there, for corruption could coexist (and, in fact, has coexisted) with substantive policies which are in the public interest. Nor have local machines always encouraged waste and corruption. . . .

There are, of course, several reasons why our attention to big-city politics is so often absorbed by reports of graft and impropriety. One may be a result of the generally accepted belief that local government is, or ought to be, that level of government "closest to the people" and thus most expressive of widely shared sentiments and fundamental principles. Dishonesty in local government is "close to home" and disturbing, while rascality in Washington or abroad is remote and, in a way, expected. Cities, after all, educate our children and police our streets. But this reason, while it may have some merit, is not completely convincing. Although local government may be close to the people in small cities and towns, it is doubtful whether the people feel that the government of a vast metropolis such as New York, Chicago, or Los Angeles is any "closer" to them than the local representatives of the federal government who collect taxes, draft soldiers, or pay benefits.

A more general reason might be that, in most cases, the activities of local government are not intrinsically interesting, at least not in the way the great, national issues of peace and war, prosperity and depression, are interesting. Local government, if it is to attract attention at all, can usually do so only when evidence of wrongdoing is brought forward. Most cities do little more than provide certain minimal, essential, public services. And, for most people most of the time, these services are provided adequately, or at least not so inadequately as to call for anything more than routine complaints. The politics and policies of big cities rarely implicate the most important interests of many powerful individuals or organizations. City politics are peripheral to the major concerns of most organized groups. . . .

. . . reform efforts in city politics have typically been aimed, not so much at altering the ends of government — reformers have usually assumed that most people were in agreement on what public services ought to be performed — but at altering the personnel of government and eliminating dishonesty and inefficiency. In this, of course, they may have been fundamentally wrong, for there are many people in big cities who prefer less, rather than more, police supervision and who care little about public education. But reform efforts have usually been led by persons with a commitment to a high level of certain "non-controversial" public services; it is the high cost or low quality of these services, rather than the services themselves, that the reformers have typically wanted to change. . . .

Reform movements are not identical, however. Although most of them have certain common features, there are local differences and, what is even more important, some have undergone a radical transformation in recent years. Generally speaking, there have been five kinds of local political reform efforts: citizens' leagues, candidate screening committees, blue-ribbon candidates, independent local parties, and intraparty factions. One variant type could be added, although it is only called into being on an *ad hoc* basis — the informal group of nonpolitical community notables who coalesce before elections, usually in nonpartisan cities, to select and raise money for local candidates. These five kinds can be conveniently categorized on the basis of whether they operate within or outside the regular political parties and whether they are interested primarily in suggesting policies and programs, selecting candidates, or winning office.

Table 1
MAJOR TYPES OF
CIVIC REFORM ORGANIZATIONS

RELATION TO PARTIES	GOALS:		
	Policies	Candidates	Organizations
Extraparty	Citizens' leagues; municipal research bureaus	Screening committees; nonpolitical elites	Independent local parties
Intraparty	[Residual category, no major examples]	"Blue-ribbon" leadership factions, and candidates	Intraparty reform clubs or factions

These kinds of reform efforts can be briefly identified:

1. Citizens' leagues. Citizens' leagues are voluntary associations, often with a paid staff executive or research director, which scrutinize local government structure, programs, and expenditures and recommend changes and reforms. The New York Citizens' Budget Commission, the Chicago Civic Federation, the Detroit Citizens' League, the Pennsylvania Economy League, the Seattle Municipal League, and the Boston Municipal Research Bureau are all examples of extraparty, policy-oriented, citizens' committees which have been the vehicle for various kinds of reform efforts. The League of Women Voters is probably the largest single organization of this kind.

2. Candidate appraisal committees. Created outside the political parties, the committees are organizations, permanent or *ad hoc,* which recommend or evaluate candidates for public office. Where the parties are weak or nonexistent (as in certain nonpartisan cities, Los Angeles, for example), these committees may be informal groups of the most influential businessmen, lawyers, and publishers who, in the absence of party control, actually select a candidate for mayor and raise the funds to hire a public relations firm to conduct his campaign. In such a case, the group will almost never be formally organized; it will usually have no name, staff, or office; and its membership will be carefully limited. Where, on the other hand, the parties are strong (as in New York, for example), no outside group can dictate the choice of candidates. Whatever committee may exist in this area will, typically, be composed of lesser business and professional people (there is too little at stake to attract top men); it will be formally organized with an office, budget, and staff; and it will confine itself to evaluating candidates for office, often by ranking them, "endorsed," "preferred," "qualified," or "unqualified." The Citizens' Union of New York City is an example of such an organization, although it also is active in other aspects of government, such as evaluating proposed legislation and scrutinizing the conduct of public officials.

3. Independent local parties. Under certain circumstances, reform-minded people will enter the elective process directly by creating a local political party, independent of the major parties, which will run slates of candidates for municipal and other local offices. The City Charter Committee in Cincinnati and the Citizens' Association in Kansas City, Missouri, are perhaps the two most important examples. The Liberal Party in New York City is an independent party of a special kind: unlike most organizations of this kind, it was formed by certain strong, Jewish-led labor unions committed to a New Deal ideology, rather than by business and professional men (often conservatives on national issues) interested in efficiency and economy in local government. . . .

4. "Blue-ribbon" leadership factions. Comprised of leaders of a regular political party, these factions seek to induce the party to nominate "good government" or "blue-ribbon" candidates for local offices. Sometimes such a leadership faction is a minority, composed of dissident reformers who happen to occupy party posts; just as often, blue-ribbon candidates may be slated at the instigation of regular party leaders who have no personal commitment to reform at all. Examples of the former would be Richardson Dilworth and Joseph S. Clark who have attempted to reform the Democratic party in Philadelphia from the top down, by fighting both to retain party support for themselves and to obtain it for like-minded men whom they endorse. Examples of the latter would be Col. Jacob Arvey and Mayor Richard J. Daley in Chicago who, although not at all interested in party reform, have, from time to time, recognized the electoral advantages to be obtained from nominating men such as Paul Douglas and Adlai Stevenson for posts at the top of the Democratic ticket. James Finnegan of Philadelphia, who before his death was an ally of Clark and Dilworth, was also a regular party man who thought "good government was good politics."

5. Intraparty reform factions. Of late, reformers have not been content with forming extraparty civic groups or with seeking nominations for blue-ribbon candidates; instead, they have entered the regular party (usually the Democratic) at its lowest levels, in the wards and assembly districts, to capture control of party posts and the party organizations. The clubs associated with the New York Committee for Democratic Voters have had considerable success with this tactic in Manhattan, coming close to winning a majority of the votes on the executive committee of the party, popularly known as Tammany Hall. In California, local political clubs have been formed, under the aegis of the California Democratic Council, which have sought to create machinery for endorsing Democratic candidates for public office that will guarantee that these nominees will be liberal, good government types.

All of these kinds of reform or good government efforts have existed for many years. With the exception of certain of the larger, better established ones, however, most are fairly short-lived. So little systematic research on city politics has been done that we know little, except in a few cities, about any causal factors which may be associated with the rise and fall of reform efforts. We have little general knowledge concerning the conditions under which one rather than another reform strategy is likely to be employed. Nor can anything be said with confidence about the relationship between the type of local political system, as described in the preceding section, and the type of reform effort which appears. What appears below, therefore, is of a very speculative nature.

First, a shift has probably begun from extraparty to intraparty reform efforts. Early in this century, there were civic groups, research bureaus, and independent local parties in many large cities. All represented efforts to reform government and politics with the power of publicity and research and by electing a few good men to top offices on independent slates. Very few made more than a monetary impression on their cities. The reasons for their limited value are well-known: their inability to sustain volunteer interest in political campaigning; their failure to create permanent political organizations which could defend the reform candidates who were elected to office; and their willingness to contest only the prestigious higher offices, leaving the minor — but often politically more important — offices in the hands of the machine. Research bureaus, of course, did not contest any offices; their decay began with the realization that the majority of the voters did not automatically respond to "objective" facts about municipal expenditures and administrative procedures by spontaneously organizing themselves in order to throw the inefficient or dishonest politician out of office. In fact, some citizens, for reasons the early reformers never really understood, seemed to prefer waste and favoritism so long as somebody in the machine was willing and able to look after a distressed voters' personal needs.

Further, except in the genuinely nonpartisan cities, the allegiance of the voters continued to be to the traditional party labels — particularly the allegiance of the lower-income, less educated voters who, in most cases, made up a majority of the electorate. Creating an independent local party led by upper-middle-class lawyers and housewives was often an excellent means for attracting the support of "independent" voters; unfortunately, these usually happened to be a distinct minority. Although exposures of shocking examples of graft and malfeasance could often give the independent party a temporary majority, these never endured as vote-getting devices when matched against the lasting power of the words "Democratic" or "Republican."

Thus, after World War II, certain young reformers in various cities and states began to think seriously of the possibility of taking over one of the major parties — of shifting from an extraparty to an intraparty strategy. This would give them the best of both worlds — reform leadership combined with control of a traditional party label. Such a strategy, of course, would be far harder to pursue, at least in its initial stages, because the regular party leaders would fight bitterly any attempt to wrest control of the organization from them. But if that battle could be won, the reformers reasoned, maintaining a reform movement would be far easier, for they would then have at their disposal the resources of the regular party, including the patronage on which conventional politicians often depended.

A second, and related, trend has been a shift from conservatives to liberals, or at least from Republicans to Democrats, as the backbone of reform efforts. The earliest independent local parties, research bureaus, and citizens' committees were often founded and financed by some of the wealthiest men in town, mostly Republicans. . . .

The new, postwar group of young reformers shares the mentality of older reformers — a belief in good government and efficiency, a dislike of machines and patronage, and a desire to see public policies set as a result of deliberate action (ideally, by "planning") rather than as the unintended consequence of struggles for power — but the difference in political strategy has meant that the new reform leaders have been drawn from a different ideological background. If one decides to be an intraparty rather than extraparty reformer, it means one must be willing to enter politics at the lowest level and spend much time and effort in the menial chores of politics — forming organizations, circulating petitions, ringing doorbells, and speaking on street corners. Such a strategy is rarely congenial to an affluent, middle-aged businessman with a secure position in society. The older reformer preferred to write a check and allow his name to be used on a letterhead; staff men were hired to do the rest, with the businessmen merely attending periodic luncheon meetings to approve high policy and hear evangelical speeches.

The intraparty reformer, therefore, tends to be young, usually under thirty-five and often under thirty and in the early years of his career. Further, the laborious nature of the work requires a high level of motivation on the part of the activist. Intraparty reform offers one inducement which is identical to that provided by extraparty reform: the opportunity to do good and throw the rascals out. But it also provides an additional incentive: the opportunity to gratify personal political ambitions. Older reformers concentrated on one or a few major offices — usually the mayor and perhaps a few city councilmen — and they were suspicious of persons who offered themselves as candidates for these posts. They preferred men who were reluctant to take on such assignments and who had to be talked into leaving lucrative law practices to serve the public. The new reformers, dedicated to taking over the entire party and all the offices it controls, can offer many opportunities for exercising power and acquiring prestige; far from being reluctant to run for such offices, the reformers often compete among themselves for the nominations.

The Democratic party dominates the politics of most major cities and, thus, intraparty reform means entering and taking over the Democratic party. As a result, the young men and women with sufficient ideological or personal motivation to undertake the difficult task are usually people who feel strongly (or who act *as if* they feel strongly) about the policies of the Democratic party, and these, of course, are usually the members of the party's liberal — sometimes even "extreme" liberal — wing. The new strategy of reform and the organizational problems it creates, therefore, virtually insure that the new reformers will be liberal Democrats while the older group were middle-of-the-road or, at best, Progressive Republicans.

If the new strategy of intraparty reform promises to be more enduring and, for young liberals, more attractive, it also has a profound disadvantage. The young reformers, although not necessarily the sons and daughters of the well to do, are at least middle class: thus, their political strength is to be found only where the middle class lives, not primarily in the central city, but in its suburbs. Where it does live in the central city, it is usually in relatively small neighborhoods, often surrounded by lower-class slums. In New York City, for example, the Democratic reformers live, by and large, in districts where they are outnumbered by Republicans. This is not a handicap so long as the reformers are struggling for control of the party in that district, for party leadership fights are waged in primary elections in which only enrolled Democrats can vote. The problems arise when these reformers attempt to extend their influence in the party; then they must contend with the fact that many, if not most, central city party officials are chosen in districts in which the middle class — and, hence, in which middle-class reformers — do not live: Negro Harlem, Puerto Rican East Harlem, the Jewish Lower East Side, and so forth.

This ecological obstacle is encountered again when reformers attempt to make their weight felt in general elections — in, for example, the election of a mayor. Here, members of all parties can vote, and in most cases the Democratic votes in reform-controlled districts are overwhelmed by the Republican votes. In the November 1961 New York mayoralty election, for example, the reform-backed Democratic candidate, Robert F. Wagner, got his strongest support from lower-income districts where the regular Democratic leaders had fought him in the primary, and little or no support from the middle-class districts where the reform Democratic leaders had backed him in the primary. Although the reformers had helped him win the nomination in the primary, the non-reform districts helped him win the general election against the Republican opposition. The reformers, as a result, could not lay full claim to Wagner's loyalties. . . .

The CDV and the CDC club members have in common at least two goals: intraparty democracy and committing the party to issues. These are the newer and, to their exponents, more sophisticated versions of such old reform slogans as "throw the rascals out" and "efficiency and honesty." Intraparty democracy means creating institutional constraints on party leaders such that party members — which usually means reform-minded, liberal, party members — can exercise a significant measure of control over them in such matters as the selection of candidates for office, campaigns, the allocation of patronage, party finance, and relations with public officials. Issue commitment means changing the party from a more or less ideologically neutral broker of competing interests into a source of positive programs; the party is to profess principles and policies, not because they are useful in winning votes, but because they are, in the eyes of the party activists, the "right" policies. The party would thus become a radically different kind of organization. Conventional local parties, based on machines, social clubs, personal followings, or interest groups, can induce their workers to contribute time and effort because of material, social, or personal interests; this leaves the party a rather considerable freedom in adopting whatever "principles" seem most expedient for winning votes. The reform-controlled party, by contrast, can only induce its intellectually oriented, liberal volunteers to work by committing itself on a wide range of issues, whether or not such positions are politically expedient. . . .

Success will probably prove to be as mixed a blessing for the CDV as it has been for the CDC. Both organizations seek to elect liberal, good government Democrats to office. In both cases, such candidates have often found club support a valuable asset in Democratic primaries, but a liability in general elections. Reformers, as mentioned before, tend to be influential precisely in those areas where few Democratic votes are to be found. Democrats who have won their primaries usually discover that they must appeal to a broad range of voters in a way which an overly close identification with ultra-liberal clubs can embarrass. And, once safely in office, they are anxious to avoid any commitments which will inhibit their ability to maintain good relations with the wide variety of interest groups and political forces which can affect their prospects for re-election. . . .

CONCLUDING OBSERVATIONS

The most general theme which appears again and again in the politics of large American cities is the importance of the class structure of the community in determining at least the broad outlines of political conflict. Although narrow conceptions of "class conflict" are — quite properly — disappearing from most of the literature of political science, the extent to which differences in income and ethnicity continue to provide the raw material of city politics is, nonetheless striking.

In partisan cities, the perennial contests between professional and reform politicians are, in large part, the political expression of fundamental differences between the conceptions of the public interest held by lower- and lower-middle class voters on the one hand, and upper-middle and upper-class voters, on the other. The former have a political ethic which places a high value on personal friendships, tangible needs, family and ethnic loyalties, and the exchange of favors; the latter an ethic which stresses the need for enacting general principles, serving city-wide rather than neighborhood interests, making policy by planning rather than by political bargaining, and rationalizing politics with law.

The organizational expression of the former ethic has been the political machine or its factional variants; of the latter, the civic associations, newspapers, reform movements, and committees of elites. The struggle between these two kinds of organizations has been surprisingly even, with the advantage shifting back and forth with pendulumlike regularity. The identity of the followers of each set of leaders has changed: in an earlier era, Irish Democrats fought Yankee Republicans; today, Italian and Negro leaders fight Yankee and Jewish Democrats. Only in those cities which have fundamentally changed their governing institutions have the reformers scored permanent gains: nonpartisanship and patronage-free administrations have largely prevented the political organization of the lower classes. Only when, as has recently happened in Los Angeles and Detroit, a widespread sense of grievance provides an issue which can activate large minorities do the community elites suffer a reverse. Otherwise, Negroes — the natural source of strength for new machines — are excluded from a share in the governing of these cities; the men who "represent" them in city hall can only be men who are acceptable to moderate white sentiments.

Shifting from an extraparty to an intraparty reform strategy has not solved this problem. Although some reformers hope that it may lessen the gulf between them and Negroes by creating the possibility of an alliance within a single party — the Democratic — it should not be forgotten that in the interwar period, reformers and many minority groups were also of the same party — the Republican. The difference, of course, is that previously the reformers sought power with leadership caucuses or independent parties, while today they seek it within the regular organization. The elimination of this organizational distinction, however, is not likely to eliminate the real grounds for the lack of rapport between lower-class voters and upper-class reformers, for that difference is far more profound than one of organizational allegiance — it is a difference in class, rhetoric, style of life, and social purposes.

73

How Tammany Holds Power

By Justin N. Feldman

TAMMANY HALL may consider the New York primary law a nuisance but never an obstacle. The long cherished hopes of Charles Evans Hughes which eventually developed into New York State's primary

Justin N. Feldman, "How Tammany Holds Power," *National Municipal Review*, July, 1950, pp. 330–334. Reprinted by permission of the publisher.

election system have been completely frustrated by failure of the law to prescribe rules for the internal management of political parties.

How does the notorious Tammany Hall organization operate to perpetuate its control of the party's machinery despite a direct primary law? It should be made perfectly clear at the outset that, while this story deals with the Democratic party organization on Manhattan Island (New York County), the techniques described and, yes, even some of the incidents, are often duplicated in the Republican party.

Tammany Hall is the popular name for the executive committee organization in Manhattan. Once the dominant influence over the party organization in the entire city, Tammany has lost much of its power in recent years. . . .

Still, it is Tammany Hall which, by controlling the party machinery, designates the party's candidates for public office. It is Tammany which sends large delegations to the all-important state and national nominating conventions. It is Tammany which dispenses whatever city, state and federal patronage falls to the Democrats. And it is Tammany which, under the election law, is authorized to make the rules by which the party in Manhattan is governed.

In Manhattan the Democratic vote regularly exceeds that of the Republican party. In most areas of the island a victory in the Democratic primary is tantamount to election. As less than 10 per cent of the Democrats in any given area of Manhattan ever vote in even the most hotly contested primary, Tammany, capitalizing on apathy, on its control of the machinery and on the obstacles it knows how to put in the way of insurgents, rules the roost.

Manhattan has sixteen assembly districts, each of which elects a representative to the lower house of the legislature. Each assembly district is divided into election districts (voting precincts) on the basis of the number of registered voters in the area. The number of election districts varies from 28 in the fourteenth assembly district to 105 in the fifth. The boundaries of the various assembly districts and of the election districts are set by the city council, which is commonly controlled by the Democratic party, and Tammany can thereby gerrymander the boundaries to suit its own convenience.

District leaders

Each of Manhattan's sixteen assembly districts has one vote in the party's executive committee and is represented there by at least one district leader and a woman co-leader, sometimes more. The co-leader is entitled to divide the district's vote and cast her portion as she likes but by force of long tradition she usually remains in the background and exercises her vote in accordance with the wishes of her leader. The value of the district's vote on this executive committee depends further upon the number of leaders there are from that particular district. For the number of leaders and co-leaders who will be recognized and entitled to sit on this party executive committee with fractional votes is determined, not by statute or by the enrolled Democrats or by the geographical size or party registration of the assembly district, but by the whim or the carefully calculated design of the executive committee itself.

Most of the assembly districts in Manhattan have thus been carefully subdivided by the executive committee to the advantage of its veteran members. An assembly district may be represented on the executive committee or "in the hall" by two, three or even seven district leaders and an equal number of co-leaders. The assembly district in which I reside, for example, has seven leaders and seven co-leaders on the Tammany executive committee; each of these leaders and co-leaders is entitled to 1/14th of a vote.

The leader is an extremely important person. Aside from his countywide power as a member of "the hall," he helps control nominations in "his" county subdivisions which elect assemblymen, state senators, congressmen and certain judges.

But how is this key leader (executive committee member) chosen? In other counties of greater New York, Democratic district leaders are elected by the voters direct; likewise in other parties. But to make boss control of the party easier in Manhattan, the leader is not voted for in a party primary directly by the voters but is selected by the members of the county committee in his portion of the assembly district.

Now, let's look at this county committee. It is a massive barrier. By state law two county committeemen must be elected from each little election district. The party may by its rules provide such additional membership on the county committee as its chairman deems desirable, so long as the additional membership for each election district is kept in proportion to the party vote for governor in the last gubernatorial race. So each election district in Manhattan elects some ten to twenty committeemen. The number of committeemen in each assembly district consequently comes to 1,125 or more!* Most of the members of the county committee are friends and relatives of the party's election district captains (whom the leader appoints) and don't even know they are on the committee, much less what its function and power may be.

---

* The whole county has about 20,000 county committeemen. Except for one occasion in 1933, however, no meeting of the entire county committee has ever been attended by more than 500 persons.

Railroaded action

In calling a meeting of the county committee members in his part of the assembly district, it is not uncommon for the leader to notify only those persons whom he knows to be friendly. Tammany Hall appoints the temporary chairman and secretary of the meeting. A script is prepared in advance and distributed to the "actors" who have been given particular parts for the evening. The chairman, working from a copy of his script, will only recognize those persons whose names appear on it although scores of other voters howl concertedly for a chance to speak or nominate. Often the meetings are held on the street. A truck is backed up in front of the local district club house. Passers-by are treated to a routine bit of mumbo-jumbo from the chairman on the truck. The stalwart Tammany committeemen who are present rubberstamp the top command's choice for leader. Who can prove that there, in the open air, no quorum of county committeemen was present?

An insurgent seeking to elect sufficient county committeemen pledged to support him for leader has an almost insuperable task confronting him.

He must print and circulate nominating petitions bearing the names of a different slate of county committeemen for each little election district. If a name is misspelled on the petition, or if the signer uses an initial in signing instead of his full given name, or if the color of the petition differs in tint from the prescribed shade, or if the petition sheet uses an abbreviation in the name of an avenue or street, or if any one of several hundred pitfalls which have been read into the direct primary law are not avoided, the petitions will be whittled down and voided by the Board of Elections.

Under New York State law the Board of Elections is composed of four commissioners, two designated by the Democratic executive committees for the counties of New York and Kings (Brooklyn) and two by the Republicans. In all internal fights whereby the control of the dominant factions of the "regular" organizations are threatened, one hand very definitely washes the other.

If the insurgent candidate for leader succeeds nevertheless in getting his slates on the ballots, he must deal with the further difficulty that his name does not appear anywhere on the ballots, and the task of informing even an aroused electorate, so that they may pick out his ten or twenty supporters on the primary ballot, is extremely difficult.

Now, assume — if you can — that you have succeeded in electing a majority of the county committee in your bailiwick! Isn't that enough? Won't your candidate then be duly elected by the committeemen who have thus been pledged to vote for him?

Surely if Tammany in calling the meeting has notified all of the persons entitled to attend, and if the persons whom you have elected attend, and if the Tammany-appointed chairman of the meeting acts fairly, and if the Tammany-appointed secretary of the meeting counts the votes accurately, and if the police repulse Tammany attempts to pack the meeting, you will elect the district leader? Oh, no! Not so simple! There are many other obstacles which Tammany may put in your way. They may do any of the following under the rules they have set up since the law empowers them to concoct their own rules:

You can't win!

Suppose you run a candidate for district leader in an assembly district which contains 99 election districts. There have always been three leaders in that district and the fellow you are anxious to oust is in charge of election districts one through 33. You file your petitions for these districts. You elect your slate for county committeemen in twenty of the 33 districts and are feeling pretty secure about the prospective meeting of the county committeemen when called to select the leader.

Tammany, however, has the right to decide *after* the primary that the man you opposed will now govern only thirteen safe districts and the remaining twenty, wherein you were successful, will be added to the territory of the fellow who previously had the 33 adjoining election districts numbered 34 to 66. You now control only twenty districts out of the revised group of 53.

Under Tammany rules, the executive committee — that is, the other leaders — may sit as judge of the qualifications of its own members and may veto the choice made by the county committeemen and substitute a man of their own selection. And this decision, again under the rules, may be made by the outgoing executive committee on which the leader you opposed is entitled to vote.

But this is not all. They have other devices! In 1947 a group of Democrats in the fifteenth assembly district organized to elect a district leader. After a hard and bitter fight waged against a leader who had been in control of that particular district for fourteen years, they elected a majority of county committeemen. Through the use of pressure on other party leaders they were able to get acceptance for their choice by the executive committee.

Some months later, however, the Tammany county leader, chairman of both the county committee and its executive committee, called a meeting of the county committeemen of that assembly district and accompanied by some of his strong-arm men, attended this meeting which was chaired by his designee. When he walked in, he distributed copies of a script for the meeting to his accomplices and the meeting went off like a well rehearsed radio program.

Following a line by line recital of the script, the assembly district, which had heretofore had only one district leader casting a full vote in the councils of the executive committee, was declared split. A second district leader was selected — someone whom nobody in the district had heard of. The meeting was declared adjourned and the master light switch was pulled so that the meeting could not continue and objectors could not be heard.

A new henchman of the dominant faction of Tammany had been installed and from that time forward the leader chosen by the county committeemen of the district no longer enjoyed a full vote in the executive committee but was relegated to a half vote, offset, of course, by the half vote of the newcomer.

Tricks of the trade

In the 1949 primary an insurgent candidate in the first assembly district filed petitions in the election districts covered by two incumbent Tammany leaders. He won a majority of the election districts in one portion of the assembly district, but not in the second. When the meeting of the county committee was called, he found that it was a combined meeting of both portions of the district and the majority he had in one section was completely swallowed up in the larger meeting.

There being sixteen assembly districts, one might think there would be a total of sixteen votes on the executive committee. But the chairman of the executive committee has an additional vote by virtue of his office. He has the further right to appoint — and remove — three subcommittee chairmen each of whom may cast a full vote in addition to his vote as a district leader. In this way the chairman controls four votes out of twenty.

All these extremely undemocratic methods are the result of a direct primary law which allows the party executive committee to make its own rules — rules that thus fortify tight clique control. It is in this way that a coterie of political leaders in Manhattan is able to frustrate insurgency, hold power for generations and select its successors. Those who are concerned with political and democratic techniques must turn their attention and that of the public to the important problem of ensuing democracy in the internal structure and machinery of parties.

74

City Politics: Free Style

By Robert L. Morlan

THE STUDENT of municipal politics in the United States today is being given an extremely one-sided picture of political organization and party activity, at least in so far as existing literature is concerned. Most of the writing on this subject seems to assume that, excepting only those cities under 100,000 population, the pattern is essentially that expounded so entertainingly by the immortal *Plunkitt of Tammany Hall* a half century ago.

The picture almost invariably presented is one of tight political hierarchies extending from a boss and the city or county central committee through ward executives, precinct leaders and multitudinous block workers, all welded into a highly efficient 365-day-a-year machine by the magic of patronage, and controlling votes largely through the familiar process of rendering personal service to the voters.

This is not to deny that extremely effective machines continue to flourish in some American cities but rather to challenge the traditional assumption that this is the way it is done everywhere. Operations of bosses and machines have often been sensational and hence have tended to attract the attention of those investigating the facts of local political life. Interesting and useful studies of bossism have resulted from these researches, but the focusing of attention in that direction has meant the virtual ignoring of cities with less spectacular politics.

Authors of general works on municipal government and politics have found their sources of material almost entirely limited to studies of highly organized cities — and have doubtless also been anxious to include in their texts as much colorful matter as possible. As a result, the politically loosely organized city has received either no attention or has been summarily passed off with a statement that in some small cities party organization is less comprehensive.

There is, in fact, a tremendous variation in the comprehensiveness of party organization and in the

Robert L. Morlan, "City Politics: Free Style," *National Municipal Review,* November, 1949, pp. 485–490. Footnote in original omitted. Reprinted by permission of the publisher.

extent of party activities in city wards. Machine strength is, of course, normally centered in the poorer wards, while in the more prosperous wards party workers rarely engage in much more than a bit of pre-election activity. The minority party frequently maintains little if any organization in wards which are overwhelmingly of the opposite political faith, but it is also true that even the dominant party is often poorly organized in certain wards. The significant fact too commonly overlooked, however, is that there are some large cities as well as many smaller ones in which *neither* party has a strong organization in *any* ward.

It is time to re-examine our traditional concepts of city political organization, to get away from the universalities in which most of the writing in this field has dealt, and to recognize the fact that even in large municipalities political organization and activity vary all the way from highly concentrated control to loose and haphazard operation.

An unorganized city

Minneapolis, with a population of over half a million and a long history of volatile politics, is an excellent example of a major city loosely organized politically. Its situation may not be widespread, but it is significant as a striking deviation from a presumed norm, and one may speculate that it is not alone.

It is often difficult for persons familiar with the politics of highly organized cities to believe that political activity in Minneapolis can actually be as "free and easy" as it is. The truth is that any interested person can step immediately into political work, that the average party ward meeting is for all practical purposes open to anyone, that in no ward is there a party organization adequately covering every precinct the year around, that many officers of both parties at the city, ward and precinct levels are practically neophytes in politics, and that the party organizations as such play minor roles in the selection and control of candidates and have almost negligible influence with city officials.

The ease with which a political amateur with a sense of direction may succeed in Minneapolis politics is strikingly illustrated by the career of former Mayor, now . . . [Vice President] Hubert H. Humphrey. As a young college political science instructor with a "gift of gab," he was expounding his views on local politics one night in a typical campus bull session when someone brought him up short: "Humphrey, why don't you practice what you're always preaching about political participation, and see what you can do in this next city election?"

The upshot was that Hubert Humphrey, with hastily collected and almost wholly amateur support, little money and organization, not only survived the nonpartisan primary in 1943 but also lost to the incumbent mayor in the final election by only 5,000 out of 115,000 votes. Gathering liberal and labor support in the interim, but still operating to a large degree with what was in effect his own organization, he came back to win in 1945 by the largest plurality any mayor has ever secured. In 1947 he swept every ward and the following year went on to defeat Senator Joseph H. Ball by a three to two margin. Never did he have behind him a tight ward and precinct organization even approximating the traditional type.

Part of the reason for this wide open situation is found in the fact that Minneapolis — as do all local units in Minnesota — elects its officials on a nonpartisan ballot, although this of course does not mean that the parties take no part in municipal politics. Party organizations would exist for state and national affairs at any rate and, since essentially the same persons are interested in politics at all levels, it is hardly to be expected that they will remain aloof in municipal campaigns.

Pressure group government

Campaigns are managed by volunteer committees for individual candidates, but the parties make endorsements instead of nominations, and in most cases they quite openly support their choices. Nevertheless, since the parties do not manage the campaigns of individual candidates and do not finance them except in the form of minor contributions, nonpartisanship in local elections is definitely a factor. It has resulted in government by pressure groups — labor unions, business associations, etc. — rather than by parties at the city level.

A further cause of party weakness is the almost complete absence of local patronage in the sense of jobs for loyal workers. The city merit system, although it has some shortcomings, covers almost all municipal employment and has been little abused in recent years.

Patronage in the sense of special favors in the expectation of future support is extensive, but it is centered almost entirely in the hands of the 26 aldermen and party officials as a rule have practically nothing to do with it. The aldermen, therefore, to that extent play the role which is normally played by party ward and precinct executives. Being relatively independent, they have tended to build up personal blocs of support with little thought for the parties whose support they receive. They consider themselves more dependent upon the support of powerful pressure groups and party organization has suffered as a consequence.

Political leaders say that a strong party organization not only lives upon patronage but cannot exist without it. Experience in Minneapolis lends credence to the argument. Persons with a sincere interest in politics and reasonably strong party convictions can be stirred by a cause long enough to work for brief periods before election, but they cannot be expected to devote themselves constantly to political activity unless the party has some control over them — or unless they are possessed of a Messianic zeal like that of the Communists.

Frank Kent, in his well known but occasionally inaccurate book, *The Great Game of Politics,* says categorically that eight out of ten ward executives are on the public payroll at good salaries. In Minneapolis, of the 26 ward chairmen serving the two major parties, only one is a city employee, and his is a position under the merit system for which he is in no way indebted to the party. Nor is it true that these officials are to any extent in businesses which stand to profit from political pull. Precinct executives in strongly organized cities often hold minor political jobs, yet in Minneapolis scarcely a handful who are public employees can be found.

One of the leading college textbooks on city government opens its discussion of party organization with a statement concerning the hierarchy of political organization, "at the base of which is the precinct committeeman or committee in each of the 130,000 precincts in the United States." This statement is misleading, since it indicates that precinct committeemen actually exist in each of those precincts. Obviously there is nowhere near the full quota.

In Minneapolis alone, except perhaps in the weeks just preceding an important election, roughly 100 of the 634 possible precinct captaincies will be unfilled and not over half the remainder are filled by active party workers who can be depended upon at all times.

Precinct captains

The precinct executive, we are told, is a person who holds that position because he can control more votes than can any competitor, and who stays in power only so long as he can "deliver the goods." In the highly organized city the precinct executive must presumably devote a major portion of his time to politics. He must have information about virtually every voter in his precinct, know many of them personally and be able to swing enough votes to carry at least his party's primary. Traditionally he has been able to control votes largely by means of giving personal service in the form of jobs, assistance to those in trouble with the police, relief for the poor, etc. Kent insists that the precinct executive functions in this manner in nine-tenths of the precincts in every city.

As many of these services are becoming institutionalized, being handled at least in part by government employment bureaus and social welfare agencies, for example, the role of the precinct executive has become more and more that of a go-between and a cutter of red tape. But in the unorganized city even this type of service is largely unknown. Minneapolis precinct captains lack the necessary political pull to do the job, even if they have the inclination. Few put any time on politics except in pre-election periods, when they distribute campaign literature from door to door, perhaps make a few phone calls on election day to remind persons to vote and assist in providing transportation to the polls. On rare occasions a few of the more earnest ones may do some doorbell ringing.

The average precinct captain has no personal political following and is unlikely to possess even such an elementary tool as a list of the registered voters of his precinct. He is not in the least concerned over the danger of a competitor developing sufficient strength to take over his job, for the job in most cases means nothing to him and he would be happy to be relieved of it.

"Every ward executive," says Frank Kent, "holds his position because he has the strength to hold it and for no other reason." He is, presumably, a little king in his ward. It is he who sits in the inner councils of the central party organization. It is he who wields influence at city hall, who appoints — or controls the election of — precinct executives and supervises their political activity. He has earned his position by hard work and fighting his way to the top.

The average ward executive in Minneapolis will hardly fit these specifications. Lawyers, labor leaders, business men, housewives — they devote only a relatively small portion of their time to politics and as a rule have but limited control over their ward organizations. As for influence at the city hall, they would be in vastly stronger positions as officers of the central labor union or the chamber of commerce. Not only do they have almost nothing to say in the selection of precinct executives but they can also do little more than request their cooperation once in office. That chairman is fortunate who is able to secure the attendance of over 50 per cent of his precinct captains at a meeting of the ward central committee.

Few ward contests

Nor have these ward executives for the most part fought their way to the top. In many cases they had no opposition and have simply been asked to serve — in some instances there are minor skirmishes. The only real battles over these positions come when there is a struggle for control of the state or county organization. After all, the ward chairman gets nothing from his job except the satisfaction of serving the party cause, although it has occasionally been used as a stepping stone toward running for elective office. Certainly he is probably one of the most politically active persons in his ward but he is only rarely a political power.

Compared to the length of service required for a person to become a ward executive in a tightly organized city, many Minneapolis ward chairmen are virtually beginners in politics. The turnover is rapid and over half the current chairmen are new to the office within the past two years, while the oldest in point of service has been a chairman for twelve years.

The writer came to Minneapolis in the spring of 1946, in a few months became a precinct captain, and in the spring of 1948 was elected ward chairman for the majority party in one of the most active and most evenly divided wards in terms of party votes. The same year he was elected a delegate to both the county and state conventions of the party — altogether a totally inconceivable series of events for a well organized city.

In the highly organized city, meetings of a ward organization are essentially closed affairs, attended only by ward and precinct officers and a few other trusted workers.

Meetings of the ward organizations of both parties in Minneapolis are open to the public. Any interested person may attend and vote on all matters, helping to elect officials or delegates and to determine party policy. To be sure, an unknown person may be questioned about his party allegiance, and known members of an opposing party would not be permitted to participate, but the individual's word on the matter is usually accepted. At most he can merely be required to state either that he voted for a majority of the party's candidates at the last election or that he intends to do so at the next.

The practice in Minneapolis is to send meeting notices to all persons in the ward who have indicated reasonably active interest. Attendance is normally low and the ward and precinct officers are likely to constitute a sizable bloc. The fact is of little significance, however, since they are rarely if ever united upon any specific course of action in advance. A highly controversial issue may and often does bring out larger crowds, when all are given a chance to be heard and to participate in decisions. Groups with pre-arranged slates or programs of action are, of course, to be expected when anything of importance is at stake, but rarely is such a group made up of ward and precinct officers.

Caucuses routine affairs

Biennial ward and precinct caucuses, the vehicle in Minnesota for election of local party officers and selection of delegates to county and state conventions, are subject to the same conditions as are regular ward meetings. Adherence to the party concerned is checked more rigidly, although legally the individual's statement is all that is required. At a time of intense factional strife these caucuses may be heavily attended, as was the case within the Democratic-Farmer-Labor party in 1948 when as many as six hundred persons jammed certain ward caucuses in Minneapolis. Normally, however, they are routine affairs, with few brisk contests.

The writer in the spring of 1948 was an observer at the precinct and ward caucuses of the Republican party in a ward where the vote is fairly evenly divided between the parties. All were held in a school gymnasium, with the ward caucus being convened after the precinct caucuses had completed their business. Out of 28 precincts there were eleven in which no one appeared for the precinct caucus. One person could have come and elected himself both precinct captain and delegate to the county convention — this happened in two other precincts. Moreover, a person with five followers could have controlled any precinct caucus, and this is not the exception but the rule.

Perhaps this loosely organized state of politics in Minneapolis is unique, or perhaps we have too long accepted the situation in a few tightly organized cities as being universal. Surely we have been too ready to accept without adequate investigation the statement that all cities are organized politically in such and such a manner. There are a great variety of local conditions existing within the pattern of certain fairly common structural arrangements. It is time to recognize the fact that there is, in larger cities as well as smaller ones, an unorganized as well as an organized style of municipal politics.

In the next selection, the head of a well-known public opinion research firm suggests a series of characteristics of American voters, determined on the basis of a number of years of election polling and research, which provide an interesting framework for discussion. Then the authors of the political behavior study which follows analyze the effect on party allegiances of shifting from urban to suburban residence, using data from the University of Michigan Survey Research Center studies of national election behavior.

75

Some Characteristics of the American Voter

By Louis Harris

. . . BROADLY SPEAKING, [survey] research has contributed most appreciably to our understanding of four areas:

1. How voters decide to cast their ballots the way they do;

2. Who votes and who does not;

3. How the social and economic structure reflects itself in elections;

4. How the events of our time affect the political complexion of America. Out of researches in these four areas have come a number of more or less hard findings which have led to some responsible generalizations.

Most voters have made up their minds well in advance of the campaign. Despite the protestations of politicians and students of politics that campaigns are "great democratic forums" the overwhelming evidence indicates that most voters have decided how to vote well before the campaign has got under way. A small group of voters may be honestly undecided and may switch in mid-stream, but not the vast majority. Campaigns may have the polarizing effect of making partisans even more partisan, but for the most part they are sound and fury affecting relatively few voters, and in many cases not affecting the ultimate outcome. (But woe betide the poll-taker who says, "There is simply no point in surveying from here on in, for no appreciable change can take place.") An exception to this rule is that larger and later shifts may be made when the voters do not feel strongly about either candidate, as in 1948. Also, the more local the election, the more likely it is that a campaign can change voting intentions.

Independent voters tend to be those who know and care the least. More and more elections in the United States are unquestionably being decided by voters who split their tickets within a given election, or who switch from one party to the other from election to election. Yet, when the much-discussed and

Louis Harris, "Election Polling and Research," *Public Opinion Quarterly,* Spring, 1957, pp. 108–116. Reprinted by permission of the author and publisher.

even glorified "independent voter" is looked at and empirical data about him are analyzed, he almost invariably tends to be a sporadic voter, to be quite poorly informed, and to have done little integrated thinking on political subjects. In fact, this slippery political animal tends to be more bored than other voters with the election process. The independents include some who are "above" politics and some who are "below" — those who are excessively ideological and those almost lacking in ideology. The people who used to be independents no longer are, and people who never dreamed of being independents have indeed become switch voters. I shall cite but two cases of this juxtaposition. First, independent liberals, such as those who kicked over Democratic Party traces in the 1930's to elect New York Mayor Fiorello LaGuardia time and again have now almost entirely joined the Democratic Party and, in many cases, have risen to positions of responsibility within it. Second, larger numbers of Irish Catholic voters, almost monolithically Democratic from 1928 through 1940, have since then gone more and more heavily over to the Republican column in national elections, and yet have by and large remained Democratic in local elections. They must now be classified as among the most "independent" of voters.

Turnout can alter the basic political balance. Who votes and who does not vote can make a critical difference in the traditionally close elections that mark American politics. The fact that proportionately more upper-income people vote gives the Republican Party an advantage in most elections. In 1952, there is no doubt that increased turnout by middle-income women heavily disposed toward Eisenhower, was an important element in changing what might have been a close election into a relative landslide. In nonpartisan local elections, where turnout is low and disproportionately of upper-income people, the results generally tend to favor a conservative victory. On the other hand, overconfidence in 1948 cost the Republicans heavily.

Voting in America is a symbol of social affiliation. Despite the traditional claim that each voter is an individual who makes up his own mind, social group pressures limit choices sharply, and are highly significant determinants of individual voting patterns. The fact is that political allegiances are a basic reflection of social allegiances. When the group tends to shift, cross-pressures on the individual may be heightened, but the pressure to shift with the group is usually dominant.

American politics tend to be highly personalized and unideological. These group patterns have much deeper roots in social and economic bases than in any firmly held ideological dogma. Americans are perhaps the least subject to ideological dogma and

integrated "lines" of political thinking than any people in the world. In election after election, whole groups of voters have reacted in a similar fashion, but almost always in terms of a protest against a specific fear (the depression, the Korean War), in terms of a man they trust to work for the things that will personally enhance their lot (Roosevelt, Truman, Eisenhower), or in terms of pocketbook self-interest. This tends to personalize American politics. American voters most nearly approached integrated mass thinking in their acceptance of the tenets of the New Deal, but even then, as was dramatically illustrated in the case of World War II, the allegiance turned out to be more a trust in Roosevelt and the Democratic Party than in a specific foreign policy program.

Class cleavages run deep, though the balance of power rests with the everchanging middle income group. Every cross-section political survey ever conducted shows the inevitable pattern of low income people being dominantly Democratic and upper-income people being Republican. Irrespective of their leadership and program at any given moment, the two parties do indeed have very different economic bases. To this extent, politics in America are a reflection of economic divisions as well as varied social affiliations. The divisions were sharpest in the depression years. Recently, however, important exceptions have arisen. For instance, the low-income Germans are more Republican today than low-income Catholics. Most of these exceptions reflect a clash between traditional economic ties and changing cultural pressures. Although the middle class may have been effectively squeezed out in Britain, it maintains the balance of power in any American election. The recent trend in American politics, however, has been toward a sharp de-emphasis of class lines and a regrouping along cultural patterns which sensitize voters to such issues as those involving civil rights and foreign policy.

Class cleavages grow more diffuse as foreign policy becomes a major issue. In the United States, as opposed to Europe, separate issues tend to cut across economic lines and make for a blurring of the traditional political structure. Surveys have provided abundant evidence that lower income groups tend to be less internationalist (rooted in the belief we have enough unsolved problems at home), while upper income groups tend to be more internationalist (though until Eisenhower's pronounced internationalism, they believed in the traditionally Republican high tariffs and non-involvement overseas). With the shift of the Republican Party, or at least of Republicans in the Executive Branch, to an internationalist position, the conflict for upper income groups tends to be resolved. At the same time, the lower income groups have tended to split. In 1956, whole segments of the lower income groups, especially those of Eastern European origins, switched to the Republican party in defiiance of their traditional economic base in politics. This switch was in response to the charge that the Democratic party was a war party. When faced with apprehensions of war, they yielded to religious and cultural, rather than to economic pressures.

Sharp and meaningful political differences emerge when an electorate is viewed in terms of the length of time particular ethnic groups have been in this country. The newer the arrivals, the more Democratic their inclinations. As time passes, and the more posperous third and fourth generations emerge, economic pressures push them toward the Republicans. This process may be accelerated, in the case of the Germans for instance, for almost entirely noneconomic reasons, and can be reversed or decelerated, as among Jewish voters, again for almost entirely noneconomic reasons. It can also be switched in one four year span, as among the Negroes in '56, and again for noneconomic reasons.

Single issues can change long time trends . . . [For example the] wholesale shifts among Negro voters . . . . The cause is clear: the Negro group is today almost wholly absorbed with a single issue . . . .

Historical issues can dominate voting long after the event. In some parts of Kentucky, vote patterns are still determined by bitter battles over road construction which took place some 70 years ago. The slavery issue has dominated southern voting patterns with regularity over the same period. The anti-Eastern tradition has been dominant in important sections in the Pacific Northwest. The indigenous radicalism of Wisconsin politics has its roots in the anti-war tradition of those who emigrated from Germany more than a century ago.

Political party images persist despite changing events. To millions, the Democratic Party is known as the party of the "working man," the "little fellow," the "common man," while to these same millions, the Republican Party is known as the party of "big business," "the bosses," "the rich." To others, however, the Republican Party is known as the "party of peace," and "the party of moderation." To these people the Democratic Party is known as "the party of war" and the "party of radicalism." For years the Republican Party suffered mightily under the impact of the "big business" image. In recent Presidential elections, the Democrats have labored under the handicap of the "war-radicalism" image. Yet even in the 1956 Eisenhower sweep, the underlying distrust of the Republicans must surely account for an important part of the electorate splitting its ticket on the Congressional and Gubernatorial level.

These are only a few of the generalizations about politics toward which survey research has made con-tributions. Many others, both more general and more specific, may be found in the growing library of election studies. . . .

76

The Suburbs and Shifting Party Loyalties

By Fred I. Greenstein and Raymond E. Wolfinger

THE IMMENSE GROWTH of suburbs is one of the most striking changes in the American social landscape of the past two decades. In 1940 9 per cent of the population of the United States lived in "satellite" communities. By 1955 this proportion had risen to 28 per cent. Most of this growing suburban population appears to be made up of people moving from increasingly congested cities. This movement is of interest to political scientists because of the marked differences between urban and suburban party identifications, with suburbanites showing a pronounced Republican preference. Suburban areas have changed from a relatively minor aspect of Republican strength in several key states to an important element in Republican pluralities.

Three different but not mutually exclusive hypotheses are advanced to account for suburban Republicanism. The simplest explanation is that it is a product of population redistribution. The upper income and status groups most likely to vote Republican have moved from the cities, taking their political preferences with them. If this were the case, there would be little reason for Democratic politicians to worry, since bigger Republican pluralities from the suburbs would be made up for by larger margins of victory in the cities. This explanation does not attribute any Republicanizing effects to the suburbs: suburbanites are taken to be more Republican because they are more likely to be in the higher income and status groups which tend to have Republican predispositions.

A number of observers have supported a second hypothesis, that a move to the suburbs is accompa-

Fred I. Greenstein and Raymond E. Wolfinger, "The Suburbs and Shifting Party Loyalties," *Public Opinion Quarterly,* Winter, 1958–59, pp. 473–482. Footnotes in original omitted. Reprinted by permission of the authors and publisher.

nied or followed in many cases by a switch from Democratic to Republican allegiance. The belief is that, in what Whyte calls "the second great melting pot," there is a social psychological climate which converts the new arrivals. Duncan MacRae, Jr., has shown that socio-economic minorities within an area tend to adopt the political responses "objectively" more appropriate to the majority group. As yet, however, little direct evidence is available on the effects on political attitudes of a move to the suburbs.

A third hypothesis, complementary to the second, is that a process of self-selection operates in the willingness to move to the suburbs, predisposing the new suburbanites to attitude change. The immigrants are upwardly mobile, newly middle class in fact or in aspiration. Their desire to move to the suburbs is considered part of a larger set of attitudes in which a shift to Republican preference is implicit.

A basic factual question underlying these speculations may be stated as follows: *Are there differences between urban and suburban political behavior which cannot be attributed to the distribution of particular social classes in the two areas, or to factors normally related to class, such as education and income?* To the degree that suburban voting is linked to factors other than membership in a social class, investigations into this problem may serve the general function of modifying sociological theories which emphasize the primacy of class as a determinant of behavior, or of refining the indices of class to include such factors as nature of residential area.

Methods

The purpose of this article is to compare political preferences of urban and suburban residents, with the customary demographic variables controlled, in an attempt to answer the question posed in the previous paragraph. In addition, the data available to the authors have been explored in an attempt to describe the differing urban-suburban social psychological environments which serve as the matrices of differing patterns of political behavior. These data were collected by the Survey Research Center of the University of Michigan in its study of the 1952 presidential campaign. The SRC gathered a wide range of information from a national sample of respondents, in one pre- and one post-election survey. A report of this survey, together with an account of the questions asked, the sampling procedures used, and the indices devised may be found in *The Voter Decides*.

The samples described by the SRC as "urban-metropolitan" and "suburban" were compared. Data from the South were eliminated, in order to avoid responses related to southern one-party conditions. The former sample (hereafter called "urban") con-

sisted of 270 respondents, the latter of 137. The urban and suburban samples are therefore smaller than is desirable for statistical comparison. However, by reporting consistent trends, even when they fall short of statistical significance, it is possible to suggest potentially fruitful lines of future inquiry.

By "suburbs" we refer to communities lying on the fringes of metropolitan cities from which large numbers of residents commute to jobs in the central city. Inspection of the communities included in the suburban sample leads us to believe that almost all of them can be classified as residential suburbs. However, the "contaminating" effect of the presence of some partially industrial suburbs in our sample would be to minimize the urban-suburban differences, since industrial workers are inclined to be Democrats. Therefore, to the extent (which we believe to be minor) that industrial suburbs are included in our sample, they have a conservative effect on the findings.

Findings

Before reporting differences in political performance, it is useful to compare city and suburb in terms of the prevalence of various characteristics customarily used to describe racial groupings. Tables 1 to 3 show the distribution of income, education, and religion in the cities and suburbs of the SRC sample.

Negroes, largely Protestant, compose 13.7 per cent of the city sample, only 3 per cent of the suburban. Distribution of age groups does not appear to differ substantially between city and suburb. On a scale subdivided by ten-year categories ranging from 12 years to 92, groups are generally equal in cities and suburbs. The major differences are in the 23 to 31 age bracket (4 per cent more in the suburbs) and 43 to 52 (5 per cent more in the cities). Virtually equal proportions of urban and suburban residents were foreign born or had one or both parents born abroad. Of the individuals who were professionals, businessmen, executives and office workers, 51 per cent of the suburbanites had fathers who were in lower-ranking occupations, while 45.8 per cent of the city sample was upwardly mobile in this sense.

As a measure of a political preference, we used the respondents' answer to the following question: "Generally speaking, do you usually think of yourself as a Republican, a Democrat, or what?" Respondents who expressed an allegiance to either of the two major parties and those who professed independence but stated that they think of themselves as "closer" to one or the other party were included in the two major political categories. Reports of statistical significance given below refer to the urban-suburban distribution of preference for the two major parties, with significance determined by the chi square test using a four-celled table of differences in party identification between urban and suburban respondents. Yates' correction for continuity was used wherever the expected frequency fell below five. The findings, in Table 4, show that Republican strength is significantly greater in suburbs than in the cities.

In order to determine whether this difference is simply the result of the presence in the suburbs of more people of higher social class levels, it is necessary to control the variables normally associated with class. When urban-suburban party identifications were controlled for education, income, or occupation, the suburban Republican tendency did not "wash-out." Dividing each of these three variables into high, medium, and low categories, we found that within such group there was a higher percentage of

Table 1
SUBURBAN-URBAN INCOME DISTRIBUTION

	Suburban		Urban	
	Number	Per Cent	Number	Per Cent
Annual income over $5,000	54	40.6	87	32.4
$2,000–$5,000	74	55.6	151	56.1
Below $2,000	5	3.8	31	11.5
	133		269	

Table 2
SUBURBAN-URBAN EDUCATION DISTRIBUTION

	Suburban		Urban	
	Number	Per Cent	Number	Per Cent
High education (Attended college)	26	19.3	46	17.0
Medium education (Attended high school but not college)	77	57.0	129	47.8
Low education (No further than grade school)	32	23.7	95	35.2
	135		270	

Table 3
SUBURBAN-URBAN RELIGIOUS DISTRIBUTION

	Suburban		Urban	
	Number	Per Cent	Number	Per Cent
Protestant	77	56.2	107	39.6
Catholic	49	35.8	112	41.5
Jewish	3	2.2	38	14.1
	129		257	

Table 4
SUBURBAN-URBAN PARTY IDENTIFICATION

	Suburban		Urban	
	Number	Per Cent	Number	Per Cent
Democratic	57	41.6	160	59.3
Republican	60	43.8	82	30.4
Independent	9	6.6	18	6.7
Other responses	11		10	
	137		270	P. 01

Republican identification for suburban respondents than for urban respondents. These differences reached statistical significance (at least the 5 per cent level of significance) for the "high" groups in both occupation and income, and for the "medium" group in education. In all other cases there was a persistent Republican trend in the suburbs. Table 5 shows the differences in party identification with occupational level controlled.

There is a possibility that different distributions of variables other than social class — for example, religion and ethnic origin — account for the greater Republicanism of the suburbs. There are virtually no Jews or Negroes in the suburban sample and there are fewer Catholics than in the urban sample. These groups have tended, at least since the New Deal period, to be heavily Democratic. Considering only white Gentiles in the sample, urban preference for the Republican Party rises from 30.4 to 37.7 per cent. The difference from the suburbs now does not quite meet the 5 per cent level of significance. Comparing only white Protestants, 63.3 per cent of the suburban sample indicated Republican preference, as against 53.3 per cent of the city group. This difference is not statistically significant, but it must be noted that as one subdivides the sample to control for

more variables, the difficulties of applying a test for significance increases; that is, as the sample decreases in size, the amount which a difference must be in order to be statistically significant increases. This made it impossible to control for national origins, although, as has been noted, it was determined that the number of foreign-born respondents or respondents with foreign-born parents did not vary in the two samples.

Clearly, part of the urban-suburban difference in party preference is due to the different distribution of socio-economic and religious-ethnic characteristics. However, these distributions do not seem to account for the entire difference. There are some indications that a process of self-selection and/or environmental conversion is taking place.

One hypothetical sequence of political conversion is as follows: upwardly mobile individuals, seeking security and recognition in their new social position by conformity to what they imagine to be its political norms, "over-compensate" by adopting strongly conservative beliefs. The data did not appear to support this thesis. Suburbanites who were "objectively" upwardly mobile (those with professional, executive, or white collar jobs whose fathers were manual workers) were more Democratic than were "stable"

Table 5
SUBURBAN-URBAN PARTY
IDENTIFICATION CONTROLLED FOR
OCCUPATION

Low Occupation

	Suburban		Urban	
	Number	Per Cent	Number	Per Cent
Democratic	7	58.3	31	63.3
Republican	2	16.7	14	28.6
Independent	3		3	
Other			1	
	12		49	Not significant

Medium Occupation

Democratic	34	51.5	67	62.6
Republican	27	40.9	31	29.0
Independent	4		7	
Other	1		2	
	66		107	
				P .10

High Occupation

Democratic	10	31.3	34	50.0
Republican	19	59.4	26	38.2
Independent	2		7	
Other	1		1	
	32		68	P. 05

suburbanites at the same occupational levels, suggesting that these individuals tend to adhere to familial party loyalties.

If the conversion hypothesis is valid, one would expect that individuals who have lived in the suburbs for a relatively short time would be less inclined to Republican allegiance than would long-term residents, all other factors being equal. While we had no direct information on this point, one item in the SRC questionnaire dealt with the length of time respondents had lived in their present county. Of our sample, twenty-six suburbanites had lived in their present county less than five years. Assuming that most of these individuals had not lived in the suburbs until moving to their present county, we examined their political characteristics. On a scale which combined our previous income, education, and occupation measures to give an index of social class, all but four of these twenty-six respondents were in the high or middle levels. Yet 57.7 per cent of them expressed a Democratic preference, compared to only 41.6 per cent of the total suburban sample. This difference suggests the likelihood of a suburban conversion process, in which urban Democrats move to the suburbs and then change as a result of exposure to environmental pressures. This hypothesis is opposed to the view that suburban Republicanism is due to self-selection in that the decision to move is part of a syndrome which includes factors leading to Republicanism.

One of the most interesting indications of the suburban interpersonal environment is in responses to the question of how each respondent's friends voted: mostly Republican, mostly Democratic, or pretty evenly split. Republican respondents in both areas appeared to associate largely with like-minded people. That is, there were no urban-suburban differences among Republicans in the distribution of their friends among the two parties, and the number of Republican respondents whose friends had mostly voted Republican was several times greater than the number whose friends had mostly voted Democratic. Suburban Democrats, however, associated with Republicans as much as with Democrats, to a statistically significant greater extent than in the city. This distribution is shown in Table 6. Statistical significance

was computed on a four-celled table based upon those individuals whose friends voted preponderantly for their party or for the opposite party.

Thus it is indicated that suburban Democrats are more prone than city Democrats to be exposed to competing political pressures. A further indication of this environment is found by comparing union members (or respondents whose families include a union member) in the urban and suburban samples. In our sample, a majority of both urban and suburban respondents were Democratic. However, suburban union members were significantly (5 per cent level of significance) less Democratic than their brothers in the city. Suburban union respondents were significantly (1 per cent level) more likely than the city union members to have Republican-voting friends. Another group which has been associated with the Democratic Party in the past, Roman Catholics, tended to be more Republican in the suburbs than in the cities, although suburban Catholics remained more Democratic than their neighbors. Unfortunately, the size of these sub-samples did not permit controlling for class-related variables.

Discussion

What accounts for the difference between urban and suburban party preference that seems to remain even when factors associated with both social class and religious-ethnic group membership are held constant? The degree to which it is a result of environmental conversion is important for reasons of political tactics. Given either of these processes, politicians might be expected to employ differing campaign strategies. There are, of course, relationships in the dynamics of the two hypotheses. For instance, the new suburbanite's perception of his environment would be conditioned by his expectations of the proper behavior for a suburban resident.

An example of self-selection might be in a mover's desire to live in the same neighborhood as his boss, and otherwise to emulate him. Republicanism might be part of the desired self-image of the individual who feels he is "on the way up." We were unable to find any firm evidence for this hypothesis, but this may be a consequence of analyzing data which were

Table 6
HOW FRIENDS VOTED, SUBURBAN-URBAN DEMOCRATS

	Suburban		Urban	
	Number	Per Cent	Number	Per Cent
All or mostly Democratic	17	29.8	77	48.1
All or mostly Republican	18	31.6	23	14.4
Evenly split	16		30	
Other	6		30	
	57		160	P .01

not collected with the purpose of answering this question in mind.

It is useful to remember that before they began to expand so enormously, suburbs were for the well-to-do to a much greater extent than they are today. People who moved to the suburbs moved into communities whose inhabitants had upper- and upper-middle-class attitudes and behavior patterns, e.g., voting Republican. Tryon's finding that neighborhoods tend to maintain the same sociological and economic characteristics in times of great population mobility suggests that the 1930 political characteristics were maintained in the 1950's. It is likely that higher status patterns will become the more dominant ones when lower status newcomers arrive, especially when these patterns are viewed as part of the "suburban way of life" which the new arrivals are presumably seeking. This interpretation is further supported by MacRae's finding that individuals of lower socio-economic status tend to accept majority viewpoints in areas where they are in the minority.

It is suggested that characteristic suburban interaction patterns help maintain the Republican predisposition which prevailed in these towns before the great migration to the suburbs began. Articles by Martin and Fava suggest that there is more informal primary group interaction in the suburbs than in large cities. While this has by no means been proven yet, it seems likely that the effects of such informal associations in a new milieu might contrast markedly with those in the old city environment. Further, the suburban town tends to be more homogeneous than a large city, where there is usually such a wide distribution of characteristics that it is not difficult to find other individuals who share one's idiosyncratic interests. In the suburbs this is not so, and this lack of diversified interaction possibilities, combined with the greater social importance and impact of one's immediate neighbors, tends to create situations where the newcomer attempts to modulate those attitudes which would impede satisfactory social participation in the smaller range of opportunities offered by the suburban environment. The familiar fact that Americans are not generally intensely concerned with politics tends to permit easy change of identifications. Our findings concerning the higher interaction rates of Democrats with Republicans and the less Republican indications of recent arrivals in the suburbs give some support to the interpretation of the environment process presented above.

Other aspects of suburban life give some reason for political change. Many new suburbanites become home owners for the first time, gaining a new interest in tax rates and other issues connected with property rights. For those residents having political ambitions, the Republican Party may offer the only path to elective office. In many communities there is a widespread belief that Republican registration will produce more sympathetic treatment on such matters as tax assessment and garbage collection.

While we found no association between "objective" upward mobility and Republican allegiance, it is likely that a more important variable is "subjective" social mobility, the individual's idea of his past and present status and his chances and desires for future ascension. Within each occupational group, it was found that suburbanites tended to have higher incomes than city dwellers. There may be political consequences of having more money than one's occupational colleagues. It may stimulate a feeling that one is destined for even higher things. Greater income may be associated with the ability to move to the suburbs and with a willingness to be converted to Republicanism.

The growth of the suburbs is one of the products of the rising American standard of living. Increasing productivity, growing specialization, and more equitable distribution of income have the effect of boosting many people into higher status brackets. As more and more Americans attain middle-class status, they strive for middle-class behavior patterns. Suburban residence is one such pattern; Republican allegiance is, at least traditionally, another. This suggests that the composition of the American electorate is changing and with it the basis of political conflict and appeal. It would be interesting to know to what degree the recent Democratic electoral success was based on Democratic responses to these societal changes, and to what degree it was simply a result of dissatisfaction with the Republican alternative to the old Democratic appeals and a possibly temporary recurrence of the image of the Republicans as "the Depression party."

The differences between urban and suburban political behavior do not appear to be completely explained by the differing distributions of socio-economic or religious-ethnic characteristics in the two populations. The additional difference may be largely a result of the self-selection of "Republican-prone" movers to the suburbs, or it may be the result of environmental conversion. It is likely that both these factors are present, but further investigation is indicated to determine which factor is more important. Democrats and union members were found to be more likely to interact with Republicans in the suburbs than in the cities. A small sample of recent arrivals in the suburbs appeared to be more Democratic than long-time suburban residents. The available evidence points tentatively to Whyte's description of the converting effects of a suburban living. It gives less support to the self-selection hypothesis. It seems likely that the current movement to the suburbs is associated with the achievement of middle-class status by large numbers of people who aspire to the attitudes and behavior of their new role. Suburban residence emphasizes and re-inforces these role patterns and in so doing may produce Republican converts. Unless the Democrats can meet this threat they may find themselves defeated by Levittown.

One of the most significant developments in political campaigning in recent years has been the growth of professional campaign management, or as some have termed it, the attempt to "merchandise" politics and candidates. While this is by no means unique to California, it has perhaps been most notable in that state which thus provides a striking case illustration, presented here by Robert J. Pitchell.

77

Professional Campaign Management — The California Experience

By Robert J. Pitchell

ONE OF THE "NEW LOOKS" in American campaigns in recent years has been the rise of professional political public relations firms which specialize in political publicity or in running virtually every aspect of a campaign for a candidate. They may raise money, determine issues, write speeches, handle press releases, prepare advertising copy, program radio and television shows, and develop whatever other publicity techniques are necessary for a given campaign. These firms have flourished in California in the past two decades and they have been used with increasing frequency by candidates for the major offices. An assessment of their influence on voting behavior would appear to be desirable. . . .

Professional campaign management firms and political party organizations

Although campaign management firms vary considerably among themselves, they have several characteristics in common which contrast with old-style party organizations. These differences lie not in their respective capabilities but rather in the basic

Robert J. Pitchell, "The Influence of Professional Campaign Management Firms in Partisan Elections in California," *Western Political Quarterly,* June, 1958, pp. 278–300. Footnotes in original omitted. Reprinted by permission of the publisher.

methods used to sway the electorate. The old-style politician uses a permanent political organization which does much of its most effective work and planning between campaigns. The campaign management firms organize particular campaigns on an *ad hoc* basis and must move into action and accomplish their missions with utmost speed and efficiency. Any major miscalculation spells disaster for them in a campaign.

The old-style politician uses personal contact and individual favors as his basic contact with the electorate. The campaign management firm depends heavily on the expert use and manipulation of the media of mass communications by professional advertising and public relations men to influence the electorate.

The professional politician frequently deals primarily or even exclusively in personal power and patronage. The campaign management man generally does not deal in these things for himself. Between campaigns he may continue to advise politicians but he normally reverts to private public relations or advertising work.

A fourth difference arises from the unpublicized work campaign management firms do in the campaign. Generally everybody knows about the political boss, but campaign management firms are just beginning to receive widespread publicity, even though they have been operating in California for more than twenty years. In this sense these firms are politically less responsible than political bosses of the old school.

On the other hand, the campaign management firms are undoubtedly less expensive to maintain than permanent political organizations. Although it is expensive to hire these firms because they must use heavy coverage in mass media to be effective, once the campaign is over the firm needs no further direct support from political sources; it reverts to its normal advertising and public relations business. The political organization must be supported between elections as well as during campaigns, usually from the public treasury.

The record of campaign management firms

No complete record of the successes and failures of campaign management firms in California elections is available. These firms do not have to register with any public agency nor report on their activities. Many of them are secretive about their record and activities and refuse to answer even the most innocuous and elementary questions.

The available data, however, indicate that campaign management firms have been enormously successful in California. Whitaker and Baxter, for example, managed seventy-five California campaigns in the years 1933 through 1955, and won seventy of them. Thirteen of the seventy-five were campaigns for major public office, a few for minor offices, and the balance for propositions. In 1956 they lost "the big one," the initiative proposition on oil and gas conservation.

Baus and Ross managed thirty-six campaigns in Southern California between 1945 and 1957. Eleven of these concerned candidates and the rest were for local and state propositions and local bond issues. In the campaigns for public office they suffered their only defeat in Manchester Boddy's campaign against Helen Gahagan Douglas for the Democratic nomination for United States senator in 1950. They have lost only three proposition campaigns, two of them bond issues requiring a two-thirds majority for approval.

Thomas S. Page broke into the business with Whitaker and Baxter in the 1947 Robinson campaign for Mayor of San Francisco. In 1952 he served as executive director of the Stevenson-Sparkman Clubs of California, which were the source of the present Democratic rejuvenation but which were unsuccessful in 1952 in gathering a favorable vote for Stevenson in California. Page then aided D. V. Nicholson's management of William Maillard's successful campaigns for Congress in 1952 and 1954. He has worked primarily in city campaigns and has managed successfully the campaigns of four candidates for the San Francisco Board of Supervisors. Page has not taken on any proposition campaigns.

Bob Alderman of San Francisco is a newcomer in the business, although he successfully managed Goodwin Knight's campaign for re-election in 1950 while serving as the Lieutenant Governor's executive secretary. After leaving Knight's office in 1954, he established his own agency and managed the 1954 campaigns of Frank Jordan for secretary of state, Charles G. Johnson for treasurer, and Alan Pattee for the State Assembly, all of whom won.

Harry Lerner has aided Whitaker and Baxter in several proposition campaigns, and he successfully managed Edmund Brown's campaigns for attorney general in 1950 and 1954. His big triumph came in his victorious campaign against the oil and gas conservation initiative in 1956.

Although the record of the total impact of the political campaign management firms is not complete as yet, it is nevertheless evident that some firms have been on the winning side in most of the campaigns they have managed. Some insight into the influential campaign factors in California voting may therefore be gained from a review of their methods, techniques, and ideas.

Methods and organization

Thomas S. Page offers a fairly complete service for his clients. He advises and counsels on issues, writes speeches as necessary, handles publicity material, re-cruits and organizes volunteer workers, determines the style and theme of advertising, and advises on how to set up an effective volunteer fund-raising organization — although he prefers to avoid direct entanglement in this.

Page directs his main attention to opinion leaders and group processes. He repudiates the view that "repetition, through mass media, and stereotypes plus mechanistic stimuli create public opinion." This conception, according to Page, improperly defines the mass as an agglomeration of people who are the recipients of communication from a central source and who are not in communication with each other.

Page agrees with Herbert Blumer's view that groups and individuals differ in terms of their strategic positions within society and consequently differ as to prestige and power. Consequently, according to Blumer, "Public Opinion consists of the pattern of the diverse views and positions on the issues *that come to the individuals who have to act in response to the public opinion.*" From this, Page concludes that the political public relations expert must analyze the value judgments of individuals who are in a position to act, and the kind of power and prestige pressures to which they are potentially responsive. Once the situation is properly analyzed, the public relations expert selects the effective groups or individuals and molds their opinions in favor of his candidate or issue. . . .

Murray Chotiner, whose views are known through his lectures at UCLA and at the Republican party's campaign school in Washington for party leaders, is a member of the "techniques win elections" school. He believes that a successful campaign can be waged by analyzing the basic desires, motivations and aspirations of the electorate and tailoring the candidate to appeal to these attitudes. The candidate only needs to use the right techniques and he will be able to defeat his opponent.

Chotiner advises against publicizing the complete voting record of a candidate. This overcomes the tendency of voters to give greater weight to a candidate's errors than to his good works. State the candidate's voting record in general terms such as "voted for military preparedness," advises Chotiner, and let the voter discover the full record if he has the time and the know-how.

It is better to have a candidate "drafted" for office than to have him impose his desire for office upon his constituents, according to Chotiner. He advises candidates to appear to be courageous in dealing with the voters. In the 1950 senatorial campaign, Chotiner had Nixon get up before an audience and say, "I have been told that I must not talk about this subject but I am going to tell the people of our State just exactly what is going on." Although this is not a new technique by any means, Chotiner claims it worked wonders for Nixon.

A candidate must take the offensive against pros-pective opponents and do so long before the cam-paign begins officially. Begin to deflate possible opponents as much as a year ahead of the campaign, advises Chotiner. A candidate should generally dis-miss with silence the deflating attacks by his oppo-nents, but if the attacks seem to be hitting home he must reply with a counterattack on the opponent for having made such an attack. This is best accom-plished by being powerfully sincere and avoiding the basic issues. Then the subject should be dropped completely. Nixon's "Checkers" speech in the 1952 campaign is a classic of this type.

Chotiner pays strong attention to the issues of the campaign, particularly to developing the one which will be most favorable to his candidate and most damaging to the opponent. The "left wing" affilia-tions of Knowland's opponent in 1946 were fully exploited and the Communist issue was effectively used in Nixon's 1946 and 1950 campaigns.

Chotiner, although a practicing attorney, has studied publicity and advertising techniques inten-sively and has become adept at some of the more effective ways of handling the mass media. Like Bob Alderman and Whitaker and Baxter, he attempts to win the favor of newspapers by notifying them at the beginning of a campaign of the political advertising which his candidate will make during the campaign.

Whitaker and Baxter — Campaigns, Incorporated

Whitaker and Baxter established the first full-fledged political campaign management firm in Cali-fornia and in the United States. In California they have become the giants of the industry, the most successful practitioners of the art of campaign man-agement and the model by which all other firms may be measured. They have written widely about their own ideas on campaign management and have been written about more than any other firm in the field. One of the most striking impressions one gets from contacts with this unusual couple is that they are a living example of the services they have to sell. It is quickly evident that they believe in the value of public relations work enough to practice it upon themselves.

Clem Whitaker served his apprenticeship as a newspaperman and as owner of the Capitol News Bureau which serviced eighty California small-town and weekly papers with political news from Sacra-mento, the state capitol. After getting to know his way around the legislative halls he became an occa-sional lobbyist, first for the barbers, and later for a bill to abolish capital punishment.

In 1933 Whitaker was hired as a publicity man on behalf of the referendum on the Central Valley Proj-ect Act. He was joined by Leone Baxter, at that time the manager of the Chamber of Commerce of Red-ding, California, which was interested in the passage of the referendum.

During the campaign Clem and Leone established Campaigns, Incorporated, and were in the political campaign management business to stay. Later they made the partnership permanent on the personal side through marriage. They also established the Clem Whitaker Advertising Agency to handle the adver-tising used in their campaign management work, and in 1936 they began the California Feature Service, a weekly clipsheet of editorials and features designed primarily for the state's small dailies and weeklies. Each of the articles in the clipsheet is more or less subtly written to enhance the interests and the gen-eral economic philosophy of the firm's clients.

Whitaker and Baxter's political opponents and some of their competitors like to charge that they win because they always have the most money — money from the big-business interests of the state. This charge has been muted somewhat, however, since they lost the oil conservation proposition cam-paign in 1956 on a budget of $3,450,000 — by far the largest amount spent for or against a proposition in California's history. Their clients include the Pacific Telegraph and Telephone Company, Standard Oil of California, Pacific Gas and Electric, and the Southern Pacific, four of the wealthiest and most conservative corporations in the state. Their Repub-lican candidates are usually well financed, too — Goodwin Knight's general election campaign for the governorship in 1954 was budgeted for almost $500,000. Yet attempts to account for their success from this source alone grossly misjudge the basis of their power and their influence over California voters.

As a matter of fact, Whitaker and Baxter have not always had large budgets or the most money to spend in campaigns. In 1933 they beat the Pacific Gas and Electric Company in the Central Valley Project Act referendum on a budget of only $39,000. In 1944, they managed the first attempt by the California Teachers Association to raise teachers' salaries and state funds for public schools on a budget of $110,-000, a figure they consider rock-bottom for state-wide proposition elections in modern California. The proposition won by a vote of 1,753,818 to 996,808 in spite of initial opposition from the State Chamber of Commerce and major taxpayer groups. Whitaker and Baxter have had their greatest suc-cesses in California with the California Teachers Association, although later campaigns for this group in 1946 and 1952 were better financed on budgets of $265,000 and $407,000 respectively.

In 1948 Whitaker and Baxter, working for the railroads, won the campaign for the initiative propo-sition amending the full-crew law, in spite of intense labor opposition and the expenditure of the same amount of money by both sides. Ironically they lost by more than three-to-one on oil conservation in 1956 when they spent two-and-a-half times more than their opponents.

It is evident that money alone does not account for Whitaker and Baxter's successes or defeats. A more thorough look at the firm's ideas and operations will give a fuller and more accurate accounting of its ability to sway the California electorate.

A successful campaign, according to Whitaker and Baxter, requires the best candidate, the best cause, the best plan of action, and the best force of volunteers. They credit much of their success to the fact that they do not accept every campaign offered to them. Pick a good candidate to work for, one whom you believe in, they advise. If none is available, take a walk. But even a good candidate must have a chance of winning. "We don't knowingly lead forlorn hopes." Winning candidates are of two main kinds, both of which serve to interest the voters in a campaign. Most Americans love a contest; hence a fighting candidate, a man who is fighting for *something,* is one type of successful candidate. Most Americans also like to be entertained. Hence if a candidate cannot fight, he must "put on a show." If he puts on a good show, Americans will listen to him. And it is of primary importance for any candidate for major office to have at least two or three years of build-up before the campaign itself gets under way.

Once they take on a campaign, Whitaker and Baxter have their staff compile complete dossiers on their own and the rival candidates. Every bit of available information on the subjects, sometimes amounting to a million words or more, is put together, digested, and analyzed by the staff. The staff then makes a précis of the data which enables Whitaker and Baxter to review and digest it with reasonable speed and comprehension.

Then Whitaker and Baxter go into seclusion in order to work out an over-all plan for the conduct of the campaign. Part of this plan is the creation of a theme or basic appeal, and this is one of the most important ingredients in their formula for success. Whitaker and Baxter maintain stoutly that this appeal must be "right" for the public because the public will not buy a dishonest issue or man. However, they claim that there is no formula for determining what this appeal should be; rather, it must be decided especially for each campaign.

Whitaker and Baxter are certain, however, that the theme must be simple and have a strong human interest appeal. It must be couched in particulars instead of generalities. It must have more "corn than caviar" in it because more Americans like corn better than caviar. It must be directed to the many-sided interests of the individual voter. The particular voter is not only a union member, but also a father, a Catholic, a veteran, a member of the PTA, and a sports fan. Each of the individual's group loyalties must be appealed to in a special way.

Whitaker and Baxter subject their first plan to an acid test. They create an opposition plan by assessing as accurately as they can the strong and weak points of the opposing candidate. Then they mentally wage the campaign and on the basis of the "experience" they make a final plan for their own candidate. This plan is worked out with considerable detail and carefully budgeted. Minimum and maximum budget figures are prepared for the candidate and it is his responsibility to raise the necessary financing.

One of their cardinal rules for a successful campaign is that there must be strong control from the top. Whitaker and Baxter insist upon full control of expenditures and operations. Every worker must be under their control, every issue must be formulated by them, every check must be signed by them, and speeches, posters, radio and TV spots, and other mass media paraphernalia must be written by their firm. The master plan must be followed as worked out in advance.

Whitaker and Baxter's emphasis upon "the best force of volunteers" as part of a successful campaign arises somewhat paradoxically from their disdain for party organizations whose precinct work is considered by them to be ineffective and expensive. According to Baxter, political campaigns in California at the time they entered the business "were the natural province of broken down politicians and alcoholic camp followers." This low view of politicians is shared by other political publicity men.

In spite of this view of permanent political organizations, Whitaker and Baxter quickly begin to set up an elaborate organization throughout the state which is really designed to do the work of a party organization without suffering its handicaps and limitations. For a gubernatorial campaign the firm's normal staff of about sixteen is enlarged to forty to eighty people, including if necessary the staffs of competitive firms which are without other commitments. Northern and southern campaign chairmen are appointed as fund-raisers and goodwill ambassadors for the candidate. Then county, district, and local chairmen are chosen. Great care is used in selecting these persons and many of them are hired for the campaign at salaries befitting the quality of work expected of them.

The next step is to set up county, district, and local volunteer committees of "enthusiastic and able men and women." These people are called the heartbeat of the organization for they are expected to do a great deal of work. The committees must accomplish specified campaign objectives: an effective endorsement or resolutions drive, an intensive local publicity campaign, a well-organized pamphlet distribution system, an energetic, carefully managed speakers' bureau, and a functioning finance committee to arrange the financing of local activities and to augment locally the work of the state committee in radio, television, newspaper advertising, and other campaign promotion.

On the state-wide scene the firm's headquarters is busy lining up natural allies. When campaigning for doctors, they enlist the support of druggists; when directing campaigns for teachers and the school system, they seek, and get, the support of school construction groups and the state and local parent-teacher organizations.

Allies are also sought among groups who are in opposition but who are potential converts. Whitaker and Baxter work hard to get Chamber of Commerce, labor, and taxpayer groups to support their education campaigns, and they usually succeed.

A classic example of Whitaker and Baxter's "allies technique" can be observed in the 1954 gubernatorial campaign on behalf of Governor Knight against Democrat Richard Graves. Early in the campaign Knight, under Whitaker and Baxter direction, bid for and received the support of the state AFL in competition with Graves' efforts to achieve the same objective, although labor groups in California are the "natural" allies of the Democrats.

Graves had hardly recovered from this setback when Whitaker and Baxter announced the public endorsement of Knight by over a hundred mayors of California cities in a Mayors-of-California Non-Partisan Committee — in spite of the fact that Graves' most recent position had been that of Executive Director of the League of California Cities and he had spent twenty years working closely with public officials of these cities.

To make it a grand coup, Whitaker and Baxter also announced the endorsement of the California Public Employees Association to Protect Civil Service — one of the *ad hoc* organizations which both sides create for propaganda and bandwagon effects in California campaigns. The inevitable California Committee of Democrats for Governor Goodwin J. Knight also appeared with an assist from Whitaker and Baxter.

For the activation and implementation of group support, they depend heavily upon the "opinion leaders" in the various groups. Some of these leaders are visited personally; others receive personal letters. Through them, arrangements are made to send members study materials and campaign literature.

As a professional public relations firm, Whitaker and Baxter are experts in the use of mass media, and this is where much of their strength lies. They not only have a skill which politicians do not usually possess but they are more adept at this end of the

business than are many of their competitors. The literature and mass media used by Whitaker and Baxter in a gubernatorial campaign are prodigious. They include a speakers' manual, a general appeal pamphlet, enclosure leaflets, special appeal leaflets, postal card mailings, "dear friend" cards (carrying a personal message from the candidate to the voter), bumper strips, windshield stickers, campaign buttons, outdoor advertising, small poster paper, headquarters posters, radio spots, TV spots, form resolutions, newspaper advertising, one-column mats of the candidate, and recordings for use before groups.

In a 1948 proposition campaign the firm used 10,000,000 pamphlets and leaflets, 4,500,000 postal cards, 50,000 letters to key individuals, 70,000 inches of newspaper display advertising in 700 papers, 3,000 radio spots and 12 fifteen-minute network radio programs, 1,000 twenty-four-sheet billboards and 18,000–20,000 smaller posters, theater slides and trailers in 160 theaters, an intensive newspaper publicity campaign conducted continuously for three months in every paper in the state, thousands of speeches delivered before civic organizations in every community in California, and sound trucks, newspaper cartoons, and a first try at television. Since 1948 television has largely replaced radio as a campaign medium. Significantly, long speeches by the candidate are scrupulously avoided. Sheer volume use of the mass media is not enough. Whitaker and Baxter insist that the proper use of words is the key to the successful use of the mass media. They like "fighting prose" and colorful, dramatic, picture-building words. Copy must be brief enough to be read and understood, dramatic enough to draw attention, and sound enough to produce action.

Generally, it is necessary to get the right issue and dramatize it in an entertaining way. The proper procedure is to draw the attention of the electorate by a gimmick or some corny entertaining, and then drive the right issue often into the consciousness of the public by a brief hard-hitting speech by the candidate. This approach differs from the hillbilly music or funny speech method of campaigning in that it attempts to add the second dimension of action, motivated by an issue, to the rapport established by entertainment alone.

It is evident that this technique must insist that the issues should not be spread too thin. According to Whitaker and Baxter, a few issues well dramatized are much superior to the dissipation of energy and attention on many issues no matter how good they may be, individually or as a whole.

Whitaker and Baxter do not leave the support of the press to chance. In addition to year-round distribution of their weekly political clipsheet "California Feature Service," they send a complete schedule of advertisements to every paper in the state at the beginning of each campaign. To enhance this good will, Whitaker and Baxter do not collect the regular 15 per cent agency fee from the papers outside the big cities. Furthermore, the firm places large amounts of advertising in the papers for its regular clients and can often depend upon this to get a favorable editorial response for its political clients. The fact that the state's newspapers are overwhelmingly Republican does not give the firm too great a barrier of resistance to the support of its invariably Republican clients.

No campaign director can allow his candidate to wage a defensive fight, according to Whitaker and Baxter rules. The candidate may be on the defensive but it must be made to appear that he is on the offensive. The classic case occurred in the recall election of Mayor Roger D. Lapham of San Francisco in 1946.

In a recall election the incumbent is necessarily on the defensive so Whitaker and Baxter adopted a two-pronged action to gain the offensive. Lapham suddenly charged his opponents with stalling in getting the necessary signatures on the recall petition so that they could prevent the recall from qualifying on the primary ballot and force it into a special election. Lapham challenged his opponents to get on with the job and promptly marched down (surrounded by photographers) to sign his own recall petition. This bold stroke was accompanied by another just as ingenious. Instead of using any identifiable person or group as the backer of the recall, Whitaker and Baxter invented "the Faceless Man" as the sinister, cowardly opposition. A picture of this faceless man was plastered on outdoor billboards throughout San Francisco and in other mass media channels. Lapham defeated the recall movement by a majority of more than 32,000 out of 185,000 votes.

Whitaker and Baxter do not subscribe fully to the theory prevalent in academic and many political circles that elections are won or lost before the campaign begins, i.e., that campaigns do not materially alter voting intentions of the electorate. They agree that many elections are won or hopelessly lost before they begin, but many others will be relatively close races and will be determined by the campaigns waged by both candidates. Because they only take campaigns with a chance of victory, they have developed a definite campaign plan based on the theory that close elections are won in the three weeks preceding election day and especially during the final week. Hence they plan a campaign to last for only 60 days prior to election day. Much of the organizing work is carried out during the first month. The development of the campaign proceeds slowly at first. It gradually builds up until three weeks before the election when it shifts into high gear and reaches peak momentum on the Friday night before election day. Fully 75 per cent of the expenditures of the campaign are made in the last three-weeks' period.

The success of the campaign depends in part upon the personality and character of the public relations personnel. Whitaker and Baxter say that they must work eighteen hours per day during a campaign and must forego their personal lives in the process. They must be adept at handling human relations problems in dealing with their candidate and his managers and the various members of the campaign committees. As they say, "It's the problem of clashing temperaments under pressure . . . the problem of keeping a sense of humor and a sense of values when your campaign committee has the jitters and your candidate is writhing under the punishing blows of his opponent."

The campaign expert must have "a strange mixture of idealism and realism" in his makeup if he is to succeed, they both believe. He must believe in his candidate and in the issues if he is to work his heart out in the campaign, but he must succeed if he is to stay in business. Hence the need to back a candidate who can get elected.

Usually Whitaker and Baxter face a tough fight because they normally would not be hired to win a campaign that appeared already won. Over-all, their work requires that they be good organizers, experts in the use of mass media, expert salesmen, sensitive and ingenious idea men, and masters of human relations.

The strength of Whitaker and Baxter springs from numerous sources. First, they probably know as much or more about California politics and have as keen an insight into what motivates the California voter as anyone else does. Like many successful advertising men and politicians, they are keen students of the "mass mind" and they claim to have "good average minds" which enable them to meet the average man at his own level and see things as he sees them.

Second, they have operated in a milieu which has been particularly favorable to the development of campaign management firms. Weak party organizations have created a need for their services and have given them little opposition during campaigns. The initiative and referendum have provided an excellent nursery for their growth, especially since California's parties have rarely taken a stand on ballot propositions.

Third, Clem Whitaker has built up an unmatchable and invaluable web of contacts and friendships during his thirty-five years of working with the political, economic and social groups in the state.

Fourth, they are accomplished experts in utilizing for their maximum effectiveness the mass media and the various social, political, professional and economic organizations in the state.

Fifth, they have usually been on the Republican side and thereby have gained the advantage of the traditional liberal Republican strength in the state especially during the Warren era, even though they have been philosophically opposed to this wing of the party.

Finally, their talents and accomplishments have attracted the big economic interests of the state and they have often had adequate financing. This has followed their successes, however, and has not always been a primary source of their strength.

Whitaker and Baxter have, in effect, created a political machine of a very delicate type. It requires a directing agent of unusual political shrewdness, of a caliber that cannot be hired and replaced at will. . . .

The organization will remain effective only as long as the directing genius behind it remains effective and the political vacuum is maintained in California. The rejuvenation of the Democrats which is now taking place may perhaps give more business to campaign management firms but will also create serious obstacles which they have not had to face before.

The comparative record of political campaign management firms

The growth of political campaign management firms in California and their many successes in state elections during the past two decades raise several important questions. Have they not, for example, blurred or destroyed issues by concentrating on mastering the technological requirements of the mass media and manipulating them for the most favorable responses by the electorate toward their clients? Samuel Yorty, after his defeat by Kuchel for United States senator in 1954, said in his congratulatory wire to Kuchel: "It seems to me that the current tendency of some candidates to rely so heavily on costly advertising agencies and techniques is contrary to the best interests of our democracy."

The question as put is, of course, partly false. It implies that parties and politicians, working without the aid of professional management men, are dedicated to the sharpening of issues and the deliberate and honest presentation of those issues for the calm, mature, and rational decision of the voters. Such is not the case. Some politicians have tried to follow this course of action; others have not. The major parties have followed neither course consistently.

The question becomes significant if political campaign management firms can deliberately prevent consideration of the political issues confronting the constituency. To affirm this proposition is to assign an influence to these firms all out of proportion to their role in the California political process. The very mass media which have been so instrumental in their rise preclude the possibility that the publicists can control the choice of the major issues which the electorate will consider in any election. Try as they might, publicists can hardly hide or dismiss issues such as the existence of wars, depressions, and gross

corruption, for example. To accomplish this would require a one-party system and a completely closed and controlled mass media system, something which certainly does not exist in California. However, as issues become less important and have less day-to-day central impact upon the public, political campaign management firms can have greater influences in selecting or disregarding issues in any particular campaign.

In practice, as we have seen, public relations firms operate along two different lines in campaigns: as publicity arms and as general campaign managers. The firms that serve as publicity arms are becoming a necessary and essential part of campaign equipage. But their role tends to be one of executing campaign policy rather than forming it.

The campaign management group has the opportunity to set policy as well as execute it. Here, too, however, these firms have tended to accentuate issues rather than to obscure them. Whitaker and Baxter have usually accepted campaigns which fit in with their own conservative philosophy. Regardless of what one thinks of the merits of this philosophy, they have usually drawn a sharp liberal-conservative issue in California politics and elections. It is probably inevitable that as campaign management firms and their campaign activities become better known to the public, they will aid the electorate in choosing among issues, candidates, and parties by aligning themselves with one party and one set of issues consistently.

The danger is that the regular clients of advertising and public relations firms will inhibit the availability of these firms for both parties. In 1956, for example, the Democrats were able to hire an advertising agency for the national campaign only after the advertising industry became embarrassed by the refusal of all the leading agencies to handle the Democratic party's account. A small and relatively new agency, Norman, Craig, and Kummel — all Democrats — finally offered their services and the industry released half-a-dozen Democratic-minded copy writers to aid the Norman firm.

The second and perhaps the most important question to be asked about campaign management firms in California is whether or not their expertise in mass media manipulation has enabled them to perfect a push-button technique for influencing and controlling elections. In a sense, every consistently successful person or group tends to employ the same techniques repeatedly. The successful teacher, businessman, military man, or advertising man tends to use repeatedly whichever "system" usually brings about desired results for him.

The consistent successes of many of the firms under consideration would indicate that they have perfected a push-button machine. Yet, they are quite aware of the limitations of their "system." Whitaker and Baxter, for example do not for a moment believe that their business is a push-button affair requiring only the injection of the most money and the grinding out of the most advertising and publicity copy. The fact that they refuse to touch a candidate they think cannot win is sufficient to refute the push-button idea of voting by mass media persuasion. . . .

It is evident from the record that the presence of professional publicity men and campaign management firms, even of the caliber of Whitaker and Baxter, has not always been the controlling factor in Republican victories in California elections. Republican candidates have won just as regularly without the aid of these firms. Significantly, too, Warren won both nominations in 1946 after he stopped using a professional campaign management firm, and Goodwin Knight won both nominations for lieutenant governor in 1950 in the only election in which he used Robert Alderman, his executive secretary, to direct his campaign.

Nor can the inference be drawn that the activities of campaign management firms on behalf of one candidate aid the other candidates of the same party in the same election. These firms, particularly Whitaker and Baxter, appeal to Democratic voters by either a bipartisan or nonpartisan campaign. Furthermore, they follow the usual California practice of specifically enjoining their workers from tie-ups with other candidates. In their instructions to the local chairmen of Knight's 1954 campaign, Whitaker and Baxter pointed out that "it is important that we do not combine the Governor's candidacy with that of anybody else. While such a procedure might help another candidate with whom the Governor may be completely friendly — obviously the Governor must not be involved in other Primary contests."

The popular conception that professional advertising men can with adequate funds merchandise any product on the market contributes to a distorted view of the power of campaign management firms in California elections. Their limitations in selling candidates are in some ways similar to the limitations of advertising techniques in selling products. Professor Neil Borden, in his monumental study of *The Economic Effects of Advertising,* drew two relevant conclusions concerning advertising's effect upon selective demand and upon primary demand. In assessing selective demand, Borden concluded: "Advertising can and does increase the demand for products of many individual companies, but the extent to which it does so varies widely and depends upon the circumstances under which the enterprises operate." Borden's conclusion regarding primary demand is even more significant: "basic trends of demand for products, which are determined by underlying social and environmental conditions, are more significant in determining the expansion or contraction of primary demand than is the use or lack of use of advertising." As examples, Professor Borden points out that demand for lettuce, sugar, green vegetables, and many professional services grew although little advertising was used, and demand for cigars, smoking tobacco, men's shoes, wheat, flour, and furniture dropped in spite of large expenditures for advertising and promotion.

Conclusions

As far as the California scene is concerned, professional publicity men and campaign management firms have added something new and significant to electoral campaigns — an expert, efficient, and economical (per voter reached) contact with the voting population. This function increases in importance with the size of the constituency and the voting population, and as the issues confronting the society become obscure and less central in the lives of the voters.

These firms have also filled much of the party vacuum in California. Parties failed to become involved in campaign management of initiative and referendum propositions, and private campaign organizations were a necessary and inevitable result. Parties, under the impact of nonpartisanship and the cross-filing system, have until recently also failed to co-ordinate the campaigns of the candidates flying their colors, and it has been necessary for resourceful candidates to look for competent management elsewhere.

The record of these firms in their management of *candidates* for political state-wide offices is not as clear-cut as is commonly believed. Certainly they have not developed a push-button technique for electing the candidate who offers the most money for their services. The voters tend to be far more impressed by the characteristics of the candidate himself, his record, the type of campaign he puts on, and the prevailing social and economic forces at the time of the election. In California, fighting reform candidates, such as Franklin Roosevelt and Hiram Johnson, leading a dramatic movement, or reform candidates such as Earl Warren and Edmund Brown, with a sustained personal build-up, have been political assets with built-in mass media antennae for broadcasting their political wares more effectively than professional campaign management and publicity men have been able to do.

One of the popular reforms promoted in the early years of this century as a means of expanding democracy was the institution of direct legislation, a way for the voters themselves to legislate or in effect to veto acts of the elected legislative body. Such provisions were never universally adopted, have been used extensively in some states and only occasionally in others, and have probably seldom if ever met fully the high hopes of the sponsors. In recent years there has been much criticism of the extreme importance of money in initiative and referendum campaigns, and of the way in which these presumed expressions of the popular will have in fact become in large measure contests between competing public relations firms. Yet the initiative and referendum have a significant record of accomplishment in some places and usually enjoy strong public support. Nowhere have they been utilized to the extent common in California, whose experience is here summarized and evaluated by Professor Winston W. Crouch.

78

The Initiative and Referendum in Action

By Winston W. Crouch

RETIREMENT LIFE PAYMENTS, old age benefits, "Ham and Eggs" and "Thirty Dollars Every Thursday" pension plans, state liquor regulation, local option, legislative apportionment, "hot cargo" labor issues, fair employment practices, and tideland oil-drilling struggles have all served to make headlines about the initiative and referendum in California. . . . California voters have had as thorough an experience with the various types of direct legislation as any group in the United States. In view of this, many persons have commented critically about the fact that the ballot is too long, the fact that California voters are faced regularly with many elaborately-drawn proposals of policy, and that large campaign funds are raised and spent to persuade the electorate to vote for or against matters of great moment put before them by petition.

It should be noted affirmatively, however, that the initiative has produced such less spectacular but nonetheless solid accomplishments as a state executive budget law, a state civil service system, and a successful method for selecting the state judiciary. . . .

Winston W. Crouch, *The Initiative and Referendum in California* (Los Angeles: The Haynes Foundation, 1950), pp. 1, 7–10, 13–15, 19–23, 25–26, 28, 30–35, 37–40. Reprinted by permission of the publisher.

the formula for state support of the public [was] placed in the constitution by the initiative. Furthermore, inspection of the state ballot at any general election will disclose that more than two-thirds of the policy propositions laid before the voters are submitted by the legislature, usually as constitutional amendments. . . .

Trends in the use of the initiative proposals

Subjects of state-wide initiative proposals have changed notably from time to time. At first they were concerned with moral and economic issues. Prohibition appeared on the ballot many times. Antivivisection, prize fighting, compulsory vaccination, the reading of the Bible in the schools, and usury were also early subjects. The eight-hour day and Sunday-closing were voted upon too. Nearly every initiative measure presented in the first eight years dealt with substantive law, although two bond issues were presented by the initiative and the single tax was initiated and defeated several times.

In the 1920's two trends began to appear. In one instance the public school people initiated a constitutional amendment to set the amount of money to be drawn annually from the state treasury for support of the public schools. This was adopted by almost a two-to-one majority. At the same time some initiatives dealt with administrative organization. The state executive budget amendment entered the field of administration and directed that the governor should have the power and responsibility to prepare a budget for the state, thereby greatly enhancing that officer's position as chief executive of the state. At the same election the voters approved initiatives creating administrative boards to examine, license, and supervise chiropractors and osteopaths. . . .

Several notable administrative matters were put before the people by petition and adopted. These included the state civil service amendment and the amendment giving the state attorney general supervision over sheriffs and district attorneys. Two amendments regarding public employment and tenure failed. Judicial administration and the rights of defendants figured on three measures. A new method for selecting the higher state judiciary was adopted by initiative during this period.

More and more, however, economic issues began to appear in the initiative process. The single tax plan reappeared. Income and gasoline taxes and increased school support were voted upon. An act to regulate picketing and boycotts was declared. The tideland oil drilling controversy figured both in initiatives and referenda.

In 1938 the first of a series of old age pension plans was projected onto the state ballot by petition. Each of these varied in amount of money to be required and in administrative detail. Each provided elaborate details of administration and sought to be self-enforcing, thus to escape the efforts of legislators to change the plans. . . .

Origins of the initiatives

Why do groups initiate legislation or a constitutional amendment? The legislature remains, as it should, the principal instrument of determining the policies of state government. What causes groups to go outside the legislature to achieve their aims? The reason most often assigned is that the legislature refuses to pass a measure that is dear to the group requesting its passage. The 1922 water and power proposition and the various chiropractor initiatives might be taken as illustrations of this reason.

On several occasions groups have been inspired to offer an initiative petition because the legislature was unable to agree upon a bill even though there had been considerable work done on it. An illustration of such an initiative is the state executive budget constitutional amendment passed in 1922. The "federal plan" of reapportioning the legislature, passed in 1926, is another.

A more significant reason than any of these is that when an initiative proposition is offered, the proponents wish to have it passed or defeated in the form they desire rather than to have it amended and transformed in the legislature. The state civil service amendment and the constitutional amendment strengthening the powers of the state attorney general, both passed in 1934, are excellent instances of this.

It must be recognized that the initiative has been given a special standing that makes it attractive to groups that have reason to distrust the legislature. An initiative proposal that has been approved by the voters cannot be amended or repealed without the consent of the voters. The state school support amendment of 1920 was offered as an initiative for just that reason and to protect it from legislators who might seek to reduce the amount of state aid. No doubt the various pension promoters had a similar notion in mind. . . .

Circulating the petition

Early in the process of circulating an initiative petition the proponents undoubtedly have decided whether to build their own organization of petition circulators or to hire a petition circulating concern. There are several of the latter in San Francisco and Los Angeles who will undertake the work on the basis of so much per name secured. The costs involved are for hire of circulators, clerical work and precincting, and profit for the firm. . . .

There is no requirement in California, as in some states, that petition signatures be obtained throughout the state. Events indicate that the bulk of signatures on most petitions are obtained in the most populous urban counties. The "Ham and Eggs" promoters, however, made considerable point of the fact that signatures to their petitions were obtained in all counties. There is some tendency for petition sponsors to circulate petitions in several counties so that they may capitalize on the publicity value accruing from having petition circulators working among the potential voters. Thus far few, if any, proposals placed on the ballot in California by initiative have been exclusively of interest to cities or city populations. Hence, the urban versus rural contention has not been raised in initiative politics, as it has been raised in the California legislature. . . .

The initiative as a political balance-wheel

Admirable as the legislative process may be when it operates as it should, there are numerous occasions when a weary public must take an emasculated, compromised substitute measure produced by the legislature because it is the best that could be had at the time — the best that could survive the gauntlet of the lobbies.

Many initiative propositions have been prepared only after the legislature has failed to settle a problem, usually after it has failed to obtain agreement to any acceptable plan. In an increasing number of instances conservatives and liberals alike have turned to the initiative when it was determined that legislators could not be persuaded to take a stand upon a measure that would have far-reaching effect. . . . The best function of the initiative has been to provide a balance wheel to correct some of the shortcomings of the legislature. . . .

Initiative educates electorate

The initiative has functioned to an unmeasurable degree as a medium for discussion and for expression of protest. This is certainly one of its most significant functions. This becomes even more important in California where political parties have played so small a role as media for discussion of political issues and for organizing the voters. Cross-filing for nominations and party factions have confused and blurred the pattern of party responsibility.

Problems of government posed by initiative petitions receive wide publicity in the newspapers, over the radio, by billboards and handbills, and in discussion meetings, as well as in the official publicity pamphlets sent out by the secretary of state at public expense. The proposals constitute topics of discussion for months before the November elections. California has developed an unusual number of organizations that have gained state-wide recognition for their analysis of ballot measures sent to members and publicized in newspapers. . . .

Initiative movements that fail at the polls are not always fruitless in the long run. They serve as vehicles for the dissemination of ideas that eventually take form in legislation. Campaigns in support of an initiative measure may demonstrate to the legislature that, with certain alterations, the program would be in accord with public opinion. They may also bring opposing groups to recognize the futility of demanding enactment of their unaltered ideas, thereby promoting compromise. . . .

THE REFERENDUM

Persons seeking to prevent a measure introduced in the legislature from becoming law have several opportunities to achieve that result. In the first place the bill may be defeated or materially altered in committee. Failing this, opponents may carry the fight to the legislative chamber. Furthermore, opposition is not confined to one house. All tactics may be duplicated as the bill proceeds through the second house. After a bill has passed both houses opponents may still seek to persuade the governor to veto it. This is the normal course of legislative opposition.

The referendum stands as the last-resort check upon the legislature. . . . The referendum is by nature a conservative process. It seeks to preserve the status quo. The procedure for circulating referendum petitions is simpler than that involved in initiative petitions because there is no question of phrasing a proposition to be put to the people by referendum. A referendum is aimed at a specific measure that has already passed the legislature and been signed by the governor; it is simply a proposition asking for a vote by the electors of the state upon that given measure. The state constitution provides that all statutes, except a few that are classified as "emergency" and "exempt," do not go into effect until ninety days after the legislature adjourns. If a referendum petition qualifies against a statute before the ninety-day period expires, the statute is suspended until the next state election. . . .

The very nature of the referendum process compels its users to develop a considerable campaign organization. This has developed to the extent that it can be generalized that the only measures that appear on the ballot by petition referendum are those opposed by substantial organized groups with sufficient financial resources to be able to organize a campaign within the ninety days required to circu-

late the petition. Furthermore, records filed with the secretary of state in accordance with the corrupt practices acts indicate that the proponents of referendum petitions normally spend large sums to present their arguments to the voters. Invariably these same groups have fought the measure while it was going through the legislature. . . .

CAMPAIGNING ON MEASURES

Campaign organization

Campaigns to convince the voters are the result of careful organization supported in turn by expenditures made on a scale that is rarely seen in states where the only policy matters presented to the voters are constitutional amendments proposed by the legislature. In California, campaigning on some hard-fought measures calls for organization and expenditure of funds equal to that customarily devoted to electing a candidate to an important state-wide office.

The chain store tax referendum brought out in startling clarity the fact that the public relations counsel and the publicity man play a very significant part in this type of campaign. Proponents and opponents of most vigorously contested measures have employed established public relations consultant firms. As the campaign gets under way the firm in charge develops campaign organizations in most counties and in the larger cities of the state. Often two separate state headquarters are established: one for the northern part of the state, one for the southern section. Some groups interested in the initiative, such as the pension-plan promoters, have had the advantage of an organization that has been built up and functioning for several years. Nearly every artifice of organized politics, including the trading of support between groups, has been used in recent years in direct legislation campaigns. . . . Candidates for governor, United States senator, and other state-wide offices have been drawn into the maneuvering over initiatives and referenda.

Campaign costs

A relatively large legitimate expenditure of money is required to carry out an effective campaign in an area as large as the state of California. Just how much is spent is not accurately known, although since 1921 state law requires that all such expenditures be reported to the secretary of state and made a matter of public record. . . . Expenditures on initiated and referred measures tend to be higher than are those on measures submitted by the legislature although there is no comparable information regarding the amount spent by groups in lobbying for or against measures before the legislature itself. There is some reason to believe that costs of lobbying often run as high as those for any direct legislation campaign. At the same time, the number of "million dollar campaigns" on direct legislation is relatively small, considering the importance of the issues involved in many instances. . . . The totals of funds spent on initiative campaigns and recorded with the secretary of state have been approximately evenly divided between opponents and proponents, although in most instances the old adage of politics that "the side that spends the most wins" has been proven true. Money is, undoubtedly, a great factor in campaigns on measures as well as on candidates.

Popular participation

Do the voters merely mark their ballot for candidates but pass up policy propositions? It is true that a number of voters mark their ballots for gubernatorial candidates and ignore some of the policy measures, although participation on direct legislation measures has been high at every election. A very significant fact is that participation in initiative and referendum votes tends to be appreciably higher than voting on measures submitted by the legislature. . . .

This higher voter participation in direct legislation may be explained in part also by the fact that a contest is usually involved, with the consequent publicity and campaign effort. Very often the electors at large have little information regarding legislative-submitted amendments other than the meager official pamphlet. Furthermore, many constitutional amendments proposed by the legislature are technical in character or are minor in significance.

Can the voter pick out the measures on the ballot that are important to him, or will he become confused by the large number of propositions and vote in some random fashion? Will he vote "no" on everything he does not feel he understands completely? Will he simply vote because he has heard of "Ham and Eggs" or "Hot Cargo" or "Reapportionment" or "22 Is a Tax on You"? The reaction of the electorate to the task of voting on large numbers of measures is a matter that has called forth much speculation. . . . On the average there have been twenty-one propositions at every general election held at two-year intervals.

The large number of proposals placed on the ballot has undoubtedly placed a burden on the electorate. Students of elections have examined the results to see if the voters cast their ballot only on measures high on the ballot or if position on the ballot had any appreciable significance. Proponents of measures have often tried to maneuver for a place on the ballot that they thought was favorable, some favoring one spot, some another. Thus far there is no conclusive evidence that place or number has any significance in California elections. The number of voters marking their ballots for Proposition Number 14 is apt to be as high or higher than that for Number 1, depending upon whether either is controversial.

Consistently the people have voted in greater numbers upon the measures submitted by direct legislation, yet they have approved a lesser percentage than of those submitted by the legislature. It would appear that where there is an issue the voters act. The record indicates, too, that they exercise discrimination and judgment. The number of measures does not seem to confuse the voter as to the real issues. In several instances, competing measures have been on the same ballot. One was approved, the other rejected; or, in a few instances, neither was accepted as a satisfactory solution. . . .

By and large the voters have been conservative in their voting upon direct legislation. The number of measures rejected has been greater than those accepted. In spite of the number of pension plans and other "panacea" proposals there has been no clear "populist" tendency in the record of measures adopted. . . . The majority of the voters appear not to be irrevocably committed to policies favorable to any one set of groups or interests. . . .

OPINIONS ON DIRECT LEGISLATION

Proposals for reform of the initiative have been numerous, but few have gained general acceptance and been written into the constitutional law of the state. . . . Numerous proposals have been made from time to time looking towards increasing the number of signatures required. Usually the thought behind such proposals has been that this would eliminate all but the most seriously considered and most widely popular proposals. . . .

Most of the suggestions for increasing the number of signatures seems to arise from opposition to the much discussed "panacea" initiatives. Yet only one of these "panaceas" that had real backing failed to win enough signatures to qualify for the ballot. In fact most of these petitions have far exceeded the required number of signatures and their backers boast of this as an indication of their strength. Increasing the percentage of signers would not eliminate the "panaceas" but it would increase markedly the amount of money that is spent in promotional work.

Other proposed restrictions

Periodically the initiative has been severely criticized because a proposal appears again and again with the same general purpose or title. In 1940 serious attention was given to a proposal to prevent a measure that had been defeated at the polls from reappearing for a number of years. Yet great difficulty was experienced in phrasing such an amendment. There appeared to be no satisfactory way to define what constituted the "same" measure as a defeated one. Most initiative "repeaters," just as repeaters in the legislative calendar, have been altered after each defeat in an attempt to overcome some estimated weakness or objection in the hope that a favorable majority can be won on the next try. Furthermore, it was pointed out that unscrupulous groups could "hijack" a measure by proposing a spurious scheme similar to one being discussed. When the false plan was defeated, the legitimate scheme could not be proposed for several years.

Another suggestion urged at that time was to prohibit the use of the initiative to propose financial schemes of such magnitude as old age pension plans. How welfare and pension matters could be excluded and support of the public schools retained is difficult to comprehend. . . .

Passage of Proposition Number 4 at the 1948 election produced in its aftermath several proposals to change the California initiative law. This proposition named the interim state administrator of social welfare, placed a very heavy charge upon the state's general fund, and sought to make the payments for aged and blind aid a prior lien on state funds, ahead of schools and other welfare and health programs. A ruling by the legislative counsel modified the matter of priority soon after the election. Legislators opposed to this scheme introduced several bills, (1) to prohibit initiatives from naming administrative officers, (2) to require that initiatives that sought to set up a program wherein state money must be spent must give an estimate of the appropriation required, and (3) to require that direct legislation proposals necessitating expenditures must designate the source of funds or to levy a new tax. Most of these restrictive proposals failed to clear from committee and only one passed either house. Undoubtedly the naming of an administrator in the statute was unsound policy and was a step backward from the long efforts to shorten the state ballot and reduce the number of elected state officials. It also breaks the very worth-while development in California that has made the governor more nearly a real chief executive of the state, responsible for appointing and removing key administrative officers. On the other hand, a requirement that petitioners must estimate the cost of a new program is likely to be an ineffec-

tual requirement. Estimates cannot be made exactly under such conditions. . . .

As to the other proposal, Colorado and Washington have had unfortunate experiences with initiatives that earmarked certain taxes for support of a program. California already has too much earmarking of funds and not sufficient flexibility in its state budget.

A proposal that has some advantage in ensuring that an initiative proposition has wide support throughout the various regions of the state is one based upon the Missouri law. This would require that a petition be signed by a percentage of registered voters, say 8 per cent, in a certain number of counties or of congressional districts within the state. . . . While petition organizers circulate their papers in several counties for a calculated advantage, the legal requirement to do so would have an advantage in indicating the state-wide nature of the successful petition and would do away with the notion that there is a sectional bias.

Initiative and referendum effectively established

While almost every election in the past twelve years has reopened a series of discussions about direct legislation, there is no indication that the majority of the voters are willing to abandon it. It has found an established place in the pattern of California politics. Unless continuous, strong leadership is provided in other channels of state government, it will have popular strength. If the legislature were to modernize and improve its processes and do an effective job of meeting the issues that arise, direct legislation would not be the formidable competitor that it is. Likewise political parties in the state must look to their own overhaul as organs of public opinion and of political leadership.

At the same time there remains the ever present need in a democracy for an intelligent, alert, and sustained interest on the part of the majority of voters whose purpose is good government. The initiative and referendum were adopted in the atmosphere of majority rule, one that sought to break minority, clique control of our instruments of government. Direct legislation was originally conceived as a "big stick behind the door," as Theodore Roosevelt referred to popular government; and its history in this state shows that it works best when used sparingly and under those conditions, as a balance wheel in state affairs.

In the final selection Professor Smallwood provides a most interesting comparison of the politics of urban change, contrasting the American "participation" model with the Anglo-Canadian "leadership" model.

The former, he suggests, puts most of the chips on the side of those dedicated to the preservation of the status quo, while the latter may in fact be a far more adequate technique for democratic decision-making.

79

"Game" Politics
vs.
"Feedback" Politics

By Frank Smallwood

DURING THE POST-WAR PERIOD, England, Canada and the United States have been forced to wrestle with many similar problems of urban change. One of the most crucial of these has been that of readjusting historic local governmental institutions to meet the challenges of modern urban life.

Because the English and Canadians have tended to emphasize a different set of decision-making priorities than have we, they have been able to make a more realistic response to the problems of institutional change without, however, sacrificing the broad ideals of democratic local self-government. Indeed, a strong argument can be advanced that the Anglo-Canadian approach to change has actually been more compatible with these local governmental ideals than our own approach.

The American "Participation" Model

In attempting to carry out institutional change in our urban areas, Americans have stressed the desirability of widespread public participation in the decision-making process. This emphasis has led to creation of a wide-open, catch-as-catch-can system in which all elements of the public are actively encouraged to intervene directly in policy formulation in an effort to assure that their individual interests are being satisfied. Indeed, as Edward C. Banfield notes, we have actually "made public affairs a game which anyone may play by acting 'as if' he has something at stake. . . . The local community, as Norton E. Long has maintained . . . , may be viewed as an

ecology of games: The games serve certain social functions . . . but the real satisfaction is in 'playing the game'. . . . The general idea seems to be that no one should govern, or failing that, that everyone should govern together."*

In addition to opening up the policy-making process to widespread public participation, we have provided procedural means to assure that participants play a crucial role in policy formation. One manifestation of this is our utilization of the initiative, referendum and recall. Although the initiative and recall may have lost some of their potency during more recent years, the referendum has become increasingly more important in our local decision-making process, especially when institutional change is under consideration. Indeed, many Americans have come to view the referendum as a sacrosanct means of resolving every issue of local governmental reorganization, no matter how complex or specialized. We have thus formulated a local policy-making process that is not only accessible to the general public but also places heavy direct demands on it.

Debate over the unsuccessful St. Louis district plan serves as an apt illustration of this model in action. Three different groups were directly involved in assuming responsibility for initiation of this reform effort. First, a Citizens Committee for City-County Coordination attempted to secure public support for the appointment of a metropolitan charter-drafting board. This committee agreed to back off temporarily when two universities in the area received grants to study the needs of the metropolitan area and recommend potential solutions. Finally, after the universities had completed their study, responsibility for formulating a concrete reform plan was turned over to a nineteen-member metropolitan charter-drafting committee, the board of freeholders, whose members were appointed by political and judicial leaders from both the city and the county (plus one member named by the governor).

The board went through a lengthy period of internal debate before it finally split ten to nine in favor of a multi-purpose metropolitan district plan for the St. Louis area. This plan was turned over to the electorate who was asked by means of a referendum either to accept or reject it. When no group stepped forward to provide leadership support for the recommendation, the Citizens Committee for City-County Coordination once again reentered the stage to assume this responsibility. Finally, one month prior to the referendum, the best-known political leader in the area, the mayor of St. Louis, announced his personal opposition to the plan. On November 3, 1959, the

---

Frank Smallwood, "Guiding Urban Change," *National Civic Review,* April, 1965, pp. 191–197. Two footnotes in original omitted. Reprinted by permission of the publisher.

---

* Edward C. Banfield, "The Political Implications of Metropolitan Growth," *Daedalus,* Winter 1961, pp. 69–70.

voters of both the city and the county rejected the plan by a three-to-one margin.

This St. Louis experience corresponds nicely to the model described by Long and Banfield. It was wide open from beginning to end, a variety of different participants were permitted to formulate initial policies, a variety of other participants were permitted to enter and reenter the political arena virtually at will during crucial stages of the contest, and, eventually, the entire affair was turned over to the general public who made the final decision.

Thus, this procedure was highly democratic to the extent that it placed a high priority on ease of access to, and unrestricted participation in, all phases of the decision-making process. The English and Canadians have stressed a somewhat different set of values in their approach.

The Anglo-Canadian "Leadership" Model

Key features of the Anglo-Canadian model have been captured nicely by Hugh Whalen of the University of Toronto. Like the American model, it is grounded on the basic assumption that authority proceeds from below. From that point on, however, the two models diverge quite markedly. As Professor Whalen goes on to observe:

This [assumption] implies a decision-making process that grows out of discussion — but, let us hasten to add, a very special type of discussion. With the assistance of their administrative specialists, political leaders propose hypothetical decisions which are communicated to the electorate and to interested groups. The public and group reactions to such proposals are, in turn, interpreted by the leaders through a complex "feedback" process and, ultimately, original proposals are modified in a manner acceptable, or judged to be acceptable, to the majority. . . . If the majority rules, therefore, it does so in a very special manner.*

Just as the St. Louis experience captures the essence of the Banfield-Long games model, both the Toronto and London metropolitan reform programs serve as apt illustrations of Whalen's feedback model.

In 1953, the Ontario Municipal Board took the initiative in proposing a metropolitan governmental solution designed to meet the needs of the greater Toronto area. It attempted to reconcile both local and metropolitan-wide interests by means of a federation scheme which preserved the identity of existing local units, while also turning over some of their powers to a new metropolitan council that was designed to serve the metropolitan community as a whole. This hypothetical solution was then communicated to all affected parties, and further adjustments and concessions were made by the provincial government in an effort to secure a consensus in favor of the plan. Only after these steps had been taken did the provincial government finally move ahead and adopt the modified plan.

The story of the adoption of the greater London program is, in many respects, identical with that of Toronto. In 1960, a special royal commission proposed a hypothetical reform program after studying the situation in detail. Once again, this solution attempted to reconcile local and regional interests by proposing a new two-tier governmental system in which 52 strengthened local borough units were designated to share their powers with a new Greater London Council designed to serve the needs of the metropolitan area as a whole. Once again, this plan was communicated to all affected parties, and further concessions and adjustments were made by the central government to gain support. Finally, the government moved ahead and approved the modified program.

Thus, the policy approach the English and Canadians utilized to secure institutional change in London and Toronto was considerably more effective in producing concrete results than the approach used in St. Louis. The key question remains as to whether this effectiveness was achieved only by limiting the role the local public played in passing upon reform to such an extent that the ideals of democratic local self-government were subverted.

Common ideals

It is hardly necessary to belabor the point that the English and Canadians place the same high value on the general abstractions of democratic local self-government that we do. Whereas we have long sung the praises of a Jeffersonian grass-roots localist mystique, in England, as W. J. M. Mackenzie observes, "Local self-government is now part of the . . . constitution, the English notion of what proper government ought to be." In a similar manner, Canadians have also come to venerate this same broad abstraction of local democracy. The ideal of democratic local self-government, thus, has come to assume an important position in English, Canadian and American political folklore.

---

* Hugh Whalen, "Democracy and Local Government," *Canadian Public Administration*, March 1960, page 5. (Like all abstract generalizations, the Whalen model does not apply precisely to all urban reform situations throughout England and Canada. In Montreal and Vancouver, for example, very little in the way of centralized leadership of the type Whalen describes has appeared to date. On the whole, however, the model does have a very widespread application, fitting extremely well such areas as Toronto, Winnipeg, London and the numerous other areas presently being reviewed by the English Local Government Boundary Commissions.)

Yet, although the English and Canadians have emphasized the values of local self-government, they also appear to have permitted their higher governmental authorities to play a dominant role in guiding institutional change in their urban areas. Many Americans have, as a result, misinterpreted their approach as being inconsistent and self-contradictory. Confusion results from a basic misunderstanding as to how the system actually works. Whereas the Anglo-Canadian decision-making process stresses a different set of priorities from our own, this does not mean that it negates the broad ideals of local democracy. Rather, it places a different interpretation on these ideals.

As Whalen notes, the public is not excluded from the Anglo-Canadian model. What does happen is that the public's direct participation in policy-making is far more restricted than in the United States. Yet, by subordinating the prerogatives of widespread public participation to those of forceful political leadership, the English and Canadians have added a number of democratic elements to their decision-making process that are usually conspicuously missing from our own approach.

1. Minimizing stalemate. First, the English and the Canadians prevent stalemate from completely clogging up the policy-making process.

The approach we have adopted, with its diffused leadership responsibilities, its wide-open accessibility and its heavy reliance on the referendum mandate, has made it exceedingly difficult for advocates of change to make any headway at all. This is especially true when "split" referenda requirements are utilized, *i.e.*, when new policies must be approved by different segments of the same electorate (city residents plus suburbanites, taxpayers, property owners, etc.), often by a two-thirds' vote. Any system as unstructured as ours must inevitably contain a built-in bias sharply favoring those interests which support the status quo. It gives them what David Truman has characterized in *The Governmental Process* as a "defensive advantage" to monopolize decision-making.

The English and Canadians, on the other hand, have tended to view the policy-making process as a more neutral one, in which both advocates of change and defenders of the status quo are granted a reasonable opportunity to have their day in court. This is because official leaders in the Anglo-Canadian process play a key role that often has been totally missing in the American approach.

Despite the fact that Americans may like to play local political games, they are inclined to do so without employing any referees who might help to assure that these games will end in something other than a draw. In Whalen's feedback model on the other hand, leaders play precisely this role in making the adjustments and concessions they deem necessary in order to secure an acceptable consensus among competing contestants. By so doing, they virtually assure that all political games will not end in deadlock.

Because the American policy-making process tends to inhibit change, it presents a severe challenge to the democratic ideal. When no action is forthcoming in a given political contest, it does not mean that no party has won the contest but, rather, that those who did not want such action in the first place are the victors. In short, just as many winners and losers emerge when political action fails to materialize as when such action is, in fact, successful. The undemocratic aspects of the American approach are to be found in the fact that it incorporates an inherently unequal bias which enables defenders of the status quo to monopolize policy formulation. To the extent that the Anglo-Canadian model is able to minimize, if not in fact eliminate this bias, a strong claim can be made that it is more rather than less responsive to the ideals of local democracy than our own system.

2. Accommodating intensity. A second valuable feature of the Anglo-Canadian model is its ability to come to grips with the problem of intensity of interests, which Robert A. Dahl analyzes in considerable depth in his *Preface to Democratic Theory*.

In addition to using the referendum device as a means of recording public reaction toward policy change, Americans have shown an equally strong propensity to encourage individuals who have little interest in or knowledge of local policy issues to record their preferences as a matter of "civic duty." In so doing, the risk is run of overloading the decision-making process to accommodate the feelings of basically disinterested and often unknowledgeable individuals, while assigning less weight to the views of those who are intensely interested in such issues.

Here, once again, leaders in the Anglo-Canadian decision-making process play a role that is missing in the American approach. After these leaders have permitted all potentially interested individuals and groups to express themselves on a hypothetical reform solution, they attempt to assign meaningful priorities to the viewpoints advanced. Thus, in addition to serving as referees to guide the reform process, they also serve as "brokers"; they attempt to weigh and assign appropriate values to the preferences that are advanced in an effort to assure that final policies will reflect a type of democratic consensus that is an accurate reflection of different intensities of preference.

The fact that these leaders serve in these twin roles explains why it is necessary for them to be drawn from higher levels of government (*i.e.*, the Canadian provinces and the English central government) rather than from local governments. Such local governments are not neutral on questions of institutional reform because they are themselves direct contestants in the struggle. Since this is the case, it is necessary to have officials from higher levels of government serve as referees and brokers. The simple point is that one cannot have such roles played by people drawn from the same stratum as the other contestants and expect the latter to accept their decisions and priorities. One might as well expect two football teams to agree that individual players should serve as the referees, timekeepers and field judges for a given game.

The English and Canadians have thus used higher levels of government in facing problems of local institutional change, not because they want to ram reform programs down the throats of local governments but because they want to incorporate elements of impartial fair play into the decision-making process.

3. Responsible commitment. The fact that English and Canadian governmental leaders are willing to serve as referees and brokers highlights a third key distinction between their policy-making process and our own. While professing vocal support for the democratic aspects of the referendum device, many American urban leaders have actually tended to hide behind the smokescreen of the referendum in order to avoid or dodge responsible commitment on issues of vital public concern.

In addition, other leaders have tended to fuzz referenda issues so completely through the use of emotional symbols that the issues have become meaningless. Thus, rather than permitting the electorate to express a clear choice on issues and to exercise a meaningful degree of control over their elected officials, in actual practice the referendum has often confused alternatives and allowed officials to escape the commitments of responsible leadership accepted by the English and Canadians.

4. Revitalizing local government. Finally, Anglo-Canadian leaders have made every effort to adopt institutional reforms that accommodate and strengthen local government.

An example of accommodation is to be found in the Toronto reform program in which every reasonable effort was made to preserve essential features of the existing governmental structure. In London, the central government went even further. The royal commission called for creation of 52 revitalized greater London boroughs (through amalgamations of existing authorities) that were designated to serve as "primary units of local government" under the new reform program. In the end, the government actually created 32 such boroughs which possessed far greater powers than the original boroughs had exercised prior to the reorganization. In addition, both of these programs created entirely new instrumentalities of

metropolitan government which actually strengthened rather than weakened the entire local governmental process.

The crucial point is not that the American approach to urban institutional change has been more democratic or more solicitous to the interests of local self-government than the Anglo-Canadian approach but rather that these two approaches have stressed a different set of priorities. The Americans have emphasized democratic participation (i.e., playing the game) as representing the essence of their approach towards reform, while the English and Canadians have emphasized democratic leadership.

Many might argue that Americans have gained something of crucial importance by emphasizing widespread public participation. This argument seems debatable on a number of grounds. First, whereas many of the newly emerging nations may find it desirable to emphasize the educational aspects of widespread participation in local government as a training ground in democracy, it is highly questionable whether the referendum performs any comparable role in dealing with complex issues of institutional reform in highly developed urban societies.

Second, despite our emphasis on such participation, public interest in referenda issues has usually been extremely low. Only about a fourth of the electorate voted down the St. Louis district plan and turnouts for similar referenda in other areas have been less impressive than this.

Finally, because the referendum procedure is so highly unstructured, diffuse and susceptible to distortion, it is very questionable whether we have actually been able to exercise as meaningful a degree of democratic control over local policy-making as the English and Canadians have by utilizing their more visible and rational leadership procedures.

In many respects, it is curious that Americans have placed so much emphasis on direct participation in dealing with issues of local institutional reform, while at the same time relying upon the feedback procedure in both national and state political arenas. We exercise indirect control over policy-making at the higher levels of government by our ability to elect (and reject) executive and legislative representatives who act as referees and brokers in very much the same manner as Whalen describes. Why we are willing to accept this procedure as being democratic at these levels of government, while tending to view it as being something less than democratic when questions of local institutional change are under consideration, is one of the deeper paradoxes of the American political process.

CHAPTER SEVENTEEN

State and Local Personnel and Finance

IN THE HISTORY OF GOVERNMENTAL INSTITUTIONS, formal civil service merit systems are a distinctly recent development. Yet in their three quarters of a century of existence such systems have become a generally accepted norm of good administrative procedure. In the first selection of this chapter one of the nation's outstanding authorities on civil service, an attorney and former executive secretary of the National Civil Service League, analyzes the progress of merit systems to date and speculates upon the kinds of developments in public personnel administration that may be expected in the next two or three decades. While the merit system has unquestionably made a significant contribution to effective government, many persons have uncritically accepted it as an unqualified blessing. In the succeeding article the case for a patronage system is vigorously and effectively stated.

The right of public employees to unionize has been commonly conceded for some time, though with only a few exceptions the patterns of collective bargaining accepted as normal in industrial relations today have not developed in the public service. The question of possible use of labor's ultimate weapon, the strike, a highly inflammable topic in many circles, is next debated by three recognized authorities — Roger Baldwin, for many years executive director of the American Civil Liberties Union; H. Eliot Kaplan, author of the first article in this chapter; and Sterling D. Spero, author of several books dealing with employer-employee relations in the public service.

80

Civil Service in the Crystal Ball

By H. Eliot Kaplan

THE 75TH ANNIVERSARY of the adoption of civil service laws of the federal government and New York State is a propitious occasion to take inventory of the accomplishments and shortcomings of the administration of the merit system and to prognosticate future developments.

H. Eliot Kaplan, "Civil Service 75 Years," *National Municipal Review,* May, 1958, pp. 220–225, 250. Reprinted by permission of the publisher.

We have come a long way in improving administration of the civil service merit system since its adoption in 1883. Like most radical reforms it started with a rush in the federal service and in some larger states and cities, halted percipitately to consolidate its gains, lagged for a considerable time and, since 1936, resumed its inevitable advance. It hesitated again during World War II but has resumed its forward march. There were only nine states operating under a formal civil service law up to 1935. There are now 24 states under merit system laws; and every state is now required to select on a merit system basis employees of their agencies paid in whole or in part out of federal funds.

At the same time the public rosters — national, state and local — have swelled at an accelerated pace . . . . The likelihood is that our public services will expand by 1975 to about eight million with an annual payroll of over $35 billion.

This huge expansion of governmental services has placed a responsibility on personnel agencies. The failure of half the states to join the merit system brigade must prove disheartening to many. They may take solace in the knowledge that even in such "non-conformist" jurisdictions the devastating influences of the patronage system have long abated in the face of obvious need for competent administrators and employees.

Much has been written of the federal civil service, and a number of plans and panaceas for its redemption have been advocated — not the least of them the Hoover Commission reports. Undoubtedly much progress in improving the federal service will result. It is in the areas of state and local government, however, that most people are more concerned and more directly affected by good, bad or indifferent service. It is here that the potentialities of the merit system vis-a-vis the patronage system have their most potent implications.

Many political scientists and public administrators may properly be criticized for whistling in the wind and Pollyannalike acclaiming that the patronage system is a dead duck! The tremendous strides made in personnel administration are heartening, even if some claims for its accomplishments are exaggerated. Yet only 25 years ago how many would have entrusted our personnel agencies with the responsibility of inventorying our personnel resources, delineating with preciseness the titles and duties of incumbents, determining the pay schedules of employees and fixing annual increments, much less with the control and direction of retirement plans, employee grievance machinery, group life, health and hospitalization insurance programs?

The temptation in observing a landmark anniversary is to point glowingly to the advances made and ignore or gloss over frustrations and weaknesses. Because the merit system is a generally accepted principle we are prone to assume that administration is more or less sound and effective.

We are likely to overlook the fact that much public support for the competitive examination system is founded on a somewhat negative attitude rather than on a conviction of its effectiveness. No one has been able successfully to defend — or rather to undertake publicly to defend — the patronage system as desirable or as effective. This has proved advantageous to complacent advocates and practitioners of the competitive examination system. Attacks on the effectiveness of the competitive system are easily thwarted by charges of partisan exploitation of the public service and other ulterior motivation. There has been lacking, therefore, an aggressive and militant approach toward determining the validity of our testing processes and improving methods and techniques of examinations.

One of the most devastating aspects of the examination process is the long delay between recruiting candidates and certifying eligibles for appointment.

No other factor is more responsible for discouraging the competent to seek careers in government service; none is more prolific of attracting mediocrity through failure of effective competition. We may even need to discard our concepts of determining comparative potentialities for successful performance on the job.

System well rooted

There need be no fear on the part of personnel administrators and technicians that weaknesses revealed in a study of testing methods would lend comfort to opponents of the merit system. The system is too well rooted in our present governmental processes to be endangered by lack of public support. Our democratic institutions have too much vitality to be shaken by pseudo claims of charlatans among professional patronage dispensers. The hesitancy of legislatures to weaken civil service laws attests to the regard the public has for the merit system.

Over the years there has been built up a congeries of local civil service agencies operating under general civil service merit laws, notably in Illinois, New Jersey, New York and Ohio. The home rule principle needs to be respected, but extension of the principle to administration of civil service laws has become a smoke screen to obscure the ineffectiveness of local administration in many smaller municipalities. In Illinois, New York and Ohio, for example, local personnel agencies are completely autonomous, with most of them acting primarily as cloaks for political exploitation of the public services rather than being concerned in staffing their agencies with competent talent. Fortunately, this has not been the experience in the large cities but in the smaller municipalities it is quite prevalent.

This may be due in part to failure of adequate appropriations for such agencies — some deliberately designed to assure innocuous application of the local civil service rules. It is questionable in light of experience whether it would be effective even if adequate funds were made available. Certainly it would be uneconomical as contrasted to centralized administration in the state personnel agency.

This is not to advocate direct administration of the civil service law by the state agency as in New Jersey. It is rather to advocate direction and supervision in the smaller municipalities by the state agency through a personnel officer in each municipality with dual responsibility to the state commission for enforcement of the law and rules and responsibility to his municipality for other phases of local personnel administration.

No longer content with or able to depend on orthodox methods of recruiting for administrative and executive talent, personnel agencies have been forced to adopt more aggressive means of attracting university graduates. Emulating private industry, the campuses have been invaded to lure promising graduates to make government their careers. To accomplish their objective of competing with private agencies for such talent, competitive examination procedures have been short-circuited. Testing methods have been geared more practically to bring candidates and positions closer. Opportunities for appointment were heightened by confining competition for internships to such graduates.

Attract college graduates

These departures from traditional policy of waiting for candidates to seek out the personnel agencies have had a salutary effect. One obstacle to greater appeal of these internships to college and university graduates is the lack of a positive program of accelerating their promotion or, perhaps more correctly, their absorption in the regular competitive service after completion of training and orientation.

This trend toward encouraging young college graduates can, however, be overdone and, in some cases, has become a fetish. The notion that only those with formal education should be inspired to seek careers in our public services, to the exclusion of others perhaps less fortunately situated, may not appeal to our democratic ideals. Nor would it be wise or politic to advance a policy of looking with a jaundiced eye on non-college-bred potential leaders. We need to have both if we are to be realistic and maintain a balanced perspective. It will be impossible to wean the American public from its deep-rooted desire for "representative government" — distinguishable from partisanship — even in the permanent career civil service.

We have gone a long way in inventorying our manpower in the public service through classification of positions based on duties and responsibilities. Salary schedules have been established on more equitable premises. But have these devices remedied the basic difficulty of leveling all incumbents in the same class, regardless of competency? Rigidity of salary classifications tends to level all in the class to a common denominator. In this respect private industry has a decided advantage over the civil service. The latter is usually inhibited from making any distinctions among its employees. Recognition of unusual talent or industry or initiative is denied the public administrator.

Salary levels in the public service have increased on an accelerated scale in the last decade even though they still lag behind private industrial levels in the higher echelons of executive posts. Technically skilled, clerical and lesser administrative positions are in most instances not far behind industrial levels. In many instances in the clerical categories salaries paid in government services, particularly federal and a few larger states and municipalities, are higher than in comparable positions in private business. In large measure this results not alone from our expanding economy. The pressure of organized labor on private industry has had its impact on public fiscal authorities.

Employee relationships in government service have also been influenced by policies and practices in private industry. Although many labor practices of private industry, of dubious application to public employment, have been resisted by public authorities, management-employee relations in government have become liberalized. Rarely does any enlightened official today resort to the shibboleth of "sovereignty of the state" to avoid his responsibility of dealing openly and fairly with his subordinates and their representatives. Likewise public employee organizations have recognized their responsibility to government management as representative of the public. Both management and employee organizations have become aware of their mutual responsibility to the public and the wisdom of collective negotiation within the framework of public law and sound policy.

These are only a few of the issues and problems which have confronted personnel agencies and public administrators. So much for the past and present.

A look to future

What apparitions appear with respect to the future of personnel administration as we gaze in the crystal ball? What developments may we expect during the next score years? One may be reasonably sure that government personnel administration will undergo vast modification. Personnel agencies as now constituted will have to measure up to much greater responsibilities or be superseded by other more dynamic and practical administrative devices.

With more and more functions placed on personnel agencies, most of them only collateral to their primary one of recruiting, examining and certifying for appointment, many agencies have been taking on responsibilities for which they are inadequately equipped. Many of these functions, such as administration of pension plans, group life insurance plans, accident and sickness insurance protections and other fringe benefits, have been dumped in the laps of these agencies because there appeared no other place to allocate them. Dealing with affairs of public employees, it would appear logical for the personnel agency to assume such responsibilities.

From a practical point of view it seems of doubtful wisdom to saddle agencies with these added functions when they have had all they can do to administer primary functions adequately, particularly with their paucity of professional technical staffs woefully unfamiliar with such new functions and inadequate appropriations. The personnel agencies will probably of necessity neglect their primary functions of staffing operating agencies, so preoccupied will they become with the new ones. This may encourage more extensive and radical reorganization of personnel functions.

If the emphasis of personnel administration as an integral part of management has the validity professed for it, the trend may well dispel the fiction of the personnel agency continuing as an independent agency of government. The multiple commission form of direction will probably be abandoned in favor of a personnel manager responsible to the "general manager," the head of a comprehensive department of administrative management. The fact is, multiple commissions have outlived their original purpose. Concern as to nonpartiality of the direction of the merit system by assurance of a bipartisan commission has been dissipated by sad experience. Impartiality has come not by such device but by the public's vital stake in its growing public service and the inherent complexities of government.

Responsible administration

Our university and college facilities will be such that none but their graduates will be among competitors for executive and administrative posts. This will probably force abandonment of our traditional "practical" examinations in favor of broad examinations to determine capacity for responsible administration. To accomplish this successfully we will need to reorient our concepts of testing techniques and procedures and drastically revamp the professional and technical staffs of the personnel agencies. More comprehensive in-service training programs must be developed.

More likely to go overboard is our present practice of filling higher executive and administrative positions by competitive promotion examinations. Appointing authorities will have far more responsibility and control over promotions, with the personnel manager having at most only a veto power over them. On the other hand, personnel managers will have added responsibility with respect to facilitating transfers from one agency to another. There will be greater flexibility in the assignment of generalists as well as specialists among the agencies of government. There will be an ever growing recognition of "expertise" in the know-how of government operation. This will perforce reduce to a minimum turnover in such personnel on change of political administration.

New concepts

With increasing public confidence in the impartiality of appointive heads of departments and agencies, with attendant more enlightened political leadership, it is likely that governmental personnel programs and policies will be decentralized and delegated to operating departments. A department of administrative management, to embrace the personnel agency, will be responsible for establishing standards of personnel practices and post audit actions of operating departments. The lessened pressure for partisan patronage will encourage public opinion to abandon the false notion that public administration needs the myopic supervision of a bipartisan independent personnel agency.

Position classification based on duties and responsibilities will take on an entirely different concept. In spite of probable short-sightedness of employee organizations imbued with the spirit of "equality of pay for equal work," more consideration will be given to superiority of performance. The era of mediocrity oozing to the top because of overemphasis on seniority and longevity is slowly waning in favor of greater incentives for those achieving unusual results. The pace in that direction will quicken as we turn more and more to government to solve our complex problems and to serve more effectively our expanding public services.

With recognition on the part of the public that a dynamic and aggressive policy of administration will make imperative greater competency and experience of its public servants, salaries of higher executive and administrative officials will be gradually increased to make them more comparable to private enterprise. The latter will find it far more difficult to "pirate" from government the more capable among public officials. The public service will be in a much stronger position to compete with industry for outstanding talent.

The crystal ball shows some shadows of possible concern, none of them, however, particularly alarming. Straining relations between public management and employee organizations appear to be lifting in growing mutual confidence and understanding of their respective responsibilities to the public. There looms on the horizon, nevertheless, a distorted view of vested rights of public employees which threatens to ripen into a festering era of costly litigation, more costly to the taxpayers than to employees. The tendency will be for legislators to continue to yield to the demands of misguided employee leaders pressured into constantly getting something more for their followers. This will be augmented by the tendency of some of the courts to approach personnel issues in terms of a sense of "justice" rather than sound principles of administrative law. These tendencies, it is feared, will add to the burdens of the courts and the taxpayers and to the frustration of public administrators.

But the crystal ball reveals such overwhelming gains for the administration of government personnel we can readily afford some of the minor retarding influences which inevitably will accompany progress.

It is safe to conjecture that there will be far greater gains in the public personnel field during the next score years than have occurred during the last 40. It is equally safe to prophesy that every state, and every municipality of substantial size, will function under a reasonably sound civil service merit system. Utopia, civil-service-wise, appears still far off on the horizon; but our sights will have been raised to much greater heights of hopeful accomplishments.

81

In Defense of Patronage

By William Turn

IN AN ERA which places a great deal of emphasis on the value of so-called "expert" opinion, there is something unreasonable in the hysterical indictments of political patronage which are made today with little or no actual knowledge of what it is about.

Almost thirty years of practical political experience have given me a real insight into the subject, and to my way of thinking, the attackers of the patronage systems are guilty of an unpatriotic act against an inherent and necessary part of our American political system. The true cause for the introduction of the spoils system was the triumph of democracy. Today it remains the one realistic device for permitting the majority of the people to mold the policies of government.

Why party workers are needed

If the people as a whole are to have a real voice in the conduct of the government, they must be organized. What is more (and this is going to be a terrible shock to the starry-eyed reformers), they have to be pushed around and coaxed or dragged to the polls to exercise the hard-won privilege of the franchise. Thousands of people never vote because the registration dates pass before the campaign gets exciting, and they are not interested enough to make the effort to qualify. Others get wildly excited about issues or candidates between election days and damn the government from first to last, but forget all about

William Turn, "In Defense of Patronage," *Annals of the American Academy of Political and Social Science,* January, 1937, pp. 22–28. Reprinted by permission of the publisher.

their objections on election day. To prod these lazy ones into action, to insure that our democratic form of government will remain truly democratic and representative of a majority of *all* the people and not just of a selfish few, militant party organizations are essential. There must be drilling and training, hard work with the awkward squad, and an occasional dress parade.

This work requires the labor of many men. There must be precinct captains and ward leaders and district representatives. On registration days and on election days there must be telephone squads and free transportation and wide-awake generalissimos. Every day of the year there must be party leaders actively concerned with the business of the organization — keeping in close touch with the great masses of "average folks" whose participation is vital to any truly democratic process, learning what they are thinking, and interpreting for them the policies which are being put into effect.

Now, some men labor for love and some for glory. But glory comes only to a few of the most outstanding leaders; it cannot serve as a general inducement, and even those who love must live. It is an essential idea of democracy that the leaders shall be of the people. They must belong to the class that makes its own living. What then could be more reasonable than for good citizens who have displayed their ability and their devotion to the principles of democracy within their party to be picked for responsible service with the government when there are positions to be filled? I have heard it suggested that we need more training in our schools in preparation for public service; but I wonder what better training there could be than the practical lessons which are a part of the orderly and disciplined advancement in the organization? Recognition in party organizations, like recognition anywhere else, comes in proportion to good service rendered.

My own experience has been a clear record of this principle. After an apprenticeship which included such routine chores as the distribution of handbills and tacking up campaign posters, I began to learn the fundamentals of party organization as a precinct leader, and I can report my activities here with no embarrassment. The idea was simply this: I went out and got acquainted with my neighbors! When a new family moved into the neighborhood, I made myself known to them at the earliest possible moment and saw to it that they got acquainted and were taken into the activities of our community. On registration days I was an early and persistent caller, ready with information about where and how to register, helping to arrange for time off if necessary, and making up schedules to take care of those who needed transportation or some one to mind the baby.

As I proved my sincerity and ability, I was allowed to sit in on the party councils. Here I found men who were leaders in the community and who honestly believed that the policies of our party would further the welfare of our people. They were frequently profane, but never treacherous. They met together and considered seriously the choice of candidates who would earnestly support the policies of the party and who seemed to have the confidence of the largest number of people in our community.

When election time approached, it was perfectly natural that my neighbors and I should talk about the candidates, and since my participation in the councils of the party had given me a better acquaintance with some of the candidates than most of them had, they were glad to hear what I could tell them. Some of the candidates spoke at meetings in our neighborhood, and it pleased both my neighbors and myself to follow these meetings with introductions and more informal conversations which gave them an opportunity to express their opinions and talk face to face with men who had their interests at heart. People in general are not very interested in just abstract ideas. But when those ideas are associated with Joe or Sam or Frank, whom they know as friends and leaders, then there is flesh upon the bones of democracy, and government is something which has interest and meaning.

The success of a candidate is much more than a chance to pull a plum out of the patronage pie; it is the satisfactory knowledge that the public affairs are in the hands of colleagues in whom it is possible to have confidence. When new policies are being developed, this is of tremendous importance. It is human nature to be suspicious of any change in the way of doing things, whether it is the way the new preacher begins the service, or a city ordinance allowing right turns on red lights. Without the confident and sympathetic support of the rank and file, there is a great deal of waste motion before people are ready to give the new ideas a fair trial.

Business methods in government

And that reminds me of the old chestnut about "What business man would run his plant like the government?" People can get pretty excited about that, but most of them don't stop to figure out that the only condition under which the question would be pat is, for example, if a private utility company were taken over by public ownership. We have all had ample opportunity during the past few years to get a reasonably clear idea of the sentiments these two camps have about each other. Keeping that in mind, I ask you to consider what the general manager for the public ownership should do about personnel. According to the reformers, he shouldn't fire any of the people in the business he took over, be-

cause some of them would have been around for thirty or forty years and knew just how their jobs should be done.

Now isn't that a pretty idea? We can assume that every employee in the business had been campaigning vigorously against the change in management. Department heads, brought up to look upon public ownership as an unwarranted invasion of private property rights, would be so hopping mad and so absolutely sure that the new plan couldn't work that they wouldn't bother to open their mail. Some of the boys who had to take salary cuts would get together on the side and start figuring out how they could spoil the show and return the business to the hands of their friends. A fine way to do business!

For the benefit of those who think "the spoils system" is something which Andrew Jackson turned loose on a previously pure and unsuspecting world, I should like to point out that the desire of leaders to surround themselves with loyal and trustworthy supporters is a perfectly natural and understandable phenomenon which is as old as time itself. The very founding of our Nation depended on the unswerving loyalty of a few daring men, and the administration of our first great President, George Washington, took into consideration the importance of placing in office those who were "supporters of the system." There is evidence, too, that this famous statesman made his appointments with an eye to geographic distribution, realizing that such action was both fair and wise. When he had appointments to make from areas in which he was personally unacquainted, he asked for recommendations from the Congressmen from those districts, because as he very properly believed, their local knowledge gave their words special weight.

Patronage appointments for demonstrated party loyalty seem to me most likely to promote efficiency. Too light weight is given to the protection which patronage gives the government against bureaucratic sabotage, which its enemies naïvely deny on the theory that "the spoils" are distributed in grab-bag fashion, with those having the longest reach taking home the prizes. The occasional administrations which have ignored the principles of loyalty and fair play in distributing patronage have been short-lived. It is only common sense for an organization which wants to maintain unity and strength in its own ranks to grant recognition on a completely democratic basis.

As for the quality of the appointments, it should be borne in mind that while patronage is a reward to those who have worked for party victory, it is also the test of a party's fitness to remain in office. Every bad appointment weakens the party's power. Dr. Carl J. Friedrich, of Harvard University, reported for the Commission of Inquiry on Public Service Personnel:

"You cannot take offices with vast powers attached to them 'out of politics' for politics is not a bottle or any other variety of container. Politics is the struggle for power. Where there is power, there is politics. What you can do, and what you must do, is to make politics responsible."

That is just what patronage does.

Civil service employees

A good measure of the value of patronage is the nature of the alternatives which are offered in its place. The greatest of these is civil service! This is a unique system under which it is assumed that people are simple organic compounds, subject to laboratory methods. Examinations are given to these specimens, and on the basis of the results they are neatly catalogued and filed until needed. Orders are filled on the general understanding that short of an Act of God there will be no returns or exchanges. The finished product is a pale, quiet individual, faithful in a dim sort of way, disinclined to originality, but capable within a limited field of an insolence that makes one wonder why it is called "civil."

The chief advantage of the civil service system appears to be that it offers regular, light employment at a moderate remuneration. This undoubtedly attracts large numbers of steady-going, unimaginative people, but I question whether their services are of any greater value to the public than the less routine but more lively efforts of patronage appointees who have a personal stake in the business. Men and women who stay in one place too long get in a rut. Like a horse with blinders, they see in only one direction, and too often that direction is not toward the taxpayers who pay their salaries. I think it is significant that when people speak of "government employees" they almost always have in mind a roomful of clerks.

It has been my experience that a dull level of mediocrity is likely to be encountered in civil service, and it was doubtless this same feeling which led Andrew Jackson to say, "I cannot but believe that more is lost by the long continuance of men in office than is generally to be gained by their experience." A more violent friend of mine refers to the "Snivel Servants" who are so afraid of doing any original thinking that it is only after long persuasion that you can get them to agree with you that Christmas will probably be on the 25th of December next year. This man is a real friend of government workers and has done a lot for them, but their shilly-shallying ways and their unwillingness to work together for any purpose whatever try his patience.

Of course the civil service policy of forbidding all political activity to government employees is largely responsible for this attitude, and I think it is a dangerous threat to democracy. Here is a large group of the very people who should have an active voice in party councils, and they are so hedged about with restrictions that they shy like a frightened horse at the mere mention of the words "Democrat" and "Republican."

This senseless insulation can have but one result —a growing chasm of misunderstanding between the government and the people it is supposed to serve. . . .

Patronage appointments are based on demonstrated ability in the organization, and they are the result of thoughtful investigation and appraisal which is strengthened by the knowledge that the record of the party is involved. . . .

Few people today subscribe to the old-fashioned doctrine that any honest fellow with ordinary horse sense can fill any job in the government. The complexity of our own invention has sufficiently impressed us all. But there are men of brains, men who are economists and planners and experts, in both parties, and their presence in the parties indicates that they have some acquaintance with the practical problems of public administration and a capacity for unselfish support of a chosen leader. . . .

Room for improvement

The enemies of the patronage system are willing occasionally to admit that their systems are not the perfect answer, and I will be equally magnanimous and admit that the patronage system could be improved. A great forward step has already been taken in the distribution of patronage. In the old days, there was an element of gamble in the assignment of jobs. There was more of the "first come, first served" philosophy, and a good-natured rivalry between leaders occasionally resulted in extra portions for the more aggressive. But closer organization and better discipline have led to a merit policy which seems to me to offer the best posssible service to the public. The most important single factor in its betterment would be a more active participation in party councils by the people who are doing most of the talking about what is wrong! Our government is not going to get any simpler as time goes on, and the need for experts in the field will increase; but if their contribution is to be realistic *and responsible*, they must first learn the elementary lessons of democratic control as exemplified in the political party.

82

Have Public Employees
the Right to Strike?

Yes

By Roger N. Baldwin

THE DISTINCTIONS commonly made between the right of workers in private industry and those in the public service to strike will not stand up under examination. They are based on no solid considerations of either the public welfare or of civil liberties. They arise from an unthinking hostility to "strikes against the government" as if all strikes of public employees are somehow or other political in motive. Along with that prejudice runs the substantial practical objection to strikes in certain essential services whose cessation would be catastrophic to the whole community — notably the firemen and police. The spectacle of this catastrophe is made to justify denial of the right to strike in the entire public service.

When the right to strike is thus denied, the argument is commonly extended against all trade unionism in the public service. It is alleged that because government does not function for private profit public employees are not exploited. It is maintained that since civil service employees enjoy pay, tenure, and pensions fixed by law, and not available to private employees, they need no other protection. Even when it is conceded that the conditions of civil service employees can be improved, the remedy is held to lie not in trade union organization but in pressure on legislative and administrative agencies.

The whole conception appears to be without substantial merit. Let us take the latter arguments first, since they can be most readily met.

While government does not function for profit the pressure for economy often produces precisely the same effects in low wages. Arbitrary authority in the hands of politicians and administrative officials bears down with the same results on public employees as on private. Protection by trade union organization is the only practicable method for counteracting such pressures.

"Have Public Employees the Right to Strike? — Yes," by Roger N. Baldwin; "No," by H. Eliot Kaplan; "Maybe," by Sterling D. Spero, *National Municipal Review*, September, 1941, pp. 515–528, 551. Reprinted by permission of the publisher.

While it is true that civil service employees enjoy advantages not commonly shared by workers in private industries, these advantages are far from meeting all needs. Practical experience with unions in the public service demonstrates their usefulness in adjusting and reforming scores of practices not covered by civil service law or regulations. Anyone with any experience in administration knows that no employer or administrator is capable of sensing from on top the needs of an army of employees. Only those who actually compose the rank and file of employees appreciate fully their own problems and are capable of speaking for themselves.

It follows that when remedies are sought from legislative bodies unions of employees are of great assistance in formulating grievances and demands. The voice of organized labor is frequently the only effective means of directing the attention of both the legislature and the public to injustices in the public service. This has been so long apparent in the relation of teachers to the school system and the community that it only needs to be stated to make the argument conclusive.

Strikes not political

As to the more dramatic aspect of trade unionism involved in the right of public employees to strike, we should dismiss at once the notion that such strikes are in any way aimed at the function of government itself. The Columbia University study of over one thousand strikes in the public services shows that not a single one of them had political motivation. They were aimed at particular politicians or administrators, not against the government as such. They are in that respect exactly like strikes in private industry.

The more substantial argument against strikes in the public service rests upon the fear that the essential functions of governments may be paralyzed, and that the government therefore has the right to insist that its services be not interrupted.

Let us at once exclude from consideration the case, so commonly cited, of policemen and firemen, for they perform a unique service in which it is not unreasonable to require that the right to strike shall be surrendered. In the comparatively few cities with unions of policemen and firemen they have commonly waived the right to strike, recognizing the exceptional character of their occupations. In a very few cities the right is denied by law. The basis for distinguishing policemen and firemen from other employees necessarily rests on the catastrophic consequences to the community of a strike, since substitutes cannot be recruited nor any emergency provision made for replacing their function.

We are met with the rejoinder that if this is true, the distinction applies equally to employees of public water works, electric light plants, hospitals, buses, street railways, subways, and a host of other services. But in all these services either emergency crews can be substituted sufficient to carry on essential functions, or, as in many strikes, the unions themselves provide for their continuance by a skeleton force to meet emergency needs.

Identical services in many communities are not in the hands of public agencies, but private utilities. Nobody, I think, argues that strikes in privately-owned utilities should be prohibited, yet the considerations of public inconvenience and danger are precisely the same. It therefore seems a reasonable distinction to place in one category, where the right to strike may be denied, those essential services which are by their nature operated exclusively by public employees — firemen and police — and to accord the right to strike in services which are variously performed by either public or private agencies.

The arguments against the right to strike in the public service tend to lose sight of one persuasive fact. That fact is the sense of community loyalty which most public employees so deeply feel. To them, as to others, a strike is a weapon of last resort. It is never lightly entered into at the behest of leaders or Communist intriguers, as is so often charged. In the public service, as the record shows, the tendency to strike to redress wrongs is far less than in private industry. Not only is this true because of the attitude of public employees to their work, but because they have channels for the settlement of grievances not open to private employees. Public attention can be aroused and support enlisted, as it cannot be for private employees.

The arguments against strikes in the public service fall a bit flat when the actual dangers are so fanciful. The Columbia University study showed only sixty-six in police and fire departments, navy yards, arsenals, and armories. Excluding the navy yards, arsenals, and armories in peacetime — where a strike could hardly be regarded as catastrophic — the dangers so commonly visualized were obviously trifling.

It remains only to note one false issue which has confused the discussion — the closed shop in government employment. It has been raised not by the unions but by public officials fearful that unions might demand it. No union whose members come under the civil service has done so. It should be clear that the closed shop is wholly incompatible with requirements that appointments be made by competitive examination and with the provisions for tenure and promotion under the merit system. Union membership in government agencies under civil service must obviously be entirely voluntary.

The controversy over the rights of government employees to organize, bargain collectively, and strike is only a phase of the larger trade union conflict rapidly nearing a stable solution. The long resistance

of private employers to trade unions is being conclusively broken. Congress has refused so far to curtail the right to strike even in defense industries, recognizing the very practical consideration that the country cannot get production by coercion. Slowly we as a nation are coming around to the concept that voluntary measures alone will settle the conflicting interests of capital and labor, employers and employees. The practice of genuine industrial democracy with free trade unions and honest collective bargaining will go a long way to avoid the desperate resort to strikes.

In the public service, as in private, unions and collective bargaining should be encouraged as essential to industrial democracy. Our democracy is incomplete so long as it is confined to the arena of politics. The public service should lead the way in model practices, adding to the guarantee of the civil service system the protection afforded only by independent organizations of employees dealing freely with their superiors.

Have Public Employees the Right to Strike?

No

By H. Eliot Kaplan

EXPANSION OF GOVERNMENT in fields viewed heretofore as within the exclusive province of private enterprise prompts the suggestion that the relationship between government and civil employees needs to be considered anew. Where employees in private industry are brought into the civil service it is not surprising that they carry over earlier precedents and customs, and with them ideas which may prove to be inimical to government administration and impractical of application in the public service. . . .

At the outset it should be made clear that the right of public employees to organize for their mutual welfare as they see fit must not be denied. The only issues that need concern us are, first, to what degree should public employees be permitted to affiliate with outside labor unions or organizations, and second, to what extent should the rights and privileges accorded to private employee unions and organizations be extended to similar associations of public employees.

Many civil service employee organizations have long been affiliated with public employee organizations of other jurisdictions. Many of them have been affiliated with labor unions — local, state, and national. Both the A.F. of L. and the C.I.O. have been vying with each other in persuading civil employees to join their ranks.

The people are generally aware of their responsibility for the economic welfare of their own employees. They are also aware that public employees owe a certain responsibility to the people.

The issue is not solely whether the public employee should be devoted exclusively to the people's interest but rather whether he should be responsible only to the people and not to a political boss, a demagogue, or a labor leader. Fundamentally, that is the crux of the problem. If we miss this concept of public employee responsibility to the people alone, under our democratic system, we are bound to misunderstand the proper relationships in public employment.

Just how far public employees should be permitted to join with outside labor unions must depend on what the purposes of such affiliation may be and the obligations assumed by public employees under such outside affiliation. Political machines and arrogant administrators have, of course, thrown many a monkey wrench into attempts of civil service employees to organize. They have sought to control employee organizations for their own political or administrative purposes — a practice which closely resembles a "company union" idea. In attempting to meet this occasional difficulty we must be careful not to permit other abuses or practices equally detrimental to the people's interests to take its place. . . .

It is one thing for civil employees in a local jurisdiction to affiliate with other civil employees in a state or national organization for their mutual welfare in educating public opinion as to their common needs and seeking to persuade the people toward certain policies affecting them. It is another thing, however, for civil employees to affiliate with outside labor unions primarily for the purpose of using their combined strength to coerce action that may be utterly inimical to the people's interests and to employ methods which run counter to orderly governmental and democratic procedure. The people must not tolerate the use of the civil service by irresponsible labor leaders for purposes that could place the people at the mercy of their very own employees, such as a sympathetic strike wherein civil employees are dragged into a situation in which they themselves have no direct interest. It is conceivable that they can be used in some cases actually to overcome the will of the majority in a community, particularly when the tactics employed to coerce action in private industry are injected to coerce administrative action. . . .

The people paramount

We must appreciate that it is for the people alone to decide what rights or privileges may or may not be granted to public employees by the people's representatives. Public officials act for the people, not for themselves — even if administrators seem to forget that elementary principle occasionally. The right to strike against themselves — the people — can be granted to public employees in given cases and under such circumstances as the people may choose. It is analogous to the privilege granted individuals by the people to sue the state. Regardless of private injury or loss, an individual may sue the state — the people — only to the extent granted by the people. In other words, not until the people recognize by law the right of public employees to refuse to obey their superior officers under specified circumstances and strike against the actions of public officials, is there any "right" of public employees to strike. No employee has the right to interfere with the orderly conduct of public affairs or to interrupt public services for the people without the people's consent. That is the difference between private and public employment.

It would be foolish to suppose that existing relationships between administrative officials and public employees are ideal even under the best administered merit system of today. Public employees should be granted the privilege to negotiate with public officials on matters of concern both to employees and the people whom they serve, such as the fixing of wages, hours, and conditions of employment, sick leave privileges, etc., or to adjust and remedy grievances. Unfortunately this privilege is too often denied them. Arrogant administrative "bosses" can be as tyrannical as the worst despot in private enterprise. But even so the civil employees may not take it in their own hands to interfere with the orderly functioning of government by striking against such a public tyrant. Do they strike against him or against the people? True, the majority of the people directly or indirectly are responsible for that arrogant administrator. But we cannot sanction the right of public employees to resort to a strike to force the people to oust the recalcitrant administrator who may have been elected or appointed for a fixed term. That is a right which the people reserve to themselves.

Who is to determine whether the particular administrator (representing the people) is right or wrong, the civil service employees? Suppose the administrator is trying to protect the public from concerted selfish action on the part of the people's employees, as in the case of an unreasonable wage demand far beyond the ability of the taxpayers to meet. Ought we permit employees to quit work and so attempt to coerce the administrator into granting their demand? Suppose an employee organization or a labor union affiliate disapproves of the dismissal of one of its number and all the employees walk out on the people in protest? This has actually occurred in more than one jurisdiction. Where does one draw the line as to just how far employees may go in attempting to coerce administrative action against the public interest? These are questions that need be given thought in any appraisal of the relationships in public employment.

Morale important

It is, of course, decidedly in the public interest that those serving the people be a satisfied and contented group. Morale of their employees is a matter of vital importance to the people. The kind of service the people will get from their public servants will depend in large measure upon the treatment the public employees get from the people.

It is essential to the people's interest, however, that conditions of employment in the civil service be remedied in more or less the same general manner and orderly means as is to be expected of any other change of public policy. Civil employees have as great, and in many respects greater, opportunities to educate public opinion toward their view of problems as has any other class of citizens. If the people do not yet see it their way, it is up to the employees to crystallize public sentiment in their direction. If the method at their disposal is too slow for them, then they may properly agitate for a change in methods and machinery for more effectively and speedily meeting their problems.

Of course, public employees have the right to strike — if by that we mean that any individual has the right to quit his job. . . . Whether or not they have the right, however, is beside the point. Unwillingness of public employees by concerted action to serve the public can hardly be condoned. There is no inherent right of public employees collectively to refuse to serve the people and still retain the privilege of continuing in the service of the people. We would not recognize the right of motorists to refuse to pay their automobile license fees but still insist upon the privilege of running their autos on the public highways merely because they did not like the gasoline tax. It is no less offensive to the public interest for an employee because of a strike to decline to run the elevators in a public office building than for a hospital nurse to leave a dying patient and join a strike parade. A motor bus operator of a city-owned transit line may no more abandon his bus full of passengers to join in a "sympathy strike," than may a fireman leave a burning building to answer a strike call.

Many mental gymnastics have been indulged in by those who should know better in attempting to distinguish between the rights and privileges of public employees in one and another type of government service. It is easy for them to postulate that a policeman or fireman or health officer should not have the right to strike because that would rob society of an imperative protection. They would distinguish the "usual" governmental function from services they consider proprietary. They seize upon the classic case of a public utility taken over by a municipality and see no reason why the employee relationship should change merely because the city operates the utility in place of the private company.

Those who argue thus forget that the people have not chosen to take over a public utility until public necessity required it. A utility or function assumed by a city becomes a service for the people. Simultaneously the relationship of employees to the people must perforce change. Many municipal functions and services of a proprietary nature have heretofore been accepted in the same light of "usual" government service as have the police, fire, and health agencies. Water supply services, collection of garbage, and similar services have been long performed by municipalities. What was not a public need yesterday may become one tomorrow. The rights and privileges of individual employees under private ownership must yield to the public interest. The people become the new "boss" and the employees the people's public servants. Attempts to distinguish between one kind of public function wherein employees may continue to have the rights accorded them as private employees, and another kind wherein such rights are denied, just begs the question.

Collective bargaining

Equally cogent issues beside the right to strike need to be weighed. Collective bargaining is one. There is no point in stressing the fact that agreements sought to be made by public officials and their employees are not legally binding on the people in the absence of express authority to make any such "contracts." Unless we have a general distrust of our public officials there seems to be no real purpose in encouraging, or rather insisting upon, formalized "contracts" of this nature. What may be informally agreed upon between administrators and employee representatives can be incorporated in a declaration of policies or rules or regulations promulgated by the agency after informal negotiation with employee representatives. Closer coöperation and better understanding between management and employees and a mutual appreciation of the problems on each side should be encouraged. This, however, is far from a system of collective bargaining such as operates in private industry, wherein negotiation may be had solely with an exclusive union or organization of employees which might bring in to represent it an outside organization or union in no wise directly concerned in the negotiations. . . .

The basic conditions that prompt necessity for a closed or union shop in private employment are generally absent in the public service. The purposes sought by a closed shop or a union shop in private employment are not suited for the people's service.

No "super-agency"

In private enterprise the relationship between employers and employees can always be subjected to government regulation, supervision, or even control. There is no "super-agency" that can step in to control, regulate, or supervise disputes between public employees and the people except the people themselves, through their representatives. Public employees, like any other class of citizens, have an equal right through orderly processes under our democratic form of government to petition the legislature and public officials for redress of grievances, adjustment of claims, and acceptance of their views. To encourage any class of citizens to ignore, or abandon in defiance of authority, such orderly procedure to gain its ends, no matter how justified its action may appear to be, would defeat our democratic process.

The public must guard against a potential danger that may be as formidable and uncontrollable as our dubious political organization machines — a self-perpetuating labor dictatorship, which could conceivably overcome the will of the people through control of governmental machinery manned by public employees. This is not a possibility to be dismissed as too fantastic. Situations have already arisen in some jurisdictions which should warn us to apply the brakes immediately.

If the two cogent issues referred to early in this article have not been adequately met and answered here it is because the relationship of public employees during this period of transition from a "policing" government to a "servicing" government is still in a state of flux, and we have yet to see and learn in just what direction it is best and safest to go. We may be reasonably sure, however, that the concepts of labor relations common to private enterprise and the practices indulged in by capital and labor are not practicable or desirable in the civil service.

Have Public Employees
the Right to Strike?

Maybe

By Sterling D. Spero

THE RIGHT TO STRIKE is regarded as so important a factor in the maintenance of human freedom that the state guarantees its exercise despite the public incon-

venience and the social dislocations which strikes frequently cause. Time and again American legislators have rejected proposals to abrogate that right. . . .

When it comes to its own employees, however, the state takes a different attitude. "The right to strike against the government is not and cannot be recognized," declared Mayor La Guardia during . . . [a] transit controversy. "No government employee can strike against his government and thus against the whole people," said President Hoover in the 1928 campaign. That government employees cannot strike, President Roosevelt told a press conference a few years ago, was "a matter of common sense." These are representative statements. . . .

What is there about government employment which makes the denial of a right regarded as so essential elsewhere so apparently simple and obvious a proposition? Can the proposition be founded on the functions which government workers perform? These, on examination, appear little different from those of other workers.

The functions of government workers fall roughly into four broad categories — administrative, industrial, service, and law enforcement. The administrative functions are similar to those which any business or institution must carry on in order to operate. They include filing, auditing, correspondence, clerical, and so-called office work of various kinds. These functions are incidental to the conduct of any establishment. Their wider importance is measured by the importance of the functions to which they are incidental.

The industrial functions of government are directly comparable with private industry. Battleships are built in navy yards and battleships are built in private plants. What logic is there in the government denying the right to strike in the former case and permitting the right in the latter? Ordnance is made at the Rock Island Arsenal which is run by the army and at the Midvale Steel and Ordnance Company's plant which belongs to a private corporation. Why is it "common sense" to deny the right to strike at the arsenal and allow it at the company?

The service functions of the government — the conduct of utilities, educational institutions, hospitals, welfare agencies — likewise parallel or compete with the work of private organizations. . . .

Those engaged in the administrative, service, and industrial functions of government account for the overwhelming majority of government employees. The comparatively small number which remain are engaged in the work of law enforcement, the only government activities not directly comparable with work outside. These are traditionally and peculiarly functions of public authority. Yet law enforcement is dependent upon far more than the work of policemen or public inspectors. Like all social processes in complex modern society it is dependent upon the running of the whole social machine. New York or Chicago could not be policed at night if employees of private lighting companies did not keep the lights on. Law could hardly be enforced and public order could hardly be maintained if privately owned transportation and communication systems ceased to operate.

The fact is that the continuity of governmental functions depends upon coöperation of society as a whole quite as much as the rest of society depends upon the functioning of government. In many instances the work of privately employed workers is actually of greater immediate social concern than the work of civil servants. Compare, for example, the immediate effects of a strike in the Department of the Interior or even a strike of public school teachers with a strike of privately employed milk drivers.

A challenge to authority

It thus becomes increasingly clear that government's denial of the right of its employees to strike cannot be based upon the ground of the harm which the cessation of their work might cause. It is based rather upon the ground that government as custodian of final authority in the land cannot permit those whom it hires to carry on its work to challenge its authority. The preservation of this concept of public authority is regarded as far more important than the immediate interests served by the functioning of particular agencies.

The famous Boston police strike in 1919 was caused because the responsible officials refused to accept a reasonable settlement which they regarded as compromising of their authority. In the same year the city of Cincinnati forced a strike of its firemen in much the same way. In Colorado Springs, in the midst of a controversy over wages, the mayor dismissed the entire fire department without making any provision for the protection of the city. In all these cases, and in many similar ones, the wrath of the community was turned against the virtually locked-out employees, while the authorities who were responsible for the protection of the community were praised for defending law, order, and public authority. . . .

No-strike policy

One of the most significant aspects of the strike question in the government services is the attitude of the employees themselves. There is not a single organization in the United States composed entirely of government employees which has a strike policy. Those affiliated with either the A. F. of L. or the C. I. O. as well as some independent unions have no-strike provisions in their constitutions. Despite such provisions there have been some municipal strikes within the jurisdiction of these unions, particularly among fire fighters. As in private industry such strikes have been for better working conditions or for union recognition. Practically all such strikes occurred in the early stages of unionization when unsatisfactory working conditions which brought the union into being were still uncorrected or when the authorities attempted to break up the movement.

Most of the membership of organizations composed wholly of public employees is in the traditional services which are non-industrial in character. These organizations have sought their objectives through legislative means. Some of these groups have lobbies of strength and influence. This is particularly true of the postal organizations, whose objective has been to carry the legislative method of fixing conditions as far as possible and to limit and narrow the discretion and authority of the supervisory officials. The postal workers feel that the influence of their lobby is substantial while their power in the department is slight. One reason for this, and this is true in some other government services also, is that the postal employee works for a government monopoly. There is no other business to which the special skills and training of a postal clerk would be of value. If he loses his government job he must seek an entirely different type of employment. This weakens him in his relations with the department.

Workers in service

Quite the opposite, however, is true of the government's industrial workers. These are organized in the regular unions of their crafts, trades, or industries. A machinist or a pattern maker can work in a navy yard or for a private firm. Washington printers or pressmen are not dependent upon even the huge Government Printing Office for employment. These workers view their governmental employer with none of the awe and respect that departmental clerks and administrators bestow upon him. They are members of their trade or industry first and government employees only incidentally. They can and do go from government jobs to private jobs and back again depending upon which employer has the better offer to make. These employees concede no special rights to the governmental employer. They insist upon their right to strike and have on occasion exercised it.

In most of these services, both federal and local, wages are fixed upon the basis of prevailing rates for comparable work through formal or informal collective bargaining or negotiation. The expansion of the public service into the field of economic activity, one of the marked characteristics of the day, will bring a larger and larger number of industrial workers into the service. Experience has already shown that they will not easily be cut to the pattern of the conventional civil servant and that they will not readily surrender methods of dealing with their employer which have proved successful. During the days of federal operation of the railroads during World War I railway workers resisted attempts to apply to them the federal rules on political activity in the civil service. They struck even during war time against the United States Railroad Administration. . . .

The right to strike

It is clear that no mere denial of the right to strike will of itself prevent strikes if workers regard their grievances sufficiently great to assume the risks. Strikes under such circumstances damage the authority of the sovereign, the very thing the denial of the right to strike seeks to preserve. The governmental employer, in order to maintain his authority in the face of illegal strikes, must demonstrate his power by punishing the offending workers and calling upon his military forces to break the strike and restore operations. The generally undesirable consequences of such procedure hardly require elaborate description.

The state, of course, has the right, where the necessity of maintaining its existence and preserving public peace, order, and safety require it, to use its military arm, but such circumstances are as likely to result through interruptions in private industry as in the public service. At any rate the use of military power is an extreme and extraordinary measure to be resorted to only under exceptional circumstances.

When the state denies its workers the right to strike merely because they are government employees it defines common labor disputes as attacks upon public authority and makes the use of drastic disciplines and armed force a method of handling otherwise simple industrial relations.

The use of the state's ultimate force for the protection of the public interest is different from the subordination of a large and growing section of the labor movement to governmental power. Such subordination is a dominant characteristic of totalitarian society. If the government services were small and inconsequential the issue would still be of importance. But with the public services in all their branches employing one tenth of all the wage earners in the land, and expanding at an ever increasing rate, the issue becomes one of major moment. A free labor movement among these millions of workers is their only effective check upon the greatly enhanced power which expanding governmental activity gives to public authorities.

The power motive, recent history teaches, is as important an exploiting force as ever was the profit motive. Labor is thus faced with a serious dilemma if the government insists upon denying it that right which is the ultimate guarantee of its freedom. An expanding public service will mean a creeping totalitarian trend as a larger and larger section of the working population is obliged to surrender its ultimate right to strike as a consequence of its public employment. This is one great danger.

There is also another danger. The labor movement may, in order to preserve its freedom, resist the expansion of government activity, thus creating a disintegrating social trend by rendering government ineffective to meet the problems of the times. Both of these possibilities present infinitely greater threats to our society than the remote possibility of a labor dispute which might result in the temporary interruption of some government service.

Public officials continually find themselves in an unpleasant squeeze between the steadily increasing public demands for new and expanded services and the at least equally loud demand for reduction or holding the line on taxes. Furthermore, in one sense, the various levels of government inevitably compete with each other for the tax dollar. In the face of widely publicized contentions that state and local governments are seriously suffering under national financial dominance, Senator Muskie, former Governor of Maine and currently chairman of the subcommittee on intergovernmental relations of the Senate Committee on Government Operations, contends that there is no significant imbalance and that intergovernmental fiscal relations are a good example of cooperative federalism at work.

The former dean of the Maxwell Graduate School, who also has wide experience as a public official, then suggests bluntly to a national convention of city officials that they cease moaning about their "hopeless" financial situations and face the fact that solutions are readily available if they are able and willing to provide first-class political leadership to their communities.

Since man first began to live in organized societies taxes have been a common and socially acceptable point of complaint — as universal a refrain as one is likely to hear. For that reason alone Herbert Coggins' method of making us stop to think a bit about what we get in return for our taxes is refreshing.

83

$ and ¢ of Federalism

By Edmund S. Muskie

THE AMERICAN FEDERAL SYSTEM is so intricate that foreign observers rarely understand it. Even Americans are frequently bewildered by its complexity. And no wonder! Federalism operates simultaneously in four spheres of political debate and action.

Theoretically, it establishes a constitutional division of powers between the states and the federal government, with local government, as a practical matter, constituting another source of independent authority.

Structurally, federalism has created three separate and autonomous levels of governmental institutions.

Functionally, it comprises a series of public-purpose programs that the nation, the states and the local governments jointly sponsor.

Administratively, it has created three layers of bureaucracy and encouraged numerous cooperative arrangements and devices.

Since the founding of the republic, the need for cooperation has battled with the opportunity for competition in each of these areas. More than three-quarters of a century ago, Woodrow Wilson set forth the basic reasons for this unending debate:

The question of the relation of the states to the federal government is the cardinal question of our constitutional system. At every turn of our national development we are brought face to face with it, and no definition either of statesmen or judges has ever quieted or decided it. It cannot, indeed, be settled by any one generation because it is a question of growth, and every successive stage in our political and economic development gives it a new aspect, makes it a new question.

More than anything else, it is the dynamic quality of federalism and of the American people that explains the continuing agitation in Congress, within the states, and by the public at large over the nature and tendency of our federal union.

Are there no stable features, however, in contemporary federal-state-local relations? A good way to come to grips with this question is to ignore the slogans and campaign oratory and focus attention on the fiscal aspects of intergovernmental relations. The dollars and cents of federalism tell us more about the essential nature of the system than many of the political arguments that clutter up the scene.

To begin with, big government at all levels has been one of the major developments of the twentieth century. Over the past 60 years, aggregate federal, state and local taxes experienced nearly a hundred-fold increase. Total governmental expenditures jumped from $1.7 billion in 1902 to more than seven times that figure in 1934 and to nearly $149 billion in fiscal 1962. Total governmental indebtedness amounted to an average of $41 for every man, woman and child in 1902. Today it comes to more than $2041 in current dollars. Past wars, the depression, the cold war, inflation, population explosion and a mushrooming metropolitan growth are basic causes for these increases. Whether we like it or not, big cities, big counties, big states and a big federal government are with us. And their emergence has occurred in Republican as well as Democratic administrations, in peace as well as war, and during conservative as well as liberal eras.

The real question raised by this development is whether any one level experienced a disproportionate growth to the detriment of another. During the '30s and World War II, federal revenues greatly overshadowed those of state and local governments. The record since the war, however, clearly demonstrates that this gap is closing rapidly. In 1944 the state and local share amounted to only one-fourth of all governmental revenues. As recently as 1954 it still came to only one-third. State and local taxes now are two-thirds as large as the federal take, and the federal government, of course, must finance defense and foreign policy commitments from its share.

The post-war federal growth rate, then, has been modest — even conservative — compared with state and local. The figures for the latter demolish the widely shared belief that these levels of government are unwilling or unable to assume their proper share of the financial responsibility for the expanding services demanded by the public since World War II. In fact, if we concentrate solely on the total direct civil expenditures for fiscal 1962 (this excludes defense, space, veterans and interest costs), we find that the federal government's proportion came to only 27 per cent, as against more than 48 per cent for local governments and nearly 25 per cent for the states.

Federal aid to state and local governments is probably the most controversial chapter of the intergovernmental relations story. In absolute terms, these expenditures have increased greatly during the past three decades. Federal grants totaled only about $200 million a year in the early '30s. Even with numerous depression programs, the figure came to

Edmund S. Muskie, "$ and ¢ of Federalism," *National Civic Review*, May, 1964, pp. 235–238. Reprinted by permission of the publisher.

only $2 billion by 1940. During World War II it slipped back to less than $1 billion per annum. Most of the real growth came after 1946 with the expansion of existing grants and the enactment of some 49 new programs.

This development has not been as dynamic as some would have it. Federal contributions to total state and local revenues averaged almost seven per cent in 1946. The federal share by 1954 had risen to a little over 10 per cent and, despite the enactment of the federal highway program and other new grants, this proportion amounted to only 13.6 per cent during the last fiscal year. If federal aid figures are examined in terms of their relationship to federal budget expenditures for civil functions, the estimated 1962 grant-in-aid share stood at 26 per cent. This represents a seven per cent increase over the comparable figure for 1948 but a four per cent drop from 1960.

Overall, these figures reveal that the proportionate growth rate of federal grants and loans during the past decade and a half has been evolutionary rather than revolutionary. In terms of dollars, of course, the federal aid figure nearly quadrupled during the 1952–1962 period. In this connection, we should recognize that the post-war growth in national production, population, urbanization and the standard of living has generated mounting demands for additional government services. Any objective assessment of the role of federal aid, moreover, must recognize the serious difficulties experienced by state and local governments in financing these expanding functions from their own limited resources.

The national government, of course, has no exclusive monopoly on the grant device. While it was dispersing $7.9 billion to state and local governments during the last fiscal year, the states allotted nearly $11 billion in grants to their own local governments. From the local viewpoint, both national and state aid is of crucial importance. The significance of these two grant sources can be better appreciated when we remember that approximately seven out of eight dollars of local revenue are provided by the much-criticized and overburdened property tax. At present, its $20-billion annual yield nearly equals the combined revenues of all state-imposed taxes. Nationwide, almost half of the greatly increased state and local tax burden required to finance the post-war demands for increased local services has been borne by this tax. In light of this performance, some experts and many local officials believe that this levy has already reached the peak of its endurance.

The equalization factor is another dimension of federal-state-local fiscal relations that is often overlooked. Since World War II, Congress has paid increasing attention to the question of whether the distribution of federal grants should take into account the difference in the ability of states to finance these grant-aided programs from their own resources. Recognition of this varying capacity has usually taken the form of attempting to compensate for the imbalance by including an equalization provision in the matching and/or apportionment formulas. Many programs do not include this feature. In some, it has been inserted in a way that fails to accomplish the objectives of Congress; in others, it has been ignored when changing conditions indicate a pressing need for its inclusion. Of all the federal grants enacted prior to 1963, only about one-third contain fairly explicit equalization provisions. This means that the distribution of funds or the proportion of federal-state sharing of costs is governed partly by the differing ability of the states to support the aided programs.

Detailed statistical analysis by the Advisory Commission on Intergovernmental Relations and others indicates that these programs have not provided the additional benefit to the less affluent states that was originally intended. To put it more bluntly, Congress' intention of leveling out some of the inequalities in grant-aided state programs has not been fully realized. Where equalization is appropriate, greater consideration should be given to a closer examination of the various indices of program need and of the states' relative ability to support grant activities. Per capita personal income, for example, has some limitations as an effective index of the relative ability of state and local governments to raise revenues. All of these findings demonstrate the need for a judicious congressional reevaluation of the equalization factor.

In brief outline, these are the significant dimensions of intergovernmental finances. But what do they tell us of federalism's essential character? The facts indicate that:

(1) Today, big government is a characteristic of all jurisdictional levels.

(2) In recent years, state and local governments have demonstrated an amazing capacity and willingness to assume a major share of the fiscal burdens imposed by demands for expanded public services.

(3) Federal revenues, debt and aid to state and local governments have expanded significantly in absolute terms over the past 15 years, but they have experienced only a modest rate of growth when contrasted with the comparable figures for the other levels of government.

(4) With soaring state and local budgets, federal aid has taken on added and crucial significance for decision-makers at these levels.

(5) Specific inclusion of an equalization factor in one-third of the existing grant programs has benefited somewhat the less wealthy states; its exclusion from the remaining two-thirds, however, hinders the reduction of inequality in program performances within the several states.

(6) If the present division of expenditures for civil governmental functions is used as an index, a rough balance exists among the federal, state and local governments; the only factor disturbing this equilibrium is the somewhat lesser share assumed by the states.

(7) In practice, a pattern of collaboration in the fiscal and program areas exists among the three jurisdictions and the federal and state grants-in-aid are the chief manifestations of this cooperation.

(8) This grand design of cooperative federalism has emerged without undermining the independence and freedom of fiscal choice of the states and local units of government; on the contrary, many authorities believe that these joint efforts have actually reinforced the identity of these governments.

Federalism still stands as a bold attempt to combine national unity with political diversity. This analysis clearly indicates that state and local governments are still playing a vital role in intergovernmental relations and that a balance of powers is still a paramount feature of the system. At the same time, these hard dollars-and-cents facts demonstrate that cooperation, not competition, is the best way to achieve national strength while preserving state and local autonomy.

84

Are the Cities Broke?

By Harlan Cleveland

It is said that the annual convention of the American Municipal Association is the occasion on which the nation's mayors get together to complain about federal intervention in municipal affairs — and demand more of it. What brings Washington into the affairs of cities is usually the simple political fact that it is easier to get money from the federal government than to raise it from the cities' own citizens.

Many people believe that local governments are "broke." It is widely reported that municipal officials are running out of tax gimmicks, or running out of property to tax, or maybe just running out of popular willingness to raise more taxes.

This worries them, as well it might; the nation's

Harlan Cleveland, "Are the Cities Broke?" *National Civic Review*, March, 1961, pp. 126–130. Reprinted by permission of the publisher.

life and livelihood are more and more concentrated in its urban areas. For 40 years past, and for 40 years into the future, all our net increases in population have taken or will take place in our metropolitan areas. Less than a hundred million people lived in metropolitan areas in 1950. In the year 2,000 the figure will be 255 million — or so the statisticians tell us.

There are two propositions that fly in the face of current comment about "the metropolitan problem."

One is that local governments are not broke; they just think they are. They are like a rich man who cannot remember where he stashed his riches. Our metropolitan cities and suburbs are bankrupt all right but not in resources. They are bankrupt, most of them, in imagination, organization, leadership and will.

The other proposition is that the federal government's task in these circumstances is not primarily to put up the money the local governments cannot find but to join in the search for more and better sources of local government funds. But this will not happen so long as most municipal government people think of the federal government as (a) the enemy, and (b) in Washington. It is neither. It is — or can be — your best friend. And it isn't in Washington, it's right across the street from city hall.

Where can you lay your hands on some more money for better services and capital improvements?

Let us start with that durable antique, the property tax. Somebody long ago told us that local governments had to subsist by taxing real and personal property and most of our communities have been doing it ever since. And the old girl has plenty of life in her yet; the fact is, the property tax has worked surprisingly well.

Between 1948 and 1959 revenue from property taxes almost tripled while gross national product was not even doubled. But to accomplish this result, the tax rates had to be hiked several times in most communities. By and large it is more the valuation of property than the willingness of the people to vote for rate increases that has prevented a more rapid growth in the "take" from the property tax during the past decade. In other words, voters in the communities tend to be more sensible and less subject to pressure than the so-called experts who assess property.

In New York State it seems that for every dollar of increase in income there is an increase of only about 66 cents in property valuations. If our municipal governments were tougher about raising assessments to match the general growth of the economy and the gradual depreciation of the dollar in real terms, they could wind up with a great deal more revenue from the property tax without going to the people as often for increases in the rates.

Even if we squeeze the most that can be squeezed out of the property tax, it probably will not be enough to provide all the public services those 255 million people in our metropolitan areas will be demanding by 1999. But local governments are not limited, except by their own mythology, to taxes on property. Income taxes and sales taxes can be mentioned only in whispers in some communities, but they are probably fairer than the property tax.

There appear to be two reasons why most cities and towns do not look more closely at the potential of income and sales taxes. One is what an African tribe would call a "taboo." There is a widespread fiction that income taxes have been "preempted" — that's the four-dollar word now in circulation — by the federal government and the states. There is also a general reluctance in the state legislatures to let cities tax people who do not live in the cities, whether with income taxes or sales taxes.

It is true there is a long tradition behind the proposition that one pays taxes where he sleeps. But the longevity of a tradition is no measure of its good sense in a world that changes as fast as ours does. What made city government well-nigh impossible was the removal of its best taxpayers — and many of its best potential political leaders too — from homes inside the city limits. What will restore the cities to good health may be the transfusion of revenue collected from people who work downtown, even if they sleep in a cornfield over in the next county. The people of every state have the power to levy an income tax or to let its municipalities levy an income tax; the same is true for sales taxes. And in most state legislatures today, if all the urban representatives got together they could easily put through the necessary amendment.

The stickiness of state legislatures on this subject is often blamed on the fact that farmers and rural towns are typically overrepresented in them. But an important part of the trouble is simply that the representatives from many of the medium-sized metropolitan areas do not yet think or vote as if they were elected by urban people; they too often vote as if Main Street were sown to legumes and the suburban shopping centers were really modernistic cowbarns.

Where I come from in Upstate New York, our legislators often act as though Syracuse were still a rural backwater of the "Big City" downstate. Whatever the Big City is for, the upstate representatives are inclined to be against. Yet Upstate New York, that is New York State excluding New York City, is as industrial an area on many of the most relevant indices as the whole states of Massachusetts, Ohio, Illinois or Michigan. When all the urban representatives learn to get together and think as city folk, a political revolution will be in the making. It may not revolutionize our party politics, since no party has a monopoly on solutions to urban problems, but it will revolutionize our thinking about the role of the state in their solution.

There is another main reason why our cities are not taking advantage of the modern kinds of taxes that don't depend so heavily on real and personal property. It is the mutual distrust among our too numerous units of local government. Every central city is afraid of chasing customers out to the shopping centers, or chasing office workers to other cities, or chasing industries out to the suburban industrial parks. Every residential town knows that nice families and smokeless, noiseless, wasteless research labs, those ideal industrial neighbors for a residential community, will refuse to move into a suburb with high taxes if other suburbs are advertising a better break for the taxpayer.

Thus in the typical metropolitan area we have the competitive coexistence of too many cities, towns and villages, not to mention districts for sewage disposal, pollution control, water supply, schools, parks, transportation and the like. The coexistence is uncomfortable and the competition is unhealthy — a booby-prize race to see which unit of government can collect the least money from its citizens.

What's wrong with this picture? The paradox is that the vast bulk of our nation's wealth and income is right there in our urban areas. Nearly all our new net investment from year to year occurs in these same urban regions for which the term "metropolitan" now seems to be favored. If the wealth is there, and if people want to buy more public services than the present governments can afford, it is surely not beyond the ingenuity of modern man to devise some way to raise the funds.

The way we are now doing it is obviously the wrong way. When we want more or better public services, we now do one of two things: set up a new kind of district or ask the federal government to help. Both solutions result in further fragmentation of the public power to act in the public interest by glorifying highly specialized solutions to particular problems at the expense of rational management of the urban region as a whole.

The special district, which has performed nobly in many vacuums, has now proliferated so that the management of our metropolitan areas closely resembles the way Chinese governments used to manage their national budgets. In old China each department had to find enough income-producing functions to finance those expenditures that were a dead loss to the department. Thus several agencies would battle for the right to manage the offshore fisheries, which were highly profitable to the government, while research in agricultural science, which produced no revenue, languished. If we have learned anything at all from a generation of systematic study of public administration it is that tying particular sources of revenue to particular kinds of expenditure is the most inefficient way to run a government.

Federal intervention is not much better organized — at least not yet. To be sure, the agencies which directly or indirectly prop up most of the so-called private enterprise in the housing field do try to condition their help on getting the city to dream up a "workable plan"; but usually this plan is for a pretty small segment of the metropolitan area involved. And overshadowing all else is $13 billion of federal highway money, described by the *Wall Street Journal* early last year as "a vast program thrown together, imperfectly conceived and grossly mismanaged, and in due course becoming a veritable playground for extravagance, waste and corruption."

This program, the largest public works effort in history, should be a centerpiece in the planning of every metropolitan area in the United States. It calls for 41,000 miles of highway — prudently bare of a single gas station, restaurant or rest room except on toll roads — connecting every city in the land. Half the expenditure will be inside the urban areas. Yet there is literally no provision for planning complementary facilities like commuter railroads and mass transit or tying highway arterials to plans for urban renewal.

The highway program is now the largest and most dynamic urban activity; it could be used to bring some order into metropolitan area planning. But, viewed in these terms, the program cannot be said to have developed any real leadership, direction or purpose other than to quiet the enormous political enthusiasm for roads by building fragments of magnificent highway here and there all over the country. . . .

The lack of coordination in the highway crusade, and its horse-and-rabbit imbalance with other forms of urban public investment, fully justifies the wry prediction of Senator Eugene McCarthy of Minnesota. Soon, he said, "You'll be able to drive 80 miles an hour along super-highways from one polluted stream to another, from one urban slum to another, from one rundown college campus to another." The American Municipal Association has been clearheaded about this problem for some time now. Yet the volume of nonsense on the subject grows louder with each year's proliferation of specialized attacks on what should be a general problem. You will have to speak your good sense louder if you expect anybody to listen.

If local governments are multiplying like rabbits and federal programs are trampling around our metropolitan areas like runaway horses, what about that forgotten unit of government, the state? The reserved powers of the states, after all, just happen to be the ultimate source of legal authority for everything that local governments do or leave undone. Shouldn't the state governments be the first court of appeals for local governments that feel broke in the midst of growing metropolitan wealth?

What it all comes down to is this:

The issue isn't between a hundred thousand local governments and a big bully in Washington. It is a more sophisticated question than that and a more interesting one. The question is whether the federal government, the states and the best and most imaginative political leadership in our local communities, working together and re-enforcing each other, are going to develop metro-wide systems of revenue for metro-wide problems, by taxing incomes and business transactions throughout the metropolitan area and spending the funds for metropolitan area improvement under local democratic controls. Failing this, our fragmented urban governments will resume their competitive inaction, our state governments will sulk and gradually wither away, and the people will insist that the federal government start setting up federal metropolitan districts to do what obviously has to be done — plan the main lines of development of each metropolitan area and collect revenue from the metropolitan region as a whole for its own development.

There is thus no longer any real nourishment in that traditional fairy tale about the big bad federal wolf and the stubborn attempt of grassroots government to avoid being ravished by federal aid. Prosperity and procreation, the internal combustion engine and the rubber-tired wheel have created the inflated metropolis whether we like it or not. Our job, the most complex and therefore the most exciting job there is in the third quarter of the twentieth century, is not to complain about the urban region but to govern it.

What faces us is not a financial crisis. The wealth is there. The crisis is of leadership and of imagination — our leadership and our imagination. The enemy is not the federal government, or the state, or those stupid planners over in the next jurisdiction. The enemy, if any, is our own incapacity to develop enough first-rate political leaders and to keep their attention focused on the problems of government in the metropolitan region as a whole. So saying, I cannot do better than to end with Walt Kelley's classic exhortation:

"Resolved, then, that we shall take our stand upon this very place, with small flags waving and tinny blasts on tiny trumpets, and meet the enemy. And may he not only be ours, he may be us."

85

I Like to Pay Taxes

By Herbert Coggins

I JUST GOT MY NEW TAX BILL. The combined city and county total for the year is $190.38. "The tax-eaters!" growled my neighbor who had come on the same errand. "Tax-eater" was his new epithet for the city and county employee. Heretofore he had referred to them more prosaically as "loafers." Whether just or not, he pricked my curiosity as to what I was getting for my money. After all, $15.86 a month is quite an expense just for staying in a house I had bought and paid for.

The city taxes were ten dollars lower than the previous year. The county taxes were higher by a slightly greater margin. For some time I have felt that the two governments were conniving against me, for my own peace of mind. One year the city tax is lower and the news thereof is heralded in the local press without any reference to the increase in the county budget. The next year the county is the low rate and gets credit in the same manner. Tricky, you would say? No, just sensitive. Tax collectors are like other business men. They are trying to make bad news look pleasant.

Anyway, let's take a ledger sheet and charge taxes $15.86 a month and see what I get for it.

Streets and sewers

First of all, on two sides of my home is a nice, clean, wide asphalt street with a concrete base. Aside from my taxes I have not spent a cent on it; but it is in better shape today than when my house was built twenty years ago. More than that, I have the use of tens of thousands of miles of similar paving all paid for by municipal, county or state tax money and extending all over the state. In not very many hours I can drive to a sunny palm and cactus-studded desert, or to snow-clad peaks, without getting off this same asphalt ribbon.

I know my street has real value for me, but how am I to figure it? As a comparison, I pay $4.25 a month for my telephone — and it is worth it or I wouldn't pay it. But if I had to surrender my telephone or the right to use the street, I would retain

Herbert Coggins, "I Like to Pay Taxes," *American City,* May, 1940, pp. 53–55. Reprinted by permission of the publisher.

the street. Anyway, let's credit the street department with $4.00 a month to offset my $15.86.

Sewerage is the same story. I should hate to do the work the sewer pipes do for me for anything less than an equal amount. But let's not be sentimental. We'll offer the tax-eater $3.00 a month. He'll accept it.

Fire and police protection

A few paces from my front door on a post is a little red box. It can bring the nearest fire engine to my door in three minutes, and a dozen others if I need them. I have never had to use it, but I know the service it has given others has protected me. In fact, the efficiency is so well thought of that an eastern insurance company has been betting on my fire service for a score of years and has been collecting its winnings from me in the form of premiums during all that time.

Nevertheless, I like the arrangement as a whole, and I much prefer it to dickering with some rugged individual when the house is on fire, either on a competitive bid or a cost-plus basis. Even if I never use it, I wouldn't part with the little red box for $4.00.

A blue-coated individual ambles about the neighborhood of my home several times a day. Sometimes there are two of them, and — worst of all — they travel about in V-8's. They are not worried-looking men like taxpayers, and apparently are not aware how expensive and useless they are in my neighbor's sight. They have a radio in the car to pick up messages from the central police station, and one time it is recorded that a message fell on the blank air because all the radios were tuned in on the world series. That has been corrected, and baseball and public safety have been synchronized.

Twice I have called on them. Once in a case of sickness, when an unknown neighbor's dog that kept the invalid awake through torturous hours was silenced without any resentful aftermath. The other time was in my absence when an uninvited guest made his exit through a rear window of my house, having been disturbed by a nosy cop. He took with him a few dollars in trinkets and change. Two suit-cases of rather worth-while furs and clothing were left beside the window, thanks to the inopportune glare of the officer's flashlight. On my homecoming the unworried official dusted some white powder on the door-knobs and pressed pieces of paper on them in a ridiculous manner. He even took my thumb-print at my request. Then, to show off, he asked my wife to go in her room and hide a ring where it would be safe from a burglar. A minute later he followed her, ran his finger around an upper molding and presented the ring to a rather chagrined lady with the remark "That's where they all hide 'em."

Later the burglar was caught and identified by the finger record from my door-knobs.

Not very much return, you will say, for years of taxpaying. Still, it is worth something; for, one time when I thought I had something worth a burglar's attention, I, with others, paid a private watchman to walk about the neighborhood at night. For this service he contracted with me at $1.00 a month, and the fact that I saw him thereafter only when he collected the dollar doesn't convince me that he wasn't worth it. On the same basis I believe that two policemen day and night, with the facilities, system and quick transportation, are worth $3.00 at least. After all, their real value was that I didn't have to call on them. Credit taxes $3.00.

Facilities for education and recreation

A nice walking distance from my house is a pleasantly planned structure surrounded by a yard and playground equipment and edged with shrub gardens. It is for the primary and grammar grades, with the high school within another short distance. While not new, they are both modern and light, and seem to reflect health and happiness, so far as school and children can be made into a harmonious combination. I will waive the extravagant claims for the value dispensed within, but it suffices that the buildings are equipped for study and recreation beyond anything I encountered in my own school days. As nearly as I recall, it cost my parents between twenty and thirty dollars a month to keep me in a private day school, which from the standpoint of investment did not compare with the tax-supported institution. There were six of us of school age in the family, but I won't be generous enough to throw the other five onto the tax-eater's side of the scale. But in view of the fact that any sum of money meant more at that time than at present, to credit the city and county with anything less than $20.00 would be cheating.

But before this goes too far, let's see what I get for my money:

Streets	$4.00		
Sewers	3.00		
Fire	4.00	Tax by	
Police	3.00	the	
School	20.00	month	$15.86
	$34.00		$15.86

Good business suggests that we don't follow this line to its finish. After all, fairness is one thing and being quixotic is another. I wouldn't tell the taxers they are giving too much for the money, any more than I would intimate to the plumber that he is entitled to more pay for hiding from his boss in my bathroom.

Other advantages for the taxpayer

But confidentially, just for the comfort of people like myself, I can't refrain from mentioning the colossal university adjacent where folks of even my vintage can accumulate hundreds of dollars' worth of education in excess of its trifling costs.

Personally, I can't claim much return from the three or four public libraries available to me. But the experience of my friends who, through the private lending libraries, have entered the race with the present-day publishers' output, proves to me that they offer a decided rebate in tax money. And when I recall the dividends that Jack London made one of these same institutions pay him finally, I have to list public library facilities as one of my lost opportunities.

Not being an esthete, I can't properly estimate the free art galleries, museums, a zoo, city parks with free band concerts, a ten-cent symphony, together with stadiums, baseball grounds, tennis courts, aquatic parks, swimming pools and picnic grounds with tables and grills. And I realize, of course, that some services such as I get are not available for taxpayers in smaller or poorer communities.

Services I don't want to see or use

I admit there are a few items where the tax-eaters have me over a barrel. In the first floor of the city hall there is an enterprising and adequate city jail with some outstanding blue-coated business-getters. It cooperates with and supplements an ample state penitentiary whose requirements are not hopelessly above the average citizen. We have an up-to-date emergency hospital served by a smooth-riding conveyance, and a mammoth county hospital that is the last word in everything that I don't want to see or use — except that it is not called a county hospital, since that name is thoughtfully reserved for a series of sunny homelike buildings that once upon a time would have been called a poor farm. Besides this, a certain amount of relief not supplied by the National Government is available to those to whom chance has not handed out the best of deals. But, as I have said, I am reconciled not to collect on these.

A camp in the Sierras

Perhaps it is bravado to say I like to pay taxes. But I prefer it to paying the hidden and unknown value of my auto repair bill, or my gas and power bills when I compare them with those of some other cities. And when I spread the facts out before me, I feel the tax-eaters are doing a good job of buying with my money.

Another thing I almost forgot. Seven thousand feet up in the Sierras, in what to my partly traveled experience is the most attractive and inspiring spot in America, is a recreation camp. It was instituted by my neighbor's tax money and mine. Here I and any other citizen can obtain good food, sleeping accommodations and entertainment at about half of its normal cost to us. Perhaps that is why I am not excited about my tax bills. For I have long ago made up my mind that when the tax-eaters start taking a page of procedure from the private corporations, and send me monthly bills for street, sewer, police, fire, school, library, recreation, hospitalization and relief services adorned with such rubber stamp suggestions as "Take it or leave it" or "Pay up or else," I will hie me to their Sierra camp and eat and sleep and loaf below cost until I get even with them.

CHAPTER EIGHTEEN

The Future of State and Local Government

STATE AND LOCAL GOVERNMENTS have had their prophets of doom, as well as many serious students concerned about the possibility of their gradual disintegration in the face of the onward march of "big government" at the national level. It would be foolish to ignore the obvious fact that most of our more critical problems today are of national and international scope, but one should hardly conclude as a result that there is no longer a place for state and local government or for interest in their continual improvement. Their many services remain as vital as ever to the public, and the demands upon them are steadily increasing rather than decreasing. In the opening article Governor Edmund G. Brown suggests a way to make the states more effective partners in the highly interdependent pattern of modern federalism. The admittedly hazardous task of predicting the conditions of urban government and administration in the year 2000 is essayed by Professor Grant. Dean Bailey then steps apart from his former role as a mayor to take a different kind of thoughtful look at the course our local governments are following and the direction they ought to take. The city which is worthy of the name, he believes, must move beyond the routine housekeeping functions to pursue a vision — to determine and achieve meaningful goals of social policy in terms of a significantly better life for its citizens. It is the role of true leadership not only to run the machinery of government but also to stimulate the initiative and cooperation of the multitude of private persons and organizations whose contributions to the finer community can be enormous.

86

How to Put the States Back in Business

By Edmund G. Brown

MOST OF THE TIME, Americans seem to thrive on change. The meadow converted to a real-estate development is regarded less as a sacrifice to progress

Edmund G. Brown, "How to Put the States Back in Business," *Harper's Magazine,* September, 1964, pp. 98–103. © 1964, by Harper & Row, Publishers, Incorporated. Reprinted by permission.

than a symbol of it. From Connecticut to California, more and more Americans change schools, jobs, and houses almost as casually as they change television channels. They accept mobility as the American way of life, like the right to boo the Dodgers, who are themselves not untypical of the nomad in us. But when it comes to government, most Americans can muster amazing resistance to change, even to modest change and even when it may be a matter of life and death for their country.

The myth dies hard, for example, that the Founding Fathers intended government to function on three rigid levels — federal, state, and local — with limited communication among them, and no fraternization.

The myth that government power must be centered at the local level where it is most responsive to the people has put down deep roots. Special interests, led these days by the mystics of the howling right, keep those deep roots well fertilized because it is precisely at the local level that they are most success-ful in preventing government from responding to needs. These notions are not only dated, but dan-gerous.

Across the nation, we breed slums faster than we can tear them down. We pour millions of dollars into air-pollution control, not to clean the air we breathe, just to keep it from getting dirtier. Many hundreds of millions of federal dollars have gone into highway construction every year, but — until the signing . . . of the transit aid bill . . . — not one federal cent had gone into rapid transit. Last winter, Boston had a grim look at what this policy is buying. Traffic in the city stopped dead for five hours when one car too many crept into the streets and locked the whole mess into place like a big jigsaw puzzle. The traffic commissioner, summoned from home, was forced to abandon his car and take the subway.

The danger of the don't-ever-change philosophy is that it insists on classifying these and other problems as the province of the city or state just because they occur in the city or the state. But these are national in scope and they cannot be solved until they are rec-ognized as such and openly dealt with as such.

After five years of struggling in California with the toughest growth problems any state faces, I am convinced that two modest revisions in present federal-state relationships will start us toward more realistic thinking and more effective action:

First, we need a Council of Governors, operating much as the President's Council of Economic Advis-ers. The Council would provide a sort of domestic hot line over which Governors could send and re-ceive suggestions and criticisms on a wide range of subjects — before, rather than after, federal execu-tive policy had been established.

Second, we need federal legislation creating formal regional structures within which states may take joint action on air and water pollution, park development, and other projects which are less than national but more than local in range.

I first suggested these adjustments in a lecture at Harvard earlier this year; and because too much of the mail I received afterward was written to con-gratulate me on my conversion to the cause of "states' rights," I want to make clear at the outset that while I believe in the rights of states, I am no states' righter. Our Constitution doesn't mention the rights of states, only the rights of people. The weak central govern-ment which states' righters pretend they want met the needs of Virginia planters, New England artisans, and New York merchants early in our his-tory, when the population of the state of New York was about that of Oakland, California, today. The Founding Fathers conceived of a nation where, as Jefferson wrote, states "were left to do whatever acts they can do as well as the national government."

Which of the forces that dominate our daily lives today could be dealt with by a single state? The company that made the clothes you are wearing? The airline serving your city? Your favorite tele-vision network? Your union or the corporation you work for? The corporation in another state whose machinery is now doing your job? Your telephone company?

Even Macy's isn't local any more, and neither are the problems with which government in this decade must deal. We need a central government powerful enough to perform the legitimate and necessary tasks of government on a national scale — to protect civil rights in every form and in every place and to regu-late big industry and big labor — and with the finan-cial resources for medical care for the elderly, aboli-tion of poverty, and increased help for schools.

This is jet-age federalism and it is here to stay, no matter how fervently its detractors invoke the Found-ing Fathers.

The people's advocate

Few people not directly involved in government realize just how tightly meshed the gears of federal and state machinery have become. It is not only hard to separate in theory what state government should do and what national government should do, it is hard to sort out what each is already doing. My Director of Employment, for example, is a state official, and a member of my Cabinet, but he ad-ministers a program that is altogether federal, with the rules written in Washington. California must fol-low those rules or risk forfeiting unemployment-in-surance checks which last year totaled $489 million and an employment service which found work for 1,060,384 people in 1963. Last year, the California Highway Department spent $612 million on building or repairing roads. More than half of the funds came from the federal government and so did the standards to which the roads were built. The national govern-ment annually sends a billion dollars to California, for which we assume administrative responsibility. The partnership reaches into every sector of gov-ernment, from desalinization to dental care, from federal aid for schools to foreign aid for Chile.

Congress was created to represent the states at the federal level, but the interests of most large states are now as diverse and divided as the nation itself. As a result, Congressmen speak primarily for their dis-tricts, rarely for the whole state. A Senator serves statewide, but his responsibility ends when policy is set, except for occasional auditing. He usually has little experience in or knowledge of the complex of administrative and fiscal details posed for the states by the national legislation on which he acts, or doesn't act.

Among state officials, only the Governor represents city and farm, suburb and slum, rich and poor, and is, at the same time, responsible for maintaining the highest level of government service for all of them. He is intimately, sometimes desperately acquainted with details of transportation, public health, welfare, crime, punishment, budgeting, and dozens of other matters as no other state official can be. The Governor of the modern American state is the people's advocate, the closest thing this country has to a King's Conscience, but he must speak at the national level through intermediaries. While an increasing number of government services are administered under joint state and federal auspices, the Governor is brought into the policy-making discussions on these programs for which he bears ultimate administrative responsibility only infrequently, informally, and haphazardly. The Council of Governors would give him a needed voice in national affairs.

Bipartisanly unhappy

Precisely how the Council would operate is open to argument and refinement. My proposal is for a Council of five Governors, with rotating regional representation on a bipartisan basis. To make its role a unifying one, rather than one producing new elements of national discord, I suggest its members be named by the President and its meetings chaired by a federal official of his choice, perhaps the Vice President.

An example of the sort of program on which the Council would work is the Kerr-Mills Act. . . . Designed to help states pay medical expenses for their indigent elderly citizens, it is an acknowledged failure. Years after its adoption, only twenty-six states have been able to implement the act at all. Of those, six spent 89 per cent of the federal funds available under Kerr-Mills — and Nelson Rockefeller and I, who spend most of that money, are equally and bipartisanly unhappy with the results. In California, we knew before the bill passed that the program would fall short of its goal. Most other Governors knew it, too, but there was no organized way for them to bring their knowledge to bear at the center of national power.

Had the Council existed when Kerr-Mills was introduced in Congress, the bill might have been handled something like this: The staff, informed of the proposal in detail, would poll the nation's Governors, gathering facts and views, not only from the Council but from all fifty states. The Council would meet, analyze the staff report, and take a policy position. The position then would be presented to the President and to Congress, and the Governors

would be available to testify where and when they were needed.

One problem we can all hope will become *more* intense with time is conversion to a peacetime economy. The Council would be an ideal source of information for the federal government on public works that could take up the slack immediately after a defense shutdown, and on civilian industry that could move to an area to start building a new economic base. I believe the Council I propose would regularly put people's needs ahead of states' rights.

More than five years ago, as Attorney General of California, I argued the *Ivanhoe* water case before the United States Supreme Court. The issue was water development, but the argument applies to other fields as well. In my brief, I contended that the "general welfare power [of the federal government] has the same attributes as any other federal power," which is to say, "it enjoys the benefit of the supremacy clause. . . ." My argument concluded: "Responsible representation of the state's interest . . . requires preservation of the power and mechanics of federal cooperative activity and resistance to fanciful constitutional objections." The Court agreed. For the first time, it gave explicit approval to federal use of the powers under Section 8 of Article I of the Constitution to promote the general welfare of the United States.

The *Ivanhoe* opinion settled the legal question of the national government's right to deal directly with national problems, but it still left us with a large body of public opinion which says national power should be used only in national emergencies. . . . During the Eisenhower Administration, a commission was appointed by the President to determine whether some jobs the federal government was doing might be turned back to the states. The study was a waste of time. The commission concluded that no state really wanted to regain a single significant function from the federal government — even those states in which "states' rights" is the best banner a politician can fly. Governor Paul Fannin of Arizona is a conservative, but he has not complained about plans to spend a billion dollars in federal funds for water development in his state. Governor John Love of Colorado believes in limiting national power but he has yet to protest because his state received more in federal farm subsidies each year than mine. Governor Ross Barnett is certainly no friend of federal power, but he has not sent back any of the Washington funds which Biloxi has received for urban planning.

Useful pilots

The second area in which reform is needed is in regional relationships among states, the dark continent of federalism. California already is involved in a pilot program of regional resource planning, and this program — if it proves out — can be used in other areas of the country. Secretary of the Interior Stewart Udall started it. Faced with a complex of bitterly argued problems of water development in the Pacific Southwest, he turned to a regional approach as a possible solution. First, he consulted all the Governors involved. Then he drafted a plan and submitted it to the states for comment. He got reams of it, including a proposal from me for a permanent regional planning commission to assist the federal government in developing water supplies for the Pacific Southwest as a unit, not state-by-state. Some people don't like commissions and councils, but as a Governor who has used a number of them to keep his information current and his analyses fresh, I am grateful to them. Without them I sometimes wonder how the revolutions of technology and information would ever get on my desk or into my briefcase.

Implicit in both of my proposals is my belief that the role of the state is changing. Lord Bryce saw states as laboratories for social progress, having in mind the eight-hour day, regulation of working conditions for women and children, workmen's compensation, public-health and welfare agencies, and other advances which were developed, tested, and passed on by states for national application. But while the states experiment with programs nowadays, they must spend increasing amounts of time on problems not of their own making. It is to help deal with emergencies which come from beyond their own borders that the Governors need their voice at the center of national government.

National problems

One of our most sweeping challenges is the open road. American mobility scatters social problems around the continent like tumbleweed in a high wind — problems of education, civil rights, employment, welfare, and others. California has been described as a window on the future, the state in which every major challenge this country must meet for the next twenty years can be found right now. One fourth of California's citizens change homes each year. One thousand people enter our state to stay every day. Some bring skills, but few bring jobs. They bring high hopes, but no classrooms, fire departments, or water. State and local government must provide those, at an average investment of $13,000 for each new family the first year. California has always drawn strength from such pioneers, whether they arrived by covered wagons or station wagons. But the investment in roads and public services for new-

comers rises each year, whether in California or New York, Illinois or Washington, D.C., and even a rich state like ours cannot go it alone indefinitely.

Education presents another major challenge to the states. Nowhere in the Free World is there a better, more broadly based public-school system than California's. But nowhere in that system is there yet a sustained and large-scale effort to make a child not only learn but want to learn. California's dropout rate is a shocking 25 per cent but it is well below the national average. We spend more on education each year than forty-three other states spend on all government services, but our classrooms are programmed for the average youngster. We cannot afford to do much more than study the plight of the young person from the poor or broken home who sees around him what looks to be good reason to doubt that a diploma will make much difference in his future. This is a national problem, rooted in poverty, and it requires a massive program which only the federal government can afford.

Not since the Civil War has the issue of civil rights dominated American life as it does today, and mobility is one of the fundamental causes. In the South, denial of the Negro's rights is backed up by open and often brutal force — clubs, guns, dogs, and the law. Elsewhere, the challenge of the minority's constitutional guarantees is more furtive than savage but its impact is no less real. The three largest Negro ghettos in the nation are in the North, not the South. . . . Here again, no state can protect its citizens without national help.

Our urban problems need national attention. One of the great ironies of our time is that we invest billions of dollars in defense to prevent the destruction of our cities and do so little to keep them from destroying themselves. This nation, with nearly 90 per cent of its citizens in metropolitan areas, is only as strong as its cities. But we have just begun to tackle slum clearance, juvenile delinquency, traffic, and smog and to encourage excellence in design. We get an astronaut around the world almost as fast as we get some fathers home from work. Modern mass transit is needed in almost every major city, but so are federal funds to build the needed systems. Unemployment is a challenge that can be met only by federal action. We may be remembered in history as a nation that could create a machine to fulfill any job but couldn't create a job to fulfill a man. The federal tax cut is expected to put more than a billion dollars in disposable extra income into my state alone, and it will generate $150 million in new revenues for state government in California with no change in tax rates. By contrast, California could wipe out personal income taxes altogether and still generate less than half the new money achieved by the cut in federal taxes. I can't think of a more dramatic example of the difference in competency to deal with truly national problems.

Our economy, like that of all other states, is tied with a thousand strings to the national economy and when a string goes slack, our economy sags. These recent challenges to the states have prompted some to recommend borrowing Dante's inscription and painting it over every Governor's office door: "Abandon all hope, ye who enter."

Difficulties know no party loyalties, moreover; they hit Republicans and Democrats alike. Governor George Romney of Michigan lost his fight for tax reforms which were almost identical to those drafted by his Democratic predecessor. Raising taxes to a level where they would sustain services cost Governor Steve McNichols of Colorado his job. Now his Republican successor finds the higher taxes were absolutely necessary after all. . . . it isn't reasonable to expect that any given tax rate will support an increasing population indefinitely. One school of political scientists interprets these breakdowns as proof that the state is obsolete. They recommend that the federal government bypass the states and deal directly with metropolitan areas. This is not the answer. For one thing, metropolitan areas have trouble enough assembling their own diverse political units into anything like a cohesive plan for growth. For another, only the state covers enough ground to provide a true balance of power to the federal government and a tax base large enough to share the burden of joint programs.

A "yes" or "no"

It is not my job to tell Congress what to do or how to do it. But as a Governor, I believe I have a right to insist on a yes or no answer from Congress on every major proposal from the executive branch and I believe a Council of Governors, making its views known — lobbying, if you will — could help force faster decisions. . . .

. . . . Right now, the legislative process is a self-conscious tug-of-war between Congress and the President in which public opinion is sometimes dimly perceived and little felt. The Council could help fill that void by speaking with authority for state needs. Following conventional approaches to government help, simply because they are time-tested, is obviously not the way. We must be as realistic about the needs of twentieth-century America as were the Founding Fathers about the needs of the 1790s. Only then will we follow Tocqueville's dictum that "the end of good government is to ensure the welfare of the people, not merely to establish order in the midst of their misery."

87

Trends in Urban Government and Administration

By Daniel R. Grant

INTRODUCTION

THE HAZARDS OF POLITICAL PREDICTIONS are well known, even when based on the highly developed science of opinion sampling to forecast voting behavior only a few days in advance of an election. To undertake a prediction of the condition of urban government and administration in the year 2000 is admittedly far more hazardous and perhaps even ludicrous, except for one important saving difference in the circumstances of prediction. The pollster must face the cold reality of actual events on election night, while the long-term forecaster may be comforted in the quite plausible hope that thirty-five years later few will note nor long remember what his predictions actually were.

Such an assignment was accepted, however, not with any thought of enjoying a brief adventure in science-fiction fantasy, but primarily in hopes that it might serve the useful purpose of compelling an examination of past and present trends in the politics and administration of the American city and a hard look at what is involved in projecting these trends into the distant future. It would be much better not to speak of this kind of analysis as "prediction," for its focus is primarily on where we have been and where we are now; but, once having agreed to make the effort, it is hardly proper to seek refuge in semantics.

SOME ASSUMPTIONS AND CAVEATS

Obviously urban governmental trends are related to other trends in the United States and the world, primarily social and economic, and many trend assumptions are required as a basis for prediction. It is

Daniel R. Grant, "Trends in Urban Government and Administration." Reprinted from a symposium, *Urban Problems and Prospects,* by permission from *Law and Contemporary Problems* (Vol. 30, No. 1, Winter, 1965), published by the Duke University School of Law, Durham, North Carolina. Copyright © 1965, by Duke University. Footnotes in original omitted.

important at the outset to make clear what these assumptions are. The assumptions listed by Catherine Bauer Wurster in the *Report of the President's Commission on National Goals* are difficult to improve on in guessing what the socioeconomic world setting for urban government will be in the future. The great bulk of future population increases will take place in metropolitan areas, and most of this will be in the suburban fringes. The core cities within the metropolitan areas will continue their population decline, sometimes only a relative decline but in many cases an absolute one, and they will become increasingly dominated by the economically underprivileged population, principally racial and national minorities. The automobile population will increase; the proportion of older people will rise; expressways will become wider and more numerous; automation will cause a decline in the proportion of industrial jobs, increase employment in the urban professions and services, and shorten the work week; and finally, increased leisure time will result in a vastly accelerated demand for recreational, cultural, and transportation services.

Some caveats are in order to accompany these assumptions. Projection of present trends obviously might be incorrect if any one of several developments might occur; and, admittedly, some of them are not entirely unlikely. Who can say now whether scientific and technological changes will make it possible within the next two or three decades for the masses of commuters to fly to and from work each day? Dramatic new breakthroughs in medical research might cause a sharp increase in the life expectancy, changing the demands on local government in a multitude of ways. Even a twenty-five per cent drop in the birth rate would have strong effects upon population trends. Many other developments, such as "hot" war, serious economic depression, a dramatic new energy discovery, and basic changes in social values and public demands, could change drastically the picture of urban government as seen in the light of current trends. Nevertheless, in spite of all these contingencies and imponderables, just so long as they are kept in mind, it should be worthwhile to review critically what political scientists and other observers seem to be saying about where our urban government is going. We are thus following the admonition of Harold Lasswell in his 1956 Presidential Address to the American Political Science Association to scan "the horizon of the unfolding future."

THE SEARCH FOR TRENDS IN URBAN GOVERNMENT

Identifying significant trends in urban government is a difficult task, but determining which trends are still "running strong" is even more difficult. For example, most textbooks in urban government speak of the beginning of the twentieth century as an important turning point in urban political history — a kind of "beginning of the end" for the "shame-of-the-cities era" which Lincoln Steffens had described so graphically. Charles Adrian expresses the textbook consensus when he states that honesty has replaced "blatant corruption and spoilsmanship" in American city government in the last fifty years. How can we know whether the strong currents which took the sting out of the muckrakers' indictments are still moving in urban government in a way that will shape the future, or whether cities have merely reached a placid end of an era? Similarly, to which trend-maker shall we listen when trying to determine the growth prospects of the manager form and the mayor form of municipal government — the spokesmen for the International City Managers Association or for the United States Conference of Mayors? Has the enthusiasm of civic leadership for the manager plan reached the limits of its expansionist capabilities or will automation technology and the electronic revolution in management give the city manager movement its "second wind?"

The search for trends in the structuring of local government for metropolitan areas, and the appraisal of the strength of such trends, present an even more tangled web. If trends or movements consisted primarily of elaborate surveys and recommendations by professional staffs and citizens' committees, then the governmental integration of the metropolitan areas would surely be one of the strongest. Literally thousands of pages of metropolitan survey reports have been published just since World War II, citing similar problems of fragmented local government and recommending one or more of several varieties of metropolitan coordination. Yet the dismal record of adoptions of survey recommendations makes it extremely hazardous to speak of any trend toward metropolitan consolidation or coordination. York Willbern's recent book entitled *The Withering Away of the City* adds further warning to any who would project such a trend. On the other hand, is there justification for projecting a strong trend of increased governmental fragmentation in the face of recent unique metropolitan government experiments in Miami and Nashville and earlier ones in Baton Rouge and Toronto? Or, to complicate the matter further, is the whole concept of metropolitan community to become obsolete in a rising tide of "megalopolis" — the polynucleated "linear city" said to be growing up both on the Atlantic and Pacific coasts, as well as at other places in the United States?

A final illustration of the difficulty of identifying and assessing the strength of urban trends is found in the area of the urban political process itself. Probably more has been written in recent years on the decline of "bossism" and old-style city machines than on any other aspect of city government, both in the political science journals and in popular magazines and newspapers. But still more recently, "second thoughts" are beginning to appear among students of the party system and of urban politics. Some studies are suggesting that the old-style, boss-controlled, city machine was not so monolithic or hierarchical in form as we had imagined; and other studies suggest that we still have and will continue to have fairly dependable, disciplined, "leader-controlled" city political machines. Persuasive revisionists add to the frustrations of any realistic projection of urban political trends.

As we turn to this puzzling maze of urban trends, it will be useful to divide them into four broad subject-matter categories: the impact of science and technology on the municipal bureaucracy, the future of metropolitan government reorganization efforts, trends in intergovernmental relations with special reference to "megalopolis," and trends in the urban political process.

I. SCIENCE, TECHNOLOGY, AND THE MUNICIPAL BUREAUCRACY

Urban needs and the electronic revolution

A kind of "revolution of rising expectations," or at least of rising demands, is taking place in our cities as they continue to swell with the population explosion. The pressure is not only for quantitative increases in such services as schools, parks, expressways, police, and water supply, but for qualitative improvements and the provision of entirely new services to meet entirely new problems and public desires. It is safe to say that, given sufficient time and the benefit of an occasional crisis situation, these pressures will become translated into new public policy for urban government, making for a larger and more burdened municipal bureaucracy.

Science and technology, especially at the level of urban government, are more often thought of as governmental "problem causers" (congestion from automobiles, noise from jet aircraft, and so on), than as "problem solvers," assisting in the executing of public policies and the provision of urban services. But one of the more dramatic technological developments of the century — electronic data processing — may well become the "wave of the future" in the planning and execution of urban functions. . . .

A few pilot projects are already underway in an effort to develop metropolitan area intelligence systems, aimed at the problem of costly, time-consuming, uncoordinated methods of collecting, recording, and analyzing information needed for making sound decisions about urban planning, renewal, and related activities. The fact that the projects are based on the

concept of the metropolitan area as a single system, even though constituent governmental units might be reluctant to concede this, has caused one writer to speak of the program as one which "has the possibility of charting a new and promising approach to metropolitan area integration."

The rewards paid by systematic decision-making based on electronic data processing have already been demonstrated in private industry and the federal government, and urban government can be expected to follow this lead. . . .

Trends in municipal manpower

Trends in population growth, urban service demands, and changing management technology, all have tremendous implications for the future of municipal manpower requirements. If the future is to consist of a projection of present trends in municipal manpower, the picture would seem to be a generally discouraging one. According to the findings of the Municipal Manpower Commission (MMC), urban government personnel are low on the totem pole in comparison to qualifications and morale of state and federal personnel. This Commission recently studied primarily the administrative, professional, and technical personnel in municipal government, and predicted serious shortages in these categories by 1980. . . .

. . . . Recruiting efforts of city governments are described as feeble, underfinanced, unimaginative, and, in the words of the personnel directors themselves, "totally inadequate for the job to be done." Only one in twenty local governments was found to have any semblance of forecast of the manpower needed for even one year into the future, much less three to five, or ten years ahead. A second criticism is aimed at the independent status of civil service commissions, which are charged with obstructing the essential personnel responsibilities of municipal executives. The Commission unanimously recommended that they either be abolished or limited to an advisory function.

While the findings of the Municipal Manpower Commission do not necessarily describe the future municipal bureaucracy for us, they tend to confirm a general proposition that "the lower the level of American government (everything else being equal), the lower the bargaining power of the unit of government seeking to recruit and keep qualified personnel." This would seem to indicate that the municipal bureaucracy will follow, rather than lead or stay abreast of, the state and federal bureaucracies in coming years. Even so, a generally rising status of public employees at *all* levels of government can be expected to improve the quality, specialization, and professionalization of the municipal bureaucracy.

Hegelian synthesis for city managers and mayors?

One of the strongest forces for reform in American government during the twentieth century has been the evangelistic fervor associated with the city-manager movement, beginning with only a few adoptions during World War I, growing to about 500 by 1940, 1,000 by 1950, and over 2,000 by 1965. Co-evangelists until recent years have been businessmen and political scientists, who promoted the council-manager plan as a means of bringing professionalism, scientific management, and non-partisanship to city government, as well as of eliminating "bossism" and the various undesirable elements commonly associated with it. During the past decade the writers of political science textbooks have been increasingly careful not to "endorse" any particular form of city government, partly because of doubts about the provision for political leadership under the manager plan, but more particularly because of a desire to distinguish the role of the political *scientist* from that of political *reformer*. Such organizations as the International City Managers Association and the National Municipal League continue to provide strong support for civic leaders interested in promoting the plan, and new adoptions continue to be reported at a rate exceeding one per week. In the population category of cities between 25,000 and 500,000, the manager form is more widely used than the mayor-council form, but only four of the twenty-one cities over 500,000 are "manager cities."

What does the future hold for the major forms of city government? It seems clear that the commission form will continue its slow but steady decline in usage by American cities. When Galveston, birthplace of the commission plan, abandoned it in 1960 in favor of the manager plan, this seemed to be a kind of symbolic *coup de grace* for the awkward "five-mayor plan," as its critics have labeled it. On the other hand, the mayor-council form in recent years has been undergoing a variety of reformations, innovations, and refurbishings, particularly in the larger cities. The changes include a more integrated administrative structure, stronger powers for the mayor, and, in some cases, a career "deputy mayor" or chief administrative officer similar in some ways to the city manager. It would be difficult to say whether these changes have taken place more as a natural outgrowth of urban pressures demanding stronger and more professional administrative direction of the city's affairs, or primarily as a strategic move to head off the growing competitive pressure to adopt the "more radical" council-manager plan. In any case, the effect has undoubtedly been to support efforts of the dominant political organizations in most of the larger cities to defeat the city-manager movement. The strengthened mayor-council form has received support from some political scientists who

suggest that the elected executive is better suited for resolving the political and social conflicts of diverse groups.

In spite of some cooling of the early ardor of the manager movement, there is little evidence of an early end to its spread among American cities and no evidence at all to indicate any reduction in the total number using the plan. At present approximately one-fourth of all cities over 1,000 in population have the city-manager plan and it does not seem unreasonable to expect this proportion to rise to one-third or even to one-half of such cities by the end of the century.

Some counter-revolution in the nature and functioning of the council-manager form can be expected, however, even as it spreads to additional cities. Partly to meet the "competition" of the mayor-council plan's alleged advantages in providing political leadership, and partly because of the liberalizing influence of an increasing number of studies showing that city managers are, in actual practice, policy leaders, the council-manager plan can be expected to evolve away from its more antiseptic, apolitical form toward a more openly politicized form. Such changes might mean still further adoptions of the manager plan in the heretofore reluctant cities above 500,000 in population. In any case, the counter trends of the mayor taking on managerial characteristics and the manager taking on mayoral characteristics would seem to call for the mayoral thesis and the managerial antithesis evolving into a Hegelian synthesis.

II. GOVERNMENTAL STRUCTURE FOR THE METROPOLITAN CENTRIFUGE

Three "isms" of population movement — urbanism, suburbanism, and metropolitanism — are all familiar terms in the modern lexicon of public affairs, but the degree of popular familiarity with each term differs considerably. The steady growth of urban population in the United States from five per cent in 1790 to nearly seventy per cent in 1960 has made the urban trend common knowledge for more than a century. Suburbanism is a newer phenomenon and our familiarity with the growth of fringe-area bedroom communities has followed only a step or two behind our familiarity with the automobile. Metropolitanism is newer and less familiar still than either of the other terms. Actually it is not a precise technical term, but is a word born out of necessity to describe the political product of urbanism and suburbanism in the larger communities — one or more core cities surrounded by a loose-joined but interrelated assemblage of incorporated and unincorporated suburbs. What is the nature of this new centrifugal creature on the American scene and, more in point for this discussion, what is the governmental future for the metropolitan area? . . . .

The metropolitan problem: diverse views

Is this fragmentation of government in metropolitan areas a "real problem" of ever increasing intensity or is it for the most part an academic issue which offends the sense of symmetry of certain reformers desiring one government for the whole metropolis? One answer to this question is found in the scores of metropolitan surveys, undertaken by both public and private groups during the past generation, which have predominantly found governmental problems of emergency proportions. These problems might be summarized as follows: (1) serious financial inequities, particularly to the disadvantage of the central city; (2) unequal services in different sections of the same metropolitan area; (3) an illogical split-up of clearly metropolitan-wide functions of government; (4) wasteful overlapping layers of local government; and (5) a weakening of democratic government at the local level by making the task of fixing credit or blame for action or inaction unduly complicated, and by permanently segregating high income suburbs and low income core cities into separate ghettos. The recommendations growing out of the surveys virtually all point toward metropolitan coordination in some form, but no single approach dominates. Generally recommended is one or more of the following proposals: annexation of the suburbs to the core city; extraterritorial powers for the core city; intergovernmental cooperation by contract; a federation of municipalities; city-county consolidation; functional consolidation; special metropolitan districts; expansion of county functions; an association of area governments; and regional planning.

In recent years, partly as a result of almost consistent failure of areas to adopt the recommendations of such surveys, "revisionist literature" in political science has begun to question some of the assumptions and findings of the metropolitan surveys. Robert C. Wood described one aspect of the re-examination as follows:

Despite our predictions, disaster has not struck; urban government has continued to function, not well perhaps, but at least well enough to forestall catastrophe. Traffic continues to circulate; streets and sewers are built; water is provided; schools keep their doors open; and law and order generally prevail. Nor does this tolerable state of affairs result from an eager citizenry's acceptance of our counsel; we know only too well that our proposals for genuine reform have been largely ignored.

Wood points to other trends running counter to the oft-predicted disaster for the metropolis: an extraordinary period of prosperity has increased core city tax returns in spite of predicted financial decline;

some core cities are finding alternative economic activities to replace departing business and industry; makeshift devices such as special districts and contractual agreements have been used to "take the heat off" of selected trouble spots; and, in less measurable ways, the trend toward deterioration of the political process seems to have been checked by more vigorous, capable leadership in some of the larger cities.

In some ways a more fundamental attack on the assumptions of the metropolitan surveys has been made by questioning the concept of "one community" when applied to an entire metropolitan area. Some have suggested that metropolitan sprawl results in a "huge mosaic of massed segregation of size, class, and ethnic groups," a "crazy quilt of discontinuities." Some use this as supporting evidence for the argument that it is unjust or at least illogical to consolidate all of the parts of a metropolitan area under a single government, but others simply use it as an explanation for the many negative votes in consolidation referenda.

Is the "metropolitan problem" real, therefore, or is it imaginary? Is it not possible to concede that many of the metropolitan survey reports, and certainly their publicists, overstated their case with the language of disaster, and yet still conclude that there is a strong case for restructuring the government of metropolitan areas? As Wood concludes, there are still metropolitan problems aplenty:

. . . ugly implications of growing segregation of classes, races, and occupations in suburban ghettos; marginal costs and wastes and inefficiencies in government finance . . . ; the overriding issue as to whether we will realize the potential, in politics, in land use, in social intercourse, in the amenities of existence which metropolitan regions promise. We may not face catastrophe, but this is no reason for countenancing one-hour commuting schedules, for permitting blight, for condoning the repellent sprawl of cheap commercial developments, inadequate parks, congested schools, mediocre administration, traffic jams, smog, pollution, and the hundred and one irritations which surround us. . . .

In the end, the case for metropolitan reform, the drive for larger governments and for one community is as strong as ever.

Charles Press comes to virtually the same conclusion after criticizing the emphasis on manhole counting and the duplication of services found in many metropolitan surveys. He commends the recent study of the New York metropolitan region by Raymond Vernon and others for its focus on the metropolitan environment as a resource for human use. The metropolitan problem is more than simply the scatteration of citizens and industry across the countryside in uneconomical and irrational ways, according to Press; it is the problem of conserving for human use the resources created by a metropolitan environment.

Trends in metropolitan reorganization

If, as this writer believes, even after a thorough re-examination of the literature on metropolitan areas, a metropolitan problem of major and expanding proportions still exists, it becomes important to consider current trends in the structure of local government in the metropolis. In the first place, what is happening in the field of annexation, the "solution" which has been pronounced "beyond hope" on so many occasions? . . . .

Annexation has been used much more vigorously during the past decade than is commonly realized, and it must not be counted out for at least some of the cities of the future. Annexations of spectacular size have taken place in some states, Oklahoma and Texas in particular, with Oklahoma City having annexed approximately 553 square miles since 1959. It now has the largest area of any city in the United States with a total land area of 641.1 square miles for its estimated population of 369,000, compared to the Los Angeles area of 458.2 square miles and a population of 2,600,000. Further evidence of confidence placed in annexation by some states has been the establishment of local boundary review boards and no-incorporation zones around municipalities. Even so, annexation's usefulness is still limited to the unincorporated areas around cities and most of the larger cities are already totally surrounded by incorporated suburbs. Annexation cannot be expected to play a significant role in most of the larger and older metropolitan areas, but it might well play a surprising role in the structuring of the future government of the presently small metropolis.

If the existence of incorporated municipal governments in the suburban fringe is the chief obstacle to the use of annexation, what is the likelihood that the more grandiose schemes of coordination by consolidation of governments, or perhaps federation of governments, may be achieved in the next generation? Neither the opinions of political scientists nor the evidence of past and present trends would seem to offer much hope for the more radical structural reorganizations commonly labeled "Metro." The legal, financial, administrative, and above all the political, obstacles involved even in the consolidation of only two units of government, seem to be simple by comparison to the obstacles involved in achieving consolidation in the larger metropolitan area with its hundreds of separate governments. . . .

A few rays of hope exist, however, for those looking for some kind of area-wide local government for the metropolis in future years. One such ray is the action of such cities as Baton Rouge, Toronto, Winnipeg, Miami, and Nashville, which in the past decade or two have adopted bold proposals for metropolitan coordination involving radical departure from the status quo. . . .

It should be remembered that the Toronto, Winnipeg, and London reorganizations were accomplished by action of the central government without a vote of the constituent local units, a method not traditionally available to metropolitan reformers (although within the state's ultimate authority) in the United States. But it is not entirely beyond the realm of realism to speculate about the possible impact of *Baker v. Carr* and of the more urban-minded state legislatures which will no doubt follow in its wake on the structure of government in metropolitan areas. Granted that legislative reapportionment will in some cases augment *suburban* power more than *core city* power, it is entirely possible that some state legislatures will become far more responsive to political forces desiring consolidation or federation of local governments in the metropolitan area. The dramatic history of the successful movement for consolidating local school districts in the United States, with its generous use of both the "carrot and the stick" by the state governments, should give pause to those who say the metropolitan consolidation in future years is either impossible or constitutes a totally unrealistic alternative. Without suggesting that there will be an epidemic of consolidated "Metro" governments within the next thirty-five years, this writer is willing to predict that there will be at least a baker's dozen among the smaller and medium-sized metropolitan areas, and certainly more than were adopted during the past thirty-five years.

A baker's dozen does not make much of a dent among the 212 metropolitan areas, however, even when reinforced by the number which may keep up with suburban sprawl by means of annexation. What, then, is to be the governmental picture for the bulk of the metropolitan areas in future years? The trends running strongest now include the creation of special districts to handle specific problems across boundary lines, an expanded role for the urban county in serving both incorporated and unincorporated areas, the development of more elaborate programs and institutions for comprehensive regional planning, and (related to the latter) the organization of voluntary associations of area governments in the various metropolitan areas. All of these devices for coping with metropolitan problems have at least one thing in common — they assume the continued existence of governmental fragmentation and even the likelihood of its increase. If the metropolitan areas in 2000 A.D. are to be larger and more numerous than they are now, with an even greater proliferation of separate governments, then is the most accurate prediction for them one of governmental paralysis and "regional chaos" . . . . [?] The answer to this question requires a consideration of the "vertical aspects" of intergovernmental relations (federal-state-local) as opposed to the "horizontal aspects" (inter-local relations) which have been our major focus thus far, and we turn to this subject now.

III. 2000 A.D.:
THE INTERGOVERNMENTAL
MEGALOPOLITY

The increasing company of authors of books and articles dealing with the "dying city" theme in recent years cannot be lightly dismissed as ivory-towered alarmists. Willbern's *The Withering Away of the City,* E. A. Gutkind's *The Twilight of Cities,* and Bernard Weissbourd's recent article in the *Saturday Review,* "Are Cities Obsolete?", are just three examples of many which, while dealing with various aspects of the city, all include a common theme: the nature of the city and of its government is changing before our very eyes and its actual survival in anything like its present form is quite doubtful. Willbern's thesis and forecast for local government are especially relevant to our discussion. The major role of the municipal corporation during the past century is seen as withering steadily in future years as its population moves outward and across county and even state boundary lines. It will become only one component among many in the new model describing American local government — the "many" consisting of a network of special districts, some single-purpose and some multi-purpose, several counties with increasing but segmental responsibilities, an assorted spectrum of public and private utility-type enterprises, and an elaborate variety of cooperative arrangements with higher governmental levels.

Where will the self-governing urban community be in this future model of local government? In view of the prospects for the development of the Gottman-style megalopolis in several regions of the United States (encompassing several metropolitan areas merged into each other), it is necessary to ask also where the self-governing *metropolitan* community will be. York Willbern considers and rejects several possible locales:

It certainly is not the traditional central city, which is largely being lost in a jumble of other units and arrangements. It is hardly to be found in new satellite suburban communities, which serve some purposes and functions but not enough. A new metropolitan-wide, self-governing community is likely to be a will-o'-the-wisp in most circumstances, beckoning the crusader, but rarely if ever attained. The . . . territorial units, primarily counties, will hardly serve as the vehicle for truly integrated communities, particularly because the territorial boundaries are largely immutable and frequently have only coincidental relationships to the areas of denser settlement.

Scott Greer and David Minar recently asked basically the same question in pointing to the explosion and disappearance of the local community as we have known it. In an era when Americans are beginning to live in many overlapping "communities," and when geographic "community" may mean less than vocational, social, or recreational community, old notions of community no longer jibe with living patterns.

The answer to the question of where the old, clearly defined, self-governing community will be in 2000 A.D. is simply that it will be lost in the shuffle of the intergovernmental megalopolity, at least for the vast majority of people. New definitions of community will have to be developed. As Willbern points out, "where patterns of urban living spread over the landscape, 'community' is hardly unitary, and self-government must probably be as complex as our interrelationships."

A word of caution is in order, lest we be carried away completely by our logic. There can be no doubt that, even while industrialization, suburbanization, and metropolitanization increasingly constitute the realities of American life, there will be a dogged persistence of the agrarian myths in popular political attitudes. As George Blair reminds us, we are experiencing a decline in rural population without much decline in the rural shibboleths about "big city government" — that it is more impersonal and less human, less subject to popular control, more "politics-ridden," more irresponsible, inflexible, bureaucratic, and less democratic generally than "rural, grass-roots government." Thus, people will continue to talk about the local community somewhere in megalopolis long after sociologists have concluded that the territorially-based local community in megalopolis has ceased to exist. For the student of political behavior, the myth may be as important as the fact, particularly as it affects the structure of local government.

It is against this backdrop of increasing fragmentation of urban government — the bad fences that make bad neighbors — and a strong tendency toward disappearance of the local community that the coordinative and leadership roles of the national and state governments become virtually if not absolutely inevitable. . . .

New and elaborate programs involving federal-state-local cooperation can be expected to seek the kind of areal coordination once provided by the municipal corporation before the suburban explosion put an end to that. Charles Adrian predicts that our tendencies toward a "mass society," with fewer regional differences, will soften the image of Washington or the state capital imposing policy on local government and will reinforce the trend toward a common set of objectives among federal, state, and local employees.

The growing influence of the career bureaucrat, the expert staff man, the professional, will be a natural result of the growing complexity of relationships, vertical and horizontal, in the "intergovernmental megalopolity." Even our comparatively brief experience with urban renewal programs, and with the newer anti-poverty program, make it abundantly clear that only highly specialized personnel can carry on the negotiations necessary to comply with the elaborate system of policies and regulations involved.

The number of urban-oriented proposals in the President's State of the Union address in 1965 can only lend support to predictions of more federal and state involvement in the metropolis and a more complex set of intergovernmental relationships. The role of the urban planner, whose training is calculated to make him concerned primarily with the *general* interest and the broader viewpoint, is being given greater influence and prestige by the various "planning strings" attached to the newer programs. This can only be augmented further as new assistance programs are added.

One other characteristic of the intergovernmental megalopoly will be the increasing reliance upon joint federal-state-local arrangements for the provision of necessary revenue to provide urban services and controls. In spite of movements in many states, which have been strongly supported by the U.S. Advisory Commission on Intergovernmental Relations, to give cities a broader tax base than the general property tax, we can expect the trends toward state grants-in-aid and shared taxes and toward increasing federal assistance to remain dominant. The obstacles to local raises in taxes include not only the difficulties of an increasingly fragmented local government structure, but the even more basic disinclination of citizens to associate taxes with services. We can expect a continuation of the trend toward levying the taxes at the higher levels of government and spending and administering the funds at the lower levels.

IV. TRENDS IN URBAN POLITICS

The preceding discussion has been concerned in large measure with the formal structure of future urban government, but any consideration of urban trends would not be complete without examining trends in urban politics — the process of influencing public decision-making. So we turn now to a consideration of the question of whether there are discernible trends in the process of urban politics which will constitute the basis for future city government.

A "new political ethos" for the city?

Edward C. Banfield and James Q. Wilson, in the concluding chapter of their *City Politics,* state that the most important changes occurring in city politics today are the changes in the urban "political ethos." They refer to the increasing absorption of the immigrant lower class into the middle class and the profound effects of this on the outlook of the electorate. The major transformation in the newcomers to the middle class is said to be their acceptance of the "middle class ideal": politics as a search for the "public" interest — the interest of the community "as a whole" — and preference for government by technical experts and statesmen, not by politicians. This new political ethos is said to provide new support for such older institutional reforms as non-partisanship, at-large elections, the city-manager plan, master planning, and metropolitan area reorganization, as well as new opposition to "bossism" and the smoke-filled room.

The one troublesome part of this analysis by Banfield and Wilson is that it seems to overlook strong evidence to the contrary in most core cities in the United States, i.e., the exodus of the middle class from core city to suburbs, leaving the core city to the swelling non-white population. They acknowledge this seeming contradiction, and the congeniality of "the old-style politics of the boss and machine" to the lower class, but contend that

. . . the nationally growing middle class has shown that it will use its control of state and federal governments — and particularly of law enforcement agencies and of special districts within the metropolitan areas — to withhold the patronage, protection, and other political resources that are indispensable to the growth of political machines in the central cities. This means that the lower class will have to play politics of a kind that is tolerable to the middle class or not play it at all.

City bossism: decline or persistence?

The decline of bossism and of old-style city politics has been widely reported by political scientists in recent decades, although it has not been explained in quite such simple terms as the lower-class absorption theory described above. . . .

But is the decline permanent? Cautious predictions of a revival of certain aspects of machine politics in certain kinds of settings are being made by some observers. Robert A. Dahl's research interest in "who governs New Haven?" resulted in his upgrading the importance of modern machine politics in that city, and Richard T. Frost's study of eight New Jersey counties revealed that party leaders were performing a great many of the traditional party services there in 1957. Still others point to the growing non-white proportion of the population of metropolitan core cities as the basis for a new, dependable political machine, as suggested above.

Two new-style urban political patterns are described by Fred Greenstein: (1) the politics of non-partisanship in approximately two-thirds of American cities above 25,000 in population, with varying degrees of conformity in actual practice, and (2) the new "party club" phenomenon, organized within some urban political parties, usually characterized by a youthful and ideologically oriented zeal. He cautions that these cannot be considered *the* future pattern of urban politics, however, but only single manifestations in a panorama of urban political practices. "The degree to which old-style urban party organizations will continue to be a part of this panorama is uncertain." Perhaps the safest prediction is that the future pattern of urban politics will be a blending of elements of the old and the new.

Rotten boroughs in 2000 A.D.

One problem of contemporary urban politics — the struggle for more proportional representation of urban citizens in the state and national legislative bodies — may well be replaced by a somewhat different version of it in decades to come. The area of greatest conflict could be the representational structure of the various area-wide metropolitan authorities, special districts, and occasional metro-type governments which will increasingly have core city and suburban clienteles. The democratic difficulties of excessive autonomy for such agencies, of equal representation for each unit of government, of representing governmental bodies rather than the electorate directly, and of excessive dominance by the core city, are just a few aspects of this problem which may move into more prominent billing in urban politics.

V. CONCLUSION: IS URBAN DEVELOPMENT BEYOND THE REACH OF GOVERNMENT?

It is presumptuous, indeed, in these concluding comments to raise such a fundamental question as whether the political variable is important in urban development, but in view of its obvious relevance it would be even worse to exclude it. On the one hand, some believe that the fate of planned urban development and redevelopment depends largely on the political system. Speaking of urban renewal, Greer and Minar recently described many of the negative effects of the political-governmental structure:

Urban renewal is limited by the dichotomy of public and private control, tension between federal and mu-

nicipal agencies, division of power between different federal agencies, and fragmentation of power at the local community level. . . .

Out of this diffusion of responsibility comes a curious rigidity, not a rigidity of program but a rigidity of process that enervates program. . . . Any one or combination of these may develop the power to revise, delay, obfuscate, or forbid action. . . . It safeguards stasis.

The clear implication of this kind of statement, and of most proposals for governmental reorganizations, is that the political variable *is* important in urban development and that alternative governmental policies and programs *do* make a significant difference. Banfield and Wilson apparently disagree, at least with respect to "the most fundamental problem of the central cities and of the older suburbs — one that constitutes a life-and-death crisis for them. . . ." The spread of lower-class slums ". . . cannot be 'solved,' or even much relieved, by government action at any level," they contend, and they downgrade the role of government more specifically by stating:

There is little that government can do about this. The forces that are at work — especially changes in technology, in location of industry and population, and in consumer tastes and incomes — are all largely beyond the control of government in a free society. Given these restraints, the future of the cities is probably beyond the reach of policy.

Greer and Minar are not so pessimistic and do not discount the possibility of radical experimentation in urban governmental structure in the future, as unlikely as it may now seem. They point out that the United States does have a tradition of experimentation, particularly in the original adoption in spectacular fashion of our "untested" organizational forms — federalism, separation of powers, the Presidency, and judicial review. Robert Wood also dissents in his *1400 Governments* from some of the economic determinism implied in the New York Metropolitan Regional Study reports, and argues that a metropolitan polity would control and guide the forces that some economists seem to regard as impersonal and perhaps even unchangeable.

Only the naïve would contend that massive change in the polity commensurate with the massive changes in urban ecology is very likely. But only the most cynical would say that the achievement of bold invention for the American metropolis is impossible. If the past generation was able to accomplish such monumental political inventions as the Tennessee Valley Authority and the Marshall Plan, is it more difficult for the coming generation to invent and achieve workable local governments for metropolitan areas? In either case, fragmentation or integration, the structure and process of urban government can be expected to play a significant role in shaping urban development and redevelopment.

88

Leadership in Local Government

By Stephen K. Bailey

SCATTERED ACROSS this vast nation are bundles of people called villages, towns, boroughs, and cities. The future of these bundles is of infinite importance to the future of the free world. For, if in these tens of thousands of smaller bundles men cannot live together in peace, order, justice, and fraternity, the larger bundles — national and international — can never be effectively shaped, integrated, or contained.

Local communities have too often been treated as problems in administrative mechanics. This is unfortunate. Like the human body, the local community is a functioning organism. It lives and breathes, grows and decays, aspires and doubts. Its viability depends not only upon the satisfactory functioning of its economic and administrative muscles, but upon the character of its will and vision; in short, upon its leadership.

In this connection, it seems to me, we need to ask and answer a few questions hoary with age. For it is only in the context of a general philosophy of leadership that the technical questions of taxation, police training, personnel ordinances, public administration, and partisan politics generally take on meaning.

Housekeeping does not make a home. Effective local government depends not so much upon the machinery we employ as the spirit we are of. We can have all the latest IBM systems, all the best personnel rating systems, the best home rule ordinances, all the latest police communication networks, and still make a flop of local government. Good municipal government is impossible unless we first discover our goals and unless we think creatively about human resources and human relations. Actually, many of our technical problems are the easiest to solve. The continuing, nagging, frustrating problems of local government involve people and the relationships among people.

Let us start by asking a rather rarefied question: What is it that most people want out of life?

Is this question really so difficult? Do they not want to love and raise their families, to choose freely their occupations and their rulers, to contemplate beauty, to sleep with the security of a child, to be valued by others, to search for truth and meaning without restraint, to laugh with the wind, and reverence the stars? Are these not the values which sages and philosophers of all ages have identified and proclaimed?

If so, then we can say of local government, as we can say of all government and of all human institutions, that they should exist in order to maximize these values. Actually, these values are assumed in the Preamble to the United States Constitution: "We, the people of the United States, in order to form a more perfect Union, establish justice, insure domestic tranquillity, provide for the common defense, promote the general welfare, and secure the blessings of liberty to ourselves and our posterity, do ordain and establish this Constitution for the United States of America." It was the sense of our founding fathers, as it should be our sense, that government exists to achieve values — to establish those conditions within which individuals and groups can achieve the good life. This is the only significant meaning of the phrase, "the good society."

As soon as we put the issue in these terms, we become instantly aware that all too many local governments set their sights too low — far too low. Far too many local governments in America behave as though their only functions were to repair a few hundred yards of streets each year, remove snow, check parking meters, direct traffic, keep vital statistics, and keep out of trouble politically. These activities may keep a treadmill running, but they will never build a civilized community. The main job of local government, like the main job of a housewife, is not to dust under the bed; it is to raise a decent family. Local government must, in short, become an effective instrument of social policy; it must dream dreams about the future, and help those dreams come true.

It is not enough to want absence of disease in our communities; we want the joy of living that comes from a positive sense of well-being. It is not enough to want a high literacy rate; we want educated citizens. It is not enough to want industry or commerce; we want industry and commerce that won't pollute our air or poison our rivers or turn us into little Hobokens. It is not enough to want streets; we want streets lined with trees. It is not enough to have sanitary jail cells; we want those cells to become increasingly unoccupied. It is not enough to double our police force; we want recreational facilities and programs which will cut our police force in half. It is not enough to paint our poor farms; we must give our older citizens something constructive to do. It is not enough to contain the ugliness of our slums;

we must destroy our slums, and build new cities in their place.

The "practical" men will say, "Ho, hum," or "Sure, sure"; the cynics will mumble "paternalism," "the welfare state," "socialism," or worse. The so-called realists will say, "Pie-in-the-sky-by-and-by." The members of the taxpayers' leagues will shudder and quietly check their wall safes. And I would agree with all of them if I were talking simply about the possibility of "City Hall" or the "State Capitol" or "Washington" doing all of these things. It is about time that we stopped thinking about special progress as the private preserve of government. It is also about time that we stopped thinking about government as an evil, disease-ridden ogre bent on destroying our liberties. It is about time that we looked at government and private agencies and individuals as useful partners in the common social enterprise of achieving a decent existence for ourselves and our posterity. America was built by this partnership. It was not built by government pretending it could or should do it all; it was not built by private enterprise operating in an antiseptic vacuum of *laissez faire*. As Walter Lippmann has pointed out, "While the theorists were talking about *laissez faire,* men were buying and selling legal titles to property, were chartering corporations, were making and enforcing contracts, were suing for damages. In these transactions, by means of which the work of society was carried on, the state was implicated at every vital point." And Lippmann does not even mention here the governmental grants to railroads, the governmental construction of highways, the governmental regulation of utilities, the governmental issuance of patents, the governmental protection of private property, the governmental training of technicians, scientists, executives, and professional men in our public school system, the governmental protection of public health — and I could go on and on with activities of government that have made our private economic progress possible.

Some of my liberal friends have assumed in recent years that government has done it all — or should do it all. They fail to realize that private economic life makes government financially possible, even if the reverse is in part also true. They fail to recognize that churches and civic clubs and voluntary agencies and dedicated private citizens do more to create civilized communities in America than all the mayors and city managers and first selectmen combined.

What I am talking about, then, is a partnership. When I use the term local government, I am talking about every possible resource, local, state, and national, private and public, which is capable of being mobilized in a common struggle to build a more prosperous, more beautiful, and more humane local society.

The first job of leadership in local government is to identify the resources of this partnership. What are some of these resources?

First and foremost, there is the resource of creative and alert individuals: the woman who sees a dangerous crossing near a school and brings this information to the attention of the common council: the businessman who notices the rubbish in back of a row of stores and stimulates a voluntary clean-up drive through the Chamber of Commerce; the worker who has a dump near his house and begins to wonder why the dump couldn't be filled over and a playground created; the church worker who finds a family in distress and is moved to organize a community chest; the industrialist, who in the course of remodeling and enlarging his plant, provides for a screen of cypress trees to hide an ugly scrap pile from public view. These are the people who give a damn. They may be private citizens or public officials, but their existence in any community is the most potent force for good that a community has.

In almost every community there are scores of men and women of this kind. The major job of City Hall is to release and harness their energies. Without so much as a nod in the direction of the general fund, these individuals will create community chests and district nurse associations, sponsor little leagues and build churches, raise money for hospitals and build YMCA's, attract new industry and decorate Main Streets with Christmas lights. They will serve for nothing on boards and commissions of the city government. They will give up the peace and quiet of their living rooms for the smoke-filled committee rooms where smoke-filled cities are scrubbed and cleaned. These are the men and women who see the world, not as it is, but as it could be, and who make their dreams come true.

A second resource for community progress is capital. This may be local, or it may come from some distance. I have already indicated that our private economy finances our government. But it can do much more than that, and actually has in hundreds of cities throughout America. Private capital has helped level slums and build low-cost housing; it has created parking lots and attractive store and office buildings; it has provided recreation facilities at a profit or as a gift of inheritance; it has built city halls and county courthouses on a lease-amortization basis; it has helped finance zoning and planning studies — and I have just scratched the surface. Actually, I should like to see private capital double and triple its activities in community development. I should like to see the Chamber of Commerce, or the NAM, or the American Bankers Association, or the life insurance companies, or our larger trade unions set up a program of rebuilding the cities of America. I should like to see them set up a community investment research staff which could work with local citizens' organizations and officials in discovering socially constructive investment opportunities in our municipalities.

To take a very modest example: one of the three movie theaters in Middletown, Connecticut, is now idle, and will continue to be unless something is done. When I was mayor, I wish I might have been able to turn to an investment consultant who could have come to Middletown to tell us how a private recreation industry could turn the inside of that theater into a skating rink or a bowling-ping-pong-dancing recreation center which could serve as a teen-age community house. I have an idea that a thing of that sort could operate at a good profit, and it would provide a facility of enormous social value in the community. I wish I could have turned to a private investment consultant to talk about urban redevelopment, housing our old people decently, remodeling a vacant factory, or polishing up our zoning laws to attract new economic ventures. If private enterprise wants to slow down the march of governmental bureaucracy, it can do no better than to run a new eye to the social and economic needs and possibilities of our cities and to invest in community development.

A third great resource at our disposal is our state and federal governments. It seems to me ridiculous to pit one level of government against another, or to attempt to work out tight jurisdictional lines. The federal government and the respective state governments have done an incalculable amount of good in our local communities: through grants-in-aid, through insisting upon high standards of administration, through uniform laws, through informational programs, through the loan of technicians, through public works, through scores of services which local communities have not been able to provide by themselves. One job of leadership at the local level is to encourage and foster programs at higher governmental levels which will help local officials do their job better. We can guard against overcentralization and bureaucratic domination, not by attempting to keep higher levels of government from concerning themselves with local issues, but by helping those higher levels of government to understand the kinds of activities which will release rather than deaden local initiative and local enterprise, public and private.

I should be less than honest if I did not at this point acknowledge that the encouraging and tapping of these diverse and partly free-wheeling resources involve substantial administrative and political risk. It is difficult enough to keep any semblance of order *within* the kaleidoscopic formal patterns of local government. Boards, commissions, authorities, special districts, utilities, staff and line agencies have grown like Topsy as horsepower has replaced the horse. Anyone who has ever worked for local government has, at one time or another, emitted an almost visceral cry for a return to the security and simplicity of the village womb of an earlier era, when, in retrospect at least, authority and responsibility seemed roughly equivalent, and governmental problems seemed capable of human solution.

In view of the terrifying complexity of modern intra- and inter-governmental relations, why complicate life still further by encouraging voluntarism and possible jurisdictional overlaps? Why not streamline administrative channels, firm up gelatinous authority, systematize a clear division of labor between private and public endeavor? Why not single out the tax and the trained administrator as the exclusive twin resource of local government and let it go at that?

The answer, I suppose, comes down to a matter of social philosophy. I am not convinced that efficient government is impossible in a pluralistic matrix. But even if I were so convinced, I think I should stick with some of the inefficiencies in order to maximize the voluntary output of private energies. A sense of community (and may I add a sense of humor) is infinitely more important in our kind of society than a sense of absolute hierarchy.

Furthermore, I am not sure that certain kinds of lateral clientele relationships are necessarily evil. A privately sponsored little league baseball club may do more to keep the maintenance operations of the park department up to snuff than the budget director, mayor, city manager, and general public combined. There are dangers in the parochial demands of citizens' groups directly interested in a part of the total governmental enterprise; but there are also enormous strengths. If local governments can do more than they have done, through charter revision and administrative improvements, to put their internal house in order, to make administrative authority and political responsibility equivalent and unambiguous in the area of formal legal power, private community endeavors can then be encouraged with a minimum danger of confusion and divided purpose.

The maximum and harmonious utilization of the resources available to local communities cannot be achieved by trusting to luck or to some "unseen hand." There is nothing automatic about the process of unleashing and, paradoxically, harnessing social power. The primary resource, without which all other resources are left inert on a centrifugal wheel, is local political leadership, what Woodrow Wilson once described as "the capacity to give sight to the blind forces of public thought." It is the job of those in local politics and administration to give direction and leadership to all the other resources at the disposal of our communities. This is a tremendous responsibility. It means not only that housekeeping functions must be run efficiently and well: police, fire, public works, health, welfare, and the rest; it means that local public officials must become major catalytic agents in stimulating constructive community activity and community planning. It is their job to set goals as well as to execute policies. It is their job to harness private energies and federal and state resources in order to create a better society. These things we cannot do unless we brighten our tarnished political instruments and raise our political sights.

In Tolstoi's "War and Peace" the Russian general Kutuzov knew, in Tolstoi's words, "that the leader existed only to give form and expression to the energy of his followers." This is a useful conception of leadership in our society only if a leader understands that he must look for the human, not the animal energies of his followers. There are warring and complex self-interests in all parts of our society, as there are in all parts of us. My own experience in Middletown taught me that people could be appealed to above the level of the belly — and would respond. I am not pretending that I was any great shakes as a mayor. I know that I made a lot of mistakes. But I know also that I was most successful where I was able to make people see the community as a total enterprise, not as a bundle of separate factions to be separately pleased.

What are the obligations of leaders at the local level, or for that matter at any level of government?

We have identified one responsibility already: to take stock of the resources at the community's disposal. A second responsibility of the leader is to search among these resources until he has found what Edmund Burke called the "permanent forces," the most common and the most ubiquitous long-range interests. Leadership involves selection. All groups and all individuals cannot have all their demands satisfied fully and simultaneously. Some demands should not be satisfied at all. The junk dealer who wants a zoning change in a restricted residential zone is defying the "permanent forces," the long-range interests of the community. So is the restaurant owner who asks a health officer to "go easy." So is the real estate entrepreneur who wants to set up jerry-built houses with forty-foot frontages in a new subdivision. So is the slum landlord who defies urban redevelopment. President Charles Eliot of Harvard once identified the prime requisite of an executive as "his willingness to give pain" — not his *desire* to give pain but his *willingness*. Almost every action of government hurts or inconveniences someone in some measure. Unless a leader can identify the "permanent forces" in a community, unless he can mobilize the will to inconvenience the transitory forces which hinder the release of these permanent forces, forward movement is impossible.

To pose a superficial paradox, however, the third obligation of leadership is self-restraint in the exercise of power. The paradox here is superficial because firmness and restraint are not antonyms. The batting average of the slugger is directly related to the control of his power. Respect for law was never increased by officiousness. If a public official has one hundred portions of authority, he should normally keep ninety-nine in reserve. One of the virtues (and God knows there are vices) of the weak-mayor form of government is that it pushes the mayor into the pursuit of consent. Insofar as a strong-mayor or manager form of government encourages a responsible leader to rule rather than govern, the soil of freedom to that extent is eroded. The potential authority of government is enormous. Our founding fathers had a healthy suspicion of corrupted power. The democratic leader must combine the resolve to move with an equal resolve to safeguard the rights of those who seem to be in the way. Negotiation and compromise are often frustrating and messy, but in a world of myopic passions they are the only real substitute for head-splitting and blood-letting.

The final obligation of the leader is vision — not just the anticipation of tomorrow but the creation of tomorrow. A public official may identify the permanent forces in his community, he may have the will to act, he may act with restraint, but unless he sets the goals of possibility, unless he sees the world not as it is but as it ought to be and can be, he will never be a true leader. Thomas Masaryk, the great Czech philosopher-king, once wrote: "You see how it is. The method must be absolutely practical, down-to-earth, realistic, but the total conception must be an eternal poem."

The central question of the leader in local government must be this: what kind of a community do we want to build? What should it look like five, ten, twenty years from now? What social tensions must be eased? What is the anatomy, the physiology, the psychology of organic community health?

These questions far transcend in their implications the local scene. Pennsylvania Avenue and the East River Drive are nothing but extensions of Main Street. If we cannot produce adequate leadership in City Hall, we will never produce it in Washington, New York, or Geneva. Unless we unleash our imaginations locally, we will never unleash them internationally. The vision of the good society is a seamless web. It is a supreme act of imagination calling for supreme acts of social invention. And vision has become the condition of our survival.

The overriding question today is whether we have lost the vision necessary for the survival of the values we hold most precious.

What is wrong with us? Have our comforts made us soft and our TV sets made us indolent? Have we become so preoccupied with the thousand and one details of building a middle-class showcase that we have forgotten Augustine's City of God — or even what Carl Becker called the Heavenly City of the eighteenth-century philosophers — the City of Man, the City of Reason? Perhaps at no time since Periclean Athens has there been an opportunity comparable to ours. We have a legacy of compassion and reciprocity in our ethical and religious heritage; we have been a nation not of squatters but of builders. And facing us is the greatest challenge ever to confront a sovereign people: a challenge to prove to the rest of the world that a sense of individual responsibility coupled with faith in each other can produce a working partnership between a free people and their government. This partnership cannot guarantee happiness, but it can establish some of the fundamental conditions of individual fulfilment. In a democracy can we ask for more? We dare not ask for less.

The two brief concluding excerpts balance each other appropriately, and are in effect the two sides of a single coin. The first, from a brochure published by the National Center for Education in Politics, states concisely the case for working in the political party of one's choice if the citizen wishes to be effective, and stresses the need for more active political participation on the part of college trained men and women. It is also undeniably true that much progress in the past in state and local government has been the outgrowth of ceaseless effort on the part of devoted individuals and associations often referred to derisively as "reformers" and "do-gooders." Probably no man has been more closely identified with municipal reform than Richard S. Childs, widely known as the "father" of the council-manager plan. His sprightly characterization of "The Reformer" provides a fitting finale.

89

Why Participate in Party Politics?

THE FUTURE OF FREE representative democracy is seriously endangered when a high proportion of men and women of character and intelligence flinch at the thought of participation in partisan politics. Some say in defense of nonparticipation that they do not wish to risk misrepresentation of their character

---

Better Minds for Better Politics, pamphlet published by the Citizenship Clearing House, New York, pp. 4–8.

and motives. Others say that they find the rough and tumble of partisan politics extremely distasteful. Still others are held back by considerations of the possible effects of political participation on their business or home life. These are mere pinpricks compared to what the citizen-soldier is called upon to endure in war for the preservation of democracy. A free and healthy system of representative government is unattainable without well-organized political parties led by honest and intelligent men and women devoted to the common good.

No generally applicable device other than political parties has yet been developed for coalescing a multitude of individual opinions to the point where democratic government becomes possible. It is true that special interest groups sometimes provide an effective means of influencing elections and the conduct of legislative bodies. But to the extent that such groups are successful it means the triumph of special interests over the general public interest. Parties represent, albeit sometimes imperfectly, the general interest. When special interest groups grow strong parties grow weak. In seeking the greatest good for the greatest number, therefore, it is essential that the strength of the parties be maintained, but the political parties cannot be more honest, more intelligent, or more patriotic than their leaders.

Many persons, including some college teachers of politics, believe that the independent citizen is more influential than the party man on the theory that the parties must woo his support to win. The independent, however, sacrifices the chance to share in the nomination of candidates and in the determination of party principles and programs. His choice at the election is too often between two evils. The machinery through which the individual voter can work most effectively for the improvement of politics is that of his political party.

No machinery, however, can be expected to operate successfully if its management is abandoned by honest, intelligent, and patriotic citizens and abused by those to whom it goes by default. . . .

In a free representative democracy a high premium must be placed on training young men and women for intelligent and effective participation in politics. Preservation of our democratic processes depends not only on knowledge and interest but also on developing a willingness among the able, well-trained, and interested students to participate in the drama and dynamics of American politics. . . . Whatever success the colleges and universities have in preparing their students for positions of prominence and leadership in the professions, they will stand to lose much if not all of their greatness as seats of learning if they fail to supply the nation with intelligent, active, and devoted participants in party politics.

90

The Reformer

By Richard S. Childs

A REFORMER is one who sets forth cheerfully toward defeat. It is his peculiar function to embrace the hopeless cause when it can win no other friends and when its obvious futility repels that thick-necked, practical, timorous type of citizen to whom the outward appearance of success is so dear. His persistence against stone walls invites derision from those who have never been touched by his religion and do not know what fun it is. He never seems victorious, for if he were visibly winning, he could forthwith cease to be dubbed "reformer."

Yet, in time, the Reformer's little movement becomes respectable and his little minority proves that it can grow and presently the Statesman joins it and takes all the credit, cheerfully handed to him by the Reformer as bribe for his support.

And then comes the Politician, rushing grandly to the succor of the victor!

And all the Crowd!

The original Reformer is lost in the shuffle then, but he doesn't care. For as the great bandwagon which he started goes thundering past with trumpets, the Crowd in the intoxication of triumph leans over the side to jeer at him — a forlorn and lonely crank mustering a pitiful little odd-lot of followers along the roadside and setting them marching, while over their heads he lifts the curious banner of his next crusade!

Richard S. Childs, "The Reformer," *National Municipal Review,* July, 1927, reverse of title page. Reprinted by permission of the publisher.